SETTING THE WORLD ABLAZE

SETTING
THE WORLD
ABLAZE

Washington,
Adams,
Jefferson,
and the American Revolution

John Ferling

OXFORD
UNIVERSITY PRESS

2000

OXFORD
UNIVERSITY PRESS

Oxford   New York

Athens   Auckland   Bangkok   Bogotá   Buenos Aires   Calcutta
Cape Town   Chennai   Dar es Salaam   Delhi   Florence   Hong Kong   Istanbul
Karachi   Kuala Lumpur   Madrid   Melbourne   Mexico City   Mumbai
Nairobi   Paris   São Paulo   Singapore   Taipei   Tokyo   Toronto   Warsaw

and associated companies in
Berlin   Ibadan

Published by Oxford University Press, Inc.
198 Madison Avenue, New York, NY 10016

Oxford is a registered trademark of Oxford University Press

Library of Congress Cataloging-in-Publication Data
Ferling, John E.
Setting the world ablaze: Washington, Adams, Jefferson,
and the American Revolution / John Ferling
p.   cm.   Includes bibliographical references and index
ISBN 0-19-513409-5
1. Statesmen—United States—Biography.
2. Washington, George, 1732–1826.
3. Adams, John, 1735–1826.
4. Jefferson, Thomas, 1743–1826.
5. United States—History—Revolution, 1775–1783—Biography.
6. United States—Politics and government—1775–1783
I. Title.
E302.5.F46   2000
973.3—dc21   99-089686

9 8 7 6 5 4 3 2 1
Printed in the United States of America
on acid-free paper

To
the predawn fitness warriors, with whom I begin my days,
and
Carol and the cats, with whom I close my days

Contents

Preface

The swift appearance of the first histories of the American Revolution eased the worries of those activists who had wondered whether the struggle would be remembered. Yet those same histories aroused fresh concerns. Some believed that the initial historians had told a story that was unrecognizable. Some leaders had been slighted, or disappeared altogether, while the role played by others had been improbably magnified. By the early nineteenth century some old revolutionaries, including John Adams and Thomas Jefferson, had come to doubt that the history of the great events of their time, as well as the portrayal of the leading figures in the American Revolution, could ever be fully and accurately told. Adams once said that the record had been so muddied by self-seeking, embroidered, and outrightly fallacious accounts that it would be impossible to write an accurate history of the American Revolution. Jefferson was no less dismayed. A factual account of the events between 1763 and 1783 was possible, he declared, but what had occurred in private within the corridors of power, which he characterized as "the life and soul of history," was lost forever because of the paucity of accurate documentation.[1]

If Adams and Jefferson could read much that has been written in recent years about early American history, they would be more bewildered than exasperated. Committed to social history, and shaped by political correctness and multiculturalism, professional historians during the past quarter century by and large have neglected the role played by leaders in important events. Indeed, they often have ignored seminal events. Today the "only creature less fashionable in academe than the stereotypical 'dead white male,'" historian David Hackett Fischer has written, "is a dead white male on horseback."[2]

Where once the likes of Benjamin Franklin and James Madison, or epic events such as the French and Indian War or the Constitutional Convention, received considerable attention in the pages of scholarly journals, today's reader is more likely to read of the plight of urban chimney sweeps or unwed mothers.3 Historical conferences have taken the same route. Only two of sixty-two papers presented at the 1999 annual meeting of the Omohundro Institute of Early American History and Culture analyzed the activities of "dead white men." An equal number, naturally, scrutinized "dead white women." These trends are also apparent in college textbooks. The text I have used in my United States History survey classes in recent years, one that hardly differs from others in today's market, devotes roughly equal space to Phyllis Wheatley and Samuel Adams, and the section on the woes of the Loyalist exiles exceeds that which dissects the content of the Declaration of Independence.4

Why, then, a book about three dead white men? Why not go with the flow? Obstinacy aside, the genesis of this book, in one sense, occurred many years ago when I was an undergraduate, adrift and trying to find both myself and the academic major that I had to declare at the end of my sophomore year. I had ruled out a history major after three semesters of mind-numbing required courses that primarily involved factual memorization. The last history course in the core curriculum, a Western Civilization Since 1600 course, had begun in the same vein when the professor fell ill. Not surprisingly, he was replaced by a junior, untenured member of the history department. Dr. William Painter tore up the course syllabi during his first day in class and sent us to the bookstore to purchase several paperbacks. Two had an incandescent impact on me: Alan Bullock's biography of Adolf Hitler and Marcus Cunliffe's analytical study of George Washington.5 After eighteen months of pre-exam stints to commit to memory the Democratic Party platform of 1828 or the terms of the Hawley-Smoot Tariff, here was history that was fascinating. I found myself puzzling over what drove these men, why they were capable of leading others, what choices they had faced, and how they met the test of war and leadership. I soon decided not only that I wanted to take more history courses, but that someday I hoped to write like Professors Bullock and Cunliffe.

In another sense, the genesis of this book was an invitation to speak at an Honors' Day Convocation at the university where I teach. Having written biographies of Washington and John Adams, I was researching a biography of Jefferson, which seemed the logical next step, when I was approached about addressing the convocation. I was asked to contrast the formative years of Adams and Jefferson, probably in the hope that the experiences of these successful young men might provide useful lessons to our students. I accepted the invitation and began to formulate my address. The results were amazing; a comparison of Adams and Jefferson, I soon discovered, prompted questions that I had not previously asked, sent me on pathways of inquiry that I might never have traveled, and led to conclusions that otherwise I probably would not have reached. I abandoned the Jefferson biography for a comparative study of Washington, Adams, and Jefferson in the American Revolution.

One other matter was crucial. Although the recent scholarship has resulted in extraordinarily enriching breakthroughs in our understanding of people too long neglected, informing us with regard to how they lived and related to the larger social structure and material processes, sight has been all but lost of the relationship between leaders and outcomes, between action and events. Military leaders in the War of Independence made strategic and tactical decisions that impacted countless lives, determined the shape of the war and to some extent its length, and certainly were important to the outcome of the conflict. Their orders sometimes had repercussions on the contours of American history for generations to come. The texture of the war, the nature of the armed forces, and the shape of the new nation emerged from decisions made in legislative halls and, as Jefferson said, in covert discussions in back-room chambers. Political leaders communicated ideas to the citizenry. At times they created new ways of thinking about old problems and shepherded the citizenry, or some of it, along unchartered paths. They gave voice and meaning to previously ill-defined or unarticulated aspirations, and on occasion painted a visionary panacea for humankind to behold. Choices were made by diplomats in paneled drawing rooms across the sea that touched untold lives in North America. Among other things, their judgments sometimes caused men to soldier or go home, decided the fate of the unfree, and determined whether frontiers were to be opened or remain closed.

I wanted to put three leading figures in the American Revolution back into the crosshairs of history. I chose Washington, Adams, and Jefferson for scrutiny because they held the most crucial posts—military, congressional, diplomatic, gubernatorial—at the most crucial times during the rebellion and ensuing war.

What follows is a study of personality, character, aspirations, drives, choices, ideas, visions, leadership, and courage. Through the medium of comparative biography, this study attempts to link personal and impersonal elements in the contours of the American Revolution and the war that accompanied it. Many questions begged for answers: What forces shaped each of the three during his youth? What was each like as a mature young man before public affairs, and fame, changed everything? Why did each become a revolutionary? How did each meet the hard tests posed by crisis, danger, and leadership? What determined the behavior of each activist?

Doubtless, some who disdain the history of "dead white men" will protest that the real story of the American Revolution lay in the actions of ordinary people, not the leaders. They are correct to suggest the importance of the year-in, year-out service of the common soldier in dreadful camps and on perilous battlefields, or of women and children who faced opportunity and despair amid their lonely struggle against wartime adversity, and of bondsmen who glimpsed a window of hope for personal independence during the hazards of Anglo-American hostilities. But before leaders are discarded as irrelevant, the lesson taught 2,500 years ago by Lao Tsu should be remembered. When adroit leadership is provided, he said, sometimes "the people say, 'We did it ourselves.'"

My scholarly debts have grown to considerable portions in the course of the time required for this book to hatch. The journey began when Dr. Painter unwittingly fueled the tank and started the ignition in that Texas classroom, as well as in many discussions in his office that undoubtedly kept him from his own work. A number of scholars and, strange as it sounds, physicians read portions of the manuscript, sometimes when it was yet in the form of conference papers, articles submitted to journals, and speeches. I am grateful for the assistance, guidance, and direction provided by Joseph Ellis, Richard A. Ryerson, Edith B. Gelles, Richard D. Brown, Lewis Braverman, M.D., Margaret Humphreys, M.D., Samuel B. Thielman, M.D., Mary Miles, M.D., Michael McGiffert, Gregg L. Lint, Donald R. Hickey, and William C. Stinchcombe.

I appreciate the assistance of the Learning Resources Committee at the State University of West Georgia, which funded research trips to Charlottesville, Mount Vernon, and Boston. Nancy Farmer, and her staff in the Interlibrary Loan Office at the Ingram Library, cheerfully obtained mountainous quantities of books and articles for my perusal. Steve Taylor, my department chair during much of the time that the manuscript was percolating, not only arranged the Honors' Day address that was mentioned earlier and helped in focusing the theme of my remarks, but arranged my first, and only, leave of absence to facilitate work on this project. Ken Noe, my friend and colleague, listened patiently to my thoughts and ideas, and read a portion of the manuscript. John Fuller and Amy Hembree provided invaluable assistance. No one has been more important than Elmira Eidson, the secretary and most valued member in the History Department in which I teach. She has helped with—and solved—at least a thousand computer problems I encountered, assisted with ordering equipment, and, with her unremittingly sunny disposition, has brought cheer to many a cloudy day.

Finally to Carol, who has always been supportive and understanding.

October 1999 J.F.

PROLOGUE

"Embarked on a Most Tempestuous Sea"

July 1, 1776

On July 1, 1776, at headquarters in New York City, General George Washington awakened in the sultry pre-dawn stillness from a fitful night's sleep. Forty-eight hours earlier a Continental soldier, armed with a spyglass and posted atop a tall building on Broadway, had spotted the lead ships in a huge British armada. The long-awaited invasion of New York was at hand. By the time he retired on June 30, Washington knew that 110 sail had been counted in the fleet. He did not realize that he was about to tangle with the largest expeditionary force sent forth in the eighteenth century, but he knew that his untested Continental army was on the verge of "a hot Campaign," as he told Congress.[1]

Washington arose on July 1 before reveille, which was always at 5:00 AM. As was his custom, he shaved and dressed himself, and before breakfast worked at his desk in the pink-blue glaze of dawn for an hour or more. He read the overnight reports and letters, discovering still more bad news from the Canadian front, where for weeks a broken American army had been retreating. Now he learned in a communiqué from Colonel Benedict Arnold that one-half the men were ill and lacked adequate food and clothing. General John Sullivan reported that there would not be enough healthy men to carry out the sick if the army did not at once fall back into New York.[2]

Washington also discovered letters from numerous public officials. Most, like Benjamin Franklin, who wrote from Philadelphia, were ebullient. They expected the colonists's new army to repulse the British regulars and their hired German allies. However, some expressed oppressive doubts. They held their breath, believing that what happened in the campaign for New York would determine the outcome of the war. Some like timorous Joseph Hawley, a member of Massachusetts's Provincial Congress and an early advocate of American independence, had grown hysterical as the Battle of New York drew near. "My soul at times is ready to die within me. . . . My blood to press out at the pores of My Body," he shuddered. "The Lord have Mercy on us," he told Washington.[3]

Washington's recent behavior hinted that he too felt the mounting pressure. Since March he had rarely summoned councils of war to consider issues, but he convened his general officers on back-to-back days at the end of June. He suddenly complained to Congress of having inadequate men and supplies, took decisive steps to sequester or impede the movement of suspected Tories, ordered extraordinarily harsh floggings for two convicted deserters, and authorized the first execution of a Continental soldier in the yearlong history of his army, a sergeant who, despite the flimsiest of evidence, had been sentenced to die by a court martial for aiding and abetting Loyalist saboteurs.[4]

On June 29 and 30 Washington had appealed to the authorities in Massachusetts, New Jersey, Pennsylvania, and New York to hurry militia units to Manhattan. He ordered his officers to allocate twenty-five rounds of powder and ball to each militiaman, and to inspect each soldier's equipment. To "be well prepared . . . is more than half the battle," Washington counseled. He advised that the first round fired by each man was to consist of buckshot, which would spray widely and lethally. That shot, he added, should not be fired until the enemy soldiers were within twenty-five to thirty yards of the American lines. If they followed his orders, the commander told his men, he did not doubt that the enemy would be repulsed.[5]

Washington issued orders on July 1 for the removal of all livestock on Staten Island and various coastal areas where the British and Germans might land. Although he had been gradually integrating work battalions into infantry units, Washington also ordered work parties to Jew's and Bayard's Hills to dig last-minute emplacements. He admonished the men to labor diligently from sunrise to sunset, yet, adhering to the work ethic of the era, Washington allotted a three-hour lunch break.[6]

Following his usual light breakfast, Washington left headquarters, a two-story, columned house situated near the Hudson River, almost a mile above the city in the lush pastures of Lispenard's Meadows. He mounted his great white horse and rode slowly under the fierce sun, through thickets of tall weeds and across barren stretches where redoubts had been constructed. He stopped now and again to remind his officers that the night sentries must now exercise even greater vigilance. Although he had done so dozens of times, he once again inspected the earthworks his army had prepared. The "hour of attack seems fast approaching," Washington reiterated throughout his ride, and indeed during the day messengers brought word that British regulars had landed on undefended Staten Island, their staging area for the assault. News also arrived that the British fleet contained several men-of-war, the largest fighting ship of the day, each armed with fifty or more cannon. It was mid-afternoon when Washington, sweaty and tired, returned to headquarters. He completed his afternoon repast more quickly than usual, then excused himself to write one more letter. With the late day's sunlight streaming into his private chamber, he wrote an acquaintance in Boston. His adversary, General William Howe, the commander of the British army in America, would attack soon, Washington said. "I am making every preparation to receive him."[7]

Philadelphia, a hundred miles further south, was hotter and stickier than Manhattan. By 9:00 on the morning of July 1 the blood-red line of Thomas Jefferson's thermometer had already climbed into the mid-eighties. Like Washington, most members of the Continental Congress rose early on this morning. Although Congress would not convene until 10:00, many members sat on committees that met daily soon after breakfast. Furthermore, every congressman understood that this was a special day. The tedium that characterized most congressional sessions was to be broken by a vote on "the great question of Independency and Total Separation from all political intercourse with Great Britain," as a North Carolinian wrote to a friend at home. Congress had drifted with painstaking slowness toward this day since the outbreak of war with Great Britain fifteen months earlier. On June 10 it had agreed to take up the question of American independence three weeks hence, on Monday, July 1. Not everyone was happy. The most conservative members yearned for reconciliation with the mother country. Others, guided by excessive caution, thought it prudent to postpone independence until considerable foreign assistance had been secured.[8]

However, no one believed that the foes of immediate independence could win this day's battle. Those whom Congressman Elbridge Gerry of Massachusetts called the "slow people" had been overcome by those whom he called the "vigorous." Three days before, on Friday, Congressman Joseph

Hewes predicted that the motion on independence "will be carried I expect by a great Majority and then I suppose we shall take upon us a New Name."[9]

No one was more delighted by the prospect of independence than John Adams, the fubsy, churlish delegate from Massachusetts. As early as February he had known that the reconciliationists in Congress could not delay the formal break with Great Britain for more than a few weeks longer. By April he believed that America in reality was already independent. Homage to the monarchy and affection for the mother country had withered. Weeks before this July morning, back in the chill of spring, Adams's barber had told him how he and his fellow artisans who drank at the Bunch of Grapes Tavern had begun to toast "The free and independent States of America." Furthermore, like a sovereign nation, Congress not only had sought trade outside the British empire, it had sent an envoy to Paris to seek French assistance. Weeks before the summer languors set in, Adams had written home that Congress was "hastening rapidly to great Events."[10]

In mid-May Adams had remarked that there was "something very unnatural and odious in a Government 1000 Leagues off." Americans deserved a government "of our own Choice, managed by Persons whom We Love, revere, and confide in," he added. He knew that America was in the midst of a great revolution, and, as a revolutionary, he understood the dangers he faced. The British had dispatched "several very powerfull Armaments against Us," he remarked. He reminded himself that courage, industry, perseverance, and prayers were essential to ride through this storm. Privately, he confronted the likelihood that his actions could lead to his death, but Adams took comfort in the sublime possibility of dying a patriot. "What a fragrant memory remains" when one dies for his country, he reflected.[11]

Adams customarily arose before sunrise. His behavior on July 1 was no different. He lodged at Sarah Yard's boardinghouse at Walnut and Second, across from the City Tavern, Philadelphia's most notable inn, and just three blocks east of the State House, where Congress met. The entire Massachusetts delegation—Gerry, congenial John Hancock, stern and opinionated Samuel Adams, and good-natured Robert Treat Paine—lived at Mrs. Yard's, a stone house that some dubbed "Liberty Hall," while other, less friendly colleagues spoke of it contemptuously as "Headquarters," for Massachusetts usually got its way.[12]

Like Washington, Adams began this day, every day in fact, at his little desk. He conducted a voluminous correspondence with family, political allies at home, and revolutionary activists throughout the colonies. On this morning, in his close, still room, straining to see by the light of a single candle, Adams composed a letter in his distinctive, stubby handwriting. He told Archibald Bulloch, his former colleague in Congress, who had recently been elected President of Georgia, that "the greatest Debate of all" was scheduled for that day. He added that the outcome was certain, and prayed that "Heaven prosper the new born Republic—and make it more glorious than any former Republics have been." The letter, like so many that Adams wrote, was lengthy. He reported the disasters in Canada and added that the new American nation must regain the lost territory. He tendered better tidings about the war at sea, where American privateers had captured numerous prizes, but Adams, who was unrelentingly candid, advised Bulloch to anticipate a long war. The "conflict must be bloody . . . and We must expect a great Expence of Blood" before victory was attained, he said. To avoid further disasters, the leaders and citizens must be wiser, more industrious, and less selfish. Just prior to leaving for the State House, Adams completed the letter: "We should always remember, that a free Constitution of civil Government cannot be purchased at too dear a Rate."[13]

Jefferson awakened that morning in an apartment across town. During the initial phase of his congressional service, between June and December 1775, he had lived only a few steps from Adams's residence. However, upon his return in May from a lengthy visit at home, Jefferson had moved to the corner of Market and Seventh Street, west of the State House. He had rented a second-floor parlor and bedroom in the narrow, three-story, red brick home of Jacob Graff, a successful mason. Jefferson moved because many summer days in Philadelphia were exactly like this torrid day, and he believed Graff's house would provide greater shelter from the city's "excessive heats."[14]

Jefferson's correspondence was minuscule compared with that of Washington and Adams. Seldom a day passed when the other two did not write at least one letter, but Jefferson customarily set aside one day each week for writing. One theme recurred in the few letters he had written during the past six weeks: he yearned to be in Williamsburg, where the Virginia Convention had begun work on the province's first constitution. Had he had his way, Jefferson would not have been in Philadelphia on July 1.[15]

Soon after rising that morning, Jefferson entered his parlor and sat in a Windsor chair that he had purchased during his stay in Philadelphia. He put across his lap a ten-by-fourteen-inch portable writing desk made for him by his previous Philadelphia landlord, an accomplished cabinetmaker, and penned a letter to an old friend, William Fleming, a Virginia judge. Canada was uppermost on Jefferson's mind. He believed the American retreat would soon end and the Continentals would make an "effectual stand." Washington and Adams did not share that view, nor did they believe, like Jefferson, that this would be a short war, lasting perhaps no more than six months. He only briefly alluded to his activities since June 10, when together with Adams and three others, he had been appointed to a committee to prepare a statement on American independence. Within a few days, he told Judge Fleming, "my political creed in the form of a 'Declaration &c.'" would be public knowledge.[16]

When his letter was written, Adams shaved and dressed, walked to a nearby tavern for breakfast, then hurried to the State House for a meeting of the Board of War and Ordinance, a congressional committee that he chaired. His three-block stroll along Walnut Street took him past family-owned shops, handsome residences with cheerful gardens, a steepled church, gambrel-roofed rowhouses, a bleak almshouse, a simple Quaker school, and gaily painted inns and taverns. Jefferson, who did not leave his residence until after 9:00, likely walked one block east to Sixth Street, then two blocks south to Walnut. Although the heat was nearly intolerable, the streets bustled with shaggy, dusty horses pulling heavy wagons, stout women, with children in tow, hurrying to street markets, and artisans and sinewy laborers carrying wares to and from businesses.

Adams dwelled in Philadelphia's South Ward, Jefferson in the Middle Ward. Nearly ten percent of Philadelphia's inhabitants, about 2,500 persons, were packed into these two small districts that comprised an area just two blocks wide and seven blocks long. Most of the residents in this part of Philadelphia were middle-class denizens—the "middling sort," colonists were wont to say—and the lion's share were skilled artisans, but members of the upper and lower ends of the social and economic spectrum dwelled here too. The governor of Pennsylvania resided near the State House, as did physicians, pharmacists, teachers, and nearly fifty shopkeepers and merchants. Franklin owned a house that fronted on Market Street, near the city post office and only a few hundred yards from the residences of Adams and Jefferson. Free servants and more than 150 impecunious unfree persons, indentured servants and slaves, lived in this section of Philadelphia as well. They were packed alongside the families of unskilled laborers in tiny apartments in the dark, mephitic back alleys.[17]

As the starting time for the congressional session neared, Jefferson and Adams were joined at the State House by most of their forty-six colleagues.

Congress had met for the past fifteen months at the Pennsylvania State House, a quarter-century-old brick structure built in the manner of a long Georgian house. Congress occupied the first floor. Its host, the Pennsylvania assembly, met simultaneously directly above. Congress's chamber, which looked capacious when empty, was close and cramped when all the delegates pressed in and took their seats on hard, wooden chairs that surrounded plain, circular tables without drawers. Tall windows, which were nearly always shut to muffle the rich cacophony of outdoor sounds and preserve the secrecy of the proceedings, ran the length of the south wall. The other walls were adorned with rich, dark paneling, and one boasted a British drum, sword, and regimental flag captured by a colonial force at Fort Ticonderoga in the first days of the war. The secretary of Congress, and its president, Congressman Hancock, occupied a dais before their colleagues.[18]

Hancock rapped on his desk at a minute or two past 10:00 to convene the session. Conversations ended, some more gradually than others, and Congress proceeded with business. First, letters from general officers, including those of Washington on the preparations in New York, were read. Congress then took up the principal issue for the day. A Virginia resolution urging American independence, which first had been presented on June 7, was reread:

Resolved, That these United Colonies are, and of right ought to be, free and independent states, that they are absolved from all allegiance to the British Crown, and that all political connection between them and the state of Great Britain is, and ought to be, totally dissolved.[19]

Congress quickly reorganized into a committee of the whole for the purpose of considering the question, but before it could proceed word arrived that the Maryland Convention had voted to instruct its delegates to vote for independence. Everyone knew that New York's delegates, who had not been authorized by its provincial assembly to vote for independence, would abstain on that day's vote. Many now assumed that Pennsylvania alone might cast a negative vote.

At last, Congress was indeed ready to formally consider American independence. Many years later Adams recalled that he had not expected any discussion on the issue of independence because the matter had been disputed in one form or another on scores of occasions during the past several months. But his recollection was probably incorrect. In his letter that morning to Bulloch, Adams had written of anticipating a grand "debate."[20]

The moment the floor was opened for discussion, John Dickinson of Pennsylvania rose to address Congress. A prominent Philadelphia attorney, he had been active in Delaware and Pennsylvania politics for a generation. He had openly denounced British taxation of America before Washington, Adams, or Jefferson took public stands. He had attended the Stamp Act Congress in 1765 and two years later authored the pre-war period's most widely read tract condemning Britain's imperial policies. Dickinson supported the war against the mother country, but did not favor independence, and on this day, in this nearly suffocating room, he spoke from prepared notes on the issue for several hours.

Dickinson knew that his opposition to independence would be futile. He was aware too that his stand would destroy what he strangely characterized as his "once too great . . . Popularity." Yet he felt compelled to speak out, for he was certain that the soon to be created nation was unequal to the exigencies of independence. For America to attempt to stand alone in 1776, he warned, was akin to sailing on stormy seas in a paper skiff. Although a hint of doleful resignation showed through, Dickinson spoke in a calm, reasoned, forceful manner.

A proclamation of independence, he said at the outset, was needless. It was not required to boost morale, which was at a fever pitch, nor was it essential for procuring foreign assistance. France and Spain would enter the war if it was in their interest to do so, regardless of American entreaties or actions. An American declaration of independence could be harmful, he cautioned. Such a step might tempt Great Britain to partition North America, purchasing French and Spanish neutrality with proffers of their former territories in North America.

It was more prudent, Dickinson went on, to fight for reconciliation on American terms. Such a war would be shorter, less brutal, and its outcome more certain. Great Britain had not succeeded in crushing the rebellion in the first year of the war. If it failed in 1776, it was likely, he said, that the mother country would "redress all the Grievances complained of" by the First Continental Congress on the eve of the war. The American colonies would then be autonomous in their domestic affairs, enjoy a freer trade than ever before, savor the economic benefits of the world's greatest empire, and rejoice in peace and security for generations to come.

No one interrupted Dickinson. His speech extended beyond 1:00 PM, until exhausted by his enterprise and the heat, he at last drew to a conclusion. In the British empire, he closed, the "commonwealth of colonies" would remain united in peace, freedom, and prosperity, but, if independent, the provinces soon would be separated into hostile unions divided at the Hudson River.[21]

Adams listened to the speech with growing impatience, thinking this "an idle Mispense of Time," for Dickinson had added nothing new. Adams's view was colored by his dislike of Dickinson. When the two first had met in 1774 at the initial Congress, Adams warmly described his colleague as friendly and intelligent. However, their relationship soured following the outbreak of the war, when Adams emerged as the leader of the faction that favored independence and Dickinson of those who sought an accommodation with Great Britain. They broke irreparably in the spring of 1775 when Dickinson, with uncharacteristic intemperance, rebuked Adams and charged that he had blood on his hands for having opposed reconciliation. Adams never forgave Dickinson, and never again spoke to him. Thereafter, he thought him weak and timid, and gave credence to the baseless rumor making the rounds that an uxorious Dickinson opposed independence because his mother insisted that he take such a stand.[22]

Because of his strained relationship with Dickinson, Adams hoped someone else would respond, perhaps someone from the committee that had crafted a declaration on independence, but an anxious silence ensued. Jefferson and Franklin, who had served with Adams on the independence committee, hated contention and rarely spoke in congressional debates; in addition, Franklin, though present, was weak from a recent affliction of the gout. When it was clear that no one would answer Dickinson, Adams rose. Dickinson, he said later, had spoken "not only with great Ingenuity and Eloquence, but with equal Politeness and Candour." Adams thought it imperative that he reply in a similarly disarming manner.[23]

Like Dickinson, Adams spoke at length, until near Congress's customary time for adjournment. He did not speak from a text. Notes were unnecessary. He had responded to Dickinson and his allies on numerous occasions. Adams reiterated familiar themes: the colonists should sever their ties with corrupt, tyrannous Britain; America could be better governed by Americans than by nabobs across the sea; once free of the empire's commercial fetters, America would prosper as never before; in a long war morale would remain higher if the object of the fighting was independence and self-government; and, victory hinged on foreign assistance, which was likely only if America declared independence.

As Adams spoke, the white filigreed clouds of early morning blackened, and thunder could be heard in the distance. In mid-afternoon the sun disappeared and Philadelphia grew quite dark. Candles were lit in the congressional chamber. The thunder grew louder. Swollen raindrops splattered on the tall windows. A flash of lightening was followed in an instant by a crash of thunder. The rain lashed in sheets.

Adams continued through the havoc of the storm. He paused only when three or four newly elected New Jersey congressmen, who had reached Philadelphia just that afternoon, entered the chamber. Richard Stockton, one of the new congressmen, pleaded with Adams to summarize his earlier remarks. Adams was reluctant, self-consciously thinking that to do so would be akin to an actor who entertained an audience by speaking memorized lines. Nevertheless, when several congressmen insisted that he "must recapitulate the arguments," he obliged, though he began by confessing that he now wished for the oratorical skills of a Demosthenes. He performed adroitly, causing Jefferson to later remember Adams's "deep conceptions, nervous style, and undaunted firmness" that made him "our bulwark" in the fight for independence.[24]

It was deep into the afternoon before Adams finished. The sudden summer storm had passed. Philadelphia was cooler and a gentle, refreshing breeze sweetened the air. The congressional chamber was almost comfortable. After Adams took his seat, one delegate after another rose to speak. Once again, however, nothing was said "but what had been repeated and hackneyed in that room before an hundred Times, for Six Months past," Adams sighed. The long shadows of early evening splayed across the State House yard by the time the debate ended. The delegates were extremely tired. Congress had not taken a moment's break since this session began. Most congressmen had last eaten twelve hours or so earlier. Some had taken no liquid refreshment since breakfast. Jefferson remarked that "all the powers of the soul had been distended with the magnitude of the object" on this day.[25]

The delegates were ready, anxious even, to vote. Two votes would be required. First, a committee vote, for Congress had met that day as a committee of the whole. Then the legislators would reconstitute themselves as Congress and the formal vote on American independence would be made. Virginia's motion was read once again.

Several candles illuminated the half-dark chamber as the voting began. The secretary, Charles Thomson of Pennsylvania, called on each colony. Nine voted yes: Connecticut, Georgia, Maryland, Massachusetts, North Carolina, New Hampshire, New Jersey, Rhode Island, and Virginia. Although some members of the delegations from Pennsylvania and South Carolina supported independence, a majority of the two delegations cast negative ballots. Only two of Delaware's three delegates were present, and they divided. That colony, in effect, had not voted. Nor did New York vote. It abstained, as expected. Some delegates were surprised, startled really, by the vote. Only Pennsylvania had been thought a likely roadblock to unanimity, and there had been considerable optimism that in the end its delegates would join in the vote for independence.[26]

At last, Congress was ready to vote. But to prevent the epic vote from falling considerably short of unanimity, Edward Rutledge of South Carolina, a twenty-six-year-old lawyer, and the youngest man in the room, rose to suggest that the vote be deferred to the next day. He said candidly that he believed his delegation would change its vote overnight. Congress quickly accepted his motion. It was 7:00 PM. Nine hours had passed since Hancock had gaveled this marathon session to order.

Although the official vote would come the next day, the congressmen viewed what lay ahead as anticlimactic. "The affair of Independency has been this day determined, Josiah Bartlett of New Hampshire wrote home shortly after Congress adjourned. Adams reflected on the sudden change in sentiment among his countrymen. He remembered that a scant thirty months earlier, before the Boston Tea Party, no one had considered breaking with the mother country. Before January 1776 none dared to openly urge American independence.[27] Other congressmen were in a reflective mood that evening as well. All knew that their difficulties had only just begun. Abraham Clark of New Jersey, the son of a farmer who grew up to be a self-taught lawyer, had arrived that afternoon during Adams's speech and a couple hours later, in his first vote as a congressman, declared for independence. Later, in the unruffled calm of his apartment following his initial day in Congress, Clark noted that the thirteen states—he believed they now had ceased to be colonies—had "embarked on a most Tempestuous Sea" with "dangers Scattered thick around us." Things could end badly, he wrote. If so, he added: "Let us prepare for the worst, we can Die but once."[28]

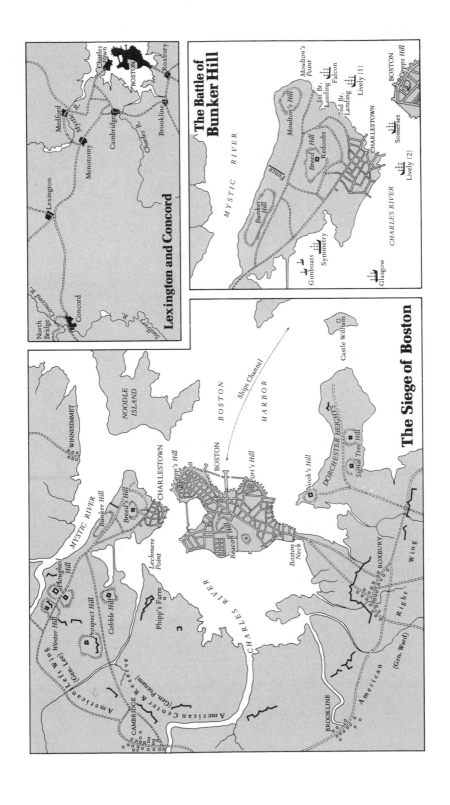

Lexington and Concord

Charles Town
BOSTON
Roxbury
Medford
Mystic R.
Cambridge
Brookline
Charles R.
Menotomy
Lexington
North Bridge
Concord
Concord R.
Sudbury R.

The Battle of Bunker Hill

MYSTIC RIVER
Moulton's Point
Moulton's Hill
1st Br. Landing
2nd Br. Landing
Falcon
Lively (1)
BOSTON
Copps Hill
Breed's Hill
Redoubt
Somerset
Fence
CHARLESTOWN
Lively (2)
Bunker Hill
CHARLES RIVER
Gunboats
Symmetry
Glasgow

The Siege of Boston

WINNISIMMET
NOODLE ISLAND
BOSTON
BOSTON HARBOR
Ships Channel
Castle William
CHARLESTOWN
Copp's Hill
Fort's Hill
Nook's Hill
DORCHESTER HEIGHTS
Signal Tree Hill
Breed's Hill
Bunker Hill
Beacon Hill
Boston Neck
ROXBURY
MYSTIC RIVER
Lechmere Point
Ploughed Hill
Prospect Hill
Cobble Hill
Winter Hill
Phipp's Farm
CHARLES RIVER
American Left Wing (Gen. Lee)
CAMBRIDGE
American Center & Reserve (Gen. Putnam)
American Right Wing (Gen. Ward)
BROOKLINE

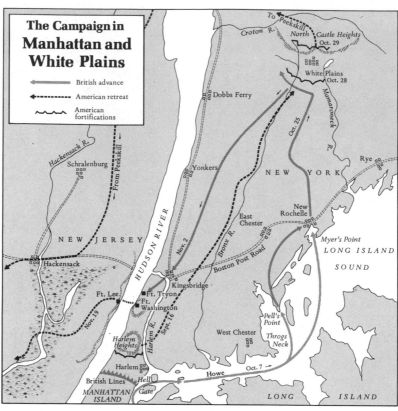

The Campaign in Manhattan and White Plains

→ British advance
→ American retreat
～ American fortifications

To Peekskill
Croton R.
North Castle Heights
Oct. 29
White Plains
Oct. 28
Mamaroneck R.
Dobbs Ferry
Oct. 25
Hackensack R.
Schralenburg
From Peekskill
Yonkers
NEW YORK
Rye
NEW JERSEY
Nov. 2
East Chester
New Rochelle
Myer's Point
LONG ISLAND
SOUND
Hackensack
HUDSON RIVER
Bronx R.
Boston Post Road
Nov. 19
Ft. Lee
Kingsbridge
Ft. Tryon
Ft. Washington
Sept. 16
West Chester
Pell's Point
Throgs Neck
Harlem R.
Harlem Heights
Harlem
British Lines
Hell Gate
MANHATTAN ISLAND
Howe
Oct. 7 →
LONG
ISLAND

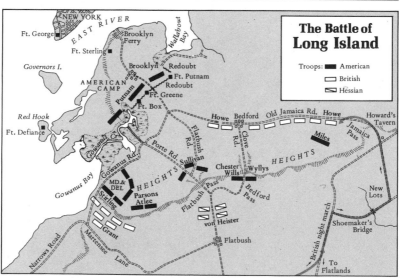

The Battle of Long Island

Troops: ■ American
□ British
▨ Hessian

NEW YORK
EAST RIVER
Ft. George
Brooklyn Ferry
Wallabout Bay
Ft. Sterling
Governors I.
Brooklyn
Redoubt
AMERICAN CAMP
Ft. Putnam
Putnam
Redoubt
Ft. Greene
Ft. Box
Howe
Bedford
Old Jamaica Rd.
Howe
Howard's Tavern
Red Hook
Miles
Jamaica Pass
Ft. Defiance
Gowanus Cr.
Flatbush Rd.
Clove Rd.
Porte Rd.
Sullivan
Chester
Wills
Wyllys
HEIGHTS
Gowanus Rd.
MD.& DEL.
Sterling
HEIGHTS
Parsons
Atlee
Flatbush Pass
Bedford Pass
New Lots
Gowanus Bay
Grant
von Heister
Shoemaker's Bridge
Narrows Road
Martense Lane
Flatbush
British night march
To Flatlands

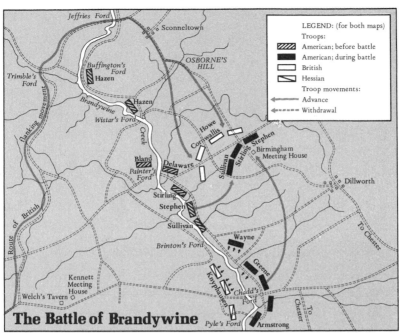

The Battle of Brandywine

LEGEND: (for both maps)
Troops:
American; before battle
American; during battle
British
Hessian
Troop movements:
Advance
Withdrawal

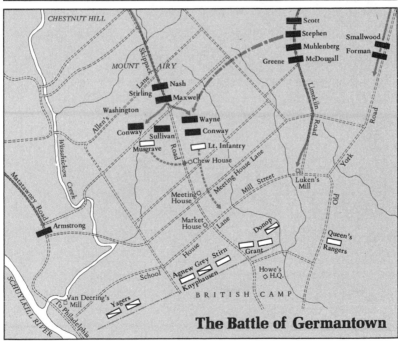

The Battle of Germantown

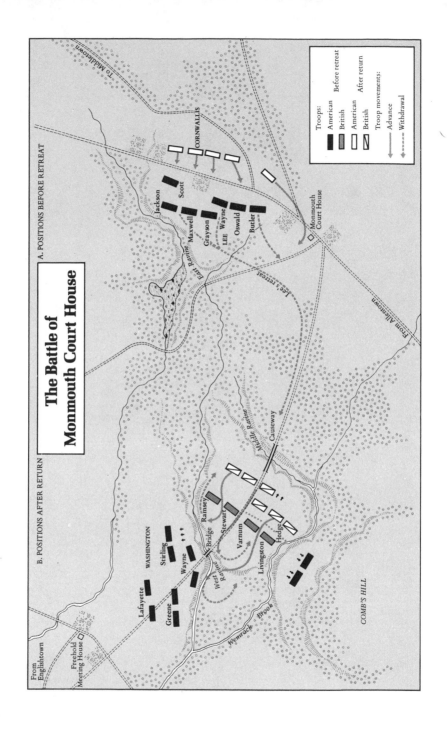

The Battle of Monmouth Court House

A. POSITIONS BEFORE RETREAT

B. POSITIONS AFTER RETURN

Troops:

American	Before retreat
British	
American	After return
British	

Troop movements:

Advance

Withdrawal

CORNWALLIS

Jackson

Scott

Maxwell

Grayson

Wayne

LEE

Oswald

Butler

East Ravine

Lee's retreat

Monmouth Court House

From Allentown

Middle Ravine

Causeway

To Middletown

Ramsey

Stewart

Varnum

Livingston

Hedge

Bridge

Westbrook

Lafayette

Greene

WASHINGTON

Stirling

Wayne

Wemrock Brook

COMB'S HILL

From
Englishtown

Freehold
Meeting House

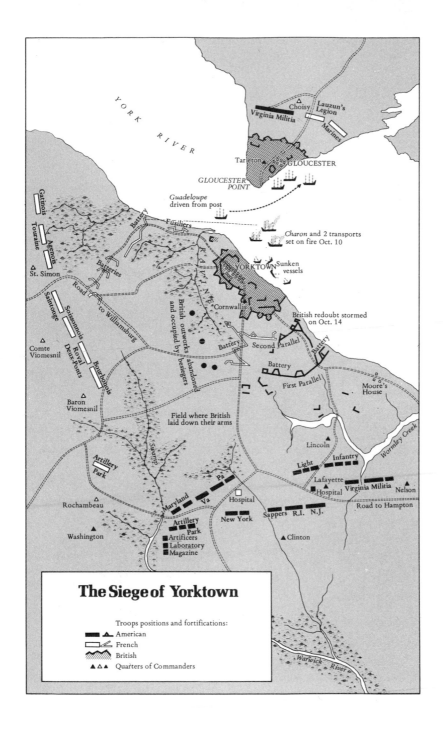

Y O R K   R I V E R

Choisy △ Lauzun's Legion
Virginia Militia

Marines

Tarleton GLOUCESTER

GLOUCESTER POINT

Guadeloupe driven from post

Charon and 2 transports set on fire Oct. 10

Sunken vessels

Gatinois
Touraine
Agenois

Battery
Fusiliers

St. Simon △

Batteries

YORKTOWN

Saintonge
Soissonois
Royal Deux-Ponts

Road to Williamsburg

British outworks abandoned and occupied by besiegers

Cornwallis

British redoubt stormed on Oct. 14

Comte Viomesnil △

Second Parallel

Battery

Bourbonois

Battery

Baron Viomesnil △

Battery

First Parallel

Moore's House

Field where British laid down their arms

Wormley Creek

Lincoln △

Swamp

Light   Infantry

Artillery Park

Lafayette △
Hospital   Virginia Militia   Nelson △

Rochambeau △

Maryland   Va

Pa

Hospital

Road to Hampton

Washington △

Artillery Park
Artificers
Laboratory
Magazine

New York

Sappers   R.I.   N.J.

Clinton △

The Siege of Yorktown

Troops positions and fortifications:

━━━ ▲ American
▭ ◁ French
〰〰 British
▲ △ ▲ Quarters of Commanders

Warwick   River

George Washington in the uniform of the Virginia Regiment. Painting by Charles Willson Peale, 1772. (Washington and Lee University)

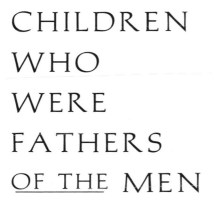

CHILDREN
WHO
WERE
FATHERS
OF THE MEN

1

"The Strong Desire of Distinction"

The Vagaries Of Youth

On a soft rainy morning in February 1760 George Washington set out to superintend the work of his slaves and artisans at Mount Vernon. He discovered that his carpenters, who had been told to saw and hew poplar trees, had made little progress. "Sat down therefore and observed," he noted in his diary later that day, knowing that his presence would make them work more diligently.[1]

A week or so later John Adams, a young attorney in Boston, sat at his desk before the fireplace in his simple, cold New England home. He wrote a friend that he feared he would be "totally forgotten within 70 Years from the present Hour." Driven by a rapturous dream of being famous throughout the ages, he told his friend that he was studying the lives of the great lawyers of antiquity for clues to their immortality. He was certain that he possessed the tools and character for greatness, he added, but wondered whether "Heaven ... [would] furnish the proper Means and Opportunities" for him to exhibit his talents.[2]

On almost that same morning, a clear winter day when the temperature never rose above freezing, Thomas Jefferson, a student in a preparatory school in Virginia, wrote to his guardian requesting that he be permitted to begin college. Not only was it an important step in his education, he said, but there was a practical factor to consider as well. He would make acquaintances who might be useful later in life.[3]

Early in 1760 Washington, Adams, and Jefferson were yet young men.

Washington was twenty-eight, Adams twenty-four, and Jefferson was on the eve of his seventeenth birthday. Washington had already "distinguished [himself] . . . from the *common run* of men," as he put it.[4] He was a military hero and a respected planter. He assumed that he had achieved the pinnacle of his ambitions. What remained was merely to grow wealthier. Adams and Jefferson were just beginning, but they too were ambitious. Adams had set his sights on a future in which he would be richly rewarded with recognition and renown. Jefferson was less certain about what he wanted. He knew only that he was unfulfilled and sought something that would bring him greater happiness.

Many years later, in 1813, Adams confessed to Jefferson that he had been an ambitious youngster, but in his greatest flights of fancy, he added, he had dreamt of a career capped by a comfortable income and election to the Massachusetts assembly.[5] Washington and Jefferson, each of whom had ties to Virginia's aristocracy, hoped for greater material rewards than young Adams knew existed. However, like Adams, neither young Washington nor Jefferson could have imagined what they would eventually achieve. Each was ambitious, but each understood there had to be limits to their aspirations, for the stage on which aspiring colonists were made to play was circumscribed by the very fact that they were colonists.

Washington and Jefferson began life in somewhat similar worlds.[6] Each was born into a wealthy and prestigious family that lived in a newly settled region of Virginia. Washington was born in 1732 at Wakefield, a planter's country home located near where Pope's Creek emptied into the wide, blue-green Potomac River in the province's Northern Neck. Jefferson was born in 1743 at Shadwell, a planter's seat nestled amid 1,400 acres in the jade green hills of frontier Albemarle County. The world that Adams entered could hardly have been more different. He was the son of farmers in Braintree, Massachusetts, a small New England village eight miles south of Boston.[7]

Each occupied a strategic point in the birthing order within his family. In an age in which the eldest son often was favored over the other children, Adams was the firstborn. Two siblings preceded Jefferson, but he too was the first son. Washington was one of seven surviving children from his father's two marriages and the third son sired by Augustine Washington, but he was the first male offspring of his father's second marriage.

While still adolescents, Washington and Jefferson lost their fathers. Augustine Washington had grown up in Virginia in comfortable circumstances and attended school in England for a few years. He married the sixteen-year-old daughter of a prosperous planter, became a successful farmer, wisely speculated in land, constructed an iron furnace that produced more wealth than the tobacco he raised, and soon held several local offices. When George was three, Augustine built a more substantial plantation, Epsewasson, situated atop a bluff overlooking the Potomac. Three years later he purchased Ferry Farm, a 300-acre tract across the meandering Rappahannock River from Fredericksburg. The Washingtons had come a considerable distance since George's greatgrandfather, a down-on-his-luck merchant seaman, had settled in America more than a century earlier. Each generation thereafter lived more comfortably than its predecessor, flourishing through industry and acumen, and advantageous marriages, until Augustine had accumulated three houses and twenty slaves. But when George was only eleven, Augustine died suddenly, likely the victim of one of the silent fevers that stalked tidewater Virginia.[8]

Peter Jefferson was also obsessed with wealth and status. Through self-study, he learned to survey, a fast track to a modest fortune in eighteenth-century Virginia, as speculators and land-hungry settlers were rapidly pushing into the western reaches of the province. Peter accumulated sufficient land and chattel to attain a planter's status. He too married well. With the aid of his wife's fortune, he built Shadwell, a gentleman's house that he modeled on the rural dwellings of the middling English gentry. With a penchant for learning, Peter accumulated a considerable library and eventually gained a reputation in Virginia as a cartographer and explorer. Like Augustine Washington, he was a large and powerful man. His son liked to tell the story of watching as a boy as three muscular slaves struggled in vain to pull down an old outbuilding. With a laugh Peter "bade them stand aside, seized the rope and dragged down the structure in an instant," Thomas recollected. By the mid-eighteenth century the Jeffersons had also come a long way since the first member of the family, a hunter and surveyor, appeared in the colony in the 1670s. Peter owned approximately six times the amount of land and vastly more slaves than his grandfather. But at age forty-nine, he fell prey to a fever and died. Thomas was fourteen when his father died.[9]

Despite their early demise, Augustine and Peter influenced their sons. The "breeching of a boy," as people said in early Virginia, occurred at age five or six. The youngster then was dressed in a man's garments for the first time and entered a masculine world. Thereafter, he spent more time with his father than his mother. The father, in fact, often sought to temper the bond that had thus far developed between the boy and his mother. The boy was taught to ride, accompanied his father on business trips and joined him at races and cock-fights, was given responsibility for delivering messages to nearby plantations, observed his father's supervision of the plantation, including the land, overseers, and chattel, and often was presented with his own slave. Most fathers fostered obedience and respect in their sons, but they also endeavored to fashion young men who would be self-reliant. Little attempt was made to eradicate willful or autonomous behavior. Indeed, these little planters learned lessons designed to serve them in a society of hierarchy and deference. They were schooled in the ways of gentility, taught the appropriate dress, demeanor, manners, and conversational style of a gentleman, learned a code of honor and dignity that would distinguish them from their social inferiors, and were made to understand that a planter aristocrat was not to be servile to others.[10]

Augustine and Peter were daring, driven men who resonated authority and mastery. Each was accustomed to having his way. Each was a man of action who introduced his son to a masculine world that extolled heartiness, resilience, courage, and resourcefulness. Washington grew up to resemble his father in significant ways, especially in seeing virtue in diligence, boldness, enterprise, vitality, and self-control. Peter Jefferson explained the mysteries of nature and the forest to his son, made a horseman of him, acquainted him with guns, and taught him to survey. Thomas would emulate his father's industry and consuming materialism, but he especially admired his father for having striven to improve himself intellectually.[11]

John Adams's father, Deacon John Adams, lived to age seventy-two, dying in 1761 when his son was a young adult. A tradition of upward mobility prevailed in the Adams clan. The first member of the family to live in America had arrived in Massachusetts a century prior to John's birth. He had earned a living as a farmer and maltster. Each generation thereafter achieved a slightly higher status. John's father was no exception. Denied a formal education, Deacon Adams earned a living from a fifty-acre farm and as a shoemaker, a trade he turned to when the long Massachusetts winters forbade working the land. Through his industry, and because he too had married into a prominent family, Deacon Adams acquired more property and achieved greater prestige in Braintree than his father. Although he was without influence beyond Braintree's borders, Deacon Adams was part of the town's elite. He was elected nine times to the board of selectmen, or city council, and was an officer in the local militia. As his title suggests, he also served often as an important lay official in his church. Deacon Adams was never a wealthy man.

At his death his estate was valued at £1,330, a comfortable middle-class level in the 1760s, yet sufficient for him to send a son to Harvard, an undertaking that cost roughly the equivalent of four years income for most skilled artisans. He was the first among the American Adamses who could afford to consider a college education for one of his sons.[12]

Deacon Adams, who was forty years old when John was born, had been reared in the late seventeenth century, before New England was transformed from a Puritan to a Yankee society. The product of an era that accented religious-based values, he did not appreciate the new Yankee ethos of the eighteenth century that placed greater emphasis on enjoying life. His son's age identified self-interest with personal independence, and legitimated the pursuit of individual objectives, including the quest of fame and fortune. The Puritans had denounced these traits as seductive vices, if they became life's driving force. Although in John's youth a sense of human self-worth and a liberation of the human will gradually replaced the foreboding sense of human depravity and wickedness that had prevailed earlier, Deacon Adams remained a Puritan among Yankees, a man tethered to the values of a bygone era.[13]

The parents were the moral custodians under Deacon Adams's roof. The Adamses almost certainly conducted daily religious exercises that included prayers and Bible readings, as well as catechetical recitation and scrutiny of the previous Sunday's sermon. Deacon Adams was the teacher. He preached the Puritan message that sloth was evil and work was to be esteemed. He taught that it was proper to enjoy the fruits of honest labor, but disparaged idolatry of wealth. He castigated ambition, pride, and longing, as well as drunkenness, swearing, lying, sex without a marriage contract, and litigiousness.[14]

An emphasis on virtue was an enduring theme in this family. The Deacon would have defined virtuous behavior, as John later interpreted it, as "a Life of Industry, Temperance, and Honour." Deacon Adams also insisted, as many ministers still did, that the Fifth Commandment mandated that virtuous behavior consisted of a becoming subordination and respect toward parents, elders, siblings, and public authority figures. The Deacon hammered into his sons that the sublimation of self-will was essential in a virtuous person. It was imperative that the individual see himself as less important than his family, and the family as secondary to the larger community. However, duty included an obligation to one's self. The Adams children were instructed in the virtue of self-mastery. They were to strive to overcome those lustful and iniquitous passions of the flesh and spirit that the Puritans had linked with corruption.[15]

Young John was raised by an authoritative and intrusive father who demanded utter submission from his children. He feared they might be spoiled by too great a display of parental affection. Nevertheless, John remembered his childhood as a happy time filled with swimming, hunting, fishing, wrestling, and skating. He recollected his father as a man who loved and nurtured his children, as kindly, benevolent, industrious, intelligent, and the most honest man he ever knew. John's upbringing instilled in him a lifelong prudishness that bordered on the pathological, but, as he later acknowledged, he also acquired traits that aided in his eventual success.

Recollections of his father predominated, but Adams later acknowledged that his mother had exerted some influence on his life. Susanna Boylston of nearby Brookline hailed from a more prestigious family. She was twenty years younger than her husband, an uncommon but not unheard of occurrence in eighteenth-century New England. John remembered her as an intelligent woman who was fond of reading. He also recollected that she shared responsibility for his education and life choices. Yet, although Adams named a child after her, his relationship with his mother was remote after he reached adulthood. After 1774, when he was almost continuously absent from Braintree, where his mother lived until her death in 1797, Adams neither wrote her, responded to communications about her, nor mentioned her in his diary or correspondence. The diary for his youthful years contains hints that he saw her as both a strong-willed individual who clashed often with her equally strong-willed husband, and as the customary instigator of these quarrels. He appears to have been uneasy with her assertiveness and unwillingness to accept without question the Deacon's paternalistic authority. Yet, without quite realizing it, young Adams was shaped as much by his mother as by his father. Whereas Deacon Adams provided a model of success through perseverance, fortitude, and integrity, Susanna Adams's stubborn willpower was to become an indelible part of her son's temperament.[16]

Jefferson experienced such an unhappy youth that he never looked with affection on this period of his life. As an old man he said he might like to repeat his early adult years, but he had no inclination to be a child ever again. He spoke of his boyhood as a time of "colonial subservience," which suggests that as a youngster he had felt fettered and constrained. Much of his discontentment must have stemmed from his parents' decision to send him away to school at the age of nine. From that point forward during his youth he endured a total separation from his parents for the better part of each year. His sense of abandonment was doubtless magnified when his father, whom he thought a giant in every sense, died in 1757.[17]

During the brief periods when Jefferson was at home following his father's demise, he lived with his mother, Jane Randolph Jefferson. His relationship with her remains a mystery. Little is now known about her, save that she was the daughter of Captain Isham Randolph, a planter, politician, diplomat, soldier, and noted American naturalist, and that she was born in England while her father served as Virginia's agent to the parent state. She grew up at Dungeness, a plantation in Goochland County, and was nineteen when she married Peter Jefferson.

Although Thomas lived on and off with her for twenty-seven years, only four references to her can be found within his voluminous papers. One was a backhand swipe against her family, toward which Jefferson evidently brooked considerable hostility. Another was an entry in his account book on the day of her death in 1776: "My mother died about eight o'clock this morning," he noted without evident emotion. He waited months before notifying her brother of her passing, then composed a letter in which he discussed Anglo-American business relations at length before matter-of-factly mentioning "the death of my mother" one hundred days before. Jefferson's punctuated silence hints at a deep-seated anger, the reasons for which can only be conjectured. Perhaps Peter Jefferson was too successful in weaning his son from his mother. It may have been that Thomas believed she had abandoned him, in as much as his earliest separation from his parents resulted in his having been sent to school at a plantation owned by his mother's family. Furthermore, while his father, the self-made man who had risen through his initiative, industry, and talents, clearly represented everything Thomas hoped to become, his mother, the daughter of privilege, indulgence, and patrician elitism, in all likelihood stood for everything that he abhorred. Or, because Jane experienced eleven pregnancies in sixteen years, she may of necessity have been so detached that she was unable to give him the love he craved. Whatever, Jefferson's subsequent remark that his father's death had left him utterly self-dependant, "without a relation . . . qualified to advise or guide me," suggests a mother-son relationship that was so troubled that the two were unable to communicate in a spirit of love, trust, equanimity, and assurance.[18]

Washington's childhood is also obscured. Nowhere in his vast correspondence does Washington reveal his feelings about his youth, other than to say that his parents sought to raise him so that he would never be in "danger of becoming indolent . . . imperious & dissipated."[19] Washington's silence toward his father may have been because he believed that Augustine had barely touched his life, inasmuch as he was yet a small boy when his father died.

He too lived for several years in a household under the sway of a widowed mother. Mary Ball Washington was the daughter of an English
immigrant who prospered as a Virginia planter. Like many Virginians, she was
orphaned as a young child. She did not marry until she was twenty-three, a
year younger than Adams's mother, but an uncommonly late age for a woman
who had inherited a modest estate and resided in a society in which males
outnumbered females. After 1743, when George was on the cusp of adolescence, she lived alone with her children at Ferry Farm, a worn-out tract near
Fredericksburg. Contemporaries described her as quiet, aloof, imperious, and
strong-willed. She frightened some youngsters, who saw her as regal and
omnipotent. It was in part from her that George likely derived his olympian
public persona of the quiet, stately, august individual.

George and his mother doubtless clashed during his teenage years. He
was eager to break away and chart his own course, and she was protective. A
great conflict likely arose when she prevented her fourteen-year-old son from
accepting a commission in the Royal Navy, which George believed his father
had wished for him. Still later she discouraged, but could not stop, her adult
son from soldiering for Virginia. However, contention between an adolescent
and his mother does not inevitably result in an unhappy childhood or a
brooding hatred, and Washington's subsequent behavior suggests that he
honored, and perhaps deeply loved, his mother.[20]

Adams alone appears not to have been influenced by his siblings. He was
sent to school while his brothers, Elihu and Peter, were trained to be farmers.
Once the Deacon and Susanna made those choices for their sons, John was
inevitably riven from his brothers by education. Little evidence exists that a
close bond ever developed between the three. Elihu died young, but Peter lived
on. John not only never wrote him—he even ignored his mother's request in
the 1780s that he do so—but in his correspondence with hometown friends,
John never inquired about his brother. Only when they were elderly did
these two grow close.[21]

Jefferson was separated from his only brother, Randolph, by age and
mental capability. Thomas was twelve and a schoolboy living away from
home when Randolph was born. Although the evidence is far from incontrovertible, some scholars believe that Randolph was mentally retarded. What is
clear is that the two boys saw little of one another and never grew close.
Thomas was distanced by age and temperament from four sisters, but was
close to Jane, who was three years older and helped raise him, and to Martha,
who was three years younger. They probably introduced him to a softer

world than their father had inhabited, accompanying him on long walks to explore the mysteries of the forest about Shadwell and spending evenings with him reading poetry and playing the violin.[22]

Three children, Lawrence, Augustine, Jr., and Jane, survived Augustine Washington's first marriage. George was the first child born to Mary Washington, followed by three brothers and a sister. A warm, familial bond developed between him and the others, but there can be no doubt that he was in awe of Lawrence, in whom he found his most profound role model. Near the time of his father's death, George who was eleven, first met Lawrence, who was twenty-five and had just returned from soldiering in the War of Jenkins' Ear, an Anglo-Spanish conflict that had erupted in 1739. Young George had never met such a man. Educated in England, resplendent in his uniform of the American Regiment, lionized in Virginia for having participated in the bloody campaign for Cartagena, Lawrence set an example of urbanity and heroism for his younger half-brother. He also filled a void left by George's absent father. The object of considerable adulation, and one who seemed to succeed at everything he touched, Lawrence appeared to be larger than life to young George. Lawrence settled at Epsewasson, which he rebuilt and renamed Mount Vernon after the admiral under whom he had recently served. To young George, who visited frequently, Lawrence must have seemed blessed. He prospered as a planter, married into the Fairfax family, the most prestigious clan in the Northern Neck, won election to the provincial assembly, and was appointed adjutant general of the colony's militia. Lawrence associated with the most powerful men in the province and with the most sophisticated women that George had ever seen. Dashing, confident, polished, valorous, and not least the object of apparently heart-felt reverence and adulation, Lawrence was everything that George aspired to be.[23]

At about the age of five or six Adams and Jefferson were told they were to receive a formal education. Adams later said that his father had yearned for him to become a minister, which meant years in a Latin academy, followed by college. Adams recalled in his memoirs that he resisted attending school. He longed to be a farmer like his father and brothers, and he recollected years of struggle against his father's designs. As he remembered the story, not even the Deacon could break his will. John changed only when he was placed in the care of Joseph Marsh, the master in a Braintree Latin academy. Young and kind, Marsh utilized blandishments and quiet encouragement to motivate, and his tactics worked with John. "I began to study in Earnest," Adams later recalled, and he slowly grew into a competent, promising student. Adams's preparatory education continued until he was sixteen, when he easily passed the entrance examination at Harvard College.[24]

Adams had blossomed under Marsh, and he flourished in college. Harvard imposed an exacting regimen on its young scholars. John and his fellow students coped with a centuries-old classical curriculum that included the study of Latin, Greek, Hebrew, rhetoric, and logic. He also studied moral philosophy, mathematics, and the natural sciences, and was additionally subjected to regular oral disputations, a crucial element in the formal curriculum. Adams relished this stressful, spartan way of life. College "invigorated my Body, and exhilarated my soul," he later wrote. The love for books and studying, awakened by Master Marsh, quickened and grew into a passion, until he not only sometimes eschewed the company of others in order to study, but found himself doing more than his professors asked.[25]

Maturation doubtless was a factor in John's transformation. In addition, just as Marsh touched him, some of Adams's college professors, mostly competent and devoted men who encouraged excellence, drew the best from him. Furthermore, college introduced him to a new world of intellectual stimulation. For the first time he studied science, read Shakespeare's tragedies, and delved into history and political theory. It was also during these years that John grew obsessed with the desire to achieve personal greatness. Striving for upward mobility was a tradition among his ancestors, a habit among Adamses that he once referred to as among the principal "virtues of the house."[26] He was aware, too, of his father's churning ambition for him. Deacon Adams's ambient hopes must have served as both catalyst and imprimatur for his son's unbridled aspirations.

Adams's experience at Harvard was so profound that it refashioned his perspective. For the first time he stood in awe of excellent students. He subsequently wrote that he began to imitate the better scholars and felt "a desire to equal them." Wishing to associate with good students, his closest friends at college were those who, like himself, eventually enjoyed extraordinarily successful careers. Adams later remarked that at least three classmates surpassed him in Latin and literature, but he thought he had no superiors in science and mathematics. He must have been near the top of a class that produced a future president of Harvard College, the last royal governor of New Hampshire, several judges, a general in the Continental army, a U.S. senator, and several successful lawyers, ministers, and physicians.[27]

John's professors gradually noticed his potential. In addition to his inten-

sity, incentive, and intellect, they probably were impressed by the skill and relish that he brought to the required disputations. The flair he displayed during
dramatic readings also convinced some of his talent for public speaking. As
John's senior year approached, both faculty members and fellow students
urged him to pursue a legal career.[28]

Jefferson painted a very different portrait of himself. He claimed to have
excelled from the outset in the one-room frame schoolhouse at Tuckahoe, the
Randolph estate, where his education began in 1748. Later, he flourished during the six years he spent in the James River Latin school of Reverend William
Douglas, a Scottish-born Anglican pastor of Dover Church. In 1757, following his father's death, he was placed in a school nearer home, the log cabin
academy of another Anglican minister, the Reverend James Maury.[29]

Young Jefferson was one of five students, all sons of planters, who studied with Maury. When he first entered Maury's academy, Thomas was so shy,
socially backward, and lacking in self-esteem that he was closer to his mentor's eleven-year-old son, three years his junior, than to those classmates his
own age. The three years with Maury were an important period for Jefferson.
He later called this the happiest time he ever knew, and acknowledged
Maury's seminal influence. Maury offered many things. He not only led the
boys through the classics, but introduced them to the best literary and scientific works of the blossoming Age of Enlightenment. In addition, Maury ran
his school out of his home, where his eight children and wife lived. This was
a family setting, something Jefferson had seldom known. In addition, Maury
was an impressive man. He farmed a bit, preached some, taught most of the
time, and wrote extremely well. Like Peter Jefferson, he was a man of many
talents. Jefferson later said that he revered Maury both as a "learned man" and
a "good man." Maury in fact was even more. He was a surrogate father at a
time Thomas desperately needed love and attention.[30]

Jefferson's guardian consented to his request to attend William and
Mary College in Williamsburg. Although his father's will stipulated that he
was to inherit roughly 5,000 acres and numerous slaves at age twenty-one,
Thomas never considered not attending college. He had discovered a sustaining joy in learning. Although he did not yet know what he wanted to do
with his life, Jefferson at age seventeen knew that he wanted more from life
than merely to be an affluent planter. He also knew that education and intellect would be powerful weapons in his arsenal if he was to rise above the status attained by his father.[31]

Tall, thin, awkward, and still-growing, Jefferson arrived on William and
Mary's tiny campus in 1760. Two brick buildings sat a few yards apart under

a canopy of tall oaks and maples. Williamsburg, a sleepy town of a few hundred souls, lay nearby. Jefferson was awestruck. While an urbanite would have thought the village the height of rusticity, Jefferson called it "Devilsburg," and portrayed it as a pit of licentiousness. Initially, Jefferson submitted to its heady temptations. He overspent his budget by one-half and enjoyed a full social life during his freshman year. However, the habits of self-discipline instilled in him by his father and Maury won out. Jefferson soon impressed his classmates as an obsessive student. To today's observer, Jefferson's behavior appears to have been that of a compulsive personality who was at war with himself and anyone, or anything, that threatened his improvement and, ultimately, his advancement. He studied several hours each day and subjected himself to an exercise regimen that included walking, swimming, and running several miles each evening in the Southern stillness.[32]

Jefferson attended classes continually for a bit longer than two years, never laying out for the customary summer hiatus. He pursued a curriculum nearly identical to that with which Adams grappled. William and Mary prepared some students for the clergy, but its primary mission was to produce an informed and well-rounded person who could manage the public affairs of the province. Most of Jefferson's classmates went on to become planters who frequently held important local offices, but between mid-century and the American Revolution, William and Mary graduated numerous future assemblymen, an Anglican bishop, a renowned political theorist, a governor, two U.S. congressmen, and a chief justice of the U.S. Supreme Court.[33]

Jefferson described himself as a "hard student" who found learning to be "the passion of my life." He astonished his classmates with his proclivity for withdrawing to read and reflect. One later remembered that Jefferson "could tear himself away from his dearest friends and fly to his studies." Jefferson's closest friend in college, John Page, himself an extraordinary student, remarked that he was "too sociable and fond of the conversation of my friends to study as Mr. Jefferson did." Another remembered that Jefferson "used to be seen with his Greek Grammar in his hand while his comrades were enjoying relaxation." Others recalled how methodically Jefferson had approached his studies. He "adopted a system" of study and would not permit "the allurements of pleasure [to] drive or seduce him" from his books, an acquaintance later wrote. In a school in which most students were carefree young gentrymen bent more on entertainment than study, Jefferson was different, and he knew it. He once contemptuously referred to most of his schoolmates as wastrels who made for "bad company" and who ultimately proved to be "worthless to society."[34]

The best of the seven faculty at this diminutive college quickly discerned Jefferson's exceptional talents. William Small, professor of mathematics and the only faculty member who was not an Anglican clergyman, took Thomas under his wing, speaking with him almost daily. An enlightened skeptic, Small brought Jefferson further down the path of eighteenth-century rationalism to which he had been introduced by Maury. In his memoirs Jefferson said that Small, together with Maury and George Wythe, were the three most influential persons in his youth. Small introduced Jefferson to Wythe, a member of the Virginia assembly and an esteemed lawyer, whose office was in Williamsburg. Small also brought Jefferson into the company of Virginia's royal governor, Francis Fauquier, whose residence was near the campus. While still a student, Jefferson on occasion dined, conversed, and played music with these three older men.[35] Not one of his fellow students, or any other student at William and Mary during the eighteenth century, ever claimed to have been regularly invited into such distinguished company.

Washington experienced a quite different classroom. The family's plan for him to study in England was aborted by Augustine's early demise, and George received no more than two or three years of formal education in Fredericksburg. He learned to read and write, and was introduced to penmanship, etiquette, and mathematics, but he was not in the habit of spending long periods cloistered in a library. He read a bit, though nothing in depth, and that which he did peruse he was drawn to by expediency. For instance, he must have carefully read the *Rules of Civility and Decent Behavior in Company and Conversation*, a compendium of over one hundred useful maxims for gentlemanly conduct, but however influential this book may have been, his most important lessons were derived from visits with Lawrence at Mount Vernon.[36]

Here, and at Belvoir, the Fairfax's nearby plantation, George discovered a wonderful and alluring new world. For the first time he entered the genteel, opulent, sophisticated world of the educated planter aristocracy. It was a transforming experience. Thereafter, he longed to live as these planters lived, aspiring to be distinguished, as they were, from the *"common run"* of humanity. Although he knew that he would never inherit a planter's fortune, he set out to improve himself. He quietly observed the behavior of those whom he encountered, and patterned his mannerisms after theirs. He read what they read, including biographies, the *Spectator*, and the translated dialogues of Seneca. He dressed after the fashion exhibited by Lawrence and Colonel Fairfax, and like them practiced fencing and dancing. He wished to embody taste and refinement in the drawing room, and to capture the qualities that would impress cosmopolitan gentlemen and cultivated women. These were unaccustomed ways to him, and he was often ill at ease. He soon learned that it was better to observe and listen than to speak. What began as a youthful strategy gradually grew to be his habitual deportment, except when in the company of those who were unthreatening. However, as cultivation would be unavailing without economic resources, George began to study surveying.[37]

Colonel Fairfax, whose daughter was married to Lawrence, saw promise in young Washington. He likely discerned qualities such as strength, sobriety, loyalty, intelligence, industry, and ambition. He not only became his patron, much as Dr. Small would be for Jefferson, but Fairfax became something of a surrogate father to George, as Maury was to be for Jefferson. Fairfax gave him his first job. At age sixteen Washington accompanied a party to survey a portion of the vast Fairfax property in western Virginia, a demanding expedition that demonstrated that Washington was not as tough as Fairfax imagined. After one cold, wet, homesick month, George deserted his colleagues and returned home. However, Fairfax stuck with him and got work for George as an assistant surveyor in the newly established town of Alexandria. When that job played out Washington worked at various sites within Fairfax's Northern Neck Proprietary, especially along the Cacapon River deep in Virginia's hilly western domain.[38]

A year later, almost certainly due to the intercession of Fairfax or Lawrence, Washington was commissioned a county surveyor in Culpepper County, a post that ordinarily required considerable experience. Altogether, Washington surveyed for seven years, spending long weeks each year in the dark wilderness forests. He slept under cold skies, lodged in the cabins of backcountry settlers, broke bread with roving bands of Indians, and supervised the hard men who composed the working parties. There was an element of danger to what he did, but it was mostly hard, lonely work. Young Washington lugubriously wrote a friend that he labored "like a Negro," and added that he seldom slept in a bed, subsisted on an execrable diet, and rarely changed into clean clothes.[39]

Washington had run nearly 200 surveys before 1753, and averaged a "tolerably . . . good Reward" for his labors, he said. While still in his teenage years, he earned an annual income that exceeded that of most successful artisans. His wages during his first year enabled him to purchase a tract of land. Each year thereafter he bought additional acreage and, like most surveyors, he sometimes received land in lieu of cash payments. Within four years he owned over 2,000 acres along a tributary of the Shenandoah River.[40] Through inheritance and industry he had begun to accumulate a modest fortune and to ascend, however gradually, in Virginia's planting society.

Washington had also grown into an impressive young man. He stood six feet and three and one-half inches tall, towering over almost every other man, for at this time native-born adult males in Virginia averaged five feet seven inches in height and the median height of European-born males in the Chesapeake was barely five feet four inches. Washington's arms were long and muscular, his shoulders broad, and other men marveled at his small, flat waist. He had light brown hair and a fair skin that sunburned easily. Handsome was not the word that came to mind when Washington was described, but he was not unattractive. Words such as rugged and strong were more descriptive of his features. There was a tough, iron-hard edge to this young man, and Washington early on learned that it often served him well to accentuate his stalwart qualities. For instance, no one failed to notice his blue-grey eyes, which, as if by design, seemed to penetrate to the inner core of those with whom he spoke. Observers spoke of him as an excellent horseman and described the supple grace of his movements, as one today might speak of a gifted athlete. People saw in him a vital, vibrant, quiet, hardy, and resolute young man, who was accustomed to the outdoors and to hard, physical work, yet who exhibited a glean of gentrified refinement.[41]

As Washington, Adams, and Jefferson reached the cusp of adulthood, each exhibited a passion for independence. Each hungered for emancipation from the entanglements of childhood and sought to carve out an autonomous existence. The handmaiden to each young man's zeal for self-mastery was a propulsive ambition that drove him to yearn for more than his father had attained, for more even than his father had ever hoped to achieve.

Ambition was not unique to these young men. Each hailed from a family in which upward mobility was accentuated. In fact, the desire to improve one's status was part of the baggage of colonial Americans, the descendants of English and European immigrants who in most instances had migrated to improve their social and economic lot. They had come to the colonies because they believed, as an English friend once exclaimed to Benjamin Franklin, that in America, as nowhere else, it had been repeatedly demonstrated "how little necessary all origin is to happiness, virtue, or greatness." Franklin in fact was the author of *Poor Richard's Almanack* and *The Way to Wealth*, works that joined a popular genre, guidebooks that were eagerly devoured by ambitious readers who hoped to rise socially and economically, or who hungered for acceptance and prosperity.[42]

This too was an age—the first age, according to Samuel Johnson, their contemporary who dominated the British literary scene—in which the "fever of renown" swept the Western world. Fame had been democratized. During most of history only members of the privileged classes had possessed a realistic opportunity to achieve majestic fame, but in the eighteenth century it had been demonstrated repeatedly, by men such as Franklin, for instance, that fame might be achieved by men born into a lesser social rank.[43]

Washington, Adams, and Jefferson were products of their time, but the aggressive ambition that propelled these three was also a legacy of their youthful experiences. It was born in a young Washington seemingly trapped on a spent farm and destined, at best, for a life as a small planter, unnoticed and without influence. Ambition germinated in an Adams held in thrall by an exacting father who demanded excellence. Jefferson's ambition was conceived in the slough of despond derived from his sense of neglect and abandonment. Washington, who sought to scale the heights attained by Lawrence, yearned for recognition and burned with a desire to be accepted as an equal in cultivated society. Adams hoped to someday be exalted as was his father, but beyond the limits of Braintree. Jefferson too craved notice, but he additionally longed for commendation and acceptance, and coveted the same love and respect that he had lavished on Professor Small and Reverend Maury.

2

"Getting under Sail"

The Decisions of Youth

Adams and Jefferson were struggling to discover themselves when they celebrated their twenty-first birthdays. Washington knew what he wanted well before he reached adulthood. He hungered for the recognition and esteem enjoyed by his older, wealthier, and better educated brothers and the men at Belvoir. He wanted it quickly too. His father had died while in his forties. Lawrence fell victim to tuberculosis and died at age thirty-four in 1752.[1] Thereafter, George was haunted by the belief that he would not live to be an old man. He feared too that his aspirations were hopelessly beyond his reach. Surveying might eventually bring him wealth, but it would be years in coming. Even then, he would not be distinguished from other planters, for he lacked the formal education that might set him apart.

Lawrence's demise had an enormous impact on young George. While he grieved for the loss of his brother, friend, mentor, and patron, new opportunities suddenly sprang out of the tragedy. Lawrence's post as adjutant general of Virginia was divided and George, probably at the behest of Colonel Fairfax, was appointed by Governor Robert Dinwiddie to be the adjutant of the southwestern quadrant of Virginia. Lawrence's death also led to George's eventual acquisition of Mount Vernon. When Lawrence's widow remarried, and their sole surviving child died in 1754, George inherited the estate.[2]

Furthermore, young Washington soon was able to play a seminal role in the diplomatic and military events that engulfed Virginia in the 1750s, a role that Lawrence likely would have filled. Great Britain had gone to war with its principal European rivals, France and Spain, three times since 1689. Although the great powers were at peace after 1748, a cold war atmosphere lingered. In America, strife centered over rival claims to the Ohio Country, the fertile land that lay west of the mountains and south of the Great Lakes. By 1750 France had dispatched troops below Lake Erie to formally stake its claim to the region. Several Virginia planters, including Lawrence, responded by forming the Ohio Company and successfully petitioned the Crown for a land grant in the region. The investors were to receive 500,000 acres if they settled 100 inhabitants in the Ohio Country within seven years and constructed a fort at the head of the Ohio River. In 1753 Governor Dinwiddie sought someone to carry to the French in the disputed area a message setting forth Virginia's claim. The person who bore the message would be a messenger of war. Twenty-one year old George Washington volunteered.[3]

Washington had twin objectives. He sought to position himself to attain a high rank in the army that Virginia would raise when war erupted. He also knew that bearing arms could result in greater notoriety than could ever be attained by toting a surveyor's instruments. Washington's mission commenced as the red and ochre leaves of autumn appeared in 1753. He crossed the Appalachians in rough weather, a long trek through country inhabited by Indians, who were more friendly toward the French than the British, but reached the French outpost of Fort Le Boeuf, just below Lake Erie, without incident. The French treated the English party of seven cordially. However, they rejected Dinwiddie's message. In essence, they instructed Washington to report that Virginia would have to fight for the transmontane West.

On the return trip, Washington twice came face-to-face with death. While rafting down the Allegheny River, he fell into the icy waters and was saved only by the quick response of Christopher Gist, an experienced frontiersman and member of the party. Later, an Indian, who had fallen in with Washington and Gist a few miles north of the Ohio at Murdering Town, tried to shoot the unsuspecting Englishmen. When his gun jammed, Gist and Washington overpowered him. Washington later claimed, somewhat improbably, that he and Gist simply disarmed and released their attacker.

Washington's exhaustive trip ended in the gloom of early winter when he reported to the governor. At Dinwiddie's behest, he wrote an account of his mission that was subsequently published in several newspapers in the colonies and London. Washington indicated that nearly 1,300 French troops near the Ohio River were busy constructing at least one additional French outpost. Dinwiddie immediately prepared for the war that would be known in American history as the French and Indian War.[4]

The educated and affluent were spared military service in eighteenth-century Europe and America, unless they volunteered to bear arms. John Adams, who was twenty years old when he completed his studies at Harvard, one year younger than Washington at the time he served as Dinwiddie's messenger, shunned a soldier's life. Although Massachusetts entered the French and Indian War and raised large armies each year, Adams's energies were consumed by his preparations for a career. Actually, he chose a career only after much indecision and vacillation, although before his graduation he had a good idea of what he wished from life. He burned with a fever for recognition and fame, and in language that was nearly similar to that of Washington, spoke of avoiding the fate of the "common Herd of Mankind, who are to be born and eat and sleep and die, and be forgotten."[5] His challenge was to discover a path that would make this possible.

Deacon Adams had never wavered in his desire that his son become a clergyman. It was a calling that might have brought John deference and respect from his neighbors, but he was not enticed.[6] He was put off by the hairsplitting disputations in which ministers often engaged. He knew too that he was temperamentally ill-suited for the profession. Gruff and self-centered, he was not likely to meet most parishioners's expectations of a cheery and congenial parson. Nor did he have the patience to listen compassionately as the anxious and grief stricken divulged their woes. Deacon Adams could not see that his son was unsuited for the pulpit, but John's mother understood and gently nudged him to consider a career in medicine.[7] John, however, found a medical career to be nearly as unattractive as that in the pulpit. Medicine was yet thought of as more an art than a science, and Adams was certain, and doubtless correct, that patients distrusted physicians who exhibited a scholarly and scientific bent.[8] The only profession that remained in Adams's day was the law, and his character, ambition, and elocutionary flair pulled him steadily in that direction.

Lawyers had been looked upon as rapacious troublemakers in Puritan New England, but the profession achieved greater legitimacy by Adams's more secular time. Whereas less than one percent of Harvard's graduates had chosen a legal career before 1700, nearly fifteen percent of Adams's classmates would do so. Nevertheless, Adams was racked by doubt. He found it difficult to defy his father, feared it would be a "dreary Ramble" to study the law; and was convinced that lawyers spent most of their time "pleading dry and difficult cases." Yet he chose the law. He made the decision because he not only found the law less objectionable than mending bones or preaching, but because he glimpsed attractive qualities to practicing law. He found it exciting to contemplate matching wits with other attorneys before a judge and jury, but he was especially intrigued by the opportunities offered by this profession to rise socially and economically, and to enter public life and sit in the provincial assembly.[9]

After graduating in 1755, Adams taught briefly in a Latin school in Worcester, about fifty miles west of Boston, in order to pay for a legal apprenticeship. Just a few weeks before his twenty-first birthday, he paid £100 in tuition to twenty-eight-year-old James Putnam, the town's only attorney, who consented to serve as his teacher. During his first year of study, Adams read and discussed with Putnam the books that his mentor assigned. Thereafter, he accompanied Putnam on the legal circuit, observing courtroom procedures and styles, and eventually assisting with the preparation of his mentor's cases. After two years Putnam signaled that Adams was ready to establish his own practice.[10]

Bright and industrious, Adams had come to the attention of several influential men in Worcester who urged him to remain and open a practice. They even offered him a small public office that would keep him afloat until he was firmly established. Adams declined. He neither wished to compete with Putnam nor to practice in a backwoods environment. He longed to be in Boston, not because he could earn a greater fortune in the city—he appears to have been almost indifferent to his income—but because an urban practice held a greater prospect of achieving notoriety. He spoke of the law as "an Avenue to the more important offices of the state." He acknowledged his "Passion for Superiority," his desire to be the best attorney, and the best-known attorney, in the colony. "Reputation ought to be the perpetual subject of my Thoughts, and Aim of my Behaviour," he scribbled in his diary. Adams knew that a learned attorney in Worcester would remain obscure outside that hamlet, but anyone who reached the apex of his profession in Boston would enjoy a reputation throughout the province.[11]

Jefferson completed his studies at William and Mary in only two years, half the time required for Adams at Harvard, probably because he was older and better prepared when he began. As graduation neared in 1762, he also faced decisions regarding his life and career, but where Adams had one goal—to be acclaimed a sagacious barrister—Jefferson wrestled with numerous tugs.

He too longed for renown, hoping to be referred to as a man of erudition. He was driven by a "little spice of ambition," he later acknowledged, to achieve the same "*very* high standing" of men such as Wythe and Dr. Small. Moreover, like Wythe and his father, Jefferson looked forward to entering public life and sitting in the provincial assembly. Jefferson additionally desired to live in the grandiose manner of a Virginia aristocrat, and even as an adolescent dreamt of the mansion he would someday build, sketching plans for a palatial dwelling fashioned after a Renaissance manor. He would have been a singular individual had he not been enthralled by the status and power that he observed in established planters. Country gentlemen were the center about which things revolved. Their neighbors acquiesced to them. They were entitled to the best pew in church, the highest rank in the local militia, and power in the vestry. Even the royal governor respected them. William Byrd II, master of Westover, a large plantation overlooking the James River, said it best when he remarked that he was independent of everyone but God. Byrd knew full well that within his bailiwick he was the one who "set all the springs in motion," as he put it. Jefferson longed for that status and power, but he also desperately yearned for the nurturing home and family that he felt he had been denied as a child.[12]

Jefferson never considered a career in any field other than the law. He held physicians in contempt. Although temperamentally suited for a career in academe, a college professor's status was hardly exalted. Besides, the nearest college was far removed from the lands he would inherit. Small and Wythe encouraged him to pursue a legal career. Jefferson was already leaning in that direction. He knew that a good law practice would provide a handsome supplemental income to that derived from his estate. Furthermore, the law would occupy him for only a few weeks annually, leaving him with abundant time both for planting and leisure. It would provide the opportunity to gain recognition within the province's elite circles and to someday hold high public office.[13]

Wythe agreed to serve as Jefferson's mentor and set him on a course of study similar to that which Adams had pursued. However, less hurried than Adams by financial necessity, Jefferson studied longer and in greater depth. He also worked with a more accomplished teacher. Wythe was seven years older and considerably more experienced than Putnam had been at the time of Adams's training. Wythe, in fact, was a man of exceptional talent. He had a profound knowledge of the law and classics, and as a member of the House of Burgesses, was acquainted with the most powerful men in the colony.

Jefferson's original intent was to learn the law through as much self-study as possible. He worked under Wythe's gaze from April until Christmas in 1762, then returned to Shadwell to complete his studies. The experiment lasted only a few months. Shadwell was filled with distractions. Visitors, often strangers passing by, dropped in and, as the man of the house, Jefferson was compelled to tend to them. Planting and labor problems occasionally required his scrutiny. Furthermore, now twenty and accustomed to living away from home, Jefferson not only must have felt uncomfortable in a house occupied by his mother and six sisters, but he found Albemarle County's frontier insularity burdensome. More than anything, however, Jefferson discovered that he required Wythe's guidance. In the fall of 1763 he returned to the capital, where he spent the better part of the next two years living and studying with Wythe, before passing a formal bar examination.[14]

Jefferson later recalled his good fortune at having had Wythe for a mentor. He called him "one of the greatest men of the age" and spoke often of his "salutary influence on the course of my life." Jefferson also spoke of Wythe as his "beloved mentor and . . . most affectionate friend," his friend "of all hours," his "earliest and best friend," and even as "my second father." Jefferson's relationship with his legal mentor was strikingly different from that which Adams forged with Putnam. Adams later complained that Putnam had not been particularly friendly, and subsequently the two had a cordial but never close relationship. Adams and Putnam certainly never developed a father–son relationship as did Jefferson and Wythe, but Adams had no need for a second father. He was struggling to become independent of the one he had.[15]

From the moment young Washington returned from Fort Le Boeuf in January 1754, Governor Dinwiddie prepared the colony for war. He asked the assembly to create an army, the Virginia Regiment, named Washington a lieutenant colonel, the second in command, and ordered him to march to the Ohio. Washington's objective was to construct a fort at the head of the Ohio River, a step that would give Virginia control of the fertile farmlands that splayed westward beyond the mountains.[16]

Washington did not remain in a subordinate position for long. When Colonel Joshua Fry died that spring in an accident, Washington, just twenty-two years of age and devoid of military experience, was appointed his successor.[17] Dapper in a buff and blue uniform of his own design, he marched his tiny army of 135 men toward the Ohio. Along the way, he received disquieting news. The French, who knew the British would be coming, had constructed Fort Duquesne at the head of the Ohio. That sturdy installation was defended by about twenty cannon and 1,000 men. Furthermore, he learned that a vastly superior French force had debouched in search of his little host.[18] Prudence dictated that he retreat and await reinforcements, but fearing that withdrawal would be seen as weakness both by potential Indian allies and officials in Williamsburg, and with his head swimming with visions of glory, Washington ordered his men forward toward almost certain disaster. He knew the hazard he ran, and confessed to Dinwiddie: "I quite despair of success."[19]

Washington acted even more irresponsibly late in May when he discovered that a small party of French soldiers was camped nearby. Moving forward quietly, he surrounded the unwary French, who were eating breakfast, and struck. Ten French soldiers were killed and twenty-one taken captive. After the ambush, Washington learned that these Frenchmen were bearing a letter to Dinwiddie, precisely as he had carried his governor's message to the French at Fort Le Boeuf. But Washington's order to fire that morning had done more. As Horace Walpole, a force in English politics, soon wrote in London: "The volley fired by a young Virginian in the backwoods of America set the world on fire."[20]

Washington's first combat experience transported him into ecstasy. "I heard Bullets whistle and believe me there was something charming in the sound," he told his brother. He knew he soon would hear more. The French would track him down. Vaingloriously, he told Dinwiddie that he would fight even if outnumbered by five to one.[21] Unfortunately, he meant what he said.

Washington prepared for the coming blow by having his men construct a tiny circular fort at Great Meadows, about twenty-five miles from the head of the Ohio. He named it Fort Necessity. He now had about 300 men under his command and felt relatively secure. He told Dinwiddie that he did not "fear the attack of 500 Men."[22] Sadly for Washington, the French force that found him consisted of 700 men. They battered the Virginia Regiment into submission in nine hours of fighting on July 3. With all his horses and cattle dead, and nearly one-third of his men casualties, Colonel Washington capitulated. By confessing that he had "assassinated" the French soldier-diplomats whom he had ambushed a few weeks before, Washington and his men were permitted to return home.[23]

Once he reached Virginia, Washington disavowed the wording of the capitulation document. He maintained that sloppy work by the Virginia Regiment's translator was to blame for his having signed such a damaging document. Not everyone believed the tale or thought that Washington's brief tenure as commander of Virginia's army had been exemplary. One of the skeptics was Dinwiddie, who told a friend that "Washington's conduct was in many ways wrong."[24] The governor soon broke up the Virginia Regiment and supplanted it with several companies of independent regulars, each commanded by a captain, the highest existing rank in the remodeled army. Although he confessed that his "inclinations are strongly bent to arms," Washington was too proud to accept a humiliating demotion.[25] He returned to a Mount Vernon that, from inattention, was in shambles, and with his military career apparently over forever, began a new life as a planter.

Adams also faced early setbacks. Having decided to practice in Suffolk County, he called on four influential lawyers in Boston. He sought a patron. To succeed, Adams later remarked, an aspiring lawyer required knowledge, a good library, time for study, and "the Friendship and Patronage of the great Masters in the [legal] Profession."[26] Two of the lawyers he approached saw considerable potential.

Jeremiah Gridley, fifty-six years old and the dean of the city's bar, advised Adams concerning further study and opened his law library to the young man. Gregarious James Otis Jr., like his father a star in the province's legal circles, barely gave John an opportunity to speak during the interview, but heard enough to ascertain that John was adequately prepared.[27]

Gridley and Otis sponsored Adams when he was sworn in at the Suffolk County bar in November 1758. Thereafter, the young practitioner immediately opened an office in Braintree and waited for clients to rush in. Only two knocked on Adams's door during his first year in practice, and he lost one of those cases by preparing a defective writ. Adams soon feared he might never succeed. Day after day he poured out his despondency in his diary: "I feel vexed. . . . I shall never shine. . . . I have not Cunning enough to cope." But he was industrious.[28] He scrutinized successful lawyers for clues about how best to comport himself. Putnam, he remembered, had succeeded with sneers and contemptuous looks. Otis, glib and facile, was a skilled actor who smiled and exhibited a casual manner. Otis's father, one of the few Boston attorneys who had not attended college, won often because he could speak to juries of farmers in a manner they could understand. There was a sense of "Grandeur" and omniscience about Gridley, he decided. Adams mimicked these styles briefly, before deciding that he had to be himself. But he did conclude that he must pursue the study regimen that Gridley had proposed.[29]

Adams had good intentions, but the loneliness that accompanied further study was depressing. He had spent seven cloistered years at Harvard and in backcountry Worcester. He was anxious to mingle with others his age, particularly young women. He did not have long to wait. Within a few weeks of returning to Braintree, he met Hannah Quincy. She was a year younger and a member of an influential local family.[30]

John called on her often. They spent cold winter evenings playing cards and backgammon. Over steaming pots of tea, they enjoyed hours of conversation. In no time Hannah so monopolized his thoughts that John made little headway with his study. "While my Eyes are on my Book, my . . . Imagination is playing and prating with her," he moaned. In the manner of a scholar, he catalogued her strengths and weaknesses. Her strong points prevailed. She was attractive, tender, intelligent, and good natured. John admitted that he was "over head and ears in love."[31]

Nonetheless, he was confounded. He cautioned himself about letting Hannah "decoy you from your Books." This could result in the "glorious Promises of Fame, Immortality" slipping through his fingers. Adams drew back. He wanted Hannah, but he did not live for her. Making a name for himself was more important. He told her that he could not marry for years, until his practice was established. He knew that his honesty would doom the relationship, and Hannah in fact began to see others. Adams's ambition had triumphed over love.[32]

Adams plunged into his studies with renewed vigor. His work habits are revealed in his diary. He excoriated himself almost daily for having failed to master a difficult task. "I have read Gilberts 1st Section, of feuds, this evening, but am not master of it," he noted matter of factly. The following day his entry read: "Am now reading over again Gilberts section on feudal tenures." He read the same text the succeeding day, and the next, and the day after that. "Read in Gilberts Tenures. I must and will make that Book familiar to me," he wrote with some despair after nearly a week of wrestling with this formidable text. He predicted it would take two additional weeks to understand the book. "I will master it," he declared. "I will . . . break thro . . . all obstructions," he pledged. On the tenth day of his labors he announced that at last he was beginning to understand the book. After two weeks he declared: "I will master it." Eventually, after nearly four weeks of daily toil, he succeeded and went on to his next assignment.[33]

Adams was acquiring a deeper understanding of the law, but after nearly eighteen months of practice he still did not have enough clients to make a living. He tried a supplemental strategy. He had to make a name for himself so that he would stand out from his competition. He took up the cause of temperance and campaigned to reduce the number of taverns in Braintree. It was a popular venture. For the first time he had gained a measure of local renown. His caseload suddenly increased. It grew even more when, twenty-four months after initiating his practice, he scored his first victory before a jury. He was giddy. "They say I was saucy," he boasted in his diary on the evening of that triumph.[34]

His self-esteem soared after that success, and other victories soon followed. He felt more "expert," as he put it, and declared that he could "feel my own strength" growing. Study came more easily. He acquired new clients and won still more cases. "My fears of failing are at last vanished," he acknowledged in June 1761. A month later, at age twenty-six, Adams was admitted to practice before the Massachusetts Superior Court. Four years after completing his studies under Putnam, Adams still had only a modest practice, consisting mostly of small farmers from Braintree, but at last his clientele was growing.[35]

After completing his legal apprenticeship, Jefferson studied for two additional years before opening his practice. During this period he found time for other pursuits—he journeyed to Philadelphia for the smallpox inoculation and traveled extensively throughout Virginia—but when he turned to his studies, Jefferson resumed the heavy regimen of his college days. He later claimed to have studied daily from 8:00 AM until midnight. Although he probably exaggerated, he was such an assiduous student that Edmund Randolph, his cousin, later wrote that Jefferson was "Indefatigable and methodical" in his studies. James Madison once said that Jefferson studied the law "to the bottom, and in its greatest breadth."[36]

Adams and Jefferson were exceptional. Few lawyers in early America devoted so many years to the study of the law. Some essentially learned on the job. Patrick Henry and Alexander Hamilton opened their law offices after about six weeks study and John Marshall devoted only three months to his legal studies. Most aspiring attorneys undertook apprenticeships that lasted a year or two, but it was a rare practitioner who thereafter continued a regular study regimen. Adams did so because the work habits instilled in him by his father had become almost second nature, and because a mere legal apprenticeship was insufficient to rise to the top in highly competitive Boston.

Edmund Randolph believed that Jefferson persisted in order to acquire "great literary endowments" that would someday enable him "to establish advantageous connections among that class of men who were daily rising in weight." In addition, Jefferson eschewed a practice in the county courts, where attorneys usually earned greater fees, in favor of the General Court of Judicature, where greater preparation was required. The trade-off was that those who practiced at the pinnacle of the Virginia judiciary enjoyed greater esteem. Furthermore, because he was a poor public speaker, Jefferson found it appealing to try cases before a panel of learned judges, as was the case in the General Court, rather than before juries, as was the practice in the county courts. Finally, the General Court was in session for only four weeks in April and another four weeks in October, a schedule that not only afforded him the opportunity to look after planting activities, but left ample time for his avocations, reading, writing, and traveling.[37]

Jefferson launched his legal practice in 1767 and succeeded rapidly. He handled sixty-eight items of business during his first year, although he earned only a modest income, about twenty percent of the income of an established weaver or carpenter, and a fraction of what Washington had made as a teenaged surveyor. However, Jefferson's practice steadily expanded. His case load doubled in 1768, increased by fifty percent during the next twelve months, and continued to grow each year thereafter until he averaged nearly 500 cases annually. Like most lawyers in early Virginia, Jefferson collected only a small percentage of his fees. Between 1770 and 1772 his income from his legal practice averaged about £175 annually, almost three times the yearly remuneration of a skilled artisan in Boston or Philadelphia, but he also accepted land and services in lieu of cash.[38]

As the first spring flowers bloomed in 1755, Washington, the ex-soldier, learned that London had sent a large army under General Edward Braddock to Virginia. With the aid of colonial forces, Braddock was to seize Fort Duquesne.

Braddock's two infantry regiments, and a train of artillery, had barely disembarked in nearby Alexandria before Washington informed British headquarters of his desire to "make the Campaigne." Braddock was pleased. Washington, who twice had journeyed through the backcountry toward the forks of the Ohio, might be of assistance. Braddock had no authority to grant commissions in the British army, but he offered Washington an unpaid position on his staff. Washington accepted, immediately donned his old Virginia Regiment uniform, and joined Braddock on May 1. He could not have imagined that he would not return to civilian pursuits for four long years.[39]

Washington ran errands for Braddock and kept his orderly book. He also met numerous British officers. Some saw promise in him and shared their knowledge of martial matters or loaned him copies of their military manuals, likely the first such books he had ever read. Given his penchant for observation, Washington learned much about the structure of headquarters and how a professional army went about its business. If Washington's later recollections can be believed—and they are difficult to accept at face value—he grew quite close to Braddock, so close that in the evenings over wine and snacks he brazenly told the general that he was going about things the wrong way. Washington claimed to have urged Braddock to abandon his European orientation and organize his force for the "American way of war," for he faced an adversary that was likely to lie in ambush for its unwary foe.[40]

By early July, Braddock's force of about 1,300 men, nearly one-quarter of whom were colonials, had painstakingly pushed almost to within sight of Fort Duquesne. On July 9, about one year to the day since the engagement at Fort Necessity, Washington experienced combat again.

The battle began not with the ambush that Washington had feared, but when Braddock's army stumbled into a force of 900 French regulars, Canadian militiamen, and Indians who were searching for the British. Braddock's adversary recovered first from its surprise discovery. The French and Indians fought in the "American manner," dispersing into the woods and firing from behind trees and ledges. Pinioned in a narrow forest defile, and unaccustomed to the method of fighting imposed on them, the British panicked. Soldiers "dropped like Leaves in Autumn," a survivor later wrote, including nearly all the Virginians. Almost three of every four Anglo-Americans were casualties, including Braddock. While Washington thought the Virginians "behav'd like Men and died like Soldiers," he could not say the same for the professional soldiers. Some, through blind fear, accidentally shot comrades, a few deliberately murdered their officers, and several fled for safety, ignoring both orders and their fallen or trapped comrades.[41]

No one questioned Washington's resolve. He remained in the fray until the very end. Bullets pierced his coat and two horses were shot from under him, yet he miraculously remained unscathed. Some British officers later said that he had fought with unflinching courage, braving death or capture. Late in the battle he exposed himself to considerable danger by attempting to prevent the chaotic, panicky retreat that followed the wounding of Braddock. Although many redcoat officers joined the flight, Washington remained on the battlefield to assist several other brave aides in carrying Braddock to the rear.[42]

Not for the last time, Washington emerged a hero from a military debacle. Friends reported that the story of his valorous behavior was the only topic of discussion in Williamsburg. Dinwiddie was forced into a corner. He reconstituted the Virginia Regiment into its original form and offered Washington his former rank as commander. Vindicated and lionized, Washington might have returned to private life, a hero whose name was known throughout, and even beyond, the province. He never considered that option. He told his mother that to refuse to serve would bring "eternal dishonour upon me."[43] But there was more. The experience of battle had touched something deep within Washington, some primal thirst for the strain of action, an aching to lead men under fire and an ineffable urge to subdue the adversary. Washington also wished to gain a commission as an officer in the British army, something that even Lawrence had failed to attain. To command the colony's army, to be successful and valorous in the fury and terror of combat, to gain the approbation of the British army by being commissioned an officer in its ranks would ennoble Washington. His reward would be an exalted reputation that would catapult him to the very apex of the postwar Virginia elite.

Colonel Washington commanded the Virginia Regiment for the next forty months. It was a dangerous and frustrating assignment. Virginia's long frontier was besieged by Indians who waged a war of attrition. They mingled guerrilla warfare with terrorism, striking both at isolated parties of Virginia's soldiers and helpless farm families. Against this, Washington faced insuperable obstacles. His army experienced chronic supply shortages and often was only at half strength. Nor was he adequately augmented by militiamen. Virginia claimed to have 36,000 militiamen under arms, but the governor, worried both about slave insurrections and the political repercussions of mobilization, hesitated to summons more than a few hundred militiamen at a time. Too weak either to contemplate a campaign against Fort Duquesne or to pacify Virginia's huge frontier, Washington was compelled to employ a strategy known in this era as "bushfighting," and what more recently has been referred to as "search and destroy" operations.[44]

His inexperience compounded the army's problems. Washington was so callow that at first he was oblivious to the magnitude of his problems. He boasted of certain victory. He was also so self-absorbed that he spent barely one-quarter of the first six months after he resumed command with his army. He scurried to Williamsburg and Mount Vernon, visited friends at Belvoir, looked into promising land transactions, and made a lengthy journey to Boston in 1756 in an unsuccessful attempt to secure the British commission that would elevate him above all provincial officers in his theater.[45]

This was a formula for ineffectuality, if not disaster. Six months after resuming command, the war was going so badly that Washington's confidence disappeared. Thereafter, conditions only worsened. By the end of two years he not only acknowledged the loss of one man in three under his command, but the loss of the Shenandoah Valley as well. The "Indians are all around, teasing and perplexing me . . . so that I scarce know what I write," he admitted. He added: "I am distracted what to do!"[46]

Washington displayed unquestioned courage, often riding dark, lonely trails in the enemy-infested woods. He imposed a harsh discipline on his army, including the copious use of the whip. An officer who implemented Washington's orders once reported that "We catched two in the very Act of desertion and have wheal'd them 'till they pissd themselves and the Spectators Shed tears for them." When the whipping post proved ineffectual, Washington approved executions. He confronted the governor with an accurate assessment of his woes. Victory could not be achieved through bushfighting. Only an invasion of the Ohio Country by a powerful army capable of seizing Fort Duquesne and destroying Native American villages, food supplies, and braves could bring this war to a successful conclusion.[47]

Dinwiddie knew the Virginia assembly would not appropriate funds for such an army, but he consented to Washington's request to be permitted to leave his army yet again, this time to journey to Philadelphia to call on John Campbell, Earl of Loudoun, the commander of the British army. The meeting was disastrous for Washington. Loudoun imperiously refused to permit him to speak, declined Washington's written entreaty for a commission in the British army, countenanced no change in Virginia's western strategy, and brusquely concluded the meeting by ordering the colonel to return to his army.[48] Loudoun's treatment of Washington, who had soldiered with valor for Anglo-American interests for three years, was inhospitable, cold, degrading, and unmerited. The British general had treated Washington with the same indifference and disdain he might have displayed in brushing a bug from his shirt.

Washington by now was drawing fire at home. An anonymous writer, who styled himself "The Virginia Centinel," blasted his repeated absences and luxurious lifestyle, and portrayed Washington as an immature, petulant, pompous martinet who owed his appointment to the "Influence of Friends, & not according to Merit."[49] Dinwiddie also lost patience. He turned savagely on Washington, criticizing him for endless complaints, and ordered him to remain with his army. "[W]ith't doubt it is the proper Place for the Com'd'g Officer," the governor wrote, the sarcasm dripping from his pen.[50]

Washington survived. Not only did his officers threaten to quit if he was removed, but he never lost the support of powerful political friends. Moreover, just as he reached the nadir of disillusionment, and briefly even contemplated quitting, William Pitt, the new prime minister, announced a new strategy.[51] He dispatched three armies to America in 1758, each of which was to be augmented by provincials. One army was to advance on Quebec up the Saint Lawrence River, a second was to drive on Montreal and Quebec through the Champlain Valley, and a third force, under General John Forbes, was to take Fort Duquesne.[52] The third element of Pitt's plan was precisely what Washington had advocated for years.

In June he marched the 1,900 men in the Virginia Regiment from Winchester to join General Forbes's regulars in Pennsylvania. This formidable Anglo-American force secured its objective within five months. On the clear, chilly morning of November 24, Forbes's forward units, now very near the Ohio, saw smoke curling above the tall Pennsylvania hills. When they drew closer, they observed the smoldering ruins of Fort Duquesne. The French had abandoned and destroyed the post without a fight.[53]

Virginia's primary objective had been realized. Washington had also accomplished his principal goal. Not only was he "distinguished from the common run," but his reputation was transformed from that of a courageous soldier to that of a legendary victor. Although Great Britain would remain at war for another five years, Washington had no worlds left to conquer in this conflict. He resigned from the Virginia Regiment just hours after Fort Duquesne was taken.[54]

Washington had made many mistakes as commander of Virginia's armed forces. However, what was most surprising was not that he had often erred, but that such an inexperienced young officer had performed so well. He had evinced striking leadership qualities. His size and strength were assets, but he came to see that other qualities were essential for winning respect. He sought to become the embodiment of honesty, prudence, fairness, dependability, guilelessness, sagacity, and, above all else, bravery. His officers, many of whom were hardened and older, and some of whom were better educated men from more prestigious families, never wavered in their support. They backed him in the face of attacks by Dinwiddie and the "Centinel," and when he retired they praised him as a leader who had "train'd us up in the Practice of that Discipline which alone can constitute good Troops." They noted his fairness, judiciousness, sensitivity, and affability, paid respect to his "renown'd . . . Courage," and applauded his eagerness to defend "King and Country."[55]

Washington's leadership qualities came not from luck, but as with Adams's and Jefferson's educations and legal practices, from a studentlike lucubration, observation, and attention to detail. He had worked diligently to discover what made an officer an effective leader. He found that he must keep some distance between himself and those beneath him. He discovered too that while it was unwise to be unfriendly, and imprudent to be acerbic, a formal demeanor set the proper tone. He never lost sight of the fact that he was their leader, not their friend. He sought their trust, even their love. Yet he never desired intimacy or real familiarity with his underlings. His aide-de-camp best described Washington. The colonel habitually manifested "a commanding countenance," he remarked.[56]

Washington left the army at the end of 1758 not just to launch his planting career, but to marry Martha Custis. It is not clear when the two met, but it is evident that he began to court her during his final year with the Virginia Regiment. Washington was twenty-six years old when the courtship commenced, not an uncommonly old age in the eighteenth century for a man, especially an ambitious young man, to first consider matrimony.

This was Washington's first serious relationship, and it occurred when he was conflicted with deep feelings for Sally Cary Fairfax, the wife of George William Fairfax and the daughter-in-law of Colonel Fairfax. He had been sixteen, and Sally eighteen, when they first met. His feelings for the next half dozen years are unknown. But by 1755, the summer he served with Braddock, George was unmistakably enthralled. He wrote her repeatedly, beginning with a missive penned only a few hours after he left for the front. He scarcely attempted to hide his love. Sally initially discouraged his overtures, but after Braddock's debacle she grew more receptive. When a camp disorder forced Washington home in the autumn of 1757, Sally came to Mount Vernon frequently to nurse him.[57]

Yet when Washington recovered from that illness, he rode for the first time to Martha Custis's elegant estate overlooking the Pamunkey River in eastern Virginia. She had married nine years earlier and borne four children, two of which—three year old John Parke and Martha, not quite two—were still alive. Two years earlier, in 1756, she had been widowed. What drew Washington to her? Her portraits suggest that she was short, plump, and plain, although by all accounts she was gracious and kind, and exuded a contagious affability. She was intelligent and experienced in managing a planter's estate. She was also probably the wealthiest widow in the colony. She owned about 100 slaves and 6,000 acres, and her liquid assets were said to be worth £12,000, more than three surveyors could earn in their lifetimes.[58]

After two overnight visits, George and Martha agreed to marry following the cessation of that year's military campaign. Whatever Washington felt for Martha, and for whatever reasons he chose to marry her, he had no more than returned to his army before he wrote to Sally, pouring out his deepest feelings for her. She was the real "object of my Love," he told her, and he confessed that he would always remember their "thousand tender passages" together.[59]

At 1:00 PM on January 6, 1759, George and Martha were married in the drawing room of her estate, the White House.[60]

Jefferson was unaccustomed to the company of young women when, at age nineteen, he met sixteen-year-old Rebecca Burwell, who lived at her uncle's estate near Williamsburg. He was too shy for the relationship to proceed very far. He asked for her silhouette. She obliged, and he carried it everywhere in a locket. But while in the capital, in the first phase of his studies under Wythe, he rarely saw her and never wrote. When he returned to Shadwell he was "wretched." He hectored Page, who had remained in Williamsburg, to report on her activities, but even after Page notified him that Rebecca had other suitors, he could not act. He admitted that he feared she would rebuff his advances. He told Page of his love for her, and even said that he wished they were engaged. Once he hinted that Page might prepare the groundwork for him. He wanted him to talk to Becca, as he secretly referred to her, and to elevate his status in her eyes. He told Page that life was not worth living without her. On another occasion, in one of the more curious letters Jefferson ever penned, he admitted that he daydreamed of building a house that he, Page, and Rebecca might share. Instead, Jefferson built a small boat to sail on the Rivanna River and named it the "Rebecca."[61]

When he returned to the capital to continue his studies, Jefferson saw Rebecca at a ball. He carefully composed his thoughts, plotted a few witty remarks, and requested a dance. However, once on the dance floor, Jefferson fell victim to a "strange confusion," as he later described it. He stammered "a few broken sentences, uttered in great disorder and interrupted with pauses of uncommon length." He encountered her again several weeks later, but his discourse was no more coherent. The following spring he learned that she was engaged to be married. The news left him with a violent migraine. During the next six years Jefferson made no attempt to squire any young lady.[62]

John Adams once remarked that he felt uncomfortable in the presence of most women because he found it difficult to make conversation.[63] Young Jefferson exhibited other difficulties. His experience with Rebecca Burwell, as well as numerous entries in his literary commonplace book, suggest that Jefferson feared women. That he hesitated to write or speak with Rebecca was hardly unusual. Timidity when in the presence of an attractive female plagues many, perhaps most, young men. The fear of failure is daunting. What set Jefferson apart from so many other aspiring suitors was that he appears to have hoped to fail.

During his second awkward conversation with Becca, he somehow managed to stammer the news that he soon would embark on a lengthy tour of Europe.[64] In fact, Jefferson planned no such journey. He faced nearly two additional years of study under Wythe. He must have known, and intended, that his remarks would be taken by Rebecca as a signal to forget him and turn to another available aspirant, much as Adams knew that his frankness with Hannah would drive her into the arms of another man. For all her charms, Rebecca posed a danger. Not that Jefferson suffered from some serious neurosis. He was a nineteen-year-old who feared that a relationship might jeopardize his long-term objectives. Many young planters deferred marriage. Peyton Randolph and George Mason, like Washington, had passed their twenty-fifth birthday when they married, and Richard Henry Lee, William Byrd II, and Peter Jefferson were in their early thirties on their wedding days.

Nevertheless, literary passages that captured young Jefferson's attention suggest that there was more to his behavior. He was conflicted with deep tensions regarding women. He copied numerous excerpts from great classics, as well as from works of seventeenth- and eighteenth-century English poets and playwrights, into his *Literary Commonplace Book*. Many of the entries made during his adolescence resonate with misogyny. Indeed, about four of every five passages that evaluate females does so in a negative manner. Jefferson repeatedly recorded lines that delineated malicious, "Destructive, damnable, deceitful Women!" Several entries reverberated with angry declamations about "how great a curse a woman is," "female Snares" that result in male privation, "Woman's pride" that ends in fiscal bankruptcy, and the "mighty ills" caused by women that have led men to ruination. Two interrelated fears permeated young Jefferson's notations. Not only did he see women as carnal temptresses who ever posed the threat of leading men into dissolute behavior, but he suspected that all females were bent on emasculating males, rendering them submissive, and controlling their very souls.[65]

Nothing similar appears in the private writings of Adams or Washington. Like Jefferson, Adams feared that love might thwart his ambition, but he never imagined that women were evil or solely to blame when sexual passion came into play. Jefferson's teeming rage suggests that he might have experienced a sex-role identification problem. Fatherless male children, as he felt that he had been since age nine when he was separated from his family to pursue an education, often struggle with their masculine identity, for their role identification has been frustrated by the want of a male model. Often boys who are raised in a matriarchal setting, as Jefferson was following his father's death, experience a cross-sex primary identification. Father-absent boys who are punished by a female for having displayed sex inappropriate behavior—that is, female modeled conduct—sometimes respond not only by denying everything that hints of femininity, but by holding feelings of hostility toward females. This is especially true when, during adolescence, they fall under the sway of older men, as was Jefferson's experience while in boarding school and college. Many such young men undergo a phase in which they are strongly attracted to other males. Jefferson lionized Maury, Small, and Wythe. He was so close to Page that he not only divulged to him his deep inner feelings, but confessed to him his most personal failures. He told Page that "No body knows how much I wish to be with you" and admitted to him that he longed to live with him as much as he yearned to live with Rebecca Burwell. Jefferson was not overtly homosexual. Indeed, there is no indication that he experienced homosexual fantasies or that he was aware of such impulses. He was a young man who displayed anxiety about his male identity, but with age and maturity he exhibited unmistakable heterosexual desires.[66]

At bottom, Jefferson struggled with the loneliness and deep hurt brought on by his childhood experiences, especially his sense of having been abandoned and stripped of the satisfaction, protection, and security of family. His childhood wishes thwarted, and grieving from a loss of care, he had failed to experience what Erik Erikson referred to as the "basic trust" essential for healthy development. A trauma of this magnitude may create havoc with the normal developmental transition from childhood to adulthood, leaving the individual suspended between the two worlds and struggling to surmount the hurdles that separate the two. Such individuals often find it difficult to leave the adolescent world, even to explore adulthood, as they lack a guide to help them cope with the incalculable vista lying before them. When childhood ends, they often feel at the mercy of a world filled with unhappy surprises. Left to fulfill the unfulfilled parental desires, they are not so much consumed with anxiety as with what has been called "unpleasure." "Abandoned" children often grow "self-centered," withdrawn, and "wholly immersed" in themselves, as did Jefferson, who developed reclusive habits. He eventually constructed a pretentious mansion befitting a mountain king, where he spent considerable time dreaming dreams of grandiose fantasy. Yet what he longed for most was emotional dependency. His pursuit of happiness was a quest for stability, roots, continuity, and endurance, all the things he had been denied as a child, and all the things that could be realized only if he found the right mate, someone filled with love who, perhaps, could become the surrogate parent he had never had.[67]

Washington, Adams, and Jefferson were so absorbed with the demands of their early careers, and so tentative and uncertain while in the presence of women, that each walled himself off from female companionship for protracted periods during his youth, or in Washington's case focused on a married woman, assured that a serious relationship could never materialize. Adams had no ongoing relationship with any young woman for thirty months following his courtship of Hannah Quincy. Nor did Jefferson express an interest in any woman for a very long time following the termination of his halting relationship with Becca. But as Adams and Jefferson's law practices stabilized and prospered, the thoughts of each young man turned increasingly to marriage and a family.

In 1761, during his third year in practice, Adams fell in love with Abigail Smith, the eighteen-year-old daughter of the Congregational minister in nearby Weymouth. At age twenty-six, with his legal practice growing, Adams was at last self-assured. Abigail, a prudent young woman with a flair for conversation and a zeal for books and ideas, intrigued him. He may also have been fascinated by the possibility of marrying above his station, as other Adams men had done, for he subsequently boasted that Abigail was the daughter of one of the most affluent clergymen in Massachusetts.[68]

They courted for a year before discussing marriage, but deferred that step for two additional years, until John's legal career flourished. He insisted it be this way, even though he had already inherited a century-old house in Braintree. On October 25, 1764, John and Abigail were married by her father in her home.[69] John was twenty-nine years old and Abigail twenty.

Adams wed shortly after Jefferson learned that Rebecca Burwell planned to marry. With Becca no longer in his life, Jefferson lived a solitary existence. His next seven years were so unhappy that his memoirs are devoid of even one fond recollection from that period of his life. He spent most of the time between 1764 and 1771 in Albemarle County, lonely and consumed with unbridled despair. He was one of the few young men in his college circle who did not marry soon after graduation. He envied his married friends, calling them the "happiest [men] in the universe" and describing himself as lonely and encumbered with the "costly apparatus of life," presumably his advanced studies and the management of his property.[70]

His rhapsodizing notwithstanding, Jefferson deliberately secluded himself from the world. It was a behavioral pattern that he practiced throughout his life. Episodically, he retreated from the dangers of discordance, alienation, and personal failings, and sought refuge at his remote asylum, as well as within his inner soul. Jefferson was a young man ensnared in an exquisite trap. He was driven to escape isolation, yet compelled to yield to it. What he yearned for above all was a partner to share his retreat and life, a companion who could accept him uncritically and provide the love and security that he had never experienced. He once confessed to a relative that nothing would give him greater pleasure than "to withdraw myself" into "domestic ease and tranquility" where he could be shielded from the dangers of the world. In a reprise of his earlier fantasy of living with Becca and Page, Jefferson even told Page of his desire to live with him and his wife, Frances, in the seclusion of the house he dreamed of building. He waxed on about his exhilaration at the thought of Frances Page's ruby lips and alluring charm. Living under the same roof, the three could "pull down the moon" in what was certain to be a "feast of the sensualist," he added. Page did not respond for a very long time and never mentioned his friend's fancy.[71]

Although he was isolated and often despondent, this was also one of the busiest periods in Jefferson's life. He studied, found time for planting and more travel, and late in 1768 was elected to the House of Burgesses to fill the seat once occupied by his father. He also began the construction of Monticello, the mountaintop home within sight of Shadwell that he had dreamt of as a child.[72]

Jefferson's busy lifestyle failed to subsume his loneliness, and this shy, reclusive twenty-five-year-old committed an unfortunate act. During the summer of 1768 he frequently visited Betty Walker, whose husband John, a friend and neighbor, was away from home on provincial business. During at least one of these visits Jefferson made improper advances, an act to which he later confessed. Whether it was also true, as her husband subsequently charged, that over a period of several years Jefferson sought to initiate a sexual liaison with her will never be known.[73]

Two years later Jefferson called on the recently widowed Martha Skelton, who lived at The Forest, her father's estate a few miles west of Williamsburg. Martha, who was twenty-one when Jefferson began to see her, had inherited some of her late husband's wealth. In addition, her father, John Wayles, a Welsh immigrant, had grown rich from speculation in the slave and land markets. One child had survived from Martha's marriage, a three-year-old son, John. Jefferson saw very little of Martha before he fell in love, or was "touched by heaven," as he put it.[74]

Little is known about Martha's appearance. Jefferson's descendants described her as slender and taller than was customary in her day, and as a beautiful young woman with abundant auburn hair and large, expressive hazel eyes. There is reliable evidence that she was bright, graceful, a skilled equestrian, played the spinet and harpsichord, was admired for her singing ability, and was an eager and eloquent conversationalist.[75]

Whatever Martha's attributes, it is not surprising that Jefferson, who was timid and inexperienced, fell in love with the first female who took notice of him. Nor is it astounding that he would be attracted to a mature, previously married woman, who likely knew how to put a timorous man at ease. On the other hand, the Jefferson who alighted at her door in 1770 bore scant resemblance to the skittish young man who had been infatuated with Rebecca Burwell six years before. He now was a mature young man who had practiced law for three years, spent two terms in the provincial assembly, and managed slaves and construction crews at Monticello.

However, Jefferson did not rush into marriage. He and Martha knew one another for about twenty months before they set a wedding date, an uncommonly long courtship for a well-established twenty-seven-year-old bachelor and a widow in eighteenth-century Virginia. A practical matter likely caused the delay. Jefferson lacked a home for his bride. Shadwell had been destroyed by fire about the time he began to see Martha and Monticello was not ready for habitation until late in 1771. By New Year's Day 1772, when Thomas and Martha married, his new residence consisted of but one room.[76]

Jefferson was married at The Forest by two Anglican priests. Just before he said his wedding vows, Jefferson told a friend that he had discovered "every scheme of happiness," for in the bliss of matrimony he believed he had found an escape from the loneliness and apprehension that had accompanied his brooding sense of neglect and abandonment.[77] The least happy of youths had, as he approached his thirtieth birthday, become the happiest of these three young men.

Following the ceremony, the happy couple and their guests feasted on a huge chocolate wedding cake. Thereafter, Thomas and Martha rode in a phaeton from eastern Virginia to Albemarle County. During the last few miles of the long journey the Jeffersons were caught in what might have been Virginia's worst blizzard of the century. The horses struggled through three-feet snowbanks to carry the shivering couple to the top of the windswept hill where the unfinished Monticello stood. It was midnight when the half-frozen newlyweds alighted at the one-room, brick bachelor's cottage in which Jefferson had previously dwelled. Martha thought it dreary, but her husband lovingly called it their "Honeymoon Lodge."[78]

3

"This Desultory Life"

Toward Mid-Life

ashington brought his bride to a remodeled house. Mansions in Virginia were ordinarily constructed after the fashion set by England's landed elite, and were meant to be showcases in which Chesapeake planters could exhibit their refined lifestyle. Thus, a planter's house was designed to be more than a house. It was a pronouncement of the owner's magisterial status, the center piece in the plantation village, the largest and most decorous structure amid dependencies. The schematization of most estates was anything but haphazard. It was carefully designed to emphasize to residents, neighbors, and visitors the authority of the planter and the subordination of all others. Some planters, taken with their suzerainty, spoke of their residences as a "Fortress."[1]

Andrew Burnaby, an English traveler who visited Mount Vernon in 1759, found the sparsely furnished, eight-room, story-and-a-half house so unspectacular that he took no note of it. However, he was awed by its breathtaking setting. "The house is most beautifully situated upon a very high hill on the banks of the Potowmac; and commands a noble prospect of water, of cliffs, of woods." Burnaby described Mount Vernon as a farmer's comfortable house, not a mansion, and thought it a good fit for Washington, the citizen-soldier.[2]

Washington had other plans. He quickly set out to make his new home the seat of a grandee. With feverish dedication, he acquired every inch of land that abutted his original tract, until the estate sprawled over 7,300 acres, stretching for nearly ten miles along the muddy banks of the Potomac, and to a depth of four miles back from the river. He commenced the expansion and remodeling of Mount Vernon even before his marriage and launched a second renovation in 1774. When the last wall had been bumped out, and the roof was raised for the final time, Mount Vernon's floor space had tripled, to nearly 4,000 square feet. Washington had made another seminal change. Whereas the dwelling had originally faced the river that led to the family's roots in England, Washington, as Robert and Lee Baldwin Dalzell have noted, reconfigured Mount Vernon so that it now faced west, toward the American frontier that he had fought to win.[3]

Washington, who was his own architect, longed for a home that would capture "the present taste in England," though on a less pretentious scale than that of the English nobility. He succeeded. Mount Vernon ultimately presented Washington as a man of power and respectability who dwelled in a fashionable house, but one in which simplicity and uncontrived eloquence prevailed. Visitors usually commented on the "picturesque" or "handsome and perhaps elegant" nature of Mount Vernon, and one remarked that "Every thing is undertaken on a great scale." Yet a striking number of visitors believed that Washington's residence was a "modest habitation." He had built a mansion that appeared to be devoid of what one guest called "any ostentatious pomp [that]would not have agreed with the simple manner of the owner."[4]

Washington may have convinced some that he lived unpretentiously, but in fact he was driven by an acquisitiveness that resulted in a patrician lifestyle matched by few contemporaries. He sent one shopping list after another to London to acquire an incredible variety of goods. In addition to clothing, carefully specified to be only that which was "agreeable to the present taste" in England, came art, crystal, silver, pewter, china, and furniture. Ship after ship docked at Mount Vernon loaded with liquor, wine, porter, light beer, guns, ammunition in ninety-pound barrels, flints, a sword, knives, and engraved whips. Exotic foods, including cheese, candy, nuts by the peck and bushel, pickles, olives, dates, raisins, currants, mangoes, anchovies, mustard, honey, tea, and coffee arrived as well. He ordered farm tools and kitchen equipment. As soon as possible he replaced Martha's carriage with one fashioned "in the newest taste, genteel and light." He bought more for Martha than for himself, and did not skimp on his stepchildren. He purchased clothes, books, toys, and musical instruments for Jackie and Patsy. During the 1760s the cost of Washington's annual acquisitions averaged approximately twice the yearly income of most successful skilled artisans.[5]

Perhaps the most surprising aspect of Washington's acquisitiveness was his frequent purchase of books. He built an extensive and varied library that included treatises on farming, atlases, histories, poetry, travel accounts, advice on behavior and etiquette, tomes on theology, law, philosophy, anatomy, and medicine, dictionaries, encyclopedias, classics, and numerous works by popular contemporary authors. Washington's library ultimately contained more than 900 titles. Although his was not the largest library in Virginia—William Byrd II accumulated 2,345 titles at Westover and by 1814 Jefferson's library consisted of over 6,500 books—Washington's collection was nearly one-tenth the size of the Harvard College library in 1790.[6]

Yet Washington was not a bookish man. Save for the agricultural and legal books, which constituted about forty percent of his collection, little evidence exists that he read many of the volumes that he owned. His active lifestyle afforded little time for reading. A creature of habit, Washington's daily routine seldom varied. Like most farmers he rose in the dark quiet just before dawn and, before breakfast, devoted up to two hours to his correspondence, diary, and financial ledgers. The sun was still low in the eastern sky when he set out on horseback to oversee the day's labor, a circuit that required roughly fifteen miles of riding. He returned to the mansion in mid-afternoon for the principal repast of the day, a large and leisurely meal that usually lasted about two hours. It was a rare occasion when there were no guests at Mount Vernon. Washington invited the visitors to his table and afterward sometimes took them on brief tours. In the late afternoon, he read or worked at his desk, pausing for a light meal of bread, cheese, or fruit. He ordinarily retired about 9 PM, after spending the early evening with his family.[7]

Washington enjoyed social contacts and found abundant time for leisure activities. As a soldier, he had been unable to establish warm relations with any other man. He had looked upon each person with whom he had come into contact as his benefactor, his follower, or his rival, and had structured each relationship accordingly. Old habits died hard. After 1759 Washington fashioned close ties only with George William Fairfax, Sally's husband, Bryan Fairfax, George William's half-brother, and Burwell Bassett, his brother-in-law. Men liked Washington and most women felt comfortable in his presence. Although restrained and formal, he could be convivial. He excelled at patiently listening to others and possessed an authentic sense of humor. People saw him as both civil and cordial, yet as tough, hardy, and dominant without being domineering. What is remarkable is that Washington won over such a diversity of acquaintances, including wily and successful older men, authoritative planters and officials who were used to having their way, barely literate frontiersmen, and the well-educated who would never be described as men of action.

He frequently attended the theater, races, and cock-fights, played cards, backgammon, and billiards, and was a member of the Masonic Order. He and Martha vacationed annually in the western mountains at Berkeley Springs, often staying for up to six weeks, and occasionally sojourned with one another's relatives in distant counties. He relished an occasional evening in a tavern and loved dances and parties. Washington found it relaxing to fish in a mountain stream, but nothing gave him greater pleasure than hunting. He bred dogs and horses, and loved to take them into the wilderness in quest of duck, pheasant, deer, and especially fox.[8]

Martha's dowry, along with Washington's energy and talent as a businessman, enabled the family to live in regal comfort. So too did the labor of his slaves, most of whom toiled in the fields of Mount Vernon. Martha brought numerous chattel to the marriage and Washington acquired others, until by 1775 he owned approximately 100 slaves, ten times the number left him by Augustine.[9]

Statues abound to Washington as a soldier or statesman, but none memorialize him as a farmer. Yet farming was the principal source of his livelihood during most of his adult life. He returned from the war aspiring to be a great tobacco planter. Problems soon arose. Not only did tobacco prices plummet just as he and Martha took up housekeeping, but Washington discovered that a superior grade of tobacco could not be grown on Mount Vernon's poor soil. His leaf in 1760 and 1761 fetched about thirty percent less than that derived by most Northern Neck planters. He briefly experimented, but after three years cut his losses. In 1764 he substituted grains for tobacco.[10]

The rolling green and amber fields of wheat were but one facet of Washington's operations at Mount Vernon. He also produced corn, garden vegetables, fruit from extensive orchards, flax, and hemp. He raised livestock, bred and sold horses, and kept poultry. A mill operated in one area, a dairy in another, a smokehouse elsewhere. Spinners and weavers toiled inside to produce cloth, much of which was sold. In 1766 he acquired a schooner, and later a brigantine, and launched a fishing business on the Potomac. By 1772 he was exporting nearly 1,000,000 shad and herring annually. He owned several flour mills in Virginia and invested in a company that sought to exploit the timber within the Great Dismal Swamp in southern Virginia.[11]

What most mesmerized Washington was the land market. Land was a good investment for a Virginian, as tobacco rapidly depleted the soil, compelling planters to search out virgin land on remote frontiers. In addition, the free population increased swiftly in the eighteenth century, resulting in a scarcity of good land east of the mountains.[12] When Great Britain acquired all the land between the Appalachians and the Mississippi River in the peace accord that ended the French and Indian War, there appeared to be nothing to stop a vast migration beyond the mountains. Anyone with capital to acquire acreage seemed certain to earn a considerable yield on his investment.

Washington had few equals as a land jobber. By 1775 he possessed title to acreage in Maryland, Pennsylvania, North Carolina, nine Virginia counties, and the unorganized territory of his province that now lies in eastern West Virginia. He had also invested in two companies with claims to western lands, the Ohio Company that Lawrence had helped establish, and the Mississippi Company, which had been awarded title to a vast empire between the Wabash and Mississippi Rivers. However, Washington's bounty lands constituted the great majority of his western holdings.[13]

When Virginia raised its army in 1754, Dinwiddie promised to divide 200,000 acres among the men who served. More than a decade passed after Fort Duquesne fell before the governor and council finally allocated thousands of acres near the Great Kanawha River in present West Virginia to Virginia's veterans. The bounty land was awarded in graduated amounts according to rank, ranging from 400 acres for a private up to 15,000 acres for the commander of the Virginia Regiment. Immediately thereafter, the veterans consented to pay Washington's expenses for a trip to inspect the region. Some came to rue their decision.

In the autumn of 1770 Washington, together with several servants and his old army doctor, descended down the Ohio and Great Kanawha to the grant lands. Upon his return, Washington used his influence in Williamsburg to secure the appointment of his friend William Crawford as the surveyor of the property, then induced the Virginia authorities to award him the best land within the tract. He also told the men that much of the land was "very hilly and broke," and hence unsuitable for farming; he offered to take it off their hands. Many veterans were happy to sell their apparently useless land for a pittance. Washington ultimately acquired 20,147 acres. Within two years some of the men began to feel they had been duped. They are "a good deal shagereend [chagrined]," Crawford told Washington, to discover that "you . . . have all the bottom . . . Land"—that is, the best land in the valleys and near the rivers and streams. None of the land "in that Country is so good as your Land," Crawford added.[14]

Washington was a success as a farmer-businessman. By 1776 at least ten great Virginia planters groaned under debts in excess of £5,000 and Virginians collectively owed British creditors approximately £1,400,000. Yet Washington, who foundered as a tobacco planter, and whose bounty land holdings proved to be of little value until more than twenty-five years elapsed, was debt-free and living resplendently.[15]

Why was he so successful? Obviously, not because he possessed a Midas touch. Washington succeeded in part because he was as daring in his business ventures as he had been on the battlefield. He was shrewd and savvy as well. He was one of the few Virginia planters before the 1770s to switch from tobacco to wheat production. Most did not act until after the American Revolution, and by then it was too late. Washington studied agrarian literature, familiarized himself with the new scientific agriculture, and often acquired and utilized new tools and machines. He was diligent and industrious, compelled his laborers to work hard, and dispatched detailed instructions to his overseers and managers that suggest he expected them to perform as efficiency engineers.[16] Nor did he indulge his bondsmen. He retained physicians and hired midwives, but his slaves dwelled in poor housing, which even Washington acknowledged to be more humble than the accommodations of the lowliest free laborers, and the chattel were given exiguous allotments of clothing.[17]

Washington decreed that his chattel were to labor from daybreak until dark, and to be "diligent while they are at it." When a slave was too idle, Washington directed his manager to "give him a good whipping." He also sanctioned the flogging of female slaves. An English traveler, who visited several plantations in Virginia, believed that Washington treated his slaves "with more severity" than any other planter he had observed.[18]

His former aide-de-camp during the French and Indian War once spoke of certain "Wshn [Washington] Principles" when it came to business and money. He did not use the expression in a complimentary sense. After his sole business transaction with Washington, he added: "I am sure I never desire to deal with him for 6 [cents] again." But for all his dexterity and industry, it was happenstance that ultimately freed Washington of debt. Following the sudden death of his sixteen-year-old stepdaughter, Patsy Custis, in 1773, Washington liquidated his portion of her assets, amounting to approximately £8,000. With this sum, probably more than John Adams's cumulative earnings in seventeen years of practicing law, Washington purged his debts.[19]

Washington lived the life he had aspired to from the moment he first glimpsed Belvoir and Lawrence's Mount Vernon. He was wealthy and respected, and after 1758 sat in the House of Burgesses.[20] He appeared to be happily married, although near the end of his life he wrote Sally Fairfax, who then lived in England, that the "happiest [moments] in my life" had been those "I have enjoyed in your company."[21]

He was disappointed that he and Martha were unable to have children, but Washington was a devoted stepfather. He provided Jackie with opportunities that he never had, hiring tutors and purchasing books for him, sending him to a Latin school, and eventually enrolling him in King's College, now Columbia University, in New York. Washington doted on Patsy. After she was stricken with epilepsy in 1768, he spared no expense in search of a cure. When she died suddenly during a seizure in 1773, Washington was so deeply moved that he virtually abandoned his supervision of Mount Vernon's business activities for several weeks.[22]

At age forty, in 1772, Washington hired Charles Willson Peale to paint his portrait. This was the first occasion on which he "sat to have my Picture drawn," as he put it. Expecting that this would be the only portrait for which he would ever pose, Washington wanted the artist to "describ[e] to the World what manner of man I am."[23] Although he was a successful planter-businessman, Washington presented himself as a soldier, posing in the Virginia Regiment uniform that he had last worn fourteen years earlier. Soldiering had been his single brush with history, the most electric and exhilarating time of his life, and the activity of which he was most proud. He did not wish to be remembered as a grain farmer and land speculator, but as a warrior.

There is no hint of husbandry in the portrait. Washington stands in the foreground. Dark, imposing mountains lurk behind him, but a cheerful blue sky beckons settlers to cross that barrier. Washington's expressionless face is that of the forty-year-old man whom Peale observed, not the mid-twenties colonel who had fought French and Indians for the Ohio Country. His hair is brown, skin slightly ruddy, and beard dark, surprisingly so for a person of his complexion. A middle-aged paunch is visible, as is the first evidence of a double chin. Today's observer is challenged with apprehending the Washington of that moment, not the man that he would become in the ensuing three decades. What Washington chose to reveal, or what Peale perceived—Washington intimated that the artist would "be put to it" to fathom his inner feelings—was a man who was solid, proud, forceful, potent, and combative.[24] What Peale captured was both a proud citizen-soldier and a citizen who missed the heady delectation that he had discovered as a soldier.

Jefferson became a rich young man on April 13, 1764, the day he celebrated his twenty-first birthday. That day he inherited more than 5,000 acres, about half of which were situated about the Rivanna River near Shadwell, as well as fifty-two slaves, considerable livestock, his father's library, and a grist mill. Even so, he had so few liquid assets that he was compelled not only to immediately sell 800 acres, but even to borrow money from his servants.[25]

Four years later Jefferson sat in Virginia's House of Burgesses, a colleague of Colonel Washington. There is no evidence that the two had previously met, nor is there any indication that Washington and Jefferson, who were separated by a wide chasm of age and temperament, fraternized during the next seven years.

Neither man possessed the flair to dominate a legislative body. Washington on occasion did not even bother to attend the assembly sessions, and when he was present he was treated as a backbencher. Always uncomfortable as an orator, and never more so than when standing before a room filled with well-educated colleagues, he seldom made a speech. Jefferson once remarked that Washington never spoke to the assembly on any issue for as long as ten minutes. On the rare occasions when he introduced legislation, it usually concerned only local or private matters. The legislative leaders reciprocated by assigning him piddling chores, such as preparing bills to regulate ferry service.[26] Fearless on the battlefield and capable of dominating dauntless military subordinates, Washington was out of his element in a legislative chamber.

Jefferson not only was better equipped for greatness in the assembly, but even better connected, as his cousin Peyton Randolph was its speaker. That he hardly shined before 1774 must have perplexed many of his colleagues. In addition to his intellect and legal training, many assemblymen would have loved to have had his physique. Jefferson was tall—probably six feet and two inches in height—and slender, with long sinewy legs and arms. Some thought him gangly and awkward, although many said he was an excellent horseman. No one described Jefferson as handsome, but many thought him pleasant looking. He had a prominent chin, high cheekbones, deep-set, nondescript hazel eyes, sandy-red hair, and skin that was so ruddy that some thought "his complexion [was] bad." Aside from taking pains to dress in fashionable, well-tailored clothing, Jefferson did little to turn his physical attributes to his advantage. His habitual poor posture, especially his tendency to slump when seated, moved one visitor to Monticello to remark on his lack of "exterior grace." Another observer said that Jefferson reminded him "of a tall, large-boned farmer."

Jefferson's manner often put off new acquaintances. He struck many who had only a passing acquaintance with him as serious and "reserved even to coldness," but once he felt comfortable with an individual, his personable side appeared. One guest at Monticello initially found his host to be "serious— nay even cold, but before I had been two hours with him, we were intimate as if we had passed our whole lives together." Those who came to know him best described him as gentle, kind, humble, charming, and affectionate, lauded his good humor, and found him to be a delightful, often provocative conversationalist. His grandson later remarked that Jefferson regarded it as an obligation to be "considerate to all persons," even listening to those who were uninformed or conversed in pedestrian ways. Whereas people wished to be with Washington because they found him to be majestic and charismatic, Jefferson attracted people because he was pleasant and interesting, and often provocative, and seemingly able to discourse in an entertaining and informed manner on almost any topic.[27]

Naturally shy and reserved, Jefferson was never entirely comfortable in a legislative setting. He loathed the arm-twisting and truckling endemic in an assembly. Furthermore, he abhorred public speaking. He could write well-crafted arguments, replete with clever and memorable phrases, but he could not effectively present those ideas as an orator. His speeches were made in a weak, barely audible voice. Not one observer at any moment in Jefferson's public career ever claimed to have heard him deliver an effective speech. Adams, who ultimately served with Jefferson in Congress for more than a year, once said that "during the whole Time I sat with him . . . I never heard him utter three sentences together."[28]

Yet the primary reason Jefferson remained a secondary figure in Virginia politics until the eve of the American Revolution was that his real interest lay in his private affairs. That was not unnatural. He passed between the ages of twenty-five and thirty-one between his first election and 1774, the years when he was preoccupied with marriage, family, and the construction of his new home. Even his zeal for the law flagged. Although he grew to be a learned and successful lawyer who won the admiration of his fellow practitioners, Jefferson never experienced a passionate joy for his calling.[29] Indeed, he never really loved the law. Early on he enjoyed the philosophy of the law, but he eventually concluded that legal literature was "Mere jargon." He grew contemptuous of lawyers, coming to believe that many were lazy, ignorant, or corrupt. He charged that by and large they were a "disagreeable crowd," mostly parasitic, "ephemeral insects" who subsisted off the malice, avarice, and mendacity of others. The lawyer's "trade is to question everything, yield nothing, and talk by the hour," he once remarked. Late in life, Jefferson confessed his embarrassment at ever having been an attorney. Even while he studied the law, he admitted to a close friend that he aspired to be a lawyer only so that he would "be admired."[30]

Jefferson almost certainly would have abandoned his legal career sooner had either his planting operations proven more lucrative or had he been willing to live on a less grand scale. Unlike Washington, Jefferson persisted in planting tobacco, a pursuit he would one day call "a culture productive of infinite wretchedness." Tobacco planters, he added, were "in a continuous state of exertion beyond the power of nature to support."[31] Nevertheless, he lived comfortably. He had the resources to build a fine library and traveled widely in Virginia. However, his most substantive indulgence in these years was the construction of his residence.

Jefferson was still a boy when he made the decision to someday build a house for himself, and to situate it on the lofty summit of a tall hill that he relished climbing on the Shadwell property. Adolescent boys are rarely concerned with thoughts of houses. That young Jefferson dreamt of building reflected his artistic urge to create and shape, his overweening desire to escape his mother and achieve independence, and his compulsion for a sanctuary within which he could withdraw. His fascination with architecture and construction was also quickened by watching his father build, or rebuild, Shadwell, and it was nourished by the realization that his mother was likely to possess Shadwell until he was in his middle years. His dream incubated throughout his youth and hatched in his early twenties. While at William and Mary, or soon thereafter, he became infatuated with the designs of Andrea Palladio, who two centuries before not only had advocated a return to classical Roman architecture, but advised building on an elevated site.[32]

Building atop a hill was not conventional wisdom among Virginia's planters. Almost all built near the banks of a river, an easily accessible thoroughfare over which tobacco could be shipped to distant markets. Other practical considerations dictated a lowland site. Building on a elevated site meant that the top of the mountain would have to be leveled, roads cut upgrade through rugged, forested terrain, and building materials hauled greater distances. In addition, not only was access to water problematical, but the likelihood of damage from wind and lightening was enhanced in an exposed, hilltop location.

Jefferson might have left his inherited property to the care of overseers and opted for a more cosmopolitan existence in Williamsburg or some other colonial city, but such a choice was rarely made in his America. Most identified farm ownership with prosperity, security, and what Jefferson called the "happiness . . . and . . . domestic enjoiments . . . and neighborly societies" of a pastoral environment. Jefferson spoke of property-owning farmers as "the chosen people of God . . . whose breasts he had made his peculiar deposit for substantial and genuine virtue." Furthermore, he was surprisingly provincial. To the end of his life he not only believed that Albemarle County enjoyed the world's best climate, but that this sleepy rural area was the virtual center of purity within Virginia.[33]

In addition, Jefferson looked on cities as centers of iniquity. His feelings went beyond repugnance. He feared cities and denigrated facets of city life that an urbanite, such as Benjamin Franklin, might have embraced. Jefferson especially belittled urban "distractions," employing the term in a pejorative sense, as if ease was a corrupting vice that resulted in inevitable and innumerable "species of misery." Cities, he ultimately concluded, added as much to human happiness "as sores do to the strength of the human body."[34]

There may have been a submerged quality to Jefferson's detestation of the city. He labeled as "treasonable" the thought of leaving his ancestral frontier lands. Jefferson's use of the word "treason," a term that suggests betrayal and treachery, suggests that he equated flight from the frontier with apostasy. Rural America had been the home of his father, whom he had ennobled as a man who "improved himself" through the opportunities afforded by the frontier environment. "Happy the man," Jefferson copied Horace into his *Literary Commonplace Book*, who "works his ancestral acres . . . [and] avoids the [urban] Forum and proud thresholds of more powerful citizens." Moreover, Jefferson looked upon the frontier as a treasure won by the toil, blood, and daring of "our ancestors," including his father, who had told him stories of the "conquest" of the "wilds of America."[35] To abandon the countryside for the city, Jefferson seemed to say, not only was to risk entrapment and degradation in the city, but to forswear the lofty heroism and sacrifices of his progenitors.

The bucolic, magisterial splendor of his ancestral lands tugged at Jefferson. Atop his mountain, he must have felt even more a part of nature. From here, Jefferson could gaze down on swirling storms that raged in the valley below, behold the grandeur of distant, green hills, and delight in the pink-blue burnish of gaudy seemingly endless, sunsets. This lofty eminence was suited for a philosopher. Indeed, a French visitor once remarked that from this "lofty height . . . [a person] might contemplate the whole universe."[36] Jefferson eventually succeeded in building one of America's most sublime houses atop this hill, a tribute to his daring and farsightedness, for many thought his dream was impractical. But if Monticello reflected its builder's intrepidity and visionary nature, it also revealed other attributes, for the house that one builds, like the clothes and mannerisms that one exhibits, can unmask hidden inner qualities.

Jefferson was only twenty-four when he proceeded with the construction of Monticello. Already leading a somewhat cloistered and insular existence, his decision committed him to an even more sequestered life. He was happy, he remarked later, to leave "the bustle and tumult of society to those who have not talents to occupy themselves." The mountain—strong, inaccessible, and foreboding—offered the refuge that this young man required. He equated heights with safety. A towering summit was a haven from the "disruption" at its base, a "placid and delightful" asylum "from the riot and tumult roaring round" below, a means of "rid[ing] above the storms," and of living as William Byrd II had at Westover, independent of others.[37] Monticello thus served twin purposes. It was designed to be what historian Rhys Isaac called Jefferson's "contemplative retreat," a site at which he could be alone in nature to dream and write. In addition, this insecure young man walled himself off from a world that he found unhappy and dangerous. There may have been a third purpose as well to Monticello. Jefferson may have constructed his own internment, the remote spot where he would sequester himself and his raging appetites.[38]

What he intended is no longer clear. However, it is known that he quickly altered his original design for Monticello, which may have been the modest dwelling he had once envisioned for himself, Page, and Becca Burwell. He soon superimposed porticoes and other features that conformed to Palladian orthodoxy, and eventually made other design changes to please Martha after she came to Monticello.[39]

Little is known of Martha, for Jefferson not only subsequently destroyed their correspondence, but said next to nothing about her. One of his slaves later described Martha as a "pretty lady." A neighbor called her "angelic." A French guest thought her "gentle and amiable," while a German soldier who visited Monticello found her "very agreeable, sensible & accomplished." Martha's brother-in-law said she was sprightly, sensible, and good natured, and one of her friends in Williamsburg characterized her as having "good Sence, and [a] good Nature." A member of Jefferson's family subsequently portrayed her as "frank, warm-hearted, and somewhat impulsive."[40]

Jefferson was inclined toward discreet and reserved women. He once remarked that he found nothing "so goading" as to witness a woman publicly "criticise and question" her husband. For any wife, he said, "all other objects must be secondary" to that of pleasing her husband. Stressing the wife's need to be submissive, he added that she must be affectionate and attentive to her husband's interests, uncomplaining, cheerfully accept his absences, never divulge to outsiders any tensions within the marriage, and take "daily care to relieve [his] anxieties." She must also soothe the passions within her husband and "teach [him] to be at peace with himself."[41]

Jefferson was married for about thirty months before the American Revolution overtook his life. He once said that the time he spent at Maury's school was the happiest period of his life, but the period between 1772 and 1774 must have been nearly as blissful, although those years were filled with numerous instances of stress and unhappiness, including one personal tragedy after another. Jack, Martha's three-year-old son from her previous marriage, died a few months after moving to Monticello, probably the victim of a fever. During the following year Martha's father died, as did Dabney Carr, Jefferson's classmate, brother-in-law, fellow lawyer, traveling companion, and dearest friend. Jefferson was so distraught by Carr's demise that, with his sister's permission, he had the body disinterred and reburied at Monticello. Early in 1774 Jefferson's mentally impaired sister, Elizabeth, died of exposure when she fled, and became lost, following an earthquake. In 1775 Thomas and Martha's second child, Jane, died at age eighteen months. The couple's first child, Martha—or Patsy, as she was called—had been born nine months following the wedding. She was sickly and not expected to survive, but after a six-month ordeal that confronted her parents with unrelenting anxiety, Martha made a striking turnabout and thereafter was robust and healthy.[42]

Like any bridegroom, Jefferson must have expected that marriage would be a transforming experience, and in one respect matrimony caused a sea change in his situation. With the unanticipated death of his father-in-law, Jefferson inherited 11,000 acres and 135 slaves. He also inherited his wife's share of John Wayles's indebtedness, but Jefferson believed he cleared that encumbrance by selling more than 5,000 acres of the bequest during the next four years. Comfortable to begin with, Jefferson now quite rightly thought of himself as very wealthy. Soon after Wayles's death, Jefferson remarked that the tragedy had "doubled the ease of our circumstances." By 1776 Jefferson owned about 5,000 acres at or near Monticello on the Rivanna, approximately 4,800 acres in Bedford County, where he would ultimately build a second residence, Poplar Forest, and Elkhill, a 266-acre island in the James River in Goochland County. His slave "family," as he called his chattel, had grown to 117 members in Albemarle County, with another sixty or more scattered about his various properties. Suddenly one of the wealthiest planters in Virginia, Jefferson immediately quit his legal practice. He was so happy to escape the burdens of a calling that he had come to detest that he relinquished his claim to nearly £1,000 in debts owed him by clients.[43]

Now a husband and father, Jefferson likely hoped to avoid protracted absences, like those that had separated him from his father, and he wished to enjoy Monticello and the extravagant lifestyle now at his fingertips. Reclusive by nature, sybaritic by choice, Jefferson seemed to have everything that he had ever desired. Wealth, ease, health—he suffered only an occasional migraine—leisure, recognition, family, and doubtless a happy marriage were his. He began to keep his Farm Book in 1774, at once signifying that he now was master of a much larger business enterprise and that he no longer was a lawyer who farmed, but he was Thomas Jefferson, planter. He must have looked forward to an uninterrupted and felicitous life of love and happiness at home, building, farming, experimenting, reading, reflecting, writing.

Adams and his bride sat for an artist in Salem two years after their marriage. At age thirty, John was overweight, pasty, and flabby. He admitted to being "thick," but Abigail said he was "so very fat." The painting confirms several contemporary descriptions of him as a formal, restrained, aloof, and somewhat snobbish and "ceremonius" individual. Adams, in fact, characterized himself as prudish, stuffy, and "stiff and uneasy."[44]

Abigail, who was only twenty-one, had put her childhood behind her. The artist portrayed her as a serious and responsible young woman. He also captured her beauty. With luminous sable eyes, silky black hair, and soft, classical features, she appeared to be at once bold, resolute, and tender.

Following their marriage, John and Abigail moved into a century-old, unpainted saltbox house in Braintree. Small by middle-class standards today, and tiny by comparison to Mount Vernon or Monticello, the dwelling was not unlike that of most comfortable New England farmers. It consisted of eight rooms, four on each floor, although three rooms in reality were only tiny cubicles. The front door and windows looked out on Braintree's busiest street, the highway that linked Boston to southern Massachusetts and Rhode Island. Through the rear windows one could see the bulk of the rolling six-acre tract on which the house sat. Adams inherited this property, as well as thirty-six additional acres in four tracts situated in different parts of the town.[45]

Adams, who professed deep ties to his Braintree property, frequently recited his love of farming, but he was not really a farmer. He hired two servants and two farmhands, and placed the four largely under Abigail's management. The farm laborers put six or eight acres into production annually, primarily planting wheat and other grains. A meadow yielded winter fodder for the livestock and an apple orchard served both family and animals. By 1767 Abigail mentioned that the farm contained three cows, two calves, twenty sheep, one rooster, and two horses, one of which was "a poor lame hip'd spavell'd, one eye'd mare."[46]

Paradoxically, while Washington and Jefferson were unmistakably farmers, Adams—a lawyer who owned a farm—almost certainly performed more physical labor in his fields and marshlands than either of the Virginians. Adams occasionally dug ditches, shoveled and transported manure, spread fertilizer, slaughtered livestock, and worked under the hot sun in his fields both at harvest time in the early autumn and in May, July, and September when the hay was stacked following the mowing of the meadows. Yet Adams devoted little thought, time, or energy to the farm. Unlike a real farmer, he kept no ledgers, read little about farming, seldom discussed husbandry with others, and engaged in virtually no scientific agricultural experimentation. He maintained the farm, which had to be worked to prevent its ruination, because it supplemented his primary income and was a hedge against both adversity and old age.[47]

Adams was one of America's earliest daily commuters. He resided in Braintree, but worked much of the year in Boston, making the roughly thirty- to forty-minute journey on horseback in every kind of weather. He often departed before 9:00 AM and did not return home until after 9:00 PM. Soon he not only wearied of his lifestyle, but discovered that he liked the city. In fact, he grew unhappy with a small town milieu and in the spring of 1768, leaving the farm in the care of his workmen, moved his family to Boston. He returned to Braintree only when war with Great Britain rendered Boston unsafe.[48]

As Adams's law practice flourished, he hired more farm workers and placed still more responsibility on Abigail.[49] John was never intimidated by his bold, resourceful young wife. He had been drawn to her in large measure because of her lively intellect and meditative cast. He admired strong, assured women, and on the eve of marriage advised Abigail to overcome her "Country Life and Education," which had accentuated feminine subservience. John eventually became something of tutor to her, but he knew that he was a pupil to her as well. Not only did he relish his dialogues with a wife who would grow to be his intellectual equal, but he wanted her to refine his manners and "banish all the unsocial and ill-natured Particles in my Compo-sition."[50] She was exactly what he wanted and believed he needed: a bright woman with whom he could erect what is now called a "companionate mar-riage," a union of friendship, esteem, respect, and love, an understanding wife who could smooth over the rough spots in his demeanor, and a sagacious person with common sense who could manage the family's affairs during his frequent absences.

John and Abigail were remarkable individuals, but in many ways their marriage was unexceptional. The couple quickly had children. Abigail, or Nabby, their first child, like Jefferson's first child, was born nine months fol-lowing their marriage. Eighteen months later Abigail was pregnant again with John Quincy. As with Martha Jefferson, who endured six pregnancies in her ten-year marriage, it must have seemed to Abigail that she was pregnant con-tinuously. Whereas most women in Massachusetts gave birth at roughly thirty-month intervals, Abigail was pregnant during about one-half the first eight years of her marriage, from which resulted five children, four of whom lived to adulthood.[51]

This marriage, like most, included strains and tensions. Abigail's world revolved about domestic concerns, while John was absorbed with his career and public affairs. As historian Edith Gelles has observed, while John called 1765 "the most remarkable Year of my Life" because of significant political events, Abigail thought it the most important year of her life because of the birth of her first child.[52] John was away on legal business when his first two children were born. He appears to have been a distant father in other respects as well. He said nothing about his children in his diary during the first sev-eral years of marriage, although his entries ramble on about myriad topics, including the children of others. When Adams finally mentioned his children, it was to complain about the distractions they caused. The Adamses' differ-ing orientations resulted in restiveness and discord, not unlike that in many modern marriages. This does not mean that theirs was an unhappy union. Each brought to the marriage deep feelings for the other, but what ultimately made it work was Abigail's willingness to accommodate her husband.[53]

Adams's self-indulgent absorption with his career was his greatest pri-ority, and the work habits that he channeled into this enterprise would have pleased the most fervent Puritan. Even after his legal practice flourished, he devoted hour after hour to the study of cannon law, English common law, feu-dal law, and tax law, and on his off days frequently attended court as a spectator, both because he enjoyed the proceedings and from the hope that it might be a learning experience. He was one of a half-dozen young attorneys in a reading club that met weekly to foster intellectual growth, and he published more than twenty newspaper essays between 1765 and 1768, many of them lengthy pieces based on extensive research.[54]

Adams chased after renown, not material wealth. He was never consumed with the desire to make a fortune, although he ultimately earned a handsome living. Within five years of opening his law practice, Adams's income exceeded that of most New England farmers and skilled artisans. After a decade in practice, he purchased a substantial house in Boston and a pew in his church, invested in land, loaned money and charged interest, and had begun to build what would become the largest private law library in Massachusetts. His income increased each year, until at its peak he earned about £900 annually, many times that of a successful craftsman in Boston. Although he lived quite comfortably, Adams hardly lived opulently. His farmhouse in Braintree, and his Boston residence, easily would have fit into one wing of Mount Vernon or Monticello. Throughout his life he preached thrift and economy. "Let Frugality, And Industry, be our Virtues," he told Abigail, and he and his wife emphasized industry and nonmaterial rewards when they trained their children.[55]

By the 1770s Adams not only had learned the law in considerable depth and breadth, but he gradually acquired a deft skill for speaking to juries. A witness to his closing argument in one of the Boston Massacre trials exclaimed that it was "the finest Speech I ever heard in my Life. He's equal to the greatest orator that ever spoke in Greece or Rome." By 1774, when he represented approximately 700 clients, Adams laid claim to the largest practice in Massachusetts, and he acted on behalf of some of the wealthiest men and largest businesses in New England.[56]

Adams had achieved virtually everything he had set out to accomplish, yet, like Jefferson, he too grew unhappy with some aspects of his career. He especially wearied of his itinerant practice. He was compelled to ride a legal circuit that extended from Maine to Martha's Vineyard, and from Cape Cod to the western frontier in Berkshire County. With each year the long horseback rides under paltry winter suns and in the heat and languor of summer, the poor food and worse accommodations, and the absences from his family, which sometimes amounted to three months annually, became steadily more burdensome. After a decade in practice he complained of "this desultory Life," of one "naked, barren journey" after another, of his "rambling, roving, vagrant, Vagabond Life." "My Brains have been . . . barren. . . . My Soul has been starved" since leaving home, he wrote Abigail from Maine on one trip. Later he moaned about still another "insipid spiritless, tasteless Journey."[57]

Adams also wearied of the petty and repetitive caseload that constituted the bulk of his practice. He practiced both criminal and civil law, and appeared in numerous cases that were both complicated and intellectually stimulating. His most famous cases were his defense of John Hancock, who in 1768 was charged with smuggling, and his representation in 1770 of the British soldiers charged with the Boston Massacre. He appeared in provocative cases that concerned imperial trade, mob activity, homicide, rape, assault and battery, slavery, larceny, defamation, counterfeiting, and prize controversies. Yet for every exciting case, Adams, like any lawyer, coped with dozens of ordinary cases. His practice was clogged with the drudgery of preparing wills, contracts, and deeds, administering estates, litigating to acquire outstanding debts, and representing clients who were bickering with neighbors over property boundaries or straying cattle. Ten years after entering the profession, Adams began to carp about the "irksome," "tedious," and "dull" nature of his daily practice.[58]

However, unlike Jefferson, Adams never despised the practice of the law, although at mid-life discontentment gnawed at him. With no mountains left to climb as a lawyer, he longed for new challenges. Furthermore, his primal aspiration remained unfulfilled. The "Course I pursue will [not] lead me to Fame, Fortune, Power," he lamented at age thirty-five in 1770. Adams was a victim of circumstances. New England had changed since he attended college and made a career choice based on the rapturous illusion of attaining glory in the courtroom. Adams now discovered that the leading politicians had surpassed preeminent lawyers in winning public acclaim.[59]

He slowly realized that "politics [was] increasingly the Subject" of discussion at social gatherings. He knew too that popular leaders in the American protest against imperial policies after 1765 had come to enjoy "the Affection and Admiration of [their] Countrymen." Adams now evaluated politicians, much as he had once assessed other lawyers. He gushed at the patriotism of Otis, calling him a man with "real Character" who exhibited a "fervent Love of . . . Country and Good will to all Mankind." Adams craved the adulation that Otis had won, dreaming that someday he might be the object of the "Illuminations, Bonfires, Piramids, Obelisks, such grand Exhibitions, and such Fireworks, as were never seen in America."[60]

Adams eased into local politics once his legal practice was established. He was selected the surveyor of highways for Braintree. Subsequently, the town chose him to be a selectman. Within a few years he was selected both by Braintree and Boston to participate in the preparation of instructions to their representatives in the Massachusetts assembly.[61]

As Adams's reputation rose in legal circles, political leaders increasingly urged him to play an active role in provincial affairs. Samuel Adams and Otis repeatedly implored him to become more active politically, but for years he declined, preferring to confine his activities to surreptitious work, such as writing propaganda pieces for newspapers or corresponding with English radicals, where he could hide under a cloak of anonymity. Otis, blunt and acerbic, grew so frustrated that he once accused Adams of heedlessness to everything but "to get Money enough to carry you smoothly through this World." That was unfair, although Adams's reluctance did stem in part from fear that political activism might prove injurious to his legal career. Nor did he quite trust himself. As much as he admired Otis and Samuel Adams, he was convinced that both men had been seduced by power. He believed that possessing authority was laden with unavoidable traps for every politician, and especially so for an ambitious, aspiring man such as himself. He pointed to Jonathan Sewall, once his closest friend among the aspiring young attorneys in Boston, as an example of how power corrupted. He believed that Sewall, who had attached himself to the Court Party, which revolved about the royal governor, had abandoned every decent principle in the pursuit of political advancement.[62]

Adams reluctantly consented in 1770 to stand for election to the Massachusetts assembly. He feared that he lacked the toughness necessary to succeed in politics. He also worried that he might succeed, for he believed that successful men, like triumphant nations, were corrupted, and destroyed, by their triumphs. Finally, he worried that the strain and tension of holding public office might ruin his health.[63] On the last count, Adams was prescient.

He fell seriously ill in the winter of 1771. He collapsed one evening in February, suffering chest pains, difficulty breathing, and probably heart arrhythmia. Adams feared that he might not survive the night. He was very ill. Indeed, this man who seldom stopped working was unable to resume work for more than four months. For much of the time he was troubled by irritability, depression, weakness, fatigue, insomnia, and what was likely either heart palpitations or a quite rapid heartbeat.[64]

Adams was thirty-five when he fell ill. He had enjoyed good health previously, although a few months prior to his collapse he had mentioned feeling weak. What neither Adams nor any physician who would ever treat him understood was that he probably suffered from thyrotoxicosis, or hyperthyroidism, the overproduction of hormones secreted by the thyroid. Hyperthyroidism can be caused by many things, but most researchers believe it is genetic in origin and considerable evidence exists that it may be triggered by stress. Adams may have experienced some mild symptoms of this malady prior to this time, but the agitation in his life in 1770 and 1771—including the death of a child, the Boston Massacre trials, sitting in the assembly, and his growing disillusionment with his calling—likely served as the catalyst for the onset of serious thyrotoxicosis. Nineteenth-century physicians, who were without modern therapies, and hence sometimes treated patients for many years, discovered that hyperthyroidism sometimes went into permanent remission, although most frequently the illness reappeared. While in remission, the patient lived without discomfort.[65] This was the case with Adams. He had improved by the summer of 1771, but on at least three later occasions he suffered protracted recurrences of likely thyrotoxicosis.

Shocked by the behavior that he observed in the assembly, and convinced, perhaps correctly, that his illness was directly attributable to the stress that accompanied his political activism, Adams announced in the spring of 1771 that he would not seek reelection. This was not the first time that he had abandoned politics. After limited political activism in Braintree, he had resolved in 1766 never again to hold public office. "Farewell Politicks," he announced. "I must avoid Politicks," he said repeatedly. However, Adams had never been happy with his decision. He could not easily lay aside his political ambitions. Adams's quandary was that he feared a life in politics, but he fully understood that political activism alone might lead to the fame for which he yearned. Some of his contemporaries fathomed his predicament, and some like Edward Trowbridge, an older friend and Superior Court justice, warned him not to "meddle with Politicks, nor think about em. . . . [Y]ou will never get your . . . Mind at ease" until you forget politics, he advised.[66]

At age thirty-seven Adams made what he doubtless thought was an irrevocable decision. He resolved to never again have anything to do with politics. Having made his decision, he declared that he "never was happier, in my whole Life. . . . I feel easy, and composed and contented," he wrote, and anticipated many pleasant, stress-free years.[67] Little did Adams know, any more than did Washington or Jefferson, that great events soon would change his life forever.

January 1774 was a dulcet moment for Jefferson. He would look back on that period in his life as a time of "unchecquered happiness," a mellow month when on sun-soft winter days he set out new trees and assisted Martha, who was deep into still another pregnancy. It was a month when Washington entertained a visitor every day, hunted fox in the cold brown fields about Mount Vernon, and rode to Alexandria for pleasure. Adams was busy. He represented thirteen clients in cases before the Suffolk County Inferior Court in Boston.[68]

That same month the *Hayley*, a three-master from Boston, sailed up the choppy Thames River and, under lowering grey skies, docked in London. The ship's captain hurried ashore. He brought dramatic tidings from America. Barely three weeks before, protesters dressed like Indians had hurled dutied tea into Boston Harbor. Whatever frustrations or joys that Washington, Jefferson, and Adams had experienced in their lives and careers, whatever they aspired to in future years, the cyclonic impact of the British government's response to the Boston Tea Party would change everything for each man, and for most Americans.

The Declaration of Independence, 4 July 1776. Painting by John Trumbull. (Yale University Art Gallery, Trumbull Collection)

WAGING WAR AND INDEPENDENCE

4

"An Epocha in History"

Revolutionaries

G reat Britain's mainland colonies boiled over in 1765 with angry protests against the Stamp Act, the parent state's first attempt to tax the provincials. Washington and Adams responded to the tumultuous events of that year in intensely personal ways. Declaring that the crisis was "very unfortunate for me," and "set on foot for *my* Ruin," Adams feared the destruction of his "small . . . Reputation" if he openly denounced the mother country.[1] Washington immediately predicted that the stamp tax would be especially injurious to the wealthier provincials.[2]

Few, if any, Americans played more important roles in the American Revolution than Washington, Adams, and Jefferson. Yet during the Stamp Act crisis, and much that followed, these three acted cautiously, often preferring not to be involved, or to be only covertly active. During the first several years of the Anglo-American crisis, none were uninhibited firebrands. Each was yet a young man in 1765—at age thirty-three, Washington was the eldest—and each, not unnaturally, was eager to begin a family and achieve financial security. Furthermore, each knew that intemperate behavior could jeopardize his aspirations. Theirs was a very human response to the often bewildering and unsettling events that roared about them in the decade after 1765.

Only Washington had truly experienced the workings of the British empire and its officials. He had fought under the British flag, served under regular officers, dealt with royal governors, pursued a commission in the British army, and marketed his crops under the aegis of British economic regulations. His experiences affected his outlook in seminal ways. Nothing in Washington's behavior suggested that he was a malcontent during the decade after his return to Mount Vernon in 1759, yet his wartime activities had opened his eyes to certain realities and provoked his anger.

By the time he left the Virginia Regiment, Washington understood that colonists were second-class citizens within the British empire. He had bubbled with fury when British regular officers expressed their disdain of provincial officers and soldiers. He had chafed at the reality that he was subordinate to lower ranking officers who possessed a royal commission, and was bitter at having been denied such a commission. He was especially galled that some had been handsomely rewarded after serving only in London, where "a field of Battle never was seen." The only explanation for such treatment, he concluded, was that native-born Englishmen were favored over provincials. Why should "being American . . . deprive us of the benefits of British subjects [or] lessen our claim to preferment," he wondered. But Washington's anger was not merely that of a spurned courtier. He believed that London had ignored the security interests of Virginia by concentrating its military prowess in other theaters, leaving the government of Virginia to cope alone with its blazing frontier, a task beyond its capabilities. Many Virginians had suffered, and some had died, because of choices made far away in London. Washington saw that what was important to Virginia, and sometimes to American colonists generally, was often distinct from British and imperial interests. Only when provincial concerns dovetailed with the interests of powerful men in England, he had come to understand, were American matters likely to be acted on by those who ran the empire.[3]

During the 1760s Washington witnessed occurrences that confirmed his wartime conclusions. When London prohibited Virginia from issuing paper money in the early 1760s, he regarded the act as in Britain's interest, but prejudicial toward Virginia. He railed that the colony had been denied a medium of exchange with which to conduct its internal trade and manage its affairs. He was angry too when the Privy Council disallowed a Virginia law that placed a prohibitive duty on slave imports. Together with many other planters, Washington had grown anxious to curtail the growth of slavery in Virginia. He feared that Virginia's slave population, which had increased from about 15,000 to nearly 190,000 since 1700, had grown to unmanageable proportions. Slave insurrections, he worried, were increasingly likely. Washington's thinking on slavery was also dictated by pecuniary interests. Now a wheat farmer, he required a smaller labor force than when he had raised tobacco; should the importation of slaves be restricted, the prices of chattel would increase, a happy circumstance for someone like himself who might wish to sell his surplus laborers. Like a growing number of Virginians, Washington additionally had come to see slavery as a damper on economic diversification. He hoped his province would develop a commercially competitive economy that would be better able to compete in the changing Atlantic market. But the Privy Council's action made it quite clear that London would neither tamper with England's profitable slave trade nor permit Virginia to grow more economically independent.[4]

But it was conditions in the West that particularly chagrined Washington. He exploded when Fort Pitt, which had been inadequately garrisoned and provisioned by Great Britain, was nearly captured by Indians in Pontiac's Rebellion in 1763. Not only had British policy left Virginia "without Money" to pacify the frontier, he railed, but London had neglected the installation that had been "the cause of the last war and which has cost . . . her Colonies so much Blood and Treasure."[5]

That was the tip of the iceberg. Washington wanted, and expected, the West to be opened quickly, so that he could begin selling his bounty lands and profit from his investments in the Ohio and Mississippi Companies. He had been cheered by the rumor that the imperial government would soon establish a new colony beyond the forks of the Ohio, for he knew that a colony would provide protection from the Indians, bring order, stimulate migration to the region, and increase the value of his land. Yet the colony never came into existence. Officials in London muddled along aimlessly, he thought, unable to formulate a coherent western policy. He railed that he had sought to make a fortune in the same manner as his predecessors in earlier generations, by "taking up & purchasing at very low rates the rich back Lands." However, his best efforts had been frustrated by officials across the sea.[6]

Greater disappointments followed. In the late 1760s the Secretary of State for the Southern Department, the ministerial official most responsible for American affairs, announced that all lands west of the mountains belonged to the Crown. The decision, made in remote London, portended disaster for the western companies. Later, John Murray, the Earl of Dunmore and the last royal governor of Virginia, disallowed William Crawford's surveys of the bounty lands on the grounds that Washington's surveyor had been improperly licensed. Washington received the news with disbelief. More than twenty years after he first had risked his life to secure the Ohio Country for Anglo-

America, Washington not only had not made a cent off his western lands, but his title to those holdings had been jeopardized by royal officials.[7]

Britain's addled western policies also played havoc with the aspirations of the Potomac Company, which hoped to dig a canal that linked East and West along the Potomac corridor. Washington had invested in the enterprise in the expectation that the canal would become "the Channel of Commerce between Great Britain and the immense Tract of Country" beyond the mountains. However, until settlers moved across the mountains, articles of commerce would never flow. By the mid-1760s Washington's ambitious western schemes were stalled and at the mercy of ministers in London whom he did not know and could not influence. Although he kept his fury in check in public, his disappointment fueled his growing conviction that colonial Virginia could never fully control its destiny within the British empire, at least as the empire was constructed in the 1760s.[8]

Jefferson saw reminders everywhere that he was a British American. As a youth he had worshiped in the Anglican Church. He had lived in Williamsburg for several years, a village given a special sheen by cosmopolitan Britains, such as Professor Small. The law that he studied and practiced was derived from English statutes and jurisprudence. He knew that someday he would make his living, as had his father, through the tobacco trade with Great Britain. Although nothing alienated Jefferson from Great Britain in these years, nothing drew him toward a close attachment with the mother country. He was born an Englishman in Virginia, but thought of himself as a Virginian. He was the fourth generation of his family to live in the colony, stretching back to Thomas Jefferson I, about a century prior to the Stamp Act crisis. His ancestors had struggled to subdue this continent, from which he had never strayed. As a young man, Jefferson thought of his province as "my country, Virginia," a sentiment he would express even after having been president of the United States.

Adams was the product of a farm family in a rustic village, where the Sunday sermon and the vicissitudes of health and weather, not politics, gave direction to life. Yet as a youth in a family that had been touched by several generations of imperial warfare, Adams was to some degree aware of the realities of life within the British empire. When an old man, he recollected how King George's War, fought when he was an adolescent, had made a "mighty impression . . . upon my little head." He especially remembered that his father and others in Braintree had cursed the British for having returned Louisbourg to France in the treaty that ended hostilities. This city-fortress, which guarded the entrance to New France, had been taken in a costly campaign by a Massachusetts army, only to be exchanged in the peace settlement for European territory coveted by powerful interests in England. Louisbourg's abandonment by London meant that New France once again was free to arm its Indian allies, enabling them to take to the warpath on the New England frontier. That Louisbourg was returned to France was a revealing indicator of where New England fit into British priorities. Nor was that all. Like Washington, Adams had been mortified by Britain's treatment of colonial soldiers in the French and Indian War. It made "my blood boil in my veins," he later recounted, to think that the provincials had been treated as unworthy soldiers suited only for menial labor. Perhaps it was not so surprising that when the war erupted, twenty-year-old John Adams told a friend that if the French should be driven from Canada, the colonies would have little need for further British protection. They could begin "setting up for themselves."[9]

Adams was a fervent nationalist during the early portion of the French and Indian War. He was exhilarated by the sight of battalions of British troops marching through New England. He thrilled when two commanders of the British army, Lord Loudoun and General Jeffrey Amherst, encamped near his home. Caught up in the war spirit that swept over his province in 1756, Adams longed to soldier. He carried a military dispatch from Worcester to Newport, Rhode Island, and later claimed to have sought a captain's commission in the army of Massachusetts, although his assertion lacks credibility.[10] Adams never bore arms in this conflict, and after he opened his legal business in 1758 paid scant heed to the war.

Soon after America's role in the war ended, Adams became aware of strains between the colonies and the parent state. Before Washington or Jefferson, he appears to have foreseen the potential for a shattering confrontation between America and Great Britain. In 1761 royal customs officials in Boston requested writs of assistance, blanket search warrants for the purpose of discovering smuggled goods in violation of imperial trade laws. When Boston's merchants sued to prevent the issuance of the writs, Adams's mentors, Otis and Gridley, represented the merchants and government respectively in the ensuing trial. Adams, therefore, had an abiding interest in the proceedings. He attended the hearings and listened with fascination as Otis argued against the writs on constitutional grounds, drawing a distinction between imperial jurisdiction and the natural rights and powers of the colonies. Years later, Adams said that the notion of American Independence was born in Otis's actions. He exaggerated, as the case attracted little attention outside New England. However, the episode made a powerful impression on him. Britain's behavior, he thought, was that of "a haughty, powerful nation, who held us in great contempt." Otis's compelling argument profoundly touched him as well, and also caused him to look differently on America's relationship with Great Britain. Thereafter Adams, who already had questioned whether it was in America's interest to be tied to postwar Great Britain, believed that Britain's powers over the colonies were not absolute. He understood as early as 1761 that "a Collision" between the provinces and London was inevitable, but he was far too absorbed with the establishment of his legal practice and courtship of Abigail Smith to pay much heed to imperial problems.[11]

However, Great Britain's implementation of a new colonial policy after 1763 affected men such as Washington and Adams. Britain had won Canada and everything in North America east of the Mississippi River in the peace accord that ended the French and Indian War, but its victory came at a staggering cost. Britain was left groaning beneath a heavy debt. Nor was it the indebtedness alone that troubled London. The ministry thought the time right to tighten its control over the colonies, a notion stimulated in part because some colonies had inadequately supported the late war, and in part from the apprehension that such lightly held, distant colonies might drift toward independence. The ministry, therefore, implemented revenue-raising measures—the Sugar Act in 1764 and the Stamp Act the following year—and strengthened the customs service to ensure that the imperial regulations would be enforced and the much-needed duties would be collected. The Stamp Act was Parliament's first attempt ever to impose a tax on the colonists.[12]

The Sugar Act provoked a flurry of pamphlets and little else. Even the pamphlets were mild, save for that of Otis, who gathered the arguments he had made three years earlier during the writs cases and published them in a tract entitled *The Rights of the Colonies Asserted and Proved*. It defiantly proclaimed that the mother country had acted in an unconstitutional manner. The Stamp Act elicited a very different response among the colonists. America blazed with an almost revolutionary fervor. Numerous pamphlets appeared that questioned the limits of British jurisdiction. Riots and street demonstrations flared in several cities, stamp distributors were threatened with violence and compelled to resign, and economic boycotts sprang up here and there. In the spring and summer of 1765 several assemblies, beginning with the House of Burgesses in Virginia, denounced the act.

Adams could not ignore the upheaval, but his response was equivocal. Although he thought the Stamp Act a grave threat to the colonists—he privately called it an "enormous Engine, fabricated . . . for battering down all the Rights and Liberties of America"—he was loath to risk his burgeoning legal practice in a dispute that would probably soon be resolved and never again replicated. In addition, Adams was both outraged and frightened by the violence that accompanied the protest in Boston. In mid-August protestors in Boston took to the streets to denounce the legislation and hang in effigy the colony's stamp collector, Andrew Oliver. That evening a second demonstration turned nasty. A mob destroyed a business owned by the stamp collector, then his residence. Another mob surged through the streets two weeks later. Its fury was not sated until it had looted and destroyed the home of Thomas Hutchinson, the lieutenant governor of Massachusetts. Adams was shaken. He agreed that the Stamp Act must be attacked, but was confident its repeal could be secured by peaceful means. He privately questioned the motives of the "designing persons" who manipulated the mobs. Not even Samuel Adams, his cousin, whom he thought was most responsible for the violence, escaped his censure. He said privately that Samuel Adams not only had schemed to attain personal power, but that he had artfully seized upon the tax as a means of fomenting revolutionary changes. Furthermore, John, who in his ambitious dreams must have hoped someday to hold a prestigious royal appointment, was shocked that Oliver, a man whom he believed had never "done any Thing to injure the People, or to incur their Displeasure," should be so vilified.[13]

Samuel Adams, who in fact emerged as the leader of the popular protest in Massachusetts, repeatedly implored John to play a more active role. Knowing his cousin well, Samuel sought to convince him that an activist role would bring him glory and renown. John finally relented, but discretion and anonymity remained his watchwords. He penned a series of unsigned newspaper essays and drafted Braintree's instructions to its assemblyman, low-profile actions that kept his name from the public. Just before Christmas, Samuel Adams also induced a Boston town meeting to elect Adams, together with Gridley and Otis, to appear before Governor Francis Bernard to urge the reopening of the provincial courts, closed because of the defiance of the Stamp Act. Dressed in a scarlet robe and powdered wig, Adams and his colleagues told the governor that the tax was unconstitutional, as it was enacted "where we are in no Sense represented. . . . A Parliament of Great Britain can have no more Right to tax the Colonies, than a Parliament of Paris."[14]

The upheaval had an enormous impact on Adams. He called 1765 the most remarkable year of his life, for the Stamp Act crisis, far more than the writs of assistance case, had caused him, and many others, to contemplate the Anglo-American relationship. He had not been transformed into a revolutionary—throughout the crisis he said that he believed the tax was only a misguided act by a poorly informed ministry—but he was adamant that Parliament's jurisdiction over America was limited. To acknowledge total parliamentary sovereignty over the colonies, he said, would result in the "Ruin of America." The crisis was crucial for Adams in another sense. Although he believed that Braintree had not festooned him with adequate laurels, and he envied Samuel Adams for the colony-wide fame and adulation he had won in leading the resistance movement, in March 1766 Adams was elected to its Board of Selectmen, a post his father had held for nine terms. After only seven years in the law, and at age thirty, Adams had begun to achieve the recognition for which he had long hungered.[15]

Washington, like Adams, was affected by the Stamp Act. News of the proposed duties had not reached Williamsburg when he and his fellow Burgesses gathered early in May 1765. He remained for only a few sessions before returning home to tend his agrarian enterprises. Washington was at Mount Vernon experimenting with the planting of wheat when official word of the Stamp Act arrived in the capital. Thus, he did not hear the speeches that denounced the tax, including a fabled verbal assault by Patrick Henry. Nor did he vote for the Virginia Resolves, the first colonial legislative enactment that denounced the act as unconstitutional.[16]

Washington subsequently agreed that the Stamp Act was "unconstitutional," but he viewed it more as an aggrieved businessman than an ideologue. He labeled the act "ill judgd," predicting that taxation would further strip the colonists of precious cash, reducing their capability to satisfy their creditors in England or to import goods from the parent state. Luxury items attained from England would have to be shunned, he cautioned. The provincials would inevitably search out cheaper necessities within the provinces, stimulating American manufacturing that would compete with English producers. Washington saw much that had escaped Adams. Whereas Adams believed London had made an innocent blunder, Washington saw the pieces of a puzzle coming together. He glimpsed a government that sought not only to tax the provinces, but to impose "restrictions on our Trade . . . to Burthen us." Having already confronted imperial obstacles both to his personal fulfillment and economic aspirations, Washington was ripe to apprehend a pattern in ministerial policy that aimed at reducing colonial independence. He was fully aware that since mid-century London had systematically enforced its commercial policies, prohibited the manufacture of some varieties of iron, which had been the principal source of Augustine Washington's fortune, denied the colonists the right to issue paper currency—which in at least one instance prevented Washington from collecting a debt—disallowed Virginia's law curtailing slave imports, and sought to tax the provincials. Britain's new colonial policy came at the very moment when Washington not only contemplated selling his surplus laborers, but when he longed for the opportunity to vend his cash crops in a truly free market and invest his profits in domestic manufacturing. Washington was inactive in Virginia's protest in 1765, but in his thinking he had outdistanced most of his fellow colonists. He beheld a design in imperial policy that most Americans would not discover until another decade passed, and he already understood that the colonists' needs were unlikely to be tended. The government in London was more devoted to serving powerful interests at home than in assisting the cause of influential provincials.[17]

When news of the repeal of the Stamp Act arrived early in 1766, both Washington and Adams were delighted. Repeal meant that "many Scenes of Confusion and distress have been avoided," Washington remarked. "Since the Stamp Act is repealed," Adams announced, "I am at perfect Ease about Politicks." With his law practice absorbing his attention during 1766 and 1767, Adams said little in his diary about politics. Washington was no less preoccupied by his businesses, including the acquisition and survey of bounty lands. His diary, silent on imperial issues, runs on with accounts of sowing crops, gathering hay, and numerous pastimes. Entries such as "Fox hunt . . . catchd nothing. . . . Hunting again. . . . Started a Fox and run him 4 hours. . . . At home all day at Cards," were not untypical. Adams believed the Anglo-American crisis was at an end and unlikely to recur soon. Washington had a better sense of the political dynamics of his time. Despair and contention were inevitable, he believed, unless London addressed the interests of the colonists.[18]

Another crisis soon erupted out of a source that neither man would have expected. The ministry once again sought to tax the colonists, this time through the Townshend Duties, imposts on glass, lead, paint, paper, and tea imported into America. At the same time the ministry not only created a board of customs in Boston to enforce the law, but it suspended the New York assembly for having failed to provide adequately for the British army quartered within the province. Word of these measures reached the colonies during the summer of 1767. Protests occurred at once, although the initial attempts at resistance in Boston were ineffectual. The assembly remonstrated against the tax, but efforts to institute another economic boycott collapsed late in the year. Disturbances were so minor, and so isolated, that Adams moved his family to Boston in April 1768, a step he would never have taken had he anticipated a massive popular upheaval. Adams had played no role in the abortive protest. His only published essay during this period was silent on the Townshend Duties, although it warned that an Anglican bishop might be appointed for America. Washington was one of the first colonists to be aware of the new taxes, learning of the legislation from his London factor, but he inexplicably ignored the matter for eighteen months, even skipping the 1768 session of the Burgesses that responded to the revenue-raising measure. While the assembly denounced the taxes as unconstitutional, Washington caulked his fishing schooner, hunted three times, attended a ball in Alexandria, and spent six days at Mount Vernon conferring with the frontier surveyor he had employed to locate the most desirable bounty lands.[19]

As Washington lived quietly at Mount Vernon, seemingly oblivious to the new ministerial act, Adams, to his surprise and consternation, found himself living in a city that became a cauldron of fury. Abigail had barely finished unpacking before Boston was swept with riots brought on by the impounding of the *Liberty*, a sloop owned by John Hancock, who was charged with smuggling. The popular leadership seized this moment, when emotions were at a fever pitch, to once again push for an economic boycott of the parent state. They were more successful. Boston agreed to join in a boycott if New York and Philadelphia also participated.

Adams once again shrank from playing a visible role in the protest, save for acting in his professional capacity, as when he defended Hancock. He refused to attend Boston town meetings and turned a deaf ear to the entreaties of those who urged him to speak out publicly against British policies. "That way madness lies," he said, a remark that suggests he still believed that the radicals secretly harbored a revolutionary agenda. Nevertheless, by 1768 Adams understood that Samuel Adams's prophesy of three years earlier was true: an activist role was essential for anyone who yearned for an important elected office. Whereas John had been elected a local selectman in 1766, in the wake of the Stamp Act protests, Samuel Adams had won election for the first time to the Massachusetts assembly and Otis had been catapulted to the speakership of the House of Representatives.

The unrest in Boston's streets forced Adams to wrestle with his choices. He was thirty-two years old with two children, ages two and three, in 1768. Was it money he sought? Was political power what he most desired? Did he even wish to maintain his private law practice? Might he not be happier as a prosecutor or a judge? He knew that if he dared to play an open, active role in the American protest, he would never receive an appointment as a royal magistrate. If he publicly attacked the mother country, the same "Curses and Imprecations" that royal officials had heaped on other activists would be directed toward him. Such attacks might impair his legal practice, as he believed had been the case with Otis's law business. Ultimately, Adams declined a visible role, telling himself that activism would "neither lead me to . . . Power Nor to the Service of my . . . Country." Nevertheless, he hoped to keep his options open. Unwilling to provoke the ire of the popular leadership, he consented to draft Boston's instructions to its assemblymen, an act that would not bring much notoriety. He wrote a muscular statement that denounced the seizure of the *Liberty* and condemned the Townshend Duties. Hancock soon thereafter retained him as counsel in the ongoing *Liberty* case.[20]

The crisis heated up as the summer proceeded, primarily because of London's addled response to the initial, and largely mild and feckless, provincial reaction to the new taxes. In a series of acts akin to throwing gasoline on a smoldering fire, Lord Hillsborough, the Secretary of State for American Affairs, ordered three regiments of British troops to Boston, demanded that the Massachusetts General Court rescind its earlier denunciation of British taxes or face dissolution, and threatened to dissolve any assembly that subsequently attacked the Townshend Duties. Hillsborough's witless edicts frightened so many colonists that new life was pumped into the protest movement. American boycotts that might otherwise never have been instituted sprang up in New York, Philadelphia, and Boston.

Nonetheless, Adams was barely more active than Washington. He continued to believe that the radical leadership "deceived the people," and vowed not to be a party to "their Crimes." But when Samuel Adams told him that some were whispering that he was more loyal to the mother country than to Massachusetts—likely a truthful statement, as it was well known that royal officials had approached John about becoming solicitor general of Massachusetts, the chief legal official in the province—Adams suddenly changed course. With some public display, he declined the royal post and attended a Sons of Liberty rally in Dorchester. He also met clandestinely with activist leaders on several occasions to prepare propagandistic newspaper essays and quietly participated in the drafting of various Boston town meeting statements, including its petition to King George III decrying ministerial acts. The year 1768 was not an easy one for Adams. He walked a tightrope. He hoped to avoid being seen by royal officials as a radical, yet he did not wish to alienate the popular leaders, for they might control Massachusetts' politics for years to come.[21]

Washington, meanwhile, finally responded to the crisis early in 1769. Actually, he had never been as indifferent as his behavior in 1767 and 1768 suggested. Because he had never been a leader in the House of Burgesses, and because the initial protest against the Townshend Duties once again took the form of legislative remonstrances, Washington had little part to play. Furthermore, both as a man of action and one who chafed at a subordinate capacity, he found it repugnant to be saddled with a passive role in a terrible crisis. His absence from Williamsburg in 1768 may even have been intended as a show of his disapproval of still another impotent legislative petition to officials in London.

Once Hillsborough's obdurate remarks demonstrated the pointlessness of further supplications, Washington seized the initiative. He sought out George Mason, his neighbor at nearby Gunston Hall, who was esteemed in Virginia as a political theorist. Washington spoke with him of creating an army—he was one of the first in America to raise the specter of taking up arms against the mother country—in order to compel Britain to repeal its new taxes. However, Washington's first choice was not armed resistance, but an economic boycott of the parent state.[22]

Although he did not ordinarily think in legalistic terms, Washington clearly believed that Parliament had no authority to tax the colonists. This was not a new way of thinking for him. Four years earlier, he had privately denounced the Stamp Act as "unconstitutional" and "a direful attack" on the liberty of Anglo-Americans. He told Mason in 1769 that he discerned a pattern in London's policies that amounted to "nothing less than the deprivation of American freedom." Britain's illegal taxation was not all that aroused him. Venom dripped from Washington's pen as he alluded to the ministerial officials as "our lordly Masters."[23] Washington's seething anger was as great as that of any American activist. Even at this early date, he may have secretly yearned for independence. If not, his predilection was for a far less dependent relationship with the parent state.

Mason shared Washington's zeal for a boycott, but hoped to return to the tranquility that had existed before 1763, changing little in the traditional connection between provinces and parent state. He hurried to Mount Vernon, where he and Washington prepared a nonimportation plan for Virginia. Washington presented the embargo scheme at the May session of the assembly.[24]

The Burgesses denounced the "ill advised Regulations, in several Acts of Parliament"—an indication that Virginia, like Washington, was anguished by more than just the Townshend Duties—before it adopted, with few alterations, the Washington–Mason boycott plan. A year later, in June 1770, the assembly created a committee to tighten the enforcement of the embargo. Washington was appointed to the panel, his most important assignment in a dozen years as an assemblyman.[25] Washington had emerged as a respected legislator. His impatience and growing disenchantment with the imperial government had become the mainstream view within Virginia. Moreover, as the province assumed a tough, defiant posture that augured a collision with London, it was natural that the status of Virginia's most notable soldier would be in the ascendancy.

Jefferson sat in the House of Burgesses during the sessions of 1769 and 1770. Although he had played no role heretofore in Virginia's protest, he had followed matters closely. He spoke often with George Wythe, who as early as 1764 had helped prepare the Burgesses' memorial against a proposed stamp tax. Furthermore, as a twenty-two-year-old law student in 1765, Jefferson had stood in a crowded hall outside the assembly chamber listening to Henry's fiery speech attacking the Stamp Act. No contemporary record exists of Jefferson's reaction to Britain's initial attempts to tax the colonies, but he must have been profoundly impressed. He immediately added works on constitutional law and ancient history to his library and later referred to Henry's speech as filled with such "torrents of sublime eloquence" that it sparked "the dawn of the Revolution."[26] Jefferson was young and without influence between 1765 and 1769, and he was just beginning his courtship of Martha Skelton in 1770. Yet from the first, he opposed parliamentary taxation and signed the boycott agreement that Washington and Mason proposed, although he was unwilling to fully abide by the embargo. He soon ordered a mahogany piano from England—he said he would store it until the embargo was lifted—and later purchased windows for Monticello from the mother country.[27]

A reader of Adams's diary for 1769 would not know that an imperial crisis festered. His interest in his legal career overshadowed his interest in public matters. But events were about to overtake his life. A series of troubling incidents shook Boston in the winter of 1770. Crowds took over the streets on several occasions to protest British policy. Late in February a mob attacked the residence of a known informer for the customs service, who fired into the crowd, killing a young boy. A week later, off-duty soldiers and dock workers brawled near the waterfront. Some feared a calamity in this tense atmosphere. "America [is] on the point of bursting into flames," the Sons of Liberty told friends in London. Combustion occurred on March 5. On that cold night British soldiers fired into a crowd gathered before the Customs House. Several people were hit, five fatally. Adams referred to what had occurred as the "slaughter in King Street." Most Bostonians called it the Boston Massacre.[28]

Although the evidence is unclear, it appears that leaders in the protest movement, including Samuel Adams and Dr. Joseph Warren, may have convinced Adams to defend the soldiers charged with the killings. Although the radical leadership believed that convictions were inevitable, they must have wished to avoid allegations that the trial was a sham. A defense team headed by a reputable lawyer, such as Adams, would militate against such recrimination. Why would Adams have accepted such a case? The soldiers could hardly pay exorbitant fees. Adams in fact later remarked that he earned only eighteen guineas off the case, barely sufficient to purchase a pair of shoes. In addition, his defense of the hated soldiers was certain to arouse skepticism among those who already suspected him of Tory sympathies. Adams took the case for numerous reasons. He believed the soldiers deserved a fair trial. He also knew that "this would be as important a Cause as ever was tryed in any Court or Country of the World." He not only wanted to be party to a historic event, but he gambled that when passions cooled, his performance as a superb defense counsel would enhance his stature and cause him to be acknowledged as one of the most distinguished lawyers in America. Moreover, defending the soldiers would not injure his standing with the government, so that in a few years, when the tumultuous times had passed, he might be amply rewarded. However, Adams had a more immediate reason for taking the case. He likely cut a deal with the popular leaders. In return for representing the soldiers, he was to be compensated with a seat in the Massachusetts assembly. Before the trials ended, in fact, one of Boston's four legislators resigned his assembly seat and Adams was elected as his replacement.[29]

Adams orchestrated a masterful defense strategy. In the face of considerable opposition by the radical leadership, he first secured a postponement of the trial until autumn, a delaying tactic that permitted some of the popular rage to subside. Next, he gained separate trials for the commanding officer, Captain Thomas Preston, and his men. This ploy enabled the defense to argue that the captain had not ordered the shooting, while in the trial of the men that followed, Adams maintained that the soldiers had followed orders. Today his stratagem would violate the American Bar Association's Canons of Professional Ethics, which prohibits a lawyer from engaging in such a conflict of interests. However, in 1770 his artifice was possible and it worked. Preston was acquitted, as were six of the eight soldiers. Two were convicted of manslaughter, not homicide, and escaped punishment by pleading benefit of clergy, a technicality for escaping the death sentence which had roots back to medieval times.[30]

Adams's victory enhanced his reputation and practice. However, his other prize, the seat in the assembly, was not the plum he had expected. For five years Adams had privately castigated the "designing persons" who orchestrated the popular protest. Now, these same men had secured his election and expected his support. In what Adams saw as a series of contrived controversies, the radical leaders in 1770 and 1771 sought to keep alive the flame of protest by demonstrating that London, and its royal officials in Boston, chiefly Lieutenant Governor Hutchinson, conspired to destroy freedom in the colonies. Adams saw no proof of such a plot. Now that he was something of an insider, what he did see more clearly than ever was that the radicals fomented unrest, hoping to maintain the colonial resistance until "Warrs, and Confusions and Carnage" resulted. He was appalled by their machinations, but cooperated and even managed some of their schemes. To have done otherwise could have harmed his career and ruined his aspirations. But he was disgusted by his complicity in their disingenuous campaign and left in "great Anxiety." Like a man riding a tiger, Adams doggedly hung on until the stress brought on by the Massacre trials and his political activism, among other things, triggered the episode of probable thyrotoxicosis early in 1771. Although he was recovering by late summer, he did not seek reelection. He used his health as an excuse to step aside. He also moved his family back to Braintree. "[S]till, calm, happy Braintree," he sighed, for he was happy to be away from turbulent Boston and the tentacles of the radical activists.[31]

Adams soon had reason to question his acumen. During 1770 Great Britain repealed all the Townshend Duties save for the tax on tea. The colonial protest movement collapsed almost immediately. Amazed at the "melodious Harmony, the perfect Concords" that suddenly prevailed, Adams predicted that the imperial crisis would never resurface in his lifetime, and he moved his family back to Boston. He suddenly realized that he might have remained in the assembly and reaped the accolades he had long sought. But he had abandoned politics. "I am for what I can see, quite left alone, in the World," Adams despaired.[32]

Historians once referred to the period between the partial repeal of the Townshend Duties and the Tea Act crisis three years later as "the lull," as if little of consequence occurred in Anglo-American relations. Washington's papers convey just that sense. After early 1770 he never again mentioned British taxation until he learned of the Boston Tea Party early in 1774. His time was consumed by his business activities and, like Adams, he appears to have thought the great imperial crisis was over, or not likely to recur anytime soon. Nevertheless, Washington was temperamentally and intellectually a radical—a revolutionary, even—by 1770, and within two or three years Adams and Jefferson shared his outlook.

Embracing a revolutionary viewpoint is something few can do. Most people, "educated in an habitual affection" for their nation, its rulers, history, heroes, and culture—as Adams remarked with regard to how he and his contemporaries had been brought up to think of Great Britain as "a kind and tender parent"—find dissent, much less rebellion, anathema.[33] Fear, or a haunting sense of futility, might deter others from protest, but moderation most often springs both from deeply subliminal and conscious fetters of responsibility, prudence, and love. Washington, Adams, and Jefferson, and most of their fellow colonials, initially found truly radical behavior and beliefs no less unsavory than would most Americans today if asked to betray or take up arms against their country. The colonials venerated Great Britain as the most free and open, and least intolerant, nation in the Western world, and one in which prosperity and opportunity abounded. A measure of the emotional and psychological magnitude of the move from a loyal mentality to revolutionary zealotry can be fathomed from the realization that it was not until the very eve of independence, ten long years after the protest commenced, that a majority of Americans were able to sever their ties with the mother country.

Washington was the first of the three to reflect on the wisdom of a union with a parent that sought to divest the colonists of the autonomy they had long enjoyed.[34] Had London not capitulated to the provincial trade embargo in 1770, Washington was prepared—if sufficient numbers of his fellow colonists agreed—to fight to force Great Britain to back down.

Jefferson later remarked that as early as 1772 or 1773 he despaired that many leaders in the assembly lacked the "forwardness and zeal which the times required." He was also disturbed by the lack of cohesion between the colonies, a disunity that had doomed efforts to build a truly effective boycott during the Townshend Duties crisis. Following the *Gaspee* incident—when London decreed that those in Rhode Island charged with the destruction of the customs vessel, *Gaspee*, be transported to England to stand trial—Jefferson joined with Henry and Richard Henry Lee to propose intercolonial committees of correspondence. Their immediate goal was to revive a colonial protest movement that had atrophied since the partial repeal of the Townshend Duties in 1770.[35]

How Jefferson got to this point in his thinking is difficult to reconstruct, for the destruction of his early papers in the fire at Shadwell, as well as his distant bearing and reticent, almost recondite manner, have made him nearly impenetrable. Late in life, Jefferson partially explained the fury that drove him to revolution by recalling that "nothing liberal could expect success" in provincial Virginia. Virginians, he recollected, had been unable to enact reforms because they groaned under a "regal government," but during his six years in the House of Burgesses after 1769, Jefferson is known to have supported only one reform measure. He backed an effort by Richard Bland, a respected member of the assembly, to secure passage of a bill that would have permitted slaveowners to manumit their chattel. The legislation failed in 1769, but its failure was due solely to opposition within the Burgesses. Neither the parent state nor the royal authorities within the province defeated the measure. No evidence exists that Jefferson was committed to any other reform endeavors.[36]

Jefferson also indicated that his revolutionary sentiments had been born out of his despair that the colonists were unable to shape their lives and destinies. His arguments on this score were more persuasive. The autonomy of the colonists, he wrote, had been "circumscribed within narrow limits." Their role as provincials was merely "to direct all labors in subservience to her [Great Britain's] interests."[37] The core of Jefferson's commitment to colonial protest did in fact arise from his belief that American subordination and dependency was unpalatable.

Jefferson has often been portrayed as an ivory-tower visionary. In fact, the historic Jefferson, the revolutionary democrat, lay in the remote future. The Jefferson of the 1770s was quite different. Self-centered and busy with the establishment of his adult life and career, he had given little thought to idealistic concerns. Like Washington, he inhabited a very real world in which ledger books were of crucial importance. He raised a cash crop in an era when serious economic woes descended on Chesapeake planters. He was aware of numerous instances in which bad markets, like a malignancy, had eaten away at prosperous tobacco producers, first causing indebtedness, then total ruin. Although Jefferson believed that he was in good shape, he worried that forces beyond his control "might sweep away the whole of my little fortune."

The natural market woes experienced by planters were exacerbated by policies enacted in London by those whom Washington had called America's "lordly Masters." When Jefferson spoke of his despair at the colonists' inability to shape their own destiny, this was what he meant. Like Washington, he was angered by the currency restrictions imposed by London. Even worse was Britain's refusal to permit the colonists to "exercise . . . a free trade with all parts of the world," an abridgment, he thought, of the "natural rights" of Americans. Confined to markets within the empire, and prohibited from vending "the surplus of our tobacco remaining after the consumption of Great Britain," Jefferson knew all too well that planters inevitably faced artificially depressed prices and the very real danger of ruin. Nor were these the only constraints that the parent state imposed on the colonists. Jefferson railed against Parliament's restrictions on certain types of manufacturing by Americans and, like Washington, castigated limitations on the colonists's access to its frontier lands. Constricted commercially, and obstructed in their opportunities to invest, Jefferson and many other planters in the early 1770s discovered that abstractions such as independence, virtue, rights, and liberty had assumed real qualities.[38]

Of course, Jefferson's outlook was influenced by Enlightenment liberalism, classical history and theory, English law, and his study of English history and government. However, every idea was first filtered through the reality that he faced both as a planter and a Virginian who yearned to control his destiny and shape conditions, especially economic conditions, within his world. After 1769, he reread John Locke and Montesquieu and, like many articulate colonists, was influenced by England's radical English Whig polemicists. These writers articulated early modern republican theory. Uneasy with the rapid commercialization of the English economy, society, and politics in their time, and fearful of the threat to conventional values posed by these new capitalistic interests, the Whig theorists produced a literature of social criticism. Equating modernization with decay and corruption, they profiled a contemporary England in which liberty was imperiled. For Jefferson, who already believed that England had been contaminated for centuries by a feudal monarchy, here not only was verification that freedom was at risk in the increasingly iniquitous parent state, but that the long arm of this old rotten state might threaten America with contamination. It was a short step to believe that England's leadership secretly plotted to curtail provincial liberties. By 1774 he was convinced that London schemed to reduce "a free and happy People to a Wretched & miserable state of slavery," in the words of Washington's nonimportation resolution that he had signed in 1769.[39] Later, in the Declaration of Independence, Jefferson would describe British policy after 1765 as "a long train of abuses and usurpations, pursuing invariably the same object . . . a design to reduce them [the colonists] under absolute despotism."

Jefferson's ability to pursue happiness within the Anglo-American world was seriously hampered. In 1774 he expressed his willingness "to establish union [with Great Britain] on a generous plan." His remark suggests that he, like Washington, already considered the old union to be obsolete. Reform alone —only revolutionary reform, in fact—could preserve America's ties to Great Britain. This was the "liberal" reform that he despaired of ever securing within the Anglo-American empire.

Even more than Jefferson, Adams attributed his radicalization to the force of ideas. He once suggested that by reading the tracts of the same English radical Whig theorists who had influenced Jefferson, he had grown aware both of the corruption eating away at England's vitals and of a ministerial conspiracy to extirpate American liberties. The truth is more complicated. As with Jefferson, ideology was not the sole trigger of Adams's behavior, but his reading and reflection, as well as the lessons of his youth, were crucial determinants of his conduct.[40]

Adams's worldview was a fusion of ideas. In part, it resulted from the somber and austere Calvinistic ideals on which he had been raised in Deacon Adams's household. It arose too out of the New Englanders unbridled despair at what they believed to be the mother country's disdain for the region's security interests. It was also the legacy of his study of history and moral theory, especially the writings of Locke and other Enlightenment writers. When barely out of college, Adams declared to a friend that to understand human behavior one had to comprehend "the passions, appetites, [and] affections in nature" that drove humankind. "An intimate knowledge therefore of the intellectual and moral world is the sole foundation of which a stable structure of knowledge can be erected," he said.[41]

The great lesson that Adams derived from such knowledge was that humankind was given to corruption. He came to see the species as driven by insatiable desires that led each person to search endlessly, selfishly, for happiness. Adams believed that the forces of reason and emotion warred within the breast of each person. Passion, greed, ambition, vanity, envy, and hatred stirred in every heart. The first urge of humankind, he thought, was to ask how each act and every occurrence would "affect my Humour, my Interest, my . . . Designs." Since the transgressions of Adam in the Garden of Eden, he said, "Mankind in general has been given up to Strong Delusions, vile Affections, sordid Lusts, and brutal Appetites." Yet he also acknowledged a brighter side to human nature. Most persons cherished sociability and played out their lives seeking an equilibrium between the natural, competing urges. The struggle was never easy, for selfish egoism was insatiable. Moreover, emotion was powerful and usually triumphed over reason. Humankind's "Imaginations are so strong and our Reason so weak, the Charms of Wealth and Power are so enchanting," he wrote, "that Men find Ways to persuade themselves, to believe any Absurdity, to submit to any Prostitution, rather than forego their Wishes and Desires. Their Reason becomes at last an eloquent Advocate on the side of their Passions and [they] bring themselves to believe that black is white, that Vice is Virtue, that Folly is Wisdom," he wrote in 1772. Such convictions led him to fear revolutionary upheaval. During revolutions, he wrote, the irresponsible and malevolent rose to seek the excision of order and moderation. When humankind moved collectively to effect revolutionary change, its actions often arose from misguided reason and too frequently culminated disastrously in licentiousness, anarchy, and tyranny. Instead of beneficial change, revolutionaries too often unloosed "deleterious distempers" that ended in the destruction of liberty and "arrested the progress of [human] Improvement."[42]

Since the Stamp Act crisis, Adams had believed that some popular leaders in Massachusetts sought revolution. He portrayed them as designing men and predicted that wickedness and calamity lay at the end of the road they wished to travel. He wrote, though he did not publish, an essay in which he assayed these men as "pretended Zealots for the public good." He suggested that they were driven by "mad Ambition" and that their "Views and Designs [were] utterly inconsistent with public Peace and Happiness." Yet while Adams distrusted the popular leadership, he did not doubt that the British policies which they attacked were illegal and threatened servility. Between 1765 and 1773 he often charged that the parent state had wrongfully sought to tax the colonists. He maintained that London hoped to render the colonists more dependent in every way and in everything, from the countinghouse to the courthouse. During these years he even came to believe that the mother country deliberately sought "to plunder our Trade and drain the Country of its money." Great Britain's policies, he declared, threatened to reduce Bostonians to slavery, rendering them "more unhappy than the basest Negro in Town."[43]

Before 1773 Adams struggled to reconcile his belief that it was imperative to oppose Britain's dangerous new colonial policy with his fear that disorder and malefaction would result inevitably from the colonists's resistance to those policies. Initially, his yearning to preserve New England society and culture from the fractious and unpredictable tumult of resistance won out. Over the years, however, he moved slowly toward the belief that resistance could be cathartic for society. Protest could "restore original virtues," as the first Puritan settlers had discovered in their fight against English tyranny and corruption. They had emigrated to America from a "love of *universal Liberty* and a hatred, an dread" of oppression, he said, and they had bequeathed liberty to their descendants. He gradually, painstakingly, moved toward the notion that his generation should exhibit similar virtues.[44]

The period between 1771 and 1773 was pivotal for Adams. "Thirty Seven Years" old, he scribbled in a birthday entry in his diary in 1772. He had reached an age when "more than half the Life of Men, are run out," he acknowledged in a saturnine mood. In the aftermath of his brush with serious illness only eighteen months earlier, Adams was more conscious of his mortality. His thoughts turned to the prospect that in a very few short years his youthful vigor would vanish. Thereafter, for the "remainder of my Days I shall decline, in Sense, Spirit, and Activity."[45]

Adams was in the grip of a mid-life crisis. He was unfulfilled and unhappy, weary with many aspects of his legal practice, but without an alternative. He lacked the wealth to retire, and had he been a man of means, he likely would have found a life of leisure and idleness unpalatable. "I was not sent into this World to spend my days in Sports, Diversions and Pleasures. I was born for Business . . . Austerity and Study. I have little Appetite, or Relish for any Thing else," he declared. Most likely, Adams hoped the time might come when his caseload would be so great that he could afford to limit his practice to the Suffolk County (Boston) district or that, if normality returned to imperial affairs, he might someday obtain a Crown-appointed judgeship. Convinced that the emotional pressures that accompanied his brief stint in the assembly had contributed to his illness, he did not see public life as an option.

When he declined Samuel Adams's invitation to deliver the address at the annual commemoration of the Boston Massacre in 1772, he resolved privately to "avoid even thinking upon public Affairs."[46]

On New Years' Day 1773, Adams proclaimed that he "never was happier, in my whole Life," and he looked forward to "a pleasant and chearfull, a happy . . . Year." It would be a good year, he told himself, because he would devote his energies exclusively to his "studies . . . Business and Duties of private Life." Four months later, he disavowed everything he had presumably learned about happiness and ran for election to the upper house of the Massachusetts assembly.[47]

The transformation in Adams's life and thought came about in part as a result of quite personal matters. During the final week of 1772, he learned that Hancock had dropped him as his counsel in favor of another Boston attorney. Adams was bitter and confused. "For about 3 or 4 years I have done all Mr. Hancocks Business, and have waded through wearisome, anxious Days and Nights, in his Defence," he said. The irony, of course, was that after years of worrying that political activism might cost him clients, the politically inactive Adams had lost his most influential local account, that of Hancock, the prince of merchant-activists. Immediately thereafter, not coincidentally, two of the most powerful members of the popular movement in Massachusetts, Samuel Adams and Joseph Hawley—the same Hawley who subsequently wrote hysterically to Washington on the eve of the Battle of New York—began a discreet courtship of Adams. Samuel Adams called often on John. He carefully utilized every stratagem in his bag of tricks to allay his cousin's fears. Mostly, he adopted the persona of a political moderate who, like John, abhorred violence and revolution. John was easily ensnared. He soon gushed that Samuel Adams was in fact "restrained [in] his Passions," "cool, genteel and agreeable," and driven by the purest motives of "public Service."[48]

Presently Hawley weighed in. Ten years older than Adams, a Yale graduate, veteran of two wars, lawyer, and powerful assemblyman, Hawley was considered an authority on constitutional questions. He suddenly consulted Adams on pressing issues. Adams was flattered by the "Attachment of Major Hawley to me." Adams was not an innocent, but throughout his career he at times exhibited incredible political naiveté. Samuel Adams discovered and exploited that weakness. So too did Hawley, who undoubtedly was acting in concert with Samuel Adams. John never suspected their motivation. Soon after each man had manipulated him, Adams noted an inexplicable change in his attitude. He was amazed at the sudden "Warmth, Heat, Violence" of his feelings toward British policies. He now felt "very free" in expressing convictions that heretofore he had discreetly suppressed.[49] By mid-March, sufficiently certain that he had been reconstructed, Samuel Adams and Hawley dared not only to bring Adams into the inner sanctum of the protest movement's deliberations, but even shared their secrets with him.

A Tory, who later was outmaneuvered in the Continental Congress by Samuel Adams, ascribed nearly superhuman political powers to him. Samuel Adams was indeed an adroit politician with a facility for intrigue and exploitation, but neither he nor Hawley were fully responsible for the changes in Adams's behavior. Three closely related occurrences after mid-autumn 1772 were also important in the reconfiguration of Adams's outlook. First, Parliament announced that henceforth it would pay the salaries of superior court justices in Massachusetts, annihilating whatever local control had previously existed. The Boston town meeting seized the issue. Adams was genuinely anxious as well, for he fervently believed that the judiciary must be independent of public opinion and political interest. He hurriedly attacked Britain's designs in seven essays that appeared in the *Boston Gazette* early in 1773.[50]

While Adams prepared these treatises, another public debate was sparked by two electrifying addresses presented to the assembly by Thomas Hutchinson, now the royal governor. Hutchinson not only maintained that Parliament possessed total sovereignty over the colonies, but that Americans did not have all the rights possessed by Englishmen living in England. He declared that Massachusetts must submit to Parliament's jurisdiction or be independent. No middle ground existed.[51]

Major Hawley and Samuel Adams shrewdly brought Adams into the deliberations of assembly committees created to draft responses to Hutchinson. They turned to Adams as a means of pulling him more deeply into the popular protest movement, but also because his published writings had established his reputation as an authority on constiitutional issues. Adams acted without hesitation, for Hutchinson's point of view was the diametrical opposite of that which he had embraced since he listened to Otis assail the writs of assistance a dozen years earlier. Moreover, to be consulted as a constitutional expert, and to sit on a panel that included Hancock, Samuel Adams, and Thomas Cushing, an influential merchant and former speaker of the house, was heady wine. Adams did not disappoint his new friends. He helped prepare a defiant assembly response to Hutchinson, one that stipulated that Massachusetts, if pushed, would choose separation from the parent state to submission to tyranny.[52]

It was the confluence of this episode and another that soon followed that was especially crucial for Adams. Just after the House published its second message to the governor, Samuel Adams brought John further into his inner circle. He divulged that he possessed a collection of purloined letters that had been exchanged between Hutchinson and a highly placed royal official in London. One letter was particularly damning. Peace and order required the curtailment of liberty in the colonies, Hutchinson had written. If the colonists refused to voluntarily acquiesce to fewer liberties, Hutchinson appeared to suggest, London must suppress by force some American freedoms. On the evening that Adams first read these letters, he ranted in his diary at Hutchinson's villainy. The letters not only proved Hutchinson's rapacity and megalomania, he said, but demonstrated the existence of a ministerial plot to abridge American liberties. Although Adams had long suspected that Hutchinson was a debased, corrupted politician who lusted after office for reasons of selfish aggrandizement, he had always attributed ministerial policy to poor judgment. No longer. He now concluded that London's deliberate objective was, and always had been, to expand its control over America. The mother country sought to restrict liberties in every sector of life in America, denying the colonists free trade, banishing their judicial autonomy, and curtailing the authority of their assemblies. If the colonists resisted the slow excision of their liberties, he now charged, London's plan was to treat them "as rebellious vassals, to subdue them, and take possession of their country."[53]

He had made a "grand discovery," Adams declared. Great Britain was bent on revolutionary change. It was seeking to restructure the Anglo-American union. More important, he now believed that Samuel Adams had been correct from the outset. He and the other popular leaders were not ambitious, destructive revolutionaries. They were defenders of freedom, like his Puritan forebearers. Throughout history, Adams wrote, "Liberty . . . has been compelled to skulk about in Corners of the Earth . . . everlastingly persecuted by the great, the rich, the noble . . . the avaricious." Now his generation faced a despotic government. The colonists, he charged, were threatened by "Egyptian Taskmasters" who sought to subject "ourselves and our Posterity . . . to Burthens, Indignities, Ignominy, Reproach and Contempt, to Desolation and Oppression, to Poverty and Servitude." The ministry, and its henchmen such as Hutchinson, he now urged, must be resisted, or American liberty would be lost forever.[54]

At the end 1773 Adams—a very different Adams from the one who had deplored active protest only a year earlier—praised the "Mohawks," the radicals who had protested Britain's latest tax, the Tea Act, by destroying the duties tea in the Boston harbor. The destruction of the tea "charms me," he wrote on the morning following the Boston Tea Party, even though he acknowledged that it might result in war. Hostilities "had better be Suffered" than to submit to oppression, he declared. Ten thousand lives lost in the defense of liberty, he added, would be lives "very profitably Spent."[55]

Adams was prepared for hostilities with Great Britain by the beginning of 1774, as were Washington and Jefferson. Each may have privately, secretly, embraced the idea that American happiness could be achieved only through separation from Great Britain. The confrontational jolts since the Stamp Act, and especially the rush of events in 1773, had brought to the surface hitherto undigested ideas in each man. Adams subsequently remarked that the American Revolution occurred prior to the outbreak of war. It occurred "in the minds and hearts of the people" between 1760 and 1775. He also said he was "surprised at the suddenness" with which the colonists' "habitual affection" for the parent state was changed into "indignation and horror." He was speaking of the rapidity of his own transformation. So too was Jefferson when he later reflected that the transition in the thought of the colonists occurred "with as much ease as would have attended their throwing off an old and putting on a new suit of clothes."[56]

By 1774 Adams and Jefferson believed that the Anglo-American union could survive only if the imperial relationship was refabricated. Although Washington said little in public, he was of like mind. Jefferson publicly denied the authority of Parliament over America, a more radical stance than that yet taken by any colonial assembly. He argued that the earliest immigrants had exercised their natural right in leaving England in quest of "public happiness." Once in America, they had erected new societies under laws of their own choosing. The earliest English immigrants had voluntarily submitted to the authority of the English monarchy, Jefferson added, but that volitional homage to the king was the only bond—he called it the "central link"—that cemented the Anglo-American union.[57]

Adams believed that the rights of New Englanders were derived both from natural law and "the compact made with the King in our charters." Adams's use of the term "compact" was crucial. Humankind, he said, possessed natural rights that they could never forfeit. This meant that citizens could never bestow upon government "unlimited and uncontroulable Powers over them." The first settlers, he believed, had contracted their allegiance to the English monarchy, although they had not surrendered their liberties to the king. They had never contracted to recognize Parliament's authority; instead they had reserved sovereign legislative authority to themselves. Parliament's authority outside England, he went on, existed where people consented, as in Scotland, or by reason of conquest, as in Ireland. America had neither consented to Parliament's jurisdiction or been conquered by Parliament. In fact, "there are 600,000 men in [the colonies] between 16 and 60 year of age, and therefore it will be very difficult to chicane them out of their liberties," he warned. Jefferson said much the same thing. Parliamentary acts were assertions of "power assumed by a body of men foreign to our constitutions." The "true ground" on which America defied British legislation, Jefferson added, was "that the British parliament has no right to exercise authority over us."[58]

Adams and Jefferson shared other beliefs. Both thought their ancestors had won control of America without the assistance of the parent state. The settlers had subdued "a dreary, inhospitable wilderness" inhabited by "wild beasts and savage men," Adams wrote. "Their own blood was spilt" in winning this continent, Jefferson wrote. "No shilling was ever issued from the public treasures of his majesty . . . for their assistance," he maintained. Adams and Jefferson also thought that England had sunk into a dark age of decadence and depravity. Adams's writings resonated with the belief that the new colonial policy inaugurated in 1763 arose from British profligacy. Adams charged that "luxury, effeminacy, and venality are arrived at such a shocking pitch in England" that the country had been reduced to "one mass of corruption." Throughout England, he charged, corruption "like a cancer . . . eats faster and faster every hour." This degeneracy was incurable. A wanton government created ever more offices for ever more debauched, aristocratic pensioners. These offices necessitated ever more revenue, which led London to seek ever more places to plunder. First the homeland had been ravaged. Next came Ireland. After 1763, it was America's turn. "[V]anity, luxury, foppery, selfishness, meanness, and downright venality" threatened to "swallow . . . up the whole society," including all of England's dominions, Adams concluded.[59]

Adams and Jefferson agreed that the parent state plotted to extirpate American liberties. As early as the spring of 1773 Adams had come to believe that a ruling clique of "cool, thinking, deliberate . . . malicious . . . vindictive . . . and avaricious" villains had set out to "ruin the country." He even thought a corrupt ministry sought to push New England into beginning a war as a means of uniting the English countryside against the colonists. Likewise,

Jefferson discerned a broad conspiracy within British ruling circles. He saw in recent parliamentary acts instances of "despotism" unequaled "in the most arbitrary ages of British history." Like Adams, he glimpsed a pattern in Parliament's conduct. "Single acts of tyranny may be ascribed to the accidental opinion of a day," he wrote, but a series of "oppressions . . . pursued unalterably thro' every" ministry demonstrated despotic intent. Both Adams and Jefferson had concluded that Britain was bent on one object. "There seems to be a direct and formal design on foot, to enslave all America," Adams wrote.[60]

Nor was it only parliamentary policy that Washington, Adams, and Jefferson resented. Each was unhappy with his status as a subordinate and dependent provincial. Washington had been driven to a cold fury by the roadblocks and disappointments he encountered, while Adams and Jefferson feared that they were subject to royal or ancestral-based dependencies that might inhibit them from reaching their full potential. Both drew especially important lessons from the experience of their mentors. Adams thought Otis the most talented man he had ever met, and Jefferson regarded Wythe as "the Cato of his country," the exemplar of the most noble Enlightenment virtues.[61] Yet Adams and Jefferson anguished that the realities of life in the provinces assured that Otis and Wythe would never attain all they deserved. Otis's ascent had been derailed by running afoul of those who were well connected with royal officials. Wythe, who was left without money or influence after his father bequeathed the family fortune to an older brother, faced severe limitations in a hierarchical society in which merit counted for considerably less than wealth and family ties.

Within a decade Washington, Adams, and Jefferson had evolved from virtually disinterested bystanders to activists who pulsated with a revolutionary mentality. No single factor can account for their transition, but one vibrant, paramount impulse was shared by each man. Each yearned for a world in which the individual enjoyed greater independence. Each had moved, and since his youth had been moving, toward a conception of freedom as an escape from dependence.[62]

By 1774 Washington, Adams, and Jefferson exhibited remarkably similar outlooks toward the conduct of the parent state and the opportunity to pursue happiness in the colonial world. A contempt for an England that was believed to have grown profligate, ravenously acquisitive, and oppressive colored their thoughts. Each considered Britain's colonial policies to be "despotick," as Washington put it. Each saw the same object in London's alleged despotism. Great Britain sought to "fix the Shackles of Slavery upon us," said Washington. It contemplated "reducing us to slavery," Jefferson thought. A debauched England wished to make Americans "the most abject sort of slaves to the worst sort of masters," Adams charged.[63]

Like snow beneath a warm sun, the reflexive loyalty toward Great Britain that had gestated within the hearts of Washington, Adams, and Jefferson had vanished by 1773. Each was outraged by British actions. Each was restive with the restraints inherent in a colonist's status. However dimly, each envisioned a bounteous new world through a restructured imperial relationship.

On the morning after the Boston Tea Party in December 1773, Adams noted that the proceedings of the previous night had inaugurated a new "Epocha in History." Adams, Washington, and Jefferson welcomed the changes that they knew would be coming to their world.[64]

5

"To Ride in This Whirlwind"

Independence

Adams and his three colleagues from Massachusetts ate breakfast in Trenton on August 29, 1774, before setting out on the twentieth and final day of their journey from Boston. Later that warm day, as the long afternoon shadows stretched from the Delaware River to the Schuylkill, they at last reached their destination, Philadelphia. Adams and his comrades had come to Pennsylvania to represent their province at the First Continental Congress.[1]

The next morning, in steamy Virginia, Patrick Henry and Edmund Pendleton arrived at Mount Vernon. They planned to accompany Washington to Congress.[2] Had the Virginia Convention also elected Jefferson, he might have joined his colleagues for the long ride north. Jefferson later remarked that he had not been chosen because his ideas were "too bold" for the times. He was incorrect. The Convention ignored him because he was only a moderately influential assemblyman.[3]

The Continental Congress had been called to determine how to respond to the Coercive Acts. News of the Boston Tea Party had provoked an angry response throughout England and in Lord Frederick North's ministry. United in the belief that further appeasement was unthinkable, and that the leadership of the colonial protest was centered in Massachusetts, the government sought to break the back of the American protest movement by singling out Massachusetts for punishment. Sever the head of the rebellion in Boston, the ministers believed, and the protest would die elsewhere. The Intolerable Acts, as the colonists called the retaliatory legislation that North's government secured, altered the government of Massachusetts and closed Boston harbor until restitution was made for the damaged tea. Like Hillsborough's misguided actions a few years earlier, these measures only fueled the resistance movement in America, for it now was clear to a majority of Americans that if the imperial government had its way, the colonists not only must submit to the fiat of Parliament, but no colonial charter was truly secure.[4]

When several colonies urged a national assembly to consider a unified response, all but Georgia agreed to participate. Massachusetts elected a four-member delegation. Samuel Adams was its most radical delegate, but the others could be counted on to support a national boycott of commerce with the parent state. The congressmen had been carefully selected. Samuel Adams aside, none was likely to frighten away potential moderate allies from the middle and southern colonies. This was a factor in John Adams's presence.[5] Many others in Massachusetts had labored longer and harder in the protest movement, but he was well educated, diligent, thoughtful, informed, and a prominent attorney who had once defended British soldiers; no one could accuse him of being an irresponsible firebrand. Samuel Adams, who was the key player in selecting the province's delegation, may have found his cousin attractive for still another reason. John was unschooled in the art of politics, having held a provincial office only once, and then for just a single year. John Adams was almost certain to be Samuel Adams's compliant student.

Washington's selection to the Virginia delegation was to be expected. His military service in the 1750s had made him the best-known Virginian throughout the colonies. Although he had never been a leader in the House of Burgesses, and it was presumed he would contribute little in Philadelphia, his leadership in Virginia's boycott movement in 1769 made it apparent that he would support a national embargo to force the repeal of the Tea Act and the Coercive Acts. If the boycott failed, and if force was the sole remedy left to the colonists, Washington would fight. He might even be asked to lead the fight. It would have been unthinkable for the Virginia assembly to ignore Colonel Washington when it chose its congressmen.

Adams carefully guarded his outlook, but this much is clear. Seeing corruption in the viscera of the parent state, and a growing pattern of tyranny in British policies, he at the very least hoped to distance America from London. He was committed to the belief that the colonies should be considered "a distinct Community" possessed of "a Right to judge for themselves." Such a view was close to an endorsement of American independence, although at this juncture he may have favored what later would be called commonwealth status, virtual independence under the aegis of the British imperial government. More likely Adams, together with Samuel Adams, doubted whether Americans ever again could enjoy the liberty and autonomy they desired under any imperial relationship.

The immediate questions that faced Congress were whether to vote a boycott and, if so, whether such an embargo would result in war. What is most clear about Adams's thought in the autumn of 1774 is that he was convinced that only the use of force could compel North's government to retreat. But he dared not express such a thought openly. Massachusetts was isolated and vulnerable and required allies. To speak publicly about the likelihood of hostilities was to risk frightening the more cautious and conservative delegates. Massachusetts would have to wait for time and events to radicalize others. As Adams remarked a few months later: "The fleetest Sailors must wait for the dullest and slowest. Like a Coach and six—the swiftest Horses must be slackened and the slowest quickened, that all may keep an even Pace."[6]

Consequently, the Massachusetts delegates came to Philadelphia prepared to ask for nothing more than a boycott of British trade. Their first objective was to find allies who would go that far. Because their new colleagues were total strangers, Adams and his comrades quickly mingled with them in taverns and at parties and meals. He wrote Abigail of attending "sinful feasts" where the tables groaned under ham, duck, chicken, beef, pork, and, "curds and creams, jellies, sweetmeats of various sorts, twenty sorts of tarts, fools, trifles, floating islands, whipped syllabubs." After a week of socializing, and gentle probing, Adams was persuaded that a majority in Congress would support an American embargo.[7]

But what if the boycott provoked Great Britain to use force? Adams gingerly endeavored to discover whether the other colonies would fight beside Massachusetts. He also assessed the character and temperament of Colonel Washington, the only congressman with much military experience. Adams was probably introduced to Washington soon after the Virginians arrived on September 4, but he did not talk to him at length until later in the month, when the two were dinner guests of Richard Penn of Philadelphia—in the house that each would occupy in the 1790s as president of the United States. Adams discovered an admirable blend of virtue and toughness in the Virginian. Although guarded as always when in the presence of a stranger, Washington must have divulged to Adams at least as much as he had recently expressed to an acquaintance in the British army. Washington believed there was ample evidence to conclude that the British government sought to destroy liberty and the constitution both in England and America. That he was prepared to take up arms to protect the colonists' "rights & privileges" was unmistakable. So was his belief that American might would prevail.[8]

What Adams heard was music to his ears. By the end of his first month in Philadelphia, he was convinced that if war came, and especially if British soldiers fired the first shot, Massachusetts would have the support of other colonies. On the day after he spoke with Washington, he wrote Abigail of his intention to move his possessions from his office in Boston to his library in Braintree. Like Washington, Adams had begun to prepare for war.[9]

Service in this congress was of crucial importance for both Adams and Washington. Inexperienced politically, Adams had come to Philadelphia doubting that he would measure up in an assembly of "the greatest Men upon this Continent." He expected the sessions to be dominated by one extraordinary leader, a provincial William Pitt, he said. He was impressed by men such as Henry and Lee of Virginia, and John Dickinson, who joined the Pennsylvania delegation in October. Nevertheless, Adams's confidence in his own abilities steadily grew that autumn, until he saw himself as the equal of the best among his colleagues. Other congressmen discovered his talents as well. Although constrained by the low profile that the Massachusetts delegation kept, Adams was elected to Congress's most important committee, a panel that prepared the Declaration of Rights, what contemporaries called the American "Bill of Rights." In fact, his colleagues on that committee asked Adams to author the Declaration's key passage, a statement in which the colonists acceded to Parliament's regulation of America's external commerce, but denied that London possessed the right to regulate trade for the purpose of raising a revenue.[10]

Washington also profited by his presence in Congress. Before September, many congressmen had heard of him, but none knew much about him. With hostilities looming, they wished to learn as much as possible. By the time Congress adjourned late in October, many of the delegates had gained considerable respect for Washington. His solemn, reserved, and purposeful manner, his industry and prudence, and his rugged appearance and intractable temperament led many to conclude that he was a man who could be depended on should war occur.[11]

The radicals secured their objectives in the Congress. A month into the session, Congress voted to prohibit British imports after December 1, to forbid the sale of all British goods in colonial retail shops after March 1, 1775, and to cease exports to the mother country after September 1, 1775. It directed each town and county to establish enforcement committees, and urged each colony to revive its militia system and commence military training.

Washington, like some of his Virginia colleagues, believed that the ship that carried the news of the boycott to London would return with word that Great Britain had repealed the Tea Act and Coercive Acts. Great Britain had backed down in every previous crisis and correspondents in London told Washington that the North government would capitulate again. Not anticipating war, Washington not only purchased still more frontier property that fall, but dispatched a party to clear a tract for settlement near the mouth of the Great Kanawha River. Washington was oddly out of step. Most Virginians acted as if war was imminent. Militia companies sprang up throughout the province, including Albemarle County, where Jefferson was a private and his overseer a sergeant. Washington also played an active role in the preparedness campaign. He and Mason raised a Fairfax County company, with Washington advancing funds to help it acquire powder, and on at least three occasions he drilled Alexandria militiamen.[12]

New England had begun to prepare for war while Adams was in Philadelphia, prompting General Thomas Gage, the commander of the British army in North America, to report to London that men throughout New England were "exercising in Arms . . . and getting magazines of Arms and Ammunition . . . and such Artillery, as they can procure." After he returned to Braintree in mid-November, Adams barely had an opportunity to visit his family before he was off to assist in readying his province for hostilities. He took a seat in the Massachusetts Provincial Congress, to which he was elected in December. His first assignment was to prepare an address to the citizenry that urged, but did not compel, each village to maintain a well-supplied and trained militia capable of responding immediately should an "arbitrary ministry" resort to arms. Adams also served on Braintree's Board of Selectmen, which enforced the national boycott and organized the village's militia units. Three companies of "Minute Men" were created and ordered to train four hours one afternoon each week. Adams understood full well that America stood "at the Brink of . . . War." He also knew that if war came, there was little likelihood that reconciliation with Great Britain could ever be achieved.[13]

Jefferson likewise understood that reconciliation was possible only if London capitulated to America's demands. Late in 1774 he publicly announced his intention of being a "conscientious observer" of the national boycott.

Three months later, in mid-March, he took his seat in Virginia's second provincial convention, where he helped "prepare a plan for embodying arming and disciplining a militia." The plan that he drafted was nearly identical to that which Adams wrote for Braintree, save for the omission of the "minutemen."[14]

Three weeks after Braintree's militia law went into effect, war erupted when General Gage dispatched a force of more than 900 regulars to seize the colonial arsenal in Concord, about twenty miles west of Boston. A bloody incident occurred in Lexington. More blood was shed in Concord, and still more along the road that led back to Boston. By twilight on that crimson April 19, over 270 British soldiers had been killed or wounded, and the colonists had suffered nearly 100 casualties.[15]

Washington and Adams were in their seats in Philadelphia when the Second Continental Congress was gaveled to order in mid-May, twenty days after the bloodshed in Massachusetts. Each was ready for war. Whatever their views before April 19, each soon thereafter crossed the chasm that divided the reconciliationists from the separatists. However, each sequestered his radical views. Adams's first task was to create a national army. Washington's first objective was to be chosen commander of that army. To publicly avow anything more radical than resistance to British policies would have jeopardized the immediate goal of each man.

Washington wore his Virginia Regiment uniform to these sessions, the one he had donned while sitting for his portrait three years before. It was a none too subtle hint of his ambitions. He and Adams almost immediately discovered "a good Spirit" in Congress, a "military Spirit" that "is truly amazing." Lee of Virginia reported "a perfect unanimity" to resist British force with force. Indeed, twenty-eight militia companies had sprung up in Philadelphia since the previous autumn, and the sound of marching soldiers eddied through the closed windows of the State House and punctuated congressional deliberations. While Congress contemplated its choices, Washington, who had been ignored by the initial Congress when it ladled out assignments, was appointed chair of committees to plan the defense of New York and procure military stores. In no time Adams sent home word that Congress would dispatch an army to New York and another to Massachusetts.[16]

Congress was moving in the right direction, Adams thought, although it was not acting as rapidly as he desired. Furthermore, there was less unanimity in the State House than Congressman Lee perceived. A moderate faction, headed by Dickinson, wished to explore every peaceful avenue. Among other things, Dickinson and his fellow accommodationists wished to petition the King, hopeful that his intervention would result in imperial reform and peace, or that the war ministry would collapse when it was discovered that the colonists were united in their commitment to bearing arms. Adams looked askance at such a step, calling it a "Measure of Imbecility" that might jeopardize the military spirit that gripped the colonies. Nevertheless, expedience required that he assent, for he feared that "Discord and total Disunion" would be the alternative.[17]

As at the initial Congress, the Massachusetts delegation again acted with consummate skill. Samuel Adams remained its adroit leader. John yet lacked the experience and stature to lead men such as Hancock, Cushing, or Robert Treat Paine, an eminent lawyer, who constituted the remainder of the delegation. The Massachusetts congressmen waited and watched as momentum built to create an American army. They bided their time, as John put it, until their colleagues discerned that London's "Designs against Us, are hostile and sanguinary, and that nothing but Fortitude, Vigour, and Perseverance can save Us." Thirty-five days after it convened, Congress created the Continental army.[18]

Immediately thereafter Adams nominated Washington to command the new army. New England was enthusiastic about Washington. It was desperate to create a truly national army, and as Eliphalet Dyer of Connecticut remarked, the appointment of the Virginian "more firmly Cements the Southern [colonies] to the Northern."[19]

Several additional factors were crucial in Washington's selection. He had soldiered for five years, prompting Adams to speak of "his great Experience and Abilities in military Matters," including the know-how to organize a European-style force. Washington was wealthy, relatively young—he was forty-three in 1775—and in good health. He was an imposing physical figure who exhibited a tough and intrepid aura. Here was a man accustomed to leading others, a man who could make life-and-death decisions, an officer who could move men to follow his orders. There was a majesty about him as well. Benjamin Rush, a Philadelphia physician who hobnobbed with the congressmen, thought Washington "has so much martial dignity in his deportment, that . . . there is not a king in Europe but would look like a *valet de chambre* by his side." Jefferson said Washington's "stature [was] exactly what one would wish, his deportment, easy, erect and noble." Jefferson was also inspired by Washington's striking athleticism. He thought his fellow Virginian "the best horseman of his age, and the most graceful figure that could be seen on horseback." Most congressmen expected much from Washington. He was to be a conqueror and a role model, a man who, as Silas Deane of Connecticut said, "Unites the bravery of the Soldier, with the most consummate Modesty & Virtue."[20]

The qualities that Washington exhibited might easily have been detrimental to his ambitions. To give over command of an army to a strong, charismatic, dignified, imposing man was to risk giving the general all that was required to become a tyrant, or a king. But Adams and his colleagues had assayed Washington's character. Washington, they were convinced, was a committed republican who understood and believed that civilian jurisdiction must hold sway over the commander and his army. "His views," as Adams put it, "are noble and disinterested."[21]

"Yesterday the famous Mr. Jefferson a Delegate from Virginia . . . arrived," one of Rhode Island's congressmen wrote five days after Washington's appointment. Late in May, when Peyton Randolph, a member of Virginia's congressional delegation since its inception, returned to Williamsburg to preside over the colonial assembly, Jefferson had been chosen to succeed him. Jefferson had catapulted into the first line among Virginia's leaders during the past nine months as a result of his radical pamphlet *A Summary View of the Rights of British America*, published in Williamsburg late in 1774, the only pamphlet attacking British policies authored by a Virginian prior to hostilities.[22]

Few congressmen in American history have been known beyond their small districts at the time of their initial election. Things were no different in 1774–1775. Samuel Adams and Washington were known outside their colonies before the First Continental Congress assembled, as were Dickinson, famous as the author of the *Letters from a Pennsylvania Farmer*, and Benjamin Franklin, the best-known American, who sat in the Second Congress. Jefferson's renown was derived from his *Summary View*. He arrived, as Adams put it, with a "reputation for literature" that included "a happy talent for composition."[23]

It is likely that the Virginia delegates, whom Adams had immediately characterized as "spirited" and "masterly," helped spread Jefferson's reputation. They were easily as adroit as the Massachusetts congressmen and no less successful. Not only had they obtained a boycott in the initial Congress, but they had postponed the embargo on American exports until after the Chesapeake planters had shipped their 1774 crop of tobacco. The Virginians had additionally attained the selection of Randolph as president of Congress in 1774 and Washington as commander of the Continental army in 1775. With the colonies at war, and Congress on the verge of once again drafting important resolutions and statements, it was in Virginia's interest to place another of its delegates on the principal committees. Thus, Virginia's congressmen made certain that their colleagues were aware of Jefferson's literary skills.[24] Less than a week after his arrival in Philadelphia, Jefferson was assigned to a committee that was to prepare what amounted to an American declaration of war. A month later he was given responsibility for drafting Congress's response to a peace proposal offered by Lord North. Perhaps never again would a newcomer in the Congress of the United States be entrusted with such important duties so soon after taking his seat.

Jefferson had indeed demonstrated a facility for writing, but before 1776 the most memorable rhetoric of the American protest came not in published writings, but in speeches, mostly by assemblymen, such as Henry. In England, where a long tradition of polemical and journalistic literature existed, an artful writer, such as Daniel Defoe or Jonathan Swift, could sustain himself with his pen. No such tradition existed in America. The colonial pamphleteers and essayists who wrote from the Stamp Act crisis onward were amateur penmen who wrote like amateurs.[25] Most were lawyers and, predictably, their essays were cast in the form of legal briefs, with arguments buttressed by legal citations and prose that often lapsed into a courtroom idiom. Schoolchildren once memorized the oratorical flourishes of the likes of Henry and Nathan Hale, but it is unlikely that anyone was ever made to learn even the best portions of the most noteworthy essays published before 1776.

Adams was a better polemicist than most. Jefferson was even better. If what Adams wrote was not rhapsodic, or especially memorable, he occasionally turned a well-crafted phrase. He wrote of how aristocratic and clerical tyrants long had kept humanity in "Sordid Ignorance and staring Timidity," and of how the colonists must take precautions not to be "driven blindfolded to irretrievable destruction." He wrote that if Americans tried and failed to resist tyranny, "nothing is lost. If they die, they cannot be said to lose, for death is better than slavery. If they succeed, their gains are immense. They preserve their liberties."[26] Too often, however, Adams never knew when to stop. His "Letters of Novanglus," which appeared in a Boston newspaper in the spring of 1775, culminated after thirteen cumbrous, repetitious essays, and ended then only because he had to leave home to attend Congress. Moreover, Adams too often wrote like a legal scholar. Here is what he wrote on the issue of parliamentary sovereignty over the colonies:

This statum Walliae, as well as the whole case and history of that principality, is well worthy of the attention and study of Americans, because it abounds, with evidence, that a country may be subject to the crown of England, without being subject to the Lords and Commons of that realm, which entirely overthrows the whole argument of Governor Hutchinson and of Massachusettensis in support of the supreme authority of parliament, over all the dominions if the imperial crown. "*Nos itaque,*" says King Ed. I. "*volentes predictam terram, &c. sicut et caeteras ditioni nostrae subjectas, &c. subdebito regimine gubernari, et incolas seu habitatores terarum illarum, qui alto et basso, Se submiserunt voluntati nostrae, et quos sic ad nostram recepimus voluntatem, certis legibus et consuetudinibus, &c. tractari Leges, et consuetudines, partum illarum hactenus usitatas coram nobis et proceribus regni nostri secimus necitari, quibus diligenter auditas, et plenus intellectis, quasdam ipsarum de concilio proceum predictorum delevimus, quasdampermisimus, et quasdam corrximus, et etiam quasdum alias adjungendas et statuendas decrevimus, et eas, &c. observari volumus in forma subscripta.*"[27]

Here is Jefferson on the same topic:

Shall these governments be dissolved, their property annihilated, and their people reduced to a state of nature, at the imperious breath of a body of men whom they never saw, in whom they never confided, and over whom they have no powers of punishment or removal, let their crimes against the American public be ever so great? Can any one reason be assigned why 160,000 electors in the island of Great Britain should give law to four millions in the states of America, every individual of whom is equal to every individual of them in virtue, in understanding, and in bodily strength? Were this to be admitted, instead of being a free people, as we have hitherto supposed, and mean to continue, ourselves, we should suddenly be found the slaves, not of one, but of 160,000 tyrants, distinguished too from all others by this singular circumstance that they are removed from the reach of fear, the only restraining motive which may hold the hand of a tyrant.[28]

Jefferson's brevity was his strength. In one-tenth the space, his *Summary View* touched upon virtually every major theme about which Adams wrote in the "Letters of Novanglus." But he too could be terribly legalistic. Writing of the outbreak of hostilities, the master pamphleteer Thomas Paine said simply: "Even brutes do not devour their young, nor savages make war upon their families." Here is how Jefferson delivered the same message: "in open violation of plighted faith & honor, in defiance of the sacred obligations of treaty which even savage nations observe . . . a body of armed men under orders from the said General . . . have proceeded to commit . . . ravages & murders."[29]

Jefferson, who in the *Summary View* had urged a hardy and militant stance, was warmly embraced by the congressional radicals in June 1775. They knew that he had supported Virginia's defensive preparations, and when hostilities commenced he appeared to suggest that no hope existed that the colonies could ever be reconciled with the mother country. Sounding very much as if he was already committed to American independence, Jefferson in May 1775 had privately attacked George III, the only British authority over the colonies whom he any longer recognized, for "blowing up the flames" of war. When he added that "a phrenzy of revenge seems to have seized all ranks of people" in America, he could not have more accurately described his own reaction to the news that the British army had fired on Americans.[30]

Jefferson's new colleagues in Congress also knew that he had been selected to write Virginia's response to the North government's peace proposal of early 1775, and that he had exposed North's plan for the sham that it was. North had recommended that the colonial assemblies be permitted to raise whatever revenue was mandated by Parliament. Jefferson charged that the scheme would impose on America "a perpetual tax adequate to the expectations and subject to the disposal of Parliament alone." He contended too that the so-called peace proposal neither extended to the colonies the autonomy over their domestic affairs that they by right possessed, nor addressed the colonists's objections to the Tea Act and Coercive Acts, and a dozen other issues that had wrecked their relationship with the parent state. Jefferson denounced the notion that Parliament could legislate for America, saying it had "no right to intermeddle" with American governance. He specifically proclaimed Virginia's right to "a free trade with all the world."[31] These ideas had been too radical for Virginia and Congress in 1774, but by the following spring, with the whiff of British gunpowder in the air, Virginia embraced what Jefferson wrote. The congressional radicals also greeted him with open arms, a man of like ideas who was a craftsman with a pen.

Two days after he arrived in Philadelphia, Congress resolved to adopt a statement explaining its reasons for fighting the parent state. Among others, the radicals elected Jefferson, and the moderates Dickinson, to the committee that was to prepare the address. Actually, little separated the two on the issue of war. Each supported hostilities, although Dickinson, to the marrow of his bones, supported war in order to achieve reconciliation in an imperial union structured along the lines that had existed before 1763. Dickinson never deviated from this position. He supported the war from start to finish, and he fought—literally fought, for he bore arms in 1777 as a private in a Delaware company during the Brandywine campaign—to compel Great Britain to negotiate a settlement that would enable America to remain within the empire.[32]

Jefferson was assigned responsibility for drafting the Declaration of the Causes and Necessity for Taking Up Arms. He catalogued a long list of grievances against Great Britain, many of which would appear a year later in his draft of the Declaration of Independence, including the charge that ministerial policy evinced the "spirit" of a design to "erect a despotism of unlimited extent" over the colonists.[33]

His muscular rhetoric frightened some in Congress. William Livingston was angered by his suggestion of British tyranny, and others thought his language pulsated with anti-monarchical sentiment. Jefferson's draft in fact exposed the hopeless illogic of the moderates' stance. Dickinson and his comrades were willing to kill English soldiers to achieve reconciliation, but feared that intemperate language might anger the King and prevent him from answering the supplications of the colonists. Congress ultimately adopted a strongly worded declaration that expressed its reasons for going to war, but softened the harshest of Jefferson's language, lest it jeopardize the Olive Branch Petition, which Congress simultaneously adopted. This was the appeal to the King that Dickinson and his compatriots had urged since the Second Congress convened. Like Adams, Jefferson voted for this entreaty with "disgust," but both knew that it could not be avoided, lest Congress be fissured and even threatened with dissolution. Nevertheless, Jefferson took pride in what had been accomplished. In its first weeks this Congress had created an American army and adopted a declaration on waging war that, as Adams put it, had "Some mercury in it."[34]

Two weeks later Jefferson wrote the draft of Congress's response to the North Peace Plan. It resembled what he had written a month earlier for Virginia's assembly, and was adopted by Congress with only modest alterations. Congress's vote that sweltering July afternoon completed the initial phase of the second Congress, a three-month period during which the colonial legislators had prosecuted the war while seeking peace and imperial reform. To Adams and Jefferson it was an exasperating, but necessary, way to proceed. Although "We cannot force Events," Adams conceded, he believed that Congress was moving steadily, inexorably, toward its next objective—independence.[35]

"I was [Jefferson's] preceptor in politics and taught him everything," Adams recalled in his latter years.[36] Adams was guilty of hyperbole, but he was not entirely inaccurate, for in the early stages of the Second Congress, he was the leader and Jefferson the follower. As spring gave way to summer in 1775,

Adams emerged as the preeminent figure within the radical faction in Congress, and he may have reached out to his younger colleague from Virginia, offering counsel. But how to explain the ascendancy of Adams, a man with little background in politics before 1774?

Adams feared that he was severely limited by his appearance. Tall men, such as Washington and Jefferson, were natural leaders, he said. Although he characterized himself as short, what he appears to have meant was that he was not tall. He was in fact a man of average size for the time, either five feet seven or five feet nine, both of which he claimed as his height on various occasions. Furthermore, while John Trumbull's famous painting of the presentation of the Declaration of Independence depicts Adams as the shortest of the five members of the committee that prepared the document, he was shown to be nearly the same height as Franklin, who was five feet nine or ten inches tall. What is clear is that Adams was in no sense statuesque. His wife described Washington as a "temple" to masculinity, but no one would have thought of Adams in those terms. Portly, balding, pallid, ungainly, and indifferent to fashionable attire—he was "careless of appearances," an acquaintance remarked—Adams did not at first blush strike any observer as a dynamic individual. "By my Physical Constitution I am but an ordinary Man," he said of himself with considerable accuracy, and added that he did not impress others as "like the Lion," strong and invincible. His deportment did little to offset his physical limitations. He characterized himself as formal in demeanor. He acknowledged that he was neither a backslapper nor a flatterer, admitted that he never learned the arts of swapping jokes or spinning off-color yarns, and never knew what to say when the conversation turned to what he regarded as men's favorite subjects: women, horses, and dogs. He antagonized some acquaintances with his penchant for argumentation, others with his unfettered candor, and a few with his sharp temper. Jefferson once said that Adams not only was vain, but blind to his vanity, "irritable" without any real understanding of how that attribute offended others. Adams, in fact, did understand. He acknowledged his "irascible" manner and admitted too that he made many enemies. If he attained the renown he sought, Adams once sighed, it would be because the "Times alone have destined me to Fame."[37]

He was too hard on himself. He in fact possessed several qualities that served him quite well in a corporate setting such as Congress. Although he was disputatious, passionate, and often too candid, many of his colleagues genuinely liked him. Jonathan Sewall, a friend and rival in pre-war legal circles in Massachusetts, said later that "Adams has a heart formed for friendship."

In 1787 Jefferson told Madison that Adams was so friendly "that I pronounce you will love him if ever you become acquainted with him."[38] Indeed, whereas Washington appears to have gone throughout life with no friends in the real sense of the term, and Jefferson seems to have been truly close only with some boyhood chums, Adams won close, dear friends at every stage of life. Many men with whom he worked, and sometimes battled, found him to be so honest, open, approachable, good-humored, and down-to-earth that they admired him immensely and enjoyed his company.

There was no more tireless worker within Congress. Between 1775 and 1777 Adams served on ninety committees, including twenty-five that he chaired, more in all likelihood than was taken on by any other congressman. As a consequence, he not only interacted closely with each of his colleagues, but he played a part, usually a major part, in shaping virtually every issue with which Congress dealt. Congress soon in fact deferred to Adams as its leading political thinker, its foremost expert on foreign affairs, even its most knowledgeable member on military matters. Historian Joseph Ellis noted that Adams's "mastery of detail was awesome," as he developed a specialist's understanding of weaponry, naval craft, and military organizational techniques. Adams "possesses the clearest head and firmest heart of any man in the Congress," one of his colleagues remarked in 1777.[39]

Adams was also a skilled debater and a more than adequate orator, the legacy of his sixteen years in Massachusetts courtrooms. He lacked Otis's flair for the dramatic, but he had developed an oratorical style that combined gravity with eloquence, and he had grown adroit in accentuating his knowledge, pragmatism, and rationality. If his dignified manner did not sweep his listeners off their feet, Adams's erudite, sedate mode of expression reassured those on guard for sophists. A Pennsylvania congressman admired Adams's courageous willingness to publicly address his convictions, and added that he was unequaled in his ability to see "the whole of a subject at a single glance." A representative from Georgia once was so moved by a speech that Adams delivered that he "fancied an angel was let down from heaven to illumine the Congress."[40]

He was deft with his pen as well. Few colonists had matched Adams's output before 1775. In addition to his "Novanglus" letters, which soon appeared in pamphlet form, Adams had published more than forty essays in Boston newspapers. He had additionally drafted important statements for Braintree, Boston, and the Massachusetts assembly. Congress immediately tapped into his talent. Not only did he draft a key passage in the Declaration of Rights that the First Congress adopted, but in 1775 he and Jefferson, and two others, collaborated to produce Congress's response to the North Peace Plan.

Adams's talents could not have been more different from those of Samuel Adams or Patrick Henry, who had risen to be legislative leaders both at the provincial level and in Congress. Samuel Adams was a tireless organizer. He was manipulative, an extrovert with an innate facility for discovering and appealing to what he called the "Humours . . . Prejudices . . . Passions and Feelings, as well as [the] Reason and Understandings" of those he wished to lead. Adams once described Samuel as a "very artful, designing man." Samuel Adams in fact combined his penchant for machination with an almost unerring political judgment. As if guided by some mysterious sixth sense, he seemed to know when to act, to pause, to move slowly, to accelerate. Men followed Henry because, as Jefferson once said, he was without a peer in his ability to electrify an audience. Jefferson described Henry's public speaking style as "impressive," "sublime," and "eloquent," and said that his audiences were unfailingly "highly delighted and moved."[41]

But neither Samuel Adams nor Henry emerged as dominant figures on the national scene. Their strengths served them well at the initial Congress in 1774, where a coalition of radicals had to be assembled to respond to the Coercive Acts. Henry's supercharged oratory won adherents for the boycott and defensive preparations, and Samuel Adams's backroom skulduggery was unsurpassed in an assembly of virtual strangers. However, in May 1775, when Congress moved from political confrontation to the management of war and diplomacy, different talents were required. "[S]ober reasoning and solid argumentation" by "an assembly . . . of cool-headed, reflecting, judicious men," as Jefferson remarked, had become the order of the day by mid-summer of 1775. Henry, whom Jefferson described as "a man of very little knowledge of any sort," and Samuel Adams were obsolete. What is more, Henry knew it, in Jefferson's estimation, and was "wonderfully relieved" to escape Philadelphia for Williamsburg in mid-1775. But John Adams, whom Jefferson characterized as "amiable," "profound in his views . . . and accurate in his judgment," and "as disinterested as the being who made him," was in his element. With a life-and-death struggle under way, Adams, according to one observer in 1775, had emerged as "the first man in the House."[42]

Adams told Abigail that the demands placed on congressmen were "as great and important as [ever were] intrusted to Man," but General Washington bore truly crushing responsibilities.[43] The Washington who departed for the military front in late June 1775 was not yet the revered Cincinnatus. He would have to prove himself. A man with some military experience, he had never commanded an army of more than 2,000 men. Nor, with the exception of the battle at Fort Necessity, which had ended disastrously, had he ever led men into battle against European regulars. In addition, more than one congressman feared that a New England army—and that was what the Continental army was in June 1775— would never follow a commander from outside the region. No one knew whether Washington would wield his awesome power responsibly.

No one was filled with more oppressive doubts than Washington himself. He told Congress that "my abilities . . . may not be equal to the extensive & important Trust." He told his brother-in-law that his inexperience might prove fatal. He confided to his brother that he feared his reputation in Virginia, built with such toil and sacrifice, might be destroyed. He was "now Imbarkd on a tempestuous Ocean," he said, and "no friendly harbour" was visible.[44]

However, Washington not only believed in the cause he had undertaken, he was not terrified by the challenge that he faced. He did not frighten easily. He had surveyed on a remote frontier, carried a governor's message into unfriendly territory, faced an intrepid foe in the wilderness, assumed a seat in a legislative hall filled with better-educated men, and hazarded his capital in slippery investments. There was a venturesome side to Washington. He relished risk-taking. When he had confessed his joy in 1754 at hearing enemy bullets, Washington was not prevaricating. He was eager to respond to this new challenge, not merely because he thrived on taking risks, but because throughout his life he had pursued recognition, admiration, wealth, and power. To command America's army was to look into the face of danger and opportunity. For a man driven by a deep-seated need to be venerated, Washington grasped the chance of a lifetime to capture enduring fame.

Washington saw his appointment as a roll of the dice. This adventure could lead to disgrace or result in opportunities that were "boundless in prospect," as he put it. This is not to suggest that Washington acted only from vainglorious and self-serving ends. He accepted this challenge from a mix of motives. He was indeed activated by very human and self-centered aspirations, but he was also impelled by what he frankly labeled "Patriotism . . . in Support of . . . the Welfare of our common Country."[45] His was a patriotism that exploded from his grandiose dreams of the expansion of Virginia's, and independent America's, hegemony over the amber prairies that spread west of the mountains. His was a nationalism that aroused him to wish to fight for the salvation of his native land. Washington long since had wearied of living in a colony whose autonomy was checked by a distant state that seemed increasingly foreign and corrupt. As with every man who served in Congress or soldiered—or refused to bear arms—Washington gambled everything out of a jumble of motives, which in his case included self-indulgent, narcissistic, pecuniary, and idealistic ends.

Before Washington arrived at the front he captured the public imagination with two announcements. First, he told Congress that he would accept no salary. He asked only that his expenses be paid by the public. It was a dramatic gesture. At a time when ordinary citizens were asked to make numerous sacrifices, Washington had renounced both compensation and the "domestk ease & happiness" of Mount Vernon. His stunning act, which resonated with the republican ethos of disinterestedness, prompted the Massachusetts assembly to proclaim his decision a noble act that proved his patriotism. Even a London newspaper applauded his virtue and wished for a few such "disinterested patriots" in the British army.[46] Ten days later, Washington told the New York Provincial Congress that he was a citizen-soldier who believed fervently in the supremacy of civilian rulers. Adams subsequently remarked that Washington was unequaled both in his ability to judge men and to understand the public temper.[47] Washington never made better use of his uncanny latter talent than by these two declarations, for he had reassured the public that Congress had selected the right commander, a man well-suited to lead a republican army.

When Washington joined the army in Cambridge, Massachusetts, he acted as had Adams in his first days in Congress. He listened, watched, and probed to understand the strangers with whom he dealt. Congress had appointed thirteen general officers under Washington. Some owed their selection to merit, but at least as many were political appointees. Washington, who had been present during the congressional debates on the general officers, knew what had occurred. He had remained silent, but like Adams he must have felt that a selection process based on privilege and preferment was a dreadful way to begin a war against a nation that often had been cast as corrupt for having erected its society along similar lines. Adams later said that the selection of the army's general officers was his worst experience as a congressman. He thought Washington was capable, and he had considerable confidence in Horatio Gates and Charles Lee, both veterans of the British army, but he was "apprehensive" of the others.[48] One of Washington's first tasks was to judge these men.

Washington also believed in Gates and Lee. He had met them while serving under Braddock, entertained each at Mount Vernon, and urged Congress to appoint them. He knew little or nothing about the other general officers, but within a remarkably brief time he had reached generally unassailable judgments regarding their talents. It took him only a few days to deduce that David Wooster and Joseph Spencer, who were sixty-four and sixty-one respectively, were useless. After two years Adams and everyone else in Congress, if Adams is to be believed, had reached the same conclusion. Likewise, Washington quickly concluded that his predecessor, Artemas Ward, was fat, lazy, inert, and incompetent. By early 1776 many authorities in Massachusetts had reached the same conclusion, although Adams never lost respect for Ward, and in fact urged his friends at home to send him to Congress. Washington also concluded that Israel Putnam, who was fifty-seven and had served with distinction in the French and Indian War and at Bunker Hill, was a good soldier, but not one who should have an independent command. Washington likely reached his conclusion because "Old Put"—a farmer and tavern-keeper who was described by one observer as "much more fit to head a band of sickle-men or ditchers, than musketeers"—lacked the polish that the commander thought essential in a high-ranking officer. Washington gave William Heath a division to command, only to be disappointed by his lack of enterprise. Thereafter, he denied him truly crucial assignments. By early 1777 Adams had reached similar conclusions about Putnam and Heath, and privately confessed that he wished both would resign.[49]

Before the foliage turned that first autumn of the war, Washington had begun to suspect that Philip Schuyler likewise was overwhelmed by the responsibilities of command. Two years later Congress removed him from command of the Northern Department. Little time was required for Washington to decide that John Sullivan was zealous and energetic, but so vain and ambitious that he was almost certain to get "into some embarrassments." His impression was unerring. Sullivan soon bungled one assignment after another. Nathanael Greene was the "rawest, the most untutored" of all the original general officers, according to some at headquarters, but Washington swiftly saw qualities in him that few discerned. Washington resisted entreaties to post Greene where he could do no harm, and kept him nearby for counsel. Within a year the commander concluded that Greene was his best qualified general officer, a view sustained by subsequent events.[50]

With Adams's help that first summer, Washington discovered Henry Knox. Adams urged that Knox, a twenty-five-year-old Boston bookseller, be appointed to the rank of colonel. Washington interviewed the corpulent young man and was so impressed with his knowledge of ordnance that he appointed him chief of the Continental army artillery. Washington also beheld a fiery zeal, indomitable spirit, and indefinable leadership qualities in Benedict Arnold, whom he met that July. Washington invested him with heavy responsibilities in a planned invasion of Canada.[51]

For all Washington knew that July, the entire war might be fought in New England and the lion's share of the men at his disposal might always be New Englanders. Therefore, it was important to win important people from this region to his side. He was more astute in this regard than General Schuyler, a New Yorker who not only failed to capture the loyalty of the Yankee soldiery, but who, when he also lost the support of New England's congressmen, lost his command as well. Washington courted the New England elite. He always found time to welcome them to headquarters, to talk with them, and to dine with them. His diligence and patience were rewarded. James Warren, a leader in the Massachusetts Provincial Congress, quickly lauded Washington's "judgment and Firmness," and called him "the best Man for the place he is in." Warren's wife, Mercy, the sister of James Otis, Jr. and a woman who was in the habit of hobnobbing with powerful men, thought Washington "the most amiable and accomplished gentleman, both in person mind and manners that I have met with." Others from Massachusetts were taken with his "vast ease and dignity," found him to be "truly noble and majestic," and applauded his efforts to shape the army. None was more impressed than Abigail Adams. She had met many of the most important clergymen, lawyers, merchants, and politicians in Massachusetts, but she had never met a man like Washington. "Dignity with ease, and complacency, the Gentleman and the Soldier look agreeably blended in him. Modesty marks every line and feature of his face." He was one of God's great creations, she added, a man of "Majestick fabric." Before Washington left New England, Harvard College bestowed an honorary degree on him.[52]

For all his talents, Washington was quite fortunate during his nine months in Massachusetts. The British army in Boston numbered about 5,000 men. Washington had 14,000 men fit for duty, a number that could have been augmented by summoning the militia in an emergency. Moreover, the siege of Boston between April 1775 and March 1776 was the sole major campaign in this war during which the Continental army was better clad, fed, and housed than its adversary. Thus, Washington not only commanded an army in which morale was high—"I never saw Spirits higher," he remarked in the dead of that winter—but he seldom had reason to fear a British attack. However, he was not free of worry. The Continental army was smaller by about one-fourth than he had expected. He was troubled too by the presence of numerous adolescents and British deserters in the ranks, and he especially wished to rid the army of blacks, whom he regarded as inherently inferior to whites. His racism was hardly unique. Each New England colony had forbidden black men to serve in its militia, although some had fought, and died, at Lexington, Concord, and Bunker Hill. Washington prohibited further enlistment of blacks, a policy that Congress upheld in September.[53]

Washington also immediately discovered an appalling lack of discipline in his army. This was to be expected, for in July 1775 the Continental army was in reality little more than a militia force. Although the men were volunteers, they—like trainbandsmen or militiamen—represented a cross section of the New England population and had signed on for short-term service, mostly six- to eight-month hitches. In the 1750s, Washington had railed that Virginia militiamen were "a poor resource, a very unhappy dependence," and he soon remarked on "the Disregard of Discipline Confusion and Want of Order among the Troops" before Boston. His men came and went freely, did not bother to salute officers, gambled, drank, and cursed openly, and took every opportunity to swim naked in the Boston-area rivers that flowed past homes inhabited by women and children. Officially soldiers, these men in reality were civilians—or citizen-soldiers, to be precise—who were on the great adventure of their lives. Washington was hardly surprised by such conduct, but there was a striking difference between what he had observed in Virginia's citizen-soldiers and what he now saw among New Englanders. Here he witnessed officers fraternizing with their men, even giving subordinates haircuts and repairing their shoes. Many were old chums from the same hometowns, or related through marriage. But Washington also beheld a New England egalitarianism that was more pervasive than he was accustomed to in Virginia. Most of these men were farmers, the poorest of whom owned about fifty acres while the most affluent possessed about eighty acres, differences that hardly resulted in a substantial dissimilarity in their standard of living. These men literally thought of themselves as the equal of one another. Washington loathed what he saw. He quietly described many of the Massachusetts officers as inept and most of the enlisted men were "exceeding dirty & nasty." Nevertheless, he thought the army would "fight very well (if properly Officered)."[54]

Two weeks before his arrival, in fact, this army had fought quite well, inflicting frightening casualties in the Battle of Bunker Hill. Over half of the

British regulars, more than 1,000 men, had been killed or wounded before they drove the colonial army from the heights in Charlestown north of Boston. To Jefferson, Bunker Hill demonstrated that "the want of discipline" could be surmounted by "native courage and . . . animation in the cause for which we are contending." Washington would have been appalled by such a remark. He knew that courage alone could not sustain an army in a long, difficult war. Strict training and discipline were imperative. "To expect the same Service from Raw, and undisciplined Recruits as from Veteran Soldiers is to expect what never did, and perhaps never will happen," he argued. In fact, what was most important about Bunker Hill to Washington was that the British had secured their objective. Colonial soldiers had displayed great courage, he acknowledged, but had the men been properly led the British would have suffered even greater losses and ultimately "met with a shameful defeat." To Washington, the lesson of Bunker Hill was that he must find good officers. He immediately promoted to officer rank several men who had performed coolly and with valor in that engagement, and he purged the army of several officers who had failed under fire.[55]

Washington, thus, had barely settled in at headquarters in Cambridge before he set out to reform the army that had been cobbled together only ten weeks earlier. He imposed draconian disciplinary measures. Men were fined, locked in the stockade, flogged, and subjected to a variety of humiliating punishments, some of which were not included in the authorized penalties listed in the Continental articles of war.[56] Men were cashiered from the service for a variety of offenses, ranging from repeatedly deserting to sleeping on duty.[57] But as much as Washington sought to make soldiers of these citizen-volunteers, he always believed that the men would be effective only if they were led by good officers.

Washington was a teacher during the initial months of the war, lecturing, explaining, and cajoling his officers, especially the junior-grade officers, mostly young men without military experience. He believed that the quality of leadership echoed down through the ranks and that the war would be won or lost by how capably the lower ranking officers performed. Nothing escaped his consideration. He taught that fraternization with the enlisted men destroyed discipline, but he also counseled that a good officer should become acquainted with his men. He told the officers to listen to their men and be aware of their mood, and to know them well enough to know what duties they could and could not perform. Some men, including married men "known to be attached" to their families, as Washington rather oddly put it, should not

be given sentry duty, as they might be weak and timorous. He advised his officers to routinely inspect the arms of the soldiery. He lectured them on the
importance of cleanliness and had them monitor the fatigue duty—sweeping
the streets, cleaning the barracks, policing the grounds, disposing the human
waste—that he required of the men each day.

He taught that preparedness was crucial. Because America had an "enterprizing enemy" that might make a sudden attack, the officers must have
their men ready for any eventuality. They must also respect the private property of nearby civilians, for if the public's morale collapsed, the cause was lost.
He urged the officers to read military manuals. He wanted each lieutenant and
captain to look like an officer as well as act like one. Each officer, therefore, was
to wear a "proper uniform." Each regiment was to have uniforms of a distinctive "Colour, Cut, and fashion" to promote kinship and pride. He
repeatedly instructed them to "appear neat, clean, and soldier-like." He had
the officers practice saluting. He forbade them to complain, for if they
appeared to be discontented, their troops would whine and the army's spirit
would be shattered. They must not fight over rank and promotions, lest
morale inevitably sink. He told the officers to be active and zealous, and their
men would be industrious. He told them that if they acted bravely in the hour
of trial, their men would take heart and fight with valor. Timidity under fire
was the greatest crime an officer could commit, Washington lectured, for "the
Cowardice of a single Officer may prove the Distruction of the whole
Army."[58]

Washington soon inaugurated the daily practice of inviting a junior officer to the mid-afternoon meal at headquarters.[59] He wished to meet them, but
he wanted them to observe the general officers. He must have lectured some
of these young men, likely telling them what he wrote to Colonel William
Woodford, one of his officers in the French and Indian War, now serving in
this conflict:

The best general advice I can give . . . is to be strict in your discipline; that is, to require
nothing unreasonable of your officers and men, but see that whatever is required be punc-
tually complied with. Reward and punish every man according to his merit, without par-
tiality or prejudice; hear his complaints; if well founded, redress them; if otherwise,
discourage them, in order to prevent frivolous ones. Discourage vice in every shape, and
impress upon the mind of every man, from the first to the lowest, the importance of the
cause, and what it is they are contending for. For ever keep in view the necessity of guarding against surprises. . . . Be plain and precise in your orders, and keep copies of them to

refer to, that no mistakes may happen. Be easy and condescending in your deportment to your officers, but not too familiar, lest you subject yourself to a want of that respect, which is necessary to support a proper command. . . . These, Sir . . . I have presumed to give as the great outlines of your conduct.[60]

Washington was not alone in reflecting on leadership qualities within the officer corps. Adams, who as the president of the Board of War was a virtual secretary of war, also gave considerable thought to the problems of military leadership. He shared Washington's idea that officers would make or break the army. Officers, Adams wrote, were the "Soul of an Army"—Washington had told his officers in the Virginia Regiment in 1757 that "Discipline is the soul of an army"—and if Congress failed to provide the officers with the means of "introducing and establishing Such a Discipline," the war was lost. "Politicks are the Science of human Happiness and War the Art of Securing it," Adams remarked. And he added: "Our Men are as good as theirs, and . . . they will follow a Spirited enterprizing Officer any where."[61]

Like General Washington, Congressman Adams emphasized the importance of discipline, the obligation to avoid disputes over rank, the crucial importance of civilian morale, and the necessity to study military manuals. Both men deplored the custom of permitting enlisted men to elect junior officers, a common practice in New England units.[62] Nevertheless, there was a significant difference in their point of view. Adams, who never served in the military, believed that a bright man of good character was certain to excel in a military command. Men of "Genius Learning, Reflection, and Address," of "Genius and Spirit," made the best officers, he wrote. Ambition, honor, and "a thirst for military knowledge" constituted the character traits that he thought essential in a good officer.[63] The highest ranking officers, he added in his most complete discourse on the subject, should understand literature, science, political theory, and human nature. They should be good judges of men and especially capable of "a deep Discernment of the Tempers, Natures, and Characters" of those with whom they had to deal. They must be unbiased and exhibit a civil disposition. They must be well-organized and capable of making decisions while under considerable pressure. And they must be robust, strong, and hearty.[64]

Adams had limned the traits of an ideal republican officer: learned, dedicated, rational, honest, methodical, just, gracious, and humane. These were the very character traits he would have deemed essential in a republican legislator, magistrate, or diplomat. No less committed to republicanism, Washington would have agreed that an experienced and pragmatic soldier who studied manuals might be a good leader. However, from experience he knew things that Adams could not know. Washington knew that there were indefinable qualities that separated success from failure, and a good officer from a great leader. There was an art to leadership. An extraordinary commander, he thought, displayed a deft touch. He knew that what moved one subordinate might fail with another. Compassion and humility were winning attributes at times. On other occasions, it was necessary to exhibit a hard, tough edge. Viciousness and cruelty were never proper traits, but sometimes a good officer had to be severe, even pitiless. The charismatic general, Washington believed, inspired both love and fear. Washington sought to capture the love of those he led not by being their brother or friend, but by winning their admiration through his unflagging dedication, integrity, industry, fairness, courage, and benign care. He prompted fear not by playing the tyrant or oppressor, but by exhibiting an air of reserve, gravity, and formality that resulted in a persona of unapproachability and an aura of peerlessness.

During that first autumn, Washington not only displayed his leadership qualities in dealing with Congress, but demonstrated how much he had learned since the days when his conduct had soured his relationship with Governor Dinwiddie. From the moment of his arrival in Cambridge, Washington inundated Congress with letters that catalogued the supply shortages his army faced. When New England evenings turned nippy, Washington's notes of foreboding increased. On the first day of autumn he told Congress that if he entered winter with "a naked Army," it "must absolutely break up." His doomsaying sounded eerily reminiscent of dozens of communiqués he had sent from his Virginia Regiment headquarters in the 1750s. This time, money and supplies soon streamed north from Philadelphia, but so too did a congressional delegation to look into matters.[65]

The congressmen dropped two bombshells on Washington. They told him that Congress not only wanted the army to assault Boston within the next ninety days, but it wanted to reduce the pay of all officers. Washington handled matters with aplomb. He did not respond directly to the delegation of congressmen. Instead, he summoned his generals to a council of war. Collectively, they rejected Congress's intrusion into strategy-making and warned that if the officers' pay was cut, there would be no army in 1776. The congressmen capitulated, and even obsequiously accepted several new demands made by Washington.[66]

Washington may have overstated his supply problems in 1775, but he did face three unmistakable crises during his first year in command. He coped successfully with each. The first came when he exposed the army to considerable danger by remodeling it in the midst of a campaign. It was a gut-wrenching step for Washington, as the reorganization came in the "face of an Enemy, from whom we every hour expect an attack," and without a good sense of how Congress—and especially the New England delegates—might respond. Less than a month after reaching the front, he explained to Congress that this was "most necessary Work" in order to secure "Regularity and due Subordination," remove cowardly and ineffectual officers, and find "useful Men." He acknowledged often that "the Experiment is dangerous." He was almost apologetic about the removal of officers, reminding Congress that "nothing can be more fatal to an Army" than incompetent leaders. As late as November he said that nothing weighed more heavily on him than this undertaking. The "trouble I have . . . is realy inconceivable." It filled each day with perplexity and confusion, and cost "So much time anxiety and pains" that he often struggled to maintain his spirits. Late in November, his spirits briefly collapsed, and he confessed to an aide that had he foreseen the mountainous difficulties he would find within his own army, "no consideration upon Earth should have induced me to accept this Command." Only when the first snow of the season fell in December, and intelligence reports reached his desk that the British were ripping up Boston's cobblestone streets to erect defensive installations, could Washington at last relax.[67]

"I have scarcely immerged from one difficulty before I have plunged into another," Washington soon remarked. His second crisis was far more alarming. It erupted in the autumn when the enlistments of those who had signed on immediately after April 19 neared expiration. General Washington appealed to his mens's sense of patriotism. Stay on, he urged. "The times, and the Importance of the great Cause we are engaged in, allow no room for hesitation and delay. When Life, Liberty, & Property are at stake, when our Country is in danger of being a melancholy Scene of bloodshed, and desolation, . . . it little becomes the Character of a Soldier, to shrink from danger." His entreaties failed. Few men wished to reenlist now that the disquieting reality of army life was evident. Separation from loved ones, harsh discipline, Spartan living, boredom, and anxiety about the farm that had been left in the care of wives caused these men to long for home. So too did the potential dangers they faced. Every soldier knew a comrade who died that summer or fall, someone such as Elihu Adams, John's brother, who was a captain in a Braintree militia company that was called to active duty in April and who perished of dysentery in August. What Washington called the "autumnal fevers"—malaria, smallpox, typhus, measles, influenza, and respiratory infections—had struck the army, not as badly as in subsequent campaigns, but with sufficient force to cause widespread alarm and misery.[68]

Washington railed at the "dirty, mercenary Spirit" of the citizenry, yet nothing was left but to recruit a new army. It was painstakingly slow work. After two months Washington had only 3,500 men committed for the 1776 campaign. He expected British reinforcements to bring the enemy's strength to near 40,000 men. "I tremble at the prospect" of the campaign season, he sighed. As January's leaden skies settled over Boston, the Continental army consisted of "a good deal less than half rais'd Regiments." How this crisis "will end God in his great goodness will direct," Washington told a young officer. "I am thankful for his protection to this time." Speaking of the "Confused and disordered State of this Army," he urged the states to resort to conscription should volunteers not step forward. Otherwise, he warned, "it will be a long time before this Army is Complete." By mid-January he had 9,600 men. The army was at half-strength. He told an aide that "reflection upon my Situation, & that of this Army, produces many an uneasy hour" and sleepless night. If he had it to do again, he said, in a melancholy moment, he would have enlisted as a private or "retir'd to the back Country, & liv'd in a Wig-wam."[69]

Washington survived the crisis. The militia, which he had often denigrated in the French and Indian War, was summoned to plug the holes left by men who headed home. In addition, many of the veterans agreed to remain on active duty for a few additional days or weeks until new recruits were garnered. General William Howe, the commander of the British army, helped as well. He could not, or would not, attack. Early in 1776 Washington, safe for the time being with a new and growing army, breathed a sigh of relief. No commander in history, he remarked, had ever had "one Army disbanded and another to raise" in the face of a powerful adversary.[70]

Washington's final crisis during his first year arose from how, or whether, to use his army. Young Colonel Washington, impatient with inactivity, had at times been reckless, impulsive, and overeager for battle. He started this war by displaying the same gambler's audacity. In September, he called a council of war and proposed an attack on the besieged British army in Boston. Joseph Reed, an aide who perhaps knew Washington better than anyone in the army, thought him "very serious." However, all but one of the general officers were aghast. The British had suffered appalling losses when they attacked an entrenched army at Bunker Hill. Washington's generals feared that the Continental army would sustain even worse losses if it attacked a fortified, veteran army possessed of naval and artillery support. Washington listened and demurred. He had consulted his generals because Congress had ordered him to do so and he abided by their advice, but he promptly told Congress that the vote of the council of war was contrary to his wishes.[71]

Many factors led Washington to this view. He felt real or imagined political pressure to use his army. He still equated inaction with debasement. In fact, he characterized Howe's failure to attack the Continental army as "disgraceful." Tactical considerations were crucial in Washington's thinking as well. His intelligence service reported—accurately—that Howe was vulnerable, that his army was weakened by Bunker Hill and camp diseases. Washington also surmised that Howe would soon evacuate Boston, reinforce his army, and attack in other colonies. He guessed—accurately, once again—that much time likely would elapse before he would again have the opportunity to attack such a large British army under such favorable circumstances. Washington believed that if he captured the entire British army south of Canada, his victory would topple the North ministry and end the war.[72]

Washington could hardly attack without the consent of a council of war, but he adroitly exercised his powers to bring his subordinates around to his way of thinking. Without consulting his generals, Washington dispatched Colonel Knox to Fort Ticonderoga to fetch artillery for his army. In the meantime, he passed on to Congress information about Howe's problems, hoping to arouse support for an assault on Boston. As soon as he learned that Knox was near Boston with fifty-two cannon and fourteen mortars in his possession, the commander summoned another council of war. This time the generals consented to a plan to fortify Dorchester Heights, which overlooked Boston harbor. The British would have to attack to keep open their Atlantic lifeline, or abandon the city. If Howe attacked, the generals agreed to land a force in his rear.[73]

Washington had obtained from his generals what he had long sought, but he could not force Howe to fight. Under cover of darkness on March 4, with temperatures below freezing and Knox's artillery pounding Howe's lines in Boston, 3,000 of Washington's men climbed Dorchester Heights. They were armed with picks, axes, and shovels. Throughout the night these hearty farm boys chipped away at earth that was frozen to a depth of eighteen inches, until after seven hours of hard labor they had constructed six fortifications. At

3:00 AM they came off the hill as 3,000 fresh troops marched to its summit. The replacements waited anxiously for dawn, and Howe's response.

Howe decided to attack. Hour by hour that day he gathered his men and prepared for an assault the following morning. But throughout that day the weather deteriorated, and that evening a fierce late-winter northeaster slammed into the region. Fighting was impossible for twenty-four hours. With time to reflect, Howe reconsidered. An attack on Dorchester Heights, he decided, would likely result in even heavier losses than he had sustained at Bunker Hill, for Washington had cannon and presumably better trained men than had defended the high ground in Charleston the previous summer.

Four days after Washington occupied Dorchester Heights, Howe offered the Americans a deal: If Washington permitted him to evacuate Boston, he would spare the city; if Washington resisted his departure, Boston would be razed. It was a Hobson's choice. Washington could seize the foe and lose a city, or liberate Boston while the enemy slipped through his fingers. He opted for the latter alternative. The destruction of Boston might cause irreparable damage to the war effort. When New Yorkers and Philadelphians learned of Boston's fate, they might press for accommodation at any cost, and this just as Congress was moving steadily closer to independence. On March 17 the British evacuation commenced. The next day the first Continentals streamed into a Boston that was devoid of British troops for the first time in eight years.[74]

Washington did not have his battle, but much had been accomplished. He had scored a great bloodless victory. Humble in public, Washington boasted in private that no general had ever accomplished so much with so little in the face of such a great adversary. He had compelled the "Flower of the British army" to leave Boston "in a shameful and precipitate manner."[75] His performance captured the public's imagination. Congress, at Adams's bequest, struck a commemorative medal honoring his "great and decisive" leadership, and John Hancock, a Bostonian and the president of Congress, commissioned Charles Willson Peale to paint still another portrait of Washington.[76]

Washington's success had not occurred by happenstance. The manner in which he had comported himself and wielded his authority was no less important than his actions that forced Howe from Boston. He had demonstrated a keen understanding of the use of power. He had profited from both his long experience as an administrator of a large plantation enterprise and from a dozen years in the Virginia assembly, where he had learned how politicians thought. He had an unerring grasp of popular opinion. Washington knew that all officers were viewed with suspicion by a colonial population weaned on the dangers posed by armies and generals. He probably would not have been surprised to discover that even Adams had exhorted friends in Massachusetts to "Spy" on him. In revolutionary times, Adams said, it was necessary "to know the Character of every Man . . . in . . . public affairs, especially in the Army."[77] Finally, Washington was careful not to repeat the mistakes he had made as a callow young officer in Virginia in the 1750s.

Remembering the charges of sybaritic behavior leveled against him twenty years earlier by the "Virginia Centinel," Washington lived in a modest manner, sacrificing the luxuries to which he was accustomed. He neither returned to Mount Vernon nor left his army during the siege campaign. He eschewed fox hunting and other familiar pastimes, and for the most part in 1775–1776 lived alone, far from his wife. Many, like Adams a bit later, concluded that "General Washington setts a fine Example" of republican simplicity.[78]

In addition, Washington was careful not to alienate Congress by becoming mired in disputes over his officers. He understood that to become enmeshed in disputes between officers over rank and promotion would be to engage in damaging—and in all likelihood—losing battles. Although he was unhappy with some general officers, like Joseph Frye, who, he remarked, merely "keeps to his Room, and talks learnedly of Emetics Cathartics, &c.," Washington kept silent. He simply posted such officers where they could do little harm and, as much as possible, assigned responsibility for important undertakings, such as the invasion of Canada in the fall of 1775, to enterprising lower-ranking officers. [79]

"It is a great stake we are playing for," Washington remarked just after his troops entered Boston. For perhaps most Americans, and certainly for Washington by the spring of 1776, the issue no longer was reconciliation. The yearning for independence had grown gradually but steadily since that cool morning when colonists had died on Lexington Green and in Concord. Quite inadvertently, Adams was the first political leader to bring the issue before the public. In July 1775 he wrote a private letter to a friend at home in which he stated that Congress should have already declared independence and written a constitution for the new nation. The letter reached Adams's friend by a circuitous route. It was intercepted by the British and printed in a Tory newspaper in Boston. Adams paid dearly. The moderates "made me as unpopular as they could," he later recalled, and Dr. Rush remembered that for a few weeks Adams, shunned by colleagues, could be seen "walk[ing the] streets alone . . . an object of nearly universal detestation." However, once the secret was out, Adams no longer was constrained. He spoke openly for independence during the closed door sessions of Congress. Moreover, now that his purloined letter had raised the matter, people throughout America quietly began to discuss the merits of independence.[80]

Nevertheless, fearful of being too far ahead of public opinion, Adams remained circumspect in what he said and wrote outside Congress. During the remainder of 1775 he seldom alluded to the possibility of a separation from Great Britain. When he did address the issue, he depicted independence as a "sad Necessity" likely to be occasioned by wartime exigency.[81] Jefferson was even more cautious, although in the autumn of 1775 he privately attacked George III as ignorant and wicked, and predicted that if Britain conducted a military campaign in 1776 the colonists would declare independence. However, he refused to make any public statements in this vein. Jefferson's timidity exasperated Adams. Although "frank, explicit" in private conversations, Adams complained, Jefferson was "a silent member of Congress" during debates. Early in 1776 Adams even suggested that the trepidation of men such as Jefferson had cost America dearly. Had Congress declared independence in mid-1775, he maintained, foreign assistance might have been received, enabling Washington to have captured Howe's entire army and preventing the Canadian debacle. Later, Adams admitted that he had been wrong and Jefferson right. Those who had counseled restraint throughout 1775 had been prudent, he said, for delaying the debate on independence allowed public opinion to coalesce around the idea of breaking away from British rule. Ultimately, it had given greater "Popularity to Our cause both at home and abroad," he acknowledged.[82]

Adams was attacked for urging independence. In 1775, he said later, the "idea of independence was as unpopular . . . as the Stamp Act itself," at least within Congress. Adams was far ahead of Congress, and even of some radical congressmen, in his thinking. He was not merely a separatist. He had grown into a true revolutionary who harbored a majestic dream for an independent America. His ideas had developed slowly. As with many other activists, he had been drawn to the protest movement not from a desire to initiate change or reform American society, but to resist what he believed to be British tyranny. London, he once said, had "driven America" to defend its liberty. When Great Britain resorted to force to suppress the colonial protest, he exhorted his countrymen to fight not to win freedom, but to save the freedom they already enjoyed. "Liberty once lost is lost forever," he told them.[83]

Adams came to believe that his generation bore a special responsibility.

Much of history, he believed, was the story of humankind's struggle to gain or maintain liberty. He believed that many generations had been called upon to do battle in defense of liberty. His Puritan forbearers had nurtured liberty in the wilds of America while those who remained in England restored it in the mother country during the Glorious Revolution. Now liberty was imperiled in America. It was the destiny of his generation, he believed, to keep freedom alive for people everywhere. As his ancestors had sought to establish a Godly "city upon a hill" that would serve as a beacon for all believers, Adams gradually came to believe that the American Revolution could serve as a shining light to the world, for it was to be "a great Revolution, in the Affairs of the World," a revolution to create a new world, a republican world.[84]

Republicanism had numerous meanings in 1776.[85] However, when Adams called himself a republican, he referred to two core beliefs that he sought to realize through this revolution. He wished to eradicate "idolatry to Monarchs, and servility to Aristocratical Pride," and in their place to cement the belief that the people were the source of all authority and power. Popular sovereignty was a radical idea in 1776. Adams said that this concept was thought by many congressmen to be a "strange and terrible" doctrine. Roughly twenty percent of the colonists must have shared the fears of those congressmen, for that percentage of provincials remained loyal to Great Britain during this upheaval. Many chose Toryism because they felt the purpose of government, as a Loyalist put it, should be "to place man . . . out of the reach of his own power." Adams could not have disagreed more. He believed government existed to secure for the citizenry "the greatest Quantity of Happiness" for the greatest numbers of people, and he was convinced that the greatest "general Happiness" would be achieved if the citizenry not only made the laws under which they lived, but if "an Empire of Laws and not of men" came into being.[86]

In addition, Adams sought through the American Revolution to enhance individual opportunity. He wished to destroy the system of privileges enjoyed by the elite in monarchical and aristocratic societies. Neither a king nor the "Dons, the Bashaws, the Grandees, the Patricians, the Sachems, the Nabobs" of society should have power as an inherited right, he said, for their first object in governance would be to serve themselves. As early as 1766 he had expressed resentment toward the British system that refused to recognize that "All men are born equal." In the British system, privilege outweighed merit, success depended on preferment, and advancement for a commoner was conditional on courting and flattering the elite. It was a system in which the best-connected trucklers rose above "much better men."[87]

No one understood better than Adams how the British political and social system operated, and no one resented it more. This descendant of a humble Braintree farming family had felt the sting of political and social elitism. He was provoked by a political system that denied sovereignty to the American citizenry. There "is something unnatural and odious in [subservience to] a Government 1000 Leagues off" that dispatched its courtiers and nobility to maintain hegemony over the colonists, he wrote. He loathed a social system in which the merit of an ancestor could pave the road to success. He decried a system in which the untalented, but well connected, whom he satirically labeled "miniature infinitesimal Deities," were regarded as his superiors. He could not be a courtier. Such behavior was terribly demeaning. He refused to go through life servilely enduring the "Passions and Prejudices, the Follies and Vices of great Men in order to obtain their Smiles, Esteem, and Patronage and consequently their favours and Preferments." He had been reduced to this shameful behavior when he started his legal practice, but he never again wanted to have to act in such a manner and he wished to save his sons from such a fate. For Adams, the American Revolution was about opportunity: the opportunity for the people to govern themselves and the opportunity for an individual to achieve whatever his merit could earn. If humankind could thus be liberated to pursue happiness, Adams believed, people at last would have before them the opportunity to achieve the "greatest Quantity of Happiness."[88]

Edmund Burke once remarked that the American Revolution was a "revolution not made, but prevented." In his judgment the American Revolution was nothing more than an upheaval in which traditionally conservative colonists had resisted Great Britain's attempts to strip them of their age-old prerogatives. But Burke's view does not adequately encapsulate Adams's revolutionary outlook. Adams did believe that Americans had become "the keeper of the heritage England had cast aside," as historian John Howe wrote, but he also dreamt a truly revolutionary dream. He spoke of the events of 1776 as only the beginning of an American Revolution that, by sweeping aside the "insolent Domination [of] a very few, opulent, monopolizing Families" that had held power through their ties to British royalty, could result in the achievement of a "more equal Liberty, than had prevail'd in other parts of the Earth." This grand achievement would bestow blessings on "future Millions, and Millions of Millions."[89]

Yet while Adams dreamt of individual opportunity and greater liberty for greater numbers, he feared unbridled individualism and untrammeled liberty. He yearned for an American Revolution that would result in a greater public good realized through the collective will of the citizenry. It was a dream born out of the practices of his native New England, which long had maintained a tradition of governance that emphasized consensus and popular concurrence. In Braintree, and countless other small villages, public policy was decided by group opinion. Once an issue was agreed upon, unanimous adherence to popular authority was expected as a matter of social propriety. The genesis of this credo lay in part in the beliefs of the early Christians, who had celebrated in the Eucharist a giving of oneself that brought the community together, and also in the practices of the New England Puritans, who had set out to erect and maintain an exclusive society, a utopian experiment that could succeed only if uniformity and conformity prevailed. They understood that the populace had to embrace the "public good." Consequently, at the local level colonial New England became a region in which accord on public policy was garnered through a corporate ethos. For the general well-being of the polity, decisions were made collectively and adherence was expected. The Puritan culture had championed the subordination of the individual to society. Self-seeking was denounced. The public welfare reigned over private interest. What John Winthrop, the early governor of Massachusetts Bay, told his fellow immigrants in 1629 resonated with New Englanders for generations: "We must be knitt together in this work as one man." Adams's New England was not the New England of Winthrop and the Puritans. In Adams's time most men—not merely those who were church members—enjoyed the privileges of citizenship, including the franchise. For many, this change only heightened the traditional aspiration for consensus. Peace and harmony did not always prevail in every community, yet the ideal of group consent and social conformity persevered. Adams's generation, like its predecessors, treated individual recalcitrance not merely as socially impermissible, but as shameless.[90]

Likewise, Adams aspired to subjugate the will of individuals to a greater public good, though a good arrived at by consensus and made by a government in which the people were sovereign. He knew full well, however, that no such polity or society could succeed if humankind's ambition and avaricious nature went uncontrolled. So compelling were greed and vaulting ambition, Adams wrote, that they could influence the selection of a marriage partner, divide families, and determine career choices. They could easily subvert the greater good. He feared too that the "Spirit of Commerce," which was fueled by avarice and, in turn, fostered an omnivorous acquisitiveness, was so far advanced in the colonies that it might be impossible to realize a republic governed by a selfless citizenry and disinterested rulers. However, Adams believed it possible that the patriotism sparked by war could trigger a moral reformation, a transformation so powerful that the citizenry would sublimate its individual desires. If this transformation, this revolution, occurred, America's republican experiment would succeed. Thus, his writings emphasized the necessity of sacrifice. Until the war was won, he said, people must live simply and renounce many material comforts, including new clothes, furniture, and houses. People must drink coffee, not tea, and they must reduce their consumption of molasses, wine, and sugar, while they abandoned hope of acquiring velvet and lace. If republicanism was to survive, men must be willing to leave home to serve the republic as soldiers, workers, and statesmen. Citizens must respect their leaders. Neighbors must act with decency and civility toward one another.[91]

Adams never imagined that sustaining a new republic would be easy. He repeatedly said that a successful republic required a knowledgeable, pious, and virtuous citizenry. Intellectual attainment was especially important to him. He once remarked that "Education makes a greater difference between man and man, than nature has made between man and brute." He championed erudition in leaders and literacy among the citizenry, and equated education with what he believed to be a flourishing liberty in New England. However, he never went so far as to suggest that schooling guaranteed successful leadership or that an untutored individual could not be a great leader. He lionized his father and lauded Benjamin Franklin, both largely self-educated men who became leaders, and he nominated Washington, who lacked a formal education, to lead the Continental army. On the other hand, he denigrated Governor Hutchinson, a man of superior intellect who had been educated at Harvard College, but whom he believed to have been undone by a flawed character. Although there were always exceptions, Adams believed that a well-educated, virtuous man who had acquired habits of discipline could become a sagacious individual, capable of growing into a discerning, farsighted public official. Adams also recognized the role of parents as educators. He urged them to foster propriety and honesty in their children, to teach their offspring to be active, industrious, and courageous, and to prevail on them to be contemptuous of prejudice and injustice, much in fact as he had been raised by Deacon Adams.[92]

He contended that piety and republicanism were inextricably linked. Without "Austere Morals" and a "pure Religion," he said, a republic could not be maintained. For Adams this was a simple matter. Private virtue was crucial for the existence of public virtue, and without public virtue any republic was doomed. In his "Novanglus" essays, Adams portrayed Great Britain as the epitome of iniquity and argued that if Americans could not discern "the difference between true and false, right and wrong, virtue and vice," they too were doomed to the same fate as the inhabitants of the parent state.[93]

Adams utilized the word "virtue" frequently in his letters and essays. He was wont to say that the people must have the acumen to preserve their liberties and the virtue to merit self-rule. His definition of virtue was crucial. He used the word to mean that citizens must subordinate their private interests to the greater welfare of the society. "Men must be ready ... and be happy to sacrifice their private Pleasure, Passions, and Interests, nay their private Friendships and dearest Connections, when they stand in Competition with the Rights of Society," he maintained. For Adams, it was a simple matter: if the peoples' spirit was not republican, republicanism could not succeed.[94]

Adams embraced a truly revolutionary ideal. He looked toward a new republican society devoid of artificial social distinctions. It would be a world in which royalty and nobility would be banished. Dependence by one citizen upon another would be ended, for a "genuine Republican can no more fawn and cringe than he can domineer," said Adams. In the republican society that he envisioned, educational institutions would exist for popular refinement, the molding of exemplary citizens, and the training of skilled leaders. Within a generation republicanism not only would inspire dignity in the people, but would produce a society of sturdy, patriotic citizens, men and women who were "industrious, sober, frugal," and ambitious to serve their brethren. Government must exist for the purpose of securing the happiness of the people. Its purpose was not to serve narrow interests of one class or to promote a ruling elite. Adams's revolutionary vision was the creation of a republican nation in which the citizenry—and none more so than the wealthiest citizens—embraced the corporate ideal of patriotism and selflessness, eschewing selfish interests in quest of a unitary common good to be achieved by a government that served the integrated parts of the community.[95]

Jefferson is almost universally thought of as having been the proponent of more sweeping revolutionary changes than Adams. Later, especially after having spent five years in France in the second half of the 1780s, Jefferson grew unquestionably more radical than Adams. However, at the time of American independence, Adams's public rhetoric was tinged with a revolutionary idealism that matched, and at times exceeded that of his Virginia counterpart. Moreover, while neither Adams nor Jefferson equaled the pulsating, paradisal spirit of Thomas Paine's *Common Sense*, Adams came closest.

To a greater degree than Jefferson, Adams—like Paine—publicly broadcast the revolutionary implications of republicanism. Paine encapsulated the idea that Adams had searched to convey: "'Tis not the concern of a day, a year, or an age; posterity are vitally involved in the contest. . . . [A] new era for politics is struck—and a new method of thinking has arisen." Adams shared Paine's belief that the world would never, could never, be the same again. A republican world no longer would tolerate the "insolent Domination [by] a few, a very few opulent, monopolizing Families," Adams predicted. Like Paine, he not only believed that the ideals of the revolutionaries would inspire Americans in succeeding generations, but he was confident that the American Revolution would "be an Astonishment to vulgar Minds all over the World." In the first half of 1776 it was Adams, not Jefferson, who was regarded as the leading revolutionary in Congress. Indeed, six weeks prior to the Declaration of Independence, Henry lauded Adams, not Jefferson, as "a democrat" to follow in the republican revolution to constrain "our opulent families" in Virginia who harbor "a strong bias to aristocracy."[96]

Jefferson likely shared Adams's outlook in this period, but was less systematic in compiling his political philosophy. Nevertheless, in his *Summary View* and other published writings, as well as in his private musings and correspondence, Jefferson plotted the rights of humankind and demonstrated how British tyranny had sought to subsume those liberties. Humankind, he wrote, possessed rights derived from the laws of nature and "natural reason." Before independence his itemization of natural rights included the liberty to: emigrate to new lands, practice self-defense against the inhabitants of that domain, establish new societies and governments in the new homeland, own new lands, renounce one's previous citizenship, marry and divorce, constitute governments that would legislate for the citizenry, tax themselves, and ascertain that their tax monies were not "wasted among the venal and corrupt."[97]

Unlike Adams, Jefferson neither dilated on America's shining future nor wrote of a dazzling new republican world. Much later, in fact, Jefferson acknowledged that before July 1776 he was so consumed with his contemplation of monarchical abuses that he had given little thought to revolutionary changes in America. However, two themes can be seen running through his writings prior to independence. Drawing on the classical literature of English common law, he rather indistinctly equated separation from Great Britain both with the establishment of greater personal freedom and the opportunity of Americans to fashion their own limited, consensual polities. In addition, whereas Adams longed to see that what had germinated in colonial New England take root throughout America, Jefferson before mid-1776 looked back wistfully to a saturnian age of liberty that had supposedly existed in Saxon England before its extirpation by tyrannical monarchs, a halcyon time in a mythic past, when humankind, in John Locke's words, was "free, equal, and independent."[98]

Adams and Jefferson faced some constraints because of the political offices they held, but General Washington had to be especially careful when he spoke in public. Washington knew that his pronouncements were often addressed both to soldiers and civilians whose support of the war sometimes was less than avid. Although he was more guarded in his public pronouncements than Adams and Jefferson, Washington's commitment to a great revolutionary cause was evident. After his first weeks in command he abandoned talk of fighting for reconciliation, although he did not openly urge independence. He portrayed the war as a struggle in defense of liberties that the colonists had long possessed. This was a "sacred cause," he said, to protect rights and freedoms that he identified at various times as "Life, Liberty, & Property," "all that is dear & valuable in Life," "everything that is valuable to Freemen," "Mankind['s] . . . Inherent Rights," "freedom and . . . privilege," the "Rights of Mankind," the "Rights of Humanity," and "all that Freemen hold dear." The only specific rights that he enumerated were the rights of self-government, freedom of religion, and the security of one's property, but he spoke obliquely of the liberty to control one's destiny. Nationalism also tinged Washington's rhetoric. Nine months before independence was declared he urged men to sacrifice for "the Welfare of [their] country." Like Adams and Jefferson, he spoke of taking up arms to maintain the right to pursue "happiness," and he frequently discoursed on resisting tyranny. For Washington, this was no ordinary war. He and his fellow revolutionaries were engaged in a "glorious & unparalleled Struggle" to save liberty for generations yet unborn both in America and throughout the world.[99]

Of the three, it was Washington who sounded most like Paine, expressing at once the towering rage, the simple yearning for autonomy, and the grandiose dream of a glittering future. On the day that Congress finally declared independence, and thousands of British regulars debouched on Staten Island, General Washington told his men:

The time is now near at hand which must probably determine, whether Americans are to be, Freemen, or Slaves; whether they are to have any property they can call their own; whether their Houses, and Farms, are to be pillaged and destroyed, and they consigned to a State of Wretchedness from which no human efforts will probably deliver them. The fate of unborn Millions will now depend, under God, on the Courage and Conduct of this army—Our cruel and unrelenting Enemy leaves us no choice but a brave resistance, or the most abject submission; this is all we can expect—We have therefore to resolve to conquer or die: Our own Country's Honor, all call upon us for a vigorous and manly exertion, and if we now shamefully fail, we shall become infamous to the whole world—Let us therefore rely upon the goodness of the Cause . . . to animate and encourage us to great and noble Actions—The Eyes of all our Countrymen are now upon us. . . . Let us therefore animate and encourage each other, and shew the whole world, that a Freeman contending for Liberty on his own ground is superior to any slavish mercenary on earth.[100]

Sentiment for American independence sprang up like the flowers that flourished in the colonists' gardens during the spring of 1776. It was an idea whose time had come. The first of several death blows that fell on those who favored accommodation came when word arrived in January that George III had recently welcomed Parliament with a speech that Washington characterized as "full of rancor & resentment." The monarch had rejected the Olive Branch Petition and denounced the colonists for waging "rebellious war."[101] One day after the monarch's bellicose speech appeared in American newspapers, *Common Sense* hit the streets of Philadelphia.

Because Adams had been the most vocal member of Congress in urging independence, many of his colleagues thought he had authored this pamphlet. Although he might have matched Paine's euphoria, and he could have tossed an equal number of barbs at the British aristocracy and the lack of opportunity for commoners and colonists within the British system, Adams could never have equaled the rage that poured from Paine's quill. Nor could he have duplicated Paine's free-flowing, excitable, and envenomed style. No one knew that better than Adams. "I could not have written any Thing in so manly and striking a style," he admitted. Paine, he said, had a flair for "clear, concise, and Nervous" composition that resulted in language that one might hear in an English gaol.[102] Perhaps, but *Common Sense* also had the ring of a Sunday sermon, with its occasional "thee" and "thou," and its equation of life under monarchies with bondage in the land of the pharaohs. Paine's style resonated with the American public as had no other political tract published between 1763 and 1776. It reached an audience 100 times larger than Dickinson's *Pennsylvania Farmer*, somewhere in the neighborhood of 150,000 readers who purchased the pamphlet and countless others—such as the soldiery in the Continental army—who listened as it was read.

Sentiment for monarchical rule, which must have been dwindling over the past few years, vanished rapidly after Americans digested Paine's philip-pic. Not only was liberty at risk under monarchy, he said, but so was peace, as monarchs had little else to do but lay "the world in blood and ashes." How-ever, the heart of his work was an assault on the idea of reconciliation. When he had finished, most readers were convinced that independence would bring them greater prospects of peace and prosperity than could be had within the British empire. But he did even more. He added a millennial quality to the colonists' struggle. This was not a revolt over taxation. The survival of liberty was at stake, he wrote, and if the American Revolution succeeded, generations yet unborn would owe a debt of gratitude to their forebearers who struggled to defend—and expand—freedom. Paine glimpsed the prospect of an Amer-ica that would become "an asylum for mankind." Henceforth, not only would America offer refuge to the world's oppressed, but like a shining beacon, rev-olutionary America would herald "the birth-day of a new world," the beginning of an epoch in which humankind across the earth could "begin the world over again."[103]

Adams once said that he believed America actually became independent on April 19, 1775, the day the war began. There can be no question that war hardened attitudes. By the spring of 1776 colonists had died fighting British regulars, British vessels had destroyed Falmouth in Massachusetts and Nor-folk on the Chesapeake, and Lord Dunmore, the royal governor of Virginia, had promised freedom to slaves who fled behind British lines. When word arrived early in 1776 that London had hired German mercenaries to help sup-press the rebellion, the colonists grew even more embittered. Adams also dated independence from March 1776, when Congress opened America's ports to the commerce of the world. That certainly affected the timing, if not the inevitability, of Congress's eventual action. So too did the failed military campaign in Canada. Thereafter, more Americans believed that the war could be won only with foreign assistance, and that French or Spanish aid could be attained only if independence was declared.

While America drifted toward independence during the first half of 1776, Adams knew that his countrymen would never be emotionally free of Great Britain, or fully able to commit themselves to anything more than a defense of their perceived rights as British colonists, until independence was actually declared. The middle colonies of New York, New Jersey, Pennsylvania, and Delaware, dominated by merchants with deep economic ties to the empire, constituted the last great obstacle to American independence, and succeeded in forestalling congressional action on independence for at least six months.

Washington was exasperated. He thought a declaration of independence was crucial to the prosecution of the war. Adams was equally vexed. He longed to play "the part of a great Politician," he said, and in this crisis he did so, albeit impatiently and reluctantly, permitting attitudes to crystallize, resisting the temptation to charge forward with public exhortations for independence that might have been detrimental to his cause. He had learned much about politics during his eighteen months in Philadelphia.[104]

A great leader must know when to act. In mid-May 1776, Adams knew the time for action had arrived. He introduced a resolution that stated the necessity for the provinces to terminate their colonial governments. Each was urged to adopt a state constitution, so that it would have a new government equal to the exigency of the times. The reconciliationists charged that this was "a Machine to fabricate Independence." They were correct. Adams in fact looked on his resolution as a declaration of independence, and its language was a harbinger of Congress's subsequent bill of indictment of the British monarch. The instant Congress adopted his resolution, Adams exulted that "the last Step" had been taken, "a total absolute Independence" had been achieved.[105]

Adams was prescient. His action had been aimed primarily at Pennsylvania, whose assembly refused to instruct its congressional delegates to vote for independence, and almost immediately thereafter that colony released its delegates to vote as they pleased. Adams's resolution had driven a stake through the heart of the foes of independence everywhere. With considerable truth he could boast that his resolution had initiated "the most important [step] that ever was taken in America."[106]

The urge to separate from Great Britain now swept across the land "like a Torrent," Adams soon noted. Within three weeks Congress had created a Committee of Five, as it soon was called, to prepare a declaration of independence. Its members included Adams, Jefferson, Franklin, Roger Sherman of Connecticut, and Robert Livingston of New York. Jefferson's inclusion on the committee may have arisen largely from happenstance. For weeks he had beseeched the legislative leaders in Virginia to recall him so that he might participate in the writing of his state's first constitution. Had they acted on his request, Jefferson would have been in Williamsburg in June 1776. Instead, Virginia summoned Richard Henry Lee, who not only had greater seniority in Congress, but had introduced the motion urging independence. Had Lee remained in Philadelphia, he might have been chosen over Jefferson to sit on this committee. Adams later offered still another explanation for Jefferson's selection. He believed that Jefferson had been chosen as a blow against Lee, who was hated by some in the Virginia delegation, but the evidence is too meager to confirm Adams's suspicion.[107]

Adams chaired the committee. How, then, did Jefferson come to draft the Declaration of Independence? When each was quite old, Adams and Jefferson offered conflicting recollections of how the Virginian came to write the draft of the Declaration of Independence. Adams remembered that the other members of the Committee of Five had requested that he and Jefferson jointly prepare the document. However, "Mr. Jefferson desired me" to perform the task. Adams offered the following description of his ensuing conversation with Jefferson:

JEFFERSON: "You should do it."

ADAMS: "Oh! no."

JEFFERSON: "Why will you not? You ought to do it."

ADAMS: "I will not."

JEFFERSON: "Why?"

ADAMS: "Reasons enough."

JEFFERSON: "What can be your reasons?"

ADAMS: "Reason first—You are a Virginian, and a Virginian ought to appear at the head of this business. Reason second—I am obnoxious, suspected, and unpopular. You are very much otherwise. Reason third—You can write ten times better than I can."

JEFFERSON: "Well, if you are decided, I will do as well as I can."

ADAMS: "Very well. When you have drawn it up, we will have a meeting."[108]

Jefferson remembered that the committee unanimously "pressed on myself alone to make the draught. I consented." His version is most likely correct, as it is supported by an entry in Adams's diary in 1779, when his memory would have been sharper. The committee turned to Jefferson because of his skills as a penman, as well as because of the uncompromisingly radical tone of his earlier writings.[109]

Adams had seniority over Jefferson and might have made an issue of it, but he did not object to his colleague's selection. In addition to the reasons he gave, Adams had still other motives for not taking on this task. Because he was already working up to twelve hours daily, and had just been added to a newly created committee to prepare instructions for the diplomats that Congress was about to send abroad, Adams had little time for still another assignment. In addition, he believed a Declaration of Independence, while necessary, was little more than "a theatrical show," a propaganda extravaganza. However, the most important factor in Adams's thinking was that he never imagined that the Declaration of Independence would be so well remembered or sanctified. He knew that the act of declaring independence would be cherished and celebrated, but he must have thought that the written declaration, like the Declaration of Rights in 1774 or the Declaration of the Causes and Necessity for Taking Up Arms in 1775, or a plethora of other resolves adopted throughout the colonies during the past decade, soon would be forgotten. Only much later would Adams discover that the author of the Declaration of Independence would run "away with all the stage effect . . . and all the glory of it," as he remarked.[110] Adams simply made a terrible miscalculation. He refused to fight for the chance to take on this chore. Jefferson accepted the opportunity.

Adams later claimed that Jefferson completed the draft in "a day or two." He was substantially correct.[111] Jefferson did not have the luxury of time. "We were all in haste; Congress was impatient," as Adams recollected. Nor did Jefferson require much time to write the draft. His ideas, which had begun to crystallize in the early 1770s, had jelled in the course of writing the *Summary View* and various legislative statements. Moreover, he had numerous guides to follow. He was familiar with the myriad declarations adopted by colonial assemblies since the Stamp Act crisis, as well as the English Declaration of Rights and countless radical polemics. He may have read some of the numerous resolutions on independence that were adopted, and in some instances published, by towns, grand juries, merchant associations, militia units, and colonial assemblies throughout the spring of 1776. Most important, the draft of Virginia's Declaration of Rights, composed largely by George Mason, appeared in a Philadelphia newspaper on the day after the Committee of Five was constituted. Mason's work began with the ringing assertion that "all men are born equally free and independent, and have certain inherent rights . . . among which are the enjoyment of life and liberty . . . and pursuing and obtaining happiness and safety." It went on to argue that the people created government for the purpose of securing their natural rights, and that governments that were inadequate to the task, or that became tyrannical, must be altered or abolished.[112]

Seventeen days after its creation, the Committee of Five presented its draft to Congress. Two days later, on that steaming July 1, Congress took up the question of independence. At day's end Congress, sitting as a committee of the whole, voted 9–2 for independence. South Carolina and Pennsylvania opposed the motion, New York abstained, and Delaware's delegation was deadlocked. Congress deferred the official vote until the following morning.

When Congress reconvened on July 2 it was immediately clear that two important changes had occurred. Two members of the Pennsylvania delegation who had opposed independence on the previous day, Dickinson and Robert Morris, were absent. In addition, the deadlock within Delaware's delegation would be broken, for Caesar Rodney, who had been absent the day before, was in his seat. Before Congress took up the momentous question on that day, it received correspondence from Washington on the military situation in New York and assigned several items of business to the appropriate committees. It then heard a report from the Committee of the Whole on the action taken the previous day and listened for final time to Lee's motion on independence. More debate occurred, perhaps lasting much of the day, if Jefferson's notes are to be taken literally. Finally, nothing was left to be said. A roll-call vote was taken. New York once again abstained, but every other colony—it was their final vote as colonies—voted for independence.[113]

That evening a jubilant Adams wrote Abigail that the "greatest question" ever debated, and the most important issue that perhaps ever "will be decided among men" in America, had been resolved. He predicted that henceforth July 2 would be commemorated annually "as the Day of Deliverance," a day to be "solemnized with Pomp and Parade, with Shews, Games, Sports, Guns, Bells, Bonfires and Illuminations from one End of the Continent to the other from this Time forward forever more."[114]

The next day, and the day after, July 3 and 4, Congress debated the draft of the Declaration of Independence. The document that Congress saw was largely Jefferson's handiwork. He had first shown his initial draft to Adams, then to Franklin, and finally to Sherman and Livingston. More than a dozen stylistic changes had resulted, two on the recommendation of Adams. He probably was responsible for changing Jefferson's charge that Great Britain sought to wield "arbitrary power" over the colonies to "absolute Despotism"; in addition, he added the charge that the Crown had compelled colonial assemblies to meet "at places unusual, uncomfortable, & distant from the depository of their public records."[115]

Jefferson's draft had contained no new or original ideas.[116] Adams later ridiculed its lack of novelty, saying that it merely reiterated what Otis and Samuel Adams had long before published, and "what had been hackneyed in Congress for two years before." But Adams missed the point. It would have been impolitic—imbecilic, in fact—for Jefferson to have introduced new notions at this juncture. Later, Jefferson said that it had not been his responsibility "to invent new ideas." His task, he said, had been "to place before mankind the common sense of the subject." He also said that Congress desired a document that would "be an expression of the American mind."[117]

In order to accurately reflect feelings in Congress, Jefferson, who had not previously kept a record of the debates in Congress, took copious notes throughout June. These show that Congress wanted a declaration that would justify the right of citizens to engage in revolution. Congress also envisioned a Declaration of Independence that would be aimed at many audiences. The Declaration was to sustain the committed. It was to convert the hesitant or undecided into supporters of the war. Knowing that the pronouncement would be read in the enemy's lair, Congress envisioned a Declaration of Independence that promoted antiwar sentiments among the disaffected within Great Britain. It also wanted to tell the world— especially France and Spain, Britain's traditional rivals—that America had repudiated reconciliation. Congress wanted foreign assistance in meaningful quantities, something that could be attained only if America's objective was to tear itself free from the British empire.[118]

The Declaration, therefore, was submitted to "a candid world," not merely to the residents of the former colonies. It asserted that the people were sovereign and that all persons have equal rights to life, liberty, and the pursuit of happiness. It urged a republican world in which self-government would prevail, fair and adequate representation would be accorded all portions of the population, justice would be impartially administered, and the citizenry would be safe both from wicked and designing rulers and the maleficence of their own governments. Finally, it indicted the King for actions inimical to the interests of the colonists.[119]

Congress devoted two days to the draft. As historian Pauline Maier has written, it proved to be "an extraordinary editor" of a document that required considerable editing. Congress trimmed the draft by about one-fourth, deleting unnecessary words and tinkering with cumbersome sentences. It cut out some baseless assertions and moderated other claims. It excised portions that were thought to be too antagonistic to America's friends in England, but the longest section to be expunged was a philippic against the monarchy for allegedly having imposed African slavery on the colonies. Not only was this bad history, but Georgia and South Carolina opposed its inclusion from fear that it smacked of abolitionism. Jefferson was mortified as the wrecking ball tore down sections of his creation. He cried that his chief editors had been the most "pusillanimous" members of Congress. They had "mangled ... the Manuscript," he declared.[120]

He should have been more thankful. The Declaration of Independence, the majestic document that inspired both contemporaries and posterity—and which, in the words of historian Joseph Ellis, has been "the core of [Jefferson's] seductive appeal across the ages"—was dramatically stylized and given its venerable sheen by its editors on the committee and within Congress.[121]

With adequate time, Jefferson might have written a more striking draft. As it was, his composition was a more polished literary effort than that which Mason composed for Virginia, or that any writer, or committee of draftsmen, produced in any town or colony. Could any member of Congress have done a better job? Adams believed that he could have written a superior Declaration of Independence.[122] While that was unlikely, he might have authored a draft that was equally good and quite similar. In a variety of writings from the Stamp Act crisis onward, Adams had articulated many of the points included by Jefferson: the sovereignty of the people, the natural rights philosophy, British designs to tyrannize the colonists, and the right and duty of the people to revolt, and the ringing assertion that "all men are born equal," which he had first written a decade earlier. He almost certainly would have included some things that Jefferson chose to omit. Jefferson never used the word "unconstitutional." The heart of any Adams statement would likely have been more legalistic. He likely would have written of the need for "a government of laws, and not of men," as he often had in previous works. He might have written, as he had a decade earlier, that British law fell especially hard on "the Multitudes of the poorer People" and threatened to "reduce them to absolute Beggary." In addition to defending the right of revolution, he might have written—as he once had—that to fail to revolt would "dishonour" the "Memory of our Fore fathers" and "our Posterity." He likely would have played on British corruption "owing to their own extravagance, and want of wisdom." He was fond of arguing that struggle toughened people and that to fight for liberty was to make liberty even more dear. He might have said, as he had only a month earlier, that to remain under British jurisdiction would be "irreconcilable to reason and good conscience."[123]

Congress adopted the Declaration of Independence on the evening of July 4 and published it two days later. Independence was officially proclaimed at noon on July 8 before a crowd of thousands assembled outside the State House. Bells pealed all that day and night, Adams told a friend, and soldiers "paraded on the common, and gave Us the *Fue de Joy*, notwithstanding the Scarcity of Powder."[124]

Philadelphians were the first to hear the Declaration of Independence, but

General Washington had it read to each brigade in the Continental army in New York on July 10. He prayed now that this ringing declaration would "serve as a fresh incentive to every officer, and soldier, to act with Fidelity and Courage." In one sense, at least, it did. That night some of his soldiers joined civilians in tearing down and decapitating the huge gilded lead statue of George III on the green at the south end of Broadway.[125]

Adams was cautiously exultant. He knew that independence would be accompanied by manifold hazards. He knew too that courage was required "to ride in this Whirlwind." Not only was victory not assured, but he trembled at the realization that "mighty Revolutions . . . sett many violent Passions at Work." The only certainty about America's future was its uncertainty. Yet his optimism surpassed his apprehension. From deep within his soul he truly believed that victory would be won, America's republican experiment would succeed, and that both his generation and posterity would benefit from what he and Congress had done. But Adams was also a hardheaded realist who knew full well that "the Toil and Blood and Treasure, that it will cost Us to maintain this Declaration" would be immense.[126]

6

"Turning the Tide of Arms"

War and Reform

General Washington remained optimistic despite the July 1 sighting of Great Britain's vast armada bobbing in the blue, sun-kissed waters off New York, a fleet so large that, to one observer, it "looked like a forest of pine trees with their branches trimmed." Every shade of rose colored Washington's pronouncements that July. His soldiers, whom he characterized as "Brave Men who love their Country," would give a good accounting when the day of battle arrived. "Freemen contending on their own land" would be superior to mechanistic regulars, he stressed. Jefferson and Adams were no less sanguine. Although Jefferson did not believe the British could be prevented from retaking New York, he doubted that the redcoats could advance much beyond the city. The Continentals "will . . . amuse [the regulars] wherever they shall go," he reflected. Adams expected Washington's army to do so well that Great Britain's European rivals would soon recognize the United States.[1]

The British were equally confident. Lord George Germain, the American secretary, and virtual secretary of war, anticipated an easy victory. Even General Howe, who habitually saw the glass as half empty, thought the pending campaign would "terminate this expensive War."[2] He was anxious to fight, something he had not yet had the opportunity to do against Washington.

Washington had little choice but to fight for New York. Congress demanded that the city be defended. It had lavished funds on the army for the past year and expected it to be used. Many believed that Europe's statesmen would be more impressed by an American army that stood and fought, and those from the middle Atlantic states, apprehensive at the prospect of British regulars on their doorstep in New York, insisted that the invasion be resisted.[3]

Washington required no prodding. He was eager to fight. He had meticulously remodeled the army during the past year. He was anxious to use it and confident that it would succeed, even that it might score such a sensational victory that the war would end in 1776. But Washington was fooled by what he saw on the parade ground. He observed a spit-and-polish army, at least in comparison to the rabble he had inherited a year earlier. He saw men filled with bravado who had begun to look and talk like soldiers. He beheld an idealistic soldiery, brimming with patriotism. How could they fail? Washington envisioned a gigantic confrontation with his adversary, a full-scale battle similar to those that routinely occurred when two great European armies clashed. He appeared heedless of the dilemma he in fact faced. Without a naval arm, he was defending islands. In the worst-case scenario, he would be left with no lane of retreat. He would be hazarding everything in this fight, committing to battle an untried army, led by inexperienced officers, with a very real possibility that if things did not go his way, he would not have a second chance.

Howe had learned a substantive lesson from his experience at Bunker Hill. He had discovered that frontal assaults were costly, even against ragged irregulars. In New York, he planned to flank the defenses that Washington had prepared. Howe knew the advantages he possessed. Not only did he have total naval superiority, but he and his men were professional soldiers. Their foe consisted of callow amateurs. Howe expected to secure his objectives with minimal cost.

Washington's first great battle in this war might well have been his last. He and his green officers committed egregious blunders. Washington's first error was to divide his army in the face of superior numbers, a violation of the most ancient tenet of war. Uncertain where the British blow would fall, he posted about 10,500 of his 24,000 men on Long Island; he kept the remainder on Manhattan Island. That was not his only mistake. He failed to use his cavalry for reconnaissance purposes and neglected to secure roads that led to the rear of his force on Long Island. Furthermore, at the very last minute, in a fit of second-guessing, Washington changed commanders on Long Island. His blundering was nearly disastrous.

The British struck in the wee hours of August 27. With thirty-seven warships escorting the invasion force, the British landed nearly 17,000 redcoats and blue- and white-clad Hessians in Gravesend Bay. One element of Britain's army, totaling about 7,000 men, assaulted an American force of about 1,600 dug in at The Narrows. Unbeknownst to Washington, this was merely a diversion. The principal British force, nearly 10,000 strong and guided by three local Tories, took a circuitous route along the unsecured roads. They were moving behind the American defenders. In mid-morning these regulars reached their objective. They struck the Continentals from the rear. This was worse than the misfortune that had befallen Braddock, on whom Washington had heaped so much abuse. Braddock had been overwhelmed in a wilderness. Washington had permitted himself to be surprised by an army so large that its column had stretched for two miles and had from time to time stopped to noisily fell trees in order to clear a path for its artillery.

Surprised and overwhelmed, order quickly broke down among the defenders. The Continentals fled into the woods, often casting away their arms to hasten their flight. Most reached the temporary safety of Brooklyn Heights, more than three miles to the rear, where formidable redoubts had been constructed during the past several months. However, many were taken captive, and others were shot down as they struggled through the swampy salt marshes or attempted to swim across Gowanus Creek. More than 1,400 men were lost, including two generals who were captured as they cowered in a cornfield.

Within a few hours of the opening of Washington's initial battle, almost one-half of his army, pinioned now against the East River, appeared to face certain annihilation. Nearly 9,500 men were trapped. Not only was it impossible for these men to fight their way out against a British army that held a three-to-one numerical advantage, but it was unlikely they could ever retreat to safety across the East River, given the Royal Navy's prowess. The British appeared to be on the verge of a crucial victory, a stunning, obliterating conquest that would threaten the survival of the Continental army and its commander—as well as the American Revolution itself. But Howe had come to New York hoping to avoid assaults on entrenched troops. He paused, convinced that the beleaguered Americans were going nowhere. He brought up additional supplies and more men. He reconnoitered and sent out patrols to gain more information. He decided to accomplish his ends through a siege operation. Howe would attack if there was no alternative, but he was taking every precaution to keep casualties at a minimum.

On August 29th an early season cold front swept across New York. The temperature plummeted and a cold rain fell. The next day was equally damp and raw, but just as the stain of night darkened the eastern sky, the rain ceased and the temperature climbed, causing a thick fog to envelop the region. Visibility was so reduced that the British withdrew their fleet from the East River, fearing the vessels would collide. Washington seized the opportunity. Gathering every imaginable boat that he could lay his hands on, he extricated his men from their snare. Howe awakened the next morning to discover that Washington's army was gone.

Washington brought his army to Manhattan Island, where he repeated the worst of his previous blunders. He once again divided his army, this time between Harlem Heights and lower Manhattan. On Long Island, his decision had nearly cost him half his army. On Manhattan, he nearly lost his entire army. Languid as usual, Howe took two weeks to regroup, but on September 15 he invaded Manhattan, landing midway between the two halves of Washington's army. Washington had posted a small force at Kip's Bay, hoping that if this was the landing site Howe chose, these men could fight a delaying action, giving him an opportunity to concentrate his forces and repulse the invasion. His strategy failed. Kip's Bay was the site of the landing, but the panic-stricken Continentals in that sector were immediately routed, fleeing in terror after a shuddering bombardment by the Royal Navy and a landing by Hessian and British regulars. The way now was clear for the British to drive rapidly to the Hudson on the west side of the island, securing every road that linked Washington's divided men. Once again, a decisive victory was within Britain's grasp, for if the two halves of Washington's army were irrevocably separated and trapped, both in time would be conquered.

The trap never sprang. The British dallied sufficiently for the Continentals in the south to escape along a road that sluiced through the hidden remoteness of the countryside. By nightfall, the two halves of Washington's army were reunited in Harlem Heights. Nevertheless, Howe still possessed the means to destroy the Continentals, as Washington remained in his island cage for another thirty days. The British commander seized this heaven-sent third opportunity to score a knockout blow. Howe landed his army at Throg's Neck, on the mainland above Manhattan Island. His plan was to follow the amphibious assault with a dash west to the Hudson. If the redcoats for once acted with dispatch, Washington's entire army would be sealed between the British army and the Royal Navy, which controlled the rivers on every side. Once again, however, Howe was undone. The landing at Throg's Neck failed. Hampered by poor maps and inadequate knowledge of the countryside, the invasion force was put ashore in an impenetrable swamp. The men had to be reloaded on their transports. Six days passed before a second landing was made at nearby Pell's Point. That operation succeeded, but by then Washington at last had abandoned Manhattan Island.[4]

Washington had been saved repeatedly by luck and his adversary's caution and languor. When young, Howe had been daring and intrepid. It was Howe in fact whom General James Wolfe had selected to lead the British landing at Quebec in 1759, the decisive act in the French and Indian War. But the Howe of 1776 had grown tentative. Washington, a novice in command of raw, ill-supplied recruits, was vulnerable to a relentless foe. Howe was not such an opponent. At the moment when it stood its best chance of winning the war, the British army was in the hands of a general who was incapable of the energized behavior that could have decimated the Continentals.[5]

If Howe had changed prior to the Battle of New York, Washington changed in the course of the many crises he faced in August and September. Where he had exuded optimism on the eve of battle, he admitted to Congress in September that his situation was "truly distressing." Where he had expected much of his soldiery, following the debacle on Long Island he confessed that he was appalled by the "infamous Cowardice" of many of his soldiers. Many had never fired their weapon, he said, and others had fled "on the appearance of a small party of the Enemy." Washington at first had sought to rally his men by appealing to their patriotism and virtue, but after the catastrophe at Kip's Bay he issued orders that any soldier who thereafter "presumes to turn his back and flee, shall be instantly Shot down." Privately, Washington spoke for the first time of his fatigue, both physical and mental. From before sunrise to well after sunset, he said, he faced every conceivable perplexity. Many nights sleep never came. During the siege of Boston, and until the British landed in New York, Washington's thoughts often drifted to Mount Vernon and his life after this war. He now worried that he might not survive the war. His fear of failure, as well as anxiety over whether his officers might lose confidence in his abilities, crept into his correspondence.[6]

Reeling under the shock of defeat, Washington's spirits sank, but he took two crucial steps in September. After his drubbing on Long Island, he realized that New York was indefensible and sought to rally support in Congress for the abandonment of the city. Prior to Howe's abortive landing north of Manhattan, Washington had received Congress's blessing to vacate the island. He was slow to act—nearly fatally slow—but he finally retreated to safety. Second, Washington once again implored Congress to require long-term enlistments in the Continental army. The present system of recruiting and training a new army each year "will totally ruin, our Cause." he warned. Green soldiers were unreliable and militiamen were next to useless, he explained. Only regulars could be counted on to "be competent almost to every exigency."[7]

However, it was a strategic decision that Washington made in September that had the most far-reaching consequences, one that ultimately saved him and the cause. Before the calamity in New York, he had believed his army was capable of inflicting sufficient pain to force the British to abandon the struggle. Now more realistic, he knew that the Continentals were unlikely to defeat a large force of British and Hessian regulars. Victory would come only through a war of attrition, what he called "a War of posts." This was more commonly referred to as Fabian tactics, after the example of the Roman general Fabius Cunctator, who in antiquity wore down a superior Carthaginian adversary by maintaining a protracted defensive presence in the field. Washington now declared that he would "on all occasions avoid a general Action or put anything to the risque unless compelled by a necessity into which we ought never to be drawn."[8] This decision meant that a long war now was inevitable. It also meant that foreign assistance was imperative.

Washington felt better once he was off the island. Not only was his army intact, but he knew that Howe, notwithstanding his conquests, had gained no "advantage which . . . can contribute much to the completion of the business he is come upon." Howe's dawdling pursuit of the Continentals made the commander feel even better. A good eighteenth-century army could easily march upwards of fifteen miles daily, but it took Howe a week to move the ten miles from Pell's Point to beyond Mamaroneck. Howe was continuing to be Howe. He finally caught up with Washington at White Plains, where Washington first put his new Fabian strategy to the test. It worked. He fought the British in a place of his choosing and employed only about fifteen percent of his army against a small portion of the enemy force. After a sharp fight, the British secured the battlefield, but what they took was of little value. To win this engagement, Howe had suffered more than 200 casualties without inflicting much damage on the Continentals. Not wishing to pay any greater price, Howe called off the chase and returned to New York. He could have taken more territory, but not "without much loss of Blood," as Washington said.[9]

Washington had no time to savor his little triumph. He correctly assumed that Howe would immediately endeavor to secure much of eastern New Jersey, a farming region that could feed his army in New York during the coming winter. Washington divided his army into three forces. He left one wing under Heath to guard the Highland passes along the Hudson River above New York. He posted another wing under General Lee at White Plains to watch for an invasion of Connecticut. Washington took the smallest portion of the army, about 2,000 men, to which he soon added about 1,000 militiamen, and set off for New Jersey. Washington knew that he was about to enter the lion's den. His situation was "critical and alarming," he acknowledged, and he told his brother that he feared his reputation was lost. If he had the decision to make again, he said in November, no amount of money could tempt him to accept his post.[10]

Already disconsolate, Washington's spirits sank even further during the next thirty days. Soon after he started south, Washington was confronted with a difficult decision regarding Fort Washington, an installation in the northern palisades of Manhattan that had been left garrisoned with 2,000 men when the remainder of the army was withdrawn from the island. Constructed earlier in the year in the spirit of what one writer called "Bunker Hillism," the belief that every British assault on Americans entrenched in hilly terrain was destined to end in bloody failure, the decision had been flawed from the outset.[11] It was a fort without a well. The British had merely to surround the installation and await the surrender of the thirsty men.

When Washington arrived at Fort Lee, directly across the Hudson from Fort Washington, he still had time to remove the men from Manhattan. Furthermore, he not only understood the danger, but had come to doubt that the installation was any longer of value. Generals Greene and Putnam had other ideas. They believed Fort Washington could be successfully defended and counseled that yet another retreat would have a corrosive effect on public morale. Washington grappled indecisively with the issue for three days, until Howe resolved the matter by attacking on November 16. Fort Washington fell in less than a day. Every man in the garrison was killed or taken prisoner. The Americans also lost irreplaceable artillery. Washington had little excuse for defending Fort Necessity in 1754. He had no excuse for defending Fort Washington.[12]

This "unhappy affair," as Washington called it, was followed by what he termed "further Misfortunes." Fort Lee, which had become more of a supply depot than fortification, and was the last installation built for the defense of New York that remained in American hands, fell five days after the loss of Fort Washington. More cannon and precious blankets were lost. Washington's indecision had led to the debacle at Fort Washington. An uncharacteristic lethargy resulted in Fort Lee's capture, for Washington waited three fatal days after Fort Washington fell before ordering the evacuation of what obviously was a doomed post.[13]

Thereafter, Washington stripped his army of its baggage, in order to move more quickly, and began a long, unbroken retreat southward across New Jersey. At times he reported to Congress that the "Enemy are fast advancing, some of 'em are now in sight."[14] On occasion, his army fled from one side of a village while the British entered the other. To be chased like a fox was almost more than Washington could bear. His spirits cascaded.

Day after day he poured out his anguish. "I have no idea of being able to make a stand." "I tremble for Philadelphia." "I see nothing to oppose" the red-coats in a campaign for the city. "[N]o person ever had a greater choice of difficulties to contend with than I have." "[L]ike a Snowball by rolling," the "Enemy are daily gathering strength from the disaffected" in New Jersey. "[M]y situation and that of our Cause is critical & truly alarming." And finally, on December 18, "I think the game is pretty near up."[15]

The last letter was written from his camp across the Delaware River from Trenton, where he had crossed into Pennsylvania on December 5. Once he was south of the Delaware, Washington took measures to make the British pay dearly should they attempt to cross in the face of his entrenched men. He seized every boat along a seventy-mile stretch of the river and trained his artillery on the Delaware. Nevertheless, he expected the British to keep coming. He knew that he could not prevent his enemy from entering Pennsylvania. He knew too that if Philadelphia fell, America's recruiting for 1777 would be decimated and the Continentals' supply lines compromised. Washington would have pressed on had he been in Howe's shoes. But Howe was not Washington. With his adversary on the ropes, Howe chose this moment to enter winter quarters. He hurried back to New York, where he learned that the King had knighted him for retaking New York.[16]

Howe had perhaps saved Washington once again, but not even his ineffectual habits could prevent the American commander from facing still another winter crisis. Late in December, Washington told Congress that "an end to the existence of our Army" will occur in two weeks. A new army must be recruited. But who would join such an ineffectual, ill-equipped band? Who would volunteer to face the prospect of a terrible winter and further defeats in the spring?[17]

In the nine months since Congress had struck a medal in his honor for liberating Boston, Washington had tumbled from the heights to the depths. He appeared more enraged than frightened by his desperate situation. He believed the leaders of New Jersey had failed to respond to the crisis and its militia had "slunk off" in the face of danger. Furthermore, Washington had summoned the army he had posted at White Plains, but General Lee had broken Howe's record for languor. A month after receiving Washington's order, Lee still had not joined with the American forces in New Jersey. Nor had Congress adequately provisioned Washington's army. It had left his men hungry and ill-clad, "much broken and dispirited," he raged. So ragged were the men that Charles Willson Peale, the artist, failed to recognize his emaciated and disheveled brother when he met him in the camp on the Delaware. Everywhere, Washington wrote angrily, "a fatal supineness and insensibility to danger" appeared to have set in. Mortification mingled with fury in this proud man's heart. He was humiliated by the necessity to retreat. It was an "unmanly" course, he thought, and yet another of the "Wounds which my Feelings as an Officer have received."[18] However, what wounded Washington most deeply was evidence of treachery by some who were close to him. He knew that the reversals in New York would cause some to doubt his competence, but as he fled across New Jersey he discovered that General Lee, whose appointment he had secured, and Joseph Reed, an aide in whom he had placed his trust, had questioned his wisdom and decisiveness.[19]

Rage, vanity, and desperation drove Washington to act late in December. He decided to attack the Hessians whom Howe had posted at Trenton. He did not act rashly. He consulted with others, and for two weeks gathered information on German behavior and customs, but the decision to act was his alone. His plan of action was designed to demonstrate his mettle and resolution. He was surfeited with being "pushed ... from place to place." Furthermore, he believed he had to act in order to save himself and his army.[20] It was a daring gamble by a man who had run risks all his life, who more than once had hazarded his fortune and his life. It was a decision reached by a man whose confidence in the soundness of his own judgment had grown, and whose trust and reliance on others had waned. It was a bold, aggressive move from which many leaders would have shrunk, but which this fierce and bitter man welcomed and embraced.

Washington struck at Christmas. He hurled his army of about 3,000 men across the Delaware, risking entrapment with his back to the river if he lost the element of surprise. Instead, he won a great victory. He attacked the unsuspecting Hessians at sunrise. He lost a dozen men. His adversary lost 939. Nor was Washington finished. He crossed back into New Jersey before New Year's. This time he sought nothing less than to drive the British and Hessian regulars from the state by destroying their supply depot at New Brunswick. He failed in this objective. In fact, this gamble almost resulted in catastrophe. The Earl of Cornwallis, with a three-to-two numerical majority, came after Washington, compelling him to fight for a second time at Trenton, on this occasion on the Assunpink Creek, with the Delaware at his back. Had Cornwallis secured Washington's flanks, the Continentals would have been trapped, with no avenue of retreat left. Instead, the British mounted several frontal assaults across the bloody stream. Washington, who had assembled numerous cannon, repulsed every charge, then wiggled out of the trap under cover of welcome darkness.

Even then Washington did not retreat from harm's way. Now behind Cornwallis, he sallied deeper into the enemy's lair, hurrying toward New Brunswick. His men marched along back roads as far as Princeton, but while skirting the eastern edge of the village they came upon three British regiments en route to Trenton. A brief, bloody engagement followed. The Battle of Princeton began on lovely, rolling land near an orchard. Portions of the two armies, barely forty yards apart, fired on one another. The Continentals held their place until the British commander ordered a bayonet charge. Washington's men broke, but the commander, astride his great white horse, regrouped them and resumed the fight. At one point the Continentals nearly surrounded their foe. But the British fought hard as well. They escaped the trap that Washington was about to spring, but once out of the snare, they broke and ran in a pell-mell retreat. This little battle lasted only thirty minutes, but it was a hot action and resulted in the loss of nearly 250 redcoats, most of whom were taken prisoner. It ended too with some of the enemy racing toward New Brunswick and some fleeing along the road to Trenton. Washington had superior numbers and might have inflicted even greater damage in a mopping up operation, but Cornwallis was expected at any moment from Trenton. The risk was too great to remain and fight on. Washington had to be content with what he had accomplished. He ended the campaign of 1776 on that frosty morning in January 1777.[21]

Washington's daring actions since Christmas had been electrifying. Not only were some heads of state in Europe impressed by his boldness and resolve, but Trenton and Princeton, as a British traveler in Virginia noted, had "given [the Americans] fresh spirits" to prolong the war.[22] This was precisely what Washington had sought. The American victories stimulated recruitment and vindicated his choice of Fabian tactics. Despite his inexperience and hesitancy, Washington had courageously abandoned a flawed strategy, replacing it with a plan consistent with the realities of his strengths and weaknesses. First at White Plains, and now in two sharp engagements in New Jersey, he had altered the course of the war and perhaps saved the American Revolution.

Adams understood before Washington that America's hope of victory lay in a strategy of attrition. From the first he had expected a long, difficult war. He knew that in such a conflict the key to victory lay with the civilian population. Victory would come if the citizenry had the staying power to fight until Britain's will to continue vanished. However, events in 1776 led Adams to wonder about the staying power of his countrymen. He first grew apprehensive when a "kind of thoughtful Melancholly" spread following the American defeat in Canada. The dire tidings from the battlefields of New York increased his concern. The loss of New York was a blow, but what most troubled Adams was what he called the "dastardly, infamous, rascally Behaviour" of the American officers and men in that campaign. He feared that a crisis of confidence would be the result.[23]

Adams was dismayed to discover that "our Generals were out generalled," but he was not too surprised. He knew they were amateurs and believed that experience and study would improve their skills. What aroused his passion were accounts that the men, and sometimes their officers, had failed under fire. He railed at their cowardice, taking a very hard line. Any soldier who fled in the face of the enemy must be shot, he demanded. He stopped just short of recommending that generals who were surprised by their adversaries should also be executed. Two things alone would save this war, he declared: good officers, who imposed an iron discipline on the troops and led intrepidly in battle, and second—in remarks that paralleled Washington's "war of posts" strategy—never hazarding the army in battle against a superior, or even formidable, British army. The spirit and ardor of the Continental army must be reformed, he warned, or "We are undone. . . . We shall perish in infamy."[24]

Adams criticized Washington for only one thing. He thought he had erred in repeatedly dividing his army between August and November. A large army had the best chance of survival, he said, for when divided into small pieces any military force was vulnerable to piecemeal destruction. He was correct about Washington's flawed strategy in the face of Howe's invasion, but thereafter Adams failed to fully understand the commander's dilemma. Washington faced a thousand difficulties that Adams could not fathom, not the least of which was how to feed a large, retreating army.

Moreover, Washington wisely hoped to avoid another large-scale clash. He merely wanted to get his Continentals through the year, and if he had to fight before year's end, he wanted to select the time and place for the encounter.[25]

However, in two crucial areas Washington and Adams agreed. The New York campaign converted Adams to Washington's belief that the army must consist of long-term enlistees. Earlier Adams had expressed horror at the thought of an army composed of men who signed on for the duration. Such an army would be a professional force consisting of "the meanest, idlest, most intemperate and worthless" sorts, he said. Now he maintained that only "a regular Army" could establish the "most masterly Discipline" essential for molding good soldiers. Adams took up this fight and subsequently, with considerable justification, claimed to have led the campaign in Congress to reform the army. In the midst of the New York disaster, Congress acted. Henceforth, men were to enlist for three years or the duration, and cash and land bounties were to be offered to encourage enlistments.

Adams and Jefferson, at Washington's behest, also played a substantive role in Congress's revision of the Articles of War. They were members of a committee that met with Judge Advocate William Tudor, a former legal apprentice of Adams, and expanded the articles by including items in the British military code. The proposed articles authorized punishments of far greater severity, including nine additional capital crimes and an increase from thirty-nine to one hundred lashes for the most serious offenses. A bruising fight ensued to secure congressional assent. The committee was accused of urging a standing army and favoring draconian punishments that many thought unseemly in a republican army. Adams later recollected that the attacks were so harsh that Jefferson was cowed into silence during the floor fight, but Congress eventually adopted the new Articles of War by a narrow vote.[26]

Although Adams delighted at the boost to morale brought about by Trenton and Princeton, he was vexed by numerous worries. He despaired of several general officers, but feared that the political cost of seeking their removal would be too high. Moreover, by early 1777 he detected signs of trouble for America's unsound currency. Adams knew immediately that new and very heavy taxes would have to be imposed to prevent disaster. He worried that public opinion would not tolerate the additional imposts, for he had glimpsed the first evidence of the erosion of the sacrificial spirit that had prevailed through the initial phase of the war. Fewer men were willing to enlist in the army, many public officials had resigned to exploit lucrative opportunities in the private sector, and increasing numbers of businessmen had begun

OPPOSITE: *Washington at the Battle of Princeton. Painting by Charles Willson Peale, 1781. (Yale University Art Gallery. Given by the Associates in Fine Arts and Mrs Henry B. Loomis in memory of Henry Bradford Loomis, B.A. 1875)*

BELOW: *Mount Vernon. Painting attributed to Edward Savage. (Mount Vernon Ladies' Association)*

John Adams. Painting by Benjamin Blythe, 1766. (Massachusetts Historical Society)

BELOW: *Adams house, Quincy, Massachusetts. Painting by Frankenstein. (Courtesy U.S. Department of the Interior, National Park Service, Adams National Historic Site, Quincy, Mass.)*

*Thomas Jefferson.
Painting by John
Trumbull. (The Met-
ropolitan Museum of
Art, Bequest of Cor-
nelia Cruger, 1923)*

BELOW: *Monticello.
Drawing by Robert
Mills, ca. 1803.
(Massachusetts His-
torical Society)*

to profiteer. Adams called this a "Spirit of Venality," and labeled avarice the "most dreadfull and alarming Enemy" that the United States confronted. Feeling betrayed by his own generation, Adams cried out that he was "ashamed of the Age I live in."[27]

Disturbed by the erosion of virtuous behavior, and alarmed for the safety of America's republican experiment, Adams had come to fear the worst in a protracted war. He called for immediate action by the Continentals. He argued that if the new army was raised quickly, Washington could march from his winter quarters at Morristown and make still more Trenton-like strikes throughout New Jersey. "Now is the Time," Adams urged. Washington could turn the war around by compelling Howe to relinquish his conquests in New Jersey, an action that might win foreign recognition and essential loans and trade.[28] But these were the musings of a man with no real knowledge of the problems faced by field commanders. It would have been imprudent for Washington to have moved his army from the safety of winter quarters, and it would have been the height of folly for him to attempt to move and simultaneously feed his army in the dead of winter.

Jefferson departed for Monticello about a week after the debacle in the Battle of Long Island. He had barely been able to tear himself away from home during much of his congressional tenure. Whereas Adams was absent less than five percent of the time when Congress was in session between September 1774 and November 1777, Jefferson was away from Philadelphia between January and early May of 1776, and after independence was declared in July he appears to have been an indifferent congressman during what remained of his time in office. He attended the congressional sessions in July and August, but contributed little. Otherwise, he read, shopped, and followed the war, occasionally dispatching commentaries that suggest that he was considerably less sophisticated than Adams with regard to military matters. He envisioned a short war, mistook minor skirmishes for major engagements, and even embraced the fantastic notion that Howe, who came to New York with nearly 30,000 men and huge fleet, planned to hide behind defensive emplacements on Staten Island.[29]

The idea of an American union was so new that most activists in the American Revolution focused primarily on events within their native provinces. Jefferson had never concealed the fact that he was more concerned about events in Virginia than those at the national level. Before independence he told a friend that for Virginians "the whole object" of the Revolution was to secure reforms in Virginia. To his mind the national struggle was but a means of securing the autonomy for each state to chart its own course. In 1776 Jefferson displayed a more provincial outlook than Washington or Adams, but he did have in mind a reform agenda for Virginia and was anxious to return to Williamsburg to seek its implementation. Jefferson also said that he had "private causes" for returning home, hinting that his wife was ill and implored his return.[30]

Jefferson had been home only a few days when word arrived that Congress wished him—expected him, Hancock's letters stated—to join Franklin and Silas Deane on a mission to Paris to seek French recognition and assistance. Richard Henry Lee, his replacement in Congress, also urged him to accept the post, telling him that the diplomatic mission would be the most important contribution that he could make to the American Revolution. With a sense of urgency, Lee told Jefferson that "every thing depends upon" bringing France into the war. Jefferson declined the post. He gave as his reason "circumstances very peculiar in the situation of my family."[31] The implication once again was that he could not abandon a wife whose health was precarious. However, Martha Jefferson not only was well enough to accompany her husband on a long, arduous journey to Williamsburg early in October, but she bore yet another child precisely nine months following Thomas's return from Philadelphia, undergoing a pregnancy apparently free of great difficulties.

Lee was not convinced by Jefferson's excuses. He accused Jefferson of an inability to eschew "private enjoyments" in this time of great crisis. Today it is difficult not to draw the same conclusion, although it is possible that Martha was ill and suffered from mental rather than physical maladies. However, it may be that she simply objected to his further absence, and that he complied with her wish that he remain at her side. Many years later Adams offered still another explanation for Jefferson's behavior. He conjectured that Jefferson lacked the courage to sail the Atlantic during wartime. Lee also hinted at that explanation in one of his letters. It is possible too that the simplest explanation may be the most accurate. Jefferson may have hungered for domestic reform in Virginia above else. Whatever the reason, Jefferson was not the only activist to decline a difficult assignment. Adams, for instance, had refused Congress's entreaties to be part of a mission to Canada early in 1776. He had wished to remain in Philadelphia and fight for independence, but he told Congress that he could not be part of the Canadian enterprise because of his inadequate knowledge of French.[32]

Jefferson's one abiding desire after July 4 was to republicanize Virginia. The first step in the process would come with the establishment of a new state government. During the late spring he had sent to friends in Williamsburg three separate drafts of a written constitution for Virginia.[33] His proposals had little impact on the Virginia Convention, which drafted the state's first constitution. Paradoxically, Adams exerted a greater influence than Jefferson, although he had never stepped on Virginia soil.

Beginning in the spring of 1775, when colonies first solicited Congress's advice on establishing new governments, Adams began to play a leading role in the congressional discussions. He had long been profoundly interested in political theory, and had read more deeply on the subject than most congressmen. In addition, during the decade before he came to Congress, Adams had published several essays on the topic in Boston newspapers. After *Common Sense* made a case for unicameral assemblies and a weak executive, Adams seized every opportunity to lecture his colleagues on political theory, telling them that Paine was "better . . . at pulling down than building" governments. Adams soon acquired a reputation as the congressman who was most knowledgeable on constitutional matters. During the winter of 1775—1776, with independence and constitution-making imminent, at least four members of Congress, including George Wythe, who now sat in Congress, requested that Adams commit his ideas to paper. He complied and in April 1776 his musings were published under the simple title *Thoughts on Government*.[34]

Adams's and Jefferson's thoughts on government were remarkably similar. That was not surprising. They drew on similar sources, especially Baron de Montesquieu, the French writer whose *The Spirit of the Laws* was a textbook for political theorists, as well as other influential figures in the English and Scottish Enlightenment. That Adams had more influence within the Virginia Convention resulted in part because George Mason, who was to play the greatest role in drafting Virginia's constitution, read *Thoughts on Government* before he began work. In addition, Adams wrote more cautiously in the *Thoughts on Government* than in his private correspondence. He perhaps chose to do so deliberately, in the hope of having greater influence within Virginia, which he believed would influence other southern states.

Both Adams and Jefferson contemplated a republic in which the supreme power resided in the people. Jefferson later said that in 1776 most people thought of republicanism as any form of government that did not include a monarch. However, he and Adams clearly understood, as Jefferson remarked, that in a true republic the government would embody, and have the ability to execute, "the will of the people."[35] Yet each was willing to permit the qualified voters only a limited voice in the selection of public officials.

Both would have restricted suffrage rights to adult white males who met property qualifications, but both hoped to expand the electorate, Jefferson by land giveaways and Adams through government assistance in reducing the price of frontier acreage. Jefferson would have reduced the suffrage requirements to ownership of a mere twenty-five acres for rural inhabitants, one-half of what had been required in colonial Virginia. Adams never listed what he regarded as a fair property requirement, but as he seemed pleased that in his lifetime Massachusetts had seldom enforced its laws in this realm, he could not have favored excessive limitations. In their schemes, therefore, few freemen would have been disenfranchised.

Both agreed that government posed dangers to the liberty and happiness of humankind. Jefferson, who thought the greatest threat came from strong executives, sought to prevent the citizenry from ever being "laid prostrate at the feet of one man!" Adams shared Jefferson's fear, but beheld an additional, and perhaps greater, danger. He believed the wealthiest citizens always succeeded in manipulating their brethren, establishing what he called "the insolent domination [by] the few" who could purchase influence and power. He sought to check this natural oligarchical propensity. Both Jefferson and Adams offered the same solution to the threat to freedom: a balanced government in which power was divided between an executive and a bicameral legislature.[36]

Each advocated that the qualified voters elect members of the lower house of the assembly, which in turn would elect the upper chamber. Both favored annual elections for members of the lower house, but longer terms for those who sat in the upper house. While Adams was not specific, Jefferson initially called for life terms, but eventually proposed a nine-year limit in order to prevent its members from "currying favor with the electors." Neither Jefferson nor Adams would have limited membership in the upper chamber to the wealthy elite. Jefferson specifically stated, and Adams doubtless would have concurred, that his object was an upper house that consisted of the state's most illustrious citizens, those whom he called the "wisest men."

Both Adams and Jefferson proposed an executive elected by the legislature. Adams preferred that the election be by the full assembly, Jefferson by only the lower house. Both favored a one-year term for the executive and both recommended against consecutive terms. Of the two, Adams favored the stronger executive, though not one who possessed the strength of the royal governors during the colonial era. Adams believed the executive, whom he called the "governor" and Jefferson titled simply the "administrator," should possess the power to veto legislation and pardon criminals. Jefferson would have curtailed the executive's war-making capabilities and his power to obstruct the legislative branch. Indeed, nearly half the charges against the British monarch in the Declaration of Independence arose from the "repeated injuries and usurpations" he had allegedly visited on colonial assemblies. Both Adams and Jefferson would have severely restricted the executive's appointment powers.

Both stressed that popular governments must be polities of law, not of men. Both provided for a separate and independent judicial branch, and each recommended that judges hold lifetime appointments following an executive nomination and legislative approval. Jefferson feared giving great latitude to judges, and warned of "whimsical, capricious, designing" magistrates; "let judges be a mere machine," he counseled. He continued to see the legislatures, not the courts, as the protectors of the liberties of the citizenry. Adams not only proposed grants of greater authority to judges, but advocated what later came to be known as judicial review, the ability of the courts to strike down unconstitutional laws. It was a radically new idea, so innovative that his countrymen would not fully embrace it for a quarter-century or more.[37]

Adams made his proposals to friends in the South who hoped to republicanize their aristocratic frames of government. What he recommended was strikingly similar to the New England colonial regimes, especially that of Connecticut, which had been a self-governing colony. Adams, who once remarked that political experimentation in the midst of a great revolution was unwise, believed that America's new governments should fundamentally resemble those of the colonial era, save for republican adjustments and modifications to fully secure popular liberties. Nevertheless, underlying his proposals was the bold and radical ideal that the people were sovereign, and that the new governments should come close to being "an exact portrait of the people at large." When he spoke of a "mighty Revolution," or asserted that "We are in the very midst of a Revolution," he was voicing his belief that great changes above and beyond mere separation from Great Britain were occurring, including the establishment of new governments based on a revolutionary concept.[38]

Some of the ideas expressed by Adams and Jefferson were out of synch with the Virginia assemblymen. There was little support in Williamsburg, or anywhere else, for a stronger executive. Many delegates also found Jefferson's views on the selection of the upper house to be old-fashioned. Still others thought his recommendations for reducing the power of the state's Tidewater aristocratic elite—to be accomplished by broadening the electorate, substituting elected for appointive officials, and awarding the backcountry a fairer and equitable representation in the lower house—to be too radical.[39]

But not all of Jefferson's ideas were rejected. The new constitution established a balanced government. The legislature held the greatest powers and the court structure was almost precisely what Jefferson had urged. Nevertheless, Jefferson was unhappy. He had hoped for a broad guarantee of freedom of religion, but the new constitution merely exempted dissenters from having to tithe to the established church. In addition, he wished that the executive and judiciary were more independent of the legislative branch, was disappointed when the electorate was not expanded, and would have given the executive greater appointive powers. Jefferson sought without success to persuade the Convention to delay a final vote on the document until the autumn, when he could be present. Even into the 1780s he labored unsuccessfully to overturn this constitution.[40]

Although a democratic reform impulse was crystallizing in 1776, spurred by the soaring rhetoric of egalitarianism and popular rights inherent in the protest and rebellion, Jefferson was more Whig than democrat. He was a radical, but as was true of most revolutionaries, an eighteenth-century radical. Jefferson did not seek to overcome economic inequalities or to level the stratified societies of his day. He was intent on redeeming a corrupt constitution and checking prerogative power. His dream for a new America was that its governors would be drawn from the "natural aristocracy" of the most talented and virtuous, replacing the old "artificial aristocracy founded on wealth and birth."[41]

Nor was Adams a democratic, as the term would be defined a half century later when suffrage rights were extended to all freemen, the line between rulers and ruled was blurred, and government was presumed to be of, by, and for the people. He was a republican who abhorred monarchy and oligarchy, was committed to the sovereignty of the people, and sought a broader participation by the people. He labeled these radical reforms "democratical," and before the end of the war rejoiced not only that this was the "predominant Spirit of every Colony," but that this fervor, "like a River changing its bed, has irresistably born away every Thing before it."[42]

Although the views of Jefferson and Adams were strikingly similar in

1776, one substantive difference existed and grew more striking over time. Jefferson's focus centered more on individualistic premises, while an air of collectivity pervaded Adams's outlook. Jefferson's emphasis on individual freedom was born not so much from the sense that each individual should be free to do as he pleased, but that each person should be free of governmental intrusion. One's pursuit of happiness should be an individual choice. He was concerned with state interposition, whether to encroach on the exercise of this freedom or to insist on the limits or terms of what he believed should be a strictly private choice. At bottom, therefore, an antigovernment bias characterized Jefferson's political thought. He sought the least possible government, and he grew steadily more distrustful of government the further it was removed from local control. Nor was he "a friend to a very energetic government. It is always oppressive," he declared.[43]

Adams, in contrast, sought a republic that would allow for the realization of a collective self-interest. He had no desire to trammel individual rights. He sought ways to protect those rights while simultaneously striving to attain and maintain the pluralistic interests that existed within a broad-based Union. Adams looked toward an inclusive government in which the branches acted in concert to achieve the greatest happiness for the largest number of citizens. The popular will was given voice in the legislative branch. The judiciary maintained the rule of law, holding some interests in check and protecting others. However, he moved steadily toward the view that the executive was the glue that held the system together, the key official who could protect and advance the interests of the greatest number of citizens. The executive played another crucial role. He protected the citizenry from the danger posed by oligarchy. At war's end, Adams authored a massive three-volume tome on political theory in which he termed the executive the "very essence of government," for the role of this office was to mediate between the "gentlemen" and the "simplemen," to be the "antidote against rivalries" inherent when a multiplicity of interests existed. Instead of the minimalist government sought by Jefferson, Adams in the course of the American Revolution came to champion an extremely strong executive. This official had to be "more wise, more learn'd, more just, more every thing," if the republican system of checks and balances was to work, and he especially had to become the "father and protector" of commoners, the defender of their rights and interests against the ever-present threat of encroachment by the elite.[44]

Jefferson's antidote was Virginia writ large, a nation in which a single interest was so pervasive that pluralistic clashes could be minimized perhaps even for centuries. This was to be a nation largely of landowning farmers. He believed that humanity would discover the greatest happiness in an agrarian setting. He knew that husbandmen who owned their own farms could live prosperously off nature's bounty, but he yearned for a system in which landowning farmers would be truly free from dependence. He was certain that if no one exercised suzerainty over them, landowning farmers would be the least corrupted, and most incorruptible, of citizens. Virtuous, free from unseemly ambition, to a considerable degree liberated from those in society who were pervasively ambitious and rapacious, and looking only "to their own soil and industry" for contentment, yeomen were the bedrock on which Jefferson sought to erect his republic.[45]

Jefferson had hoped the new constitution of Virginia would allocate land to the landless, creating a society in which every freeman owned his farm. The idea was too radical for the Revolutionary generation, which in Virginia and elsewhere was willing to give away land only as a reward for military service. Thereafter, Jefferson sought to make land more readily available through other means. He played a key role in making Kentucky a county in Virginia, the first step in opening the region to settlement, the goal Washington had hoped for since the early 1760s. He also endeavored, though without much success, to thwart powerful speculative land companies and open the west directly to consumers, a move that would have reduced western land prices and brought land within the reach of a larger percentage of the free population. The land reform for which Jefferson is best remembered was his campaign to abolish entail and primogeniture, ancient practices that restricted a property owner's freedom in conveying his land. Jefferson depicted his efforts as both an attempt to enable wealthy planters to bequeath their property to a far larger number of persons and as a means of gradually eroding the base of aristocratic hegemony. Late in life, he claimed that his strategy had worked. He told Adams that his assault on entail and primogeniture had "laid the axe to the root of Pseudo-aristocracy" and paved the way to the republicanization of Virginia. Jefferson exaggerated. The law of primogeniture applied only if a person died without a will, a rare occurrence among Virginia planters. Nor did Jefferson face a fierce struggle against a recalcitrant power structure that resisted his attempts to banish entails. Historians long ago discovered that entail was often bothersome to aristocrats, as it obstructed their efforts to sell unwanted property. Entail was so unpopular with the Virginia aristocracy that Jefferson's bill was passed into law two weeks following its introduction. Planters saw this reform as one in which they were the principal beneficiaries, although some benefits may have trickled down to the general citizenry.[46]

In the autumn of 1776 Jefferson also proposed that Virginia's legal code be reviewed and "adopted to our republican form of government." The assembly named him to a committee of five to consider the state's existing laws and recommend their continuation, repeal, or revision. Because of the death or inactivity of the other members, Jefferson and Wythe soon became the key members of this panel. Jefferson never intended "to abrogate our whole system" of laws from the colonial era, but he saw this as the means through which he could achieve many of the reforms that he cherished. Nearly three years passed before he and Wythe completed their assignment, and another six years elapsed before the legislature took up the last of their recommendations. About half of their proposals were eventually enacted.[47]

The measure that was closest to Jefferson's heart concerned religious freedom. He subsequently referred to pre-Revolutionary Virginia, a province in which the Anglican Church was the established church, as a land of "religious slavery." However, change was in the air prior to the Anglo-American difficulties, and independence made change of some sort virtually inevitable. Virginia's large population of Methodists, Presbyterians, and Baptists, a citizenry being asked to soldier in defense of the Revolution, was ardent in its demands for greater individual freedom against the religious claims of the state. Thus, the state's Declaration of Rights, adopted in 1776 while Jefferson was yet in Philadelphia, asserted "the free exercise of religion" to all citizens.

Many Virginians, including Jefferson, had hoped for more. He believed the Declaration of Rights should have protected nonbelievers. He said it was proper for the state to concern itself with injuries that one person caused to another, but an affront to God was a matter between the offender and the deity. It "does me no injury for my neighbor to say there are twenty gods, or no God," he remarked. He thought each individual should have the right of "free inquiry" in matters of religion, as in matters of science and government. Although Jefferson was later attacked as an atheist, what he in fact sought was not so much freedom from religion, as the freedom for each person to pursue whatever beliefs his or her study and thought led them to, including the decision to believe in nothing. Therefore, in 1779 Bill No. 82, in the legal code that Jefferson introduced, provided that "no man shall be compelled to frequent or support any religious worship, place, or ministry," and that no person could be made to "suffer on account of his religious opinions or belief." His proposed legislation passed with slight modifications that did no damage to the sense of the original bill. Nothing that Jefferson accomplished in his public life gave him greater satisfaction, and little else that he touched has been of such lasting importance. He justly felt that he had acted to secure for each man the right to use his powers of reason in "the formation of his own [religious] opinions." He lived to see his statute serve as a model for legislation in other states and, ultimately, for the First Amendment to the U.S. Constitution.[48]

Jefferson also proposed a series of educational reforms. He advocated three years of public education for all white children in Virginia, male or female. He also called for the establishment of college preparatory schools throughout the state. These institutions, similar to the Latin school in Worcester in which Adams had taught, were to provide a free education to poor male youths who had exhibited extraordinary skills during their three years of required schooling. Finally, he proposed that the very best poor students be selected annually—"raked from the rubbish" was how he put it—for a free education of three years' duration at the College of William and Mary. Jefferson had several objects in mind: conveniently situated schools for the children of the affluent; the preparation of a literate and responsible citizenry; and the extension of the opportunity of education to the neediest talented young men, a step that would serve the poor and become an additional bedrock for his cherished "aristocracy of virtue and talent." It was a noble proposal that would have simultaneously opened opportunities for the disadvantaged and served the common interest. Jefferson later remarked that "a nation [which] expects to be ignorant and free . . . expects what never was and what never will be." He also sought an informed citizenry that might ride herd on those in power. If citizens "became inattentive to public affairs," he warned, the officeholders "shall all become wolves." His education proposals, too visionary for the time, were not approved. Nor did the assembly accept his recommendation that a public library system be established or that the governing body and curriculum at William and Mary College be reorganized.[49]

Although he pushed for progressive changes in the state's land, religious, and educational statutes, Jefferson's record on the enhancement of civil liberties in Virginia during the American Revolution was dismal. It should be remembered, however, that Revolutionary Virginia was also wartime Virginia, and during hostilities civil liberties frequently bow to the exigencies of the times. Jefferson urged legislation that severely restricted free speech and sought to coerce adherence to the Revolution by instituting a loyalty oath. He even supported a move to intern suspected Tories who had not been convicted of any crimes. In 1778 Jefferson introduced a bill of attainder against a renegade Loyalist who employed guerrilla tactics to terrorize the revolutionary citizenry. An attainder, which a few years later would be made illegal by the Bill of Rights, is an act under which a legislature can order the execution, without due process, of a suspected criminal. Long after attainders had become illegal, Jefferson continued to defend the wisdom of his action. He believed that each step he took to limit civil liberty was undertaken in order to win a long, grim war. Had the War of Independence, which ultimately hinged on a final, determinative campaign in Virginia in 1781, been lost because he had protected the rights of a few individuals at the expense of the greater common good, Jefferson today would almost certainly be seen as a myopic, incompetent visionary whose softness had sown an American tragedy.[50]

However, it was Jefferson's actions concerning the treatment of criminals and slaves, not his wartime indifference to civil liberties, that is most troubling. Jefferson proposed numerous changes in Virginia's criminal code that were out of step with the ideas of liberal reformers of his age. He later said that his objective was to make the punishments proportionate to the offense, to reduce the severity of some punishments, and to inaugurate the practice of rehabilitating criminals. Although he urged a reduction in the number of offenses punishable by death, he proposed that treason, murder, the second conviction on a charge of manslaughter, and the killing of another in a duel were to be punishable by execution. He also proposed that all condemned criminals were to be executed on the second day following their conviction, which was customary in his time.

Jefferson proposed that most executions be by hanging. However, he recommended that those convicted of murdering by poison, a fear that haunted slaveowners, be executed by the administration of poison. He proposed horrific punishments for several crimes. Rape, polygamy, buggery, and sodomy, including acts of homosexuality, were to be punished by castration and, for females, "cutting thro' the cartilage of her nose a hole of one half inch diameter at the least." Those convicted of maiming another were to be similarly maimed and to forfeit one-half their property to their victim. Counterfeiters were to serve six years at hard labor, thieves three to five years depending on the offense, arsonists three years, and larcenists two. Under his proposed code, sorcerers, conjurers, and witches would have faced punishment. Slaves convicted of noncapital offenses were to be sold out of the country, "there to be continued in slavery." Jefferson may be excused his ignorance of reforms in the treatment of criminals that already circulated in enlightened circles in

Europe, but the fundamental humanitarianism of any individual who could have embraced such a reprehensible code as that proposed by Jefferson is open to question. Jefferson had retreated to the Mosaic principle of "an eye for an eye," in some instances even proposing torturous mutilations. Young James Madison, who in 1785 agreed to introduce these so-called reforms as a courtesy to his friend, was embarrassed by the proposals. The Virginia legislature, hardly a bastion of liberality, rejected Jefferson's proffered criminal code, in part because of its repulsive harshness. When an old man, Jefferson confessed that many of his proposals had been "revolting."[51]

Slavery had been legal in Virginia for more than a century by the time of the American Revolution. Not only had no sentiment to liberate Virginia's slaves crystallized before 1776, but no movement had germinated to rethink the abiding racism on which the province's socioeconomic system was constructed. The American Revolution brought little in the way of substantive change in Virginia. Revolutionary Virginia may have been engaged in a struggle to throw off the shackles of what many believed to be British slavery, but it was simultaneously committed to the preservation of African-American slavery. Few Virginians suggested otherwise. Jefferson was one of the exceptions. He claimed to be a dedicated foe of slavery. In his memoirs, he strove to leave the impression that he had labored to secure "a plan for a future and general emancipation" to be effected over time. He looked toward the day, he wrote, when "the evil will wear off insensibly" and the descendants of the slaves of the Revolutionary era would be "a free and independent people." Toward the end of the war Jefferson asked what kind of nation permitted some in society to daily tyrannize others? To "degrade a whole race" was unconscionable, he declared. African Americans had been wronged "ten thousand" times over. They had experienced "misery enough." No other important leader in Revolutionary Virginia portrayed himself as so filled with rage by the evils of slavery. Nor did any other claim to be so zealously committed to slavery's abolition.[52]

During the American Revolution, Virginia took two important steps with regard to slavery. First, it prohibited the African slave trade to Virginia. This measure, which had been enacted previously, but disallowed in London, was widely supported by slaveowners, more from pragmatic and economic considerations than from humanitarian impulses. Many planters feared that the slave population had reached dangerously unmanageable proportions. Furthermore, faced with collapsing tobacco prices and increasing indebtedness, most slaveowners understood that ending the importation of slaves would drive up prices, not an unhappy prospect for those who might wish to sell their surplus chattel to booming markets in the Caribbean or rice-producing South Carolina. Jefferson backed this legislation.

Second, Virginia revised its laws to make it easier for slaveowners to manumit their slaves. In the late colonial era manumission had required the assent of the governor and assembly, and could be granted only for meritorious service. Together with other assemblymen, Jefferson had sought unsuccessfully to change the law as early as 1769. In 1782, when he no longer was politically active, the legislature enacted a law that permitted private manumissions for slaves under forty-five years of age. Virginia's new law did not compel those who were liberated to leave the state, a stipulation in the legislation that Jefferson had supported earlier.[53]

Jefferson later claimed that during 1777 or 1778 he had drafted a bill that provided for the emancipation of all slaves born after the passage of the legislation, but that the bill had never been introduced because "it was found that the public mind would not yet bear the proposition." Instead, he said, he had prepared legislation that would have provided for the liberation of all children born to slaves, followed by the forced colonization of these freedmen, but he shrank from introducing that legislation as well. Although Jefferson appears to have saved virtually every scrap of paper that he touched, these purported bills have never been found. The legislation concerning African Americans and slavery that Jefferson is known to have written would have compelled every manumitted slave to leave Virginia within a year, denied citizenship to free blacks, virtually prevented free blacks from entering the state, exiled from Virginia any white woman who bore the child of either a mulatto or African American, and banished from the state any child born to a white mother and African-American father. So harsh were his proposals that free blacks who violated the legislation would have been placed "out of the protection of the laws," thus opening the door to legalized lynching. Not a single one of these measures ever became law, not because they were too progressive, but because they were excessively restrictive even for Jefferson's time. Near the end of the war, Jefferson privately urged that all children born to slaves in Virginia after January 1, 1801—seventeen years in the future—be free at birth. However, he neither publicly advocated such a law nor had it introduced in the legislature, and ultimately nothing came of his idea.[54]

During the American Revolution, Jefferson did nothing to ameliorate the burdens imposed on slaves or extend the rights of citizens to free blacks. The lustrous statements on human rights and equality in the Declaration of Independence caused many contemporaries to rethink their racist convictions, but that had not been Jefferson's intent. Indeed, he accepted, and advanced, every element of racist dogma then in fashion. He admitted his abhorrence of the color black and thought it "markedly inferior to the beauty of a red and white complexion." He was repelled by the "wooly hair" and the "ungainly" physique of blacks. He wrote that blacks perspired more but urinated less than whites, emitted "a very strong and disagreeable odor," and tolerated heat better than whites, but coped less satisfactorily with cold weather. He thought blacks innately lazy and slow. He asserted that blacks required less sleep than whites. He portrayed African Americans as carefree sorts who were inclined to play all night following a full day's labor. To his way of thinking, blacks were more driven by sexual urges than whites, but were incapable of feeling the depths of love that whites experienced. He thought blacks were unable to grieve as deeply as whites. Jefferson described blacks as unimaginative and inferior to whites with regard to critical reasoning faculties. Only as musicians did blacks exhibit superiority to whites, he said. Jefferson categorically rejected environmental explanations for the perceived differences that he beheld between whites and blacks. He was certain that nature had made whites superior to blacks and that neither time nor freedom would erase the differences between the races.[55]

Jefferson's attitude and actions cannot be attributed to the times in which he lived. Many of his contemporaries, especially religious dissenters, including Quakers, Baptists, and Methodists, more zealously opposed slavery. Several Virginia planters, such as Robert Carter and John Randolph of Roanoke, liberated dozens, even hundreds, of slaves, sometimes purchasing land for those whom they freed. Moreover, numerous enlightened contemporaries, such as Benjamin Rush and Benjamin Franklin, concluded that the perceived character and habits of blacks were attributable to the malicious environment of slavery, not to race.[56] Jefferson hoped to convince those who lived outside the South—and perhaps himself as well—that he was an advanced thinker in matters of slavery and race. Nothing could have been further from the truth. Although he contemplated measures that would have put Virginia on an abolitionist course, he shrank from introducing such legislation, much less fighting for its enactment. Once Jefferson's self-serving cant is set aside, his views and behavior were exceptional principally for their backwardness and faintheartedness.

Washington had bought and sold slaves to the very eve of hostilities. If he ever reflected on the morality of slavery prior to 1775, and for some time thereafter, there is nothing in his papers to substantiate it. At the time the war broke out his attitude concerning racial matters was quite conventional for one who had been raised in a family of Chesapeake slaveowners, and in some ways it never changed. Throughout his life he spoke of blacks as innately ignorant, shiftless, careless, deceitful, unconscionable, untrustworthy, and dishonest. In one significant way, however, Washington changed during the course of the Revolution. He meditated on slavery, perhaps for the first time, pondering its economic wisdom and ethicality. No one factor caused him to assay the institution. Revolutionary rhetoric and the sight of African Americans soldiering with valor were important, but so too was the fact that he was surrounded by persuasive young aides and officers who detested slavery, men such as Joseph Reed, Alexander Hamilton, the Marquis de Lafayette, and South Carolina's John Laurens. These men formed a close bond with Washington, and in numerous candid conversations must have persuaded him to contemplate slavery and slaveowning. Like Jefferson, Washington during the American Revolution pondered slavery, but like his fellow Virginian he took no decisive steps with regard to his chattel.[57]

Like many northern politicians, Adams feared that raising the slavery question would antagonize southerners and jeopardize the Union. He once inveighed against an abolitionist scheme in the Massachusetts assembly lest it sow sectional differences in Congress. His primary concern was to make the thirteen clocks strike simultaneously, as he put it, so that the war could be won. Adams kept his views on slavery so hidden, or made such contradictory statements, that it is impossible to discern his real feelings. For instance, he once claimed that he had never given the slavery question much thought, yet on another occasion he said that even as a young man he had "adore[d] the ideal of gradual emancipation." Adams's views on race are no less difficult to construct, but like Washington and Jefferson he likely accepted much of the racist logic of his age. While a congressman, for instance, he opposed permitting African Americans to serve in the Continental army and when he practiced law he had never scrupled about representing slaveowners against their slaves. On the other hand, he was married to a woman who denounced slavery as an unchristian abomination, and who wrote her husband in tones that suggested that she believed he shared her outlook. Furthermore, John and Abigail, unlike many of their affluent friends in Massachusetts, refused to own slaves, even though bondsmen would have provided more economical labor than the free workers they used on their small farm.[58]

In areas other than slavery and race, Jefferson embraced a reform agenda whose twin objects were to prevent the inheritance of power and to open new opportunities to the white population. His most significant reform efforts were characterized by his dreams of containing governmental power, rendering officeholders accountable to the people, securing the natural rights of all free persons, and extirpating artificial aristocracies, in part by banishing the superstition and ignorance that ruling elites had utilized throughout history. Had all his proposals in this vein been enacted, Virginia would have been substantively altered in its political, educational, and social spheres. Even so, the Jefferson of this era was a conservative reformer. To read Thomas Paine is to feel a supercharged radicalism. It is to sense the energy of a man who, to the very bottom of his soul, sought to overthrow and refabricate the world into which he had been born.[59] To read the Jefferson of the 1770s is to confront a man who had been drawn to radical ideas that addressed his personal anger and despair. He saw himself as the provincial in an empire dominated by unseen and unworthy noblemen, the westerner in a colony ruled by a Tidewater elite, the erudite and scholarly lawyer-philosopher rendered servile to less able men who hailed from more exalted families, and the free thinker in a society yet given to medieval habits of religious practice and thought. His reformist zeal stopped when his hurt ended.[60]

Adams has often been thought of as dedicated only to independence, while Jefferson has been hailed as a great reformer who seized the moment to push for sweeping change after 1776. It is true that Jefferson sought to bring about greater changes in Virginia than Adams desired in Massachusetts. However, Massachusetts was a quasi-republic long before the American Revolution, whereas Virginia was a bastion of aristocratic domination and excessive socioeconomic inequality. Whether or not he realized it, what Jefferson sought was to make Virginia more like Massachusetts.

In reality, both Adams and Jefferson chased the dream of a new, transformed, republicanized America. In 1776 their constitutional views and their aspirations to more fully empower the people were nearly identical. Jefferson recognized this and spoke of the "perfect coincidence of principles and of action" between himself and Adams in 1775 and 1776. Each looked optimistically toward a future in which the American experience, the American character, and the American people—not a foreign dominion, or its provincial satraps, or an artificial aristocracy—would shape America's destiny. And ultimately Adams and Jefferson agreed that their similar aims had effected beneficial change. Forty years after independence they told one another that the American Revolution had ushered in numerous reforms that had elevated human dignity both in America and western Europe.[61]

Between 1777 and 1779 Washington and Adams, and numerous others, beseeched Jefferson to leave Virginia and add his talents to the struggling new nation. "We want your Industry and Abilities here," Adams wrote from Philadelphia. Through intermediaries, Washington said much the same thing. Jefferson was not swayed. He never left Virginia during the six years following his return from Congress in 1776. He seldom left Monticello before 1779. When he descended from his mountain, it was to attend the assembly for a week or two of a legislative session that ordinarily lasted for about eight weeks.[62]

Jefferson hurried home from Williamsburg in the spring of 1777 to be present at the birth of another child, a son who was born in May. However, like the couple's second child, who had been born in April 1774 and died eighteen months later, this infant who was never named died after only three weeks of life. Martha was pregnant again almost immediately and in August 1778 gave birth to Mary, who would always be called Maria, or Polly, by members of the family. Building a family was not Jefferson's only preoccupation. He supervised the ongoing construction at Monticello, and by 1779, eleven years after work had commenced, all six rooms of the original house were habitable, although the finish carpentry work remained. By this time Monticello had taken on the look of a small village. More than eighty slaves and approximately thirty overseers and free laborers, and their dependents, lived and worked on the estate. Buildings dotted the landscape and the air hummed with industry.[63]

A French visitor in 1782 was struck by the serenity atop the mountain, remote from the swirling events of the world, including the anguish and suffering experienced by most Americans during this long and desperate war. Jefferson received and entertained frequent visitors, including several German and British officers who were confined in Charlottesville as prisoners of war. He also devoted much of his time to music and study. Public affairs outside Virginia barely aroused his attention. In 1777 he wrote Adams about his concern over Congress's difficulty in preparing a national constitution, expressing his fear for the safety of the Union once the war ended. He said little about the war, save for its impact on monetary affairs, which of course directly affected a planter-businessman such as himself. Otherwise, he so rarely commented on the war in 1778 and 1779 that it seems likely that Jefferson must have concluded that victory was assured, even imminent.[64]

In mid-1778 Jefferson hinted that his public service left him with little time for himself. This was untrue. In the midst of a great war that he had helped to bring on, a conflict that separated soldiers from their families and spread terror and suffering throughout the land, Jefferson chose not to endure the hardships or make the sacrifices he expected of others. He even spoke of retiring from the limited public activities of which he was a part.[65] His behavior during the three years after the Declaration of Independence sheds light on his temperament. This was a man who indulged himself throughout a long life, content to live amid the affluence provided by the toil of his slave laborers. In the late 1770s, unmoved by the entreaties of others, he was happy to remain on his mountain while thousands of his fellow citizens bore the burden of winning this republican revolution.

Adams, on the other hand, carried self-sacrifice to excess. He was away from home attending his congressional duties during thirty of the forty months after August 1774. He made five round-trips from New England to Pennsylvania, most on horseback. Each journey required more than two weeks of riding in every conceivable kind of weather. After each exhausting day of travel he lodged and dined in taverns that seldom offered the least luxury. Once he reached Philadelphia, Adams lived for months on end in a small room in a boardinghouse. He thrived on this spartan life. Jefferson not only dreaded absences from the sumptuous pleasures of home, but found the legislative regimen, with its tedious committee meetings and hour after hour of repetitive debates, to be nearly unbearable. Both Jefferson and Adams were contemplative men who relished the opportunity to escape to the privacy of their chambers, but of the two Adams most successfully relinquished his old habits in favor of the newer demands imposed by public service.

In part, Adams adapted better because his churning ambition, always greater than that exhibited by Jefferson, made his personal sacrifices seem sufferable, even remunerative. In addition, Adams's lifestyle in some respects did not change that much after he entered Congress, for he was accustomed both to coping with heavy caseloads and to living away from home. Adams may even have welcomed the escapes from the tensions within his marriage that protracted residencies in Philadelphia made possible. What is clear is that his unabated public service produced new strains between Adams and his wife. Abigail embraced his congressional service between 1774–1776, and encouraged him to remain in Congress until the struggle to secure independence was won. However, she hated living alone and expected him to come home once independence was declared. She worried about the economic ramifications of her husband's public service, fearing that his congressional salary, which was modest in comparison to the legal fees he had once earned, would harm the family. She also anguished over the potential harm to her children from growing up without a father.[66]

During 1775, probably in December when John came home briefly during a congressional recess, he and Abigail appear to have agreed that he would serve only until independence was declared. Adams probably expected to resume his legal practice, or accept a state office in nearby Boston, once he left Congress. However, he stayed on until the end of 1776, then after a few days at home, returned to Congress early in 1777, pleading that public affairs "wore so gloomy an aspect" that he could not yet abandon his congressional responsibilities. Abigail was grief stricken. She repeatedly asked her husband to come home. "If you will come Home and turn Farmer, I will be dairy Woman, " she promised. Abigail even permitted herself to become pregnant, although she was thirty-three and the mother of four children, and during the previous five years had never expressed a desire to have an additional child. It was almost certainly a stratagem designed to keep her husband at home, but John was not moved. In fact, he may have resented her behavior. Although he knew that she was experiencing difficulties with this pregnancy, he neither returned home nor wrote consoling letters. When the pregnancy terminated in a miscarriage in July 1777, he expressed his sorrow, but in his very next letter, written within the week, he did not inquire about his wife's health. In fact, his missive began: "I am sorry to find by your late Letter what indeed I expected to hear, that my Farm wants manure."[67]

By 1776—though she did not yet dare speak her mind—Abigail deduced that John's ambition was the primary driving force behind all that he did, including his public service. Unlike Washington and Jefferson, who as adults had enjoyed deference in aristocratic Virginia, Adams experienced real renown and acclaim only after his election to Congress. He soon desired even greater recognition, often pouting privately about not receiving his fair share of praise. Throughout the Revolution he was bothered by the adulation bestowed on Washington and Franklin. Although he conceded that Washington was a "wise, virtuous, and good" man, he sulked when the public treated him as "a Deity or a saviour." He admired Franklin as an essayist and scientist, but thought himself a better congressman. Adams feared that future generations would never know what he had done. The "History or our Revolution will be one continued lie," he once raged. Posterity's understanding of the American Revolution was likely to be "that Dr. Franklin's electrical Rod smote the Earth and out sprung General Washington. That Franklin electrized him with his Rod—and henceforth these two conducted all the Policy, Negotations, Legislatures and War."[68]

Adams always denied any linkage between his ambition and his public life. He portrayed his political activism as selfless and sacrificial, and empha-sized the difficulties he experienced from public service. "I live like a Miser, and a Hermit," he said. To live at home "would be to me Paradise," he went on. "Poor, unhappy I," he was fond of saying. Sometimes he limned himself as a "poor Creature [who was] worn out with scribbling, for my . . . Liberty . . . [but who] must leave others to wear the Lawrells." Adams found it nec-essary to say these things, for otherwise the guilt that flowed from his ambitious nature was too much to bear. Yet he did make sacrifices. He forfeited his considerable legal income. He missed his library, home-cooked meals, comfortable bed and familiar chair, and dozens of additional domestic luxu-ries. He wished to spend more time with his children and he, like Abigail, feared that his continued absence might have a detrimental impact on them. He also exposed himself to uncommon stresses and strains, which he sus-pected were damaging his health and perhaps shortening his life.[69]

Yet he was happy in Congress. The one alternative duty that he longed for was soldiering, if only for a brief moment in one campaign. He was guilt-ridden over his failure to bear arms, and reproached himself for having been the first member of his family to never have served in the militia. He was besieged by feelings of worthlessness as he watched congressmen such as Henry and Dickinson return home to soldier. Adams was haunted by the real-ization that although he had helped bring on this war and asked other men to fight, he was never near the front lines. His dilemma was made more difficult because he had always admired soldiers and thought them the embodiment of "true manliness." He especially revered General Lee, whom he thought combined the attributes of a "Scholler and a Soldier." He confessed to Abigail that when young he had longed to soldier more than he had wanted to study law. Now he wished again to soldier. "Oh that I was a Soldier!—I will be.—I am reading military Books.—Every Body must and will, and shall be a sol-dier," he wrote. But he never became a soldier. Instead, he tried to convince himself that he was too old to soldier, or that his health was too frail for bear-ing arms, or that he was in fact a civilian-soldier "running dayly Risques of my Life" through a backbreaking load of congressional duties. He even per-suaded himself that serving in Congress was more hazardous than fighting at the front.[70]

Preposterous as Adams's comment sounds, he may have reached this con-clusion because he was in poor health, especially in 1775 and 1776. In fact, he was far more ill than he realized. Adams had gradually recovered from the ill-ness that had caused his collapse in February 1771. He remained in good health until shortly after his return from the First Continental Congress. The first sign of renewed problems occurred early in 1775, on the day he and his fellow Braintree selectmen voted to prepare the militia for war. That evening Adams noted in his diary that he had begun to experience discomfort in his eyes. A month later, soon after learning of the bloody incidents at Lexington and Concord, he collapsed with "an allarming illness." He was bedridden for several days and unable to travel to Philadelphia with the Massachusetts delegation to the Second Congress.[71]

A few weeks after he arrived in Philadelphia in the spring of 1775, he told a friend that he had come "from home Sick and have been so ever since." In letter after letter during the next year he complained that he was "miserable," "completely miserable," "not well," "quite infirm," "wasted and exhausted," and "weak in health." "I am always unwell," he despaired at the conclusion of his first full year in Philadelphia.[72] Adams enumerated several symptoms of his illness. He suffered from "smarting Eyes," eyes that were "so weak and dim that I can neither read, write, or see without great Pain." He was acutely sensitive to heat and frequently experienced night sweats, even on cool evenings. He was treated for a skin disorder. He complained of suffering from anxiety, spoke of coping with depression, and acknowledged periods of mental confusion. He suffered insomnia, weakness, and fatigue. He experienced tremors. He admitted to being more irritable than ever before and to having difficulty controlling his temper.[73]

Physicians in Adams's time had no knowledge of thyroid disease, but today a patient suffering the cluster of symptoms that Adams mentioned, together with the heart palpitations or extremely rapid heart rate that he had exhibited during his 1771 illness, would be evaluated for hyperthyroidism. If he did suffer from this malady, it had gone into remission following his collapse four years earlier. Today many medical specialists believe that stress may trigger the onset of this disease in susceptible patients, and it is likely that Adams's illness resurfaced as a result of the enormous stress that he endured in public office, especially following the outbreak of war.[74]

If Adams in fact suffered from thyrotoxicosis, he was afflicted with a very serious malady. Evidence from the nineteenth century, before surgery, drugs, or irradiation were utilized as therapies, suggests that patients often lived several years without treatment, although the malady eventually proved fatal for the overwhelming majority of the afflicted. Adams was one of the fortunate. He survived the ravages of hyperthyroidism through 1775 and 1776, until the disease once again went into remission during 1777. By understanding that some sort of relationship existed between stress and health, Adams may have helped himself by devising strategies for dealing with the adversities in his life. He believed that a good diet, adequate sleep, and considerable exercise were effective antidotes for his stressful lifestyle. He may even have found that living apart from his family was less stressful than dwelling in Braintree. Furthermore, the level of stress in his public life was reduced once independence was declared and Washington won his magnificent victories at Trenton and Princeton. Soon after those victories Adams reported "tolerable Health," the first indication that his health had improved since the onset of hostilities. Thereafter, he improved rapidly. During the three years that followed he "enjoyed uncommon Health," as he told his wife.[75]

Unlike Adams, neither Jefferson nor Washington experienced serious health problems during the war. Washington had been selected to command the Continental army in part because he was young and robust, and his health endured despite the enormous burden that he bore. Washington experienced only three minor illnesses between 1775–1783, each a two-or-three day malady due in all likelihood to food poisoning or some form of infectious disease. However, he aged considerably during the war. His hair turned grey, he lined deeply, and once past fifty he was compelled to wear reading glasses. But he remained remarkably fit. In middle age Washington boasted a physique that many younger men coveted. Tall and muscular, Washington at age fifty weighed 209 pounds.[76]

Washington endured numerous sacrifices during the War of Independence. He fashioned a lifestyle to comport with the prevailing mood of republican simplicity. When he took his army into winter quarters, Washington sometimes lived in a tent until housing had been constructed for all his men. Thereafter, he always selected a modest habitation for headquarters. At Morristown he took only a room in a tavern. Elsewhere, he dwelled in unpretentious farmhouses, seldom setting aside more than a bedroom and parlor for his own use. He eschewed pleasures that he had enjoyed in civilian life. On rare occasions he attended a play or tossed a ball with the younger officers. Sometimes he accompanied riding parties at the completion of the workday, and now and then he relaxed on a picnic in some bucolic spot. However, he did not hunt, fish, play cards, shoot billiards, or seek amusement in taverns.[77]

Washington's normal workday was as lengthy as that of Adams. He too arose before sunrise and, save for a hurried breakfast, worked steadily until the midday repast at about 3:00. Washington was joined at this mess by his aides, several officers, and visiting dignitaries. The fare was less sumptuous than what Washington was accustomed to at home, but the cuisine at headquarters was exquisite in contrast to what was available to the men. Meat, vegetables, and desserts were always on the table, as was wine. On occasion, Washington and his guests beheld an abundance of delicacies. During one month in 1781 Washington's large "household" consumed sixty-two turkeys, thirty-nine ducks, 102 chickens, four dozen trout, three dozen perch, twenty-nine bushels of oysters, one goose, one lamb, two sheep, 138 pounds of pork, fifty-four pounds of ham, 261 pounds of mutton, thirty-six pounds of veal, and a vast assortment of fruit and vegetables. Following the afternoon meal, Washington returned to his desk for two or three additional hours. His workday ended about 7:00 PM, when he ate a light evening meal, often consisting of bread, fruit, and cheese. Afterwards, he frequently relaxed with his aides, drinking a glass or two of claret or madeira and consuming a bowl of nuts, his favorite snack. As had been his custom at Mount Vernon, he retired early, usually around 9 PM.[78]

Washington never returned to Mount Vernon during the initial six years of the war. However, Martha joined him at headquarters each year soon after the army entered winter quarters. She normally remained for five or six months, until the eve of the next year's campaign.

Those who encountered Washington most often described him as reserved, formal, and aloof, a man of "mild gravity" and "stately bearing" who was habitually wary of strangers. Visitors never portrayed him as curt or inhospitable, but none ever said that they felt completely at ease with Washington or claimed to have grown close to him. However, there were two groups with which Washington developed close relationships. He grew near to several of his aides and the Marquis de Lafayette. All were young enough to be his sons and all venerated him. These young men posed no threat to Washington. Blindly loyal, they were acquaintances with whom he could relax and speak with candor. Washington was also quite comfortable in the company of women. Perhaps because they too posed no threat to his public position, he permitted women to see a side of him that few men ever witnessed. Several women described Washington's manner in ways that no man ever suggested. Some commented on his sense of humor, others said he listened to them more attentively than most men, and some portrayed him as cheerful, even playful.[79]

Some visitors to headquarters noted a hard, violent side to Washington. Others used words such as vain, petty, coarse, or insensitive to characterize him. One man who met Washington was struck by his "repulsive coldness . . .

under a courteous demeanor." The brother of one of his aides said Washington was "better endowed by nature in habit for an Eastern monarch, than a republican general." Yet numerous visitors spoke of his "virtue," usually mentioning qualities such as his selflessness, courage, dedication, integrity, calmness, firmness, industry, and honesty. Lafayette gushed that he "had never beheld so superb a man." No one described Washington as a genius, but some said that he understood his limitations and sought out and listened to good advisors. Virtually everyone agreed that he reached important decisions slowly and after great deliberation. Adams and Jefferson reached identical conclusions about his decision-making process. Washington was "slow, but sure," Adams concluded, while Jefferson thought his fellow Virginian "slow in operation, being aided little by invention or imagination, but sure in conclusion."[80]

Washington entered the campaign of 1777 with his new, though unseasoned, regular army and with an adequate supply of arms, munitions, uniforms, and shoes, a harvest of secret French aid that had slipped into American ports during the winter. The campaign developed slowly. Howe, languid as ever, did not sally forth from New York until mid-June. He moved about eastern New Jersey in an attempt to lure the Americans into a fight, but Washington held to his Fabian tactics and declined the challenge. Frustrated, Howe pulled back, his mission a failure. An aide noted that the mood at British headquarters was "much dejected," "very melancholy," and "pensive."[81]

Nevertheless, Howe had a plan for 1777 that slowly crystallized over the winter. While a British army under General John Burgoyne descended on Albany from Canada, Howe would transport his army by sea to the Chesapeake, then march the final few miles to Philadelphia. Howe thought the loss of the city would result in a terrible blow to American morale. The Americans knew better, as few yet perceived the city as a true national capital. Some, like Adams, immediately concluded that Howe's plan was flawed. Philadelphia would capture Howe, Adams wrote, for the British would be immobilized by their efforts to retain their newly won prize. Although Adams was correct, Howe's notion was not entirely misguided. The British commander surmised that Washington could not permit Philadelphia to fall without a fight. Here was the means by which Washington could be compelled to hazard his army, and the fight would take place on terrain favorable to the British—the level, coastal littoral.[82] Howe was correct. Washington did have to fight.

When Washington learned that Howe's army was boarding transports in

New York, he suspected that the redcoats were about to sail up the Hudson to act in concert with Burgoyne. That would be "good policy," he ruminated. When he discovered that the armada had sailed on a southward course, and that Howe was "abandoning Genl. Burgoyne," as he put it, he was amazed, but delighted. Washington put his army in motion. The Continentals marched south from New Jersey and crossed the Delaware at the same spot where Washington had passed over the river on that fateful Christmas night eight months earlier. On August 29 the Continental army paraded through Philadelphia, with Washington, aboard his great steed, riding at the head of his men. Virtually every resident turned out for the spectacle. It took two long hours for the army to file past. They marched with "a lively step," observed John Adams, who stood under a warm sun with the other bystanders. He thought it a "fine Spectacle." The men were "well armed . . . and tolerably disciplined," he added, but the "soldiers have not yet, quite the Air of Soldiers. They dont step exactly in Time," or hold their heads just right, or cock their hats as they should. As soon as the parade ended, Adams sought out a church to offer prayers for what lay ahead.[83] As he prayed, Howe's 16,500 men debouched ashore only sixty miles away. Washington would have to defend Philadelphia with about 11,000 men.

Washington hurried ahead to select an advantageous site on which to meet the enemy. Believing there was little time, he did not adequately reconnoiter the area. Ultimately, he placed his army on the green, sloping terrain behind the Brandywine Creek, about twenty-five miles west of Philadelphia, posting his men at what he believed was the only possible crossing that Howe could utilize. Washington assigned Pennsylvania and Maryland militia to his left flank, the area in which he thought fighting was least likely to occur. General John Sullivan, whose record had been spotty, commanded the right wing of the American forces; he too was situated where Washington thought it was impossible for the British to ford the creek. The cream of the American army, under General Greene, defended the center of the Continental lines. This was where Washington expected the blow to fall.

Plagued by poor maps, stormy weather, and a dearth of horses—scores had perished in the suffocating holds of the transports during the monthlong voyage south—the British required nearly two weeks to march approximately twenty-five miles to the Brandywine. On the morning of September 11, unusually warm for so late in the summer, Howe at last was in place. At 8:00 AM the stillness was broken by the thunderous blasts of the British artillery. A few minutes later, Hessian infantry moved down the slope west of the creek, precisely where Washington had expected the attack to come, and peppered the American lines with small arms fire. By mid-morning the Germans had moved to the edge of the stream, but still made no move to wade across the creek and assault the Continentals's lines.

Washington was perplexed. Why was the enemy not struggling across the creek? Around 9:00 his puzzlement grew as word reached headquarters that a large British force had been spotted moving north, toward Sullivan's men on the American right. Washington discounted the intelligence. Shortly after 11:00, Sullivan dispatched a similar report. Two witnesses later said that Washington had laughed at the tidings. It was unlikely that Howe would divide his army and attack both the American center and right. He would prefer a massed attack, Washington remarked.

An hour passed. Then another. Slowly the early afternoon melted away. From headquarters, about three miles behind the center of the American lines, Washington could hear sporadic cannon fire. There was no indication of major attack. Why was Howe waiting? More reports reached Washington. As always in these circumstances, they were sketchy and contradictory, and nothing shook him from the conviction that Howe yet would attack the American center.

At 3:30 an artillery barrage opened to the north of headquarters, in the direction of the American right. Immediately, fresh cannonading commenced on the American center. The bombardment was so massive that it could be heard in distant Philadelphia. Shortly thereafter a neighborhood farmer was shown into headquarters. He claimed to have seen a large British force crossing the Brandywine well to the north, where Washington had believed a crossing was impossible.

Washington once again discounted the intelligence. This could only be a feint, a move designed to induce him to reassign men, until the center was fatally weakened. Washington wanted more intelligence. Four o'clock passed. Then 5:00 PM. Washington appeared confused. As the long shadows of late afternoon fell over the Brandywine, he wrote Congress. About fifteen percent of the enemy had crossed at Jones' Ford on his right, he said. It was merely a diversion. He awaited the primary assault in the center of his lines.

Shortly before 5:30 incontrovertible evidence reached headquarters, brought by another local resident, that the main British blow was falling on the American right. Sullivan, in fact, was in the fight of his life, and had been for some time. If Howe, with incredibly superior numbers, rolled up the American right, the remainder of Washington's men would be vulnerable.

Howe had replicated his Long Island tactics, and Washington once again had fallen for the bait. He had mistaken a feint for the principal assault, and ignored an action that threatened a fatal envelopment.

But at last Washington understood the peril he faced. He detached the bulk of Greene's men and sent them double-timing to rescue Sullivan, who was four miles away, and indeed his entire army. Sullivan's men were posted atop a rolling green bluff known as Birmingham Meetinghouse Hill, the site of a Quaker place of worship. Although outnumbered two to one, and confronted with what some veterans later described as the most savage fighting they had experienced in this war, Sullivan's lines held just long enough. Once they sagged in the face of a Hessian bayonet charge, but when men from other sectors of the hill were plugged into the gaps, the withdrawal was stanched. "We broke and Rallied and Rallied and broke," one of the men later remarked. These men, the three-year-or-during-the-war men that Washington had sought, and Adams had struggled to persuade a reluctant Congress to provide, stood "as firm as a rock in the middle of a wild ocean of carnage," according to a subsequent battle report. Sullivan simply described them as "Exceedingly Brave." Other factors also influenced this fight. Because he sailed to Pennsylvania, Howe left two cavalry regiments in New York, fearing the horses could not endure the voyage. With them, he would have quickly overrun Sullivan. Furthermore, even before the fighting commenced, the wool-clad regulars were exhausted by their long march on this warm summer day. Nevertheless, at about 5:30 the British had launched their largest attack of the afternoon, and the American lines at last broke.

Greene's reinforcements, taking a shortcut shown them by a local farmer, arrived just as the withdrawal threatened to become a rout. Washington reached the battle site at about the same time. He directed the American defense, moving regiments here and there. He rode about the battlefield for nearly ninety minutes, oblivious to the danger. Soldiers near him were cut down and one of his staff officers, only a few yards away on horseback, was seriously wounded. Meanwhile, as Greene and Washington raced to rescue Sullivan, the assault on what once had been the American center at long last began. Hessians splashed across the shallow creek and easily subdued the remnants of the Continenals. The enemy was across the Brandywine and striking at the American center and right flanks.

Greene's fresh men, hiding behind houses and ditches, made their final stand about a mile from the site of Sullivan's lengthy fight. The bloody contest raged for nearly forty-five minutes. This time the Americans repulsed several bayonet charges, one of the few times in this conflict that the Continentals successfully defended against such an attack. At times it appeared as if the American resistance would collapse, but the breakthrough that would have enabled the British to envelop the Americans never occurred. Instead, dusk fell over the battlefield and the fighting gradually ceased. Howe later said that he was on the cusp of victory and that darkness had saved Washington. A Hessian officer, perhaps more accurately, raged that Howe would have had his victory had he commenced the attack two hours earlier. As it was, Washington had lost about 1,200 men, killed, wounded, and captured, nearly one-tenth of his army.[84]

Howe hoped for another opportunity the following morning, but there was not to be a second day on the Brandywine. Soon after night descended, Washington's sweaty, exhausted men retreated to safety. Thereafter, Washington fell back on his Fabian tactics and avoided another major encounter. His light infantry units merely harassed the British until they entered Philadelphia near the end of the month.

Washington sought to put the best possible face on this engagement. He referred to the Battle of Brandywine as a "misfortune" attributable to a "series of unlucky incidents," especially "uncertain" intelligence. He accepted no blame for the events of that day. Washington also claimed that the British had sustained heavier losses than his army, when in fact the Americans had suffered twice the number of casualties as their adversary. Howe, the professional, once again had exposed Washington as an amateur general, and once again he had narrowly missed scoring a decisive victory. A wag writing in a London newspaper soon after Brandywine declared that only Howe could have failed to defeat Washington, and only Washington could by now have failed to finish off Howe. In fact, had Howe possessed Washington's character and temperament, the likelihood is great that he would have inflicted a mortal defeat on Washington sometime in 1776. No one knew this better than Washington. With "a little enterprise and industry," he once remarked, Howe would have defeated him long before anyone thought of fighting on the Brandywine.[85]

As the British closed in on Philadelphia, Washington alerted Congress that it soon would have to quit the city. Each congressman packed, in order to hasten his getaway when the inevitable alarm was sounded. Some destroyed sensitive papers, lest they fall into British hands. Adams spoke for a time of remaining and fighting alongside Washington, but that was bluster and he knew it. "I shall run away ... with the rest," he ultimately admitted to

Abigail.[86] That was precisely what he and each of his colleagues did when Washington's messengers arrived in the dead of night on September 19.

The knock at Adams's door came at 3:00 AM. In March he had moved from Mrs. Yard's to another boardinghouse, and only a week earlier he had moved again, this time to the home of Reverend James Sproat, minister of the Second Presbyterian Church in Philadelphia. Startled awake, Adams struggled to his senses. When he opened his door he discovered that it was James Lovell, his colleague from Massachusetts, with word that the British regulars were coming. Haste was imperative, he said. Messengers dispatched by Alexander Hamilton, an aide to General Washington, had arrived moments before and begun to alert the congressmen, Lovell reported. The British had secured the boats and a ford on the Schuylkill River, on the west end of Philadelphia, perhaps within three miles of the State House. The enemy might get advance units into the city within the hour, Hamilton cautioned. Now fully awake, Adams hurried down the hall to the room occupied by Henry Marchant, a congressman from Rhode Island, the only other congressman who lodged at the Sproat's, and alerted him to prepare to ride to safety. Adams sent someone—it might have been Lovell or Reverend Sproat, who had been jarred from his sleep by the din inside his home—to fetch his and Marchant's horses. Meanwhile, by the half-light of a solitary candle, Adams dressed quickly, fumblng to retrieve his possessions, especially his papers. When he emerged from his room, he reminded Sproat that by prior agreement he was leaving in his care a trunk crammed with many items, including some clothing and his account books."[87]

Just after Brandywine, Adams had reflected that the "Prospect is chilling . . . Gloomy, dark, melancholy, and dispiriting."[88] This was worse. Not only did Adams and Marchant have little knowledge of the whereabouts of the British army, but this was a fluid situation. Howe's mounted patrols could stab deep into American territory moving twenty or thirty miles in a day. The risk of being captured, though not great, had to be considered.

Congress had agreed to reassemble in a few days in Lancaster, about fifty miles west of the Brandywine. But to reach that town, Adams and his colleagues, probably according to a prearranged plan, rode north to Trenton, hugging the Delaware River in order to stay as far east of the advancing British regulars as possible. Their first object was to avoid escape. This journey to Lancaster would be three times its normal length.

That first night was the worst. Adams and Marchant clattered out of town on Philadelphia's barely lit cobblestone streets, following the same route Washington had taken when he left Congress to assume command of the

Continental army in Cambridge twenty-seven months earlier. In no time, the congressmen were beyond the edge of the city, riding in the dark, remote countryside. Adams had ridden this way before, but never at night, and never with the possibility of encountering enemy soldiers. He was shaken. "Ruin . . . seems to await" this great cause, he thought as he rode in the stygian darkness. "We have as good a Cause, as ever was fought for. We have great Resources. The People are well tempered." Why, he wondered through this forlorn night, did one military disaster after another befall the American army?[89]

As the first purple streaks of dawn showed in the eastern sky, after about two hours of riding, Adams relaxed considerably. He and his colleague continued on to Bristol, where they paused to rest and eat breakfast. Soon they were riding again. Late in the afternoon, they crossed into Trenton, where they remained for two nights. A grueling journey of more than 150 miles by horseback lay ahead, but the worst danger was past. Indeed, on Sunday, two days after Lovell awakened him, Adams learned that Howe had not yet entered Philadelphia.

At month's end Adams arrived in York, near Lancaster, which Congress finally selected as its new—and, it hoped, temporary—home. Because accommodations were lacking in this small village, Adams was compelled to share a room with Samuel Adams and Elbridge Gerry.

Adams was in a melancholy mood when he unpacked. He had expected a better showing from Washington's legions. He believed the Continental army, which had grown throughout the year, should have improved on its performance in the New York campaign. Throughout the summer, in fact, he had boasted to Abigail that the American army would perform ably when tested. Furthermore, he believed that Howe had blundered by not cooperating with Burgoyne's invaders. "Now is the Time to strike," he had exulted in August, for both British armies might be defeated before winter. He thought it within Washington's grasp to "crush that vapouring, blustering, Bully [Howe] to Attoms," he said. Thus, on the eve of Brandywine, he thought that it would be better for Washington to risk all than to continue his Fabian tactics. Even if defeated, the Continental army would be able to inflict severe losses, casualties that the British could not endure. However, once Brandywine was fought, he never blamed Washington for the lack of American success on that bloody day. He knew that Washington not only had faced the cream of the British army, but he had received little or no help from civilians in southeastern Pennsylvania.[90]

Adams's dark mood stemmed from more than just the missed opportunity on the Brandywine Creek. The concerns he had expressed in 1776 over

the erosion of the currency, and the decline in the public's willingness to sacrifice for the cause, had grown throughout 1777. Nowhere was this more
evident than in Congress, which many had quit to chase after acquisitive pursuits at home. Only eight of the fifty-five congressmen who had served with
Adams at the First Continental Congress were with him in York. Even many
who came later, like Jefferson, who had not arrived until mid-1775, had long
since departed. Adams also discovered unhealthy signs among those who
remained active. The army's officers fought "like Cats and Dogs . . . Scram-
bling for Rank and Pay," he said heatedly. Adams feared this selfish behavior,
which he labeled as "vicious and luxurious and effeminate," threatened the
very superstructure of the revolutionary movement. Likewise, Adams was
outraged by self-serving pressures on Congress from the states and from special interests, as well as by businessmen who had turned price gouging into
an art form.[91]

But Adams's tortured gloominess fell away in a flash in October as a
result of two stunning military engagements. Within a week of Adams's
arrival in York, Washington struck suddenly at detachments of about 9,000
British regulars that Howe had posted—but not yet entrenched—at Germantown, seven miles from Philadelphia. Washington hoped to complete the
year with an assault that might demoralize his adversary, as had occurred at
Trenton and Princeton at the conclusion of the previous campaign. Adams
knew something was coming. After Brandywine, Washington had told him
that he would "exert every nerve to collect, without loss of time, all the force
we can get together, to endeavor to compensate for the loss we have sustained." The general brought down reinforcements from New York and
secured militiamen from Pennsylvania, New Jersey, and Maryland. By early
October, he had about 11,000 men, three-fourths of whom were regulars.[92]

Washington proposed a surprise attack at Germantown, but just as during the siege of Boston, two councils of war voted against his plan, one by a
two-to-one margin. This time Washington refused to be stopped. He spoke
with each officer privately, utilizing every ounce of persuasiveness that he
could muster. Some reconsidered and consented to his proposed attack,
enough that he felt free to act. The gambler in Washington propelled him to
act, but his yearning for another fight was also brought on by his insecurities.
He knew that his failure at Brandywine, and his inability to hold Philadelphia,
would inevitably result in carping, perhaps even an inquiry by a congress that
was radically different from the one that had appointed him twenty-eight
months before. By early October, Washington also knew that the American

army under General Gates, which had resisted Burgoyne's invasion, had performed brilliantly. Although Washington did not yet know the outcome of the
campaign in New York, he was aware that Burgoyne faced "circumstances that
threaten his ruin." In fact, Gates's Continentals and militiamen had already
inflicted heavy losses on Burgoyne in the Battle of Freeman's Farm, leaving
the besieged British unable to advance or retreat. If Gates accomplished more
than Washington, tongues were certain to wag.[93]

Washington prepared a complicated plan for his callow army. On October 4, one week after the redcoats marched into Philadelphia, Washington
divided his men into four columns. Each faced a long march down a different
road toward Germantown, and each was to be in position to launch a bayonet
assault at 5:00 AM. Inevitably, problems arose. The marches were made on a
foggy, moonless autumn night down unfamiliar roads. Several units lost their
way. Nearly two-thirds of Washington's men arrived after the battle began.
Furthermore, the element of surprise, which had been critical to the success at
Trenton, was lost when pickets discovered some of the advancing Continentals. Despite these glitches, Washington's men fought well. So did the British.
After three hours the Americans broke down, falling apart after two Continental units stumbled into one another in the smoke and fog, and fired on
their comrades. That horrible mistake triggered an inexorable panic in one
sector of the battlefield, which in turn unnerved the tired, edgy men in other
units. Washington rode into danger again—General Sullivan later said that
the commander exposed himself to "the hottest fire"—desperately attempting to stop the retreat and prevent a rout. At last, he succeeded in restoring
order so that a retreat was completed in a generally disciplined manner.[94]

Washington must have felt as Howe and Cornwallis had on so many
occasions. Although another success such as that at Trenton had been unlikely,
Washington had come close to scoring a victory similar to his triumph at
Princeton. Furthermore, a smashing victory in this sector, coupled with the
destruction of Burgoyne's army in the north, might have induced London to
end the war. Instead, while Washington acted boldly and unpredictably, his
losses at Germantown, and at Brandywine, were twice those of his enemy.

Yet Germantown proved to be an instance of a general losing a battle but
winning the war. Adams subsequently discovered that French officials had
been as impressed by Washington's spunk and determination as by Gates's
substantial victory, which was accomplished in mid-October when Burgoyne
surrendered his trapped and starving army at Saratoga. Versailles appreciated
Washington's willingness to fight. French leaders admired his planning, think-

ing Washington's preparations had been worthy of a competent European general. They were impressed too by Washington's ability to hurl his green army into a second engagement so soon after Brandywine. Gates and Washington had brought the British army in America to the "moment of crisis," as the French foreign minister put it. Saratoga and Germantown would bring France into this war, a struggle that France believed it could win with only a commitment of naval forces, for America's army was commanded by a daring and resourceful general.[95]

Washington had preserved his army and, together with Gates, brought about a great turning point in this war. Nevertheless, as 1777 closed, General Washington was overcome with despair while Adams, who had been despondent in September, radiated joy. Washington lauded Gates, but was bitterly disappointed that he had been unable to score an equally significant victory. He was driven to act once again in the hope of achieving a similarly magnificent triumph. Washington summoned another council of war and proposed an attack on Howe's entrenched army in Philadelphia. The generals rejected the scheme. The risk was too great, especially as Saratoga might lure France into the war. This time Washington adhered to their vote. However, he ordered General Greene to attack a British force that was attempting to destroy American forts on the Delaware below Philadelphia. It too was a misguided notion, as Greene would possess only about sixty percent as many men as his adversary. Usually the model of compliance, Greene objected. He candidly told Washington that he was permitting himself to be driven into unwise moves. Some would now think Gates was the better general, Greene appeared to suggest, but he advised Washington not be swayed by "an ignorant and impatient populace." To act imprudently, and to fail, Greene warned, would result in Washington being "condemned . . . by all military Gentlemen of Experience." It was better not to act until the campaign season of 1778, when he might fight in a more advantageous situation. Washington mulled over Greene's unadorned counsel and, in a sober light, rescinded his order. Shortly thereafter Howe, perhaps sensing Washington's despair and hoping to propel his foe into a reckless act, or perhaps out of his own sense of desperation, brought his army out of Philadelphia in an effort to entice the Continentals into one additional battle, albeit on terrain that the British had chosen. Whatever Washington's personal perplexities, his reason prevailed. Washington did not take the bait. As Washington watched and waited, resisting the temptation for one final gamble, the campaign of 1777, like a flickering candle, slowly burned out.[96]

While Howe returned to the warmth and safety of Philadelphia, Washington's men set off for winter quarters at a site on the west bank on the Schuylkill about twenty miles from Philadelphia, a place the local inhabitants called Valley Forge. This had not been the commander's choice. He had wished to divide his army between several posts, reasoning that each camp could more easily be supplied by the nearby populace than could one large cantonment that was dependent on shipments from throughout the United States. But congressmen from Pennsylvania, New Jersey, and Delaware hectored Washington to find quarters near Philadelphia. They wanted him to harass any British attempts to forage in their districts. Washington, bitter, frustrated, and seething with anger, wrote the strongest note he ever dared send to Congress. It was far easier for congressmen to fight a war from a desk "in a comfortable room by a good fire," he said, than for his soldiers to "occupy a cold bleak hill and sleep under frost and Snow without Cloaths or Blankets."[97]

Adams, meanwhile, was ecstatic with the sudden shift in America's military fortunes. He believed the "turning [of] the Tide of Arms" had occurred. Expecting France to enter the war soon, he was confident that an American victory was inevitable. If Britain had been unable to suppress the rebellion when America stood alone, he reflected, it could hardly hope to win a war against Franco-American forces. Adams was secretly happy too that it was Gates who had scored the great triumph. A colossal victory at Brandywine might have resulted in such "Idolatry and Adulation" that Washington's head would have been turned, as had happened with some many conquerors throughout history.[98]

Adams was happy for another reason as well. He resigned his seat in Congress late in November and began the slow journey home. He had long promised Abigail that he would leave Congress when "Our Affairs are in a fine prosperous Train."[99] That time had come. But whereas Abigail thought her husband was coming home for good, Adams knew differently. He knew that Congress had recalled Silas Deane from Paris. He was too savvy not to know that Congress would select him for the vacant diplomatic post.

Jefferson, far from the war at Monticello, was equally delighted. He too believed an American victory had been sealed by Burgoyne's surrender. Many citizens shared this view. During the ride to Braintree, Adams discovered that he was lauded as one of the "Saviours of [his] Country" by a populace that believed that the worst was behind them.[100] It was a potentially fatal sentiment, as Washington, Adams, and Jefferson would discover during the three long years of war that lay ahead.

American Commissioners at the Preliminary Peace Negotiations with Great Britain. Painting by Benjamin West, ca. 1783. (Courtesy: Henry Francis du Pont Winterthur Museum)

PART THREE

*"It Is Impossible
to Exceed This"*

FROM
DESPAIR
TO TRIUMPH

7

"A Fatal Crisis"

The Great Peril, 1778–1780

There was much to celebrate at Valley Forge in early May 1778. Warm, sunny days heralded the end of a long, besetting winter. Not only were the men better clothed and fed than they had been during the gloom of early year, but the army was intact and, in General Washington's estimation, better prepared than ever before to fight effectively. Washington also believed that he enjoyed more support in Congress than when he had brought his army to this bleak encampment. Furthermore, he radiated a confidence that his staff had seldom observed during the past two years. Only a few days earlier *La Sensible*, a French brig, had brought glad tidings to America. While the men had shivered and starved at Valley Forge, France had recognized the independence of the United States and emissaries of the two nations had concluded treaties of alliance and commerce.

Washington had feared problems even before his soldiery shuffled into Valley Forge. Since late in the previous summer he had known that southeastern Pennsylvania had been picked clean both by Howe's army and his own Continentals and militiamen. Furthermore, as chaos had reigned in the quartermaster corps since early 1777, Washington suspected that even if supplies could be found, most would never reach Valley Forge. Even so, Washington had never anticipated the adversity he encountered during that terrible winter.

Over 3,000 men died at Valley Forge. Food was always scarce. Housing was inadequate, consisting of jerry-built huts that were crowded, drafty, and cold. Nearly one-third of the men lacked shoes, and almost all were without blankets and sufficient clothing. Inevitably, disease—smallpox, typhus, dysentery, and scurvy—swept through Valley Forge. By late January, with every bed occupied in the log cabin infirmaries within the camp, local churches and taverns were converted into sick bays. The few who were healthy, and had not deserted, spent much of their time burying their less fortunate comrades. Washington quickly complained to Congress that his army was "uncomfortably provided" for. By mid-February he warned that the army was confronted by "a fatal Crisis." In February 1778, 3,989 men in camp were listed as unfit for duty. Altogether, less than one-third of the men on the rolls of the Continental army were recorded as effective rank and file. If the army survived at all, Washington warned, a general mutiny was possible.[1]

The mutiny never occurred, although on many days ten to fifteen men deserted. For the most part this vexed soldiery served with stoicism, or with what Washington, Adams, and Jefferson called virtue. It was the officers, a class that never endured the deprivation of the men, who came closest to decimating the army. Upwards of 300 officers quit before winter ended, fifty from the same division on one gray day late in December. Although their pay was munificent in comparison to that of the enlisted men, the officers demanded that at war's end they be given a lifetime pension equivalent to one-half their annual salary. They threatened to resign unless Congress acquiesced. Such naked self-serving flew in the face of everything that Washington believed about sacrificial service, but he backed his officers and became their principal advocate with Congress. Otherwise, the Continental army might have disappeared or—and Washington feared this just as much—new officers elevated from the ranks, and consisting primarily of men from the lower socioeconomic strata, would have supplanted the original officers. The crisis was resolved in May when Congress voted half-pay for the officers for seven years following retirement.[2]

After Gates's great victory at Saratoga, and his own lack of success at Brandywine and Germantown, Washington had entered winter quarters expecting that some would question his abilities. Inevitably, some did express doubts. Unavoidably, too, word of the second-guessing reached headquarters. All Washington knew for certain was that some distrusted his abilities, including his alleged proclivity for listening to supposedly bad advice, especially that proffered by General Greene. Washington did not know how many had reproached his leadership. Nor did he know exactly who had reproved him. Nevertheless, troubled, tired, and overworked, and in the slough of despondency brought on by the misery at Valley Forge, Washington succumbed to his many anxieties. He convinced himself that he was under widespread attack for surrounding himself with sycophants who offered misguided counsel. With little or no evidence to substantiate such a conclusion, Washington came to believe that some officers in Gates's orbit had allied with disenchanted congressmen to topple him. His actions in fact make it readily apparent that Washington suspected that Gates himself was the driving force behind a subterranean plot to overthrow him.[3]

The alleged conspiracy, often called the Conway Cabal, likely never amounted to more than some caviling by a few disgruntled officers. If a group dedicated to securing Washington's removal actually existed, it had few adherents, either inside or outside Congress. Washington, in fact, was quite popular. His birthday was already widely celebrated and for the first time that winter he was called the "father of his country." Many congressmen admired Washington and spoke of him as the "first Man in this World" and the "first of the Age." Most understood that he had been confronted by a much stronger British adversary in Pennsylvania than Gates had faced in New York. When Dr. Rush complained to Adams about Washington, suggesting that a new commander was needed to save the American Revolution, Adams ridiculed his criticism. The "Idea that any one Man, alone can Save Us, is too Silly . . . to harbour for a Moment," he retorted. Furthermore, whether or not they liked Washington, virtually everyone in Congress understood that he had to remain, unless he suffered a cataclysmic defeat or engaged in improper behavior. Any attempt to remove Washington would be immeasurably divisive, perhaps fatally so.[4]

In the midst of his greatest trials that winter, Washington welcomed to Valley Forge Frederick Steube, who called himself Baron von Steuben and claimed to be a Swabian nobleman who once had been a general officer in the Prussian army. Steuben exaggerated greatly, but Washington and everyone else was taken in. Steuben, who was put to work training the Continentals, introduced a drill program modeled on the Prussian system. Although he spoke little English, Steuben succeeded in making the soldiers at least look like soldiers. It was just one of many changes that Washington implemented that winter. By the spring the Continental army included an engineer corps, companies of sappers and miners, who specialized in digging entrenchments and tunnels, troops of light dragoons, a Corps of Invalids for guarding prisoners, a mounted police unit, and a reorganized medical department. In addition, Washington, in collaboration with Congress, overhauled the supply system and induced General Greene, who was honest and industrious, to surrender his field post and become quartermaster general. Greene's appointment had the additional merit of removing from headquarters the favorite whipping boy of Washington's critics.[5]

One other substantive change had its origin that winter. General James Varnum of Rhode Island proposed to the commander that African Americans, who had been prohibited from joining the army since soon after Washington took command, be permitted to enlist. Varnum suggested that Rhode Island's two depleted battalions be combined and that the extra officers be sent home to recruit a new battalion composed of black soldiers. Washington, who two years earlier had wished to remove all African-American soldiers from his army, was inclined to agree. He not only needed men badly, but once Lord Dunmore had armed slaves in 1775, Washington understood that African Americans would fight in this war. He knew that unless the United States relented on its discriminatory policy, most blacks would fight for the enemy. If this war turned "on which side can arm the Negroes the faster," he warned, Great Britain would be the victor. Thus, in the spring of 1778 Washington sent Varnum's proposal to the governor of Rhode Island without comment, save to urge the state to meet its quota. He could do no more, as Congress had never altered its position on African Americans in the Continental army. However, no one could mistake Washington's feelings. Rhode Island quickly enacted legislation enabling slaves to serve in the army, and decreed that those who enlisted were to be freed and their owners compensated. By mid-year 755 African Americans from Rhode Island, Massachusetts, and Connecticut served in fourteen brigades in the Continental army.[6]

By the time the maples and oaks displayed the first evidence of spring, Washington was exultant. Not only would the Franco-American allies be a formidable force, but he believed French recognition would spur other powers to assist the United States. The "game is verging fast to a favorable issue," he rejoiced, and added that there could be no doubt that America was on the "plain and easy road to independence."[7]

Washington designated May 6 as a *feu de joie*, a day to celebrate the army's, and the American Revolution's, deliverance. The festivities commenced with sermons by the brigade chaplains. At 10:30 a single cannon blast announced Washington's appearance. He rode before his assembled army, then from a reviewing stand watched his men parade. When the last company received his salute, thirteen cannon roared. "Long live the King of France," the soldiers shouted in unison. Thirteen cannon fired again; "And long live the friendly European powers," the men chanted. After still another cannonading, the men cried: "To the American States." When the celebration ended and the commander mounted his white horse to depart, the men spontaneously threw their hats in the air and cheered: "Long live General Washington."[8]

Adams also bubbled with enthusiasm that spring. On learning of Saratoga, he proclaimed that "the great Anxiety . . . concerning the Issue of the Cause . . . is now done Away." Yet while Adams thought victory assured, he did not believe the end of the war was imminent.[9]

In mid-February 1778, while Washington experienced his darkest moments at Valley Forge, Adams boarded the frigate *Boston*, anchored off Mount Wolleston, near Braintree. Accompanied by eleven-year-old John Quincy, he was sailing to France to join Franklin and Arthur Lee as American commissioners charged with securing French recognition. The journey lasted six weeks and was filled with danger.

At one point the *Boston* overtook a British merchant ship. Adams came on deck to watch the taking of the prize. Suddenly, unexpectedly, the British vessel fought back, firing on the *Boston*. A cannonball whizzed just over Adams's head and tore through the mizzen yard behind him. Adams volunteered to help with one of the guns, but the captain, more shaken than his important passenger, ordered him below deck. On another occasion, the *Boston* became the hunted. British vessels suddenly appeared and chased their prey, confronting Adams with the likelihood of capture and, at the very least, a dangerously long and unhealthy incarceration. However, fortune smiled. A terrific storm blew up and dispersed the vessels, but the tempestuous weather system posed perils of its own. The ship was tossed about like a toy. At the height of the gale, lightening struck the foresail, killing one crewman. Adams and his son, who were confined to their tenebrous, unventilated cabin throughout the tempest, thought death was imminent. They prayed, held on to their bunks in a vain effort to prevent being hurled about, and without much success fought to stay warm and dry. At last, seventy-two interminable hours after the storm blew up, the wind died and the foam-green sea ran more quietly. Adams came topside at once and breathed in the clean air. He was exultant and dared to believe that he might live to landfall. Several additional days of sailing lay ahead, but the remainder of the journey was calm and uneventful, and late in March, Adams stepped ashore in Bordeaux.[10]

When he reached Paris a week later, Adams learned that the American commissioners had concluded the treaties with France just about the time he sailed. His perilous voyage had been unnecessary. He considered returning home immediately, but when he discovered that Franklin and Lee were so deeply divided temperamentally and philosophically that they could not agree on any issue, Adams opted to stay on and await orders from Congress. In the meantime, he realized, his vote would be decisive.[11]

Adams's stay in France lasted twelve months, until April 1779. He might have spent the time traveling and sightseeing, visiting as much of Paris and western Europe as possible, for he had few official responsibilities and this was likely to be a once-in-a-lifetime opportunity. But that would have been out of character. Adams preferred to work. After enrolling his son in an academy, he moved into a garden apartment at the Hotel Valentinois, a hilltop château in suburban Passy, and got down to business. Six months before, Adams had been the most important member of Congress. Now he served as a virtual clerk. He kept books for the delegation and looked after the commissioners' correspondence. But he took on other duties as well. He met frequently with influential private citizens and minor government officials. He kept Congress informed on affairs in France, England, and Europe, writing nearly a score of letters for every one dispatched by Franklin or Lee. He devoted several hours each day to his French lessons, and within six months conversed comfortably in his second language, better in fact than Franklin, who had lived in France two years longer. Together with Franklin and Lee, Adams additionally handled problems concerning American prisoners of war incarcerated in England, as well as issues that arose from the activities of the U.S. navy and privateers.[12]

Adams had exuded optimism when he sailed from Massachusetts, but crucial changes occurred in his outlook during 1778. Two years earlier when he had prepared the Model Treaty to guide America's first diplomats, Adams envisioned only a commercial connection with France. Trade with France, he had believed, would give the United States the tools it required to win the war. Besides, he had feared a military pact with France. Not only did he distrust the French, but he was apprehensive that an alliance might someday drag America into Europe's wars. However, when Adams discovered in 1778 that Franklin, Lee, and Deane had no choice but to sign a military alliance, he acquiesced and warmly embraced the compact.[13]

His principal concern was that his countrymen might grow too dependent on France and lose their fighting edge, but that worry soon vanished. During his first months in France, Adams came to see the alliance as crucial for winning the war and maintaining the postwar security of the United States. In mid-1778 he told correspondents at home that the interests of the United States were in no way jeopardized by the French alliance. Both sides were well served, he said, because Great Britain was the implacable foe of each. "The United States . . . will be for Ages, the natural Bulwark of France against the Hostile designs of England . . . and France is the natural Defence of the United States against the rapacious Spirit of Great Britain," Adams declared.[14]

However, in the course of 1778 Adams's outlook grew more jaded. Not only did he come to believe that the United States was developing an unhealthy dependence on its ally, but word from home confirmed his early fears that the alliance had eroded his countrymen's fighting spirit. Many Americans were now inclined to let the French win the war for them. Simultaneously, Adams discovered from contacts in England that France's entry into the war had not frightened the ministry into peace talks. Great Britain, these correspondents said, would not abandon hostilities until it was decisively beaten. Adams, who unlike Washington and Jefferson, had never expected an early end to the war, once again had every reason to believe that hostilities would continue for a very long time. The prospect of a protracted war placed America's growing financial woes in a new light. Indeed, the American economy worsened dramatically in 1778. By year's end the continental currency had depreciated so badly that it was worth about one-eighth its value at the outset of the war. Sound money, desperately needed for the acquisition of essential commodities overseas, could be found only through additional loans from France.[15] Adams was growing to fear that if the United States was compelled to fight a lengthy war while both its dollars and fighting resolve eroded, his country would inevitably become a satellite of France.

By autumn Adams perceived signs that the French also recognized the changing relationship with its struggling young ally. Increasingly, French officials treated the United States as a client state, not as an equal partner. Not only did a hauteur now characterize the attitude of the highest French officials, but they increasingly turned a deaf ear toward the entreaties of the American diplomats. Near the end of the year Adams, for the first time, cautioned that the French alliance was "a delicate and dangerous Connection." He warned Congress to be alert to French efforts to shape American foreign policy "by Attaching themselves to Persons, Parties, or Measures in America."[16]

Adams soon concluded that the United States was verging on a great crisis. He apprehended that the United States might secure its independence from Great Britain, but emerge a retainer, a virtual colony, of another great power, the very danger that Dickinson had warned of in 1776. The only solution, he concluded, was to bring the war to a rapid end through a quick military victory. Not only must the leadership at home restore the fighting mood that had prevailed at the beginning of the war, but France must make a greater military commitment. Simply sending its fleet to the West Indies, as it had done that autumn, was not enough. It must be more aggressive. In December, Adams importuned Franklin and Lee to join him in exerting pressure on France to do more. He wanted France to dispatch more privateers to prey on British merchant shipping, unleash squadrons against the English fishing fleet, and commit its navy to convoying vessels engaged in Franco-American commerce. Above all, he believed that France must send as many as a dozen heavy warships to American waters. If given a naval arm, Washington could take the offensive against an undersupplied British army. That, and that alone, Adams asserted, could bring Britain to its knees.[17]

Franklin balked. He was loath to accost his ally, fearful that Versailles would take umbrage. If France interpreted the commissioners' entreaties as a criticism of its policy, it might retaliate by denying the United States a desperately needed loan. However, Adams and Lee outvoted Franklin. Early in 1779 the American envoys urged on the Comte de Vergennes, the French foreign minister, the recommendations that Adams had developed, including an appeal to send to America "a powerfull Fleet sufficient to secure a naval Superiority." Vergennes, who was focused on an invasion of England, brushed aside the commissioners' request in a terse note, but within ten months the French government reconsidered and committed a larger fleet to American waters.[18]

Franklin's behavior provoked still another change in Adams's thinking. By year's end he questioned Franklin's efficacy as a diplomat. Privately, Adams portrayed Franklin as a hedonist whose indolence and debauchery affected the day-to-day conduct of the commissioners' business. Adams, who had shared quarters with Franklin at the Valentinois since April, had observed that his colleague lived what he thought was the grand life of a sybarite. Franklin was attended by nine servants, driven about in an elegant coach, feasted daily on every imaginable delicacy, and held the keys to a wine cellar stocked with more than a thousand vintage wines; Franklin played every night—he "comes home at all hours," even as late as 9:00 o'clock, Adams complained—and did not arise until well into the day, sometimes as late as 8:00 in the morning. Franklin had little time for work, Adams charged. When the Doctor found a few minutes for his diplomatic responsibilities, he often was too fatigued to concentrate. Adams cried that Franklin lacked time for his colleagues, was inattentive to detail, and caused interminable delays in the work of the commissioners. But that was not Adams's most substantive complaint. He questioned Franklin's style of diplomacy. He "hates to offend," Adams told friends at home. He was correct. Franklin disliked confrontation, and had always sought to avoid it in his private life. What America needed at Versailles was a strong, assertive voice, Adams said. Franklin could never be such a diplomat, he added. "He may be a Philosopher, for what I know, but he is not a sufficient Statesman."[19]

Adams was consumed with envy. Franklin was adored by the French. Streams of Parisians called on him each day. Many women loved being in his presence, laughing and joking with him, and sometimes sitting on his lap, and the illuminati were just as eager to share his company. Meanwhile, Adams was largely ignored. Initially, several Frenchmen had been excited to meet him, thinking he was "*le fameux* Adams," Samuel Adams. When they discovered their error, John found himself treated as "a Man of no Consequence." Nevertheless, Adams's complaints cannot be dismissed entirely as the result of jealousy. Franklin aroused the enmity of virtually every American diplomat with whom he served during the war, and both Vergennes and British envoys with whom he subsequently dealt, complained that he displayed a regrettable apathy toward his responsibilities. Yet, whatever Franklin's foibles, even Adams admitted that he had strengths as a diplomat. He was honest, devoted to the American cause, "a Great Genius," and beloved by the French. Thus, despite the Doctor's faults, Adams urged Congress to appoint Franklin as the first U.S. minister to France, a post he coveted for himself. He told one congressman that Franklin's "Character, has excited such an Enthusiasm, that it would do us great Harm to recall him."[20]

The genesis of every change in Adams's outlook sprang from the allies' lack of military success in 1778. The disappointments of that year, and the next, also transformed General Washington's perspective. Washington began the campaign season in 1778 with the intention of resuming his Fabian tactics, unless a large French fleet arrived. However, when Washington learned in June that the British army would soon abandon Philadelphia, he suddenly altered his plans. The British army was to march to New York, where some would be garrisoned and others—about one-half the regulars in America—would ship out to the Caribbean to defend imperial holdings against the possibility of a French assault. Washington saw an opportunity to strike at the redcoats as they crossed New Jersey and, at the same time, test his army of newly trained veterans. The odds appeared to be favorable. Washington had about 13,000 men under his command, most of whom were regulars. The

British force barely totaled 10,000. Furthermore, the Royal Navy was not likely to be a factor in any engagement fought deep inside New Jersey. Washington believed that if he could inflict heavy losses on the British so soon after their humiliating surrender at Saratoga, London might cut its losses and end the war before France could inflict further harm. Washington's army departed Valley Forge on June 20 and began to shadow the British as they marched toward New York, looking for an opportunity to strike.[21]

The Continentals doggedly trudged after the British for nearly a week, covering five or six miles each day in the midst of a severe June heat wave. Marching under a mottled blue sky, with temperatures above 100 degrees by noon, soldiers in both armies suffered terribly and many men fell victim to heatstrokes. On June 26 Sir Henry Clinton, who during the winter had replaced Howe as the commander of Britain's forces in America, paused near Monmouth Court House to await cooler weather. At last, Washington had the chance he had sought. He seized the moment.

During the march across New Jersey, Washington had summoned a council of war to discuss a plan of action. Several officers, led by Charles Lee, opposed any attack, preferring to hazard nothing before the arrival of French aid. Some of the foreign officers, notably von Steuben and the Marquis de Lafayette, advocated an assault. General Greene was between the two poles. He urged a harassing action, lest Washington expose himself to the charge that "our courage faild and we halted without attempting to do the enemy the least injury." Greene's philosophy was always to preserve the army and prolong the war, and Washington always listened to Greene.[22]

Washington later insisted that he intended to provoke a full-scale battle. That may have been his intention when he left Valley Forge, but the evidence suggests that on the eve of the attack Washington, in keeping with his Fabian tactics, merely sought to make "a serious impression without any great risque," as Greene put it. Indeed, on the morning of the engagement Washington spoke of his desire to "harass" Clinton; he wanted to demonstrate the improved quality of the Continental army and prove to the British that they could not defeat their Franco-American adversaries. Washington's caution at Monmouth was a mistake, the first of three major blunders he committed during this enterprise. His sudden chariness was his most surprising error, as it was quite out of character for this man of action who had always been an aggressive risk-taker. In fact, had Washington in this instance moved intrepidly and sealed off Clinton's avenues to a coastal rescue by the Royal Navy, he might have inflicted debilitating damage on his foe. Instead, Washington eschewed the gamble. Several factors led to his decision. His advisors were divided. France's entry into the war appeared to him to promise imminent victory and militated against injudicious riskiness. Finally, because of the alleged winter conspiracy against his command, Washington must have feared another great failure. He committed only 5,500 men to action, about one-third of his army, holding the remainder in the rear for use in the event of an emergency.[23]

Washington's second blunder was his choice of a commander for this operation. After General Lee declined the opportunity to lead the attack—he thought commanding such a small force was beneath the dignity of someone of his rank—Washington passed over two senior officers and offered the post to Lafayette. The Frenchman, only nineteen years old and sporting a major general's commission that he had pried from Silas Deane, had arrived in America a year earlier. He had been merely a captain in the French reserve. Furthermore, not only was he almost devoid of command experience, but Lafayette had never tasted combat until the Battle of Brandywine. Thereafter, he had been in only one small encounter. But Washington was captivated by this young man. Lafayette was sober, industrious, shy, ambitious, eager to learn, committed to republicanism, and courageous, very much as young Colonel Washington had been when, at nearly the same age, he had commanded the Virginia Regiment. It is not unlikely that Washington in fact saw a mirror image of himself when he observed Lafayette. Furthermore, Lafayette, like young Washington, had a facility for winning over older men. Skilled in the arts of ingratiation, Lafayette immediately adapted to the role of Washington's son, much to the satisfaction of the commander.[24] Lafayette exhibited many fine qualities and doubtless was an excellent soldier, but he was not sufficiently experienced to be entrusted with command responsibilities at such a critical moment.

Predictably, Lafayette performed poorly. He led his force on a night march, planning to attack at dawn on June 27. The Frenchman soon lost his way and had no idea of his whereabouts, much less where either Washington or the enemy were situated. Had Clinton discovered what his adversary was up to, and exploited the situation, he might have inflicted an egregious defeat on the Continentals. During the long, restless night Washington received one alarming report after another of Lafayette's blind wandering. He finally deduced what had occurred and rescued his young protégé just as the advance units under the American flag stumbled within a few hundred yards of the British lines. Thereafter, General Lee, probably encouraged by other officers who feared that Lafayette would prove their ruination, suddenly offered to accept the command he had initially spurned. Washington, doubtless relieved to be let off the hook, accepted. However, serious damage had already been done. Near dawn Clinton had discovered Lafayette's blind roving. He did not have time to prepare an attack, but he now knew what Washington intended. Lafayette not only had cost the Americans the element of surprise, but Clinton readied a surprise of his own.[25]

Washington's final mistake was similar to the error he had committed at Brandywine. He sent his army into battle on terrain that had not been properly reconnoitered. As Lee led the American forces toward the British on June 28th, he discovered that his men were crossing a landscape punctuated by two large ravines. A hurried retreat would be stymied by such obstacles. Nor was that the end of Lee's problems. Before he could strike at the British, Clinton suddenly, surprisingly attacked him, and with a numerically superior force.

Lee's left wing, which was commanded by Lafayette, buckled almost immediately. Lafayette ordered a retreat, which exposed the American center under Anthony Wayne to the danger of envelopment. Lee had no choice but to order his entire force to fall back behind the first of the ravines. His retreat assuredly was not born of a disinclination for battle. He was still full of fight, and fashioned a sound plan. He intended to make a stand behind the ravine. However, the French engineer who was assigned responsibility for selecting a proper site, chose terrain that left the British in command of high ground. Lee took a look and ordered a second hurried withdrawal. His intent now was to position his force on an eminence behind the final ravine. Had he not retreated before the British resumed the attack, he almost certainly would have been compelled to fall back during the attack, which could have left his men pinioned against the last ravine.[26]

Around noon Washington learned that Lee was retreating. According to several witnesses, the commander was fuming as he hurried toward the battlefield in search of Lee. Even before he knew what had happened, Washington apparently had already concluded that Lee, who had counseled against a battle, had sabotaged the Continentals' assault. Washington found Lee just beyond the second ravine. A heated discussion occurred, and some observers later said that Washington cursed him. Startled and appalled, Lee for perhaps the first time in his life was speechless. Momentarily, he stammered incoherently, leading some to believe that he had lost control of his wits under the stress of command. When Lee finally recovered sufficiently to explain what had happened, Washington refused to listen. Having worked himself into a purple fury—Jefferson once said that Washington sometimes "got into . . . passions when he [could] not command himself"—the commander removed Lee, sent him to the rear, and assumed command. He then gave the same order that Lee had given. Washington put the army in defensive positions behind the final ravine.[27]

A few minutes later the British assaulted. The battle raged for an hour, often with men fighting, and killing, at close quarters. But the American defenses held until the sun sank, mercifully bringing cooler temperatures and a suspension in the bloodletting. Washington expected another round the next morning, but overnight Clinton took a page from the American's book. He disengaged and fell back, hurrying to the coast, where the Royal Navy fetched his army to New York. The Battle of Monmouth was at an end. Washington sought to put a happy face on the encounter. "We forced the Enemy from the Hill," he trumpeted to Congress. With "Zeal and Bravery," he added, the army had scored a "Victory over the Arms of his Britanick Majesty."[28] In fact, the battle ended indecisively and did nothing to change the course of the war.

Although no one knew it as the blood-red sun set on that brutally hot day, Washington would not command his army in another major engagement against the British for three long years. A golden opportunity had been lost that day in the New Jersey countryside. Just how much had been squandered became evident within a few days. Soon after Clinton unloaded his last soldier in New York City, a French flotilla under Vice Admiral Comte d'Estaing arrived off the New Jersey coast. It consisted of twelve ships of the line and four frigates, and carried 4,000 soldiers. Had Washington contained the British for only a few days, d'Estaing might have prevented their retreat by sea. What was accomplished years later at Yorktown might have occurred in July 1778 in the flatlands about Sandy Hook. This war had taken a bizarre turn. Washington had survived in 1776 because of Howe's excessive caution. Now Clinton may well have survived in 1778 because of Washington's guarded behavior.[29]

Nor was Monmouth the only disappointment that the United States experienced in 1778. Even before leaving the battle site, Washington drafted plans for a Franco-American attack on Manhattan, but the scheme was thwarted when d'Estaing's pilots discovered that the channel in New York was too shallow for the French vessels. Thereafter, Washington and d'Estaing concocted a scheme for flushing the enemy from Newport, Rhode Island, which the British had seized eighteen months earlier. As d'Estaing's fleet drifted to the northeast, Washington wrestled with the choice of a commander for America's ground troops in that operation. Gates coveted the post and, given his rank, record of success, and enormous popularity in New England, should have been chosen. However, Washington named General Sullivan to command the American forces, claiming that he was reluctant to supersede him. Greene offered a better explanation. He candidly acknowledged that Washington was loath to give Gates another shot at glory. Sullivan, whose record included egregious failures at Brooklyn and in Canada, and whom Washington had once characterized as so anxious to succeed that he was wont to act injudiciously, remained in command. Washington dispatched Greene and Lafayette to serve under him. Sullivan and d'Estaing were to besiege Newport, defended by 3,000 British regulars and a slightly superior royal fleet.

The operation's chances appeared promising. Sullivan had started with 1,000 Continentals, but his appeals to the New England states procured 9,000 militiamen, more than the region had committed to Gates before Saratoga. If all went well, these men would be joined by the 4,000 French soldiers in d'Estaing's flotilla. However, the auspicious start to this undertaking soon was literally blown away. Before it saw any action, d'Estaing's fleet was badly damaged by a sudden, violent Atlantic storm, what may in fact have been a late summer hurricane. With numerous vessels impaired, d'Estaing had no choice but to limp into Boston for repairs. Left without a naval arm, Sullivan quickly compounded his difficulties. He imprudently castigated his ally for refusing to leave behind his soldiers to cooperate with the New Englanders and Continentals. Things rapidly fell apart thereafter. The militiamen, disheartened by the disappearance of their powerful ally, deserted in record numbers. Almost 5,000 men in Sullivan's force vanished within a week. Greene wrote Washington that Sullivan's improper behavior was in large measure responsible for the gathering crisis. Lafayette agreed, and pleaded with Washington to hurry to Rhode Island and take command of the army. While their messages were en route to the commander's headquarters, the British emerged from Newport and attacked Sullivan's emaciated force. The beleaguered American army barely escaped.[30]

Washington's worries did not end with Sullivan's narrow deliverance. He was left in what he called a "disagreeable state of suspence" for several days, for Clinton suddenly possessed the means to attempt a *coup de main* against the disabled French fleet in Boston. The new British commander had been presented with a golden opportunity to inflict terrible damage on his vulnerable adversary and at the same time wreak havoc in the city. Clinton considered an attack, but paused until his rare mood for action passed. For the second time within sixty days a commander had let escape an opportunity to score a substantial, perhaps even decisive, victory.[31]

What Clinton did do later that autumn changed the course of the war forever. He abandoned Britain's initial design of achieving victory by suppressing the rebellion in the north, especially in New England, substituting a southern strategy. He had little choice. Clinton saw the futility of attempting to win the war in the northern theater, especially with an army only half the size that Howe had possessed in 1776–1777. In addition, because of the South's close mercantile ties to Great Britain, a large percentage of southerners had remained loyal to the crown. Clinton planned to tap into this residual loyalty, raising and arming Tory regiments in the South, and utilizing them to assist in the pacification of Georgia, the Carolinas, and Virginia. Furthermore, half or more of the inhabitants of the South were slaves. Many of the chattel owned by revolutionaries might be enticed to flee behind British lines, a threat that would likely lure numerous slaveowners into the Loyalist camp. Furthermore, the runaway bondsmen could serve the British army as laborers, teamsters, spies, and farmers.[32]

Clinton commenced his southern strategy in December, just as Washington reentered winter quarters. Two days before Christmas, British regulars disembarked on the marshy Georgia coast. Before sunset on the first day of fighting, the British flag once again flew over Savannah. Within a month Augusta was also in British hands, prompting a regular to boast that the redcoats had taken "the first stripe and star from the rebel flag." Although weeks would pass before Washington learned of Clinton's success, the ebullience he had radiated six months earlier had vanished. His mood once again had plummeted to the darkest depths. In addition to the failures at Monmouth and in Rhode Island, Washington was troubled by two dangerous tendencies that he had observed in 1778. For the first time he saw signs of war weariness spreading across the land. Saratoga had raised hopes too high. When victory and peace did not occur in 1778, a letdown followed. By late 1778 Washington understood what Adams had discovered. The war was likely to continue for a long time. Furthermore, its outcome was no more evident than it had been in 1776. Washington also saw evidence of another dangerous mood that had grown suddenly. A "lax of public virtue" stalked the land, he said, perceiving at last what Adams first had noted two years before. Washington warned of a "general wreck" of the American Revolution unless the nation witnessed the "Spirited exertions of her Sons."[33]

Washington's spirits tumbled throughout 1779. The only good news he heard was that Spain had entered the war against Great Britain. Otherwise, bad omens lurked at every turn. Too many of his countrymen believed that France and Spain would win the war for America, he said that spring, and too many others were "laughing at the impotence" of Great Britain, having mistakenly concluded that London was "on her knees, begging mercy of us."[34] Britain was yet strong, Washington warned. In 1779 Washington had come to see what Adams had seen much earlier. Washington now understood that the greatest threat to the Revolution was posed by Americans themselves. He too believed that a venal, mercenary spirit had seized the populace. A "decay of public virtue," characterized by "Stock jobbing," "avarice," "rapacity," and an "abominable lust of gain" had replaced the mood of sacrifice that had colored the early months of the struggle. In despair, he asked: "Is the paltry consideration of a little dirty pelf to individuals to be placed in competition with the essential rights and liberties of the present generation, and of Millions yet unborn?"[35]

Other problems surfaced during 1779. America's economy verged on total collapse. A "waggon load of money will scarcely purchase a waggon load of provision," Washington remarked in April. A month later he told a Pennsylvania congressman that the crumbling economy posed a greater threat than the British armed forces. In October he confided to a friend that Great Britain might not have to fight to win this war. It could bide its time until the economy of the United States imploded. If the economic woes were not corrected, Washington warned in November, "every other effort is in vain."[36]

Morale suffered as never before. A "general languor . . . has seized the people at large," Washington announced during the summer. Later he spoke of "the extinction of public spirit" as evidenced by the failure of the states to meet their manpower quotas for the Continental army. At mid-year Massachusetts, which faced one of the largest quotas, had dispatched barely thirty percent of its assigned share. Many states had not done that well. Entire battalions "scarcely deserve the name," Washington told Congress, and he added that in an emergency militiamen would greatly outnumber regulars.[37]

Then there was the French fleet. Once the repairs were completed in Boston's shipyards, d'Estaing's flotilla sailed for the West Indies. Washington never saw it again in 1778. Nor did he see it the following year. During the second year of the alliance, as in the first, no Franco-American offensive occurred. In the fall of 1779 Washington was led to believe that d'Estaing was coming north to cooperate with him. He summoned 12,000 militiamen to active duty and waited. But the French fleet never arrived. After thirty days, during which the militiamen stripped the Continentals' pantry bare, Washington sent them home. On the cusp of another winter, Washington now was confronted with the same logistical predicament he had faced on the eve of marching into Valley Forge. D'Estaing meanwhile had not been inactive. He had indeed sailed north from the Caribbean, but instead of joining Washington, he had headed instead for Savannah, where in September he participated in an unsuccessful joint venture to retake that Georgia city. Savannah was of little concern to Washington. He longed to act in concert with the French in New York. A victory there, and virtually only there, he told the French minister to the United States, would be decisive, although he allowed that something useful might be accomplished in Rhode Island. Somehow, somewhere, he told Lafayette, his army and the French navy had to act in concert or civilian morale would erode even further.[38]

Early in 1780 Washington's spirits reached low ebb. He understood that what Adams had initially feared seventeen months earlier had in fact occurred. America's cascading willpower and disintegrating economy had rendered it incapable of winning the war without still more French assistance. Two years after the alliance had been consummated, the United States had grown utterly dependent on France. America could no longer raise an effective army without French economic assistance. Once raised, the Continental army would do nothing unless it was assisted by the French navy. In fact, the American army was so debilitated that even with the support of a French fleet it might no longer be insufficient to score a great victory. Many now believed that France must send an army to America. The United States, Washington declared at the end of 1779, had entered on "a wide and boundless field, puzzled with mazes and o'er spread with difficulties."[39]

Adams soon saw at firsthand what Washington had bemoaned, for much against his will he returned to Braintree from France in the summer of 1779. In mid-February word had arrived in Paris that Congress had named Franklin to be the U.S. minister to France. Adams had anticipated as much, but he thought he would be given a diplomatic assignment, perhaps in Austria, or more likely in Holland, where he could seek recognition and a loan. Instead, Congress had ignored him. Adams was furious, and with good reason. After risking his life crossing the Atlantic, and enduring his lengthiest separation to this point from his wife and three of his children, Congress appeared to have forgotten him. Like Washington a year earlier, he suspected that his reprehensible treatment had been the result of a cabal of his enemies in Congress. Embarrassed and fuming, Adams packed his bags and left Passy. He and John Quincy returned home on *La Sensible*, the same vessel that a year earlier, almost to the day, had brought word of the French alliance to America. The voyage required six weeks, rather long by the standards of the time, but it was a pleasant trip aboard a large and powerful vessel. On August 3 Adams at last glimpsed the familiar sights of Boston harbor, which he had not seen for eighteen months. Before sunset on that mellow afternoon he was home and reunited with Abigail and the children.[40]

Adams thought his diplomatic career had ended almost before it began. He also believed it unlikely that he would ever again hold a national office. However, he did not ignore politics. He had barely unpacked before a Braintree town meeting asked him to serve as its delegate to a Massachusetts constitutional convention scheduled to meet the following month in Cambridge. He accepted and eventually, and almost singlehandedly, authored the draft of the constitution that the convention considered. Adams produced a document that closely resembled the ruminations on government that he had presented to several congressmen in 1776. It was subsequently only slightly altered by the constituent assembly and ultimately ratified by a popular vote. Today, it remains the oldest constitution still in use in the United States.[41]

Adams was not present for the final debates on the constitution. In mid-October he learned that Congress had selected him to be America's sole minister plenipotentiary to negotiate peace with Great Britain at the conclusion of hostilities. Much to the dismay of Abigail, who was loath to endure still another separation from her husband, Adams accepted the appointment on the very day that Congress's message arrived. His acceptance came after what must have been a stormy and painful clash between the Adamses. Abigail believed that she and the children had already paid a heavy price in the public cause. Why, she demanded, must she be called on "so often . . . to struggle" with the pain of losing her spouse? John answered by speaking of sacrifice as a public virtue. He also said that he was serving in order to build a better world for his children and grandchildren. Abigail knew that was true. She also knew that her husband, driven by vanity and ambition, hungered for recognition and the opportunity to achieve immortality. This drive was greater than any other need felt by Adams. Abigail realized that she and her husband were consumed by irreconcilable urges. "Honour and Fame" moved him. "Domestic happiness" was paramount for her, she said. But Adams had his way. Only seventy-one days after disembarking in Boston, Adams, under an ashen autumn sky, reboarded *La Sensible* and sailed again for Paris, leaving behind a wife who thought of herself as a widow, and three children who thought their father a stranger.[42]

Adams had come home convinced that victory was possible only if America's ally made a greater military commitment. By the time he sailed again in November 1779, Adams was positive that France must do more. During his ten weeks at home Adams had seen nothing but parlous omens. The collapsing economy, scarcity of labor, and dearth of drudge animals was ruining New England farms. Boston harbor was nearly empty. From time to time the city's residents suffered from food shortages.[43] Morale was plummeting. It was next to impossible to secure volunteers for the Continental army. He knew it would be no easier in 1780, for just before he sailed he learned not only of d'Estaing's failure to liberate Savannah, but of France's inability to secure control of the English Channel, a requisite step for his ally's invasion of England.

As *La Sensible* weighed anchor, Adams hardly displayed the ebullience that he had radiated on his initial voyage. A dark, pessimistic mood had taken root in him. He knew that the War of Independence was stalemated. He knew too that France would seek to escape this interminable war as soon as it concluded that victory was impossible, leaving an eviscerated America to stand alone once again, or to accept disappointing terms at the peace table. Yet, for all his oppressive gloom, Adams believed that victory was still possible, but only if France and Spain rethought their strategy and objectives. He hoped to persuade the French that while it was unrealistic to believe any longer that territorial concessions in Europe or the Mediterranean might be won from Great Britain, Versailles might yet attain other ends through the successful prosecution of this war. With American independence, France would continue to enjoy a profitable trade with the United States. Furthermore, Britain would be weakened considerably by the loss of its mainland colonies, thus providing greater security for France, and especially its interests in the Caribbean.[44]

Although Washington and Adams believed that victory hinged on French actions, each continued to argue that America could do more to help itself. Each in fact offered the same prescription for the ailing country. The virtuous spirit that had prevailed in 1775–1776 must be rekindled and, as Adams put it, "Foppery . . . Avarice . . . [and] Vanity" banished, or at least restrained. Only "a virtuous few struggle" any longer, Washington acknowledged a week before *La Sensible* cleared Boston harbor, and he added that "virtue and patriotism are almost kicked out" of the United States.[45] In addition, Washington and Adams realized that extraordinary leadership was required in the present crisis. Each lamented the diminution of talent in Congress. Two years earlier Adams had concluded that only five or six truly gifted men remained in Congress. Some talented men had died and a few had been "cutt up into Governors &c," he remarked, but most had resigned to chase after wealth or luxuriate in the comfort of their homes. Washington made the same charge a year later. "[T]oo many of [the] ablest men [have] withdrawn from the general Council for the good of the common weal," he remarked. He wished the best men could be compelled to serve in Congress, just as the physically fit were made to serve in the army. Like Adams, he believed that too many had renounced public service to chase after "their own private emolument." The nation required the services of its "first Statesmen . . . to give energy to the whole." When Washington and Adams thought of men of talent who refused to sacrifice to sustain the American Revolution, each thought of Jefferson.[46]

Adams had written Jefferson as early as 1777 beseeching his return to Congress. Two years later, in March 1779, Washington urged a mutual acquaintance to nudge Jefferson to do more. It was time, the general said bluntly, for patriots to banish their "idleness and dissipation," lest "our . . . noble struggle end in ignominy."[47]

The war was far from Monticello and it was often almost forgotten by Jefferson, except as hostilities affected the completion of his residence. The importation of materials for the house was out of the question and the scarcity of labor brought on by the war had led the few remaining workers to charge exorbitantly for their services. Nevertheless, little by little the house took shape. Jefferson kept some of his slaves at work under the supervision of a brickmason, while other bondsmen toiled under the watchful eyes of the two skilled carpenters who had deserted from the British army.[48]

Jefferson tried not to let the war interfere with his pursuits. One has to search carefully through his correspondence during the crisis-laden year of 1778 to discover that a war was in progress. No evidence exists that he was moved by the tribulations of the soldiery at Valley Forge, angered by the missed opportunity at Monmouth, alarmed at the dangers that faced d'Estaing's crippled fleet, or concerned by Sullivan's narrow escape in Rhode Island. He constructed his house, oversaw the normal farming operations on his estate, put in new gardens, explored ways to obtain salt at Monticello, and engaged in carefree dialogues with correspondents on questions of science and philosophy. When his thoughts turned to national affairs, a pecuniary interest often showed through. For instance, he importuned Congress to explore opening trade with southern Europe, a region he said that might provide cheap "skillful labourers" for American entreprenuers, as well as "important markets for our great commodities," including tobacco. Jefferson was now the titular commander of the Albemarle militia, but there is no indication that he devoted any time to his duties. His biographer, Dumas Malone, noted that Jefferson, almost alone among the men of his time who qualified to be addressed by their military title, was never called "colonel." Malone suggested that this was due to his habitually unmilitary bearing, but it as likely resulted from a reluctance among his acquaintances to debase the title.[49]

"Where is Jefferson?" Some Virginians who soldiered in this war asked that question. Many believed that Jefferson, who was thirty-three when he returned to Monticello following his stint in Congress, shirked his military obligations.[50] If Jefferson's fellow legislators did not condemn his refusal to bear arms, many regarded him as an unenthusiastic assemblyman. Jefferson devoted little time to his legislative duties. He attended fewer than one-quarter of the legislative sessions in the fall of 1778 and spring of 1779; at one point, he left Williamsburg early to return home so that he might have a better vantage point from which to observe a solar eclipse. He was absent so often during the autumn 1779 session that the sergeant-at-arms took him into custody at least twice, compelling him to pay fines to secure his release. When friends nominated him to be speaker of the house in 1778, he was defeated by a three-to-one margin, voted down by colleagues who thought him unsuited for such a responsibility.[51]

It may have been Washington's prodding that caused Jefferson to assume a more active public role. Immediately on learning of Washington's denunciation of those who shirked their duties, Jefferson signaled his willingness to serve as governor. Other factors may also have influenced him. Jefferson was under pressure from numerous influential Virginians "to suffer every thing rather than injure the public cause," as Lee told him in May, to sacrifice for "the rising Generation," as Edmund Pendleton pleaded a few days later. His old friend Judge Fleming candidly remarked to him: "I have heard much, but seen little, of patriotism and public virtue. If there is any remains of it in America, this is the season for calling it forth, and for its utmost exertions."[52] These men pressured Jefferson in the spring of 1779 because Governor Henry's third successive term would end in June and he was ineligible to serve again. They doubtless believed that Jefferson possessed the talent to be an effective governor, and they probably hoped the example set by his re-emergence from the shadows might rekindle the spirit of sacrifice in their countrymen.

Jefferson was aroused as well by the emergency brought on by Clinton's new southern strategy. In May 1779, at the tag end of Henry's administration, a British force of 1,800 men and twenty-eight ships landed on the Virginia coast. It burned Suffolk and occupied Portsmouth. The redcoats wrecked several tobacco warehouses and shipyards, seized or laid waste to numerous large vessels, plundered civilians, liberated nearly 100 Tories and over 500 slaves, and captured so much booty that seventeen ships were required to carry it back to New York. Virginia was plunged into a crisis the likes of which it had not seen in the war. But a great opportunity was at hand as well. As Lee told Jefferson: "If we can baffle the Southern invasion," the "game will be presently up with our enemies."[53]

Very personal reasons may also have persuaded Jefferson to seek the governorship. With Monticello now habitable, his daily supervision of the workers was no longer required. Furthermore, in the spring of 1779 Martha was not pregnant, almost the first time since the day of their marriage more than seven years before that she was well, unencumbered, and able to join her husband in Williamsburg.

Jefferson's election was not assured. On June 1 the assembly balloted and gave him only about one-third of the votes. The remainder were divided between General Thomas Nelson of Yorktown, the commander of the state's militia, and John Page, the lieutenant governor and Jefferson's longtime close friend. On the second ballot Jefferson gained a six-vote majority out of 128 votes cast. Because of the threat of British invasion, most assemblymen preferred a man with military and administrative experience and a person with a proven record of commitment to the daily rigors of a difficult job. Jefferson hardly fit such a description. He was backed by a faction that desired domestic reform and further western expansion. His supporters also were impressed with his striking intellectual capabilities. He ultimately prevailed largely because Page, who had little stomach for running against his old friend, encouraged his supporters to vote for Jefferson.[54]

Whereas Washington and Adams had been eager to serve, to take command and confront new challenges, Jefferson's tone in 1779, and indeed throughout his twenty-four months in office, was that of a man who did not want to be governor and who chafed miserably under the responsibilities that he bore. He confided that he accepted the post because "it would be wrong to decline." After only thirty days in office he wistfully remarked that the "hour of private retirement . . . will be the most welcome of my life." Early in his second term he said that he wanted to quit and return home to write a book on Virginia. Unlike Washington and Adams, who had assumed office at the high

tide of American optimism and confidence, Jefferson took the oath as governor at a time when all America faced crushing problems. Virginia's financial
disarray was as bad as that facing any state. When Jefferson took office,
agents from the state were fecklessly poking around Europe in search of a loan
of £1,000,000. Trade had fallen away, inflation was rampant, and half the
counties were unable to meet their obligations. Virginia's large militia had
performed well during the May invasion—at least 3,000 men had been mus-
tered in the threatened region—but over the long haul it was risky to place
much reliance in the trainbands. The militia was poorly equipped because
much of Virginia's military hardware had been shipped to the Continentals.
In addition, its manpower base was likely to shrink because the state was
under enormous pressure from Congress to bring its eleven battalions in the
Continental army up to full strength.[55]

In virtually every subsequent American war executives have played substantive roles in shaping the course of the conflict, often determining both
strategy and tactics. Neither Jefferson nor any other state governor wielded
such power during the War of Independence, largely because the first state
constitutions had dramatically limited executive authority. The governor of
Virginia was elected by the assembly and existed almost solely to execute legislative enactments that he was powerless to veto. When he had to make a
decision, such as whether to summon the militia to active duty, the governor
was compelled to do so in collaboration with an eight-member Council of
State. Moreover, the governor of Virginia was the executive in a state inhabited by "a People not used to war and prompt obedience," Jefferson once
explained. The chief executive, he added, could only "temporize." In fact, he
could do somewhat more. Governor Henry, a strong, assertive personality
who was immensely popular, induced the assembly to grant him greater latitude in raising and equipping Virginia's soldiery. In the crisis that ensued
when General Howe invaded nearby Pennsylvania in 1777, Governor Henry
relished the opportunity to at last "act with Vigour." Jefferson never asked for
greater authority. He in fact criticized the assembly for having "create[d] a
Dictator" when it complied with Henry's requests, a charge so preposterous
that it calls into question the wisdom of entrusting an important office to a
person of such temperament, especially in this crisis-laden moment.[56]

Although Jefferson was unhappy and unwilling to request greater powers, he was an industrious governor who tended his duties and eschewed the
self-indulgent propensities that had characterized his behavior for the past
several years. He lived alone in miasmic Williamsburg during his first sum-

mer in office, but was joined at the Governor's Palace, where as a youth he had been entertained by Fauquier, by Martha and the girls as soon as the first cool days of autumn arrived. Aside from one hurried trip to Monticello to fetch his family, and another to enjoy a brief holiday at home in August 1780, Jefferson remained at his desk in Williamsburg or Richmond, which became Virginia's new capital late in his first term. He conferred with legislators and other officials, grappled with considerable paperwork, and if the scant surviving record is accurate, met almost daily with his Council of State.[57]

Jefferson took office just after the British invasion force had withdrawn from Virginia, but everyone expected the enemy to come back. The assembly quickly took steps to improve the state's defenses. Tough new laws governing militia service were passed. Cash and land bounties were introduced to entice men to enlist in Virginia's little army, but in the event that volunteerism proved unavailing, conscription was legalized. None of the legislation did much good. At the end of 1779 Jefferson confessed to Washington that "we find it very difficult to secure men." In fact, the state furnished less than one-half its quota for the Continental army.[58]

What role, if any, Governor Jefferson played in shaping these military responses is not clear. However, it is known that he ordered the state Board of War to prepare a plan of defense, and by the end of 1779 Jefferson and the Council had implemented most of its recommendations. Steps were taken to establish armories, procure weapons, powder, and equipment, find workers for the shipyards, erect coastal batteries, appoint express riders and coastal sentinels, and even to prepare vessels to house British prisoners of war.

However, Jefferson failed to heed the Board of War's recommendation in one key area. The Board exhorted the governor to immediately appoint "at this critical juncture a General Officer ... to direct such military operations as circumstances may call forth." Jefferson, the commander-in-chief with constitutional authority to muster the militia, clearly had the authority to comply, but he was extraordinarily cautious. He took the position that he possessed the constitutional authority to appoint a military commander only after an invasion actually occurred. He also proved hesitant to summon the militia. When word arrived from Washington just before Christmas in 1779 that another British invasion was imminent, Jefferson refused to act until he had secured legislation that permitted him to mobilize the militia and post it at designated locations in the state. In this instance, Jefferson's caution spared Virginia's taxpayers, for the British target proved to be Charleston, not the Chesapeake. The one thing Jefferson possessed absolute power over was his pen, but he did not use it during this crisis. His Declaration of Independence and Thomas Paine's *American Crisis,* which had appeared during the dark days of late 1776, had stirred deep emotions. Jefferson might have mobilized his literary talents in this emergency to arouse a people unused to the suffering spawned by war, but no ringing pronouncements issued from the governor's office.[59]

Once it was clear that the British objective was Charleston, Jefferson sent an artillery regiment and a small detachment of cavalry to South Carolina, then turned to resolving Virginia's economic woes, which he believed posed a more serious threat than British arms. Governor Jefferson's immediate object was to raise a revenue. With George Mason serving as his legislative leader, Jefferson obtained legislation that abolished Virginia's historic headright system, under which the affluent had obtained free land during the past 150 years. Virginia's western lands would now have to be purchased. It was a step that General Washington counseled against; he feared—correctly as events proved—that cheap western land would induce thousands of Virginians to set out for the frontier, depleting the state's manpower pool without raising much revenue. The assembly also reformed the tax code. Not only was a poll tax levied on slaves, but property was subjected to new evaluations. Finally, Jefferson drafted, and the assembly passed, legislation that enabled the state to seize Tory properties; Virginia raised more than $3,000,000 through the confiscation and sale of Loyalist estates.[60]

However, Jefferson's initiatives failed to solve Virginia's fiscal problems. Traditionally, the state's revenue had been derived almost entirely from commerce, but Great Britain's naval blockade impaired the tobacco trade from 1776 onward. Jefferson was powerless to challenge the Royal Navy. In fact, Virginia could not even sell tobacco to its neighbors; a drought plagued the state throughout 1779, resulting in what Jefferson called the worst harvest that planters had ever experienced. At the end of his first term, Jefferson reported that "our trade has been almost annihilated." The state's printing press operated day and night churning out currency, although each new dollar was less valuable than its predecessor. Inflation soared to unprecedented levels, compelling Jefferson to pay late twentieth-century prices for bonnets that he purchased for Martha and his daughters, and for new shoes for himself.[61]

Like every governor, Jefferson faced constitutional restraints and economic maladies that made his job more difficult. Nevertheless, he waged war over a vast territorial expanse. While Virginia prepared for another British invasion in the east, its soldiers were also fighting in the remote west. The state had committed an army to the frontier in the fall of 1776 after the Cherokees—who had been armed by the British—attacked backcountry settlements from Georgia northward into Virginia. One of the loudest voices urging retaliation had been that of Jefferson, who demanded that the Cherokees be expelled from their ancestral lands east of the Mississippi River. Virginia's inevitable counterattack succeeded. Acting in concert with soldiers from the Carolinas and Georgia, Virginia's army destroyed numerous villages and brought the Indians to heel. In July 1777 the Cherokees not only ceded thousands of acres in present Virginia and West Virginia, but pledged their neutrality for the duration of the Anglo-American war.[62]

That quick victory whetted the appetite of those who hungered for further western adventures. Six months after the Cherokees capitulated, the assembly authorized Governor Henry to send an army into the Ohio country. The action was prompted by intelligence reports that Britain had concentrated its forces to protect Detroit, leaving present Ohio, Kentucky, Indiana, and Illinois poorly defended. Those same reports also suggested that the French-Canadian inhabitants in the northwest would welcome the Virginians, who soon were to be allied with France, as liberators. Thus, while Washington's men shivered and starved at Valley Forge, Henry appointed George Rogers Clark to lead a force of 350 men into present Indiana and Illinois.

On the day Jefferson observed the solar eclipse from his mountaintop estate, Clark set out from near the current Cincinnati with an army about one-half the size he had been authorized to raise. He succeeded beyond all expectations. Before the summer ended, Clark had conquered British outposts at Vincennes and Kaskaskia. Early in 1779 he not only repulsed a British counterattack, but captured its leader, Lieutenant Colonel Henry Hamilton, the royal governor of Detroit. Hamilton, whom Clark, and soon every Virginian, called the "Hair-Buyer" because of his role in arming Indians who scalped their victims, was perhaps the most despised British official in America. The frontier inhabitants thought him solely responsible for having incited the Native Americans in the Northwest. Clark sent his famous prisoner, and twenty-six other captives, under guard to Williamsburg. The prisoners arrived in the capital two weeks after Jefferson's inauguration.[63]

No other British officer who fell captive was made to suffer as Colonel Hamilton was. Governor Jefferson flung him into the dank Williamsburg jail, where he was shackled in eighteen pounds of iron, denied the opportunity to converse with the other prisoners or even correspond with his family or British officials. Hamilton soon was so emaciated that he could slip his hands and wrists in and out of his irons at will. Jefferson was not solely responsible for this outrage. The brutal terms of Hamilton's confinement were consented to by the Council, but Jefferson's contemporary comments leave no doubt that he approved of Hamilton's treatment. The illiberal and medieval usage that Jefferson imposed on Hamilton, like the prescriptive and harsh criminal code that he had recently drafted as a "reform" measure, is a dark stain on his character and reputation as a humane and enlightened person.[64]

Emotion—the heart, as Jefferson liked to say—had triumphed over reason. Jefferson did not hate all British officials, as his close relationship with many officers interred near Monticello indicates. However, his loathing for Colonel Hamilton knew no bounds. Perhaps because he had grown up near the frontier, and was the son of a man who had frequently lived and worked in Indian territory, Jefferson was keenly sympathetic toward the western inhabitants who fell victim to what he called the "barbarity practiced by the Indian savages." He genuinely hated Hamilton, whom he thought responsible for unleashing the "cruel and cowardly warfare of the savage." Jefferson was blind to evidence of outrages committed by frontier settlers and could find no justifiable explanation for the assistance that London provided to the Indians who were defending their homeland.[65]

Jefferson agreed to soften Hamilton's treatment only when General Washington protested. The commander initially applauded Jefferson's behavior, but on reflection Washington, who had been treated quite liberally by his captors at Fort Necessity, concluded that it was wrong to treat Hamilton with "uncommon severity." He recommended that he be placed under house arrest while attempts were made to secure his exchange. Washington saw the matter in broader terms than Jefferson. He not only understood that the British reaped a propaganda bonanza from Hamilton's shameful treatment, but feared British retaliation on American prisoners. Early on, Washington also saw the opportunity to exchange Hamilton for Virginians who had endured lengthy captivities as prisoners of war. When Washington first expressed misgivings, Jefferson immediately removed Hamilton's irons, but would go no further. Hamilton languished in despicable circumstances in his Williamsburg cell for thirteen months. In August 1780 he was sent to a more commodious facility in Chesterfield County. Finally, in the spring of 1781, he was exchanged.[66]

Jefferson probably gave little thought to Hamilton's plight during the winter and spring of 1780. The British invasion of South Carolina occupied his attention. Washington urged Jefferson to send assistance to beleaguered

Charleston, telling him that there had never been a moment in this war when the southern states needed to do more. Jefferson acted with dispatch, then told the commander that he had sent "all the little aid in our power."[67] That was not quite true. The assembly had granted Jefferson considerable discretionary powers in responding to the crisis further south. He was authorized to send up to 1,500 militiamen, and several hundred state troops, to assist in the defense of Charleston, but he dispatched only about twenty percent of those who could have been sent. They did not set off until weeks after word of the emergency in South Carolina reached the governor's desk.

Jefferson was not solely responsible for Virginia's inadequate response. The war on the frontier siphoned off the state's soldiery, which hampered recruiting. Logistical problems compelled Virginia to proceed slowly, until it was more or less able to supply the men it raised. Furthermore, Jefferson, aware that Virginia had already been the target of one sizeable British raid, had to be ready to meet any emergency that arose at home. Ultimately, Virginia was fortunate to have committed so few troops, for Charleston—besieged by naval and land forces that possessed a two-to-one numerical superiority over the city's defenders—was doomed by the time Washington's plea reached Williamsburg. In mid-May, just as the advance units that Jefferson had dispatched were nearing the hopeless city, Charleston fell. The United States lost over 5,500 men in the campaign.[68]

The deteriorating military situation had grown vastly darker and more gloomy. Savannah and Charleston were in British hands. The pacification of all South Carolina seemed at hand. Once that state was secured, it would be North Carolina's turn and, when it was subdued, the British would surely muscle into Virginia. Jefferson now feared the worst. "North Carolina is without arms [and] We do not abound with weaponry," he anguished, as news of the debacle in Charleston arrived in Richmond. "There is really nothing" but the militia, which he had always regarded as undependable, "to oppose the progress of the enemy Northward," he sighed. Nor was that all. The defeat at Charleston, Madison reminded Jefferson, was not only "disgraceful" to Americans, it was certain to be "disgustful to our Allies."[69] The same question was on everyone's mind: How would France respond to the ominous tidings from America?

No one worried more than Adams about what the French might do in this seemingly endless war. Adams had sailed for France in November 1779, just as Washington alerted Governor Jefferson about the likelihood of a British invasion in the Chesapeake. His second Atlantic crossing was an augury of the difficulties that lay ahead. The first journey had been long and precarious. His second trip was rapid, but filled with even greater peril. Eleven days into the cruise, *La Sensible* was struck by a savage storm that terrified the passengers for three interminable days. Soaked to the skin and unable to eat, Adams was confined to his unlit cabin for the duration of the gale. When the tempest at last ended and the ship could be inspected, it was discovered that the vessel had sustained heavy damage. Dangerous amounts of water were remorselessly seeping in below deck. For the next two weeks each passenger, including Adams, took his turn manually operating pumps during four daily shifts. Only by that expedient could the ship remain afloat. Their toil in the dark, damp oubliette below was rewarded. Although too damaged to risk running the gauntlet of Royal Navy frigates near France, the ship limped safely into port in Spain a few days before Christmas. Soon thereafter Adams, together with eight other Americans, including his sons John Quincy and eleven-year-old Charles, commenced a thirty-day journey by mule over treacherous mountain roads. Often the party lodged at night with residents who lived in rude huts along the route, sleeping in beds infested with fleas and lice. Once across the French border, the weary travelers faced an additional ten days of travel via chaise in gloomy winter weather.[70]

Almost ninety days after leaving home, Adams alighted in Paris. Good news awaited him. France not only had sent naval reinforcements to America, but it had dispatched an army of 5,500 men under Comte de Rochambeau to assist Washington. Adams's gloom vanished in a flash. He once again felt that victory was at hand. He believed that France's resolve would induce other maritime powers to act against Great Britain, and he prayed it would rejuvenate the peace faction in England. Mostly, however, Adams anticipated a vigorous military campaign in 1780 that would destroy Clinton's army.[71]

Adams's bubble began to burst after only three days in Paris. Believing that the British peace faction would be strengthened if word of his mission was made public, he asked Foreign Minister Vergennes's consent to inform the British ministry of his powers to engage in peace negotiations. Vergennes coldly refused. He lectured Adams that such an announcement would lead Whitehall, the British foreign ministry, to conclude that the Allies were desperate for peace, a surmise that would only stabilize the North ministry. Adams, who had also been directed by Congress to seek an urgent loan from the Dutch, next applied for a passport to travel to the Netherlands. Once again, Vergennes refused, offering an implausible excuse. What the French really feared, and Adams suspected, was that the American envoy might succeed at The Hague, provoking Great Britain to declare war against Holland. An Anglo-Dutch war, which would adversely affect French commerce, was the last thing Versailles wished. The conflict between American and French interests had never before seemed so apparent, or so dangerous, to Adams.[72]

Left with no official responsibilities, Adams nevertheless remained busy. He wrote numerous anonymous essays for a weekly Paris newspaper, *Mercure de France*, propaganda pieces designed to counter British efforts to undermine support for the war among Parisians.[73] In addition, he dispatched essays to known foes of the war in England, who in turn had them published in anti-ministerial newspapers. None too discreetly, Adams used this medium to surreptitiously reveal to British readers the purpose of his mission, an act that was not lost on the French foreign minister.

Late in the spring, when he learned of the pamphleteering of Joseph Galloway, Adams once again called on the assistance of friends in London. Galloway, who had attended the First Continental Congress as a representative from Pennsylvania, turned Tory and defected late in 1776. Before fleeing to exile in London, he served the British as an intelligence official and police commissioner of occupied Philadelphia in 1777–1778. By 1780 Galloway was turning out pamphlets at a feverish pace in an effort to maintain Britain's resolve to continue the war. Adams believed that this challenge could not be permitted to go unanswered. Writing under the pseudonym "Probus," he responded with one essay after another. Adams maintained that France, Spain, and the United States, blessed with greater resources than Great Britain, could hold out longer. He sought to convince London of the futility of its attempt to reassert authority over the former colonies. Americans would never again submit to British rule, he asserted. British attempts to exercise hegemony would result in never-ending American rebellions and ceaseless costly wars. Britain was doomed to fail. America had the advantages of youth on its side. Its power was growing rapidly, while an aging Britain was declining. But it was not pugnacity that lay at the core of Adams's message. More than anything, he sought to reassure London about its relationship with the United States in the postwar era. The United States, wishing only peace and prosperity, he declared, would not fight in European wars on the side of any nation. Furthermore, wrote Adams, Britain could coexist and prosper through free trade with an independent America.[74]

While Adams churned out these essays, uniformly bad news trickled into the French capital. Although Rochambeau arrived safely in Rhode Island, the

French fleet, now larger and more formidable, once again sailed for the West Indies. Even before the last jonquil gave way to Paris's late spring flowers, Adams knew that Washington's Continentals and the French regulars would be inactive throughout the summer of 1780. This would be the third campaign season since the conclusion of the French alliance and, like its predecessors, it too would witness no decisive allied victories. More bad news followed. First, Adams learned that the Royal Navy had recently scored a great victory over the Spanish fleet blockading Gibraltar. Alarm spread in Paris that Spain soon would make peace. Adams had to wonder whether France would remain at war without a European ally. Next, just as Paris basked in the first warm days of spring, Adams received the initial dire tidings of the campaign for Charleston. He knew that if South Carolina was conquered, as Georgia had been during the previous year, American prestige would plunge and all hope would be dashed that any European neutrals might enter the war against Great Britain. Already, in fact, informants in England were telling him that Clinton's vigorous action in the south had stimulated hope in London that the rebellion would be smashed. The English peace movement, which had appeared so promising in 1778 and 1779, now languished.[75]

While Britain's will to fight grew stronger, Adams received fresh evidence from correspondents at home that war weariness was spreading. It was fed by a growing skepticism whether this war could be won. Some, anticipating a worsening military situation, believed that the optimum moment for securing favorable peace terms had arrived. The most disturbing tidings came from Arthur Lee, who returned home in the summer of 1780. From Boston, where he disembarked, Lee wrote that the mood was growing that America's military and economic woes might soon result in an "inevitable necessity to [reach] an accommodation" short of independence. Adams remembered only too well that many in Congress in 1776 had resisted independence. Nor did he doubt that these "artful" sorts, as he labeled the reconciliationists, yet lurked in the dark corners of American politics, waiting and hoping to seize the first opportunity to negotiate peace and return America to the British empire.[76]

Adams heard and saw much that also convinced him that the French government likewise was growing war-weary. He knew that France's involvement in this war had resulted in mushrooming economic problems. He knew as well that Vergennes had pressed Congress to reduce its territorial ambitions in Canada and the West, and to renounce its claims to the Newfoundland fisheries, and he suspected that the foreign ministry had taken that step in order to make a negotiated peace more palatable to Great Britain. Had Adams been privy to what was being said behind closed doors at Versailles, his concern would have ballooned into hysteria. The French economics minister feared collapse and urged Louis XVI to end the war. Vergennes, who did not wish to fight on without a European ally, was aware that Spain would almost certainly drop out of the war after 1781. He knew too that if the Franco-American allies did not soon gain victory, France likewise would have to consider leaving the war and accepting the best possible peace terms.[77]

Adams correctly believed that France wished to fight on to compel Great Britain to recognize American independence. It not only wanted America to be its postwar commercial partner, but it wished to permanently strip Great Britain of its ties to its former mainland colonies. But Adams also believed, once again correctly, that France would not be unhappy if the independent United States was shorn of the fisheries, the transmontane west, and perhaps even one or two southern states. Such a United States would be too weak to stand alone. Nor would it be truly independent. Of necessity, it would be a French vassal. More than any other American diplomat or statesman, Adams divined French intentions. He saw clearly that Vergennes aspired to "Keep us poor. Depress Us. Keep Us weak. Make Us feel our Obligations. Impress our Minds with a Sense of Gratitude."[78]

Knowing that France had not yet reached the breaking point, what Adams most feared was that Europe's neutral nations, weary of having their trade violated by both the French and British navies, would offer a mediation proposal that would result in an international conference. Adams saw the danger. Not only would this provide France the face-saving mechanism it required for exiting the war, but a peace conference was certain to be preceded by an armistice. Adams knew full well that his war-weary countrymen would never resume fighting once a cease-fire took hold. "We are in a safer way at war," he said. "If we go out of it we may be lost."

There were other dangers too. Europe's monarchical states could not be expected to be charitable toward a republican people who, as Paine had declared in Common Sense, hoped to set an example for the oppressed round the world. In addition, in a mediated settlement the major territorial issues might be resolved on the basis of uti possidetis. That is, each belligerent would retain what it possessed at the moment of the armistice. If such terms took hold in the autumn of 1780 the independent United States could be denied Canada, Nova Scotia, the fisheries, upper Maine, Georgia, much if not all of South Carolina, portions of New York, and most, perhaps all, of the trans-Appalachian lands. If France accepted peace on such terms, the United States would face a choice of agreeing to independence on malodorous conditions or of fighting on alone and risking defeat and the reinstitution of British hegemony. Little wonder that Adams said he dreaded "a truce ten times more" than a continuation of the war.[79]

Two months after he reached Paris, in the early summer of 1780, Adams, like Washington, had concluded that the time of greatest peril had arrived in the War of Independence. The course of the war had to change or potential disaster confronted the United States. However, if Washington lacked the power to break the stalemate, Adams appeared to have even less capability of impacting the course of the war. He was trapped in France and had not been in contact with Vergennes since the week of his arrival.

Then, suddenly, on June 21 Vergennes wrote to Adams. Mystery, and a patina of deviousness, shrouded Vergennes's action, as he approached Adams about monetary policy, not diplomatic concerns.[80] Ordinarily, the foreign minister would have consulted with the U.S. minister to France about such a matter. It is possible that Vergennes simply believed that Adams, who had served in Congress much longer than Franklin, would have a better understanding of congressional policies. However, Vergennes's penchant for Byzantine, and often devious, practices invites skepticism. With France looking longingly toward peace negotiations, Vergennes naturally would have desired a compliant American envoy. Adams clearly was not such a person. Vergennes was only too aware that Adams had defied him by revealing the purpose of his mission in London newspapers. He suspected too that in 1778 Adams had been the instigator behind the American commissioners' expression of displeasure with French military efforts. Vergennes had still another reason for wishing to be rid of Adams. He had been informed by the French minister in Philadelphia that Adams had been a member of a pro-British party in the American Congress that secretly fancied a separate peace with Great Britain. The tale was preposterous, but Vergennes accepted it.[81] Thus, there is reason to suspect that he approached Adams with the first available issue in the hope that the American minister plenipotentiary would respond in a self-destructive fashion, affording the French foreign minister the opportunity to tell Congress that he could not work with Adams.

If Vergennes was baiting Adams, the envoy did not at first fall into the trap. He prudently confined his reply to Vergennes to the monetary issues raised by the foreign minister. However, almost immediately after dispatching his response, Adams received two important pieces of information, one dark and foreboding, the other containing the barest possibility of hope. First he learned of the egregious American defeat at Charleston, news that was much worse than he had expected. It came as a "rude shock," he told Jefferson, for he knew that South Carolina now lay open to British conquest. A day or two later Adams received tidings that brought a glimmer of hope. He learned that London had been rocked for ten days by massive riots early in June. The disturbances came hard on the heels of a bruising debate in the House of Commons on a resolution to limit the monarch's power and by implication—at least in the minds of some members of Parliament—to end the war in America. Considerable property damage had occurred. The British ruling elite emerged badly shaken by the disturbances.[82]

Adams was convinced that he must act, and act boldly. He believed that the Gordon Riots, as the London commotions were called, had made it imperative that France formally announce his mission and make a public commitment to do more toward winning the war. Each, or both, might stimulate the British peace movement, he believed. Furthermore, the deteriorating military situation confronted Adams with the very real likelihood that his countrymen's dreams for the American Revolution would be shattered unless something was done immediately to enable Washington and Rochambeau to take the offensive. When Vergennes responded to his communiqué concerning fiscal matters, Adams decided, probably much as the French foreign minister had hoped he would, to undertake a dangerous gamble. Adams knew that he had no authority to approach the French government with impassioned entreaties. He risked angering Vergennes, even hazarded his recall and the destruction of his reputation. Adams gambled because he was convinced that time was running out and no one else, least of all Franklin, would confront the foreign minister.

Adams dispatched several letters to Vergennes over the next month. From the outset he stressed his commitment to the French alliance. He called it a "rock of defense" for the United States, spoke of his "great confidence in the sincerity of France," and pledged never to make a separate peace with Great Britain. Then he got down to business. Adams passed along intelligence, obtained from his sources in London, that Great Britain intended to enlarge its army in the United States in 1781. He insisted that London would never consider peace until its military forces had been utterly defeated in America. A victory over British arms either in New York or in the South would compel London to end the war, but he stressed that Washington and Rochambeau would go on the offensive only when they could act in concert with the French navy. He contended that any allied military activity would strengthen the peace faction in England. His most dangerous gambit was to advise that if his countrymen concluded that France was not doing all it could to win the war, the reconciliationists in America might regain control of Congress and restore the Anglo-American union.[83]

After Adams's fifth letter in July, Vergennes broke off the correspondence, but not until he had flayed the envoy for his brazen conduct. Henceforth, he said, he would deal only with Franklin. Vergennes then took two steps of which Adams was unaware. He secretly launched a campaign to have Adams removed as minister plenipotentiary. He directed his minister in Philadelphia to lobby Congress for Adams's recall. He also enlisted the services of Franklin in securing the removal of Adams. Vergennes passed on to Franklin his recent correspondence with Adams, requesting that he transmit it to Congress. Franklin, who had never displayed much pluck with Vergennes, not only complied, but apologized for Adams's behavior. He then wrote Congress that "Mr. Adams has given Offence to the Court here." Without a shred of evidence to warrant such a remark, Franklin even told Congress that Adams had sown the impression that the United States sought reconciliation with Great Britain. Vergennes's second step came a few weeks later. He did what Adams had requested. He secured the dispatch of additional warships to North America, with orders to the Comte de Grasse, the commander of the French fleet, to proceed north if he believed he could not succeed in the West Indies.[84]

Vergennes disliked Adams, but he feared him more than he hated him. He knew that Adams had fathomed the postwar aims of France. He was aware that Adams was a fiercely independent man who could not be manipulated. Adams, he knew, would accept nothing less than the peace terms that Congress had instructed him to secure. Adams would never surrender to Versailles. To Vergennes, who hoped to end the war quickly on terms satisfactory to France, Adams constituted a danger. He had to be removed.

As the hot, humid summer of 1780 neared an end, Jefferson understood—seemingly for the first time—the great peril that the United States faced, but even so he did not fully grasp the magnitude of the crisis as did Washington and Adams. He still blindly trusted France, whereas Adams, and Washington to a growing degree, were better versed in the realities of national self-interest. Jefferson yet spoke of the "disinterested exertions of France for us," and even remarked that "What is best for [France] is best for us also." Although

Jefferson understood his country's economic woes and admitted that Virginia faced the "utmost distress" in its attempts to raise and supply a military force, an air of unreality sometimes characterized his outlook concerning the potential threats to Virginia and the United States. Washington and Adams knew that American morale was disintegrating, yet Jefferson continued to believe that the will of the citizenry remained "unshaken." Furthermore, although the Continentals had failed to save Charleston, Jefferson was dreamily assured that a new American force, commanded by Horatio Gates and posted in South Carolina, could keep the British regulars out of Virginia.[85]

Adams saw events in a dark, yet clearer, light, and risked a career that he had painstakingly, and painfully, constructed since 1773. Rebuffed and castigated by Vergennes, he told Franklin that "something must . . . be done to render us less dependent on France." His solution was to strike out for Holland, which was made possible when the French government at long last granted him the passport he had sought for six months. As he traveled for Amsterdam, Adams noted in his diary his conviction that it was the goal of France to "Let Europe see our dependence" and to discourage "other nations . . . from taking our Part." Adams was ready to exert every fiber of energy in his body to break America's dependence on France and to bring Holland and other neutral states into the war.[86]

Washington shared Adams's concerns and attempted to persuade Jefferson of the magnitude of the danger. Virginia must do more to defeat the British in South Carolina, he wrote the governor in August. The "absolute safety and existence of America demands it," he lectured. If Virginia did not do more, and if a negotiated settlement ended the war, Americans would face the "loss of our liberties and Independence." Washington sounded the same theme as Adams. He too stressed that America could not rely entirely on France. It must fight this war as if it no longer had an ally. "The politics of Princes are fluctuating, more guided often by a particular prejudice, whim, or interest," he warned Congress. "The change or caprice of a single minister is capable of altering the whole system of Europe."[87]

Adams saw promise in Holland. He was cheered too by France's greater naval commitment. Washington discerned hope as well. "The fairest prospects are held out to us," he wrote in August 1780, but he cautioned that America must seize the opportunity within the next year. Thereafter, it will never again have the chance to win the war. He expected the army to be depleted at year's end as the earliest long-term enlistments expired. Soldiers, he said, "will have every motive except mere patriotism to abandon the Service." Congress must attempt to keep these men in the army and, at the same time, raise a new army of long-term volunteers and conscripts. America had multitudinous problems and faced manifold dangers, but Washington knew that Great Britain faced difficulties as well. Merely keeping the Continental army intact might be enough to force London to end the war, he counseled, but if the army melted away as it had in 1775 and 1776, "it would be the strongest temptation they [the British] could have to try the experiment a little longer." Furthermore, if the army dissolved, the hope of French support would be lost. However, Washington's emphasis was on victory. With a strong Continental army, and with Rochambeau's men at last on American soil, the possibility of an American triumph loomed as had not been the case for two long years. Yet Washington, like Adams, knew that the United States was at the crossroads. What occurred in the coming military season, in the twelve months beginning in the autumn of 1780, would decide the outcome of the war and the fate of the American Revolution.[88]

8

"The Womb of Fate"

Victory

In the summer of 1780, when Adams told Vergennes that the war could be won only if the French fleet acted in concert with the armies of Washington and Rochambeau, the French foreign minister had seen matters differently. He placed much of the blame for the military stalemate on General Washington. Writing to Lafayette, Vergennes revealed his unhappiness at "the inactivity of that American Army who before the alliance had distinguished themselves by their spirit of enterprise." Not only was Washington's army doing nothing, he said with some heat, but each year it somehow managed to consume more *livres* than would have been devoured by a French army four times its size. The foreign minister grumbled that he now had only "feeble confidence" in the ability of Washington and the United States to wage the war with zeal and energy.[1]

Three days after Adams sent his last communiqué to Vergennes, General Washington acknowledged to Congress that there is "a total stagnation of military business." He attributed his inactivity to the absence of the French navy, but added that he could do nothing because only 6,000 of the 16,500 men whom Congress had sought to raise that year were under arms.[2]

Washington had a point, but so did Vergennes. The American commander had grown cautious since the Valley Forge winter. Once the alliance was consummated, Washington was unwilling to risk his army when the likelihood existed that he soon would be able to act in concert with the French. In 1779 he had ordered daring, but small-scale assaults, as when he sent crack troops under General Wayne to assault the British post at Stony Point above New York City. The only large campaign that he approved that year was against the Indians on the New York frontier, an operation that he assigned to General Sullivan. These initiatives produced some successes, but they were designed as much to bolster public morale as to substantively affect the course of the war. Washington was even less active in the first half of 1780. At the beginning of the year he had learned that a French army was being sent to America. He decided to embark on no adventures prior to its arrival.

However, caution is only a partial explanation for Washington's behavior after Monmouth. He had grown obsessed with driving the British from New York. He posted his army near the city and waited, and hoped, that the allied forces might launch joint operations against New York. He turned a blind eye toward every alternative. Washington had become convinced that a great victory in New York—and probably only in New York—could end the war. He was tied to the belief that wars almost always ended with a great climactic victory.

That often had been true both in Europe and America, as when the British victory at Quebec in 1759 determined the outcome of the French and Indian War. Thinking along these lines was not new for Washington. He had objected to Dinwiddie's "string of forts" concept in the 1750s, arguing relentlessly for a decisive assault against Fort Duquesne. Washington's fixation on the theme of scoring a climactic victory underscores his shortcomings as a strategist. He had wisely embraced a Fabian strategy in 1776 and 1777, but once the Franco-American alliance was consummated, and he possessed a more veteran army, Washington reverted to his original notion of hoping to risk everything on one grand, dramatic showdown with a large enemy force. He no longer seemed to understand the wisdom behind fighting a war of attrition. Moreover, when Great Britain shifted to a southern strategy after 1778, he appeared incapable of devising a realistic response.[3] His unremitting focus on New York was a blind spot that prompted Jefferson, who otherwise never criticized Washington, to complain. While the "Northern States are safe" and "our Enemies have transferred every expectation from that Quarter" to the South, Governor Jefferson cried out in exasperation, Washington remained in the North, his gazed locked on New York. Jefferson equated Washington's compulsion to retake New York with Spain's undying preoccupation with Gibraltar, and he predicted that the American commander would be no more successful than the Spanish.[4]

There can be no doubt that Washington faced multitudinous problems after 1778. Nevertheless, alternatives existed to the course he pursued. One option was to have resisted the British invasion of the South. Prior to the arrival of the French army in mid-1780, Washington might have proposed to Congress that the militia in the northern states be mobilized to confine the small British army that occupied New York City, as New England's soldiery had contained General Gage's army in Boston in the months that followed Lexington and Concord. Or, after August 1780, the French army could have been utilized to that end. Washington could then have led his regulars into the southern theater. After his experience in the New York campaign of 1776, Washington knew better than to gamble everything on the defense of Charleston. However, he might have campaigned in the interior of the Carolinas, where the British army would have derived little or no benefit from the Royal Navy. Furthermore, Washington's Continentals might have drawn assistance from southern partisans, who later emerged and fought effectively after the British army plunged into the backcountry. Indeed, ragtag bands of New Englanders had demonstrated on the first day of the war in 1775 how much damage could be inflicted on regulars who ventured into an inhospitable country, a lesson that New York frontiersmen provided anew during Burgoyne's invasion in 1777.

Washington had a second option. He might have urged a campaign to take Canada, a course that had widespread support as early as 1778. Soon after his victory at Saratoga, General Gates had sent scouts to Canada and determined that the region was poorly defended. Thereafter, Gates became the principal advocate of the Canadian option. After France entered the war, he produced intelligence reports indicating that the French-Canadian inhabitants, who had refused to aid the American invaders in 1775–1776, would now provide assistance. Gates further argued that this invasion, unlike the initial attempt three years earlier, would be undertaken by veteran soldiers who were better supplied than their predecessors, for much of their equipment would be supplied by France. Finally, Gates stressed that success in Canada would neutralize the Indians along much of the northern frontier, and perhaps even in the Ohio country, for they were armed by the British in Canada. With considerable insight, he maintained that military success in Canada would remove the need for campaigns such as Sullivan's expedition against the Iroquois in 1779, ventures that were costly and seldom terribly successful. As with most wartime operations, there were attendant risks to an invasion of Canada, the chief being that failure would further erode America's will to continue. Yet success might end the war, either by toppling the North ministry or by furnishing the United States with a bargaining chip it could use to gain independence and other concessions from London. In 1778 both the Board of War and Congress endorsed an invasion of Canada. In January 1779 Congress once again called for a Canadian invasion.[5]

However, Washington, who early in the war had expressed his desire to "run all risques," not only counseled against an invasion, but fought tenaciously to prevent such an enterprise. He argued that a Canadian campaign would result in manpower shortages in the Highlands, the Hudson River area above Manhattan Island, exposing that vital region to the risk of British seizure. He predicted that both the vastness of the Canadian countryside and logistical difficulties would inevitably doom a Canadian enterprise, as had occurred during the first invasion in 1775. He warned that French participation in such a campaign might result in France's eventual reacquisition of Canada. He painted a picture of a postwar world in which Spain was "possessed of New Orleans, on our Right" while France held "Canada on our left," and both were "seconded by numerous tribes of Indians on our Rear." This was a vision of a postwar world in which the independent United States not only was encircled, much as the colonies had been prior to 1763, but friendless and isolated. Swayed by his objections, Congress vetoed the project.[6]

Many of the qualms raised by General Washington in 1778–1779 were chimerical. Militia units might have successfully guarded the Highlands, as they had in 1777, when Gates fought further to the north and Washington campaigned before Philadelphia. Furthermore, vast expanses of Canada need not have been conquered. The conquest of Quebec would have won the campaign. Washington's fears of France's reacquisition of Canada were phantasmal. The invasion plan that Congress envisioned was for an American army, unassisted by the French, save for a handful of volunteer officers such as Lafayette, to undertake the operation; in fact, Rochambeau's army was not even in America, and would not arrive for nearly eighteen months, when Congress proposed this alternative. It required a great leap of imagination to believe that Canada, acquired by U.S. blood and muscle, would somehow be lost to France following the war. Moreover, Adams, who had an excellent understanding of French war aims, knew that Versailles had no desire to regain Canada, and had communicated this knowledge to Congress. As Adams suspected, and as is now known, Vergennes hoped that Great Britain would retain Canada. The French foreign minister understood that if France possessed Canada, America would be driven back into the arms of Great Britain, but if London retained Canada, the United States would remain dependent on France so long as it was weak and vulnerable.[7]

Washington's opposition to a Canadian venture arose in part from his fetish with New York. It also resulted from a newfound wariness on his part, an attitude that arose from his belief in 1778 and 1779 that victory was imminent, unless the United States blundered into defeat through imprudent undertakings. But his opposition also stemmed from his fear of General Gates, which burned at a fever pitch in the aftermath of the "Conway Cabal." Washington realized that Gates, who was the principal proponent of the plan, would inevitably be chosen to command any Canadian adventure. He also knew that if Gates, the hero of Saratoga, succeeded in Canada, he would be viewed as the new nation's greatest war hero. Yet Washington, who had fought against a Canadian venture in 1778 and again in 1779, suddenly championed such an expedition in 1780. How can his about-face be explained?

When the French army at last arrived in Rhode Island in July 1780, Washington had conceived of no plan save that of a joint campaign to liberate New York. On learning that his ally had landed, the American commander quickly dispatched Lafayette to Rochambeau's headquarters to explain his thinking about a siege operation in New York. The French general was not swayed. He quickly sent young Lafayette back to American headquarters bearing a polite note rejecting Washington's proposal. A month later Rochambeau learned that French reinforcements might arrive in October. He requested an immediate conference with his counterpart to discuss options. Doubtless the Frenchman also wished to evaluate the American commander. Washington and Rochambeau met for the first time at Hartford on September 22.[8]

On their first afternoon together Washington feted Rochambeau lavishly. There were many toasts and awkward attempts at conversation. Rochambeau confessed to his staff that evening that he had been impressed by Washington. He found the American commander to be cold and aloof, but businesslike, competent, and learned in his discussion of the problems and realities he faced. Once the lengthy afternoon meal was over and the tables had been cleared to make room for maps, the two commanders talked of possible operations. Washington immediately proposed siege operations against Clinton's army in New York. Rochambeau demurred. To achieve success, the Frenchman explained, too many obstacles would have to be overcome. The French navy must have undisputed superiority, but no assurance existed that a flotilla of such magnitude would arrive that autumn. Furthermore, the siege of New

York would require a very long time, perhaps as long as eighteen months. Should an enormous French fleet come north, it was unlikely to remain for such a period. It would have urgent business to attend in the Caribbean, defending French possessions and possibly moving against Britain's lucrative sugar islands. In addition, the siege armies would have to maintain a considerable numerical superiority, something that could be achieved only if the Americans augmented their regulars with militiamen. Rochambeau pointed out that trainbandsmen customarily served for only ninety days or so at a stretch.[9]

Washington, who had never displayed any inclination for fighting in the South, next proposed a southern campaign. If the Franco-American armies were transferred to South Carolina, Clinton would be compelled to come south in an attempt to rescue the Earl of Cornwallis, who commanded the redcoat army in the southern theater. This likely would produce the first major clash of arms since Monmouth. Rochambeau rejected that idea as well. Without naval superiority, the allies would accomplish nothing, he counseled.[10] Washington would not campaign in the South without his French ally.

Thereafter, Washington, the foe of a Canadian expedition for the past two years, proposed a joint invasion of Canada. His about-face on the Canadian issue was the result of several factors. Aware that time was running out, Washington was desperately anxious to take the offensive, and spoke of the need to do something to end the "disgraceful and fatal inactivity" that he had so long endured.[11] In addition, a joint invasion by an exiguous Franco-American force would have diminished the logistical and manpower problems that had troubled him in the past. Perhaps most important, however, Gates was removed from the picture by September 1780. Only days before Washington met with the French at Hartford, the commander learned that Gates had suffered a terrible defeat in the Battle of Camden in South Carolina. Washington's *bête noire* was in disgrace and would never again be considered to command an army that invaded Canada. However, Rochambeau ruled out a Canadian operation, telling Washington that his orders were to act only in concert with the French navy.[12]

The meeting ended with an exchange of pleasantries. Early the next morning Washington began the long dusty ride back to the Hudson. Neither the agreeably cool weather nor the first signs of autumn's beauty cheered Washington. His ebullience at the arrival of the French army had vanished. "I see nothing before us but accumulating distress," he remarked, for the dispiriting reality of the Hartford conference was that the allied commanders had made a decision to do nothing. No campaign was in the offing for the remainder of 1780, nor was anything planned for the next year. The United States was "tottering on the brink of a precipice," Washington lamented. But if Washington believed that low ebb had been reached, he was wrong. When he arrived back at West Point he learned of Benedict Arnold's treason. The turncoat had attempted to hand over West Point to the enemy. Luck alone had prevented the British from gaining control of the Hudson River. Bitter and melancholy, Washington reflected that if resolute and virtuous men did not emerge "to rescue our affairs," all might be lost "in the general wreck" wrought by inactivity and betrayal.[13]

As 1780 waned, Washington and Adams anguished that a stalemated war would cheat the Americans out of the great revolutionary ends for which they had struggled so long. Jefferson faced a more immediate threat. He looked toward the chilling prospect of an imminent British invasion of Virginia. The governor was delighted that more than half the 2,500 militiamen he had sent in the early spring to relieve Charleston had arrived late, thus avoiding capture. During July they straggled into General Gates's hurriedly assembled army in South Carolina. Jefferson quickly sent equipment, including tomahawks, but Gates needed more of everything. A week after taking command, he begged Jefferson to send livestock, flour, and men. If relief was not forthcoming, Gates warned, his army would be destroyed and no Continentals would remain in the South to defend Virginia. Jefferson expressed his "wish to do every thing to second your enterprizes," and he might have done more had Gates waged his own war of posts, avoiding a confrontation until a more advantageous moment.[14]

Instead, Gates cast aside the prudence that had brought him glory at Saratoga. He put his army in motion in search of the enemy. He found them at Camden. In what Jefferson later called "an unlucky affair," Gates blundered into a superior force, two-thirds of which consisted of British regulars. The Americans were crushed. Gates fled with his men, riding like the wind to avoid capture. He did not stop until he reached Charlotte, 200 miles away. His flight resulted in ridicule and censure, and ultimately his end as a field commander in this war.

Jefferson was stunned by the defeat, which was made all the worse by word that Gates's undoing was partially the result of the panic and flight of Virginia's militia. Now only North Carolina stood between Cornwallis and Virginia. Jefferson hurriedly called up nearly one-third of the state's militia units and sent roughly 5,000 trainbandsmen and 300 state regulars south in September. In addition, he impressed wagons and other essential items, and demanded the arrest and punishment of those who had deserted at Camden. His energetic response soon paid dividends. On October 7 a wing of Cornwallis's army was defeated at King's Mountain in western South Carolina, the single glint of sunlight that fell on America's military efforts in 1780. Nearly a quarter of those who fought under the American flag that day were raw militiamen from Virginia.[15]

Jefferson had no time to enjoy the tidings from the Carolina backcountry. In mid-September he had learned from Washington that a British naval force was about to embark from New York. Common sense suggested that its destination would be Virginia or North Carolina. If Virginia, the state would be defended largely by inexperienced militiamen. Jefferson feared that "calamity" faced his state.[16]

The blow fell on Virginia. A British force of 2,200 under General Alexander Leslie sailed into the Chesapeake in mid-October. Jefferson summoned 6,000 militiamen and awaited the worst, but good fortune smiled on him. Leslie caused little damage. Jefferson at first thought the enemy had staged a diversion as part of a greater campaign to secure Baltimore, but in actuality Leslie's mission was to pin down Virginians in Virginia, affording Cornwallis an even freer hand to mop up in the Carolinas. Leslie took control of some territory south of the James, but before long he was ordered south to reinforce Cornwallis's army, which was somewhat tattered after King's Mountain. The last British sail disappeared from view after only a thirty-day stay in Virginia.[17]

No one knew better than Jefferson how fortunate Virginia had been. Nevertheless, fifteen months of terrible stress and anxiety—his first real experience of coping with the loneliness of exercising power and responsibility in a time of crisis—had exacted a heavy toll on Jefferson. That autumn he told Washington that his greatest frustrations had been caused by Virginia's economic difficulties. The people remained zealous and anxious to fight, he remarked, but they were "reduced to fold their Arms for want of the means of defence." Jefferson grew so depressed that he considered resigning as governor, a step that neither Washington nor Adams contemplated in their darkest hours. Jefferson even approached his old friend John Page, the lieutenant-governor, about replacing him. Friends urged Jefferson to stay on. With some heat, Page even admonished Jefferson to "Deny yourself your darling Pleasures" and see the task through.[18] He understood, if Jefferson did not, that flight by the governor would have a toxic effect on public morale. It would also end Jefferson's public career forever.

Jefferson did not resign. In fact, throughout the autumn he acted with considerable vigor. He told the assembly that the lesson to be learned from Leslie's invasion was that the state must hasten its military preparations. Although he downplayed the possibility of another invasion anytime soon, he emphasized the woeful state of Virginia's readiness. Virginia was safe for the moment, but only for the moment, he told the legislators. The states to the south were occupied or exhausted. Virginia could not escape this war, he added. Either its armies would battle in the Carolinas or on Virginia soil. Jefferson preferred that they not fight at home. He sent units to North Carolina and urged the Virginia assembly to meet the needs of the Continentals to the south, now being restructured under General Greene, Gates's successor.[19]

However, events did not unfold as Jefferson had anticipated, and he was ill-prepared when the crisis came. On December 30 the invaders came again, not across the North Carolina border, but, as before, through the Chesapeake. Six weeks earlier Washington had again cautioned Jefferson that the enemy in New York was preparing another expedition. Washington warned that its target might be Virginia and that the strike might be timed to coincide with the expiration of enlistments at the end of December. Jefferson paid little heed. On December 11 he told the assembly that he would not summon the militia. His focus remained on the Carolinas.[20]

But Washington was prescient. On the last day of the year, a Sunday, Jefferson learned that a British force under Benedict Arnold, now commissioned a colonel of cavalry in the British army, had been spotted off the Virginia coast. The governor did not act quickly. On that Sunday, he neither summoned the militia nor informed the Council of State of the threat. By Tuesday, the day after Jefferson finally acted, Arnold was at Jamestown, a stone's throw from Williamsburg, and only fifty miles from Richmond. Panic erupted in the new capital. The wealthy set off for the safety of remote plantations, after loading their treasures in wagons and carriages. Jefferson ordered the removal of public records and military stores, and called up the militia in two areas, the Richmond area and, oddly, Albemarle County, far to the west. After he sent Martha and the children to Tuckahoe, Jefferson hurried to safety across the river. According to the subsequent allegations of his political enemies, he observed Arnold's unopposed arrival in Richmond on January 5, as well as the destruction of the capital, from a hiding spot in a barn.[21]

Arnold commanded about 1,600 green-clad men and a flotilla of twenty-seven vessels, including five heavy warships. His force destroyed a foundry, twenty-six cannon, about 300 small arms, 150 wagons, five tons of powder, stores of salt and grain, and half a dozen buildings, including two tobacco warehouses. His men found Jefferson's residence and quickly stripped bare the wine cellar, pilfered some of his books, and took away ten of his slaves. However, Arnold caused remarkably little destruction. He was gone as quickly as he had come, plundering several plantations along the James before he settled into winter quarters at Portsmouth. The emotional damage wrought by Arnold was greater than the physical destruction, but psychological warfare was part of his intent, and he had succeeded in frightening and demoralizing many Tidewater Virginians.[22]

Jefferson's leadership in this crisis had been deplorable and it was not long before he was publicly upbraided by critics at home and in Philadelphia. Charges of negligence and incompetence were hurled at him. Some said that after eighteen months on the job he should have had Virginia better prepared to cope with what, in reality, had been a small raid. He was heavily criticized for having failed to listen to Washington's admonition and for his languid response to the first sightings of the enemy flotilla. Even Madison, who defended Jefferson in Congress, privately reproached his friend's behavior during the emergency. Jefferson responded by heaping the blame on poor intelligence, and when that defense proved unconvincing to almost everyone, he vented his rage toward Arnold. Frustrated and humiliated, the violent fury that lurked deep within Jefferson burst forth, as it had in his adolescent misogynist rantings and his reprehensible treatment of Colonel Hamilton. He badly wished to capture Arnold, even offering a substantial reward for his apprehension out of his own pocket. When the turncoat was in his hands, Jefferson said longingly, he would first make a "public spectacle" of him, after which he would see to his execution.[23]

Governor Jefferson's shortcomings during that autumn's emergency were not due to lack of industry. He was anchored to his desk. Nor was he distracted by his penchant for study and intellectual inquiry. Indeed, his correspondence in this period is virtually devoid of literary, philosophical, or scientific ruminations, as if he deliberately walled himself off from his customary habits. Nevertheless, Jefferson fell short as a leader in this crisis. As Washington's mesmerization with New York caused him to slight other theaters, Jefferson had permitted himself to become so bewitched by the threat in the Carolinas that he was blind to the dangers at home. Washington's warnings failed to make him see the peril, and even when his sentinels sighted the enemy, Jefferson's captivation with Greene's campaign obscured the grave hazard that was upon him. Had he not been so shortsighted, Jefferson could have had the militia in place before Arnold arrived. There were other failures as well. Weeks before Arnold's flotilla arrived, General von Steuben, posted in Virginia by Greene, had urged Jefferson to erect a redoubt at Hood's Point, a narrow channel on the James below Richmond. A strong defensive installation at that site might have kept Arnold from Richmond. At the very least, it would have slowed his progress, giving additional time for the militia to muster before the capital. However, Jefferson had responded indifferently to von Steuben's counsel, with the result that Arnold easily brushed past the unfinished rampart and entered an undefended capital city. Nor had Jefferson utilized what Adams once had called his "happy talent for composition" to rally the public. Nothing in Virginia's constitution prohibited him from communicating directly with the public. Instead of bemoaning the lack of martial spirit in his state, he might have mobilized his pen to rekindle the zeal and energy that had slowly ebbed during the previous three years.[24]

While Arnold awaited the warmer days and drier roads that would come with spring, Jefferson, stung by those who questioned his performance, suddenly appeared inclined to take the initiative. He summoned the assembly into a special session and, despite some equivocation, urged the creation of a large regular army, akin to the Virginia Regiment that Washington had once commanded. He also implored Congress to send aid of every kind to Virginia. He was only partially successful. The assembly thought the state too poor to create an army. The militia would have to do. However, Washington took steps to aid his stricken state. He sent the Pennsylvania line and considerable materials to Virginia, and he devised a bold plan to capture Arnold's army, one that bore a resemblance to his attack on Trenton more than four years before. Virginia was to raise nearly 3,000 militia. Most were to be posted before Arnold's army, together with 1,200 Continentals under Lafayette, whom Washington sent south. The remainder of the Virginia militia, about 800 men, were to be posted below Portsmouth, where they could prevent the redcoats' escape into North Carolina following the American attack. The entire scheme hinged on the French High Command's consent to send two men-of-war and two frigates from Newport to the Chesapeake. That little flotilla would have an excellent opportunity to succeed, Washington believed, for the British fleet had been severely damaged in a winter storm and was idled for repairs.[25]

Everything was in place by February except the French fleet. It never reached the James. This plan, like so many other attractive plans during this war, came to naught. Washington's scheme was undone by interminable delays. The French agreed to act, and even consented to dispatch a force of 1,100 regulars and a larger fleet than Washington had proposed. However, nearly eight weeks elapsed between the moment that Washington first broached the subject to Rochambeau and the arrival of the French armada off the Chesapeake. By then, the royal naval craft were repaired and awaiting the Gallic force. In a sharp encounter near the entrance to the Chesapeake, both navies sustained damage, but the outgunned French fleet suffered the heaviest impairment. It retreated to Rhode Island, signaling the end of what had appeared to be an excellent opportunity for a decisive Allied victory.[26]

Soon thereafter, more British arrived in Virginia. A flotilla bearing 2,000 reinforcements for Arnold under General William Philips, whom Jefferson had befriended while he was confined as a prisoner of war near Monticello, docked at Portsmouth in late March. Without a naval arm, Lafayette retreated immediately to Maryland and the Virginia militia units abandoned all hope of attacking the entrenched lines at Portsmouth.

However, the Virginia militia might have been put to good use in another capacity. A plan to march the militia into North Carolina, where it would aid Greene in contesting Cornwallis, was developed and supported by the militia leadership, von Steuben, Lafayette, and the speaker of the Virginia assembly. The plan had merits. The British were reeling in the Carolinas. Ninety days after their thrashing at King's Mountain, the redcoats had suffered another heavy defeat in an engagement at Cowpens in South Carolina. The British, who had seemed invincible in the early autumn of 1780, were now in desperate straits. Cornwallis, who was far from his supply base in South Carolina, and deep in the hinterland where the Royal Navy would be of no assistance, was vulnerable. Reinforced by the Virginia militia, Greene would have possessed numerical superiority. At the very least—and this was the scenario that von Steuben imagined—Philips and Arnold would have been compelled to abandon Virginia in order to save Cornwallis. It is conceivable too that an attack by Greene might have resulted in the climactic victory in this war. Although Washington was not privy to this plan, there can be little doubt that it would have had his support. He had repeatedly reminded Jefferson that Virginia's primary objective must be to support Greene. The "predatory incursions" into Virginia paled in comparison to "the injury to the common cause" that would result "from the conquest of those states southward of you," Washington had advised Jefferson.[27]

Jefferson and the Council of State debated the alternatives. Ultimately, they rejected the plan, fearing that the state would be defenseless before Arnold and Philips should they not rush south to aid their comrade. It was a decision that rightly outraged the architects of the plan, some of whom pointed out that Virginia had been defenseless in the face of Colonel Arnold's force in January, even when the militia was available. The commander of the militia, General George Weedon, roared that Jefferson was a petty figure who was incapable of comprehending the full scope of the war. General Greene agreed. He complained that the war could be won only if continental officials, whose national outlook superseded local interests, were empowered to direct every state militia. Greene's anger ran deep. To this beleaguered officer, who had dealt with numerous state executives, Jefferson was the least capable of understanding the depth of the American crisis. It was a sentiment shared by von Steuben.[28]

The simmering outrage of these soldiers was merited. The times required daring and intrepid leadership. Jefferson had acted cautiously and timorously, but predictably. Since Arnold's invasion he had hoped to be seen as a man of resolution, vigor, and enterprise, but he was not, and seldom had been, the man the public believed him to be. Jefferson wanted to be esteemed as a radical reformer, but he was in fact a cautious and conservative man. He longed to be seen as liberal and enlightened, especially on the issue of slavery, but his racial views were unilluminated. He permitted himself to be named a militia colonel, but he had no zeal for soldiering. He was Virginia's chief executive, but it was a post he had never wanted and one that he wished to quit in the midst of travail. In the spring of 1781 Jefferson wished to be seen as brave and venturesome, but he was not a risk-taker. At the darkest moment of the war, Washington had hazarded all in the strikes at Trenton and Princeton. Believing that the American Revolution hung in the balance, Adams had risked his career in the confrontation with Vergennes. Their gambles substantively shaped the successful outcome of the War of Independence. Jefferson's caution in April 1781 ruined a possible opportunity to inflict a fatal blow on Cornwallis, one that might have broken the military stalemate. Nor was that all. Jefferson's decision to safeguard Virginia ironically exposed the state to the greatest peril it would face during the war.

Less than three weeks after Jefferson's fateful decision, British raiders in Virginia were on the move. Left with no reason to move south to protect Cornwallis, the British instead sailed up the unobstructed James once again, this time in fourteen naval vessels. One column under General Philips caused damage around Williamsburg, burned the shipyards on the Chickahominy

River, and captured Petersburg, where ships, warehouses, and tobacco were torched. About fifteen miles below Richmond, at Coxe's Dale, a second column under Arnold destroyed nine Virginia warships, captured a dozen commercial vessels, and burned 2,000,000 pounds of tobacco. Richmond was more fortunate. The two British columns did not reunite before the capital until ten days into the operation, at a moment when Richmond was defended by only 500 militiamen, barely half of whom possessed arms. However, on the very evening that Philips and Arnold rendezvoused before Richmond, 900 Continentals under Lafayette arrived from Baltimore. The British were numerically superior, but they knew their advantage would be brief, as von Steuben was marching on Richmond from Petersburg with about 900 militiamen. The redcoats contented themselves with the destruction of an additional 1,200,000 pounds of tobacco at nearby Manchester and Warwick, then sailed back down the James, wreaking havoc and liberating scores of slaves.[29] Although no one publicly faulted Jefferson for the losses sustained in this incursion, the raid demonstrated that the state was largely defenseless against a professional army augmented by naval power. Virginia's best defense, as Washington had advised, would have been to compel the enemy to fight in North Carolina.

Jefferson immediately sent Washington a glowing account of Virginia's preparations and the conduct of its militia. Toward the conclusion of his note, almost as an aside, he mentioned that Cornwallis was moving north with the intention of "forming a Junction" with Arnold and Philips. Thus, the union of enemy forces would occur in Virginia, not in North Carolina. "This . . . we consider as most perilous in its Consequences," Governor Jefferson added. Not until three weeks later, and then under pressure from members of the assembly to do so, did Jefferson urge Washington to bring his army from New York to save Virginia. By then several legislators had importuned his assistance and one, Richard Henry Lee, even proposed that General Washington be given dictatorial powers when he set foot in the state, thus emasculating both the assembly and the governor.[30]

The "Times are pregnant. . . . [W]e are in the Moment of a Crisis," Adams remarked from Amsterdam at the outset of this crucial year. He had arrived in the United Provinces, the Netherlands, in the summer of 1780, soon after Governor Jefferson began his second term. Although he was not recognized by the Dutch government, Adams soon found private businessmen and financiers who were willing to talk. He rented a large house on the Kiezersgratz, in which he entertained Dutch notables, and obtained a chaise, team of horses, and coachman to deliver him to their residences in the proper European style. Adams's immediate goal was to smooth the way for Henry Laurens, whom Congress had appointed as its commissioner to Holland. His long-range objective was a Dutch loan, which would at once ease America's financial burdens and reduce its dependency on France. Adams did not anticipate immediate success, and it did not come. Vergennes not only did everything in his power to ruin his efforts, but as Adams knew from the outset, the Dutch would never be inspired to act on America's behalf until the allies scored victories on America's battlefields.[31]

Adams faced disappointments, but while the spirits of Washington and Jefferson sank in the latter half of 1780, his mood improved once he escaped Paris. He believed that the Dutch would eventually assist the United States. Working tirelessly toward that end, he stressed in meeting after meeting that his countrymen had much in common with the Dutch, including their Protestant outlook, faith in republican government, and yearning to escape British commercial restraints. In addition, Adams now believed that Europe's neutral states, several of which had entered into a League of Armed Neutrality in 1780, were as likely to someday join the fray against Great Britain as to demand a mediated peace. He was buoyed too by news of the victory at King's Mountain, the first American military success of much consequence in the three years since Saratoga. Adams, who believed that small victories paved the way to grander triumphs, was confident that the British army in the Carolinas might be smashed. At the outset of 1781 he predicted Cornwallis's imminent defeat, and even greater victories if only the French fleet and the Franco-American armies could act in concert.[32]

Adams's newfound optimism quickly vanished when word reached Amsterdam in March that the Continental army had recently been rocked by mutinies. This was what Washington had most feared since his earliest days as commander. The anguish and despair of men with too little food and clothing, and no pay, sparked rebellions on New Years' Eve, and in the days that followed, within units from Pennsylvania and New Jersey. Negotiations in Princeton—on the fourth anniversary of Washington's important little victory in that college town—terminated the first insurrection, but the New Jersey mutiny was suppressed by force. Washington sent troops from West Point to crush the rebellion, and ordered them to "instantly execute a few of the most active and most incendiary leaders."[33]

Washington soon was able to report that "every thing is now quiet," but Adams knew that great damage had been done. Whereas he had discovered in

1778 that Gates and Washington had been America's most effective "diplomats" in persuading the French to ally with the United States, Adams knew that a mutinous Continental army would thwart his efforts in Holland and perhaps furnish France with the excuse it needed to drop out of the war. Maybe "we can carry on the war forever, [but] our allies cannot," he moaned. Nor did he any longer really believe that the United States could fight for more than one additional campaign, for in January and February friends at home informed him of a further decline in the will of his countrymen. The people had begun to complain openly about this never-ending war, a former law clerk wrote from Boston. Benjamin Rush sent similar tidings from Philadelphia, and a Virginian notified Adams that an ineffectual Congress had squandered its credibility with the people. The American Revolution was nearly lost, Lovell, the Massachusetts congressman, told him. "[W]e are bankrupt with a mutinous army," he added.[34]

Adams had seldom been so alarmed. The loss of a people's will to fight was a more pernicious enemy than all the King's soldiers and ships, he declared. In addition, his nagging fear of a European mediation conference, almost dormant in late 1780, resurfaced as an all too real danger in the late spring of 1781. Just as word of the Continental mutinies eddied across the Atlantic, Russia and Austria proposed a conference of the great European powers to end the war through mediation. Their proposal also spoke of resolving the status of the American "colonies." Once again, Adams was confronted with the threat that the great powers would succeed in their "most insidious and Dangerous Plot . . . to ensnare and deprive us of our Independence."[35]

Three times in the previous thirty months mediation proposals had been broached. They had gone nowhere, in part because of France's lack of interest. However, this time Vergennes summoned Adams to France to respond to the Russo-Austrian initiative. Adams interpreted this as a sign that the foreign minister had warmed to the notion of terminating the war at the conclusion of this season's military campaign. Adams hurried south from Amsterdam and met twice with Vergennes at Versailles. Thereafter, working from his lodging in the Hôtel de Valois in Paris, Adams crafted his response. He demanded that Great Britain recognize American independence as a precondition to talks. He also rejected a peace based on the principle that the United States and Great Britain would retain possession of the territory that each held at the instant of the armistice that would likely precede the conference. All decisions with regard to territory, he insisted, must be the subject of negotiation.[36]

The European conference never met, but not because of Adams's stance or Vergennes's wishes. Great Britain rejected the co-mediator's entreaties.

Given America's mounting problems, London believed it could profit by continuing the war. Nevertheless, this alarming episode, coupled with the steady drumbeat of bad news from home and the mounting tension that accompanied his confrontational diplomacy, produced an unbearable strain on Adams. By the spring of 1781 he had begun to display signs that hyperthyroidism, in remission for the past three years, had recurred. It is probable that the stress he had endured since his clash with Vergennes during the previous summer had caused this malady to resurface. In fact, during that spring he protested to his wife that he lived "with more cares" than he had ever endured.[37]

Adams complained of an extraordinary nervousness, beyond anything he had ever experienced. He evinced signs of paranoia, speaking to acquaintances of his fear of assassination, even of being set upon by mobs in the streets of Amsterdam. He once again experienced ophthalmic difficulties. A Massachusetts physician who lodged briefly with him in the spring of 1781 described Adams's health in alarming terms. His host was uncommonly irritable and somewhat confused, according to Dr. Benjamin Waterhouse. He also spoke of Adams's "protuberant eyes." Adams referred to his sensitivity to heat and said that he felt unusually weak, conditions he had last mentioned nearly five years earlier. His secretary described a "tumor" in Adams's neck, possibly a reference to a goiter, a diffusely enlarged thyroid. If Adams in fact exhibited a goiter, he displayed the classic triad of signs—exophthalmos, goiter, and a constellation of symptoms of thyrotoxicosis—existent in Graves' disease, or hyperthyroidism.[38]

Adams was already quite ill when he journeyed to France in July to consult about mediation, and he evinced signs of confusion in his responses to Vergennes. He disavowed his initial written statement and prepared a second reply, only to subsequently scuttle that response and once again embrace his original position. Adams was very sick when he returned to Amsterdam. His condition soon worsened. He had no more than unpacked his bags when he received alarming tidings that aroused even greater stress. From Abigail and friends in Congress he learned not only that Vergennes had sought his removal as the U.S. peace commissioner, but that Franklin had written Congress a year earlier to complain of his behavior toward the French foreign minister. A day or two later Adams received a letter from Franklin informing him that Congress had stripped him of his powers as the sole peace commissioner. Congress had created a five-member commission, of which Adams was to be a part.[39] Adams felt betrayed. He was certain that Vergennes, with the help of Franklin, whom he now regarded as the very personification of treachery, had won the battle. His aspirations for fame and heroism were dashed. He even believed that the American Revolution was threatened by the cunning French statesman and his Janus-faced American satrap.

Soon thereafter, in August 1781, Adams collapsed. His Dutch physicians alternately diagnosed his illness as malaria and scurvy, maladies whose signs include jaundice, extreme weakness, exhaustion, swelling in the extremities, ulceration of the skin, fever, and sweating. However, the same symptoms may appear in those who suffer from hyperthyroidism. In all likelihood, Adams had suffered his most serious recurrence of this disease.[40]

Adams later said that he had been afflicted with "a nervous Fever, of a dangerous kind, bordering upon putrid." He was "insensible" for five or six days and remained seriously ill for weeks thereafter. For more than six weeks following his collapse, he was too sick to write even a brief letter to his wife. A year after the onset of what he called his "great Sickness," Adams not only exhibited what may have been a goiter, but he continued to experience painful dermatological problems and suffered from sensitivity to heat, lameness, feebleness, and depression. He also complained of memory loss, once remarking that his affliction had "burnt up half [my] Memory and more than half [my] Spirits." Two years after he collapsed, Adams said that the illness had "broken me very much." He wondered if he would ever be well again. At the end of 1784, forty months after his collapse and approximately four years after the illness recurred, his wife said that he was yet "infirm."[41]

Adams's physicians administered quinine, a drug that would have had no therapeutical value for someone afflicted with hyperthyroidism, but they likely also kept him warm and comfortable, and took pains to see that he did not suffer dehydration. Their ministrations must have shepherded Adams through the first terrible days of the emergency.[42] Thereafter, weeks of rest—he did virtually no work for months—and his ability, based on ample experience, to cope with anxiety likely further reduced the danger. For instance, by the fall of 1781 he not only had persuaded himself that he and his country were better served by a team of commissioners, but he had come to believe that the attacks on him by Vergennes and Franklin would do little harm and might, in the long run, backfire on them and prove beneficial to him. Someday, he hoped, everyone would see that he had sought nothing but the security interests of the United States.[43] It is also likely that a natural diminution of the malady occurred during the months following his collapse.

General Washington bore up well despite the heavy burden he carried. He may have labored under a greater strain in the summer of 1781 than at any other moment in this war, for like Adams he had come to believe that victory must be gained that year or it probably would be lost forever. He had also concluded that if the military stalemate was not broken soon the European belligerents would demand a diplomatic resolution of the conflict. Moreover, Washington, who like Adams apprehended the collapse of popular will, feared that 1781 might be the last year in which an American army could be raised. Nor was he even certain that the army could be kept together beyond the autumn. He told a congressman that he did not know if the soldiers would again enter winter quarters if they were unpaid and inadequately clothed, and if they knew that the hospitals were without medicine.[44]

What gave Washington the most pain was his steadfast belief that victory was yet possible, if only the French navy would cooperate with the Franco-American armies. However, he had been repeatedly frustrated on this score. For months after his meeting with Rochambeau in the autumn of 1780, he spoke of how "the promised succor from France" had "prov'd delusory." When his plan for a campaign against Arnold's force on the James was thwarted, due to French indecision and dalliance he believed, Washington was livid. He knew that he had contrived a bold plan, and had all gone well the allies might have scored such a colossal victory that it would "have given a decisive turn to our Affairs in all the Southern States." Washington wrote at least five letters in which he complained of the indolence of his allies. One miscarried and, to the commander's mortification, soon was published in a Tory newspaper in New York.[45]

While in the thicket of despond, Washington received alarming news from Mount Vernon. At the same moment that Arnold and Phillips had raided along the James, the British sloop *Savage* had cruised the Potomac, sowing destruction at several large estates. It had visited Mount Vernon. Seventeen slaves had fled to the enemy, but unlike some of its neighbors, Mount Vernon had not been burned. Lund Washington, the commander's nephew who managed the property in Washington's absence, had boarded the *Savage*, serving food and beverages and pleading that the estate be spared. Lund's supine behavior had saved Mount Vernon, but when General Washington learned of his nephew's conduct, he flew into one of his towering rages. He wrote Lund a long letter, rebuking him for toadying to "a parcel of plundering scoundrels" and advising him that his actions invited the public to conclude that he cared more for his private concerns than for the national cause.[46] Washington's anger was genuine. It was as if, perversely, he harbored the wish that Mount Vernon had been razed.

The bad news from Mount Vernon mingled with better news from the military front. Two months after Cowpens, in mid-March, Greene had inflicted heavy damage on Cornwallis in a battle at Guilford Court House in north central North Carolina. For the third time in six months Cornwallis had suffered costly losses. This was good news for Washington, but it raised difficult questions. Was Cornwallis vulnerable? Should the southern theater now take precedence over New York? Jefferson pleaded with Washington to choose the South. Otherwise, Cornwallis soon would be in Virginia, where he could "waste an unarmed Country." If Cornwallis succeeded in sowing terror and destruction across the state, Jefferson appeared to suggest, those who desired peace at any price might gain the upper hand. Come to Virginia and take command, Jefferson pleaded. "[Y]our appearance . . . would restore full confidence of salvation" and would enable Virginia to recruit an army, the governor appealed.[47]

Rochambeau had begun to think along the same lines. Early in May he learned that naval reinforcements might be available during the summer or fall. The French general thought the Virginia theater offered the greatest promise for successful allied land and sea operations, and he asked to meet with Washington, obviously hopeful that the American commander would consent to a campaign in Virginia or the Carolinas.

The two commanders met for three days in mid-May at Weathersfield, Connecticut. At times the sessions were stormy. Rochambeau opened with an argument for operations in the South, which Washington had proposed a year earlier. Washington now rejected such a course, and countered with a proposal that they plan a siege of New York. He maintained that to march the armies into the miasmic southern climate would be to risk heavy losses due to desertion and disease. Washington fancifully predicted that up to one-half the men would be lost before the army reached the lower Chesapeake. He also argued that the South could be saved by acting against New York. Once imperiled, Clinton would have to order Cornwallis, Philips, and Arnold to come north to assist in the defense of the city. Washington proposed that Rochambeau join him outside New York, where they would be poised to strike if a French armada indeed arrived.[48]

Washington's position mixed flimflam and myopia. He exaggerated the dangers of illness and defection. He also failed to see the opportunities that existed in the South. Hope and wishful thinking aplenty existed in Rochambeau's outlook, but realism and common sense were present as well. At bottom, Rochambeau understood better than Washington the difficulties that confronted Cornwallis. The British army in the South was vulnerable. If the French fleet participated, conditions would be more favorable for a major allied victory in the Chesapeake than in New York, for in the South the allies would face only a portion of the British army, while seeing little or nothing of the Royal Navy. Any action in New York would be a contest against the entire British armed forces in America. Even if the allies failed to destroy Cornwallis, they might inflict sufficient damage to compel him to abandon the South, a factor that could be crucial in the post-armistice diplomacy.

As Rochambeau listened to Washington's objections to a southern campaign, he struggled to maintain his composure. Already angered by Washington's unkind remarks that had spilled into the press, Rochambeau seethed at what he regarded as his counterpart's strategic shortsightedness and inflexibility. One observer later said that the French general let his annoyance show, but it did not budge Washington. Instead, it was Rochambeau who relented, or so it seemed, when he consented to link his army with the Continentals outside New York. However, once the Americans were gone, Rochambeau wrote Admiral de Grasse and urged him to bring the fleet to the Chesapeake, not New York. It was the only way around Washington, and the only realistic prospect for breaking the stalemate during this pivotal year. Rochambeau had obviously consented to bring his army to New York in order to shorten the distance he might eventually have to cover to reach Virginia. Not until three weeks later did he divulge to Washington the action he had taken.[49]

If Washington was furious at having been duped, he hid his anger. In fact, by the time he discovered what Rochambeau had done, Washington had begun to rethink matters. Many years after the war, in virtually the only public comment he ever issued about his command decisions during the conflict, Washington maintained that he and Rochambeau had agreed as early as the Hartford Conference in September 1780 to conduct joint operations in the South, either in the Chesapeake or against occupied Charleston. He also claimed that New York had never been considered as the target for an allied campaign.[50] That he took a public stand on this matter, and distorted the facts in the process, suggests that in later years he was uncomfortable with the role he had played in planning the campaign against Cornwallis.

Yet Washington may have been too hard on himself. Three weeks after the Weathersfield Conference in early May, he wrote to Rochambeau questioning their decision to focus on New York to the exclusion of other opportunities. He urged that de Grasse be notified that he was free to decide whether to sail to New York or the Chesapeake, according to "which will be the most advantageous quarter for him to make an appearance in." Washington as much as said that he now preferred a southern campaign. What had changed his mind? The abortive campaign to capture Arnold's army in January had awakened him to the possibilities of a dramatic, even climactic, victory in the South. Furthermore, he had received the pleas of Jefferson and other Virginians that he hurry south. He now knew too that Cornwallis's army was at "full liberty to go wherever they pleased" in Virginia, so that if peace was forced on America in the near future, the British might retain possession of his native state. Since the previous fall, moreover, Washington had understood that time was running out. He had even referred to the American war effort as an "expiring effort."[51] Washington understood the imperative need for an immediate victory, and he came to see that there was a greater likelihood of a rapid, decisive triumph in the Chesapeake than in New York. As during his darkest days in 1776, and as was true of Adams in the most desperate moments of 1780, Washington met the test of wartime leadership. He switched course. He acted boldly, backing away from the campaign he so long had fancied to advocate an alternative course that held out a glimmering hope of success. Once he and Rochambeau were in agreement that the Chesapeake offered the greatest promise of victory, they sought to "misguide & bewilder" Clinton about their plans, as Washington later remarked. The allied armies rendezvoused outside New York. They gathered boats and built field ovens, the sorts of things an army about to besiege a port city might do. They wrote letters containing references to a pending campaign for New York, and made certain that these communiqués fell into British hands. Clinton took the bait. Convinced that a land-sea assault on New York was imminent, he directed Cornwallis to "take a defensive position in any healthy situation you chuse (be it at Williamsburg or Yorktown)" and send reinforcements northward.[52]

While Washington and Rochambeau waited for word from de Grasse, and long before he received Clinton's orders, Cornwallis acted. He crossed into Virginia with 1,500 men on May 20, the day before the allied generals met at Weathersfield, and twelve days before the expiration of Jefferson's second, and last, term as governor. Cornwallis was joined immediately by the British forces in Virginia and reinforcements from New York. The British commander soon had about 7,000 men.[53]

Historians have often excoriated Cornwallis for invading Virginia, but his plan had merits. Indeed, Britain's southern strategy might have enjoyed greater success had it commenced in 1778 in the upper South rather than in Georgia. Not only might the pacification of Virginia been easier than that of South Carolina, but once it had been conquered all supply routes from north to south could have been closed. Cornwallis knew in 1781 that Virginia could not be subdued in one campaign, but he could interdict some supply lines and at the same time cause serious injury to the state's tenuous will to continue. It was a plan that held forth a reasonable promise of scoring substantive gains that year and of inflicting crucial, even fatal, damage on the Americans during 1782, especially if the Continental army was weakened still further by another ghastly winter.

On his third day in Virginia, Cornwallis unleashed Colonel Banastre Tarleton's cavalry on a destructive raid into Chesterfield County. Soon thereafter Cornwallis set out after Lafayette, whose force of regulars and militiamen barely totaled 2,000 ragged men. Lafayette had no choice but to run. He abandoned Richmond and withdrew northward across the Rapidan. Governor Jefferson had already left the capital, as the assembly had agreed earlier to meet in remote, and presumably safe, Charlottesville on May 24, a week before the end of his term.[54] Jefferson retrieved his family at Tuckahoe and rode to Monticello, relieved to be escaping public office, happy to be a comfortable distance from the regulars, and anticipating a long and happy residence at home.

Cornwallis soon unleashed his cavalry once again. The Queen's Rangers, a Loyalist force composed mostly of Virginia Tories under Colonel John Graves Simcoe, drove for Point of Fork. Colonel Tarleton, with 180 men, rode hard for Charlottesville. His orders were to capture Jefferson and the assembly. He nearly succeeded, for chaos prevailed in the state. Jefferson had already confessed to Lafayette that he could not guarantee that the militia would respond to his calls.[55] It was soon apparent as well that communications, for some time tenuous at best, as the success of Arnold's raid had demonstrated, had now completely broken down.

Tarleton's dragoons set out from Hanover before sunrise on Sunday, June 3, the day after Jefferson's term as governor expired, although in the prevailing turmoil the legislature had not yet elected his successor. The British force moved incredibly swiftly, covering over seventy miles in a bit more than twenty-four hours. In the enveloping confusion no one had posted patrols. Not only did Tarleton advance to the Rivanna without opposition, but officials in Charlottesville had no idea that the enemy was coming.

They were saved by valorous Jack Jouett, a militia captain who was languishing in the Cuckoo Tavern, forty miles southeast of Monticello, when Tarleton's troop rode past. Jouett, a native of Charlottesville, sprang into action. He raced toward his hometown to warn the state officials, taking short cuts and driving his steed at a dangerous pace. He reached Monticello in total darkness a couple of hours before sunrise. After awakening the inhabitants of Jefferson's mansion, Jouett hurried to the nearby town to alert the sleeping legislators.[56]

Jefferson's heart must have raced when the knock sounded on his door so deep in the night. Adams and his congressional colleagues in beleaguered Philadelphia four years earlier had known for days that the British army was en route, but Jefferson had no prior warning that he was in the least danger. He immediately arranged to have Martha and the girls driven to Blenheim, a neighbor's house, but several hours passed before he left home. He secured important state papers, probably burned materials that he did not wish the British to see, and may have hidden some personal valuables that his wife and daughters had been unable to carry away. Jefferson had posted lookouts following Jouett's arrival, and remained at home until they reported that a white-coated party of dragoons was ascending the hill to the estate. Jefferson then ran for his life, and escaped only minutes before the enemy reached the front door of Monticello. Under a mottled blue sky, he fled down the other side of the hill, galloping toward Blenheim. Jefferson remained there only briefly before fleeing a second and, ultimately, a third time. He eventually found a safe haven in Bedford County. Like Washington, who had dashed from New York in 1776, and Adams, who had fled Philadelphia in 1777, Jefferson had good reason to run like a frightened hare. To be captured meant, at best, a lengthy confinement in conditions that might be as reprehensible as those he had imposed on Henry Hamilton.[57]

As Jefferson rode to safety over Virginia's dust-choked roads, he likely had already decided that his political career was at an end. He soon announced that he would never again accept even limited public responsibilities. "I have taken my final leave of every thing" concerned with politics, he announced that summer. He had "retired to my farm, my family and books from which I think nothing will ever more separate me."[58]

In the summer of 1781 Jefferson's faith in public service had been shattered and Adams, the victim of a dangerous illness, barely clung to life. Only Washington's spirits were ascendant. Rochambeau's army completed its march to

New York in late June, just as Washington learned that Clinton had sent nearly a quarter of his army on a foraging raid in New Jersey. The allies suddenly had a numerical edge. Washington wanted to strike against the British perimeter forts in the northern reaches of Manhattan Island. If he succeeded, and if de Grasse came to New York, a siege operation against Clinton's interior defenses could be immediately initiated. Rochambeau consented to the enterprise.

Washington prepared a plan of attack that was every bit as complicated as the operation he had planned at Germantown four years earlier. As with that previous endeavor, success hinged on the element of surprise. But, once again, Washington's hopes were dashed. Clinton, who had captured Washington's correspondence that waxed on about a Franco-American attack on New York, was prepared. The allied commanders aborted the assault as soon as they realized that the British had not been caught off guard.[59]

Washington was disappointed. He was anguished too by the almost simultaneous tidings from Virginia of the recent humiliating events in Charlottesville. However, a week later better news reached headquarters. General Wayne, who commanded the Pennsylvania line, had linked his force with Lafayette's men, and they had been joined by several hundred Virginia militiamen. The little army under Lafayette had grown quite quickly to 4,000 men, forcing Cornwallis to suspend operations. The British commander had recalled Simcoe and Tarleton, and retreated to Williamsburg. Washington immediately pronounced this a "Happy Turn [in] our Affairs." Not only had the ravishing of interior Virginia ended, but Washington now glimpsed the faintest prospects of a major turn of events. If de Grasse did come to the Chesapeake instead of New York, and if Lafayette, with help from Virginia's militiamen, could contain Cornwallis on the York peninsula until the primary allied armies arrived, the possibilities were stunning. Washington immediately ordered Lafayette to strengthen his cavalry. Almost breathlessly, he also told the young Frenchman to stand by for messages "of very great importance." To almost everyone else that he could think of Washington wrote that his army would not come to Virginia. New York was the only object on his mind. Some of the letters fell into British hands, as Washington doubtless planned. To General Greene he wrote: "I have a great many things which I want to commit to you, *confidentially*, to paper I dare not trust them."[60]

Then Washington waited. It was not an uncommon experience. He had been awaiting the French fleet since the day he left Valley Forge nearly forty months earlier. He did not know whether de Grasse would come to New York or to the Chesapeake, or what his strength would be, or if he would come northward at all. He had often been disappointed by the French. While he waited, he was informed by Greene that Cornwallis's army was so ill-supplied that it could be defeated in three weeks by an army supported by a naval arm.[61]

Greene's message only heightened Washington's impatience. Not since Howe had been trapped in Boston in March 1776 had Washington been so close to the possibility of a truly great victory. The hazy summer days dragged by without news. July passed. The first week of August, then the second, slipped by without word from the French fleet. Then it was August 14, near the day— perhaps the very day—that Adams fell deathly ill in Holland. For Washington, this day began as had every other during the past several anxious weeks, and as had virtually all his days for six years. He arose in the quiet, pre-dawn darkness and worked by candlelight at his desk for an hour or more. Following his customary light breakfast, he rode slowly about the camp, enjoying the mellow warmth of this soft summer morning, inspecting the grounds, and pausing briefly from time to time to speak with a sentry and to acknowledge officers. In mid-morning he returned to his office for his usual daily round of conferences.

Sometime during that bright, warm day, a dispatch rider galloped into camp. He was quickly shown to headquarters. He bore crucial tidings. De Grasse was coming! The French fleet had sailed for the Chesapeake with twenty-eight warships and 3,000 men. Still later that same day Washington learned from Lafayette that Cornwallis had posted his army at Yorktown.[62] Within five days Rochambeau and Washington—who left a small force under General Heath to guard the Highlands—were on their way to Virginia.

The British in New York did not follow. By now Clinton guessed that de Grasse was sailing for the Chesapeake, but he was confident that the French admiral possessed only a small fleet. He was wrong. De Grasse had sailed northward with a fleet that was larger than anything the Royal Navy could dispatch to Virginia. In fact, the French fleet soon would become even more formidable, for early in September it would be augmented by French vessels posted in Rhode Island, giving the allies a two-to-one majority in ships-of-the-line. On September 5 de Grasse and a British fleet sent to rescue Cornwallis fought for control of Chesapeake Bay. De Grasse won. The British fleet limped back to New York on September 13, leaving Cornwallis without hope of escape by sea.

The following day, one month to the day after learning that de Grasse was en route, Washington arrived in Williamsburg. He had accompanied his army on its march to the top of the Chesapeake, where on September 7 he supervised the loading of his men onto vessels that would complete their transferral to the York peninsula. Then, with a few days to spare before all of his men would be in place near Williamsburg, Washington hurried to Mount Vernon to look in on his home and farms. It was his first trip home in more than six years.

In the last lingering moments of daylight on September 9, General Washington, accompanied by a few aides and French officers, rode up the long gravel driveway to the front door of Mount Vernon. Everything was as he remembered it, but everything looked different. The children of the chattel had grown. The faces of Lund and the laborers had aged. The grounds displayed a worn appearance, brought on by wartime shortages and the lengthy absenteeism of its owner. The house looked very different. About eighteen months before the war Washington had begun a considerable rebuilding project that included, among other things, doubling the length of the house.[63] When Washington left only about one-half the framing had been completed and nothing had been done inside. During the war work had proceeded, but slowly. The additional rooms were dried in, although none were yet habitable in 1781. The area near the construction site looked like a war zone. Familiar trees and shrubs were gone, lumber and equipment was piled everywhere, and mud, sand, and green thickets of weeds stood where once a lush lawn had lapped to the foundation of the dwelling.

Washington relaxed at home for two nights and one blithe, sunny day that he spent escorting his guests on a tour of the property. The next day he rode for Williamsburg. Cornwallis, as Washington had known all along, was still encamped in Yorktown, less than ten miles removed from the former Virginia capital. The allied generals must have wondered why the British had not by now attempted to fight their way out by land, especially as Cornwallis for weeks had possessed a considerably larger force than that under Lafayette. Indecision, and an abiding confidence in the Royal Navy's capability of dealing with any French fleet, were partly responsible for Cornwallis's inactivity. In addition, he had received bewildering and contradictory orders from Clinton. Once he had been ordered to march to Pennsylvania. Another communiqué mentioned bringing his army to New York. Still another told him to stay put in Virginia. Clinton clearly was uncertain of the best course of action. Just as clearly, he believed that Cornwallis was safe in Virginia.[64]

On his arrival, Washington found that the allied soldiers were still trickling in, but he also learned that his fears of massive desertions while the

Continentals marched southward—of which he had warned at Weathers-field—had been unwarranted. He discovered too that French ships from Rhode Island had brought Rochambeau's siege guns, more than forty in all. Washington met with de Grasse almost immediately. He was rowed out to the *Ville de Paris*, the flagship of the flotilla, where he enjoyed one of his more pleasant conferences during this war. De Grasse informed him that he could remain through the end of October. Rochambeau told Washington that six weeks should be sufficient to compel the British to surrender, inasmuch as the allied armies, like the navy, had a two-to-one numerical superiority and ample artillery. "What may be in the Womb of Fate is very uncertain," Washington told another general when he returned to headquarters, "but we anticipate the Reduction of Ld Cornwallis with his army."[65]

At the end of the month the Franco-American armies advanced from Williamsburg to Yorktown and took up positions about two miles outside the sleepy little village. The Americans were posted on the right, the French on the left. Whatever chance Cornwallis once had of escaping by land was gone.

The fighting at Yorktown commenced with a struggle to dislodge the British from their forward redoubts, about half a mile from the village of Yorktown. The allies secured their objective in less than a week. Next the French and American sappers, working under a warm autumn sun that reminded Rochambeau of the time he had been posted in Algiers, dug their first parallel, a trench three-quarters of a mile long. It was only 600 yards from Yorktown. One day Washington came to watch. To his surprise, an audacious soldier handed him a pick. But the commander good-naturedly chopped briefly at the sun-baked earth while the men laughed and cheered.[66]

On October 9, when the first parallel was completed and the siege guns were in place, Washington was given the honor of firing the first round into Yorktown. The large gun roared and the shell whistled toward its target. Seconds later the men heard a muffled explosion. Later they learned that the shot had struck a house, collapsing the roof and heavy beams onto several unsuspecting British officers who were dining inside. One man had been killed.[67]

Within a week the allies were digging a second parallel only 300 yards from the village. More than 100 artillery pieces soon fired red hot metal into the midst of the British defenders. Each day Cornwallis's position grew less tenable. Fifty of his men died during the first day's fusillade. Another 500 died or were wounded by the shelling during the next five days. Nor were allied cannon balls Cornwallis's only source of woe. By the time Washington ignited the first siege gun, the British, who had been unable to forage for weeks, were running low on food. Disease soon erupted within the ranks of Cornwallis's weary, malnourished soldiery. As his army diminished and his artillery was destroyed, Cornwallis's chances of fighting back decreased almost hourly.

On October 16 Cornwallis made his only attempt to escape. Under cover of darkness he sought to get his men across the York River and make a run for it, but the endeavor was foiled by a storm that broke after sunset. It had been a mere gesture anyway, a forlorn attempt to appear to be enterprising. The next morning at 10:00 AM Cornwallis sent a messenger under a white flag to Washington's headquarters. The commander heard the words he had waited years to hear: Cornwallis requested a meeting "to settle terms of the surrender."[68]

Twenty-one days had passed since the allied armies had arrived before Yorktown. Washington had been in command of the operation, but in actuality he had deferred to the French engineers, for a siege operation was a science. Near the outset of the operation, in fact, Washington had remarked that the besieged British were "reducible to calculation." Washington met frequently with Rochambeau during the investment, often in the latter's tent, and he kept a close eye on every aspect of his army's behavior.[69]

Washington anticipated success, but he had learned many times over that in war no outcome was guaranteed. He could never rest easy as long as the British resisted. A British fleet might arrive unexpectedly and alter the balance of power. A storm might blow up and drive de Grasse away, as d'Estaing had been flushed from Rhode Island three years earlier. The siege operation might take longer than Rochambeau envisioned, and longer than de Grasse could remain. Cornwallis might escape, as Washington on three occasions had fled traps. Thus, when Cornwallis indicated that he was ready to talk surrender terms, Washington was not inclined to permit the negotiations to drag on too long.

Washington had negotiated his own surrender at Fort Necessity twenty-seven years before, but in more than a decade of soldiering in two wars he had never arranged the capitulation of a foe. These talks moved rapidly to a conclusion. The two sides parlayed under a flag of truce for only forty-eight hours, much of which was consumed in making translations for Rochambeau. While the talks proceeded, the environment on what had been the battlefield was surreal. The shooting stopped. British bagpipers serenaded the three armies. Men who had been hidden in bunkers for days emerged to walk, exercise, even play amid the carnage and stench that pervaded the area.

Most of the surrender terms were easily negotiated, but there were two troubling points. Washington wanted the British to surrender every Tory and American deserter in Yorktown, and he asked that all fugitive slaves with Cornwallis's army be handed over as well. In fact, the moment negotiations began, Washington posted units along the beaches to assure that no slaves escaped. Cornwallis was unwilling to relinquish either the Loyalists or slaves. Both had helped him and both would face a bleak future if they fell into American hands. After two days it appeared that Cornwallis felt so strongly about the issue that he would attempt to string out negotiations indefinitely. Two days was as long as Washington wished to gamble. He had done enough to assure his fellow Virginians that he had tried on their behalf, but bagging Cornwallis's army was worth infinitely more to him than seizing a few dozen defectors and runaways. The negotiations concluded when Washington agreed to permit Cornwallis to send "letters" to New York via the H.M.S. *Bonetta*. The commander knew that its real cargo would consist of former slaves, Tories, and turncoats.[70]

At 2:00 PM on October 19, a pleasantly warm, sunny, fall day in Yorktown, the British and their Hessian allies appeared on the surrender field. Cornwallis was absent. He pleaded illness. Washington was present, sitting atop his white horse, while Rochambeau sat nearby on his mount. As a British band played a popular tune of the day, "The World Turned Upside Down," Washington, betraying no emotion, watched silently as his foes laid down their arms. By the time the last of the 7,241 enemy soldiers had surrendered his weapons, a gaudy red and gold autumn sunset colored the sky, and the long shadows of late afternoon stretched across bucolic fields that only two days before had been a killing ground.[71]

On the day of the surrender, which he simply called "this Important Event," Washington told Congress that his victory was the result of the "unremitting Ardor" of his officers and soldiers. A week later, a bit more jauntily, he spoke of his victory as a "glorious event." However, in the midst of the celebrations Washington was anxious to seize the opportunity and score additional glorious victories. He remained apprehensive that Britain would yield to America only the territory it did not control. Furthermore, past successes had sometimes resulted in unexpected troubles. The victory at Saratoga, for instance, had led many to mistakenly conclude that the war was all but over. If Cornwallis's surrender led the citizenry to a similar conclusion, there could be such a diminution of public support that Washington might soon find himself without an army. Thus, he hoped to immediately clear Georgia and South Carolina, including Charleston, of the British army. The victory festivities had hardly ended before he dispatched Lafayette and Wayne to join Greene's army in South Carolina, and he sought to persuade de Grasse to sail for Charleston, where still another siege operation could be instituted. But as so often occurred in this war, Washington met with frustration. Explaining that his orders were to return to the Caribbean in early November, de Grasse refused to participate in a campaign for Charleston.[72]

Personal tragedy soon afflicted Washington as well. Jackie Custis, Martha's twenty-six-year-old son, had come from Mount Vernon with Washington to serve as his stepfather's aide during the siege. Just after Cornwallis's capitulation, he fell ill with a camp fever and was moved to his uncle's estate about thirty miles away. Soon thereafter complications set in. Washington was packing at headquarters for another trip to Mount Vernon when word arrived that Jackie's condition had worsened. The general hurried to his side, but the young man died only minutes after his arrival, one of the last casualties of the last great engagement of the war. Washington was "uncommonly affected," according to an observer. He remained at Martha's side for five days, grief stricken and unable to tend his duties. Eventually, Washington rode to Mount Vernon, where he spent a week with Lund carefully planning operations at his estate for 1782. Then he journeyed to Philadelphia to plan with Congress military operations for 1782, if in fact another campaign was required.[73]

While victory was being won at Yorktown, Jefferson was under siege in Virginia, reeling under charges that he was responsible for the debacle that had befallen Virginia between January and June. As Rochambeau and Washington mounted their siege, Jefferson told a friend: "I . . . covet [a] large . . . share of the honor in accomplishing so great an event."[74] If Jefferson believed he had helped in some way to shape the triumph over Cornwallis, it is unlikely that anyone else in Virginia shared his feelings. In fact, when the assembly finally met a week after Tarleton's raid on Charlottesville, George Nicholas urged his colleagues in the House of Delegates to investigate the conduct of Jefferson and the Council during the past twelve months. Patrick Henry supported the inquiry, which was approved and scheduled for the fall session of the legislature.

Several members of the assembly sought an explanation for the "numberless miscarriages and losses," the "omissions, and other Misconduct" that had, among other things, resulted in the "total want of opposition" to two British incursions during the year. Charges were made that Jefferson had mishandled the militia, failing to mobilize it in several important counties, ignoring offers by militia commanders to recruit volunteer units, and tardily calling up inadequate numbers of the soldiery. It was also alleged that Jefferson had failed to post sentinels, developed a poor signal system for relaying information regarding enemy movements, ignored General Washington's warnings, and responded to Arnold's invasion with inexcusable dilatoriness.[75] Despite Jefferson's vow to turn his back forever on public service, he successfully ran for election to the assembly in order to defend himself. When the legislature met in December, Jefferson for once scrupulously attended each session so that he might respond to the inquiry into his conduct. However, the inquest never occurred. After Yorktown few assemblymen thought it worthwhile to pillory someone who had little interest, and little future, in politics. Near the end of the session, Jefferson took the floor and defended his conduct, after which both houses adopted resolutions that lauded his integrity. Pointedly, neither house commended any act that Jefferson had undertaken as governor of Virginia.[76] Most assemblymen likely saw the resolution as a valedictory for a man who had been their colleague for many years and who had authored the Declaration of Independence. Once the resolutions were passed, Jefferson went home and never again attended the assembly.

The news of what had occurred at Yorktown reached Europe five weeks after Cornwallis's surrender. When Lord North learned of the debacle on the Virginia peninsula, he took the news as if he had been shot in the chest, according to the messenger, exclaiming: "Oh God. It is all over." He was correct. Although the British possessed New York and parts of the South, and did not lack favorable prospects should they choose to campaign for still another year, Yorktown immediately enfeebled the national will to continue. Within six weeks of learning of Cornwallis's surrender, the House of Commons passed a resolution against "the further prosecution of offensive warfare on the Continent of North America." Although not everyone understood it as such at the time, this action was tantamount to a grant of American independence, for if London was no longer prepared to fight, it no longer was capable of dictating the terms under which the residents of the United States would live.[77]

Word of Yorktown arrived in Amsterdam on or about November 26, while Adams was still recovering from his recent brush with death. Late the previous month, about ten weeks after his collapse, he at last had felt strong enough to dictate his first letter to Abigail. He now was able to write his own letters, though he said it "fatigues me more to write one letter than it did ten" a year earlier. However, he was still too weak to conduct much business, and too feeble even to celebrate the joyous news from Virginia. This passionate man, who had so often roared with anger when stymied, or sprang with joy at his triumphs, and who had risked so much to achieve the concerted action by allied land and sea forces that had at last occurred at Yorktown, received the news quietly. He merely wrote a friend that the "infant Hercules . . . [has] tryumphantly . . . strangled . . . Cornwallis." Curiously, Adams, who had been correct about so much, misjudged the magnitude of the allies' victory. He knew that the triumph meant that Virginia and North Carolina were safe. He knew too that the United States would be larger than it might have been had mediation occurred in 1780 or early 1781. However, Adams did not foresee an early peace. In fact, he told his wife that peace would not come "for several years." He was not alone. Neither Washington nor Vergennes thought peace was at hand.[78]

The war did continue, but not as Adams, or Washington, had envisioned. Adams believed that the British army would have to be driven from South Carolina and Georgia, and from New York as well, before the ministry would consider peace. He did not immediately understand how drastically Yorktown had changed everything. For instance, it reversed the relationship between the allies. In the dark days from the spring of 1780 onward, Adams and others had worried that France would betray the United States, making peace when it was in her interest to do so. Yorktown made France fearful that it would be betrayed by an ally that would immediately make peace if enticed with an offer of independence. It now was France that feared being left to fight alone. Furthermore, from the moment that news of Yorktown reached London, a majority in Parliament was resigned to peace with America, though not necessarily accompanied by a recognition of the independence of the United States.[79]

Yorktown also sparked movement at The Hague. During the previous spring, soon after Congress had formally commissioned him to seek a treaty of amity and commerce with Holland, Adams had urged the Dutch government to recognize the United States, grant it a loan, and open its ports to American ships. The French resisted his action to the end. In fact, the French minister to Holland even hurled nebulous threats at Adams, but French cajolery only made Adams more certain that his behavior was in the best interest of the United States. Adams did not expect swift success. Dutch officials "will deliberate, and deliberate and deliberate," he had predicted. They did just that, until word of Yorktown arrived. Then they acted. In a ceremony set for April 19, 1782, the seventh anniversary of the war's origin at Lexington and Concord, Holland recognized the United States. Six months later it extended a loan to the United States.[80]

If Jefferson craved some credit for Yorktown, Adams longed to be lauded for his years of sacrifice and anguish as a diplomat, service that he believed had destroyed his health. While Jefferson endured the scent of failure, Adams's success in Holland brought the rewards he had sought. It was very sweet, all the more so because both Vergennes and Franklin had attempted to block him from ever going to Amsterdam. His Dutch mission, he said that spring, was the greatest triumph of his career, and his achievement was the "happiest Event" of his life. It was therapeutic as well. "Mynheer Adams" was feted throughout Holland, he told Abigail. After laboring in the shadow of Franklin, and suffering the wrath of Vergennes and the disdain of Congress, his triumph provided an emotional boost that aided in his slow recovery from his debilitating illness.[81]

Yorktown also brought down the North ministry. It tottered into the spring of 1782 before collapsing, ending a dozen years of governance that spanned the period from just before the Boston Massacre to just after Cornwallis's defeat on a distant battlefield. In May the new ministry sent Richard Oswald, an elderly retired businessman with an interest in philosophy and an avocation for diplomacy—a man chosen because of his obvious similarities to Franklin—to Paris to open negotiations with the American commissioners. Franklin summoned Adams from Holland and John Jay, who had been sent as the United States plenipotentiary to the Spanish court in 1779, then added to the peace commission when it was expanded by Congress. Adams declined to come immediately. He believed he was close to success in negotiating the loan and commercial treaty with the Dutch. He also doubted that the negotiations would proceed quickly.[82]

Adams was correct. The early negotiations in Paris moved at a snail's pace. The British envoy probed to determine whether it was likely that America would agree to any terms that would keep it within the empire. Two months passed before the discussions moved off dead center. By then the British understood that American independence was inevitable, although the ministry had not decided on the conditions on which independence would be offered. Franklin acted alone during this early phase. Adams was absent and Jay, who had rushed to Paris, fell ill with influenza and was bedridden for weeks. Franklin proved to be an adroit diplomat, convincing London that if it offered bountiful terms, America would threaten to make a separate peace, thus enabling the British to conclude a satisfactory settlement with Versailles.[83]

Thereafter, talks between Oswald and Franklin, then between Oswald and Jay, after Franklin fell ill with a kidney stone, progressed rapidly. The British were generous, as they wanted the United States out of the war. Indeed, the Americans might have gotten more—what today is southern Ontario, for instance—had they understood just how munificent London was willing to be. The final break in the early discussions came in September when Jay learned, with British help, that Vergennes's secretary had made a secret trip to London. For some time Jay had suspected that France desired to prevent the United States from obtaining the transmontane West and rights to the Newfoundland fisheries. He now was convinced of French duplicity. Fearing that Versailles was attempting to abandon its ally by reaching a separate accord with London, Jay informed the British that the commissioners would betray France in return for a treaty with favorable terms. Great Britain leaped at the opportunity. To this point, London had consented only to parlay with the commissioners of the "colonies or plantations." Now it agreed to treat with "the Commissioners of the United States of America." On September 28 Jay wrote Adams to come "soon—very soon."[84]

Adams did not reach Paris until October 26. He refused to leave The Hague until the commercial accord was signed and, because of his delicate health, traveled slowly from Holland to France. On his arrival, Adams spoke with his fellow commissioners and learned that to this point the negotiations had resulted in a mixed bag of accomplishments and disappointments. Franklin and Jay had already relinquished Canada, but as the U.S. invasion in 1775 had failed, and no attempt had been made subsequently to conquer the region, Adams never expected to secure this territory. However, he was happily surprised to discover that Great Britain had already conceded the West to the Mississippi River. The worst news was that New England had not done well. His fellow commissioners not only had agreed to a United States-British Canada boundary line well below what Massachusetts had historically regarded as its northern limits, but terms had been agreed to that were detrimental to the New England fishing industry. Finally, Adams learned for the first time that Congress had stipulated in 1781 that the commissioners were to adhere to the "advice and opinion" of France in making agreements with London. He was outraged at such a thought, but relieved to find that Jay and Franklin shared his unwillingness to be bound by such a directive.[85]

Adams met with Jay soon after he reached Paris. He and Jay had often clashed in Congress. Anticipating that he might side with Franklin on every issue, Adams expected to dislike him, maybe hate him. Instead, Adams discovered that Jay not only agreed with him on every substantive issue, but that the two shared a mutual suspicion of France. "Our Allies dont play us fair," Jay carped. The French were "endeavoring to deprive Us of the Fishery, the Western Lands, and the Navigation of the Mississippi. They would even bargain with the English to deprive us of them," Jay railed. By the time he left the meeting Adams knew that he and Jay would, if necessary, outvote Franklin on every crucial point.[86]

As he prepared to enter negotiations, Adams's principal concern, aside from securing good terms for his native New England, was to obtain a treaty that would permit the United States to be truly independent. If it was left weak and powerless, Adams knew his country would inevitably become a satellite of France, for relations between the United States and Great Britain were certain to remain strained for generations to come. Adams, in fact, referred to Britain—a commercial rival and the possessor of Canada—as the "natural enemy" of the United States. But if the United States was sufficiently strong to be truly independent of both France and Britain, its future promised peace and prosperity. Adams focused on two items that were crucial to these ends. The territory west of the Appalachians had already been obtained, but he wished to gain the right of navigation on the Mississippi River. If denied the use of that mighty river, western farmers would be unable to get their goods to eastern and foreign markets. If denied access to markets, the western farmers would be ripe for the machinations of the European power that controlled the Mississippi. Adams was also prepared to fight for full rights to the fisheries. This was crucial to New England, but important to the United States too, he said, as a fishing industry would be "a Nursery of Seamen and a source of naval power" for the young nation.[87]

Adams was confident that these concessions could be won from Great Britain, but he worried about Franklin, whom he thought no better than "a willing auxiliary" of Vergennes. He had no intention of calling on Vergennes, who did not even learn that he was in town until he saw Adams's name in the "Returns of the Police" two weeks later. Nor did he plan to visit Franklin, whom he had not seen for more than two years, and toward whom his fury knew no bounds. Since learning that Franklin had told Congress that he had injured America's relationship with France, Adams had spoken often of the Doctor's deceit, treachery, and malevolence. Adams was certain that Franklin and Vergennes had acted in concert to "demolish me" and "crush me," and that little effort had been required of Vergennes to persuade Franklin to act against him. Franklin's tactics, he charged, had "ever been to Sweep Europe clear of every Minister, that he might have a clear unrivaled Stage." Franklin was "cunning," Adams said, and he now feared that the Doctor would stop at nothing to win. "[H]e will provoke, he will insinuate, he will intrigue, he will maneuvre" to "divide" Jay and himself in order to get the American commissioners to act as France desired.[88] Adams had no intention of making a long carriage ride to Passy to call on a man he hated with every fiber in his body.

However, Adams relented after a friend convinced him that it might prove to be quite unfortunate if the British realized that fissures existed within the American negotiating team. Thus, on his third day in Paris Adams called on Franklin. He managed to be cordial and Franklin, though still recovering from the stone, appeared to be "merry and pleasant."[89]

Later that same day the members of the British negotiating team called on Adams at his customary Parisian lodging, the Hôtel de Valois. This was only a social call. They drank tea and chatted informally, but never discussed diplomacy. Henry Strachey, a proper, dignified undersecretary of state, was now in charge of the British team. Strachey's colleagues were Oswald, Benjamin Vaughn, a Jamaican gadfly whose mother hailed from Boston, and Alleyne Fitzherbert, a 29-year-old career diplomat. It was not a strong delegation. Fitzherbert was the best of the bunch, but he devoted most of his energies to the negotiations with Spain and France, which were preceding simultaneously. There was no plausible reason for Vaughn's presence. Strachey had some experience in foreign policy matters, but almost no background in day-to-day diplomacy, and poor Oswald was in the clutches of dementia, perhaps the early stages of Alzheimer's disease.[90]

The next morning, October 30, the men on both sides, dressed in finery—Adams had purchased new clothing, shoes, and a wig upon arriving in Paris—alighted from handsome carriages at Jay's lodging, the Hotel de la Chine at the Palais Royal. The final negotiations, what Adams called "this great Affair," were at hand.[91] For years men had served, and many had suffered and died in squalid camps and on lonely battlefields, in order to decide this terrible war. The soldiers had now done all they could. From this moment forward everything was in the hands of diplomats and politicians, who in the elegance and comfort of paneled drawing rooms would make the final decisions in a war spawned by the American Revolution.

That Wednesday morning Franklin, Jay, and Adams were together for the first time. The delegation was to have consisted of two additional members. Jefferson, who had been appointed to the expanded commission twenty months earlier, nine days after Tarleton chased him from Monticello, had declined the assignment. He wished to remain in Virginia to fight the scheduled legislative inquiry into his gubernatorial conduct, but even more he steadfastly maintained that he had "taken my final leave" of public affairs.[92] Furthermore, by the time he declined the post, he knew that Martha once again was pregnant, and did not wish to leave her side. Henry Laurens, a South Carolina planter and former president of Congress, was to have been the other member of the American team. He had accepted and sailed for Europe during 1781, but was captured on the high seas. Although the British released him on the eve of Oswald's initial meeting with Franklin, Laurens's health had suffered terribly during nearly two years incarceration in the Tower of London and he played no role in the negotiations until the next to last day.

The three American commissioners were superior to their counterparts. Each was an experienced diplomat and skilled politician, and Jay and Adams were veteran lawyers, adept at disputation and repartee. Furthermore, it soon was apparent that Adams's fears that Franklin might prove a liability had been misplaced. He was "very able" at the bargaining table, Adams subsequently remarked. Not only was Franklin not a burden, he said, but he contributed to the commissioners' success "both by his Sagacity and Reputation." However, Adams believed that Jay was the superior negotiator and the most capable member of the American team.[93] The three commissioners worked together in a spirit of harmony, even conviviality. Although they disagreed on the details of many issues, their differences did not result in disruptive strains. On the most substantive issue of all, Congress's directive that they be governed by the advice of the French foreign ministry, they unanimously agreed to disregard their orders. In fact, at the first negotiating session after Adams joined his colleagues, Franklin openly stated that the commissioners would proceed without consulting the French, although the Treaty of Alliance had stipulated that neither signatory would agree to a separate peace.[94]

Although much had been accomplished prior to Adams's arrival and that of the entire British delegation, much remained to be done. Issues relating to debts, fisheries, New England's boundaries, and the Loyalists were still on the table. Adams quickly made a decision on the debt question without prior consultation with his colleagues, one of the few instances of such an occurrence during these final talks. The British had pressed to recover debts incurred prior to 1775. Franklin and Jay had insisted that Congress had not granted them power to treat the issue, but Adams believed the honorable course was to pay the debts. "I have no Notion of Cheating any Body," he declared. This was a moral issue for Adams, but he also feared that without such a provision, British creditors would wreck the treaty in Parliament, perhaps causing the fighting to resume in America in 1783. Adams also knew that nonpayment would unavoidably damage postwar relations with Great Britain. As most prewar debts were owed by southern planters, Jefferson and Laurens might have seen things differently, but they were not present, and Jay and Franklin immediately conceded the point. A provision was added to the treaty stipulating that "Creditors on either side shall meet with no lawful impediment to the Recovery of the full Value in Sterling Money of all bona fide Debts" incurred prior to the war.[95]

Adams took an active role in seeking a treaty that guaranteed Massachusetts the territory that it had traditionally claimed on its frontier with Nova Scotia. After lengthy bargaining, he scored a considerable, but not total, victory, securing most of what had been relinquished earlier. The U.S.–Canadian boundary west of Maine also grew from Adams's proposal that it follow the forty-fifth parallel from the Connecticut River to the Mississippi River. As a result of this agreement the United States forfeited southern Ontario and gave the Canadians access to the Great Lakes, but acquired the northern reaches of present Minnesota, in which the Mesabi Iron Range is located. As both sides mistakenly believed that the Mississippi River originated in Canada, the agreement that both Great Britain and the United States would enjoy the right of navigation on the river came easily.[96]

No issue in these negotiations was of greater importance to Adams than the fisheries. He spoke of trying to acquire "Tom Cod" for his countrymen, but because fishing was big business on both sides, Adams was compelled to make more concessions than he would have liked. At one point Adams announced that he had "laid down a Line, and beyond that I will not go," though he later conceded still more. Nevertheless, Adams secured much more than Franklin and Jay had obtained prior to his arrival, especially in the Newfoundland Banks. Ultimately, U.S. fishermen received the "liberty" to fish on the Newfoundland Banks and the "right" to fish in the Gulf of St. Lawrence, as well as the right to dry their catches on the uninhabited coasts of Nova Scotia, Labrador, and the Magdalen Islands. The distinction between a "liberty" and a "right" would cause problems for American fishermen for the next century. Many years later Adams remarked that "We did not think it necessary to contend for a word," although the contemporary evidence suggests that he clearly understood the distinction between the terms, but agreed to such wording as the only hope of immediately extending America's fishing jurisdiction.[97]

The last great issue that produced incessant bickering, and no little acrimony, concerned the Loyalists. Tories had been the victims of violence and social ostracism since before the outbreak of the war. Hostilities worsened their situation. Late in the war, faced with a collapsing economy, virtually every state had confiscated and sold Loyalist properties as a revenue-raising measure. The British demanded that the United States indemnify the Tories for their lost property. Adams, who was touched by the plight of these unfortunates, some of whom were friends from his days as a provincial attorney, would have agreed to compensation had he been the sole negotiator, but Jay and Franklin—whose son had remained loyal to the Crown—were intransigent. The best the British team could get was a meaningless provision stipulating that Congress was to recommend that the states make remuneration to the Loyalists.[98]

Negotiations seemed to Adams to drag interminably. Paris had luxuriated under a pleasant autumn sun when he joined the talks, but as they drew to a conclusion in late November, the city lay beneath gray scudding clouds that announced the coming of winter. In reality, the talks had moved quickly, requiring barely a month to complete. Many substantive points were agreed on within the first ten days of discussion. On November 10 Strachey hurried to London for instructions. When he returned two weeks later he was prepared to overcome the last stumbling blocks, the Loyalist issue and the fishing questions. Thereafter, matters sped to an end, concluding after only five days of further bargaining. The fishing question was the last matter to be resolved, although on that same day, at the next to last session, an issue not previously raised was introduced and quickly accepted, almost as an afterthought. Laurens attended for the first time that morning and proposed the inclusion of an article that prohibited the British army from taking American "Negroes or other property" from the United States when its army left America. The British negotiators agreed with seeming indifference.

All that remained was to sign the Preliminary Articles. On November 30, a cold Saturday, the four Americans met at Jay's lodging, then proceeded to Oswald's apartment in the Grand Hotel Muscovite. What followed was not a ceremony. The signing did not take place in a grand hall before the press and a vast, beaming audience. Instead, in a spacious hotel suite the diplomats, with a few aides looking on, simply signed the accord, then rode in several carriages to Passy, where they dined as the guests of Franklin.

To the surprise of some, Adams had performed ably. His friend Mercy Warren had believed that Adams, a small-town New Englander who had never shed his simple proprieties, was "deficient in the *je ne scai quoi* so necessary in highly polished society," and was doomed to fail as a diplomat. Another friend, Jonathan Sewall, who had remained loyal to Great Britain, also expected that Adams would be wanting as a diplomat. He will be "quite out of his element," Sewall predicted, for he "cannot dance, drink, game, flatter, promise, dress, swear with the gentlemen, and talk small talk or flirt with the ladies." Both underestimated Adams. In fact, his comments suggest that he delighted in the "surfeit of feasting, fatigue, and ceremony" that accompanied the negotiations. Always a competitor, Adams also doubtless prospered on the sparring and the challenge.[99]

It was true that Adams, and every other American envoy, lacked Franklin's skills to soothe adversaries and cultivate friends. However, those talents that had helped Adams win success as a lawyer and congressman—industry, intelligence, preparation, persistence, and frank honesty—served him well in diplomacy. Adams probably won his point on the Maine boundary question not only because he had done considerable research on the matter, but because he had with him maps and documents that he had the foresight to bring from home in 1779. He presented so much evidence on the fisheries question that he literally wore down his counterparts; at one point an exasperated Fitzherbert conceded an issue, sighing wearily that the "argument is in your favor." Rather than the stuffy prig whom Warren and Sewall limned, Adams repeatedly demonstrated that he could be an excellent companion and good conversationalist. He was well-read and could address numerous subjects. Furthermore, as a lawyer, politician, and diplomat who had lived away from home in the company of other men for extended periods, Adams had grown more dexterous in swapping stories and—perhaps a greater skill—listening to others talk. Not that Adams had abandoned his well-known irascibility. When the French told the Americans that British "national honor" dictated that the United States must compensate the Loyalists, Adams roared: "National honor, bosh!" In heated tones he went on to argue that Great Britain had been dragged to defeat and disgrace by listening to the half-truths of the Tories. "Very true," Vergennes's secretary acknowledged, and dropped the issue.[100]

Franklin and Vergennes, and some in Congress, had feared that Adams was too inflexible to be an effective diplomat. He proved them wrong. Throughout these talks he was ready to make concessions. He saw that a good treaty was the sum of all its parts. He was not about to let the gains that had been achieved slip away through his intransigence. But he could be patient, which is always a virtue in a good diplomat. During the negotiations on the fisheries, the British attempted to bluff him by claiming they could not make an agreement without London's assent. Adams called their bluff. "That is perfectly all right," he told the British. "We can wait. Send a courier back to London." His British counterparts subsequently accepted what Adams had demanded. Some had also feared that Adams could not work with others, but they too were wrong. "We lived together in perfect good humour," he said of his relationship with Franklin and Jay, adding that "nothing could have been more agreeable." Franklin and Jay never disagreed with his assessment.[101]

With good reason, Adams was delighted with what the American commissioners achieved. It was an excellent treaty for the United States. Adams had sought a pact that would enable his country to be truly independent, and that had been accomplished. Nothing in this accord, he rejoiced, would make the United States "a Football between contending Nations." He was especially happy with the provisions that granted the right of navigation on the Mississippi and opened the fisheries to the United States. To have been denied those rights, he said, would have been "sure and certain Sources of a future War."[102]

He breathed a sigh of relief when all was done. On the eve of negotiations, Adams reflected that he and fellow activists in Massachusetts in 1775 had, "with the best Intentions in the World, set the World in a blaze." It was a conflagration that had resulted in the death of at least 25,000 Americans, and probably as many as 35,000; that many, or more, British soldiers had died in service, as well as nearly 5,000 Hessians. Adams had no misgivings about his participation in what he called a "mighty Trajedy." Nor was he disappointed in its outcome. Both militarily and diplomatically, the war "has unravelled itself happily for Us," he remarked just after the preliminary articles were signed.[103]

One other matter especially delighted Adams. During the mid-November lull in the talks, he learned from Lafayette that Vergennes wished to see him. Adams glumly rode out from Paris, expecting the worst. Not only had Vergennes caused him considerable pain over the years, but the foreign minister was livid with the commissioners for having agreed to a separate peace with

Great Britain. However, he arrived at Versailles to discover that Vergennes and his wife had prepared an elaborate formal dinner for him. When the dishes were taken away, and the guest and company raised a last glass of wine, Vergennes, who all along had known that Adams was fiercely independent and indomitable, toasted him as *Le Washington de la Negotiation*. Adams was enraptured. He felt vindicated. His sacrifices, his daring, his suffering had not been in vain. "This is the finishing Stroke," he wrote that evening in his diary. "It is impossible to exceed this."[104]

Signing the Preliminary Articles did not end the war. Great Britain did not reach preliminary accords with France and Spain until early in 1783, and the work of the diplomats on all sides had to be approved by their respective governments. Yet while the United States technically remained in a state of hostilities, the nature of the war that followed Yorktown was quite unlike that which had preceded it. Britain and France fought on the high seas and in the Caribbean, but neither undertook land operations in mainland North America. Washington did not even rejoin his army until six months after Cornwallis's surrender, and he did not confer again with Rochambeau before the summer of 1782. He spent from November to April in Philadelphia, occasionally consulting with Congress. They agreed to attempt nothing risky. Their object was simply to keep the army together in the event that the peace talks collapsed and fighting resumed on the continent. The potential for danger persisted, but when London did nothing after the Royal Navy scored a considerable triumph over the French fleet in April in the Caribbean, it was evident that Great Britain had no stomach for further warfare against its former colonies.

After Yorktown the greatest danger to the American Revolution was posed not by the British armed forces, but by officers in the Continental army. With peace on the horizon and the economy in shambles, many officers grew apprehensive that Congress would not honor its commitment to provide them a pension of half-pay for seven years. On at least seven occasions during the autumn of 1782 Washington told Congress that an ugly mood was growing among the officers. Just after Christmas the officers petitioned Congress for compensation.[105]

What followed is one of the most mysterious events in U.S. history. In all likelihood nationalists in Congress, men such as Hamilton, Robert Morris of Pennsylvania, and Gouverneur Morris of New York, saw an opportunity to use the officers' disaffection to strengthen the powers of the national government. They recognized that the army could be used as leverage to frighten Congress into agreeing to a constitutional amendment granting the national government the power to levy imposts. Secret talks doubtless took place between conspirators in Philadelphia and Newburgh, New York, the principal cantonment of the Continental army. How much Washington knew of these machinations will never be known, but it stretches credulity to believe that he knew nothing. He not only had kept his antennae raised throughout this war for evidence of conspiracies, but he was extremely close to General Knox, who had authored the petition to Congress. Furthermore, in February Washington received a remarkable letter from Hamilton that all but said that the army was about to be used to sow alarm in Congress.[106]

The officers' protest burst into the open on March 14, 1783, a few days before anyone in America learned that the Preliminary Articles had been signed in Paris. That day at Newburgh the plotters published an unsigned statement urging a meeting of all officers the following day. Their address proposed that if Congress betrayed them, the officers must either resign en masse should the war continue or refuse to disband the army should peace occur. Only a congressional vote to fund their pensions would stay their hand. To take the first option would leave the United States at war without an army. The second option would confront civilian authority with a defiant, even revolutionary, army, raising the specter of a coup d'etat.[107]

Only General Washington commanded the respect to head off the cabal, and he acted immediately. Whether Washington acted spontaneously or on cue will probably never be known. However, as Hamilton had told him three weeks earlier that in the event this "suffering army" threatened illegal action, the commander must take steps to "bring order perhaps even good, out of confusion," it is likely that Washington was not taken by complete surprise.[108] What is certain is that Washington required no prompting to act. He had labored tirelessly to establish the prestige of the Continental army and he was a devout republican, committed to the military's subordination to civilian authority. He would not stand by and permit the conspirators to misuse this army. Washington summoned the officers to a meeting in the Temple of Honor at Newburgh at noon on March 15.

The Temple, which the soldiery used for social purposes and worship services, was new and still smelled of fresh-cut green wood. Although a blanket of newly-fallen snow covered the landscape, the hall was warm and stuffy, as fires roared in several fireplaces and hundreds of officers crowded inside. Near noon some of the men stood in clusters talking loudly, but most were in their seats, waiting quietly, or conversing in low tones with friends seated nearby. Tension filled the air. Opinions were many and varied about how to respond to the unsigned statement. No one knew what would transpire at this meeting, or even precisely what was planned either by Washington or those who had written the address. The officers knew only that the order of the day indicated that the senior officer, General Gates, would preside at this gathering, and he, together with several aides and high ranking officers, were seated at a table in the front of the hall.

Precisely at noon a door adjacent to a small dais suddenly opened and General Washington, looking grave and "agitated," according to one observer, strode into the Temple. He walked directly to a rustic podium near where Gates was seated. Conversations ended abruptly. Men hurried to their seats. Washington waited patiently until the scraping of chairs and all commotion ceased. When the room fell totally silent, he slowly unfolded a sheaf of papers, looked up one last time, then gazed at his notes and began to read. The men strained to hear him. Washington, who was never comfortable making speeches, spoke in a quiet, almost inaudible voice. He stumbled over a few sentences, then gained his rhythm.

He told the officers that he had been with them since the first, and that he had never left their side, save for times when Congress called him away. He spoke lovingly of the army, and of how his reputation was inextricably tied to it. The course that had been proposed for the army, to "sheath your swords" or to refuse to disband—whichever path was contrary to the wishes of the civil leaders—was "so shocking . . . that humanity revolts at the idea," he said slowly, forcefully. The author of the address, he charged, was "an insidious foe" both of his army and his country, and unless foiled would destroy both. Congress, he promised, would act. Legislators moved slowly, but Congress would act and "act justly." He closed his prepared address by asking the officers to remember "your sacred honor," your country, the "natural character of America," and the "rights of humanity." Reject this wicked appeal, and posterity will say that the officers in the Continental army had attained "the last stage of perfection to which human nature is capable of attaining."

Washington was at the end of his prepared statement. He paused. Not a sound was heard in the great room. He sensed that his remarks had failed to move many in this audience. After a moment, he spoke again. He wanted to read a letter from a congressman. He slowly removed the missive from his inside coat pocket and began to read. Once again he stumbled, apparently having difficulty seeing the letter. He paused. Slowly he reached again in his pocket. He extracted a pair of glasses, and slowly put them on. The men had never seen General Washington in spectacles. He very slowly adjusted the tiny wire-rimmed glasses, took up the letter once again, but stopped after a long pause. Looking over his glasses at the packed room, Washington begged their indulgence at his wearing glasses. In a soft voice that resonated with anger, fatigue, and unbridled despair, he told the officers: "Gentlemen, you must pardon me. I have grown gray in your service and now find myself growing blind."[109]

Washington read the letter. It was meaningless, but he had made his point with clever theatrics. With the assurance of an accomplished actor, he now had the audience in the palm of his hand. Throughout the hall men were weeping, tough men who had witnessed much carnage and had grown accustomed to life-and-death decisions. Washington completed the congressman's letter, carefully, slowly, removed his glasses, and strode from the Temple of Honor without another word. He knew that one more word would be anticlimactic. With the adroitness of a skilled dramatist, he sensed when, and how, to stop, to leave. He had defused the threat in an instant. After Washington departed, men from headquarters, leaving nothing to chance, obtained the floor and pushed to adoption a statement of loyalty to Congress.[110]

Three days later word of the Preliminary Articles arrived at headquarters. Soon thereafter both General Guy Carleton, now the commander of the British army in North America, and Washington issued orders for a cease-fire.[111] Their orders were issued just before the eighth anniversary of that chilly April morning in 1775 when the stillness in Lexington, Massachusetts, had been shattered by British gunfire.

Washington was anxious to return to Mount Vernon, leaving behind his cares as commander and resuming his civilian pursuits. However, the army had to be kept intact until word of the definitive peace treaty arrived and the British army at last sailed from New York. Washington faced a busy schedule in the eight months before the commissioners in Paris were heard from again. He spent some of his time lobbying Congress on behalf of his officers. His efforts succeeded when Congress voted full pay for five years to each officer. Washington never requested, and Congress never provided, any bonus for the enlisted men, who had not been paid for months. Washington issued a valedictory address to the citizenry. His theme, uttered publicly for the first time, was one that he had often reiterated in private since 1779. Unless the national government was granted additional powers, "the Union cannot be of long duration."[112]

Washington also negotiated directly with General Carleton on two important matters. One issue concerned the exchange of prisoners of war. The capture of Cornwallis's army gave Washington the leverage he required to arrange the speedy liberation of virtually all American soldiers who languished in captivity within the United States. However, Washington could not win on the second issue, which concerned the treaty provision that prohibited the British from carrying away American property. Washington insisted that the British commander surrender all fugitive slaves who had fled behind British lines. As Washington was aware that the British had taken away more than 10,000 fugitive slaves from Charleston and Savannah prior to the arrival of the preliminary treaty, he was not surprised when Carleton refused his demand. Carleton took the position that the African-American fugitives had ceased to be property when they made the decision to escape to the British. After only one day of negotiation, Washington knew it was hopeless. That same evening he wrote a friend in Virginia that the fugitive slaves still within the United States would never be returned. He was correct. The British eventually shipped about 4,000 African Americans from New York to Canada and the Caribbean in 1783.[113]

Washington spent little time with his army during the final months of the war. He undertook a summer trip to northern New York, partly to enjoy a vacation from headquarters, partly to search for suitable land that he might purchase. He succeeded on both scores. It was a vacation for a hardy individual. Washington traveled over 750 miles in less than three weeks, hiking, portaging, riding, sailing, canoeing, and camping both in the Lake Champlain wilderness and the green New York forests west of Albany. He vigilantly watched for choice available land and eventually acquired a lush tract in the Mohawk Valley. Soon after he returned to the Hudson, Congress summoned him for consultation on the postwar army and Indian relations. He hurried to Princeton, where Congress now met, and remained there from August into November. The leaves had fallen and winter was in the air by the time he returned to West Point. In every village along his route the citizenry turned out in the bleak town squares and browned commons to cheer him and, if he would submit, to fete him. Sometimes he made a little speech, almost always a homily about virtue, sacrifice, and strengthening the national government.[114]

Washington had left Congress as soon as word arrived that the final peace accord, the Treaty of Paris, which was identical to the preliminary pact, had been signed in early September. Washington remained at West Point for only a week before he learned that the British were evacuating New York. He hurried to the metropolis that he had so longed to take in battle and, at noon on November 25, led his army down Broadway into the heart of the city. It was a cold day, but thousands lined the streets to cheer Washington and the soldiers.

Washington remained for several days of wearying festivities. He was anxious to be gone, and did depart on December 4, but not until one last ceremony was completed. On his final day in New York, Washington invited his highest officers to a noon luncheon at Fraunces Tavern. His intention was less to dine than to say farewell. It was an emotional meeting. Most of the men were middle aged. The war was over. The great epoch of their lives was at an end. Each man knew that his life now would change in ways that he could not foresee. Yet each knew that he would probably never again savor the intimate pleasures of camaraderie, never again experience the pulsating thrill of danger, or ever again glory in the elation of military victory. These men ate together one final time. They talked, a bit awkwardly now, and there were long pauses when they did not know what to say. When it was time, Washington rose. He would deliver no speech. Nothing was left to be said. He could not put into words what he and these men felt. He simply asked that each man come forward individually to say goodbye. Each came in his turn. In a public ceremony they would have bowed politely, stiffly. In the privacy of this room every man embraced Washington, and he in turn held them. Every man in the room wept, including Washington.[115]

When the final goodbye was said, he was abruptly gone, rushing out the door to the great horse that awaited in the street. It was cold, as on other wintry days during this war, as it had been on afternoons in Cambridge in 1775 when he rode through the army that was disappearing before his eyes, as it had been on that terrible black Christmas night when he had led his men across the Delaware at Trenton, as it had been on bitter days when he had made the lonely ride past the squalid huts in Valley Forge. Washington hurried through the streets of New York, riding to the Hudson, the river he had fled across in 1776, the sluicing blue-green waterway that Arnold had tried to relinquish to the British. This time Washington crossed by barge, with citizens standing and cheering when he embarked on the eastern shore, and applauding and hurrahing when he alighted on the Jersey shore.

He did not pause. He was on his way home. He traveled the same road between New York and Philadelphia that he had taken when he left Congress to assume command of the army more than eight years before. Now well into middle age, just shy of his fifty-second birthday, Washington made part of this journey on horseback, but most of it while seated in a carriage. Behind him a team of horses pulled a wagon laden with his personal possessions, including seemingly numberless boxes that contained his papers.

He stopped briefly in Philadelphia to say goodbye to old acquaintances and to shop a bit. A civilian at heart, if not in fact, Washington had turned into a consumer again. He purchased lockets, sashes, hats, and hose for his wife, and books and toys for his grandchildren. He bought a hunting rifle, several bottles of wine, and many delicacies for himself, including nuts, olives, and anchovies.[116]

Then he was away to Annapolis, where the peripatetic Congress now held its sessions. The legislators honored Washington at a dinner attended by upwards of 300 on December 22. It was a stately occasion, with thirteen nearby cannon booming salutes and thirteen toasts made, and so formal according to a Delaware congressman that "not a soul got drunk." Three days earlier, when Washington arrived in this charming little village, he had presented to Congress the expense account he carefully kept throughout the war. The legislators painstakingly scrutinized it and concluded that it contained one error—Washington had shortchanged himself by a single dollar. Congress ultimately awarded him $64,335.30 in public securities, a larger sum than he would have had by accepting a salary.[117]

Washington's final act as a public official came at a ceremony held at noon on December 23. He surrendered the power that Congress had bestowed on him in June 1775. The amenities were brief and simple, yet "solemn and affecting," according to one congressman. Washington walked before Congress and slowly read a brief final address, which an observer characterized as "worthy of him." Washington was immediately overcome with emotion. His hands shook so badly that he had difficulty seeing the paper. His voice choked and was barely audible. Few in the audience could hear as he told Congress that he was surrendering a command that he had "accepted with diffidence." It was proper, he said in low tones, that he should lay down his weapons, for the United States now was independent and sovereign, "a respectable Nation." Congressmen strained to hear his last words: "I retire from the great theater of Action."[118]

When Washington completed the address, he "drew out from his bosom his commission and delivered it up to the president of Congress," as one congressman described the scene. Immediately thereafter Washington hurried from the chamber to compose himself. A few minutes later he returned to take his leave of the congressmen. He did not know many of these men. Only two had served in Congress with him in 1774 or 1775. One was Thomas Mifflin of Pennsylvania, who had also been one of his first aides-de-camp and now was the president of the Congress. The other was Jefferson, who despite his earlier pledge to never again hold public office, had been elected to Congress earlier in 1783, in time to vote for the ratification of the Treaty of Paris.

The congressmen who were bidding farewell to the commander were deeply moved. They, like their countrymen, appreciated Washington's long years of sacrifice and dedication, but he had won their affection, and that of the world, by relinquishing his power. The painter John Trumbull soon thereafter said that Washington's act "excites the astonishment and admiration of this part of the world. 'Tis a Conduct so novel, so inconceivable to People, who far from giving up powers they possess, are willing to convulse the Empire to acquire more." About this time the King, George III, asked Benjamin West, the artist, what Washington would do when he learned of the peace. West said he believed Washington would retire to Mount Vernon. "If he does that" the monarch responded, "he will be the greatest man in the world."[119]

Many congressmen and spectators were weeping as Washington donned his greatcoat for his departure. The "past—the present—the future—the manner— the occasion—all conspired to make it a spectacle inexpressibly solemn and affecting," Maryland's James McHenry noted of the day's events.[120] When the last goodbye was said, Washington hurried away on the final leg of his last journey in the American Revolution. He had promised Martha that he would be home for Christmas dinner. He kept his word.

On Christmas Eve, as the last mellow light of day pierced a soft linen blue sky, George Washington, the planter, spotted Mount Vernon. In the half light of late day he paused to gaze lovingly on his house and grounds. There was no longer any need to hurry. He never again expected to leave home on public business.

9

*"Who Shall Write the History
of the American Revolution?"*

Memory and Meaning

J efferson once used actuarial tables to calculate
that nineteen years was the span of a generation.[1] If true, less than half the residents of
the United States in 1799, when Washington died, had been alive that day a
quarter century before when British troops landed in New York and Congress
debated American independence. By the time Adams and Jefferson perished
in 1826, not one American in ten could remember the War of Independence.
With stunning swiftness, the American Revolution became a distant historical event for most Americans.

It was always the central event in the lives of Washington, Adams, and
Jefferson. Of the three, Washington appeared the least interested in the
history of the American Revolution. When he left the army his reputation
was so secure and unassailable that he had little to gain by retelling the
events of his lifetime. Furthermore, he died before the emergence of a post-
Revolutionary generation that sought to understand what the Founders had
accomplished. Nevertheless, Washington hardly ignored the great epoch of his
time.

In his final years he visited a few battlefields, including Lexington, Camden, and Guilford Court House, where he had not fought, and Trenton,
Princeton, and Germantown, where he had commanded. Once or twice he was
in the vicinity of Yorktown, the scene of his greatest triumph, and Saratoga,
where Gates's victory had helped entice France to enter the war, but did not
visit either site. When the Constitutional Convention, of which he was a

member, took a long recess in the late summer of 1787, he visited nearby Valley Forge and was disappointed to find it neglected and overgrown with tall weeds. During his presidency, Washington neither attended celebrations commemorating Revolutionary events nor published proclamations on July 4 or other Revolutionary anniversaries. Yet, although he did not publicly reminisce about the war, he assisted David Humphreys, a former-aide-de-camp, who hoped to write his biography.[2] He also owned several histories of the American Revolution, aided and encouraged at least three individuals who were chronicling the history of the rebellion, and endowed John Trumbull, who was painting the most significant events of the era.[3]

Washington's behavior offers clues to what the American Revolution meant to him. His passion to preserve the Union that had been created by the American Revolution led him to abandon an easy, fulfilling retirement in 1789 and assume the presidency. He believed that the new, stronger national government was essential for saving a Union, which he told his countrymen was the "Main Pillar in the Edifice of your real independence," the source of domestic tranquility, peace, safety, prosperity, and "that Liberty which you so highly prize." As president, he exhorted his fellow citizens to think of themselves as Americans and to "always exalt the just pride of [American] Patriotism" over and above all "local discriminations." He encouraged them to see that there were few differences, and numerous similarities, between northerners and southerners. All free Americans, he said in his Farewell Address, shared a mutual ideology and similar religious and cultural outlooks, but above all they were bound by the shared experience of the American Revolution. "You have in a common cause fought and triumphed together. The independence and liberty you possess are the work of joint councils, and joint efforts, of common dangers, sufferings and successes," he reminded his countrymen.[4]

Although President Washington comported himself with something of the majesty and formality of a monarch, no doubt existed that he cherished the national commitment to republicanism secured by the American Revolution. He scoffed privately at those who longed to imitate the "high-toned" manner of European courts. He denounced those Americans who yearned for monarchy, calling them "disciples of despotism." When Washington was urged by one of his officers to become America's king at the conclusion of the War of Independence, he replied in the most acrimonious language that he found such an idea repugnant.[5] The meaning of republicanism was clear and simple to Washington: the people possessed ultimate power. He was comfortable with the concept of the people as governors, and once even privately criticized Massachusetts for disenfranchising so many of its citizens. Washington was confident that the citizenry would exercise good judgment, although from time to time he warned the people of that "proneness to abuse [power] which predominates in the human heart," and advised them to maintain "a uniform vigilance" against charlatans and despots.[6]

The American Revolution also left Washington deeply troubled about the institution of slavery. Even before the war he had come to see that slavery was a notoriously inefficient system of labor, especially for a wheat farmer such as himself. When he returned to Mount Vernon, he found that his problems had deepened. By 1784 he owned approximately 250 chattel, scattered about the five separate farms that comprised his estate.[7] He possessed a surplus of laborers, including many who were too young, too old, or too ill to work, and others who could not labor because they were pregnant or recently had borne children. In addition, unlike free laborers who hoped for promotions or pay raises, Washington's bondsmen, like slaves everywhere, lacked any incentive to toil with enterprise.

Furthermore, in the course of the war he pondered the impropriety of bonded labor, especially race-based subjugation. Soon after hostilities ended, Washington for the first time spoke of his "regret" that the institution existed and indicated his hope that it would eventually be abolished. Pecuniary considerations had shaped his views, but moralistic concerns nurtured by his experiences in the American Revolution also played a role in his new thinking. The Revolutionary egalitarian and natural rights ideals impacted him, but his new perspective also stemmed from his surprising discovery that African Americans could match the industry, dedication, and courage exhibited by the white soldiers in the Continental army.[8]

Yet Washington found it impossible to cut his ties to slavery. When he left the army he had already outlived his father, and many other males in the Washington family, and believed that he had but a scant few years remaining. He was eager to enjoy those material accouterments he had relished before 1775, and eschewed during the long war years, and which of course hinged on the productivity of his chattel. Furthermore, Washington wished to bestow a handsome inheritance on his step-grandchildren.[9] Hesitant to cut his personal ties to slavery, he was also unwilling to speak out against slavery. He was urged to do so by many activists in America's first antislavery movement, who hoped to build on their successes in winning the gradual abolition of slavery in Pennsylvania in the mid-1780s. Washington demurred. Not only did he wish to keep the slavery question out of national politics, but he fully under-stood the potential volatility of any abolitionist remarks he might make. He had spent a lifetime dreaming and struggling to achieve ends that could be realized only through a strong national Union. The safety of that Union, not the end of slavery, was his guiding principle during all his years after the War of Independence. Slavery could be dealt with in the future, he thought, but there might never again be an opportunity to forge the Union.

However iniquitous his silence may have been to those who lived as slaves and saw their offspring born into servility, it should be kept in mind that during the last decade of his life Washington believed that southern slavery was dying. Tobacco prices had plummeted in the mid-eighteenth cen-tury and never recovered. Although the cotton gin was invented in 1792, few in Washington's lifetime understood how it would transform the South. Instead, Washington glimpsed the infant Industrial Revolution in the North and imagined—and hoped—that it would take root in the South as well. He looked toward a time, perhaps within the next half-century, when free labor-ers, black and white, would work in northern and southern mills and factories, and free farm workers, black and white, would cultivate tobacco and rice in southern fields. With good reason, Washington believed that this evil insti-tution could not long survive. But the survival of the Union, with all its potential benefits, was uncertain, and many contemporaries, including Wash-ington, believed its endurance hinged in part on the actions of the master of Mount Vernon.

In his final years Washington was clearly troubled by his station as a slaveowner. He understood only too well that he was complicit in a pro-foundly shameful enterprise. Indeed, some abolitionists did not hesitate to explain that to him. Robert Pleasants, a Virginia Quaker who had liberated his slaves, asked Washington in 1785 to imagine "how inconsistent . . . will it appear to posterity, should it be recorded, that the great General Washington . . . had . . . at the expence of much Blood & treasure been instrumental in relieving those States from Tyranny & oppression: Yet after all had so far countenanced those Evils, as to keep a number of People in absolute Slavery, who were by nature [as] equally entitled to freedom as himself."[10] Washing-ton need not have been told. As he anticipated the extinction of slavery, he also suspected that future generations would judge harshly both slavery and all who were inculpated in having sustained it. Yet, vexed though he was, Wash-ington did virtually nothing in the first fifteen years after the War of Independence to sever his ties to slavery.

In the early 1790s he looked into the possibility of simultaneously liberating his slaves and leasing to English farmers all of Mount Vernon, save for
the lands that immediately surrounded his residence. The terms of the lease
would have required that the tenants employ Washington's former slaves as
free laborers.[11] The plan was improbable and never materialized. However,
Washington might simply have done what he expected of his tenants: emancipate, then hire, his slaves. No evidence exists that he seriously considered
such an option. Nor is there reason to believe that at any time after Washington returned home in 1784 he lightened the regimen imposed on his
bondsmen. Their workload remained heavy, their living conditions squalid,
and the discipline under which they lived and worked severe. He refused to
purchase additional slaves after 1784, but, surfeited with laborers, Washington's behavior was merely pragmatic.[12] His lone sacrificial act following the
war was his refusal to sunder slave families through the sale of its members,
an instance in which his humanity triumphed over his business instincts.

Washington ultimately sought to resolve his dilemma over slavery by
preparing a new will in 1799. It stipulated that his slaves were to be manumitted on Martha's demise. However, he did not stop there. He also directed
that those who were too young or too old to look after themselves, were to be
cared for indefinitely. The younger freedmen were to be taught to read and
write, and "brought up to some useful occupation," presumably a skilled
craft. He explicitly stated that none were to be compelled to leave Virginia,
"under any pretense whatsoever." There was great poignancy in what Washington had done, for as Robert and Lee Dalzell have pointed out, his will
condemned Mount Vernon to ruin.[13] His will was an act of atonement for a
lifetime of concurrence in human exploitation. He hoped his example would
lead other great planters to take a similar step, hastening the day when the
scourge of slavery was effaced throughout America. If successful, his act
would extend to a generation yet unborn still another legacy of the American Revolution: the extirpation of a horrid institution that stretched back to
a distant past long before the Revolutionary era.

As Adams had read history all his life, it was not surprising that in his latter
years he devoted considerable thought to the momentous Revolutionary
events of which he had been a part. Defeated by Jefferson in his bid for reelection to the presidency in 1800, Adams had been hurt and angry at the time of
his return home. He told friends that he was happy. Swapping the cares of the
presidency for the quiet of Peacefield, as he had named the residence he had

purchased in Quincy following the war, was a good bargain, he said. But Adams was a poor fibber. He could not hide his despair. His long public career had ended ruinously, not only in his rejection by the voters, but in the cold enmity of many members of his own Federalist Party. "Ennui, when it rains on a man in large drops is worse than one of our North East storms," he confided to a friend in a candid moment. He lamented that he was "buried and forgotten."[14]

Stricken with such a profound melancholy that he was reduced to inactivity during his first several months at home, Adams in 1802 emerged from his cocoon and set out to rehabilitate his reputation. Since before the end of the War of Independence, he had feared that his contributions would be eclipsed in the public mind by those of Washington and Franklin. When Jefferson's reputation soared, as a result of his popular presidency and his links to the sustaining and ascendant Democratic Party, Adams grieved that Washington, Franklin, and Jefferson had come to be seen as the great triumvirate responsible for American independence. He labeled them "the American untouchables," and once predicted, only half in jest, that the eighteenth century would be named "le Siecle Franklinnien."[15] Adams was anxious to tell his side of the story.

He began work on his autobiography, which he expected to be published posthumously by his children. He had carried his life story to the beginning of his second mission to France when he read the three-volume history of the American Revolution written by his friend, Mercy Otis Warren. He was appalled to discover that she portrayed him as having abandoned his republican beliefs as a result of his residency in Europe. Adams forsook his memoirs to answer her in a series of lengthy, passionate letters that he also expected would someday be made public. A year later, in 1809, Adams went public for the first time. Responding to an attack on his character by a Baltimore newspaper, he published essay after essay in a local newspaper, the *Boston Patriot*, in which he defended his wartime diplomacy as well as his presidency. In these three endeavors, as well as through a voluminous correspondence with numerous individuals, Adams defended himself and assessed Washington and Jefferson. He carefully preserved copies of his letters, knowing full well that all that he wrote would eventually be published.

Adams never wavered in his admiration of Washington's service during the American Revolution. He once said that he "loved and revered the man," praised his integrity, industry, courage, administrative skills, and sagacity, and predicted that Washington's performance as commander of the Continental army would "command the esteem of the wisest and best men in all ages." However, he did not believe that Washington's generalship had been without error. He criticized Washington's vanity and powerful ambition, and wrote that the general's many mistakes had been concealed from the public. Those around Washington had struggled to gloss his generalship, Adams contended, and Congress too, in the darkest times, had conspired "to blow the trumpet of panegyric . . . to cover and dissemble all [his] faults and errors, to represent every defeat as a victory and every retreat as an advancement, to make that Character . . . [the] center of union, as the center stone in the geometrical arch." Adams's purpose was not to destroy Washington, but to make him human, and in the process to demonstrate that while the general should be esteemed, even venerated, no one should believe that the American Revolution had succeeded because of him alone. The respect he felt for Washington was never more evident than in his last public appearance. In August 1821 the West Point corps of cadets marched from Boston to Peacefield to honor the ex-president. The once voluble Adams, now so frail that he required assistance standing, was able to utter only two sentences. He urged the aspiring soldiers to model themselves on the character of Washington.[16]

Adams knew Jefferson far better than Washington. He had served with him in Congress and in France, where he and Abigail had frequently entertained and grown to love him. However, their relationship cooled in the course of the party battles of the 1790s, particularly when Adams learned that Jefferson had privately uttered censurious remarks about his political philosophy and presidency. Adams blamed the breach on Jefferson's propulsive ambition and insatiable quest for acclaim. Early in his retirement Adams, filled with self-pity and rancor, privately excoriated President Jefferson as an unduly partisan chief executive who ultimately left the state of the Union in far worse shape than he had found it.[17]

Everything that Adams said about Jefferson in the period between his return to Quincy in 1801 and their reconciliation in 1812 was colored by the deep hurt that lingered from his final, bruising years in public life. Yet his object was never the destruction of his old friend's reputation, but the elevation of his own reputation to a par with that of Jefferson, and the only means to that end was to bring the Virginian down from his lofty perch as a demigod.

Some of Adams's claims were preposterous and others were uninformed. Yet a solid substructure existed to his overall assessment. He understood that Jefferson was a terribly complex person, a "shadow man," he said. Like "the great rivers, whose bottoms we cannot see and make no noise," Adams added,

Jefferson exhibited a public persona, but kept his real self secreted beneath impenetrable layers of prophylactic sheathing. Adams believed that Jefferson was the most honest and straightforward person he had met in public life. He acknowledged too that Jefferson had been blessed with numerous gifts. Nevertheless, Adams judged his talents as a public official to be merely ordinary. Adams was impressed with Jefferson's intellect, although he did not think him the equal of James Otis, whose original, imaginative, and penetrating mind set New England on a new way of thinking about its relationship with the mother country. He touted Jefferson as a scholar of political philosophy, but thought him unsophisticated in his attempts to link theory to day-to-day politics. Part of his problem, Adams concluded, was that Jefferson's extraordinary talents were corroded by insuperable limitations of personality. For instance, Adams rated Jefferson only an ordinary congressman because of his inability to join in debates and reluctance to take a stand on volatile issues, and he was struck by the Virginian's chronic unwillingness to commit himself to public service.[18]

Once he and Jefferson were reunited by mutual friends, and commenced a lively, warm correspondence in 1812, Adams appeared to be happier. Thereafter, he not only said little of Washington and Jefferson, but abandoned the defense of his own conduct and focused on leaving posterity with a historically accurate understanding of the American Revolution.

Adams was troubled by some of the earliest histories of the rebellion, especially those of Mercy Warren and William Wirt's biography of Patrick Henry, which was published soon thereafter. He charged that Warren's study was the work of a Democratic Party idealogue, not a dispassionate historian. He thought that Wirt, a young Virginia lawyer, had authored a filiopiestic life of a fellow Virginian, rather than an honest search for the truth. "Who shall write the history of the American Revolution? Who can write it? Who will ever be able to write it," Adams wondered in 1815. He believed the best historians would face a daunting task. They would have to rely on the flawed recollections of participants, for much had been suppressed at the time and had never, and would never, be made public. The habitual silence of some participants, notably Washington and Franklin, would hamper future students of the Revolution, he added. Furthermore, he had seen Samuel Adams burn many of his papers before fleeing Philadelphia in 1777, and he suspected that other precious materials had been, or would be, destroyed, either by accident or design. These losses would be a formidable obstacle to the truth. As a result, Adams declared that he had come to have "little faith in history. I read it as I do romance," for pleasure, not elucidation.[19]

Nevertheless, Adams knew that future generations would read and write histories of the American Revolution and he set out to influence their assessment. In letters to numerous correspondents, including a magazine editor who was gathering materials on the Revolution, he offered explanations for the onset of the rebellion and appraised the roles played by many of the principal participants. Whereas Wirt had amplified the theme that the American Revolution originated in Virginia in Henry's spirited assault on the Stamp Act in 1765, Adams saw deeper roots to the upheaval. He viewed the American Revolution as an evolving epoch that grew from the transformation of Europeans into republicanized Americans, a metamorphosis that had occurred by degrees in the 150 years since the arrival of the earliest colonists. Thus, the rebellion awaited only a catalyst. He variously dated the rebellion's origin to 1760, when France had been driven from Canada, or 1761, when the Writs of Assistance controversy flared, both earlier than Henry's eloquent actions in Virginia. Nevertheless, Adams argued that the rebellion might never have occurred in his lifetime had the British Crown and ministry abandoned its misguided colonial policies before 1775.[20] This was Adams's frame of reference when, in 1818, he wrote of the mother country's misguided colonial policies in the aftermath of its exquisite victory over France:

The Revolution was effected before the war commenced. The Revolution was in the minds and hearts of the people. . . . The people of America had been educated in an habitual affection for England . . . and thought her a kind and tender parent. . . . But when they found her to be a cruel beldam, willing . . . to 'dash their brains out,' it is no wonder if their filial affections ceased, and were changed into indignation and horror.

The radical change in the principles[,] opinions, sentiments, and affections of the people, was the real American Revolution.[21]

Adams additionally championed the roles played by numerous figures in the rebellion, especially those who, like himself, were often overlooked. He acknowledged the contributions of several Virginians, including Richard Henry Lee, Francis Lightfoot Lee, and Arthur Lee, his diplomatic colleague. He applauded the efforts of John Dickinson, once an acrid congressional rival, whom he now portrayed as responsible for the success of Pennsylvania's prewar protest movement. He thought the efforts on behalf of independence by congressmen Robert Livingston of New York and John Rutledge of South Carolina had been largely ignored, as was John Jay's contribution to the peace settlement. He was anxious that New Englanders receive their fair share of credit. He depicted John Hancock as the glue who had held together the protest in Massachusetts. He paid tribute to Roger Sherman of Connecticut as a sensible, earnest, and influential figure in numerous congressional deliberations. He wanted people to remember the role General Artemas Ward had played in the siege of Boston and the Battle of Bunker Hill before Washington took command of the Continental army.[22]

Adams maintained that Samuel Adams and James Otis were more responsible than any others for the American Revolution. He called Otis "the Father of the American Revolution" for having built the intellectual superstructure on which the rebellion's design would be erected. However, he labeled Samuel Adams the greatest man of the era, the politician who had sculpted the protest movement in Massachusetts, influenced the resistance elsewhere, and both openly and covertly led the First Congress to embargo the mother country and the Second toward independence.[23]

When Adams conveyed to Jefferson his apprehension for the memory of the American Revolution, the Virginian responded indifferently. He "liked the dreams of the future better than the history of the past," he remarked. If he read history, he told Adams, he was satisfied to read only ancient history. This was mere dissimulation. It is true that in his final years Jefferson wrote less about the American Revolution than did Adams, but that was not due to lack of interest. Like Washington, Jefferson was not driven to vindicate himself. He enjoyed "Unbounded Popularity" when he left office, as Adams once reminded him. When he at last retired to Monticello in 1809, Jefferson knew that together with Washington and Franklin he would be remembered as a giant of his age.[24] Not only was he acclaimed as the author of the Declaration of Independence, but the political party that he had founded, and that controlled the presidency and Congress, had a vested interest in enhancing his stature.

Nevertheless, Jefferson was hardly disinterested in the history of the American Revolution. Although he claimed to have no time for writing history, he authored his memoirs, taking pains to chronicle his Revolutionary achievements. While in Paris in the 1780s, he appears to have taken steps to let the world know that he had been the principal author of the Declaration of Independence, not a well-known fact at the time. After 1813, when he and Adams were the lone survivors of the committee that had drafted the Declaration, Jefferson took exceptional steps, as Pauline Maier has noted, to make the document "the defining event of a 'Heroic age.' "[25]

Like Adams, he argued that the Revolution arose from the colonists' deep-seated republican spirit, but he located the epicenter of the rebellion in

Virginia. However, Jefferson broke with those from his state who had lionized Henry as virtually the lone instigator of the American rebellion. He, in fact, shared Adams's disdain for Wirt's biography of Henry, snickering privately that the author was "one of our fan-colouring biographers, who paints small men as very great." Jefferson emphasized the role of many assemblymen, especially younger burgesses, in the crystallization of Virginia's protest. He thus misleadingly placed himself at an early moment at the center of the Revolutionary struggle in Virginia. He wrote of how "we"—he and Dabney Carr, the Lees, and Peyton Randolph—had shaped the province's response to British policies in the early 1770s. Jefferson also sought to diminish Henry's place in history. He never forgave Henry, a one-time friend who had endorsed the movement in 1781 to investigate, and possibly censure, his behavior as governor. During his retirement years Jefferson not only was mute on many of Henry's alleged triumphs, but portrayed him as intellectually shallow, avaricious, materialistic, and egomaniacal.[26]

One significant difference separated how Adams and Jefferson viewed the American Revolution. Adams believed that an earlier revolutionary transformation had preceded the revolutionary events of his time. He concluded that a revolution had occurred in the course of the century after the beginning of the English settlement of America. During the seventeenth century the colonists had conceived and infixed their liberties, and gradually embraced a republican outlook. He saw his generation's struggle with the parent state as a battle for the preservation of long-cherished liberties and republican ideals. Furthermore, Adams argued that the American Revolution culminated on July 4, 1776, with the decision to separate from Great Britain.

In contrast, Jefferson saw the Revolution as part of a flow of history that had originated in the sixteenth century. He believed that the Renaissance, Reformation, and the Age of Enlightenment had expanded individual opportunities and freedoms, ushering in an "honorable" epoch in which humankind had become better educated and "soften[ed] and correct[ed]." He argued that the American Revolution had been brought on by these trends, and it in turn had advanced these same currents by sparking new reforms after 1776. Moreover, while Adams was largely indifferent to the example set for others by the American Revolution, Jefferson boasted that the strife in America had inspired revolutionary struggles elsewhere. The "flames kindled on the 4th of July 1776," Jefferson gloried, had sparked the French Revolution in 1789 and the Greek Revolution that raged in the 1820s. Like the "city on a hill" that Adams's forbearers had set out to erect in New England, the Revolutionary

United States, Jefferson hoped, would inspire people everywhere to believe that the "engines of despotism" could not prevail forever. In the last letter he wrote, Jefferson reiterated his belief that the American Revolution would prove to be "the signal of arousing men to burst the chains under which monkish ignorance and superstition had persuaded them to bind themselves, and to assure the blessings and security of self-government."[27]

Although Adams and Jefferson steadfastly applauded the legacy of the American Revolution, both in their latter years, like Washington, were beset by a brooding apprehension for the survival of the Union that they had hazarded their lives to create. Each saw the American rebellion and the American union as inextricably linked, for the United States was the superstructure on which rested the great gains made by the American Revolution: national security, republican government, expanding prosperity, and the endurance and extension of human liberty. By 1815 America's future presaged peace and prosperity to a degree unimagined since independence, yet it was in this most hopeful of times that a new and menacing storm gathered. As never before, Adams and Jefferson despaired because each understood that the Union might be wrecked on the shoals of southern slavery. The American Revolution, which had held the promise of natural rights for humankind, had not ended slavery in the United States. Within a few months of Washington's death every northern state had abolished slavery, either gradually or immediately. However, not only had no southern state terminated slavery, but beginning in Washington's presidency the institution had expanded with unparalleled rapidity, sweeping first across the Appalachians into Kentucky and Tennessee, and later throughout the burgeoning cotton kingdom in the lower South. Abolitionism had been unwelcome in the Continental Congress, the Constitutional Convention, and the halls of Congress in the new national government in the 1790s. Lest southern slaveowners be offended, the very northern representatives who had been hospitable to antislavery in their own states happily consented to sacrifice abolitionism at the national level for the sake of preserving the Union. During the American Revolution, some had willingly demurred in the belief that the post-Revolutionary generation of southerners would act to end slavery. However, by 1815 no southern state had yet acted, and both Adams and Jefferson understood that the slavery issue could not be kept out of national politics much longer. In addition, both knew that the issue held the potential of becoming an abiding political menace that could divide, and ultimately destroy, the national house.

As a younger man Adams, probably like most white colonists, unthinkingly assimilated much of the racism of the time. His occasional references to blacks in his diary and correspondence hint at bias. Later, as a congressman, he resisted the enlistment of blacks in the Continental army, expressing doubts that they could become effective soldiers. Yet however bigoted Adams may have been, he hated slavery. He thought it a crime against humanity that begat multiple horrors, including sexual exploitation. He once remarked that he believed every Virginia planter, presumably including Jefferson, had fathered children through his female chattel. Adams never considered purchasing slaves, although by the early 1770s he possessed the financial means to do so. He later remarked that those had been times "when the practice was not disgraceful, when the best men in my vicinity thought it not inconsistent with their character, and when . . . I might have saved by the purchase of negroes at times when they were very cheap," utilizing slave labor rather than more expensive free labor to work his farm.[28]

Adams never publicly expressed his feelings about slavery during the American Revolution. His first object was to win the war and maintain the fragile Union, not to interject an issue that might imperil both goals. Like most in his generation, he thought slavery an issue that had to be dealt with by each state, and he was confident that Virginia, in due time, would emancipate its slaves. He also appears to have believed that Jefferson would play a leading role in the destruction of slavery in Virginia. In the 1780s Adams praised what his friend had written about slavery in *Notes on the State of Virginia*. "The passages upon slavery, are worth Diamonds," he exclaimed. "They will have more effect than Volumes written by mere Philosophers."[29]

Adams remained silent on slavery issues during his vice presidency and presidency. He once suggested that he had not spoken out because he feared that abolitionism would trigger slave insurrections in the southern states. He said that he was "terrified" by the prospect of "Armies of Negroes marching and countermarching in . . . shining . . . Armour." He also explained his silence by saying that because he had never lived in the South, or ever been south of Washington and Baltimore, he felt that he did not adequately understand the many ramifications of emancipation. Once he pledged to Jefferson never to support legislation affecting southern slavery to which his friend objected. "I must leave it to you," he added.[30] Adams also remained silent during much of his retirement, at first probably from fear that he might damage the ascendant political career of his son, John Quincy.

But Adams's silence, and that of many other Founders from northern states, had arisen from the misguided belief that the South was making progress toward the eventual termination of slavery. Some changes in fact had occurred. In the course of the American Revolution several southern states banned the foreign slave trade and made it easier for slaveowners to manumit their chattel. As a result, between 1776 and 1810 the percentage of the free black population increased sevenfold in Virginia and tripled in the Lower South. Furthermore, in 1808 the South consented to federal legislation—enacted during Jefferson's presidency and with his blessing—that prohibited slave imports. Otherwise, the signs were disappointing. Not only did private manumissions decline after 1790, but no southern state acted to abolish slavery. By early in the nineteenth century the Revolutionary generation's attack on slavery was being replaced by the South's first sustained defense of its peculiar institution.[31] As hope waned that the South would eradicate slavery, some in the North grew restive.

Adams was among the first to discern the gathering storm clouds. He told Jefferson that the slavery question would give his son's generation greater difficulty in sustaining the Union than the Revolutionary generation had faced in creating it. He even told Jefferson that he feared the Union would survive only if slavery was abolished. Before 1819, however, Adams always told Jefferson that he did not know how to deal with slavery. Adams claimed that he had wrestled with the issue for half a century without discovering an acceptable solution for eradicating slavery, save for abolition at the behest of the white South. He only knew, he said, that if and when the South turned to abolition, the rights of the emancipated should be protected. This led him to oppose colonization, as he thought it unconscionable to contemplate the exile of unwilling African Americans.[32]

The tempest that Adams divined burst in 1819. When Missouri applied for entry into the Union as a slave state, a New York representative introduced an antislavery amendment to the statehood bill. His proposed legislation would have prohibited the further introduction of slaves into Missouri and required that after admission all children born of slaves be set free at age twenty-five. This was radically new. Congress had previously prohibited slavery's expansion into federal territories, but it had never before attempted to eradicate its existence within a state. The slavery question had been plunged into mainstream politics.

Adams exulted, confident that the time at last had arrived when the slavery issue might be resolved. If the amended Missouri bill passed, the precedent would be established for prohibiting slavery in all new states. He even dared to hope that the spirit of abolitionism might swell in the South, sparking the end of this "evil of Colossal magnitude." His comments during the Missouri Crisis were nearly identical to those of free-soilers a generation later. Adams maintained that the Founding Fathers had never intended slavery's expansion. He said that its growth must be stopped to protect whites who wished to migrate to the western frontier, but moral considerations also decreed an end to its dispersion. Adams thought "the turpitude, the inhumanity, the cruelty, and infamy" of human slavery must be terminated. Finally, he wrote, slavery must end, lest it inevitably "rend this mighty Fabric [the Union] in twain." In this milieu of fear and hope, Adams did something that he had seldom done. Very gently and subtly, he raised the issue with Jefferson. Adams hoped his friend might utilize his exalted reputation to accommodate the South to a stoppage of slavery's expansion and start Virginia down the path toward emancipation.[33]

But, like so many others, Adams misjudged Jefferson's commitment to the eradication of slavery. Had Jefferson been the foe of slavery that he claimed to be, or had he practiced at Monticello the manumission that he wrote about with such grace, he might have achieved much. Had he emancipated his own chattel at any time after 1776, and especially during his presidency, his action might have produced an electrifying effect within Virginia. On several occasions after 1776 conditions in Virginia were favorable for a campaign pledged to gradual emancipation. What was most urgent in each instance was extraordinary leadership. Characteristically, Jefferson was unable to provide that guidance.

The first propitious time for making inroads against slavery arose in the immediate aftermath of the War of Independence, at a moment when America's first abolitionist movement gathered strength, tobacco prices were depressed, and the cotton bonanza was unforeseen. Although Jefferson reentered public life in 1783, and even privately drafted a scheme for the gradual abolition of slavery in Virginia—a plan that would have left intact the slave labor force at Monticello during his lifetime—he refused to make his ideas public. Ambitious to hold public office once again, Jefferson shrank from a fight over slavery. He proposed legislation in Congress that would have abolished slavery in all western territories after 1800, but by deferring abolition for nearly twenty years, Jefferson's bill was seriously compromised. Kentucky and Tennessee were certain to be in the Union as slave states by 1800. Moreover, by 1800 such large numbers of slaves would have been introduced into the southwest territories that slavery's extension to the Mississippi would be assured. Congress rejected his bill.

A second instance when slavery might have been weakened or destroyed in Virginia occurred during Jefferson's presidency. Following the discovery of planned slave insurrections in Richmond and around Petersburg, the Virginia assembly after 1802 contemplated legislation that would have urged the United States to set aside western lands as an asylum for emancipated slaves. Governor James Monroe appeared to believe that the idea might succeed with the staunch support of the president, but Jefferson refused to entertain such a notion. He believed the West existed for white yeomen. The plan of the Virginia assembly died. President Jefferson's lone antislavery stand was his support of congressional legislation to terminate the African slave trade. Although he grounded his opposition to the further importation of slaves on humanitarian grounds, Jefferson had a pecuniary interest in such a law. He knew that under the laws of supply and demand, the price of chattel would rise dramatically once the slave trade ended. A debtor, he was also aware that someday he might have to seek capital by selling his bonded labor. In fact, ten years after the termination of the foreign slave trade, Jefferson sold a large number of slaves to his grandson in order to satisfy his creditors.[34]

Although Jefferson's support for ending the foreign slave trade earned the applause of antislavery adherents, he did nothing to cut his personal ties to the institution. His chattel more than doubled in the half-century after 1776, until he owned an "enormously large family," as he put it, of nearly 250 slaves. Just as Mount Vernon groaned under a surplus of laborers in Washington's latter years, Jefferson's chattel swelled inexpediently. Unlike Washington, who refused to sell his slaves if it resulted in the sundering of a family, Jefferson often sold his surplus laborers. However, he gave little thought to liberating his slaves.[35]

Jefferson had still another opportunity to use his influence against slavery during his first decade at Monticello following his presidency. In 1814 Edward Coles, a Virginian who once had been Madison's private secretary, appealed to Jefferson to add his lustrous name to the cause of antislavery. Coles, like Adams a few years later, thought a commitment from Jefferson, even at that late date, might cause Virginia to abandon slavery. He told Jefferson that the eradication of slavery would forever destroy the last "degrading feature of British colonial policy" that yet haunted their state. Coles planned to liberate his chattel and establish them on land he had purchased in Illinois, but he did not ask Jefferson to follow his example. He merely requested that Jefferson support his action with a ringing endorsement that would resound throughout the slave South.[36]

Had Jefferson denounced slavery in 1814 in a vibrant, graceful pronouncement that approximated the literary qualities of the Declaration of Independence, the antislavery forces in his state, and throughout the Upper South, might have drawn sufficient sustenance from his words to coalesce. Furthermore, in 1832, when the Virginia assembly debated the future of slavery in the aftermath of the Nat Turner insurrection, Jefferson's rhetoric and commitment might have boosted the abolitionists to success. However, Jefferson refused to act on Coles's appeal. He rehearsed to Coles his now conventional litany of half-truths and exculpatory tales. He claimed that as a youth before the American Revolution his efforts to eradicate slavery had been thwarted by elders habituated to that "degraded condition." The golden moment for ending slavery in Virginia, he said, had been immediately after the war, but he had been prevented from acting by his diplomatic missions. He claimed that by the time he returned home from Europe the burden for ending slavery had fallen to the "younger generation," forgetting that for nearly all the twenty years that followed 1790 he had held the most important offices in the land. Thus, he shifted the blame for slavery's survival to the generation that succeeded his. The men who dominated Virginia in the 1790s should have been animated by "the generous temperament of youth," he disingenuously asserted. They should have risen "above the suggestions of avarice," he charged. Instead, he claimed to have heard nothing from that generation, once again disregarding that generation's interest in suppressing the African slave trade and in emancipating and colonizing slaves on federal lands in the West.[37]

Not only would Jefferson not help Coles, he reproached the young man for his abolitionist spirit and advised him to "reconcile yourself to your country [Virginia]." Jefferson lectured Coles on the evils of emancipation. He claimed that African Americans "are by their habits rendered as incapable as children of taking care of themselves." Free blacks would inevitably become "pests in society," he stated. Liberation would be followed by race mixing and race pollution that would weaken the white race, "a degradation to which . . . no lover of excellence in the human character can innocently consent," he cautioned. One additional fear haunted Jefferson. He had long been troubled by the prospect of a race war. Thirty years earlier Jefferson, who so often expressed his faith in humanity's ability to triumph over superstition and ignorance, had exclaimed that "Deep rooted prejudices" would not cease with emancipation, but would continue until "the extermination of the one or the other race." Not long after writing Coles, Jefferson wrote another acquaintance that "We have the wolf by the ear, and we can neither hold him, nor safely let him go. Justice is in one scale, and self-preservation in the other." Thus Jefferson refused to take a stand. He admonished Coles to abandon his imprudent idea. Coles did not listen. Instead, he moved west, freed his slaves, gave each family 160 acres, and in 1822, as governor of Illinois, successfully fought a powerful pro-slavery element that hoped to legalize slavery in that state.[38]

Jefferson's long, sophistic reply to Coles exposed the depths of his hypocrisy on the issue of slavery. It also destroyed the hopes of abolitionists everywhere that Jefferson—like both Washington and George Wythe, his beloved legal mentor, who had died in 1806—would provide for the posthumous liberation of his slaves. Jefferson's final will manumitted only five slaves. Previously, he had freed three slaves, two in the 1790s and one in 1822, and permitted two others to escape. All ten slaves set free by Jefferson between 1764 and 1826 were mulattoes from the Hemings family and, hence, blood relatives of Jefferson's late wife, for they were descendants of Martha's father, John Wayles, and one of his female slaves, Betty Hemings. The remainder of his chattel, as Jefferson well knew, would be bequeathed to relatives or sold following his death.[39]

Jefferson's attitude and behavior were especially bizarre in light of the protracted intimate relationship that he almost certainly maintained with one of his female slaves, Sally Hemings. In the racial classification of the day, Hemings was a quadroon, born in 1773 to Wayles and his slave mistress, Betty Hemings, herself the daughter of an African slave woman and an English seafarer. Born at The Forest, Sally became Jefferson's property following her father's demise and came to Monticello by 1776. She was nine years old when Martha Jefferson died and eleven when her owner sailed for France on a postwar diplomatic mission. In 1787, at age fourteen, she accompanied nine-year-old Maria Jefferson on an Atlantic crossing that culminated at the Hotel de Langeac, Jefferson's Parisian residence.

It is unclear when Jefferson and Hemings first became intimate. One of Sally's sons, Madison Hemings, and Jefferson's biographer, Fawn Brodie, believed their relationship commenced in Paris in 1788. Others doubt that it began before 1794, when Hemings was twenty-one and Jefferson, now fifty-one, retired to Monticello after serving for four years as secretary of state in Washington's administration. Although the evidence is scant, some scholars believe that Hemings was pregnant in 1789 when she returned to America with Jefferson and his daughters. However, there is no disputing that she bore six children between October 1795 and May 1808.

Recent DNA testing of descendants of Jefferson and Hemings has provided the most conclusive "probabilistic" evidence yet offered that Jefferson fathered the children that Sally Hemings bore after 1795.[40] A mountain of additional circumstantial evidence also points to his paternity. Contemporary inhabitants of Charlottesville gossiped about it. A strong oral tradition among Sally Hemings's descendants attests to her long sexual liaison with Jefferson. Furthermore, although Jefferson was absent from Monticello much of the time while he served as vice president and president from 1797 to 1809, "for fifteen years through six children," as historian Annette Gordon-Reed has observed, he was always at home "when [Sally Hemings] conceived, and she never conceived when he was not there." Numerous visitors to Jefferson's home were struck by the resemblance that Sally's children bore to Jefferson. His grandson, Thomas Jefferson Randolph, once remarked that her offspring "resembled Mr. Jefferson so closely that it was plain that they had his blood in their veins." Finally, although it was rare for Jefferson's slave runaways to succeed in fleeing Monticello, several of Sally's children "escaped" around the time of their twenty-first birthday. All of her remaining offspring were legally freed by their owner on reaching adulthood, instances of largess that Jefferson did not extend to his other chattel during more than sixty years as a slaveowner.[41]

The nature of their relationship remains a mystery. He may have forced himself on Hemings, but it is more probable that the relationship was consensual. Hemings may have acquiesced primarily as a means of securing preferential treatment for herself and her children, including their liberation on reaching adulthood, or the two may have shared a passionate love. It is possible as well that the liaison may have begun in one way, but with time undergone gradual transformations. Given the complexity of most intimate relationships, that between Jefferson and Hemings must have been extraordinarily multifarious and confounded. In addition to their age, educational, and racial differences, one was free and the other unfree, one legally owned the other, and Hemings was the half-sister of Jefferson's late wife. In all likelihood they shared a relationship so labyrinthian that no outsider will ever hull away the layers of feelings these two held for one another.

However, it is not inexplicable that Jefferson would have been involved in such an ongoing relationship. Hemings, who was fair-skinned—"mighty near white," a slave at Monticello said of her—with abundant dark hair, struck Jefferson's grandson and several slaves at Monticello as an extraordinarily beautiful young woman. She may even have born a resemblance to

Martha Wayles Jefferson, either physically or in her mannerisms. In addition, having lived in Paris for two years, Hemings was more widely traveled than most women in Virginia. Evidence exists, moreover, that she received some formal instruction while in France, and her education may have continued at Monticello, given the special status of the Hemings family. One thing is clear. She did not spend her days chopping tobacco or plowing the brown, dusty fields of her owner.[42]

Although Jefferson faced considerable danger from public disclosure of his links with Hemings, the relationship also afforded uncommon safety and security. Following the shattering of his connection to his parents, Jefferson's adolescence and early adult years had been filled with painful, fruitless searches for affectionate relationships. His dreams came true when he discovered Martha, only to have his happy marriage abruptly severed by her premature death. Once again abandoned, Jefferson withdrew in mournful despair, convinced that he could never replicate the idyllic life he believed he had shared with his wife, and unwilling to risk a recurrence of the grief that had accompanied his every intimate bond.

The difficulty that Jefferson faced in establishing an indelible loving relationship was apparent in his behavior with Maria Cosway, an unhappy married woman whom he met in Paris on one warm August day in 1786. He was introduced to her by John Trumbull, the American artist, and immediately fell in love. A "mass of happiness," as he put it, descended on him at the first sight of this charming and attractive twenty-seven-year-old Englishwoman who had been educated in Florence. A talented musician and artist, she resembled Martha in many ways, though she was considerably more cosmopolitan and far more accomplished and better educated. She excited a fire within Jefferson that had been banked since his wife's demise four years before. They saw one another almost every day for six weeks. "Every moment was filled with something agreeable," he later reflected, and he told her that she had restored gaiety to his life. Their relationship stopped abruptly in October when Maria's husband took her home to London, but she returned the following August and the couple enjoyed more than three months together, revisiting the sites they had seen the previous summer and meeting discreetly at dinners hosted by friends. Once again, their relationship was cut off when Maria and her husband returned to England.[43] They never saw one another again. But Richard Cosway, the cuckold of the piece, appears to have been less responsible than Jefferson for having placed an insuperable obstacle between the two lovers. At the very moment that Jefferson confessed his abiding love for her, he in effect also acknowledged to Maria his inability to contemplate carrying matters beyond a furtive entanglement.

In one of the longer letters he ever penned, Jefferson confessed to Maria that the "human heart knows no joy which I have not lost, no sorrow of which I have not drank." He had initially believed that Maria, herself grieving and melancholy, was the balm to "softly bind up the wound of another . . . who has felt the same wound himself." He may never have doubted that she possessed the magic to heal his heart, but prudence and experience caused him to be wary of any relationship, and certainly one as awkward as this inevitably would have been. However, it was not her marital status that deterred Jefferson. While the "pleasures" she offered were innumerable, he explained, the "pains which are to follow" would of necessity be greater. "The art of life is the art of avoiding pain," and the "most effectual means of being secure against pain is to retire within ourselves," he remarkably confided.[44] In short, Jefferson had grown incapable of surrendering his heart to any other person who possessed the means and self-command to cause him heartache.

With Sally Hemings, however, the emotional risks that Jefferson hazarded were minimal. She not only lacked autonomy, but her self-will was severely circumscribed. That she might abandon him through flight was unlikely, given the cruel world that even free blacks faced in her day. He had told Maria Cosway that he would seek happiness only in what was inviolable. The "only pleasures a wise man will count on," he had said to her, were those that no other "may deprive us of."[45] No one could deprive him of servile Sally Hemings. Virtually alone, a person in Hemings's situation offered Jefferson, dispossessed as he was of the ability to engage in a lasting, loving relationship with an unimpeded equal, the best hope of achieving a gratifying intimate bond.

Jefferson likely commenced his relationship with Hemings in the mid-1790s and fathered the last child with her in 1808, six years before Edward Coles beseeched his assistance in the cause of abolitionism. Five years after he coldly rebuffed Coles, the Missouri crisis erupted. It afforded Jefferson a final opportunity to use his influence against slavery. Adams longed for Jefferson's eloquent voice to warn the South that slavery's continued existence posed great danger for the future of the American Union. He and Washington, and Jefferson, had dared to speak out during the great Anglo-American crisis of their youth. Now Adams wanted Jefferson to do no less in this crisis. Adams had good reason to think that Jefferson might respond favorably to his supplication. He not only believed Jefferson's repeated protestations about the evil of slavery, but Adams must have presumed that the most noted apostle of agrarianism and yeomanry would eagerly embrace his vision of limitless free-soil in the American West. Adams ever so gently raised the matter with his friend, believing that the Virginian's majestic reputation, both as a Revolutionary and as the founder of America's triumphant political party, might be the important first step in the resolution of America's greatest dilemma. But Jefferson refused to denounce the further spread of slavery. In private, in fact, he made it clear that he would stand with the slave South in defense of slavery.[46]

The opportunity was lost. As historian William Gienapp has written, with the Missouri Crisis "the South had reached the point of no return." Slavery's expansion, and slavery itself, were assured for another generation. Only the "perpetual duration of our vast American empire," as Adams referred to the Union, was left in question.[47]

But Jefferson knew the answer to that question. He had reacted to the Missouri situation as he would to "a fire-bell in the night," he said. Word of the crisis had "awakened and filled me with terror," he told an acquaintance, for he knew immediately how he and the South would respond, and he knew that because of their response the "knell of the Union" had been sounded.[48] With the nation divided between free and slave states, and with the slavery question throbbing in the political arena, Jefferson knew in his heart of hearts that the Union was doomed. That realization left him trembling in dark despair, for he never doubted that when the American house was destroyed, most of the benefits won through the American Revolution would also be eradicated.

In time the legend grew that Adams and Jefferson lived to regret the American Revolution. In fact, in 1816, at age seventy-three, Jefferson gushed at the liberating times in which he had lived. In the eighteenth century, he said, "the sciences and arts, manners and morals, [had] advanced to a higher degree than the world had ever before seen." The American Revolution witnessed the flowering of the most progressive political ideals of this "Heroic age," as he labeled his century. The true meaning of the great epoch was that a break had been made with the past. The Revolution was not won until his election and subsequent presidency, what he called the "revolution of 1800." Only then had monarchy, with its distasteful royal prerogatives and limitations on personal freedoms and rights been quashed, and only then had a republican system that hinged on a "direct and constant control of the citizens been firmly established."[49]

Adams and Jefferson supposedly represented the "North and South Poles of the American Revolution," as a contemporary remarked. The two did differ in their understanding of the Revolution. More fervently than Jefferson, Adams insisted that the real merit of the American Revolution stemmed from its salvation, and institutionalization, of the best features of the pre-1776 colonial world—those advances made in America by emigres from English tyranny and persecution. Nevertheless, in his old age the core of Adams's feelings about the legacy of the American Revolution hardly differed from those of Jefferson. In 1821, at age eighty-six, Adams, sounding quite Jeffersonian, boasted that the Revolutionary generation had left "a better world than we found." Not only had much of the rampant superstition, prejudice, and religious and political persecution of the pre-1776 era been scotched, or at least ameliorated, he said, but succeeding generations faced fewer barriers to their realization of personal opportunities.[50]

It has also been alleged that Jefferson became disillusioned, not because the American Revolution failed, but because it had "succeeded only too well" and eventually resulted in "a democratic world."[51] Dramatic changes occurred in the half-century that followed 1776, yet Jefferson coped reasonably well with the new world of the nineteenth century. He in fact was far less concerned by the emerging democratic character of the United States than by what he perceived were the limitations on popular sovereignty inherent in the constitutional settlement of 1787–1788. He was never comfortable with federal hegemony over state and local interests, and he especially disliked the growing power of the federal judiciary, the least democratic element in the national government.[52]

Still, Jefferson's final years were sadly troubled. Like all mortals who live long enough, he discovered a haunting despair brought on by the deaths of the friends of his youth. But he also faced an added source of melancholy. Jefferson was afflicted by a wrenching awareness that he had lived to witness the sour fruit of his lifelong hesitancy, even antipathy, toward undertaking the difficult steps that might have resulted in the eradication of slavery. The Missouri Crisis had been resolved, but the slavery issue persisted and was certain to intensify. After 1819 Jefferson came to fear that his public life had been for nothing, as indeed could well be the case if the new United States foundered on the issue of slavery. "I regret that I am now to die in the belief, that the useless sacrifice of . . . the generation of 1776, to acquire self-government and happiness in this country, is to be thrown away by the unwise and unworthy passions of their sons," he mourned in one of the last letters he wrote on the slavery issue.[53] To the end, he was incapable of accepting the reality of his culpability in the perpetuation and expansion of African slavery and the danger it now posed to the achievements of the American Revolution.

EPILOGUE

The "Sword" and the "Bulwark"
of the American Revolution

P resident Washington and Robert Morris, the national treasurer during the last years of the war, made a compact to live into the nineteenth century. Morris carried out his bargain; Washington did not.

As if crossing into the next century somehow loomed as an insurmountable hurdle, Washington grew haunted by the prospect of death as 1799 proceeded. Reflections on health, and death, crept into his correspondence with increasing frequency. One night that summer he dreamt that he and Martha were sitting together when an angel appeared and whispered in her ear. Martha immediately turned pale and vanished. The next morning Washington told her of the dream and explained that he interpreted it as a warning of his imminent death. Washington was so disturbed by the dream that "he could not shake it off," Martha subsequently recollected. She thought it was the nightmare that had led him, perhaps on that very day, to prepare the new will that provided for the emancipation of his slaves.[1]

Washington remained in excellent health until December 13, when he awakened with a sore throat. Unconcerned, he spent some time that day outdoors in a swirling snow and bitter temperatures marking trees for pruning. He fell asleep that night expecting to be better in the morning. Instead, he awakened about 3:00 AM desperately ill, likely suffering from a streptococcus infection. His life strength had vanished during the five hours that he had slept, as pulmonary edema and distension in his throat diminished his capacity to breathe. Physicians were summoned, but their ministrations, which included rigging a vaporizer, applying a blister of Spanish fly, administering a purgative, and carrying out three phlebotomies, or bleedings, failed. At 5:00 PM, as winter's darkness fell over Mount Vernon, he told an aide that he knew he was dying. Thereafter, he slipped in and out of consciousness. At about 10:30 on the night of December 14, 1799, Washington died quietly. He was sixty-seven years old.[2]

Adams lived in retirement at Peacefield for a quarter-century. Initially bitter at having been forced from office in the election of 1800, he gradually adjusted and grew happy and contented. He filled his days with small amounts of physical labor on his farm, visits with his brother and old acquaintances, long walks throughout his bucolic neighborhood, and even hikes into the rugged, green hills west of Quincy that he had climbed as a boy. Typically, however, he spent the greatest portion of each day in his study, reading and writing.

During his first fifteen years at home Adams remained in remarkably good health. At eighty his mind was sharp and eyesight sufficient, if not especially good. The thyrotoxicosis, which had last seriously plagued him in the early 1780s, remained in remission. He attributed his remarkable health to the tranquility of retirement, adherence to a strict diet of porridge, gruel, mutton broth, and lemonade, and daily walks of four miles. The gradual rehabilitation of his reputation, which had been tarnished in the course of a rough-and-tumble presidency, also added a healthful buoyancy to his spirits. With Abigail and numerous grandchildren at his side, and the family dog scurrying through his home, Adams lived in a happy household. He also had something to live for: his obsession with vindicating his name.[3]

Although he relished the cheers of friendly crowds that greeted him during infrequent trips to Boston, and exulted when deferential public officials occasionally called on him, he essentially made peace with himself. He told others—and possibly even believed it to be true—that he was a man of average talents who, through "the severest and most incessant labor," had overachieved. He took enormous pride in having never violated the public's trust, and was equally gratified that after having held office for a quarter-century not the least whiff of scandal was attached to his name.[4]

After a dozen years at home, Adams's troubles mounted. A son, Thomas Boylston, who struggled with alcoholism, was a disappointment. In 1813, his daughter, Nabby, succumbed to breast cancer, dying slowly and painfully, with her father seated at her side. By then Abigail's health had deteriorated. She was so crippled by rheumatoid arthritis that she often was unable to come downstairs for days at a time. In 1818 John lost her as well, to typhoid fever.[5]

By then, Adams himself had declined perceptibly. Although he remained alert, Adams was racked by chronic aches and pains. His hearing and eyesight had badly deteriorated. He dictated letters to relatives whom he pressed into service as his amanuenses, and listened as they read sermons, poetry, fiction, history, or newspapers to him. He described his home as a place of sorrow, and after Abigail's demise he said that he too simply waited to die.[6]

Jefferson's retirement was similar in many ways to that of Adams, except that he left public life voluntarily and happily returned to Monticello in 1809. Once at home, Jefferson, like Washington, managed the ongoing business operations at his estate. Even into his eighties, Jefferson spent six to eight hours daily on horseback superintending his laborers.[7] Aside from visits to Poplar Forest, a getaway house in Bedford County that he had constructed during his presidency, Jefferson seldom left Monticello. It was not that he was immobilized by poor health—he was simply where he wanted to be.

During his second year in retirement, when he was sixty-seven, Jefferson called his health "perfect." One of his overseers, in fact, later recollected that about this time Jefferson invented a strength-testing machine and that he was able to better every visitor who competed with him, though in truth many were probably compliant losers. Like Adams, Jefferson attributed good health to a good diet and daily exercise. He adhered to a largely vegetarian regimen, though poultry and shellfish were on his menu. He drank coffee, tea, malt liquor, hard cider, and wine in moderation, rarely touched red meats, and virtually eschewed desserts altogether. He began each day by soaking his feet in cold water, and if the weather permitted, walked, rode, and worked in his gardens.[8]

Debilities eventually sprang up, and at an earlier age than they afflicted Adams. The "hand of age is on me," Jefferson announced in 1811 at age sixty-eight. Not long thereafter he mentioned, somewhat hyperbolically, that his memory, hearing, and eyesight were declining. Worse followed. After 1818, when he turned seventy-five, his complaints multiplied. He spoke of his "shattered" health and "feeble" condition. One adversity after another befell him. Walking became a problem because of chronic pain in his lower back, hip, and legs. He was afflicted with a broken left arm, arthritic right wrist, boils, an abscess on his jaw, an enlarged prostate gland, frequent bouts of diarrhea, and numerous brief illnesses likely attributable to food poisoning or viruses. At age eighty Jefferson told Adams that he longed for the days of "youth and health" which had "made happiness of every thing."[9]

With each year Jefferson's thoughts turned increasingly to the prospect of death. He regarded his body as a ticking watch that was winding down. He had "one foot in the grave, and the other uplifted to follow it," he quipped a year before his death. During his last two years Jefferson was largely confined to his house, barely able to walk from one room to another. He spoke of meeting death "with good will," of not wishing to live on after his faculties were gone and all his friends had perished. He spoke to Adams about "the friendly hand of death" that would liberate him from the "heavy hours" of old age. He told his daughter that he was ready to die, for he had done all that he had dreamed of doing. He looked forward to being reunited with Martha and old friends in "an ecstatic meeting" in an afterlife, an ethereal reconciliation with those "we have loved and lost and whom we shall still love and never lose again."[10]

However, declining health alone cannot account for the atrabiliousness that often gripped Jefferson during his final years. He faced mounting financial problems, even catastrophe, arising from mountainous debts. His problems arose in part from his unfettered, and seemingly ungovernable, habits of consumerism. In addition, his difficulties stemmed from a decision made long before. When John Wayles, his father-in-law, died in 1773, Jefferson had the choice of accepting or rejecting what he had bequeathed to his daughter. To accept his wealth meant to also take on the considerable debts that he owed overseas creditors. Jefferson made a calculated decision. He believed that Wayles's indebtedness could be retired easily through the profits generated by the tobacco grown on the Wayles lands. What seemed a prudent decision was, in reality, an egregious blunder. The outbreak of war in 1775 wrecked Virginia's tobacco trade. Furthermore, the Treaty of Paris, which stipulated that creditors were to meet with no impediment in the recovery of pre-war debts, left Jefferson and numerous other planters groaning under heavy, and mounting, obligations.

As early as 1787 Jefferson spoke of the "torment of mind" adduced by his indebtedness. Four years later he remarked that his financial difficulty "cripples all my wishes." Thereafter, his problems only worsened. When he left the presidency he commented on "the gloomy prospect" that faced him. He was, he said, "loaded with serious debts." He was compelled to dispense with land and slaves, but his greatest sacrifice was to sell his huge private library to the federal government. That transaction, arranged by political and personal friends, brought him nearly $24,000. However, these painful steps only scratched the surface of his problem. At a time when most workers earned a few hundred dollars a year, Jefferson owed in excess of $1,200 annually in interest alone. By 1819 his indebtedness exceeded $40,000. Had Monticello been owned by anyone else, his creditors would have seized the estate. Jefferson knew this. During the last five years of his life, he was saddled with the sad realization that there would be nothing to leave to his sole surviving child, not even Monticello, which would probably go to ruin.[11]

Although Adams and Jefferson were ready to die, each longed to live to the fiftieth anniversary of the Declaration of Independence, July 4, 1826. Each made it by sheer willpower. Adams's physician doubted that he would live through May, but he fought to stay alive. Jefferson was lucid and continued his correspondence until June 24, when his final illness, probably congestive heart failure, commenced. Both lapsed into a coma on July 2, but swam in and out of consciousness during the next forty-eight hours. In their final hours each frequently asked in a low whisper whether July 4 had dawned. In Quincy, at noon on July 4, Adams proclaimed in quiet tones: "Thomas Jefferson survives."[12]

These were his final words. Immediately thereafter he lost consciousness for the last time. Adams died about 6 PM, as the long shadows of a warm summer afternoon enveloped Peacefield.

Adams's last thought had been incorrect. Jefferson had not outlived him. At almost precisely the moment when Adams had murmured that his friend and rival in Virginia lived on, Jefferson died at Monticello.[13]

When Washington died, his countrymen mourned the loss of a man they admired and trusted. He was seen as "the man who unites all hearts," as a eulogist put it, the cement of the Union during the long war and in the first trials of the new government. In solemn ceremonies throughout the land Washington was celebrated as the courageous hero and savior of liberty and republicanism, as well as a general and statesman who was neither northerner nor southerner, but American.[14]

The striking coincidence of the deaths of Adams and Jefferson on the fiftieth anniversary of the Declaration of Independence astonished and moved all Americans. Many thought it a providential occurrence. Even John Quincy Adams, who was not given to a belief in divine intervention, pronounced it "a strange and exciting" happening. Word of the death of these two Founders sparked a genuine outpouring of love and reverence across the nation. Farmers and artisans momentarily laid aside their tools to mourn at mock funerals conducted in dusty village greens. Throngs numbering into the thousands lined the streets in the largest cities to pay their final respects to their "political parents," as one clergyman called Adams and Jefferson. There was a greater outpouring of love for these two men than there had been for Washington, as if this generation considered Adams and Jefferson as having been more human, more approachable, more vulnerable. Their humanity enhanced their achievements, for as a New England eulogist stated, what Adams and Jefferson had accomplished had been due to their "intellectual and moral energies," and hence had stemmed from among the greatest qualities and virtues that humankind could develop. In tribute after tribute their achievements were chronicled: they had founded the nation, preserved liberty, helped win the war, established religious freedom, and made possible the "diffusion of knowledge through the community, such as has been before altogether unknown and unheard of."[15]

Fifty years after that hot, expectant summer of 1776, the American citizenry gloried in the republican Union. Americans believed that Adams and Jefferson, together with Washington, had been instrumental in securing their nation's destiny. Not one American in twenty in 1826 remembered the time when the British army landed in New York and Congress declared independence, but they were mindful both of the actions of the Revolutionary generation and the presidencies of Washington, Adams, and Jefferson. These three had come to be seen as the grand triumvirate of the Revolutionary era. Washington, it was believed, "is in the clear, upper sky," but Adams and Jefferson "have now joined the American constellation." To this generation a half-century removed from 1776, Jefferson was the eloquent "pen" of the American Revolution, Adams the resounding "tongue" of the rebellion, and Washington its mighty "sword."[16]

Washington never adumbrated the Revolutionary actions of which he was most proud, but there can be little doubt that he took the greatest pride in his tireless service as commander of the Continental army. When he posed in 1772 for what he believed would be his only portrait, he chose to be remembered in a military uniform. Even after his presidency he still hoped to be remembered most for his contributions to the American triumph in the War of Independence. Military success not only had required resolution, industry, courage, daring, and resourcefulness, the virtues that he most admired, but the very survival of the American Revolution and all that followed hinged on military victory.

Jefferson told the world how he wished to be remembered. He left directions to have an inscription placed on a tall stone obelisk that would serve as his tombstone in the quiet, shaded family burial plot at Monticello:

Here is buried Thomas Jefferson, author of the Declaration of Independence, of the Statute of Virginia for Religious Freedom, and Father of the University of Virginia.

During his retirement Adams wrote voluminously on the American Revolution, but in one, small passage in an unpublished letter written eight years after he returned to Quincy, he came closest to professing how he hoped to be remembered. He told a friend that had

I ... omitted to Speak and write ... this Country would never have been independent; Washington would not have been Commander of the American Army; three hundred Millions of Acres of Land which she now possesses would have been cutt off from her Limits; the Cod and Whale Fisheries ... would have been ravished from her; the Massachusetts Constitution, the New York Constitution, the Pensilvania Constitution[,] the Maryland Constitution, the Constitution of the United States would never have been made; Our Armies, for a long time at a most critical period could never have been fed or cloathed, ... an American Navy would not have existed.[17]

Adams once mentioned to Jefferson an additional matter of which he was quite proud. Jefferson and Washington would have concurred. Looking back on his life at age seventy-eight, Adams told Jefferson that when he began his legal career in colonial Massachusetts the most a young man could ever hope for was to someday "be worth ten thousand pounds Sterling, ride in a Chariot, be a Colonel of a Regiment of Militia and hold a seat in his Majesty's Council. No Mans Imagination aspired to any thing higher beneath the Skies."[18] Never in his wildest dreams could Adams have imagined the life that lay before him. Nor could Washington and Jefferson have foreseen the heights they would attain. Each had been driven by ambition, and each had accomplished what he had set out to achieve, and so much more. Each knew too that his sacrifices had paved the way for young people in subsequent generations to dream grandiosely and, if meritorious, to anticipate that their hopes would be fulfilled.

Little separated Washington, Jefferson, and Adams in the great ends they sought from the American Revolution. Each had set the world ablaze praying that the conflagration would change the course of history and form a new epoch, as Adams prayed in the aftermath of the Boston Tea Party. They sought to cast off the long arm of foreign governance, as each by 1774 thought of British rule. Each yearned for a new world that was less hierarchical, cruel, and bellicose, and which brimmed with greater opportunities for the meritorious. Each yearned for a republican America in which political power was derived from the people. For Washington that meant the American Revolution was "a noble cause" that would determine "whether Americans are to be, Freemen, or Slaves." For Adams it meant protecting the liberties enjoyed by earlier generations of colonists, but in time it also increasingly meant living in a land in which the oppressive hand of wealth and privilege was kept at bay. For Jefferson it meant "a hope that light and liberty are on a steady advance" toward a world in which the "misery of the lower classes will be found to abate."[19]

Jefferson was the least committed to service and sacrifice, and in some ways the least certain in 1776 where the American Revolution should take the new nation. In every way he was the least capable of fully and adequately filling the great offices he held. Perhaps things had come too easily for him. At an age when Washington endured grim dangers on a wartime frontier and Adams struggled with an uncertain future as an attorney, Jefferson, with his inherited wealth, constructed a mountaintop mansion and contemplated retirement. Adams spoke often throughout his life of having been improved by being thrust into the "furnace of affliction." The term would have resonated with young Washington. Jefferson would not have understood its meaning.

Washington, through protracted service and myriad economic enterprises, and Adams, through the enrichment of a vibrant professional and urban cauldron, as well as the guidance of skilled political minds and operatives, were prepared for the American Revolution and knew where they wished to lead it. Each was deeply committed to the American struggle. No sacrifice was too terrible, no adversity too daunting, no danger too dismaying to deflect their dedication to the rebellion and war or to suppress their quest for a place in history.

Jefferson's behavior was at once more tarnished and more bewitchingly human. His inner needs diffused his desire to serve the rebellion he had helped to set in motion. He was temperamentally unsuited for the invidious battles that faced every political leader and too inexperienced, and shortsighted, to measure up to the vexatious challenges demanded of a wartime executive. His earlier secluded existence robbed him of the enriching experiences that might have fleshed out his reform impulses. A deeply ingrained and insuperable racism prevented him from making what might have been his greatest contribution to the American Revolution and to humanity, a truly genuine and concerted effort to extirpate African-American slavery in Virginia. It is paradoxical, therefore, that while Jefferson's contributions to the success of the American rebellion and military victory were the least vital of these three Founders, his ringing phrases concerning liberty and equality in the Declaration of Independence, as well as his initiatives on behalf of religious freedom, may have directly touched more lives than any single action that may be attributed to Washington or Adams during the long course of the American Revolution.

The greatest contributions made by Washington and Adams resulted not from a lone act, but from their unflagging and altruistic dedication to the long struggle for independence. Washington, in many lonely army camps and dark, foreboding battlegrounds, and Adams, both in Congress and far from home amid the shoals of European diplomacy, were the bedrock of the American Revolution. Through the long years of war, Washington and Adams, time and again, displayed incredible personal valor, extraordinary qualities of leadership, admirable selflessness, indomitable will, and remarkable insight and sagacity.

Neither Washington nor Adams was flawless. Washington was an amateur soldier who made numerous military mistakes in the early going. Later, when he should have improved with experience, he grew insalubriously cautious and his strategic judgment became steadily more cramped and circumscribed. Thinskinned and insecure, he committed what could have been a fatal blunder of permitting personal jealousies and emotional weaknesses to intrude on his tactical, strategic, and personnel considerations.

However, he counterbalanced these weaknesses with numerous strengths. He grew accustomed to power and to making difficult decisions, and most who observed him, including both Adams and Jefferson, believed he usually made the correct decision. He could be admirably daring. He was incorruptible. He exhibited a noble and virtuous behavior that set a noteworthy example about which the citizenry could rally. He was an excellent administrator and an extraordinary judge of other men. He sought good advice from good advisors. He was a man of fierce courage who set an admirable example for his officers and men. He was a good diplomat who generally worked well with his French counterparts. His political astuteness cannot be underestimated. Dealing with myriad state officials, and especially with Congress, required enormous skill and tact. Overall, his efforts were crowned with success. For the most part he got what he wanted from Congress and kept the legislators happy in the process.[20] Washington, it must be said, passed the test of war.

Despite what he acknowledged to be a long list of personality flaws, Adams was a sagacious, tireless, and courageous congressmen during the crucial first thirty months of the war, and later, during the second and perhaps gravest crisis of the American Revolution, an intrepid and farsighted diplomat. No other American envoy displayed such an incisive grasp of the war and its relationship to diplomatic imperatives. To a degree unmatched by any other American envoy during the American Revolution, Adams not only came to an astute understanding of America's ally, but he saw clearly the military role that France had to play if the allies were to win this war.

Jefferson understood better than most the real significance of the contribution made by Adams and Washington. Both in Congress and in diplomacy, he once remarked, Adams was "profound in his views and accurate in his judgment." He thought Washington "incapable of fear," prudent, and perceptive. He was, Jefferson added, "a wise, a good, and a great man." Indeed, in his final years Jefferson concluded that "it may truly be said" of Washington "that never did nature and fortune combine more perfectly to make a man great."[21]

Adams often remonstrated that no one man had been responsible for the success of the American Revolution. In his last years he rebuked those who venerated him as the "Godlike Adams" or "The Founder of the American Republic," and likewise chastised those who honored Washington as "The Father of His Country." Such titles, he declared, "belong to no man, but to the American people in general."[22]

Adams was correct. The American Revolution had been secured by the War of Independence, a terrible eight-year ordeal that was won by a people's struggle and sacrifice. Almost every freeman of military age soldiered in some capacity in the course of the war. More than 25,000 in the Continental army, roughly ten percent of those eligible to have borne arms, died. Countless others died in the course of militia service. Nor were young men the only ones who sacrificed to win this war. Many older men served on local committees and boards that pertained to the war effort. Every family paid higher taxes. Many women made bullets, sewed shirts and uniforms for the soldiers, worked in clothing drives to secure blankets and uniforms for the men at the front, and acted as spies and gathered intelligence. Perhaps as many as 20,000 women accompanied the army, cooking, washing, nursing the men, and helping to keep the camps clean. Furthermore, it would have been difficult to find a family that was untouched by the conflict, whether through the long absences of one of its own, the death of a loved one, or economic and emotional travail induced by the war. Even civilians sometimes made the supreme sacrifice. In the South many fell victim in the raging civil war after 1779. In the North many found themselves in harm's way when the British conducted military raids, especially on coastal areas. Civilians everywhere succumbed to disease spread by nearby armies or brought home by the soldiers on leave.[23]

However, as Abigail Adams remarked in the course of the war, "Great necessities . . . wake into Life, and form the Character of the Hero and the Statesman" who would lead.[24] The thousands who struggled in the American Revolution required direction. John Adams had never doubted this. In the first days of the war he had declared that leadership was imperative if thirteen disparate colonies that constituted such "a vast, unwieldy Machine" were to gain victory. General Washington, with his mettle, management, acumen, enterprise, and sacrificial example, came closer than any other participant to providing the indispensable leadership that was crucial to the success of the American Revolution. No congressman played a more important role than Adams in 1775 and 1776 in seeing to it, as he later remarked, that "Thirteen clocks were made to strike together."[25] Leadership was crucial to unify the provinces, rally them when despair set in, direct them through the brightest days and darkest nights of the long struggle, and to brazenly face every danger, whether posed by foreign soldiers or America's powerful ally.

Washington and Adams achieved historical greatness in the American Revolution. In some ways, Adams's achievement was the more impressive. His was the more lonely struggle. Before 1778 he battled for unpopular, but necessary, ends against a recalcitrant Congress. Later, when faced with a menacing isolation in Europe, he struggled against America's most popular diplomat and citizen and refused to quail before an imperious ally in whose clutches the very survival of the American Revolution seemed to rest. He was a "bold spirit," as Daniel Webster stated in an address at Faneuil Hall in Boston shortly after Adams's death, a "manly and energetic" leader who possessed the qualities of "natural talent and natural temperament" which the Revolutionary crisis demanded.[26] The Revolutionary generation was indeed fortunate to have had Washington and Adams as its greatest stewards and shepherds.

Abbreviations

The following abbreviations are used in the notes to designate frequently cited publications, libraries, and individuals.

AA	Abigail Adams
AFC	L. H. Butterfield, et al., eds., *Adams Family Correspondence*. 4 vols. Cambridge, Mass., Harvard University Press, 1963–.
AFP	Adams Family Papers. Boston, Massachusetts Historical Society, 1954–1959. Microfilm edition.
AJL	Lester J. Cappon, ed., *The Adams–Jefferson Letters: The Complete Correspondence Between Thomas Jefferson and Abigail and John Adams*. 2 vols. Chapel Hill, University of North Carolina Press, 1961.
DAJA	L. H. Butterfield, et al., eds., *The Diary and Autobiography of John Adams*. 4 vols. Cambridge, Mass., Harvard University Press, 1961.
DGW	Donald Jackson, et al., eds. *The Diaries of George Washington*. Charlottesville, University Press of Virginia, 1976–1979.
FLTJ	E. M. Betts and J. A. Bear, Jr., eds. *The Family Letters of Thomas Jefferson*. Columbia, University of Missouri Press, 1966.
GW	George Washington
JA	John Adams
JCC	Worthington C. Ford, et al., eds. *The Journals of the Continental Congress*. 34 vols. Washington,D.C., Library of Congress, 1904–1937.
LDCC	Paul H. Smith, *Letters of Delegates to Congress, 1774–1789*. Washington,D.C., Library of Congress, 1976–
LPJA	L. Kenvin Wroth and Hiller Zobel, eds. *Legal Papers of Adams*. 3 vols. Cambridge, Mass., Harvard University Press, 1965.

MHS	Massachusetts Historical Society
PGW:Col Ser	W. W. Abbot, et al., eds. *The Papers of George Washington: Colonial Series*. 10 vols. Charlottesville, University Press of Virginia, 1983–1995.
PGW: Confed Ser	W. W. Abbot, et al., eds. *The Papers of George Washington: Confederation Series*. Charlottesville, University Press of Virginia, 1992–
PGW: Pres Ser	Dorothy Twohig, et al., eds. *The Papers of George Washington: Presidential Series*.Charlottesville, University Press of Virginia, 1987–.
PGW:Rev War Ser	Philander Chase, et al., eds. *The Papers of Washington: Revolutionary War Series*. Charlottesville, University Press of Virginia, 1985–.
PGW: Retirement Ser	Dorothy Twohig, et al., *The Papers of George Washington: Retirement Series*. Charlottesville, University Press of Virginia, 1997–.
PJA	Robert J. Taylor, et al., eds. *Papers of John Adams*. Cambridge, Mass., Harvard University Press, 1977–.
PTJ	Julian P. Boyd, et al., eds. *The Papers of Thomas Jefferson*. Princeton, Princeton University Press, 1950–.
TJ	Thomas Jefferson
VMHB	*Virginia Magazine of History and Biography*
WJA	Charles Francis Adams, ed. *The Works of John Adams, Second President of the United States:With a Life of the Author*. 10 vols. Boston, Little, Brown and Company, 1850–1856.
WMQ	*William and Mary Quarterly*
WPUV	Washington Papers, George Washington Papers Project, Alderman Library, University of Virginia.
WTJ	Paul Leicester Ford, ed. *The Writings of Thomas Jefferson*. 10 vols. New York, G. P. Putnam's,1892–1899 [cited as Ford, *WTJ*] and A. A.Lipscomb and A. E. Bergh, eds. *The Writings of Thomas Jefferson*. 20 vols. Washington,D.C., The Thomas Jefferson Memorial Association of the United States, 1900–1904 [cited as Lipscomb and Bergh, *WTJ*].
WW	John C. Fitzpatrick, ed. *The Writings of Washington*. 39 vols. Washington, D.C., U.S. Government Printing Office, 1931–1934.

Notes

Preface

1. JA to TJ, July 30, 1815, *AJL* 2:451; TJ to JA, Aug. 10 [–11], 1815, ibid., 2:452–53.
2. David H. Fischer, *Paul Revere's Ride* (New York, 1994), xiv.
3. Between the 1960s and the 1990s the number of articles that dealt with the lives of important leaders declined by about one-half in the *William and Mary Quarterly*, the leading scholarly journal in early American History. Fewer than twenty percent of the articles between 1990 and 1998 were devoted to recognizable leaders.
4. Carol Berking, et al., *Making America: A History of the United States* (First Edition, Boston, 1995), 129–58.
5. Alan Bullock, *Hitler: A Study in Tyranny* (New York, 1952); Marcus Cunliffe, *George Washington: Man and Monument* (New York, 1959).

Prologue

1. GW to James Clinton, June 29, 1776, *PGW: Rev War Series,* 5:147; GW to John Hancock, June 30, 1776, ibid., 5:169–70; Bruce Bliven, *Under the Guns: New York, 1776–1776* (New York, 1972), 318; Richard Brookhiser, *Founding Father: Rediscovering George Washington* (New York, 1996), 18.
2. Douglas S. Freeman, *George Washington: A Biography* (New York, 1948–1957), 4:116–19; Arnold to GW, June 25, 1776, *PGW: Rev War Ser,* 5:96; Sullivan to GW, June 24, 1776, ibid., 5:92.
3. Franklin to GW, June 21, 1776, *PGW: Rev War Ser,* 5:64; Hawley to GW, June 21, 1776, ibid., 5:71.
4. Freeman, *GW,* 4:115, 119, 121,127; GW to Hancock, June 28, 1776, *PGW: Rev War Ser,* 5:135; GW to Essex County Committee of Safety, June 21, 1776, ibid., 5:53–64; GW, General Orders, June 26, 27, 28, 1776, ibid., 5:109, 112,128–29, 130n; Joseph Reed to Henry Remsen, June 26, 1776, ibid., 131n.
5. GW to James Wadsworth, June 27, 1776, *PGW: Rev War Ser,* 5:127–28; GW to Massachusetts General Court, June 28, 1776, ibid., 5:138; Reed to Samuel Tucker, June 28, 1776, ibid., 5:137n; GW, General Orders, June 29, 30, 1776, ibid., 5:142–44, 155.

6. Council of War, June 27, 1776, ibid., 5:114; GW, General Orders, July 1, 1776, ibid., 5:164.

7. Freeman, *GW*, 4:635; John A. Kouwenhouen, *The Columbia Historical Portrait of New York* (New York, 1953), 91; GW, General Orders, June 28, 1776, *PGW: Rev War Ser*, 5:129–30; GW to Artemas Ward, July 1, 1776, ibid., 5:178–79.

8. Joseph Hewes to James Iredell, June 28, 1776, *LDCC* 4:332; Edward Rutledge to John Jay, June 8, 1776, ibid., 4:174.

9. Gerry to James Warren, June 11, 1776, ibid., 4:187; Hewes to Iredell, June 28, 1776, ibid., 4:332.

10. JA to Richard Henry Lee, June 4, 1776, *PJA* 4:239; JA to AA, April 12, 14, 23, 28, 1776, *AFC* 1:377, 382, 392, 401.

11. JA to AA, April 28, May 17, June 2, 16, 1776, *AFC* 1:401, 411, 2:3, 12; JA to Samuel Cooper [?], June 9, 1776, *PJA* 4:242–43.

12. *ADA* 2:115n.

13. JA to Bulloch, July 1, 1776, *PJA* 4:352.

14. TJ to Thomas Nelson, May 16, 1776, *PTJ* 1:292, 293n; Nathan Schachner, *Thomas Jefferson: A Biography* (New York, 1951), 118.

15. TJ to Nelson, May 16, 1776, *PTJ* 1:292; TJ to Edmund Pendleton, June 30, 1776, ibid., 1:408.

16. TJ to Fleming, July 1, 1776, ibid., 1:411–13; TJ to John Randolph, Nov. 29, 1775, ibid., 1:269; Frank Donovan, *Mr. Jefferson's Declaration* (New York, 1968), 41.

17. James A. Bear, Jr. and Lucia C. Stanton, eds., *Jefferson's Memorandum Books: Accounts, with Legal Records and Miscellany, 1767–1826* (Princeton, 1997), 1:432; Sam Bass Warner, Jr., *The Private City: Philadelphia in Three Periods of its Growth* (Philadelphia, 1968), 3–21.

18. *LDCC* 4:xv–xxi.

19. *JCC* 5:424.

20. *JCC* 5:504–505n; *DAJA* 3:396; JA to Chase, July 1, 1776, *PJA* 4:353.

21. John Dickinson, "Notes for a Speech in Congress," [July 1, 1776], *LDCC* 4:351–57; John Dickinson, "Notes on Arguments Concerning Independence," [July 1, 1776], ibid., 4:357–58.

22. JA to Chase, July 1, 1776, *PJA* 4:353; *DAJA* 2:137, 146, 151, 162, 173–74; 3:316–19; Milton E. Flower, *John Dickinson: Conservative Revolutionary* (Charlottesville, 1983), 145.

23. *JADA* 3:396.

24. JA to Mercy Warren, Aug. 17, 1807, in Charles Francis Adams, ed., "Correspondence between John Adams and Mercy Warren Relating to Her History of the American Revolution," Massachusetts Historical Society, *Collections*, 5th Ser., Vol. 4 (Reprint, New York, 1972), 467; *DAJA* 3:396; TJ to Samuel Wells, May 12, 1819, Ford, *WTJ* 10:131.

25. JA to Chase, July 1, 1776, *PJA* 4:353; TJ, To the Editor of the *Journal de Paris*, August 29, 1787, *PTJ* 12:63.

26. Merrill Jensen, *The Founding of a Nation: A History of the American Revolution,*

1763–1776 (New York, 1968), 700; Edmund C. Burnett, *The Continental Congress* (New York, 1941), 181–82.

27. Bartlett to John Landgon, July 1, 1776, *LDCC* 4:351; JA to AA, July 3, 1776, *AFC* 2:28.

28. David F. Hawke, *Honorable Treason: The Declaration of Independence and the Men Who Signed It* (New York, 1976), 146; Clark to Elisha Dayton, July 4, 1776, *LDCC* 4:379.

Chapter 1

1. *DGW* 1:232–34.
2. JA to Jonathan Sewall, Feb. 20, 1760, *PJA* 1:41–42, 45n.
3. TJ to John Harvie, Jan. 14, 1760, *PTJ* 1:3; *DGW* 1:223.
4. GW to John Stanwix, April 10, 1758, *PGW:Col Ser* 5:17.
5. JA to TJ, Nov. 15, 1813, *AJL* 2:402.
6. Washington and Jefferson are the subject of numerous biographies. On GW see: Douglas Southall Freeman, *George Washington: A Biography*, 7 vols. (New York, 1948–1957); James T. Flexner, *George Washington*, 4 vols. (Boston, 1965–1972); Rupert Hughes, *George Washington*, 3 vols. (New York, 1926–1930); John Ferling, *The First of Men: A Life of George Washington* (Knoxville, 1988); John R. Alden, *George Washington: A Biography* (Baton Rouge, 1984); Willard Sterne Randall, *George Washington: A Life* (New York, 1997); Paul L. Ford, *The True George Washington* (Philadelphia, 1898); John C. Fitzpatrick, *George Washington Himself: A Commonsense Biography Written from His Manuscripts* (Indianapolis, 1933). On GW's character see Brookhiser, *Founding Father*. On TJ see: Dumas Malone, *Jefferson and His Times*, 6 vols. (Boston, 1948–1981); Merrill D. Peterson, *Thomas Jefferson and the New Nation: A Biography* (New York, 1970); Henry S. Randall, *The Life of Thomas Jefferson*, 3 vols. (New York, 1858); Fawn Brodie, *Thomas Jefferson: An Intimate History* (New York, 1974); Page Smith, *Jefferson: A Revealing Biography* (New York, 1976); Alf Mapp, *Thomas Jefferson*, 2 vols. (New York, 1987–1991); Noble E. Cunningham, Jr., *In Pursuit of Reason: The Life of Thomas Jefferson* (Baton Rouge, 1987); Joseph J. Ellis, *American Sphinx: The Character of Thomas Jefferson* (New York, 1997); Willard Sterne Randall, *Thomas Jefferson: A Life* (New York, 1992); Schachner, *TJ*; Andrew Burstein, *The Inner Jefferson: Portrait of a Grieving Optimist* (Charlottesville, 1995). For additional works on TJ see Frank Shuffleton, ed., *Thomas Jefferson: A Comprehensive, Annotated Bibliography of Writings About Him (1826–1980)* (New York, 1983); Frank Shuffleton, *Thomas Jefferson, 1981–1990: An Annotated Bibliography* (New York, 1992).
7. For biographies and other important works on the life of Adams see: Gilbert Chinard, *Honest John Adams* (Boston, 1933); Page Smith, *John Adams*, 2 vols. (New York, 1962); Peter Shaw, *The Character of John Adams* (Chapel Hill, 1976); John Ferling, *John Adams: A Life* (Knoxville, 1992); Joseph Ellis, *Passionate Sage: The Character and Legacy of John Adams* (New York, 1993), C. Bradley Thompson, *John Adams and the Spirit of Liberty* (Lawrence, Kan., 1998), which unfortunately appeared too late to be utilized in this study. For additional works, see John Ferling, ed., *John Adams: A Bibliography* (Westport, Conn., 1993).

8. Freeman, *GW*, 1:32–35, 37–42, 55–58, 71–72; Flexner, *GW*, 1:14–15.

9. TJ, "Autobiography," in Saul K. Padover, ed., *The Complete Jefferson* (New York, 1943), 1119–20; TJ, *Notes on the State of Virginia*, in ibid., 577; Randall, *Life of TJ*, 1:13; TJ to Thomas Jefferson Randolph, Nov. 24, 1808, in *FLTJ*, 363; Cunningham, *In Pursuit of Reason*, 2.

10. Daniel Blake Smith, *Inside the Great House: Planter Family Life in Eighteenth-Century Chesapeake Society* (Ithaca, 1980), 48–49, 51, 57, 82–85; Jan Lewis, *The Pursuit of Happiness: Family and Values in Jefferson's Virginia* (Cambridge, Eng., 1983), 21; Rhys Isaac, *The Transformation of Virginia, 1740–1790* (Chapel Hill, 1982), 131–35.

11. TJ, "Autobiography," Padover, *Complete TJ*, 1119; Sarah N. Randolph, *The Domestic Life of Thomas Jefferson* (New York, 1871), 23; Randall, *TJ*, 9–14; Silvio Bendini, *Thomas Jefferson: Statesman of Science* (New York, 1990), 9–10.

12. *DAJA* 3:256–60; *PJA* 1:51–53; James Axtell, *The School Upon a Hill: Education and Society in Colonial New England* (New Haven, 1974), 214–15. All estimates of earning and income are based on data contained in Jackson T. Main, *The Social Structure of Revolutionary America* (Princeton, 1965), and Billy G. Smith, "The Material Lives of Laboring Philadelphians," *WMQ* 38 (1981): 163–202.

13. Richard Bushman, *From Puritan to Yankee: Character and Social Order in Connecticut, 1650–1765* (New York, 1967), 3–21, 267–88; Jack P. Greene, "Autonomy and Stability: New England and the British Colonial Experience in Recent Historiography," in Jack P. Greene, ed., *Interpreting America: Historiographical Essays* (Charlottesville, 1996), 126–55, 240–80.

14. Bushman, *From Puritan to Yankee*, 3–21, 267–88; Steven Mintz and Susan Kellog, *Domestic Revolutions: A Social History of American Family Life* (New York, 1988), 1–23; Larzer Ziff, *Puritanism in America: New Culture in a New World* (New York, 1973), 14–18, 24, 27, 122, 184, 260, 269, 295.

15. *DAJA* 1:72–73, 217; Edmund S. Morgan, *The Puritan Family* (Boston, 1956), 28–61; John Demos, *Past, Present, and Personal: The Family and the Life Course in American History* (New York, 1986), 45, 47; Philip Greven, *The Protestant Temperament: Patterns of Child-Rearing, Religious Experience, and the Self in Early America* (New York, 1977), 151–261.

16. *DAJA* 3:257–58; 1:65–66, 79–80.

17. Brodie, *TJ*, 23, 51.

18. TJ to JA, Aug. 1, 1816, March 25, 1826, *AJL* 2:483, 614; Brodie, *TJ*, 22, 41–42; TJ to William Randolph, June 1776, *PTJ* 1:408–09; TJ to TJ Randolph, Nov. 24, 1808, *FLTJ* 362–63. On Jane Randolph Jefferson, see Malone, *TJ*, 1:37–38; Mapp, *TJ*, 1:12.

19. Rosemarie Zagarri, ed., *David Humphreys' "Life of General Washington" with George Washington's "Remarks"* (Athens, Ga., 1991), xiii, xx, 5–6.

20. George Washington Parke Custis, *Recollections and Private Memories of Washington* (New York, 1860), 131; Flexner, *GW*, 1:11–12, 19–20; Alden, *GW*, 34; Freeman, *GW*, 1:193; Zagarri, *David Humphreys' "Life of General Washington,"* 7.

21. *DAJA* 1:36–37n; 3:227, 237, 255; Mary Smith Cranch to AA, Dec. 18, 1785, *AFC*

6:494, 495n; Richard Cranch to JA, Nov. 19, 1785, ibid., 6:458, 459n. For profiles of Elihu and Peter Adams see *PJA* 1:36–37n.

22. Randall, *TJ*, 1:41; Smith, *Jefferson*, 12–13; Randall, *TJ*, 83.

23. Zagarri, *David Humphreys' "Life of Washington,"* 8; Flexner, *GW*, 1:24–26; Freeman, *GW*, 1:70–71, 77.

24. Ibid., 3:257–60.

25. Ibid., 3:259–64; Shaw, *Character of JA*, 7; Lawrence A. Cremin, *American Education: The Colonial Experience, 1607–1783* (New York, 1970), 212–19, 330–31, 466–68, 509–15, 553–54; Axtell, *School Upon a Hill*, 201–45.

26. JA to John Trumbull, March 9, 1790, AFP, reel 115.

27. *DAJA* 3:261–62; Shaw, *Character of JA*, 7–8, 12; JA to Trumbull, March 9, 1790, AFP, reel 115. JA ranked fourteenth in a class of twenty-five, but Harvard's ranking system was not meritocratic. Student ranking was based primarily on the Puritan concept of duty and service, so that the sons of magistrates and Harvard graduates outranked the offspring of farmers, shopkeepers, and artisans who had not attended college. See Clifford Shipton, "Ye Mystery of ye Ages Solved, or How Placing Worked at Colonial Harvard & Yale," *Harvard Alumni Bulletin* 57 (1954): 258–63. JA's closest friends at Harvard included John Wentworth, later the royal governor of New Hampshire, Samuel Locke, who became president of Harvard College, Samuel Parsons, a lawyer and general in the Continental army, and Tristram Dalton, who eventually was elected a U.S. senator. See *DAJA* 3:260–61.

28. *DAJA* 3:259–64; Shaw, *Character of JA*, 8; Charles R. McKirdy, "Massachusetts Lawyers on the Eve of the American Revolution: The State of the Profession," in *Law in Colonial Massachusetts, 1630–1800: A Conference Held 6 and 7 November 1981 by The Colonial Society of Massachusetts* (Boston, 1984), 339.

29. Malone, *TJ*, 1:40.

30. On TJ's experiences in Maury's school, see TJ to Harvie, Jan. 14, 1760, *PTJ* 1:3; TJ to Maury, April 25, 1812, Lipscomb and Bergh, *WTJ* 13:149; Carl Binger, *Thomas Jefferson: A Well-Tempered Mind* (New York, 1970), 24; Randall, *TJ*, 11–25; Malone, *TJ*, 1:42; Marie Kimball, *Jefferson: The Road to Glory, 1743–1776* (New York, 1943), 30.

31. Peterson, *TJ*, 7–8; Randall, *TJ*, 22–24; TJ to Priestley, Jan. 27, 1800, Lipscomb and Bergh, *WTJ* 10:147; TJ to Harvie, Jan. 14, 1760, *PTJ* 1:3.

32. Dumas Malone, "Jefferson Goes to School at Williamsburg," *Virginia Quarterly Review* 33 (1957): 483–86; Malone, *TJ*, 1:56–57; Randall, *TJ*, 37, 41–42; TJ to John Page, Oct. 7, 1763, *PTJ* 1:11.

33. Malone, *TJ*, 1:49–61. James Madison was the bishop, John Taylor of Caroline the political philosopher, Thomas Nelson the governor of Virginia and congressman, TJ's close friend John Page was also a congressman, and John Marshall served as Chief Justice of the United States.

34. TJ to Vine Utley, March 21, 1819, Ford, *WTJ* 9:126; TJ to William Duane, Oct. 1, 1812, Lipscomb and Bergh, *WTJ* 2:420–21; Malone, *TJ*, 1:56–57; Randall, *TJ*, 37, 41–42; TJ to John Page, Oct. 7, 1763, *PTJ* 1:11.

35. Malone, *TJ*, 1:53–55; TJ, "Autobiography," in Padover, *Complete TJ*, 1120.

36. Flexner, *GW*, 1:18; Longmore, *Invention of GW*, 6–9; Freeman, *GW*, 1:57–58, 70–71;

Charles Moore, ed., *George Washington's Rules of Civility and Decent Behaviour in Company and Conversation* (Boston, 1926).

37. GW to John Stanwix, April 10, 1758, *PGW:Col Ser* 3:117; Flexner, *GW*, 1:23–24; Freeman, *GW*, 1:64n 76; Ford, *True GW*, 60–75; Fitzpatrick, *GW Himself*, 40.

38. *DGW* 1:6–23; "GW's Professional Surveys," in *PGW:Col Ser* 1:8–9.

39. GW to Richard ?, [1749–1750], *PGW:Col Ser* 1:44.

40. Ibid., 1:44; "GW's Professional Surveys," ibid., 1:8–37.

41. "GW's Professional Surveys," ibid., 1:8–37; Samuel E. Morison, "The Young Man Washington," in Samuel E. Morison, *By Land and By Sea: Essays and Addresses by Samuel Eliot Morison* (New York, 1953), 169; Flexner, *GW*, 1:80; Hughes, *GW*, 1:37–38; Fitzpatrick, *GW Himself*, 147; Bernhard Knollenberg, *George Washington: The Virginia Period, 1732–1775* (Durham, N.C., 1964), 87; William S. Baker, *Early Sketches of George Washington* (Philadelphia, 1893), 13–14. On the height of colonial males, see John Ferling, "Soldiers for Virginia: Who Served in the French and Indian War?," *Virginia Magazine of History and Biography*, 94 (1986): 312–13; Kenneth L. Sokoloff and George C. Villaflor, "The Early Achievement of Modern Stature in America," *Social Science History*, 6 (1982): 435–81.

42. Gordon S. Wood, *The Radicalism of the American Revolution* (New York, 1992), 18–35; Douglass Adair, *Fame and the Founding Fathers: Essays*, ed. Trevor Colbourn (New York, 1974), 6; [Benjamin Franklin], *Poor Richard Improved*, 1758, in Leonard W. Labaree, et al., eds., *The Papers of Benjamin Franklin* (New Haven, 1959–), 7:340–55; Timothy Breen, *Tobacco Culture: The Mentality of the Great Tidewater Planters on the Eve of the Revolution* (Princeton, 1985), 125.

43. Leo Braudy, *The Frenzy of Renown: Fame and Its History* (New York, 1986), 368, 371.

Chapter 2

1. *DGW* 1:43–116; Freeman, *GW*, 1:43–83, 256–66; *PGW:Col Ser* 1:52n; GW to William Fitzhugh, Nov. 15, 1754, ibid., 1:226.

2. Freeman, *GW*, 1:266–70; Flexner, *GW*, 1:53; Charles Cecil Wall, *George Washington: Citizen-Soldier* (Charlottesville, 1980), 17.

3. For general accounts of the intercolonial wars, see Douglas Edward Leach, *Arms for Empire: A Military History of the British Colonies in North America, 1607–1763* (New York, 1973) and John Ferling, *Struggle for a Continent: The Wars of Early America* (Arlington Heights, Ill., 1993). On Dinwiddie's role in the precipitation of hostilities in 1753–1754, see John R. Alden, *Robert Dinwiddie: Servant of the Crown* (Charlottesville, 1973), 38–44; James Titus, *The Old Dominion at War: Society, Politics, and Warfare in Late Colonial Virginia* (Columbia, S.C., 1991), 5–28.

4. *DGW* 1:154–56, 161n; William M. Darlington, ed., *Christopher Gist's Journal, with Historical, Geographical and Ethnological notes* (Pittsburgh, 1893), 83–87.

5. JA to Sewall, Feb. 1760, *PJA* 1:41–42.

6. For a good account of the lifestyle of a parson in a New England village, see Harriet Beecher Stowe, *Oldtown Folks* (Cambridge, Mass., 1966), 52–53, 55, 88, 101–02.

7. JA to Charles Cushing, April 1, 1756, *PJA* 1:13; *DAJA* 3:262–63; Stowe, *Oldtown Folks*, 53, 55.

8. JA to Charles Cushing, April 1, 1756, *PJA* 1:13.

9. *DAJA* 3:263–64; JA to Cushing, April 1, 1756, *PJA* 1:12–13; Richard D. Brown, *Knowledge Is Power: The Diffusion of Information in Early America, 1700–1865* (New York, 1989), 83, 87; John Murrin, "The Legal Transformation: The Bench and Bar of Eighteenth-Century Massachusetts," in Stanley N. Katz and John M. Murrin, eds., *Colonial America: Essays in Politics and Social Development* (New York, 1983), 541–42, 548–53; G. W. Gewalt, *The Promise of Power: The Emergence of the Legal Profession in Massachusetts, 1760–1840* (Westport, Conn., 1979); Gerard W. Gewalt, "Sources of Anti-Lawyer Sentiment in Massachusetts, 1740–1840," *American Journal of Legal History*, 14 (1970): 238–307; McKirdy, "Massachusetts Lawyers," *Law in Colonial Massachusetts*, 326n, 333–36; Cremin, *American Education*, 554.

10. *DAJA* 1:42–44, 63; 3:264–65; McKirdy, "Massachusetts Lawyers," *Law in Colonial Massachusetts*, 350; Brown, *Knowledge Is Power*, 91. On Putnam, see "James Putnam," in John L. Sibley and Clifford K. Shipton, eds., *Biographical Sketches of Those Who Attended Harvard College* (Cambridge, Mass., 1873), 12:57–64.

11. *DAJA* 4:269–70; 1:24–25, 78, 118, 132, 168, 337–38. On JA's fear of wealth, see Ellis, *Passionate Sage*, 52.

12. Brodie, *TJ*, 71; Malone, *TJ*, 1:114; Adair, *Fame and the Founding Fathers*, 7, 13–16, 19; Kenneth A. Lockridge, *The Diary, and Life, of William Byrd II of Virginia, 1674–1744* (Chapel Hill, N.C., 1987), 23.

13. TJ to Page, Jan. 20, 1763, *PTJ* 1:8.

14. Randall, *TJ*, 47, 51, 53, 55–58, 66–68.

15. TJ to Ralph Izard, July 17, 1788, *PTJ* 13:372; TJ to TJ Randolph, June 14, 1806, Lipscomb and Bergh, *WTJ* 12:197–98; TJ, "Autobiography," in Padover, *Complete TJ*, 1120; Randall, *TJ*, 47; Brodie, *TJ*, 61; Smith, *Jefferson*, 23; *DAJA* 1:63; McKirdy, "Massachusetts Lawyers," *Law in Colonial Massachusetts*, 350.

16. Dinwiddie to GW, March 15, 1754, *PGW:Col Ser* 1:95.

17. On prerevolutionary society and culture, see Wood, *Radicalism of the American Revolution*, 3–168.

18. GW to Dinwiddie, May 9, 18, 27, 1754, *PGW:Col Ser* 1:94, 96, 105–6; GW to Joshua Fry, May 23, 1754, ibid., 1:101.

19. GW to Dinwiddie, April 25, May 18, 1754, *PGW:Col Ser* 1:88, 99.

20. GW to Dinwiddie, May 29, 1754, ibid., 1:107–13; *DGW* 1:195; Thomas A. Lewis, *For King and Country: The Maturing of George Washington* (New York, 1993), 147.

21. GW to John Augustine Washington, May 31, 1754, *PGW:Col Ser* 1:118; GW to Dinwiddie, May 29, 1754, ibid., 1:112.

22. GW to Dinwiddie, June 3, 1754, ibid., 1:124; Dinwiddie to GW, June 2, 4, 1754, ibid., 1:121, 126; Lewis, *For King and Country*, 150.

23. "The Capitulation of Fort Necessity," *PGW:Col Ser* 1:157–59; "Account by GW and James Mackay of the Capitulation of Fort Necessity," July 19, 1754, ibid., 1:159–61; "Articles of Capitulation," July 3, 1754, ibid., 1:165–68.

24. Lewis, *For King and Country*, 156; "GW's Account of the Capitulation of Fort Neces-

sity," 1786, *PGW:Col Ser* 1:172–73; "Account by GW . . . of the Capitulation of Fort Necessity," July 19, 1754, ibid., 1:159–64; Alden, *Dinwiddie*, 96.

25. GW to William Fitzhugh, Nov. 15, 1754, *PGW:Col Ser* 1:226; Lewis, *For King and Country*, 158–62.

26. JA to Cranch, Oct. 18, 1756, *PJA* 1:20; *DAJA* 1:58–59.

27. *DAJA* 1:54–57; 3:371–73.

28. Ibid., 1:45, 50, 54–55, 58–60, 63–65, 73–74, 77; 3:270–73.

29. Ibid., 1:51, 52, 59–60, 63, 64, 68, 69, 71, 73–74, 78, 80–81, 83, 84, 86, 87, 93, 95–97, 100, 106, 118, 131, 133, 168, 207, 227, 236, 317; 3:269–70; Shaw, *Character of JA*, 27; Hiller B. Zobel, *The Boston Massacre* (New York, 1970), 10; McKirdy, "Massachusetts Lawyers," *Law in Colonial Massachusetts*, 327; Brown, *Knowledge Is Power*, 93.

30. *DAJA* 1:57, 71n, 77.

31. Ibid., 1:68–73, 100, 104, 108, 114; JA to John Wentworth, Oct. [?], 1758, *PJA* 1:26.

32. *DAJA* 1:53, 72–74, 77, 104.

33. Ibid., 1:45–48, 174.

34. Ibid., 1:52, 63, 68, 73, 78, 84, 95–96, 98, 100, 106, 118, 128–30, 135–38, 168.

35. Ibid., 1:100, 193, 217–19, 224n; 3:276; *LPJA* 1:lviii; Brown, *Knowledge Is Power*, 96.

36. Randall, *TJ*, 58–65; Edward Dumbauld, *Thomas Jefferson and the Law* (Norman, Okla., 1978), xi.

37. Dumbauld, *TJ and the Law*, 66–83; Dewey, *TJ, Lawyer*, 9–14; Edmund Randolph, "Essay on the Revolutionary History of Virginia," *Virginia Magazine of History and Biography*, 43 (1953), 123; Randall, *TJ*, 85–86.

38. Malone, *TJ*, 1:122–23; Cunningham, *In Pursuit of Reason*, 12–13; Dewey, *TJ, Lawyer*, 29, 34, 35, 44, 90–91; Randall, *TJ*, 95, 102, 104.

39. Robert Orme to GW, March 21, April 3, 1755, *PGW:Col Ser* 1:241, 249; GW to Orme, March 15, April 2, 1755, ibid., 1:243, 246–47.

40. Orme to Gov. Robert Morris, July 18, 1755, *LGW* 1:71; Oliver L. Spaulding, "The Military Studies of George Washington," *AHR*, 29 (1924), 677; Zagarri, *David Humphrey's "Life of General Washington,"* 15.

41. GW to Dinwiddie, July 18, 1755, *PGW:Col Ser* 1:339–40; GW to John Augustine Washington, July 18, 1755, ibid., 1:343.

42. Paul E. Kopperman, *Braddock at the Monongahela* (Pittsburgh, 1977), 32–93; Lewis, *For King and Country*, 176–90; Titus, *Old Dominion at War*, 64–71; Flexner, *GW*, 1:119–31; Stanley Pargellis, "Braddock's Defeat," *American Historical Review*, 40 (1936): 259–62; Freeman, *GW*, 2:104–14; GW to Dinwiddie, July 18, 1755, *PGW: Col Ser* 1:339–40; GW to Mary Ball Washington, July 18, 1755, ibid., 1:336–37; GW to J. A. Washington, July 18, 1755, ibid., 1:343; GW, "Biographical Memoranda" [Oct. 1783], *WW* 29:44–45. The casualties in this engagement were officially listed as 456 killed and 520 wounded out of a force of 1,469. See *PGW:Col Ser* 1:338n.

43. Philip Ludwell to GW, Aug. 8, 1755, *PGW:Col Ser* 1:356–57; Charles Lewis to GW, Aug. 9, 1755, ibid., 1:357–58; Warner Lewis to GW, Aug. 9, 1755, ibid., 1:358–59; Dinwiddie to GW, Aug. 14, 1755, ibid., 2:3–8; GW to Mary Ball Washington, Aug. 14, 1755, ibid., 1:359.

44. GW to Dinwiddie, Oct. 8, 1755, ibid., 2:83.

45. Titus, *Old Dominion at War*, 77–78, 90; Lewis, *For King and Country*, 197, 205; Freeman, *GW*, 2:151–64; Flexner, *GW*, 1:145–47, 174–75; GW to Dinwiddie, Oct. 8, 11 1755, *PGW:Col Ser* 2:83, 101–03; GW, "Notes of Journey to Boston," *WW* 1:298–99.

46. GW to Dinwiddie, Feb. 2, April 7, 24, May 3, Aug. 4, 1756, April 16, Sept. 24, 1757, *PGW:Col Ser* 2:313–15, 332–35; 3:44–45, 81; 4:136, 420; GW to Robert McKenzie, Aug. 5, 1756, ibid., 3:336; 4:334–35n; Adam Stephen to GW, July 25, 1756, ibid, 3:294.

47. Adam Stephen to GW, July 25, 1756, ibid., 3:294; GW to Dinwiddie, Oct. 11, 1755, April 16, 18, 19, 24, May 3, 23, June 25, Aug. 4, Sept. 8, Oct. 10, Nov. 9, 1756, ibid., 2:102–03; 3:1–3, 13–15, 20, 44–46, 81–84, 171–73, 222–25, 312–18, 396–400, 430–34; 4:1–6; GW to Adam Stephen, Nov. 18, 1755, ibid., 2:172–73.

48. Freeman, *GW*, 2:234; Flexner, *GW*, 1:174–75.

49. *PGW:Col Ser* 3:411–12n.

50. Dinwiddie to GW, Nov. 16, 1756, Sept. 2, 24, 1757, ibid., 3:25, 397, 422.

51. Dr. James Craik to GW, Nov. 25, 1757, *PGW:Col Ser* 5:64–65 GW to Stanwix, March 5, 1758, ibid., 5:102.

52. Leach, *Arms for Empire*, 415–19; Ian K. Steele, *Warpaths: Invasions of North America* (New York, 1994), 207–10; Ferling, *Struggle for a Continent*, 170–72.

53. GW to Governor Francis Fauquier, Nov. 28, 1758, ibid., 6:158–60; Freeman, *GW*, 2:360–66; Flexner, *GW*, 1:206–23; Lewis, *For King and Country*, 269–70; Leach, *Arms for Empire*, 438–45; Titus, *Old Dominion at War*, 122–24.

54. GW to Richard Washington, Sept. 20, 1759, *PGW:Col Ser* 6:359.

55. "Address from the Officers of the Virginia Regiment," Dec. 31, 1758, ibid., 6:179–80; Longmore, *Invention of GW*, 29–31, 43, 232n.

56. GW to Charles Lewis, Jan. 27, 1756, *PGW:Col Ser* 2:297; Freeman, *GW*, 3:6; Flexner, *GW*, 1:191–92.

57. GW to Sally Fairfax, Nov. 15, 1757, Feb. 13, 1758, ibid., 5:56, 93.

58. Freeman, *GW*, 2:277–78, 298–301; Anne Wharton, *Martha Washington* (New York, 1897), 3–24; Eugene E. Prussing, *The Estate of George Washington, Deceased* (Boston, 1927), 96; Knollenberg, *GW*, 26–28.

59. GW to Sally Fairfax, Sept. 12, 25, 1758, *PGW:Col Ser* 6:10–13, 41–43.

60. Freeman, *GW*, 2:302; Flexner, *GW*, 1:227.

61. TJ to Page, Dec. 25, 1762, Jan. 20, Feb. 12, July 15, 1763, *PTJ* 1:5–10.

62. TJ to Page, Oct. 7, 1763, Jan. 19, 1764, ibid., 1:11, 13–14; TJ to William Fleming, March 20, Oct. ?, 1763, ibid., 1:13, 16.

63. JA to Francis Vanderkemp, April 18, 1815, AFP, reel 122; AA to William Shaw, Feb. 2, 1799, Shaw Papers, LC.

64. TJ to Page, Jan. 19, 1764, *PTJ* 1:13–14.

65. Kenneth A. Lockridge, *On the Sources of Patriarchal Rage: The Commonplace Books of William Byrd and Thomas Jefferson and the Gendering of Power in the Eighteenth Century* (New York, 1992), 47–102; Douglas L. Wilson, ed., *Jefferson's Literary Commonplace Book*, in *Papers of Thomas Jefferson*, 2d Ser. (Princeton, 1989), 70–71, 73, 76–77, 82, 98–99, 117–18, 126–27 (hereafter cited as Wilson, *PTJ*); Brodie,

TJ, 68–69; Rhys Isaac, "The First Monticello," in Peter S. Onuf, ed., *Jeffersonian Legacies* (Charlottesville, 1993), 82–83.

66. Jefferson to Page, Jan. 20, Oct. 7, 1763, *PTJ* 1:8, 11. On TJ's sexuality, see Barbara Far-isha-Kovach, *The Experience of Adolescence: Development in Content* (Glenville, Ill., 1983), 260; F. Philip Rice, *The Adolescent: Development, Relationships, and Culture* (Boston, 1981), 313; Robert Grinder, *Adolescence* (New York, 1973), 85; G. Kriegman, "Homosexuality and the Educator," *Journal of School Health*, 39 (1969): 305–11; K. A. Adler, "Life Style, Gender Role, and the Symptoms of Homosexuality," *Journal of Individual Psychology*, 23 (1967): 67–78; David B. Lynn, *Parental and Sex-Role Identification: A Theoretical Formulation* (Berkeley, 1969), 23–25, 62–64; L. Ovesey, *Homosexuality and Pseudohomosexualty* (New York, 1969), 11–31, 57; A. G. Barclay and D. Cususmano, "Father-Absence Cross-Sex Identity, and Field-Development Behavior in Male Adolescents," *Child Development*, 38 (1967): 243–50; R. V. Burton and N. W. M. Whiting, "The Absent Father and Cross-Sex Identity," *Merrill Palmer Quarterly*, 7 (1961): 85–95.

67. Erik Erikson, "Growth and Crisis of the Healthy Personality," in Milton Senn, ed., *Symposium on the Healthy Personality* (New York, 1941), 101, 105–6; Daniel J. Levinson, *The Season's of a Man's Life* (New York, 1978), 48–49, 73–76, 80; Alexander Mitscherlich, *Society Without the Father* (New York, 1970), 137–64; D. W. Winnicott, *The Maturational Processes and the Facilitating Environment* (Madison, Conn., 1965), 83–92; Anthony Storr, *Churchill's Black Dog, Kafka's Mice, and Other Phenomena of the Human Mind* (New York, 1965), 45, 87, 99, 101, 115, 148; George Pollock, "Childhood Parent and Sibling Loss in Adult Patients: A Comparative Study," *Archives in General Psychiatry* 7 (1962): 295–305; Martha Wolfenstein, "Effects on Adults of Object Loss in the First Five Years," *Journal of the American Psychoanalytic Association* 24 (1976): 659–68; John Bowlby, "Grief and Mourning in Infancy and Early Childhood," in Ruth Eissler, et al., eds. *The Psychoanalytic Study of the Child* 15 (1960): 9–52; John Bowlby, "Separation Anxiety," *International Journal of Psycho-Analysis* 41 (1960): 105–9; Robert Furman, "Death and the Young Child: Some Preliminary Considerations," ibid., 19 (1964): 321–33.

68. L. H. Butterfield, ed., *The Earliest Diary of John Adams* (Cambridge, Mass., 1966), 12; *DAJA* 1:108–09; Levin, *AA*, 4, 10, 27, 496n; AA to JA, May 9, 1764, *AFC* 1:46–47; JA to Rush, Aug. 25, 1811, Schutz and Adair, *Spur of Fame*, 188.

69. JA to Zabdiel Adams, July 23, 1763, *PJA* 1:95; JA to Abigail Smith, April 7, 13, 26, 1764, *AFC* 1:16–18, 24, 38; *DAJA* 3:280.

70. TJ to Page, Feb. 21, 1770, *PTJ* 1:36; TJ, "Autobiography," in Padover, *Complete TJ*, 1120–24.

71. TJ to John Randolph, Aug. 25, 1775, *PTJ* 1:241; TJ to Page, Feb. 21, 1770, ibid., 1:35–36; Ellis, *American Sphinx*, 34–35.

72. TJ to John Minor, Aug. 30, 1814, Lipscomb and Bergh, *WTJ* 2:420–21.

73. TJ to Francis Willis, July 23, 1766, *PTJ* 1:21; Malone, *TJ*, 1:448n, 450n.

74. TJ to Page, Feb. 21, 1770, *PTJ* 1:36.

75. Mapp, *TJ*, 65; Randall, *Life of TJ*, 1:63.

76. Randall, *Life of TJ*, 1:63; Randall, *TJ*, 156; Robert Skipwith to TJ, Sept. 20, 1771, *PTJ*

1:84; TJ to Skipwith, Aug. 3, 1771, ibid., 1:78; TJ to James Ogilvie, Feb. 20, 1771, ibid., 1:63; Jack McLoughlin, *Jefferson and Monticello* (New York, 1988), 161–63. Historian Rhys Isaac has argued persuasively that TJ fell in love as early as February 1770. See Rhys Isaac, "The First Monticello," Onuf, *Jeffersonian Legacies*, 88.

77. TJ to Skipwith, Aug. 3, 1771, *PTJ* 1:78.

78. Randall, *Life of TJ*, 1:64; Petterson, *TJ*, 27; Randall, *TJ*, 160.

Chapter 3

1. Isaac, *Transformation of Virginia*, 34–42; Breen, *Tobacco Culture*, 37, 86, 105; Jack P. Greene, *Pursuits of Happiness: The Social Development of Early Modern British Colonies and the Foundation of American Culture* (Chapel Hill, 1988), 92–94.

2. *PGW:Col Ser* 6:381n; Robert F. and Lee Baldwin Dalzell, *George Washington's Mount Vernon: At Home in Revolutionary America* (New York, 1998), 30–31.

3. Dalzell and Dalzell, *GW's Mount Vernon*, 47–73.

4. *DGW* 1:239–42n; 2:30–31n; Elswyth Thane, *Potomac Squire* (New York, 1963), lx; Flexner, *GW*, 3:20, 40; Zagarri, "*David Humphreys' Life of Washington*," 39–40; Wall, *GW*, 149, 176.

5. GW to Richard Washington. Dec. 6, 1755, *PGW:Col Ser* 2:207. On GW's acquisitions, see the following sample of invoices from his consignment merchants: *PGW: Col Ser* 7:22–29, 124–30, 191–99, 253–56, 287–95, 327–28, 353–57, 402–04, 418–23, 447–49, 470–75; 8:12–14, 44–50, 100–02, 130–36, 231–33, 372–74, 503–11, 558–66; 9:103–109, 273–75. The interest that Washington paid is discussed in Bruce Ragsdale, "George Washington, The Tobacco Trade, and Economic Opportunity in Prerevolutionary Virginia," *VMHB*, 97 (1989): 143.

6. "List of Books at Mount Vernon," c. 1764, *PGW:Col Ser* 7:343–50; Longmore, *Invention of GW*, 213–26; Harry M. Ward, *Colonial America, 1607–1763* (New York, 1991), 312; Cunningham, *In Pursuit of Reason*, 332. The JA quotation can be found in Marcus Cunliffe, *George Washington: Man and Monument* (London, 1959), 32.

7. Longmore, *Invention of GW*, 218; Thayer, *Potomac Squire*, 243; Freeman, *GW*, 6:54; Fitzpatrick, *GW Himself*, 147; Flexner, *GW*, 1:284; Hughes, *GW*, 2:91; Francis R. Bellamy, *The Private Life of George Washington* (New York, 1951), 140–43; *DGW*, 1:256–58, 263, 266, 283.

8. *DGW:Col Ser* 1:238; 2:32, 38–39, 67, 73, 91, 120, 139, 148, 154, 157, 203, 209, 219; Paul L. Ford, *Washington and the Theater* (New York, 1899), 20–21; Fitzpatrick, *GW Himself*, 459; Flexner, *GW*, 1:239.

9. GW, "List of Titables," July 16, 1770, *PGW:Col Ser* 8:356–37; GW, "Cash Accounts," ibid., 7:10n, 110n, 233n 332; 8:154–55; *DGW*, 1:240, 252, 276, 296; 2:37, 77, 164–65; GW, "Lease to Samuel Johnston, Dec. 25, 1761," ibid., 7:100–02; Ford, *True GW*, 138–45; Wall, *GW*, 56; Worthington C. Ford, *Washington as an Employer and Importer of Labor* (Brooklyn, 1889), 8–10, 25; Donald M. Sweig, "The Importation of African Slaves to the Potomac River, 1732–1772," *WMQ*, 42 (1985): 507–24; Freeman, *GW*, 3:88, 179, 186, 243; Ragsdale, *A Planter's Republic*, 68.

10. Ragsdale, "GW and the Tobacco Trade," *VMHB*, 92:140, 143, 146; Ragsdale, *A*

Planter's Republic, 34–35; Breen, "The Culture of Agriculture: The Symbolic World of the Tidewater Planter, 1760–1790," in David Hall, John M. Murrin, and Thad W. Tate, eds., *Saints and Revolutionaries: Essays on Early American History* (New York, 1984), 255–56; Longmore, *Invention of GW*, 84; GW to Cary & Co., May 28, 1762, Aug. 10, 1764, *PGW:Col Ser* 7:135–37, 323; GW to Stewart & Campbell, Sept. 4, 1766, ibid., 7:462; Freeman, *GW*, 3:42–44, 43n; Thane, *Potomac Squire*, 76.

11. *DGW* 1:319–26; Charles Ambler, *George Washington and the West* (New York, 1936), 137–40; Freeman, *GW*, 2:102n; 3:94, 101–03, 116, 141, 153, 162–63, 175, 179, 238–40, 242–43, 319–26, 345, 348; Hughes, *GW*, 2:91, 116–17; Ford, *True GW*, 112–37.

12. U.S. Bureau of the Census, *Historical Statistics of the United States from Colonial Times to 1970*, 2 vols. (Washington, 1975),DC, 2:1168.

13. *PGW:Col Ser* 7:43, 211, 219–25, 437; 8:218, 283; Thomas P. Abernethy, *Western Lands and the American Revolution* (New York, 1937), 48.

14. GW to the Officers of the Virginia Regiment of 1754, Jan. 20, 1771, *PGW:Col Ser* 8:428; GW, Memorial to the Governor and Council, Nov. 1–4, 1771, ibid., 8:534–40; GW to George Mercer, Nov. 7, 1771, ibid., 8:541–44; GW to Robert Adam, Nov. 22, 1771, ibid., 8:550–53; GW to Charles Washington, Jan. 31, 1770, ibid., 8:300–03; Crawford to GW, Nov. 12, 1773, ibid., 9:380–82; GW to Charles Thurston, March 12, 1773, ibid., 9:194–98; *DGW* 2:277–328; Knollenberg, *GW*, 96–100.

15. GW to Cary & Co., May 1, 1764, *PGW:Col Ser* 7:305; Breen, *Tobacco Culture*, 127–28; Ragsdale, "GW and the Tobacco Trade," *VMHB*, 92:149.

16. Breen, *Tobacco Culture*, xiii–xiv, 31, 46, 55, 160; GW to Cary & Co., Feb. 13, 1764, *PGW:Col Ser* 7:286; GW, "A View of the Work . . . , " [1789], *WW* 30:175–76; GW to Thomas Green, March 31, 1789, ibid., 30:262–64; GW, "Agreement with Philip Bater," April 23, 1787, ibid., 29:206–07.

17. GW, "Cash Account," *PGW:Col Ser* 7:4, 7, 262, 268, 276, 308, 352, 482, 515; 8:20, 169, 221, 250, 521; James Hill to GW, July 24, Aug. 30, and Dec. 13, 1772, Feb. 5, May 11, July 2–3, 23, 1773, ibid., 9:72–73, 84–88, 138–39, 171–73, 231–33, 254–57, 284–86; Joseph Valentine to GW, Aug. 24, 1771, ibid., 8:519–20; GW to Anthony Whiting, Oct. 14, 1792, May 12, 26, 1793, *WW* 32:184, 458, 474–75; GW to William Pearce, Dec. 22, 1793, ibid., 33:205; GW, "Estimate of the Cost. . . , " [1790?], ibid., 33:186–87; GW to Tobias Lear, Oct. 7, 1791, ibid., 31:385; Julian Ursyn Niemcewicz, *Under Their Vine and Fig Tree: Travels Through America*, translated by Metchie J. E. Budka (Elizabeth, N. J., 1965), 100.

18. GW to Whiting, Nov. 4, Dec. 9, 1792, Jan. 6, 20, Feb. 23, March 3, May 19, 1793, *WW* 32:205, 256–57, 293, 295, 307, 358, 366, 465; GW, Memorandum, Nov. 5, 1796, ibid., 35:265; GW to James Bloxham, Jan. 1, 1789, ibid., 30:175n; GW to Alexander Spotswood, Sept. 14, 1798, ibid., 36:445; GW to Pearce, Oct. 27, Dec. 18, 1793, Jan. 19, 1794, Jan. 25, March 1, Dec. 13, 1795, ibid., 33:33, 142, 191, 243; 34:103, 128, 193, 393; GW to the Overseers at Mount Vernon, July 14, 1793, ibid., 33:11; Richard Parkinson, *A Tour of America*, 2 vols. (London, 1805), 2:121–23. The English traveler's view of Washington as a harsh master—not "of a humane disposition," as he put it—should be contrasted with that of a Polish military officer who visited Mount

Vernon and concluded that "Washington treats his slaves far more humanely than do his fellow citizens of Virginia." See Niemcewicz, *Under Their Vine and Fig Tree*, 100–01.

19. Hugh Mercer to James Mercer, March 11, 1764, *PGW:Col Ser* 8:545n; GW to Cary & Co., Nov. 10, 1773, ibid., 9:374–75; Longmore, *Invention of GW*, 85; Flexner, *GW*, 1:287n.

20. Freeman, *GW*, 2:241–42, 242n; *PGW:Col Ser* 5:263n; 7:6n, 8n, 43n, 84n: "Frederick County Poll Sheet, [July 24], 1758," ibid., 5: 334–43.

21. GW to Richard Washington, Sept. 20, 1759, *PGW:Col Ser* 6:359; GW to Sally Fairfax, May 16, 1798, *WW* 36:262–64.

22. GW to Jonathan Boucher, May 30, 1768, May 13, Dec. 16, 1770, June 5, July 9, 1771, *PGW:Col Ser* 8:89–90, 333–35, 411–12, 476–78, 494–97; GW to Boucher, Jan. 7, 1773, ibid., 9:154; GW to Myles Cooper, Dec. 15, 1773, ibid., 9:406–07; GW to Burwell Bassett, June 20, 1773, ibid., 9:243–44; *DGW* 2:31, 45, 47, 54, 68, 76, 108, 120, 122–23, 128, 141, 168, 177, 195, 197, 201, 209, 257, 272; 3:1, 2, 7, 9, 71, 114, 188–205.

23. Ibid., 3:108–09; GW to Boucher, May 21, 1772, 9:49.

24. GW to Boucher, May 23, 1772, ibid., 9:51.

25. Malone, *TJ*, 1:114, 437–39; McLoughlin, *Jefferson and Monticello*, 34; Lucia Stanton, "'Those Who Labor for My Happiness': Thomas Jefferson and His Slaves," Onuf, *Jeffersonian Legacies*, 148; Randall, *TJ*, 82, 111; Mapp, *TJ*, 1:43.

26. Carl Van Doren, *Benjamin Franklin* (New York, 1938), 529; Knollenberg, *GW*, 103–06.

27. Randall, *Life of TJ*, 1:34–35; 3:364; Ellis, *American Sphinx*, 120; Peterson, *TJ*, 10; Malone, *TJ*, 1:48; Cunningham, *In Pursuit of Reason*, 22; Padover, *TJ*, 180, 334–35, 339, 411–12; James A. Bear, Jr., "Monticello," in Peterson, *TJ: A Reference Biography*, 438–39; Bedini, *TJ: Statesman of Science*, 303–04; Randall, *TJ*, 100; McLoughlin, *TJ and Monticello*, 4; Randolph, *Essays on the History of Virginia, 1774–1782*, in *VMHB*, 43 (1953): 115; Noble Cunningham, ed., "The Diary of Frances Few, 1808–1809," *Journal of Southern History* 29 (1963): 350–51; Randolph, *Domestic Life of TJ*, 238, 337, 366; James A. Bear, *Jefferson at Monticello* (Charlottesville, 1976), 71, 74; Marquis de Chastellux, *Travels in North America in the Years 1780, 1781 and 1782*, ed. Howard C. Rice, Jr. (Chapel Hill, 1963), 2:389–95; William Howard Adams, *The Paris Years of Thomas Jefferson* (New Haven, 1997), 17–18, 160.

28. *DAJA* 3:335–36; Gaillard Hunt, ed., *The First Forty Years of Washington Society Portrayed by the Family Letters of Mrs. Samuel Harrison Smith* (New York, 1906), 26; Charles Francis Adams, ed., *Memoirs of John Quincy Adams*, 12 vols. (Philadelphia, 1874–77), 1:373; Arthur H. Shaffer, ed., Edmund Randolph, *History of Virginia* (Charlottesville, 1979), 182–83, 213.

29. Randolph, "Essays on the History of Virginia," *VMHB*, 43:115; John W. Davis, "Thomas Jefferson: Attorney at Law," *Proceedings, Virginia State Bar Association*, 38 (1926): 369.

30. Randall, *TJ*, 98, 109; Kimball, *Jefferson: Road to Glory*, 134; TJ to Page, Dec. 25, 1762, *PTJ* 1:5; TJ to Fleming, [Oct. 1763], ibid., 1:13; Davis, "TJ," *Proceedings, Va. State Bar*,

38:368; Dewey, *TJ, Lawyer,* 83–93; Main, *Social Structure of Revolutionary America,* 77, 102.

31. TJ, *Notes on the State of Virginia,* in Padover, *Complete TJ,* 680; Malone, *TJ,* 1:115–16; Albert J. Nock, *Jefferson* (New York, 1926), 60; GW to William Tilghman, July 21, 1793, *WW* 33:26; GW to William Pierce, Dec. 18, Dec. 18, 1793, ibid., 33:192.

32. McLoughlin, *Jefferson and Monticello,* 34, 35, 39–41.

33. TJ to Maria Cosway, June 23, 1790, *PTJ* 16:550–51; TJ, *Notes on the State of Virginia,* in Padover, *Complete TJ,* 678; Charles A. Miller, *Jefferson and Nature: An Interpretation* (Baltimore, 1988), 13–14.

34. TJ to Daniel Williams, Nov. 14, 1803, Lipscomb and Berg, *WTJ* 10:428–31; TJ, *Notes on the State of Virginia,* in Padover, *Complete TJ,* 679.

35. TJ to Page, Feb. 21, 1770, *PTJ* 1:35; TJ, "Draft of Instructions to the Virginia Delegates to the Continental Congress" [July 1774], ibid., 1:122; TJ, "Autobiography," in Padover, *Complete TJ,* 1119; TJ to T. J. Randolph, Jan. 3, 1809, Betts and Bear, *Family Letters of TJ,* 375; Randall, *TJ,* 141; Isaac, "First Monticello," in Onuf, *Jeffersonian Legacies,* 81, 94–95.

36. Chastellux, *Travels in North America,* 2:397.

37. Tj to Maria Cosway, Jan. 30, 1787, *PTJ* 11:509; TJ to Fleming, March 20, 1764, ibid., 1:16; TJ, *Notes on the State of Virginia,* in Padover, *Complete TJ,* 578; McLoughlin, *Jefferson at Monticello,* 135n; Miller, *Jefferson and Nature,* 102.

38. TJ to Page, Feb. 21, 1770, *PTJ* 1:35–36; Page to TJ, March 6, April [?], 1770, ibid., 1:38, 41; Isaac, "First Monticello," in Onuf, *Jeffersonian Legacies,* 77–108.

39. TJ to Page, July 15, 1763, *PTJ* 1:11.

40. Randall, *Life of Jefferson,* 1:63; Chastellux, *Travels in America,* 2:391; Kimball, *Jefferson: Path to Glory,* 171–72; Cunningham, *In Pursuit of Reason,* 21; McLoughlin, *Jefferson and Monticello,* 183, 187; Mrs. Drummond to TJ, March 12, 1771, *PTJ* 1:66; Bear, *Jefferson at Monticello,* 5; Randall, *TJ,* 156.

41. TJ to Martha Jefferson Randolph, April 4, 1790, *FLTJ* 51; TJ to Mary Jefferson Eppes, Jan. 7, 1788, ibid., 152.

42. Ibid., 1:158; Randall, *TJ,* 181.

43. Peterson, *TJ,* 28, 40, 161–62; Malone, *TJ,* 1:441–45; Stanton, "Those Who Labor for My Happiness," in Onuf, *Jeffersonian Legacies,* 148; Randall, *TJ,* 168.

44. JA to William Tudor, March 29, 1817, *WJA* 10:245; ibid., 1:57–58n; JA to Skelton Jones, March 11, 1809, ibid., 9:612; AA to Mary Cranch, Oct. 6, 1766, *AFC* 1:56; AA to JA, April 30, 1764, ibid., 1:42; *DAJA* 2:76; JA to Mercy Warren, Nov. 25, 1775, *PJA* 3:318.

45. "Will of Deacon John Adams," *PJA* 1:33–35.

46. JA to AA, July 6, 7, 1774, *AFC* 1:129, 131; AA and JA to Mary Cranch, Jan. 12, 1767, ibid., 1:58; *DAJA* 1:330.

47. *DAJA* 1:1, 229–30, 284–85, 322; 2:41, 48–49. JA mentions a "Common Place Book of Husbandry and Gardening" in his diary, but if he kept such a book it has not survived. See ibid., 1:88–89. On farming in Massachusetts during JA's time, see Howard S. Russell, *A Long Deep Furrow: Three Centuries of Farming in New England* (Reprint, Hanover, N.H., 1982), 71–120.

48. *DAJA* 1:307, 339n; 2:6–7, 12, 53, 63, 68; 3:286.

49. JA to AA, June 30, July 1, 1774, *AFC* 1:117, 119.

50. JA to AA2d, April 18, 1776, *AFC* 1:388; JA to AA, May 3, Sept. 30, 1764, June 29, 1777, ibid., 1:45, 47; 2:271; *DAJA* 1: 108, 234.

51. John D'Emilio and Estelle B. Freeman, *Intimate Matters: A History of Sexuality in America* (New York, 1988), 39–54.

52. Gelles, *Portia*, 28; *DAJA* 1:263; Charles W. Akers, *Abigail Adams: An American Woman* (Boston, 1980), 18–19.

53. *DAJA* 2:6–7; AA to JA, Aug. 11, 1763, *AFC* 1:6; Gelles, *Portia*, 24–26.

54. *DAJA* 1:251–54, 270, 273, 299, 314, 316–17, 320–21, 333–36, 338n; *PJA* 1:103–28, 146–47, 155–214.

55. JA to Rush, Aug. 25, 1811, Schutz and Adair, *Spur of Fame*, 189; *DAJA* 1: 286, 294; 2: 64, 67, 73; 3:286; *LPJA* 1:lxii–lxiii, lxix–lxxiv; Brown, *Knowledge is Power*, 99; JA to AA, June 29, 1769, *AFC* 1:66.

56. *DAJA* 2:44–45; JA to AA, June 29, 1774, *AFC* 1:113; *LPJA* 1:lix, lx–lxiii, lxxi. For an excellent treatment of how JA prepared for some of his most important and exotic cases, see Daniel R. Coquillette, "Justinian in Braintree: John Adams, Civilian Learning, and Legal Elitism, 1758–1775," *Law in Colonial Massachusetts*, Col. Soc. of Mass. *Pubs.*, 62 (1984): 359–418.

57. *DAJA* 2:33, 43; JA to AA, June 30, July 1, 5, 1774, *AFC* 1:117, 118, 123.

58. JA to AA, June 29, 1769, June 23, 30, July 3, 9, 1774, *AFC* 1:66, 109, 115, 123, 134. For the nature of JA's legal practice, see *LPJA*.

59. *DAJA* 1:337–38.

60. *DAJA* 1:271, 285, 294, 306, 327, 330; JA, "Clarendon to Pym," *PJA* 1:161.

61. Ibid., 3:278–80; *PJA* 1:54–57, 216–18.

62. *DAJA* 1:222; 2:7, 20, 54–55, 65–66, 73–74, 76.

63. Ibid., 3:294–95; Ellis, *Passionate Sage*, 45–46.

64. *DAJA* 2:5–7, 9. 15–33, 37; 3:296; JA to Catherine Macaulay, July 19, 1771, *PJA* 1:250.

65. Lewis E. Braverman and Robert D. Utiger, "Introduction to Thyrotoxicosis," in Lewis E. Braverman and Robert D. Utiger, ed., *Werner and Ingbar's The Thyroid: A Fundamental and Clinical Text* (Philadelphia, 1991), 6454–57; Sidney Werner, "History of the Thyroid," ibid., 3–5; Robert Volpe, "Graves' Disease," ibid., 648–50; Peter C. Whybrow, "Behavioral and Psychiatric Aspects of Thyrotoxicosis," ibid., 865; Leslie J. De Groot, et al., *The Thyroid and Its Diseases* (New York, 1984), 2–42, 136–44; Rene Mornex and Jacques J. Orgiazzi, "Hyperthyroidism," in Michael De Visscher, ed., *The Thyroid Gland: Comprehensive Endocrinology* (New York, 1980), 279–91, 306–17; Brita Winsa, et al., "Stressful Life Events and Graves' Disease," *Lancet*, 338 (Dec. 14, 1991): 1475–79; Paul J. Rosch, "Stressful Life Events and Graves' Disease," *Lancet*, 342 (Sept. 4, 1993): 566–67; A. Horsley, "On the Function of the Thyroid Gland," *Proceedings of the Royal Society of London*, 33 (1885): 5.

66. *DAJA* 2:38, 67.

67. Ibid., 2:76.

68. Mapp, TJ, 1:73; DGW 3:225–30; *PJA* 2:8n; *LPJA* 3:346.

Chapter 4

1. *DAJA* 1:264–65. Emphasis added.
2. GW to Francis Dandridge, Sept. 20, 1765, *PGW:Col Ser* 7:395–96; GW to Cary and Co., Sept. 20, 1765, ibid., 7:401–02; *DGW* 1:337–38.
3. GW to Dinwiddie, March 10, 1765, *PGW:Col Ser* 4:113; Longmore, *Invention of GW*, 52–53. On the haughty attitude of British officers toward provincial soldiers, and the damage it caused in terms of the colonists' growing disdain for Great Britain, see Douglas Edward Leach, *Roots of Conflict: British Armed Forces and Colonial Americans, 1677–1763* (Chapel Hill, 1986), 107–33, and Gwenda Morgan, "Virginia and the French and Indian War: A Case Study of the War's Effects on Imperial Relations," *Virginia Magazine of History and Biography*, 81 (1973): 23–48.
4. Robert Stewart to GW, Sept. 3, 1763, *PGW:Col Ser* 7:241; GW to Burwell Bassett, July 5, 1763, ibid., 7:230–31; Ragsdale, *A Planter's Republic*, 111–29; Longmore, *Invention of GW*, 74.
5. GW to Stewart, Aug. 13, 1763, *PGW:Col Ser* 7:237.
6. GW to John Posey, June 24, 1767, *PGW:Col Ser* 8:1–4; GW to William Crawford, Sept. 21, 1767, ibid., 8:27–29; GW to Gov. Baron de Botetourt, Dec. 8, 1769, Sept. 9, Oct. 8, 1770, ibid., 8:272–77, 378–80, 388–93; GW to James Wood, March 13, 30, 1773, ibid., 9:199, 205–06; *DGW* 2:133; 3:37; Longmore, *Invention of GW*, 52–53. On Great Britain's western policies, see Ambler, *GW and the West*, 132–51; Francis S. Philbrick, *The Rise of the West, 1754–1830* (New York, 1965), 1–52; Jack M. Sosin, *The Revolutionary Frontier, 1763–1783* (Albuquerque, 1967), 20–38; Thomas P. Abernethy, *Western Lands and the American Revolution* (New York, 1937), 14–97.
7. Abernethy, *Western Lands and the American Revolution*, 48; *PGW:Col Ser* 7:43, 211, 219–25, 437; 8:218, 283; GW to Dunmore, April 3, 1775, ibid., 10:320–22; Dunmore to GW, April 18, 1775, ibid., 10:337–38.
8. GW to Thomas Johnson, July 20, 1770, *PGW:Col Ser* 8:358–60.
9. JA to Mercy Warren, July 20, 27, 1807, Adams, "Correspondence between John Adams and Mercy Warren," MHS, *Colls*, 4:339–40, 455; JA to Nathan Webb, Oct. 12?, 1755, *PJA* 1:5.
10. *AJA* 3:266–67; JA to AA, Feb. 18, 1776, *AFC* 1:347.
11. *DAJA* 3:275–76; JA to Mercy Warren, July 20, 1807, Adams, "Correspondence between John Adams and Mercy Warren," MHS, *Colls.*, 4:343; LPJA 2:106–44; *PJA* 1:xxv-xxvi.
12. Lawrence Henry Gibson, "The American Revolution as an Aftermath of the Great War for Empire," *Political Science Quarterly* 55 (1950): 86–104; Jack P. Greene, "An Uneasy Connection: An Analysis of the Preconditions of the American Revolution," in Stephen G. Kurtz and James H. Hutson, eds., *Essays on the American Revolution* (Chapel Hill, 1973), 32–80; Merrill Jensen, *The Founding of a Nation: A History of the American Revolution, 1763–1776* (New York, 1968), 36–69.
13. *DAJA* 1:259–60, 263, 271, 274, 352.
14. John Adams, "A Dissertation on the Canon and Feudal Law," *PJA* 1:121, 130n; "Argument before Governor Bernard and the Council in Favor of Opening the Courts," Dec. 20, 1765, ibid., 1:152; *DAJA* 1:266–68, 274; *WJA* 1:259–61.

15. *DAJA* 1:263, 264, 272, 301–05, 312–13, 304n.

16. *DGW* 1:337. Only 39 of 116 assemblymen were in Williamsburg when the terms of the Stamp Act arrived.

17. GW to Francis Dandridge, Sept. 20, 1765, *PGW:Col Ser* 7:395–96; GW to Cary and Co., Sept. 20, 1765, July 21, 1766, ibid., 7:401, 457; GW to Capel and Osgood Hanbury, July 25, 1767, ibid., 8:15; George Mason to GW, Dec. 23, 1765, ibid., 7:424–25n; Longmore, *Invention of GW*, 79, 253n.

18. GW to Capel and Hanbury, July 25, 1767, *PGW:Col Ser* 8:15; *DGW* 2:4–32; JA to Cranch, June 29, 1766, *AFC* 1:52.

19. Shaw, *Character of JA*, 57; *Boston Gazette*, May 23, 1768, *PJA* 1:211–14; *DGW* 2:51–53; H. R. McIlwaine and John Pendleton, eds., *Journals of the House of Burgesses of Virginia, 1766–1769* (Richmond, 1915), 165, 168.

20. *DAJA* 1:331, 337–38; 3:290–91, 306; "Instructions of Boston to its Representatives in the General Court," June 17, 1768, *PJA* 1:216–18; *LPJA* 3:173–84.

21. *DAJA* 3:289–91; 1:52, 294, 324, 331, 337–38, 341–43, 349; *LPJA* 2:103, 183; Boston Sons of Liberty to John Wilkes, June 6, Oct. 5, 1768, Nov. 4, 1769, *PJA* 1:214–15, 220–22, 232–35; Boston Town Meeting Petitions to George III, July 24, 1769, ibid., 1:223–24; Instructions to Boston Representatives in the General Court, May 8, 1769, ibid., 1:224–29; Boston Town Meeting to Dennys DeBerdt, Oct. 23, 1769, ibid., 1:231–32; Jensen, *Founding of a Nation*, 289–90.

22. GW to Mason, April 5, 1769, *PGW:Col Ser* 8:177–80.

23. GW to Dandridge, Sept. 20, 1765, ibid., 7:395; GW to Cary and Co., Sept. 20, 1765, ibid., 7:400; GW to Mason, April 5, 1769, ibid., 8:177–80.

24. Mason to GW, April 5, 28, 1769, ibid., 8:182–83, 187, 181n, 187–90n.

25. GW to George William Fairfax, June 27, 1770, ibid., 8:353, 354n; GW to Jonathan Boucher, July 30, 1770, ibid., 8:361.

26. TJ to William Wirt, April 12, 1812, Ford, *WTJ* 9:338–41; TJ, "Autobiography," in Padover, *Complete TJ*, 1121; Smith, *Jefferson*, 51.

27. "Resolutions for an Answer to Governor Botetourt's Speech," May 8, 1769, *PTJ* 1:26–27; "Virginia's Nonimportation Resolutions," 1769, ibid., 1:27–31; TJ to Thomas Adams, June 1, 1770, ibid., 1:71; Malone, *TJ*, 1:132; Ellis, *American Sphinx*, 28.

28. Boston Sons of Liberty to Wilkes, Oct. 5, 1768, *PJA* 1:220; JA to William Tudor, April 15, 1817, *WJA* 10:251–52.

29. Zobel, *Boston Massacre*, 32, 41, 49, 214, 217–21; *DAJA* 3:292–94; *PJA* 1:238n.

30. *DAJA* 3:293; Zobel, *Boston Massacre*, 26–94, 242, 267–94. For the lawyer's notes and minutes for both trials, see the entire third volume of *LPJA*.

31. JA to AA, Jan. 29, 1774, *AFC* 1:114; *LPJA* 1:lix–lxxxv; *DAJA* 2:7, 35; 3:295. JA's suspicions were warranted. For an excellent account of how the ringleaders in the popular movement in Boston not only planned and managed their opposition to the mother country, but carefully crafted their public persona, see William M. Fowler, Jr., *Samuel Adams: Radical Puritan* (New York, 1997), 55–127.

32. *DAJA* 2:35; JA to Isaac Smith, Jr., April 11, 1771, *AFC* 1:74.

33. JA to Hezekiah Niles, Feb. 13, 1818, *WJA* 10:282.

34. GW to George William Fairfax, June 10, 1774, *PGW:Col Ser* 10:95–98.

35. TJ, "Autobiography," in Padover, *Complete TJ* 1122; Lawrence Henry Gibson, *The Coming of the Revolution, 1763–1775* (New York, 1954), 210.

36. TJ to Edward Coles, Aug. 25, 1814, in Merrill Peterson, ed., *The Portable Jefferson* (New York, 1975), 544; TJ, "Autobiography," in Padover, *Complete TJ*, 1121; Paul Finkleman, "Jefferson and Slavery: 'Treason Against the Hopes of the World,'" in Peter Onuf, ed., *Jeffersonian Legacies* (Charlottesville, 1993), 188–89.

37. TJ, "Autobiography," in Padover, *Complete TJ*, 1121.

38. TJ to Thomas Adams, Feb. 20, 1771, *PTJ* 1:61; [Thomas Jefferson], *A Summary View of the Rights of British America* (Williamsburg, 1774), ibid., 1:123–24, 133, 135; Breen, *Tobacco Culture*, 127–28, 159.

39. Ellis, *American Sphinx*, 32–34; Peterson, *TJ*, 45–65; H. Trevor Colbourn, *The Lamp of Experience: Whig History and the Intellectual Origins of the American Revolution* (Chapel Hill, 1965), 3–56, 158–60; John Howe, "Republicanism," in Merrill D. Peterson, ed., *Thomas Jefferson: A Reference Biography* (New York 1986), 59–61; Malone, *TJ*, 1:173–79; Daniel T. Rogers, "Republicanism: The Career of a Concept," *Journal of American History* 79 (1992): 11–38; Joyce Appleby, "Republicanism and Ideology," *American Quarterly* 37 (1985): 461–73; Robert Shallope, "Toward a Republican Synthesis: The Emergence of an Understanding of Republicanism in American Historiography," *WMQ* 29 (1972): 49–80; Bernard Bailyn, *The Ideological Origins of the American Revolution* (Cambridge, Mass., 1967), 55–143; J. G. A. Pocock, *The Machiavellian Moment: Florentine Political Thought and the Atlantic Republican Tradition* (Princeton, 1975), 506–52; Gordon Wood, *The Creation of the American Republic, 1776–1787* (Chapel Hill, 1969), 10–45; Wood, *Radicalism of the American Revolution*, 97–107. The text of Virginia's non-importation resolution that TJ signed in 1769 can be found in *PGW:Col Ser* 8:187–189n. On how this generation sensed conspiratorial tendencies behind every conceivable act and occurrence, see Gordon S. Wood, "Conspiracy and the Paranoid Style: Causality and Deceit in the Eighteenth Century," *WMQ*, 39 (1982): 401–402.

40. JA to Hezekiah Niles, Feb. 13, 1818, *WJA* 10:285–86; JA to Tudor, June 1, 1817, July 9, 1818, ibid., 10:259, 327; JA to Tudor, Nov. 16, 25, Dec. 7, 1816, AFP, reel 123; JA to Skelton Jones, March 11, 1809, ibid., 118; John Howe, *The Changing Political Thought of John Adams* (Princeton, 1966), 43.

41. JA to Jonathan Sewall, Oct. 1759, *DAJA* 1:123–24.

42. Ibid., 2:54; JA to Sewall, Oct. 1759, ibid., 1:123–24; JA to TJ, July 15, 1813, Aug. 15, 1823, *AJC* 2:237, 594; "U" to *Boston Gazette*, Aug. 1, 29, 1763, *PJA* 1:72–73, 79–81; "Clarendon to William Pym," *Boston Gazette*, Jan. 27, 1766, ibid., 1:169; "Replies to Philanthrop," (1766–1767), ibid., 1:179, 187; Zoltan Haraszti, *John Adams and the Prophets of Progress* (Cambridge, Mass., 1952), 192; Howe, *Changing Political Thought of JA*, 15, 17–19.

43. JA, "Dissertation on the Canon and Feudal Law," *PJA* 1:114, 120, 122, 127, 128; *Massachusetts Gazette*, Oct. 10, 1765, ibid., 1:141; JA, "Clarendon to Pym," ibid., 1:158–60, 165, 169–70; JA, "Replies to Philanthrop," ibid. 1:185, 187, 189, 195, 200; Instructions of Boston to its Representatives in the General Court, June 17, 1768,

May 8, 1769, ibid., 1:217, 226–27; Boston Sons of Liberty to Wilkes, Nov. 4, 1769, ibid., 1:233; *Boston Gazette*, Jan. 11, 18, 25, Feb. 1, 8, 15, 22, 1773, ibid., 1:256–309.

44. JA, "Dissertation on the Canon and Feudal Law," ibid., 1:114.

45. *DAJA* 2:64.

46. Ibid., 2:74, 82.

47. Ibid., 2:63, 64, 67, 76, 82, 63–64n, 83n.

48. Ibid., 2:72, 74.

49. Ibid., 3:305; JA to Tudor, March 8,1817, *WJA* 2:311; *PJA* 1:311n. This is the same Hawley who wrote General Washington the hysterical letter on the eve of the British invasion of New York in 1776.

50. [Joseph Galloway], *Historical and Political Reflections on the Rise and Progress of the American Rebellion* (London, 1780), 67–68; *Boston Gazette*, Jan.11, 18, 25, Feb.1, 8, 15, 22, 1773, *PJA* 2:256–309, 252–56n.

51. *Speeches of His Excellency Governor Hutchinson, to the General Assembly of the Massachusetts Bay ... With the Answers* (Boston, 1773); Bernard Bailyn, *The Ordeal of Thomas Hutchinson* (Cambridge, Mass., 1974), 207, 209.

52. *DAJA* 2:76–77; 3:305; *PJA* 2:252–56n.

53. *DAJA* 2:34–35, 55, 80, 119, 80n; JA, "The Letters of Novanglus" (Jan. 23–April 1775), *PJA* 2:256, 257, 277–78, 284, 370.

54. JA to Rush, Feb. 27, 1805, May 1, 21, 1807, Schutz and Adair, *Spur of Fame*, 35–36, 80, 88; JA, "Dissertation on the Canon and Feudal Law," *PJA* 1:106, 108, 103–04n; JA, "Novanglus Letters," ibid., 2:242.

55. JA to James Warren, Dec. 17, 1773, April 9, 1774, *PJA* 2:1–2, 83; JA to James Burgh, Dec. 28, 1773, ibid., 2:206; JA, "Novanglus Letters," ibid., 2:232, 285; *DAJA* 2:85–86.

56. JA to Niles, Feb. 18, 1818, *WJA* 10:282; JA to TJ, Aug. 24, 1815, *AJC* 2:455; JA to AA, July 3, 1776, *AFC* 2:28; TJ to Benjamin Franklin, Aug. 3, 1777, *PTJ* 2:26.

57. TJ, *Summary View*, in *PTJ* 1:121–23.

58. JA, "Novanglus Letters," *PJA*, 2:129–31, 309, 328, 355, 358, 366–67, 370, 380–84; JA, "Reply to *A Friendly Address to all Reasonable Americans* (Nov. 1774 [?]), ibid., 2:195; TJ, *Summary View*, in *PTJ*, 1:122–23, 126.

59. JA, "Dissertation on the Canon and Feudal Law," *PJA* 1:126–27; JA, "To a Friend in London," Jan. 21, 1775, ibid., 2:215; TJ, *Summary View*, in *PTJ* 1:122.

60. JA to Joseph Palmer, Sept. 26, 1774, *PJA* 2:215; JA, "Novanglus Letters," ibid., 2:255, 370; *DAJA* 2:80; TJ, *Summary View*, in *PTJ* 1:122, 124–25.

61. *DAJA* 3:2565; TJ, "Autobiography," in Padover, *Complete TJ*, 1119–20, 1143, 1143–44n; "Biographical Sketches," ibid., 927–28; JA to Rush, Nov. 11, 1807, Schutz and Adair, *Spur of Fame*, 97–98; JA to Wirt, Jan. 5, 1818, AFP, reel 123; JA to Vanderkemp, April 23, 1807, ibid., reel 118, JA to Morse, Nov. 29, 1815, ibid., reel 122; JA to Niles, Jan. 14, 1818, *WJA* 10:275; JA to Cranch, Aug. 2, 1776, *AFC* 2:74; Wood, *Radicalism of the American Revolution*, 169–89; Hawke, *Honorable Treason*, 121–22.

62. Jack P. Greene, "All Men Are Created Equal: Some Reflections on the Character of the American Revolution," in Jack P. Greene, ed., *Imperatives, Behaviors, and Identities: Essays in Early American Cultural History* (Charlottesville, 1992), 263–66; Edmund S. Morgan, "Slavery and Freedom: The American Paradox," *Journal of American*

History 59 (1972): 7; Wood, *Radicalism of the American Revolution*, 172–89, 200–01.

63. GW to Fairfax, June 10, 1774, *PGW:Col Ser* 10:96; GW to Mason, April 5, 1769, *PGW* 8:178; TJ, *Summary View*, in *PTJ* 1:125; TJ to Charles Bellini, Sept. 30, 1785, ibid., 8:568; JA, "Novanglus Letters," *PJA* 2:195, 242; JA, "Dissertation on the Canon and Feudal Law," ibid., 1:113.

64. *DAJA* 2:86.

Chapter 5

1. *DAJA* 2:114.

2. *DGW* 2:271–72.

3. TJ, "Autobiography," in Padover, *Complete TJ*, 1124–25; Cunningham, *Pursuit of Reason*, 31. TJ fell ill during the journey to Williamsburg for the meeting of the Virginia Convention in August 1774 and was not in attendance when the congressional delegates were selected.

4. Jack Sosin, "The Massachusetts Acts of 1774: Coercive or Preventive?" *Huntington Library Quarterly* 26 (1963): 236; Allan J. McCurry, "The North Government and the Outbreak of the American Revolution," ibid. 34 (1971): 141–57; David Ammerman, *In the Common Cause: American Response to the Coercive Acts of 1774* (New York, 1974), 1–17.

5. Benjamin W. Labaree, *The Boston Tea Party* (New York, 1964), 219–26; Stephen E. Patterson, *Political Parties in Revolutionary Massachusetts* (Madison, Wisc., 1973), 71–88; Jensen, *Founding of a Nation*, 467–69; John C. Miller, *Sam Adams: Pioneer in Propaganda* (Boston, 1936), 301–02.

6. JA to AA, Sept. 6, 8, 9, 14, 1774, June 17, 1775, *AFC* 1:127, 135, 150, 155, 158, 216; JA to James Warren, May 18, 1776, *PJA* 4:193; JA to William Tudor, Sept. 29, 1774, ibid., 3:177.

7. JA to Cranch, Sept. 18, 1774, *AFC* 1:160; *DAJA* 2:121; JA to Tudor, Sept. 29, Oct. 7, 1774, *PJA* 2:177, 188.

8. *DAJA* 3:308; GW to Robert Mackenzie, Oct. 9, 1774, *PGW: Col Ser* 10:171–72.

9. JA to AA, Sept. 29, Oct. 7, 1774, *AFC* 1:163, 165; JA to Tudor, Sept. 29, 1774, *PJA* 2:177; *DAJA* 2:147.

10. *PJA* 2:147n; *JCC* 1:63–73; *DAJA* 2:119; 3:309–10.

11. *DAJA* 3:308; Silas Deane to Elizabeth Deane, Sept. 10–11, 1774, *LDCC* 1:61.

12. GW to John Connally, Feb. 25, 1775, *PGW:Col Ser* 10:273–74; *DGW* 3:304, 321, 323, 325; Ambler, *GW and the West*, 152–58; Freeman, *GW*, 3:398–99; Peterson, *TJ*, 77.

13. Gage to Lord Darmouth, Sept. 12, 1774, in Clarence E. Carter, ed., *The Correspondence of General Thomas Gage with the Secretary of State, 1763–1775* (Reprint, New York, 1969), 1:374; [Massachusetts Provincial Congress], "To the Freeholders and Other Inhabitants of the Towns and Districts of Massachusetts Bay," Dec. 10, 1774, *PJA* 2:198; "Report of the Braintree Committee respecting Minute Men," March 15, 1775, ibid., 2:402–03; JA to James Burgh, Dec. 28, 1774, ibid., 2:206; JA to Warren, Jan. 3, 1775, ibid., 2:209.

14. TJ to Archibald Cary and Benjamin Harrison, Dec. 9, 1774, *PTJ* 1:154; "Report of a Committee to Prepare a Plan for a Militia," March 25, 1775, ibid., 1:160–61.

15. David H. Fischer, *Paul Revere's Ride* (New York, 1994), 321.

16. JA to AA, May 29, June 10, 1775, *AFC* 1:207, 213–14; JA to Isaac Smith, Jr., June 7, 1775, ibid., 1:212; Lee to William Lee, May 10, 1775, *LDCC* 1:337; *JCC* 2:59–60, 67.

17. *DAJA* 3:314, 318–19, 321; "John Dickinson's Notes for a Speech," May 23–25, 1775, *LDCC* 1:373; JA to AA, June 17, 1775, *AFC* 1:216; JA to Warren, July 6, 24, 1775, *PJA* 3:62, 89.

18. JA to AA, June 17, 1775, *AFC* 1:216.

19. *DAJA* 3:321–24; Dyer to Joseph Trumbull, June 17, 1775, *LDCC* 1:499.

20. JA to AA, May 29, 1775, *AFC* 1:207; Rush to Thomas Rushton, Oct. 29, 1775, L. H. Butterfield, ed., *Letters of Benjamin Rush* (Princeton, 1951), 1:92; TJ to Skelton Jones, Jan. 2, 1819, Lipscomb and Berg. *WTJ* 14:49; Deane to Eliz. Deane, June 16, 1775, *LDCC* 1:494.

21. JA to Elbridge Gerry, June 18, 1775, *PJA* 3:26; Dyer to Trumbull, June 17, 1775, *LDCC* 1:499.

22. Samuel Ward to Henry Ward, June 22, 1775, *LDCC* 1:535; TJ, "Autobiography," in Padover, *Complete TJ*, 1125. *A Summary View of the Rights of British America* (Williamsburg, 1775) can be found in *PTJ* 1:121–25. In March TJ had been chosen as an alternate by the Virginia Convention.

23. JA to Pickering, Aug. 6, 1822, *WJA* 2:512.

24. *DAJA* 2:120; 3:321.

25. Bailyn, *Ideological Origins*, 1–21.

26. JA, "Dissertation on the Canon and Feudal Law," *PJA* 1:109, 127; JA, "Letters of Novanglus," ibid., 2:232.

27. JA, "Letters of Novanglus," *PJA* 2:339–40.

28. TJ, *Summary View*, in *PTJ* 1:126.

29. [Thomas Paine], *Common Sense*, in Philip Foner, ed., *The Complete Works of Thomas Paine* (New York, 1945), 1:19; "Declaration of the Causes and Necessity of Taking Up Arms," June 26–July 6, 1775, *PTJ* 1:202.

30. TJ to William Small, May 7, 1775, *PTJ* 1: 165.

31. "Virginia Resolution on Lord North's Conciliatory Proposal," June 10, 1775, ibid., 1:170–74, 174n; TJ, "Autobiography," in Padover, *Complete TJ*, 1125.

32. *PTJ* 1:187–88n; Milton E. Flower, *John Dickinson: Conservative Revolutionary* (Charlottesville, 1983), 168–86.

33. TJ, "Composition Draft," *PTJ* 1:193–98.

34. Livingston to William Alexander, July 4, 1775, ibid., 1:189n; "Declaration of the Causes and Necessity of Taking Up Arms," June 28–July 6, 1775, ibid., 1:193–224; JA to Moses Gill, June 10, 1775, *PJA* 3:61; JA to Warren, July 6, 1775, ibid., 3:61; JA to Tudor, July 6, 1775, ibid., 3:59; TJ, "Autobiography," in Padover, *Complete TJ*, 1126–27. For a contrary view of the moderates' peace initiative, see Jerrilyn Greene Marston, *King and Congress: The Transfer of Political Legitimacy, 1774–1776* (Princeton, 1987), 210–13.

35. *PTJ* 1:225–33; JA to Gill, June 10, 1775, *PJA* 3:21; JA to Warren, May 21, 1775, ibid., 3:11.

36. JA to Rush, Oct. 25, 1809, Schutz and Adair, *Spur of Fame*, 158–59.

37. JA to Shelton Jones, March 11, 1809, *WJA* 9:612; JA to Tudor, March 29, 1817, ibid., 10:245; JA to AA, Feb. 9, 1799, AFP, reel 393; JA to Vanderkemp, April 18, 1815, ibid., reel 322; Ferling, "Soldiers for Virginia, *VMHB*,94:312; Carl Van Doren, *Benjamin Franklin* (New York, 1938), 191; *DAJA* 2:362–63; TJ to Madison, Jan. 30, 1787, May 25, 1788, *PTJ* 11:94–95; 13:201–02; AA to JA, July 16, 1775, *AFC*, 1:246–47.

38. Carol Berkin, *Jonathan Sewall: Odyssey of an American Loyalist* (New York, 1974), 142; TJ to Madison, Jan. 30, 1787, *PTJ* 11:94–95.

39. Shaw, *Character of JA*, 95; Ellis, *Passionate Sage*, 42–43.

40. Conner, *Autobiography of Rush*, 299; David F. Hawke, *Benjamin Rush: Revolutionary Gadfly* (Indianapolis, 1971), 164–65; G. S. Rowe, *Thomas McKean: The Shaping of a Republican* (Boulder, Colo., 1978), 164–65.

41. Pauline Maier, *The Old Revolutionaries: Political Lives in the Age of Samuel Adams* (New York, 1980), 18, 20, 21; JA to Pickering, Aug. 6, 1822, *WJA* 2:512n; TJ, "Biographical Sketches," in Padover, *Complete TJ*, 902, 904.

42. "Character Sketches," in Padover, *Complete TJ*, 900, 904; TJ to James Madison, Jan. 30, 1787, *PTJ* 11:94–95; George W. Conner, ed. *The Autobiography of Benjamin Rush; His Travels Through Life Together with His Commonplace Book for 1789–1813* (Princeton, 1948), 140.

43. JA to AA, May 26, July 7, 1775, *AFC* 1:206, 241.

44. GW, Address to Congress, June 16, 1775, *PGW Rev War Ser* 1:1; GW to Bassett, June 19, 1775, ibid., 1:13; GW to John Augustine Washington, June 20, 1775, ibid., 1:19.

45. GW to John A. Washington, June 20, 1775, ibid., 1:19; GW to Bassett, June 19, 1775, ibid., 1:13; GW to John Parke Custis, June 19, 1775, ibid., 1:15; GW, Address to Congress, June 16, 1775, ibid., 1:1; GW, Address to the New York Provincial Congress, June 26, 1775, ibid., 1:41; GW, Address to the Massachusetts Provincial Congress, July 4, 1775, ibid., 1:59; GW to Gen. John Thomas, July 23, 1775, ibid., 1:160.

46. Quoted in Longmore, *Invention of GW*, 177.

47. GW, Address to NY Prov. Cong., June 26, 1775, *PGW:Rev War Ser* 1:41; JA to AA, Dec. 27, 1796, AFP, reel 382.

48. JA to Gerry, June 18, 1775, *PJA* 3:25–26.

49. JA to AA, Feb. 21, 1777, *AFC*, 2:165–66; Samuel Cooper to JA, April 22, 1776, *PJA* 4:138; JA to Warren, July 26, 1776, ibid., 4: 413; Freeman, *GW*, 4:101, 367; Page Smith, *A New Age Is Now Begun* (New York, 1972), 2:1134.

50. Freeman, *GW*, 4:101; GW to Schuyler, Aug. 20, Oct. 6, Nov. 5, 1775, *PGW:Rev War Ser* 1:331–33; 2:120, 302; GW to Charles Lee, May 9, 1776, ibid., 4:245; GW to John Hancock, Jan. 30, June 17, 1776, ibid., 3:217; 5:21; Richard K. Showman, et al., eds., *The Papers of Nathanael Greene* (Chapel Hill, 1976–), 1:211n; Theodore Thayer, "Nathanael Greene: Revolutionary War Strategist," in George A. Billias, ed., *George Washington's Generals and Opponents* (New York, 1994), 109, 111.

51. North Callahan, "Henry Knox: American Artillerist," in Billias, *GW's Generals and*

Opponents, 240; Willard M. Wallace, "Benedict Arnold: Traitorous Hero," ibid., 169–72; JA to Warren, July 23, 1775, *PJA* 3:87.

52. John H. G. Pell, "Philip Schuyler: The General as Aristocrat," in Billias, *GW's Generals and Opponents*, 62; Warren to JA, Nov. 14, 1775, *PJA* 3:306; ibid., 4:111n; Mercy Warren to JA, Oct. [?], 1775, ibid., 3:269; AA to JA, July 16, 1775, *AFC*, 1:246–47; Freeman, *GW*, 3:504–05.

53. GW to Richard Henry Lee, July 10, 1775, *PGW:Rev War Ser* 1:99; GW to President of Congress, July 10, 1775, ibid., 1:90; Philip S. Foner, *Blacks in the American Revolution* (Westport, Conn., 1975), 42–44; Benjamin Quarles, *The Negro in the American Revolution* (Chapel Hill, 1961), 15–17; Walter H. Mazyck, *George Washington and the Negro* (Washington, 1932), 37–43.

54. GW to Richard Henry Lee, July 10, Aug. 29, 1775, *PGW:Rev War Ser* 1:99–100, 372; GW to Joseph Reed, Feb. 26 [-March 9], 1776, ibid., 3:374; GW, General Orders, July 4, 5, 6, 7, 10, 11, 14, 16, 18, Aug. 11, 18, 1775, ibid., 1:58, 62–63, 71–74, 82, 106, 114–15, 122, 127–28, 287, 321–22; Don Higginbotham, *George Washington and the American Military Tradition* (Athens, Ga., 1985), 65–66.

55. TJ to Givanni Fabbroni, June 8, 1778, *PTJ* 2:1918n; GW to Hancock, July 10–11, 21, 1775, Feb. 9, 1776, *PGW:Rev War Ser* 1:90, 138; 3:275; GW to Lund Washington, Aug. 20, 1775, ibid., 1:336; GW, General Orders, Aug. 9, 1775, ibid., 1:277–78, 285–87n.

56. For the use of fines, see the following examples: GW, General Orders, Aug. 9, 18, Sept. 13, 1775, *PGW:Rev War Ser* 1:278, 322, 455. For the incarceration of offenders, see: "Proceedings of Committee of Conference," Oct. 8–24, 1775, ibid., 2:195–96. For the use of corporal punishment, see GW, General Orders, July 10, 14, 23, 29, Aug. 18, 21, Sept. 15, 1775, ibid., 1:82, 115, 159, 191, 321, 322, 340, 465.

57. See the following examples of the cashiering of men and officers during the first weeks of GW's command: GW to Hancock, July 21, 1775, ibid., 1:138; GW, General Orders, Aug. 2, 9, 16, 19, 1775, ibid., 1:212, 278, 312, 325.

58. GW to Col. William Woodford, Nov. 10, 1775, ibid., 2:347; GW, Address to Massachusetts Provincial Congress, July 4, 1775, ibid., 1:60; GW, General Orders, July 7, 24, Nov. 17, Dec. 11, 1775, Jan. 3, 5, April 17, 25, May 5, 6, June 9, 1776, ibid., 1:71, 73, 163; 2:389–90, 529; 3:13, 28; 4:75, 123, 216, 468; GW to Gen. Spencer, Sept. 26, 1775, ibid., 2:55; GW to Jonathan Trumbull, Jr., Oct. 29, 1775, ibid., 2:255; GW to Gen. Sullivan, June 16, 1776, ibid., 5:12. For an excellent discussion of GW's efforts to mold his officers, see Higginbotham, *GW and the American Military Tradition*, 16–19, 70–76.

59. GW, General Orders, Sept. 6, 1775, *PGW:Rev War Ser* 1:419.

60. GW to Woodford, Nov. 10, 1775, ibid., 2:346–47.

61. GW to Company Captains, July 29, 1757, ibid., *PGW:Col Ser* 4:344; GW to Knox, Aug. 25, 1776, *PGW:Rev War Ser* 4:497; Ford, *JCC* 5:438; Shaw, *Character of JA*, 101; Chinnard, *Honest JA*, 109–10; JA to Sullivan, Feb. 22, 1777, *PJA* 5:89; JA to Heath, Aug. 3, 1776, ibid., 4:426; JA to Tudor, Nov. 14, 1775, ibid. 3:296; GW to Greene, March 9, April 13, 1777, ibid., 5:106, 151.

62. JA to AA, April 28, May 22, Aug. 8, 1777, *AFC* 2:227, 245, 304; JA to Greene, May 9, 1777, *PJA* 5:185.

63. JA to Hawley, Aug. 25, 1776, *PJA* 4:495–96; JA to Knox, Aug. 25, 1776, ibid., 4:497–98; JA to Tudor, Aug. 24, 1776, ibid. 4:491.

64. JA to Tudor, Aug. 24, 1776, ibid., 491.

65. GW to Hancock, Sept. 21, 1775, *PGW:Rev War Ser* 2:29; President of Congress to GW, Sept. 30, Oct. 3, 1775, *LDCC* 2:82, 105.

66. Freeman, *GW*, 3:355–56; *JCC* 3:270–71; "Conference Minutes," *LDCC*, 2:233–38.

67. GW to Richard Henry Lee, July 10, Aug. 29, 1775, *PGW:Rev War* Ser 1:99–100, 372–73; GW, General Orders, July 22, 1775, ibid., 1:153; GW to Hancock, July 21, Aug. 4[-5], Nov. 11, 19, Dec. 14, 1775, ibid., 1:138, 140, 225, 229; 2:350, 398, 548; GW to Joseph Reed, Nov. 8, 28, 1775, ibid., 2:335, 449.

68. GW to Reed, Jan. 4, 1776, ibid., 3:24; GW, General Orders, Oct. 26, 1775, ibid., 2:235–36; *DAJA* 3:326.

69. GW to Reed, Nov. 28, Dec. 15, 1775, Jan. 4, 14, 1776, *PGW:Rev War Ser* 2:449, 252; 3:24, 89; GW, Circular to the New England Governments, Dec. 5, 1775, ibid., 2:492; GW to the Massachusetts Council, Jan. 10, 1776, ibid., 3:61; GW to Hancock, Dec. 11, 1776, ibid., 2:533. On enlistments, see ibid., 3:3n.

70. GW to Reed, Nov. 28, 1775, Jan. 4, 14, 1776, *PGW:Rev War Ser* 2:449; 3:24, 88–89; GW to Hancock, Dec. 4, 11, 1775, 2:484, 533–34; Christopher Ward, *The War of the Revolution* (New York, 1952), 1:120–21.

71. GW, Circular to General Officers, Sept. 8, 1775, *PGW:Rev War Ser* 1:432–34; "Council of War," Sept. 11, 1775, ibid., 1:450–51; GW to Hancock, Sept. 21, 1775, ibid., 2:28; Instructions from Congress to GW, June 22, 1775, ibid., 1:22; Reed to Thomas Bradford, Sept. 14, 1775, Joseph Reed Papers, New-York Historical Society; Reed to [?], Sept. 29, 1775, Reed Letterbook, ibid.

72. GW to Artemas Ward, Nov. 17, 1775, *PGW:Rev War Ser* 2:392; Reed to Esther Reed, Reed Papers, N-Y Hist. Soc.

73. GW to Knox, Nov. 16, 1775, *PGW:Rev War Ser* 2:384–85; GW to Hancock, Jan. 4, 1776, ibid., 3:19–20; Council of War, Feb. 16, 1776, ibid., 3:320–22. On the plans for an assault on Boston, see ibid., 3:333–34n.

74. Freeman, *GW* 3:28–57; Ward, *War of the Revolution*, 125–34.

75. GW to John A. Washington, March 31, 1776, ibid., 3:567–69; GW to Ward, Nov. 17, 1775, ibid., 2:392; GW to Reed, April 1, 1776, ibid., 4:11–12.

76. Hancock to GW, March 25, 1776, ibid., 3:533; *LDCC* 4:9n; JA to GW, April 1, 1776, *PJA* 4:101. For details on the medal that Congress awarded Washington, see *PGW:Rev War Ser* 4:2–4n and *PTJ* 16:53–79.

77. GW, Address to the Massachusetts General Court, April 1, 1776, *PGW:Rev War Ser* 4:8; GW to Richard Henry Lee, Aug. 29, 1775, ibid., 1:375; JA to Tudor, July 23, 1775, *PJA* 3:85.

78. JA to AA, Sept. 1, 1777, *AFC* 2:335–36.

79. GW to Hancock, July 10–11, 1775, *PGW:Rev War Ser* 1:89; GW to Reed, Feb. 26 [-March 9], 1776, ibid., 3:375; *JCC* 3:344–45.

80. GW to John A. Washington, March 31, 1776, *PGW:Rev War Ser* 3:569; JA to Warren,

July 24, Oct. 7, 1775, *PJA* 3:89, 90n 188; JA to Josiah Quincy, Oct. 6, 1775, ibid., 3:187; *DAJA* 3:317, 319; JA to Pickering, Aug. 6, 1822, *WJA* 513n; Conner, *Autobiography of Rush*, 142.

81. JA to AA, Oct. 7, 1775, *AFC* 1:295–96; JA to Warren, Oct. 1, 7, 1775, *PJA* 3:178, 188.

82. TJ to John Randolph, Nov. 29, 1775, *PTJ* 1:269; JA to Pickering, Aug. 6, 1822, *WJA* 2:514n; JA to AA, July 3, Aug. 10, 1776, *AFC* 2:28, 30, 83–84; JA to John Winthrop, May 12, 1776, *PJA* 4;184; JA to TJ, Nov 12, 1813, *AJL* 2:293.

83. JA to Pickering, Aug. 6, 1822, *WJA* 2:512n; JA to AA, July 7, 23, Oct. 7, 1775, May 17, 1776, *AFC* 1:241, 253, 295, 410.

84. JA to Josiah Quincy, Oct. 6, 1775, *PJA* 3:186; *DAJA* 1:282; 2:58, 93; JA to Niles, Feb. 13, 1818, *WJA* 10:284; JA, "Clarendon to Pym," *PJA* 1:163, 164; Bailyn, *Ideological Origins*, 81–83, 140; Wood, *Creation of the American Republic*, 23–24.

85. The literature on republicanism is enormous. For essays that provide introductions to the topic, and that served as a basis for a portion of this paragraph, see the following: Robert Shalhope, "Republicanism and Early American Historiography," *WMQ* 39 (1982): 334–58; Robert Shalhope, "Republicanism, Liberalism, and Democracy: Political Culture in the Early Republic," in Milton Klein, et al., eds., *The Republican Synthesis Revisited Essays in Honor of George A. Billias* (Worcester, Mass., 1992), 37–90; and Lance Banning, "The Republican Interpretation: Retrospect and Prospect," ibid., 91–117. See also W. Paul Adams, "Republicanism in Political Rhetoric before 1776," *Political Science Quarterly* 85 (1970): 397–421.

86. JA to Henry, June 3, 1776, *PJA* 3:186; JA to Josiah Quincy, Oct. 6, 1775, ibid., 3:186; JA to Jonathan Dickinson Sergeant, July 21, 1776, ibid., 4:397; *DAJA* 3:352; [JA], *Thoughts on Government....* (Philadelphia, 1776), in ibid., 4:86–87; JA to William Hooper, ante March 27, 1776, ibid., 4:73, 74; JA to Warren, July 20, 1807, Massachusetts Historical Society, *Collections*, 5th Ser. (1878): 4:353; JA to J. H. Tiffany, April 30, 1819, *WJA* 10:378; [John Jacob Zubly], *A Sermon on American Affairs* (Philadelphia, 1775), 6–7.

87. JA to Henry, June 3, 1776, *PJA* 4:235; JA, "Clarenden to Pym," ibid., 4:168; *DAJA* 1:306.

88. *DAJA* 1:207; 2:7, 38, 53, 93; JA to AA, May 17, July 10, 1776, *AFC* 1:411; 2:42; Wood, *Radicalism of the American Revolution*, 70–75.

89. Russell Kirk, *The Conservative Mind: From Burke to Eliot* (New York, 1953), 78; Howe, *Changing Political Philosophy of JA*, 44; JA to Henry, June 3, 1776, *PJA* 4:235; JA to Trumbull, Feb. 13, 1776, ibid., 4:22; JA to AA, Feb. 11, Ap. 14, 1776, *AFC* 1:346, 382.

90. Michael Zuckerman, "The Social Context of Democracy in Massachusetts," *WMQ* 25 (1968): 523–44; Michael Zuckerman, *Peaceable Kingdoms: New England Towns in the Eighteenth Century* (New York, 1970), 5, 51, 65–72, 94, 187; Stephen Innes, *Creating the Commonwealth: The Economic Culture of Puritan New England* (New York, 1995), 217–19. JA believed that the New England towns were principally responsible for the development of a republican tradition in the region. See JA to Hooper, ante March 27, 1776, *PJA* 4:74.

91. JA to Mercy Warren, Jan. 8, April 16, 1776, *PJA* 3:398; 4:124; JA to Warren, Oct. 19,

20, 1775, April 22, 1776, ibid., 3:215; 216–17; 4:137; JA to Sullivan, May 26, 1776, ibid., 4:210; JA to AA, April 15, July 3, 1776, *AFC* 1:384; 2:28.

92. JA to Mercy Warren, April 16, 1776, *PJA* 4:124; JA "Dissertation on the Canon and Feudal Law," ibid., 1:114; JA to Hawley, Aug. 25, 1776, ibid., 4:496; JA to AA, Aug. 28, Sept. 19, 1774, Oct. 29, 1775, April 15, 1776, June 18, 1777, *AFC* 1:145, 160, 317–18, 384; 2:268; *DAJA* 3:256, 367, 392; 4:118–20; JA to Tudor, Nov. 25, 1816, AFP, reel 123.

93. JA to Mercy Warren, April 16, 1776, ibid., 4:124–25; JA to Benjamin Kent, June 22, 1776, ibid., 4:326; JA, *Letters of Novanglus*, ibid., 2:229; JA, *Thoughts on Government*, ibid., 4:86; Nathan O. Hatch, *The Sacred Cause of Liberty: Republican Thought and the Millennium in Revolutionary New England* (New Haven, 1977), 48, 157.

94. JA to Mercy Warren, April 16, 1776, *PJA* 4:124; JA to Hooper, ante March 27, 1776, ibid., 4:74–75; JA, *Thoughts on Government*, ibid., 4:86–93.

95. JA to Mercy Warren, Jan. 8, 1776, *PJA* 3:398; JA to Hooper, ante March 27, 1776, ibid., 4:77; JA to John Penn, ante March 27, 1776, ibid., 4:79, 83; JA, *Thoughts on Government*, ibid., 4:91; JA to Tudor, Nov. 14, 1776, ibid., 3:296; JA to AA, *AFC* 2:28; Wood, *Creation of the Republic*, 58–60.

96. Paine, *Common Sense*, Foner, *Writings of Paine*, 1:17; JA to Warren, March 31, 1776, *PJA* 5:137; JA to Henry, June 3, 1776, ibid., 4:235; Henry to Richard Henry Lee, May 20, 1776, in William H. Wirt, *Patrick Henry, Correspondence and Speeches* (New York, 1891), 1:411.

97. TJ, *Summary View*, in *PTJ* 1:121–25, 134; TJ, "Fair Copy ... Declaration of Causes and Necessity of Taking Up Arms," June 26–July 6, 1775, ibid., 1:199–200; TJ, "Draft Resolution of Congress on Lord North's Conciliatory Proposal," July 25, 1775, ibid. 1:225; TJ, "First Draft Virginia Constitution," ante June 13, 1776, ibid., 1:338–41; Gilbert Chinnard, ed., *The Commonplace Book of Thomas Jefferson: A Repertory of His Ideas on Government*, Johns Hopkins Studies in Romance Literatures and Languages (Baltimore, 1926), 322; Dewey, *TJ, Lawyer*, 57–72; Charles A. Miller, *Jefferson and Nature* (Baltimore, 1988), 157–88; Garrett Ward Shelton, *The Political Philosophy of Thomas Jefferson* (Baltimore, 1991), 19–40.

98. TJ to Samuel Kercheval, July 12, 1816, Ford, *WTJ* 12:4; Sheldon, *Political Philosophy of TJ*, 27–35, 41.

99. GW to John Thomas, July 23, 1775, *PGW:Rev War Ser* 1:160–61; GW, General Orders, Aug. 10, Oct. 26, 31, Nov. 12, 1775, ibid., 1:282; 2:235, 269, 354; GW to Arnold, Sept. 14, 1775, Jan. 27, 1776, ibid., 1:456; 3:198; GW Circular Instructions for the Seizure of Certain Royal Officers, Nov. 5–12, 1775, ibid., 2:301; GW to Hancock, Jan. 3, July 10, 1776, ibid., 3:20; 5:258; GW to the First Church of Woodstock, March 24, 1776, ibid., 3:531; GW to Richard Henry Lee, May 9, 1776, ibid., 4:244; GW, Address to Massachusetts General Court, April 1, July 11, 1776, ibid., 4:9; 5:270; GW to Schuyler, July 17–18, 1776, ibid., 5:363; GW to Samuel Miles, Aug. 8, 1776, ibid., 5:636.

100. GW, General Orders, July 2, 1776, ibid., 5:180.

101. GW to Hancock, Jan. 4, 1776, ibid., 3:20.

102. *DAJA* 3:333; JA to AA, March 19, 1776, *AFC* 1:363.

103. On the decline of monarchy in America, see Pauline Maier, *From Resistance to Revo-*

*lution: Colonial Radicals and the Development of American Opposition to Britain,
1765–1776* (New York, 1972), 287–95. *Common Sense* can be found in Philip S.
Foner, ed., *The Complete Writings of Thomas Paine* (New York, 1945), 1:4–46.

104. JA to Warren, March 21, April 16, 1776, *PJA* 4:56–57, 122; JA to Mercy Warren, Jan.
8, 1776, ibid., 3:398; JA to AA, April 12, 14, 1776, *AFC* 1:377, 382; GW to Reed, April
1, 1776, *PGW:Rev War Ser* 4:11.

105. JA to AA, May 17, 1776, *AFC* 1:410–11; *JADA* 3:335, 352. The resolution as adopted
by Congress is printed in *PJA* 4:185.

106. *JCC* 4:342–58; JA to AA, May 27, 1776, *AFC,* 1:420; JA to Warren, May 15, 1776, *PJA*
4:186.

107. JA to Warren, May 20, 1776, *PJA* 4:195; JA to Lovell, June 12, 1776, ibid., 4:250; *DAJA*
3:336.

108. JA to Pickering, Aug. 6, 1822, *WJA* 2:514. JA offered a similar explanation in *DAJA*
3:335–37.

109. TJ to Madison, Aug. 30, 1823, Ford, *WTJ* 10:267–69; *DAJA* 2:392. The best accounts
of what likely occurred, and the reasons for the confusion, can be found in Pauline
Maier, *American Scripture: Making the Declaration of Independence* (New York,
1997), 99–105, and Robert E. McGlone, "John Adams and the Authorship of the Declaration of Independence," *Journal of American History* 85 (1998): 411–38.

110. JA to Rush, June 21, 1811, Schutz and Adair, *Spur of Fame,* 182. On TJ's "coup de
theatre" in writing the Declaration of Independence, see Jay Fliegelman, *Declaring
Independence: Jefferson, National Language, & the Culture of Performance* (Stan-
ford, 1993), 79–94.

111. *DAJA* 3:336; Maier, *American Scripture,* 102–105.

112. *DAJA* 3:336; Maier, *American Scripture,* 50–105; Ellis, *American Sphinx,* 54–59. On
the background of the Declaration of Independence, see also Julian P. Boyd, *The Declaration of Independence: The Evolution of the Text as Shown in Facsimiles of Various Drafts* (Princeton, 1945) and Carl Becker, *The Declaration of Independence: A
Study in the History of Political Ideas* (New York, 1922), 142.

113. TJ, "Notes of Proceedings of the Continental Congress," [June 7–August 1, 1776],
PTJ 1:314–15.

114. JA to AA, July 3, 1776, *AFC* 2:30.

115. Maier, *American Scripture,*110, 137; *PTJ* 1:404–06; *PJA* 3:342–43.

116. For influences on TJ's thinking, see Cunningham, *In Pursuit of Reason,* 48–49; Wills,
Inventing America, 170, 174, 192–255; Ronald Hamowy, "Jefferson and the Scottish
Enlightenment: A Critique of Garry Wills's *Inventing America: Jefferson's Declaration of Independence,*" *WMQ* 36 (1979): 503–23; Becker, *Declaration of Independence,* 24–134.

117. JA to Pickering, Aug. 6, 1822, *WJA* 2:513–14; TJ to Henry Lee, May 8, 1825, Ford,
WTJ 10:343; TJ to Madison, Aug. 30, 1823, ibid., 10:267–68.

118. TJ, "Notes of Proceedings in the Continental Congress," June 7–August 1, 1776, *PTJ*
1:310–15.

119. For excellent summary analyses of the Declaration of Independence, see William
Pencak, "The Declaration of Independence: Changing Interpretations and a New

Hypothesis," *Pennsylvania History* 57 (1990): 225–35; Dennis J. Mahoney, "Declaration of Independence," *Society* 24 (1986): 46–48.

120. Maier, *American Scripture*, 143–53; Ellis, *American Sphinx*, 51.

121. Ellis, *American Sphinx*, 9.

122. JA to Rush, Sept. 30, 1805, *Old Family Letters*, 86; Ellis, *Passionate Sage*, 64.

123. *PJA* 1:133, 134, 136, 233, 326; 2:232, 242, 255, 267, 314; 4:185.

124. TJ, "Notes," *TJ* 1:314–15; Charles Warren, "Fourth of July Myths," *WMQ*, 2 (1945): 237–72; JA to Samuel Chase, July 9, 1776, *PJA* 4:372; Jensen, *Founding of a Nation*, 701–02.

125. GW, General Orders, July 9, 10, 1776, *PGW:Rev War Ser* 5:246–47, 256–57; ibid., 5:257n.

126. JA to AA, April 28, July 3, 1776, *AFC* 1:401; 2:30–31.

Chapter 6

1. GW to Samuel Miles, Aug. 8, 1776, *PGW:Rev War Ser* 5:636; GW to John A. Washington, July 22, 1776, ibid., 5:428; GW, General Orders, Aug. 20, 1776, ibid., 6:88–89; TJ to Eppes, July 15, 1776, *PTJ* 1:459; TJ to Pendleton, Aug. 13, 1776, ibid., 1:493; JA to AA, July 3, Aug. 10, 1776, *AFC* 2:71, 83; JA to Reed, July 7, 1776, *PJA* 4:364; Benson Bobwick, *Angel in the Whirlwind: The Triumph of the American Revolution* (New York, 1997), 206.

2. Ira D. Gruber, *The Howe Brothers and the American Revolution* (New York, 1972), 100, 104.

3. Jonathan Trumbull, Sr. to GW, June 22, 1776, *PGW:Rev War Ser* 5:76; GW to William Livingston, June 28, 1776, ibid., 5:136–37; GW to Gen. Lee, Aug. 12, 1776, ibid., 5:682; Russell Weigley, *The American Way of War: A History of United States Military Strategy and Policy* (New York, 1973), 9–10.

4. Freeman, *GW*, 4:176–231; Ward, *War of the Revolution*, 1:208–209, 215, 216, 219, 231; Marcus Cunliffe, "George Washington's Generalship," in George A. Billias, ed., *George Washington's Generals* (New York, 1964), 9; GW to John Augustine Washington, Nov. 6 [–19], 1776, *PGW:Rev War Ser* 7:102–03.

5. Ward, *War of the Revolution*, 1:261. For more flattering portraits of Howe, see Maldwyn A. Jones, "Sir William Howe: Conventional Strategist," in Billias, *George Washington's Generals and Opponents*, 39–67; Troyer S. Anderson, *Command of the Howe Brothers During the American Revolution* (New York, 1936).

6. GW to Hancock, Sept. 2, 16, 25, 1776, *PGW:Rev War Ser* 6:199, 313–14, 393, 400; GW, General Orders, Sept. 3, 19, 20, ibid., 6:204, 340–41, 348; GW to Massachusetts General Court, Sept. 19, 1776, ibid., 6:344; GW to Lund Washington, Sept. 20, 1776, ibid., 6:442.

7. GW to Hancock, Sept. 2, 1776, ibid., 6:200; GW to John A. Washington, Sept. 22, 1776, ibid., 6:374.

8. GW to Hancock, Sept. 8, Oct. 7, 1776, ibid., 6:249, 499; GW to Robert Morris, Feb. 5, 1777, *WW* 7:108; James Kirby Martin and Mark Edward Lender, *A Respectable Army: The Origins of the Republic, 1763–1789* (Arlington Heights, Ill., 1982), 79.

9. GW to John Hancock, Oct. 11 [-13], Nov. 6, 1776, *PGW:Rev War Ser* 6:534–35; 7:96–97; GW to John Augustine Washington, Nov. 6 [–19], 1776, ibid., 7:102–05.

10. GW to Hancock, Nov. 9, 1776, ibid., 7:121; GW to Livingston, Nov. 7, 1776, ibid., 7:110; GW to Massachusetts General Court, Nov. 6, 1776, ibid., 7:100; GW to John A. Washington, Nov. 6 [–19], 1776, ibid., 7:102–03.

11. Thomas Fleming, *1776: Year of Illusions* (New York, 1975), 374–75.

12. GW to Greene, Nov. 8, 1776, *PGW: Rev War Ser* 7:115–16; GW to Hancock, Nov. 16, 1776, ibid., 7:162–64; Greene to GW, Nov. 9, 1776, ibid., 7: 119–20; Freeman, *GW*, 4:242–51.

13. GW to Hancock, Nov. 19 [-21], 1776, *PGW: Rev War Ser* 7:180–83.

14. GW to John A. Washington, Nov. 6 [-19], 1776, *PGW:Rev War Ser* 7:102–05; GW to Hancock, Nov. 19 [-21], 30, Dec. 1, 3, 5, 8, 1776, ibid., 7:180–83, 232–33, 243–44, 255–56, 262–64, 273.

15. GW to Lund Washington, Dec. 10 [-17], 1776, ibid., 7:289–90; GW to Samuel Washington, Dec. 18, 1776, ibid., 7:370; GW to Hancock, Dec. 20, 1776, ibid., 7:382; GW to Gen. Heath, Dec. 21, 1776, ibid., 7:397.

16. GW to PC, Dec. 3, 8, 20, 1776, ibid., 7: 255–56, 273, 381–86; Bobwick, *Angel in the Whirlwind*, 222; Gruber, *Howe Brothers*, 148.

17. GW to PC, Dec. 20, 1776, *PGW:Rev War Ser* 7:381–86.

18. GW to Samuel Washington, Dec. 18, 1776, ibid., 7:370–71; GW to Gen. Lee, Nov. 21, 27, Dec. 1, 3, 10, 11, 14, 1776, ibid., 7:193–95, 224–25, 249, 257, 288, 301, 335–36; GW to Hancock, Dec. 5, 16, 1776, ibid., 7:262–64, 351–52; GW to Reed, Nov. 30, 1776, ibid., 7:237; GW to Hancock, Sept. 25, 1775, ibid., 6:400; Brookhiser, *Founding Father*, 28.

19. Gen. Lee to Reed, Nov. 24, 1776, *The Lee Papers [1754–1811]*, New-York Historical Society, *Collections* (New York, 1872–75), 2:305–06.

20. GW to Hancock, Dec. 27, 1776, *PGW:Rev War Ser* 7:454–58; William S. Stryker, *The Battles of Trenton and Princeton* (Boston, 1898), 64–65, 86–88, 112–13.

21. Stryker, *Trenton and Princeton*, 255–98; Freeman, *GW*, 4:343–57; Ward, *War of the Revolution*, 1:306–18; Alfred Hoyt Bill, *The Campaign of Princeton, 1776–1777* (Princeton, 1948), 95–123.

22. Nicholas Cresswell, *The Journal of Nicholas Cresswell, 1774–1777* (Port Washington, N. Y., 1968), 179–81; Charles Royster, *A Revolutionary People at War: The Continental Army and the American Character* (Chapel Hill, 1979), 119; Gruber, *Howe Brothers*, 191–93.

23. JA to Warren, April 20, Oct. 5, 1776, *PJA* 4:132; 5:46; JA to AA, Feb. 11, June 26, Sept. 4, 1776, *AFC* 1:345–46; 2:23–24, 118.

24. JA to AA, Oct. 8, 1776, *AFC* 2:140; JA to Henry Knox, Sept. 29, 1776, *DAJA* 3:441–42; JA to Col. Daniel Hitchcock, Oct. 1, 1776, ibid., 3:442–44; JA to Gen. Samuel Parsons, Aug. 19, Oct. 2, 1776, ibid., 3:444–46, 448–49.

25. JA to Mercy Warren, Nov. 25, 1775, *PJA* 3:319; JA to Hitchcock, Oct. 1, 1776, *DAJA* 3:443; JA to Parsons, Oct. 2, 1776, ibid., 3:445.

26. Don Higginbotham, *The War of American Independence: Military Attitudes, Policies, and Practice, 1763–1789* (New York, 1971), 390; *DAJA* 3:409–10, 434–35; *PJA*

5:38–40n; JA to Knox, Aug. 25, 1776, ibid., 4:498; *JCC* 5:762–73, 788–807; JA to Elbridge Gerry, Dec. 31, 1776, ibid., 5:56; JA to AA, Sept. 22, 1776, *AFC* 2:131; *JCC* 5: 788–807; Robert K. Wright, Jr., *The Continental Army* (Washington, D.C., 1983), 92.

27. JA to AA, Oct. 8, 1776, Feb. 7, 1777, *AFC* 2:140, 153–54, 165; JA to Tudor, Feb. 25, 1777, *PJA* 5:94; JA to Warren, Feb. 3, 12, 17, 1777, ibid., 5:75–76, 80–83, 87.

28. JA to AA, Jan. 20, 1777, *AFC* 2:147; JA to Warren, Feb. 3, 1777, *PJA* 5:74.

29. TJ to Nelson, May 16, 1776, *PTJ* 1:292; TJ to Eppes, Aug. 9, 1776, ibid., 1:488; TJ to Pendleton, Aug. 26, 1776, ibid., 1:506; Cunningham, *In Pursuit of Reason*, 53.

30. TJ to Nelson, May 16, 1776, *PTJ* 1:292; TJ to Pendleton, June 30, 1776, ibid., 1:408; TJ to Richard Henry Lee, July 29, 1776, ibid., 1:477.

31. Hancock to TJ, Sept. 30, 1776, ibid., 1:523–24; Lee to TJ, Sept. 27, 1776, ibid., 1:522–23; TJ to Hancock, Oct. 11, 1776, ibid., 1:524.

32. Lee to TJ, Nov. 3, 1776, *PTJ* 1:590; JA to AA, Feb, 18, 1776, *AFC* 1:348–49.

33. TJ, "First Draft by Jefferson" [Before June 13, 1776], *PTJ* 1:337–47; TJ, "Second Draft by Jefferson" [Before June 13, 1776], ibid., 1:347–55; TJ, "Third Draft by Jefferson" [Before June 13, 1776], ibid., 1:356–64; Leonard W. Levy, *Jefferson and Civil Liberties: The Darker Side* (Cambridge, Mass., 1963), 42.

34. *DAJA* 3:351–60; JA to AA, March 19, 1776, *AFC* 1:363; JA to Warren, April 20, 1776, *PJA* 4:130–32.

35. TJ to Samuel Kercheval, July 12, 1816, Ford, *WTJ* 10:37.

36. JA to Penn, April 28, 1776, *PJA* 4:149; JA to Henry, June 3, 1776, ibid., 4:235; TJ, *Notes on the State of Virginia*, in Padover, *Complete TJ*, 563.

37. On JA's and TJ's thoughts on government in 1776 see JA to Sullivan, May 26, 1776, *PJA* 4:210–11; JA to William Hooper [ante March 27, 1776], ibid., 4:73–78; JA to John Penn [ante March 27, 1776], ibid., 4:78–84; [JA], *Thoughts on Government* (Philadelphia, 1776), ibid., 4:86–93; TJ, "First Draft by TJ" [Before June 13, 1776], *PTJ* 1:337–47; TJ, "Second Draft by TJ" [Before June 13, 1776], ibid., 1:347–55; TJ, "Third Draft by TJ," [Before June 13, 1776], ibid., 1:356–64; TJ to Pendleton, Aug. 26, 1776, ibid., 1:503–06; Daniel N. Mayer, *The Constitutional Thought of Thomas Jefferson* (Charlottesville, 1994), 53–66; Robert E. and B. Katherine Brown, *Virginia 1705–1786: Democracy or Aristocracy?* (East Lansing, Mich., 1964), 288; John Zvesper, "Jefferson on Liberal Natural Rights," in Gary L. McDowell and Sharon L. Noble, eds., *Reason and Republicanism: Thomas Jefferson's Legacy of Liberty* (Lanham, Md., 1997), 15–30; Robert K. Faulkner, "Jefferson and the Enlightened Science of Liberty," ibid., 31–52; Paul A. Rahe, "Jefferson's Machiavellian Moment," ibid., 53–84. JA was apprehensive of constitutional departures during the war, fearing they might be divisive. As he put it: "unanimity in this Time of Calamity and Danger, is of great Importance." He specifically mentioned his apprehension about making significant changes in suffrage requirements before the end of the war. See JA to Hichborn, May 29, 1776, *PJA* 4:218.

38. JA, *Thoughts on Government*, in *PJA* 4:88; JA to Cushing, June 9, 1776, ibid., 4:245; JA to Mercy Warren, April 16, 1776, ibid., 4:124; JA to Warren, April 22, 1776, ibid., 4:135, 137; Howe, *Changing Political Thought of JA*, 66–101; Wood, *Creation of the American Republic*, 150–61.

39. *PJA* 4:70; *PTJ* 1:334–35, 369; TJ to Pendleton, Aug. 26, 1776, ibid., 1:503–06; Selby, *Revolution in Virginia*, 119–20.

40. *PJA*, 4:70; *PTJ* 1:334–35, 369; TJ to Pendleton, Aug. 26, 1776, ibid., 1:503–06; Selby, *Revolution in Virginia*, 119–20; Malone, *TJ*, 1:237–39; Peterson, *TJ*, 100–107.

41. Merrill Jensen, *The American Revolution Within America* (New York, 1974), 40, 44, 50–51; Elisha P. Douglas, *Rebels and Democrats: The Struggle for Equal Political Rights and Majority Rule During the American Revolution* (Chapel Hill, 1955), 287–316; TJ to JA, Oct. 28, 1813, *AJL* 2:388; Bailyn, *Ideological Origins of the American Revolution*, 282–84.

42. JA, Letter No. XII, in James H. Hutson, ed., *Letters from a Distinguished American: Twelve Essays by John Adams on American Foreign Policy, 1780* (Washington, 1978), 48.

43. Ellis, *American Sphinx*, 293–300; TJ to Madison, Dec. 20, 1787, *PTJ* 12:442; J. David Greenstone, *The Lincoln Persuasion: Remaking American Liberalism* (Princeton, 1993), 73–94.

44. JA, *The Defence of the Constitutions of Government of the United States of America . . . .*, in *WJA* 4:271–6:220. See especially 4:289–91, 585; 5:473; 6:73, 97–99, 186–87. See also JA, "Discourses on Davila," ibid., 6:241–48, 252, 254, 256, 323; JA to Thomas Hollis, June 11, 1790, ibid., 9:570; Howe, *Changing Political Thought of JA*, 96; Wood, *Creation of the American Republic*, 578–80; Ralph Ketchum, *Presidents Above Party: The First American Presidency, 1789–1829* (Chapel Hill, 1984), 57–68, 93–99.

45. TJ, *Notes on the State of Virginia*, in Padover, *Complete TJ*, 678–79.

46. TJ to JA, Oct. 28, 1813, *AJL* 2:389; TJ, "Autobiography," in Padover, *Complete TJ*, 1140; Malone, *TJ*, 1:257–59; Randall, *TJ*, 288–90; Cunningham, *In Pursuit of Reason*, 55–56. The literature on TJ as a land reformer is vast. Richard Hofstadter's "Thomas Jefferson: The Aristocrat as Democrat," in his essays on *The American Political Tradition* (New York, 1948), provides a good starting place, but for a conflicting view one should consult C. Ray Keim, "Primogeniture and Entail in Colonial Virginia," *WMQ* 25 (1968): 545–86.

47. TJ, "Autobiography," in Padover, *Complete TJ*, 1144–45; Malone, *TJ*, 1:261–63.

48. TJ, *Notes on the State of Virginia*, in Padover, *Complete TJ*, 675; TJ, "Bill No. 82," *PTJ* 2:545–47, 549–50n; TJ to Madison, Dec. 16, 1786, ibid., 10:603–04; Malone, *TJ*, 1:274–80; Isaac, *Transformation of Virginia*, 243–95; Merrill D. Peterson, "Jefferson and Religious Freedom," *The Atlantic Monthly* 272 (December 1994): 113–24.

49. TJ, "Bills No. 79, 80, 81," *PTJ* 2:526–45; TJ to Edward Carrington, Jan. 16, 1787, ibid., 11:49; TJ, *Notes on the State of Virginia*, in Padover, *Complete TJ*, 667; TJ to JA, Oct. 28, 1813, *AJL* 2:389; Shelton, *Political Philosophy of TJ*, 65; Malone, *TJ*, 1:285–86.

50. Levy, *Jefferson and Civil Liberties*, 25–41; TJ, "Bill to Attaint Josiah Philips and Others," May 28, 1778, *PTJ* 2:189–91.

51. TJ, "Autobiography," in Padover, *Complete TJ*, 1146–47; TJ, "Bill Nos. 64–76," *PTJ* 2:492–522, 505–06n; John Selby, *The Revolution in Virginia* (Charlottesville, 1980), 160.

52. TJ, *Autobiography*, in Padover, *Complete TJ*, 1149–50; TJ, *Notes on the State of Virginia*, ibid., 661, 665. On racism and slavery in Virginia, and in the eyes of the Revo-

lutionary generation, see Edmund S. Morgan, *American Slavery, American Freedom* (New York, 1975),316–37, 363–87.

53. *PTJ* 2:22–23, 23n, 471, 472–73n; John Shelby, *The Revolution in Virginia, 1775–1783* (Williamsburg, 1988), 160–61; James C. Ballagh, *A History of Slavery in Virginia* (Baltimore, 1902), 116–23; John Miller, *The Wolf by the Ears: Thomas Jefferson and Slavery* (New York, 1977), 5, 21–22. .

54. TJ, "Autobiography," in Padover, *Complete TJ*, 1149–50; TJ, "Bill No. 51: A Bill concerning Slavery," *PTJ* 2:470–72; TJ, "Draft of a Constitution for Virginia [1783]," ibid., 6:298; Paul Finkelman, "Jefferson and Slavery: 'Treason Against the Hopes of the World,'" in Onuf, *Jeffersonian Legacies*, 194–99; Paul Finkelman, "Thomas Jefferson and Antislavery," *Virginia Magazine of History & Biography*, 102 (1994): 193–208; Miller, *The Wolf by the Ears*, 12–22; David B. Davis, *Was Jefferson an Authentic Enemy of Slavery?* (Oxford, Eng., 1970); Winthrop D. Jordan, *White Over Black: American Attitudes Toward the Negro, 1550–1812* (Chapel Hill, 1968), 430–36; William Cohen, "Thomas Jefferson and the Problem of Slavery," *JAH* 56 (1969): 503–26; Howard Temperley, "Jefferson and Slavery: A Study in Moral Perplexity," in McDowell and Noble, *Reason and Republicanism*, 85–99; Conor Cruise O'Brien, "Thomas Jefferson: Radical and Racist," *The Atlantic Monthly*, 278 (Oct. 1996), 53–74. Another view of TJ and slavery can be found in Douglas L. Wilson, "Thomas Jefferson and the Character Issue," ibid., 270 (Nov. 1992), 57–74. While TJ's purported emancipation legislation have not been located, he did discuss these plans in *Notes on the State of Virginia*, which he authored in 1782 and which was published during that decade.

55. TJ, *Notes on the State of Virginia*, in Padover, *Complete TJ*, 661–66.

56. Finkelman, "Jefferson and Antislavery," *Virginia Magazine of History and Biography*, 102:221, 226.

57. GW to Lund Washington, Feb. 24 [26], 1779, *WW* 14:147–49; GW to Oliver Wolcott, Sept. 1, 1796, ibid., 35:201–02; GW to Joseph Whipple, Nov. 28, 1796, ibid., 35:296–98; GW to Fielding Lewis, Nov. 13, 1797, ibid., 36:70; GW to Anthony Whiting, Jan. 6, Feb. 17, 1793, ibid., 32:293; GW to Henry Lewis, Aug. 18, 1793, ibid., 35:53; GW to James Anderson, Dec. 21, 1797, ibid., 36:114; GW to Alexander Spotswood, Sept. 14, 1798, ibid., 36:445; GW to Charles Vancouver, Nov. 5, 1791, ibid., 31:410; GW to William Pearce, Feb. 9, July 13, 27, 1794, June 7, July 5, Oct. 25, 1795, May 1, 1796, ibid., 33:267, 447; 34:212, 231, 343; 35:34; GW to Tobias Lear, June 19, 1791, ibid., 31:302; GW to Arthur Young, Nov. 9, 1794, ibid., 34:21; GW, Last Will and Testament, ibid., 37:276–77.

58. JA to Niles, Feb. 13, 1818, *WJA* 10:283; JA to Warren, July 7, 1777, *PJA* 5:242; JA to Jeremy Belknap, March 21, 1795, MHS, *Colls.*, 5th Ser., 3:40; AA to JA, Sept. 22, 1774, March 31, 1777, *AFC* 1:163; 2:369; Donald L. Robinson, *Slavery in the Structure of American Politics, 1765–1820* (New York, 1971), 468n.

59. Lipscomb and Berg, *WTJ* 13:123; TJ to JA, Jan. 21, 1812, *AJL* 2:291–92; Paine, *Common Sense*, in Foner, *Writings of Paine* 1:17–31.

60. On the Enlightenment critique of slavery, see: David B. Davis, *The Problem of Slavery in Western Culture* (Ithaca, 1966), 391–445; David B. Davis, *The Problem of Slav-*

ery in the Age of Revolution, 1770–1823 (Ithaca, 1975), 255–342; John P. Diggins, "Slavery, Race, and Equality: Jefferson and the Pathos of the Enlightenment," *American Quarterly* 28 (1976): 206–28.

61. JA to TJ, Nov. 13, 1815, *AJL* 2:456; TJ to JA, Jan. 11, 1816, ibid., 2:458–59; Greenstone, *Lincoln Persuasion*, 72.

62. JA to TJ, May 26, 1777, *PJA* 5:204; GW to Harrison, Dec. 18–30, 1778, *WW* 13:467; GW to Mason, March 27, 1779, ibid., 14:301; Malone, *TJ*, 1:286–87.

63. McLaughlin, *Jefferson and Monticello*, 74, 84–85, 87, 158, 166–68, 170–71; Stanton, "'Those Who Labor For My Happiness,'" in Onuf, *Jeffersonian Legacies*, 148.

64. Chastellux, *Travels in North America*, 2:397; TJ to JA, May 16, Dec. 17, 1777, *PTJ* 2:1819, 120; TJ to Henry, March 27, 1779, ibid., 2:238; TJ to Fabbroni, June 8, 1778, ibid., 2:195; Malone, *TJ*, 1:293–97.

65. TJ to Fabbroni, June 8, 1778, *PTJ* 2:195; Pendleton to TJ, May 11, 1779, ibid., 2:266.

66. AA to JA, July 10, 1775, May 7, 1776, *AFC* 1:247, 402.

67. AA to JA, Sept. 20, 1776, June 1, July 23, 1777, ibid., 2:128–29, 250–51, 288; JA to AA, Jan. [?], July 28, 30, 1777, ibid., 2:150, 292, 296–97.

68. AA to JA, Jan. 21, 1796, AFP, reel 381; JA to AA, June 23, 1775, *AFC* 1:226; JA to Rush, Feb. 8, 1778, *PJA* 5:403; JA to Rush, April 4, 1790, Biddle, *Old Family Letters*, 1:168–70.

69. JA to AA, June 10, 1775, Feb. 10, May 14, 15, June 29, July 26, Aug. 3, Oct. 25, 1777, *AFC* 1:213; 2:159, 238, 239–40, 271, 289, 298–99, 360.

70. Shaw, *Character of JA*, 46–47; JA to Mason, July 18, 1776, *PJA* 4:391; JA to Chase, June 14, 1776, ibid., 4:313; JA to Warren, June 25, 1774, Sept. 26, 1775, July 27 1776, ibid., 2:100; 3:170; 4:414; JA to Mercy Warren, Nov. 25, 1775, ibid., 4:318; JA to Gen. Lee, Oct. 13, 1773, ibid., 3:302; JA to AA, June 23, July 24, 1775, Feb. 13, March 19, April 28, May 2, 22, 29, July 11, 1776, Feb. 17, July 26, Sept. 2, 1777, *AFC* 1:191, 207, 226, 255, 347, 363, 399, 412–13; 2:44, 131, 163, 289, 336; *DAJA* 1:26, 87; JA to Parsons, Aug. 19, 1776, ibid., 3:448. Also see: John Ferling, "'Oh that I was a Soldier': John Adams and the Anguish of War," *American Quarterly* 36 (1984): 258–75.

71. *DAJA* 2:156; 3:314; JA to Warren, March 15, 1775, *PJA* 2:404.

72. JA to AA, May 29, June 10, July 12, 1775, *AFC* 1:207, 213, 243; JA to Warren, May 21, 1775, May 21, 1776, *PJA* 3:11; 4:181.

73. JA to AA, May 25, 29, June 2, 10, 23, July 8, 12, Sept. 26, 1775, May 15, 1777, *AFC* 1:206, 207, 208, 213, 226, 243, 285; 2:238–39, 276; JA to Warren, May 12, 1775, May 21, June 27, July 23, 27, 1776, *PJA* 3:11, 39, 87; 4:181, 413–14.

74. Braverman and Utiger, "Introduction to Thyrotoxicosis," in Braverman and Utiger, *Werner and Ingbar's The Thyroid: A Fundamental and Clinical Text*, 6th ed., 645–47; Volpe, "Graves' Disease," in ibid., 648–54; Robert Volpe, "Autoimmune Thyroid Disease," *Hospital Practice* 19 (1984): 141–43; Winsa, "Stressful Life Events and Graves' Disease," *Lancet*, 342:566–67; S. G. Dortman, "Hyperthyroidism: Usual and Unusual Causes," *Archives of Internal Medicine*, 137 (1977): 995–96; Peter C. Whybrow, "Behavioral and Psychiatric Aspects of Thyrotoxicosis," in Lewis E. Braverman and Robert D. Utiger, eds., *Werner and Ingbar's The Thyroid: A Fundamental and Clinical Text*, 7th ed. (Philadelphia, 1996), 697.

75. A. Horsley, "On the Function of the Thyroid Gland," *Proceedings of the Royal Society of London,* 33 (1885): 5; JA to AA, June 15, Aug. 30, Sept. 30, 1777, *AFC* 2:262, 310, 350.

76. *WW* 6:106n; 7:268n; 11:342n; GW to Lund Washington, Dec. 25, 1782, ibid., 25:472; Freeman, *GW,* 4:453; JA to Skelton Jones, March 11, 1809, Adams, *Works of JA,* 9:612; JA to Tudor, March 29, 1817, ibid., 10:245.

77. Freeman, *GW,* 3:290; 4:413; 5:44, 408, 443.

78. GW, "Military Expenses," *George Washington Papers: Presidential Papers on Microfilm* (Washington, 1961), Ser. 5, reel 17, nos. 281–82; GW to Livingston, Gerry, and Clymer, July 19, 1777, *WW* 8:439–40; Freeman, *GW,* 5:483; Flexner, *GW,* 2:283; Chastellux, *Travels,* 1:117–28.

79. James Thacher, *A Military Journal of the American Revolution . . . to the Disbanding of the American Army* (Hartford, 1862), 30; Claude Blanchard, *Journal* (Albany, 1876), 67, 89, 117–19; Chastellux. *Travels,* 1:119–26, 137; Evelyn M. Acomb, ed., *The Revolutionary War Journal of Baron Ludwig von Closen, 1780–1783* (Chapel Hill, 1958), 64, 241; North Callahan, *Henry Knox: George Washington's General* (New York, 1958), 32; Freeman, *GW,* 3:370n; 4:343n, 413, 496, 519n, 581n; "Mrs. Theodorick Bland's Reminiscences on George Washington," *New Jersey Historical Society Proceedings,* 51:250–53.

80. Hamilton to Philip Schuyler, Feb. 18, 1781, Harold C. Syrett and Jacob E. Cooke, eds., *The Papers of Alexander Hamilton* (New York, 1961–1979), 2:567; Silas Deane to Elizabeth Deane, Sept. 10–11, 1774, Smith, *LDC* 1:61; Chastellux, *Travels,* 1:113, 129; Flexner, *GW,* 2:372, 406; Charles Royster, *Light-Horse Harry Lee and the Legacy of the American Revolution* (New York, 1981), 199–204; Mathieu Dumas, *Memoirs of His Own Time; Including the Revolution, the Empire, and the Restoration* (Philadelphia, 1839), 1:29; Cunliffe, *GW,* 153, 160, 162–63; John Alden, *General Charles Lee: Traitor or Patriot?* (Baton Rouge, 1951), 2236, 297; Smith, *JA,* 2:1084; JA to AA, June 18, Sept. 1, 1777, *AFC* 2:268, 335; JA to TJ, May 1, 1812, *AJL* 2:301; TJ to William Jones, Jan. 2, 1814, Lipscomb and Berg, *WTJ* 14:48.

81. Ward, *War of the Revolution,* 1:321; GW to Board of War, June 30, 1777, *WW* 8:318–19; Wright, *Continental Army,* 104; Edward Tatum, ed., *The American Journal of Ambrose Serle* (Los Angeles, 1940), 234.

82. Gruber, *Howe Brothers,* 156–57, 179–80, 188–89; Anderson, *Command of the Howe Brothers,* 214–22; JA to AA, March 7, 1777, *AFC* 2:335.

83. JA to AA, Aug. 24, 1777, *AFC* 2:327.

84. Ward, *War of the Revolution,* 1:341–54; Alan Valentine, *Lord Stirling* (New York, 1969), 208–10; Paul David Nelson, *Anthony Wayne: Soldier of the Early Republic* (Bloomington, Ind., 1985), 55; Piers Mackesy, *The War for America, 1775–1783* (Cambridge, Mass., 1965), 127–29; Theodore Thayer, *Nathanael Greene: Strategist of the American Revolution* (New York, 1960), 196–98; Charles Wittemore, *A General of the Revolution: John Sullivan of New Hampshire* (New York, 1961), 56–64; Higginbotham, *War for American Independence,* 185; Wright, *Continental Army,* 118.

85. GW to PC, Sept. 11, 1777, *WW,* 9:206–08; GW to Heath, Sept. 30, 1777, ibid., 9:287; Ward, *War of the Revolution,* 1:344–53; Freeman, *GW,* 4:471–89; Jones, "Sir William

Howe," Billias, *GW's Opponents*, 61; GW, "Circular to the States," Oct. 18, 1780, *WW* 20:206.

86. JA to AA, Aug. 19, 1777, *AFC* 2:318–19.

87. *JADA* 2: 117, 118n, 256n, 262; JA to AA, March 16, Sept. 30, 1777, *AFC* 2: 176–77, 349.

88. *JADA* 2: 264–67.

89. Ibid., 2:265.

90. JA to AA. April 13, 19, Aug. 26, 23, 26, 1777, ibid., 2:208, 213–14, 325, 329, 350; JA to Gordon, Aug. 31, Sept. 2, 8, 1777, *PJA* 5:276, 336, 337; JA to Rush, Feb. 8, 1778, ibid., 5:403.

91. JA to AA, Feb. 18, March 14, 16, April 13, 28, May 17, 22, 28, Sept. 8, 30, Oct. 15, 1777, *AFC* 2:163, 175, 177, 209, 227, 240, 245, 250, 338, 350, 353.

92. GW to Board of War, Sept. 28, 1777, *WW* 9:277; Mackesy, *War for America*, 130.

93. "Councils of War," Sept. 27, 28, 1777, *WW* 9:259–61, 277–79; GW to Heath, Sept. 30, 1777, ibid., 9:287.

94. GW, General Orders, Oct. 3, 1777, ibid., 9:305–06; Ward, *War of the Revolution*, 1:362–71; Freeman, *GW*, 4:502–19; Thayer, *Greene*, 201–02; Whittemore, *Sullivan*, 69–75; Higginbotham, *War for American Independence*, 187.

95. JA to Lovell, July 26, 1778, *PJA* 6:318–19; Orville T. Murphy, "The Battle of Germantown and the Franco-American Alliance of 1778," *Pennsylvania Magazine of History and Biography*, 82 (1958): 55–64; Brookhiser, *Founding Father*, 32.

96. GW to Gates, Oct. 30, 1777, *WW* 9:465; "Council of War," Oct. 26 [29], 1777, ibid., 9:441–42, 442n, 461–64; GW to Green, Nov. 22, 25, 1777, ibid., 10:96, 104–05; Greene to GW, Nov. 24, 1777, in Showman, *Greene Papers*, 2:208–9, 217.

97. *LDCC* 8:381n; Congress to GW, Dec. 15 [?], 1777, *WW* 10:162–63; GW to PC, Dec. 22, 23, 1777, ibid., 10:186–88; Freeman, *GW*, 4:561–63.

98. JA to AA, Oct. 28, 1777, *AFC* 2:361.

99. JA to Warren, May 15, 1776, *PJA* 4:187.

100. TJ to Fabbroni, June 8, 1778, *PTJ* 2:195; JA to AA, Dec. 15, 1777, *AFC* 2:374.

Chapter 7

1. Charles H. Lesser, ed., *The Sinews of Independence: Monthly Strength Reports of the Continental Army* (Chicago, 1976), 54–61; Erna Risch, *Supplying Washington's Army* (Washington, 1981), 17–18, 80–84, 188–219; James A. Huston, *The Sinews of War: Army Logistics, 1775–1953* (Washington, 1966), 6–12, 27–36; Louis C. Hatch, *The Administration of the Revolutionary Army* (New York, 1904), 92–97; Victor Johnson, *The Administration of the American Commissariat During the Revolutionary War* (Philadelphia, 1941), 82–102; E. Wayne Carp, *To Starve the Army at Pleasure: Continental Army Administration and American Political Culture, 1775–1783* (Chapel Hill, 1984), 20, 43–45, 56–72, 89, 92, 116–24; Jean Edward Smith, *John Marshall: Definer of a Nation* (New York, 1996), 62–63; GW to John Parke Custis, Feb. 1, 1778, *WW* 10:414; GW to Henry Champion, Feb. 7, 17, 1778, ibid., 10:425, 474; GW to William Buchanan, Feb. 7, 1778, ibid., 10:427; GW to Henry, Feb. 19, 1778, ibid., 10:483.

2. GW to PC, March 24, 1778, *WW* 9:139; GW to Committee of Congress with the Army, Jan. 29, 1778, ibid., 10:362–65. On the officers, see Royster, *Revolutionary People at War*, 190–254.

3. Craig to GW, Jan. 6, Jan. 6, 1778, WPUV; Paul David Nelson, *General Horatio Gates: A Biography* (Baton Rouge, 1976), 48, 55, 73–77, 102–03, 163–64; Jonathan Rossie, *The Politics of Command in the American Revolution* (Syracuse, 1975), 188–202; Higginbotham, *War of American Independence*, 216–22; Bernard Knollenberg, *Washington and the American Revolution: A Reappraisal* (New York, 1941), 65–77; Royster, *A Revolutionary People at War*, 179–89.

4. Henry Laurens to John Laurens, Oct. 16, 1777, Smith, *LDCC* 8:125–26; Gouverneur Morris to Richard Peters, Jan. 21, 1778, ibid., 8:650; Peters to Morris, Jan. 21, 1778, ibid., 8:651n; Abraham Clark to William Alexander, Jan. 15, 1778, ibid., 8: 597; Robert Morris to Richard Peters, Jan. 21, 1778, ibid., 8:649; Rush to JA, Oct. 21, 1777, *PJA* 5:316–18; JA to Rush, Feb. 8, 1778, ibid., 5:403.

5. Rudolph Cronau, *The Army of the American Revolution and its Organizer* (New York, 1923), 13–30; John M. Palmer, *General von Steuben* (New Haven, 1937), 3–22, 137–72; Hatch, *Administration of the Revolutionary Army*, 66; Wright, *Continental Army*, 91–119; Royster, *Revolutionary People*, 213–54; Thayer, *Greene*, 224, Risch, *Supplying Washington's Army*, 40–44.

6. Robinson, *Slavery in the Structure of American Politics*, 115–16; Quarles, *Negro in the American Revolution*, 72; Sylvia R. Frey, *Water from the Rock: Black Resistance in a Revolutionary Age* (Princeton, 1991), 78.

7. GW to Richard H. Lee, May 25, 1778, *WW* 11:450; GW to Robert Morris, May 25, 1778, ibid., 11:453; GW to J. A. Washington, May 16, 1778, ibid., 11:315; GW to Board of War, May 16, 1778, ibid., 11:395.

8. GW, General Orders, May 5, 7, 1778, ibid., 11:354–56, 362–63; Royster, *A Revolutionary People*, 250–54; John Laurens to Henry Laurens, May 7, 1778, in *The Army Correspondence of Colonel John Laurens in the Years 1777–1778* (New York, 1969), 169–70.

9. JA to Gerry, Nov. 19, 1777, *PJA* 5:331; JA to Samuel Cooper, Aug. 6, 1778, ibid., 6:368.

10. *DAJA* 2:274–93; 4:7–34.

11. Ibid., 2:293, 296, 346–47; 4:43, 46, 106; James H. Hutson, *John Adams and the Diplomacy of the American Revolution* (Lexington, Ky., 1980), 38.

12. *PJA* 4:xxiv; *DAJA* 4:77, 99–100, 125–26, 136–37, 164; 2:296–317, 354.

13. *DAJA* 2:236; 3:337–38; JA to Warren, April 16, 1776, May 3 [?], 1777, July 26, 1778, *PJA* 4:122; 5:174; 6:321–22; JA to John Winthrop, June 23, 1776, ibid., 4:331; JA to Henry Laurens, July 27, 1778, ibid., 6:323; JA to Edme Jacques Genet, July 12, 1778, ibid., 6:286.

14. JA to Warren, Aug. 4, 1778, *PJA* 6:348–49; JA to Samuel Chase, July 1, 1776, ibid., 4:354; JA to President of Congress, Aug. 4, 1779, ibid., 7:111–12; JA to Samuel Adams, July 28, 1778, ibid., 6:326; JA to Comte de Vergennes, March 30, May 12, 1780, ibid., 9:99, 303–05; JA to Genet, May 17, 1780, ibid., 9:321–24; TJ, "Notes on Proceedings in the Continental Congress," June 7-Aug. 1, 1776, *PTJ* 1:325.

15. JA to President of Congress, Dec. 3, 1778, *PJA* 7:247–48; R. H. Lee to JA, Oct. 29,

1778, ibid., 7:175–76; Elizabeth Cometti, "The Labor Front During the Revolution," in John Ferling, ed., *The American Revolution: The Home Front*, West Georgia College's *Studies in the Social Sciences*, 15 (1976): 83–84.

16. JA to President of Congress, Dec. 3, 1778, *PJA* 7:247; JA to Samuel Adams, Nov. 27, 1778, Feb. 14, 1779, ibid., 7:234; 8:413; JA to Gerry, Dec. 5, 1778, ibid., 7:248; JA to Roger Sherman, Dec. 6, 1778, ibid., 7:254.

17. JA to President of Congress, Dec. 3, 1778, ibid., 7:247; Commissioners to Vergennes, April 19, 1778, ibid., 6:42; Commissioners to Antoine de Sartine, May 16, 1778, ibid., 6:123; Franklin and JA to Sartine, Oct. 30, 1778, ibid. 6:197–98.

18. Commissioners to Vergennes, [Dec. 20-Jan. 9], 1778–1779, *PJA* 7:294–309; Vergennes to the Commissioners, Jan. 9, 1779, ibid., 7:348–49.

19. JA to Samuel Adams, Dec. 7, 1778, ibid., 7:256; JA to James Lovell, Feb. 20, 1779, ibid., 7:420; JA to Thomas McKean, Sept. 20, 1779, ibid., 7: 162; *DAJA* 2:367, 391; 4:118–20; Gerald Stourzh, *Benjamin Franklin and American Foreign Policy* (Chicago, 1954), 154–66; Jonathan R. Dull, "Franklin the Diplomat: The French Mission," *Proceedings*, American Philosophical Society, 72 (1982): 10–17.

20. *DAJA* 2:302, 347, 351–52, 367, 391–92; JA to Samuel Adams, May 21, 1778, ibid., 4:106–08; *Boston Patriot*, May 15, 1811, in *WJA* 1:655; JA to Lovell, Jan. 3, 1779, *PJA* 7:336. On Franklin's popularity and unpopularity, see Esmond Wright, *Franklin of Philadelphia* (Cambridge, Mass., 1986), 288–89; Stourzh, *Franklin and American Foreign Policy*, 133, 153; Dull, "Franklin the Diplomat," *Proceedings*, Am. Phil. Soc., 72:65; William C. Stinchcombe, *The American Revolution and the French Alliance* (Syracuse, 1969), 140; Robert Middlekauf, *Franklin and His Enemies* (Berkeley, 1996).

21. GW to R. H. Lee, May 25, 1778, *WW* 11:451; GW to Gen. Philemon Dickinson, June 5, 1778, ibid., 12:19; GW to PC, June 18, 28, 1778, ibid., 12:84, 128; Council of War, June 24, 1778, ibid., 12:116.

22. Councils of War, June 17, 24, 1778, ibid., 12:75–78, 115–17; Greene to GW, June 24, 1778, Showman, *Papers of General Greene*, 2:447.

23. Greene to GW, June 24, 1778, Showman, *Greene Papers*, 2:447; GW to Lafayette, June 25, 1778, *WW* 12:117; GW to Gates, June 28, 1778, ibid., 12:127; GW to Charles Lee, June 30, 1778, 12:133; Alden, *General Charles Lee*, 213–14.

24. John Shy, "Charles Lee: The Soldier as Radical," in Billias, *Washington's Generals*, 41; GW to Lafayette, June 25, 1778, *WW* 12:117; Lee to GW, June 25, 1778, ibid., 12:119n. On Lafayette, see Howard H. Peckham, "Marquis de Lafayette: Eager Warrior," in Billias, *Washington's Generals*, 212–38; Louis R. Gottschalk, *Lafayette Comes to America* (Chicago, 1935); Louis R. Gottschalk, *Lafayette Joins the American Army* (Chicago, 1937).

25. Theodore Thayer, *The Making of a Scapegoat: Washington and Lee at Monmouth* (Port Washington, N. Y., 1976), 31–33; GW to Lafayette, June 26, 1778, *WW* 12:119, 121–23.

26. Lee to Robert Morris, July 3, 1778, *The Lee Papers*, in New York Historical Society, *Collections* (New York, 1871–1874), 2:458.

27. Alden, *General Charles Lee*, 222; Thayer, *Making of a Scapegoat*, 52; George E.

Scheer, ed., *Private Yankee Doodle: Being A Narrative of Some of the Adventures, Dangers and Sufferings of Revolutionary Soldier, by Joseph Plumb Martin* (Boston, 1962), 127.

28. GW to PC, June 29, 1778, *WW* 12:128, 145; GW, General Orders, June 29, 1778, ibid., 12:130; GW to J. A. Washington, July 4, 1778, ibid., 12:156–57.

29. Ward, *War of the Revolution*, 2:587.

30. GW, "A Plan of Attack on New York," ibid., 12:135–38; GW to Sullivan, July 17, 22, 27, 1778, ibid., 12:184, 201, 237; GW to Lafayette, July 22, 1778, ibid., 12:203; GW to Hancock, June 17, 1776, *PGW:RW Ser* 5:21; Paul F. Dearden, *The Rhode Island Campaign of 1778: Inauspicious Dawn of Alliance* (Providence, 1980), 38–39, 105, 107–108, 116; Ward, *War of the Revolution*, 2:587–93.

31. GW to d'Estaing, Sept. 11, 1778, *WW* 12:425–28; GW to J. A. Washington, Oct. 26, 1778, ibid., 13:156; William B. Willcox, *Portrait of a General: Sir Henry Clinton in the War of Independence* (New York, 1964), 249–54.

32. Henry Lumpkin, *From Savannah to Yorktown: The American Revolution in the South* (Columbia, S. C., 1981), 27–29; War, *War of the Revolution*, 2:679–84; Higginbotham, *War of American Independence*, 353–54; Mackesy, *War for America*, 214, 222, 226–34.

33. GW to Benjamin Harrison, Dec. 18 [-30], 1778, *WW* 13:464; Higginbotham, *War of American Independence*, 355.

34. GW to Mason, March 27, 1779, ibib., 14:299; GW to Harrison, May 5–7, 1779, ibid., 15:6.

35. GW to James Warren, March 31, 1779, ibid., 14:312–13; GW to Gouveneur Morris, May 8, 1779, ibid., 15:75.

36. GW to Jay, April 23, 1779, ibid., 14:437; GW to John Armstrong, May 18, 1779, ibid., 15:98–99; GW to Harrison, Oct. 25, 1779, ibid., 17:20; GW to Pendleton, Nov. 1, 1779, ibid., 17:52.

37. GW to G. Morris, May 8, 1778, ibid., 15:24–25; GW to PC, Aug. 11, 1779, ibid., 16:78–79.

38. GW to Conrad Gerard, May 1, 1779, ibid., 14:471–72; GW to Govs. Trumbull, Clinton, and Livingston, Sept. 27, 1779, ibid., 16:344–45; GW to Govs. Trumbull and Clinton, Nov. 16, 1779, ibid., 16:107–10; GW to Lafayette, March 8 [-10], 1779, ibid., 14:219.

39. GW to PC, Dec. 15, 1779, ibid., 17:272; GW to Gerry, Robert Livingston, and John Mathews, Jan. 23, 1780, ibid., 17:432; GW to Gerry, Jan. 29, 1780, ibid., 17:463; GW to von Steuben, Feb. 8, 1780, ibid., 17:504; GW to Harrison, Oct. 25, 1779, ibid., 17:21.

40. JA to Lovell, July 26, Sept. 26, Nov. 27, 1778, Feb. 20, Aug. 13, 1779, *PJA* 7:77, 237, 318, 419; 8:121; JA to Cushing, Feb. 24, 1779, ibid., 7:424–25; JA to Vergennes, Feb. 11, 16, 1779, ibid., 7:401–403, 416–17; JA to Cooper, Feb. 28, 1779, ibid., 7:432–33; *AFC* 3:188n; JA to AA, Dec. 3, 30, 1778, Jan. 18, Feb. 13, 20, 28, 1779, ibid., 3:129, 142, 149, 169, 175, 181. On JA's voyage home see *DAJA* 2:381–400.

41. On JA's draft and an excellent essay on his role in the preparation of the Constitution of 1780 see: "The Massachusetts Constitution, ca. 28–31 October 1779," *PJA* 8:228–71. See also Robert J. Taylor, "Construction of the Massachusetts Constitu-

tion," in American Antiquarian Society, *Proceedings*, 90 (1980): 317–46; Howe, *Changing Political Thought of JA*, 67, 83, 88, 90, 94–96.

42. Laurens to JA, Oct. 4, 1779, *LDCC* 14:17–19; JA to AA, Nov. 13, 1779, [post May 12], 1780, *AFC* 3:224, 342; AA to JA, Nov. 14, 1779, ibid., 3:233–34; AA to Lovell, Nov. 29, 1779, ibid., 3:240; Gelles, *Portia*, 37–49.

43. Robert A. Gross, *The Minutemen and their World* (New York, 1976), 140–43; "Instructions to Elbridge Gerry and Samuel Osgood from the State of Massachusetts," Jan. [?], 1780, Elbridge Gerry Papers, MHS.

44. JA to Rush, Sept. 19, 1779, *PJA* 8:153.

45. GW to PC, Nov. 5, 1779, *WW*, 17:73; JA to Warren, Feb. 25, 1779, *PJA* 7:429.

46. JA to Warren, Feb. 17, 1777, *PJA* 5:87; GW to Harrison, Dec. 18 [-30], 1778, *WW* 13:464; GW to Mason, March 27, 1779, ibid., 14:300; GW to G. Morris, May 8, 1779, ibid., 15:26; JA to J. A. Washington, May 12, 1779, ibid., 15:59.

47. JA to TJ, May 26, 1777, *PJA* 5:204; GW to Mason, March 27, 1779, *WW* 14:301.

48. John Harvie to TJ, Sept. 15, 1778, *PTJ* 2:212; McLoughlin, *TJ and Monticello*, 166–69.

49. TJ to R. H. Lee, Aug. 30, 1778, *PTJ* 2:210–11; Malone, *TJ* 1:140, 291.

50. Albert Beveridge, *The Life of John Marshall*, 4 vols. (New York, 1916–1929), 1:126–30.

51. Mapp, *TJ* 1:128–29.

52. Lee to TJ, May 3, 1779, *PTJ* 2:262–63; Pendleton to TJ, May 11, 1779, ibid., 2:266; Fleming to TJ, May 22, 1779, ibid., 2:269.

53. Lee to TJ, May 3, 1779, ibid., 2:262; Selby, *Revolution in Virginia*, 204–08.

54. Selby, *Revolution in Virginia*, 209; Malone, *TJ* 1:303.

55. TJ to William Phillips, June 25, 1779, *PTJ* 3:15; TJ to R. H. Lee, June 17, 1779, Sept. 13, 1780, ibid., 2:298; 3:643; Selby, *Revolution in Virginia*, 176–83; Peterson, *TJ* 170–72.

56. TJ to Lafayette, March 10, 1781, *PTJ* 5:113; Peterson, *TJ*, 173–74; Selby, *Revolution in Virginia*, 127–30; Richard R. Beeman, *Patrick Henry: A Biography* (New York, 1974), 115; TJ, *Notes on the State of Virginia*, in Padover, *Complete TJ*, 653.

57. Malone, *TJ* 1:307; Peterson, *TJ*, 201.

58. Bill for Establishing a Manufactory of Arms, Oct. 30, 1779, *PTJ* 3:131–47; TJ to GW, Nov. 28, 1779, ibid., 3:205; TJ to Samuel Huntington, Dec. 16, 1779, ibid., 3:225–26; Selby, *Revolution in Virginia*, 201–11; Peterson, *TJ*, 184; Malone, *TJ* 1:321n.

59. TJ to Board of War, Nov. 9, 13, 15, 18, *PTJ* 3:171–72, 182, 186, 187, 193–04; Board to War to TJ, Nov., 11, 13, 16, 20, 24, Dec. 1, 11, 14, 17, 23, 1779, ibid., 3:124, 182, 183–87, 190–91, 195, 199, 209–10, 215, 221, 229, 238–40; GW to TJ, Dec. 11, 1779, ibid., 3:217. On the governor's military authority under the Virginia constitution of 1776, see ibid., 1:381.

60. TJ to R. H. Lee, June 17, 1779, ibid., 2:298; TJ to George Muter, Feb. 18, 1780, ibid., 3:301–02; GW to La Luzerne, May 31, 1780, ibid., 3:578; Selby, *Revolution in Virginia*, 230–36; Malone, *TJ* 1:315; Randall, *TJ*, 316–17; Peterson, *TJ*, 124.

61. TJ to Bernardo de Galvez, Nov. 8, 1779, *PTJ* 3:168; Nathan Schachner, *Thomas Jefferson, A Biography* (New York, 1951), 181.

62. TJ to Pendleton, Aug. 13, 1776, *PTJ* 1:494; Selby, *Revolution in Virginia*, 184–88.

63. Selby, *Revolution in Virginia*, 192–97.

64. TJ to Bland, June 8, 1779, *TJ* 2:286; Peterson, *TJ*, 179; Selby, *Revolution in Virginia*, 197.

65. TJ to Bland, June 8, 1779, *PTJ* 2:286–87.

66. GW to TJ, July 10, Aug. 6, Sept. 13, Nov. 23, 1779, *PTJ* 3:30, 61, 86, 198–99; TJ to GW, Oct. 8, 1780, ibid., 3:104; GW to Abraham Skinner, Oct. 7, 1780, *WW* 20:144; GW to Charles Dubysson, Oct. 20, 1780, ibid., 20:144; Selby, *Revolution in Virginia*, 197.

67. GW to TJ, April 15, 1780, *WW* 18:263; TJ to GW, Feb. 17, 1780, *PTJ* 3:297; Malone, *TJ* 1:321.

68. Ward, *War of the Revolution*, 2:697–703.

69. TJ to GW, June 11, 1780, *PTJ* 3:433; Madison to TJ, June 23, 1780, ibid., 3:461.

70. *DAJA* 2:403–04; 4:191–203; *AFC* 3:238n; John Thaxter to AA, Dec. 15, 1779, ibid., 3:251; JA to AA, Feb. 12, 1779, ibid., 3:271; Thaxter to John Thaxter, Sr., Nov. 20, Dec. 15, 1779, Jan. 15, Feb. 14, 1780, Thaxter Mss, MHS.

71. JA to William Carmichael, April 8, May 12, 1780, *PJA* 9:113–14, 302–03; JA to Genet, April 29, May 9, 1780, ibid., 9:249–50, 290–91.

72. JA to Vergennes, Feb. 12, 19, 1780, *DAJA* 4:243–45, 250–51; Vergennes to JA, Feb. 15, 1780, ibid., 4:245; *PJA* 8:334n; JA to President of Congress, Feb. 20, 27, 1780, ibid., 8:346; JA to Gerry, Oct. 18, 1779, ibid., 8:213; JA to Lovell, Jan. 29, 1780, AFP, reel 96; Samuel Flagg Bemis, *The Diplomacy of the American Revolution* (Bloomington, Ind., 1935), 176–77; Hutson, *JA and Diplomacy*, 66; *JCC* 15:1196–1198, 1210–1211.

73. *PJA* 9:231n; JA to Genet, May 15, 1780, ibid., 9:314–15.

74. On Galloway's pamphleteering, see: John Ferling, *The Loyalist Mind: Joseph Galloway and the American Revolution* (University Park, Pa., 1977), 46–64. For JA's essays in the British press, see Hutson, *Letters from a Distinguished American*. JA's essays, written in the summer of 1780, were not published for nearly two years.

75. JA to President of Congress, March 12, April 18, 1780, *PJA* 9:37–40, 148–50; JA to Vergennes, July 13, 1780, ibid., 9:520–28; JA to President of Congress, July 23, 1780, ibid., 10:26–27; JA to William Lee, July 20, 1780, ibid., 10:14–15; JA to Jay, May 15, 1780, ibid., 9:315–16; JA to Genet, May 9, June 1, 1780, ibid. 9:290–91, 365; JA to James Wilson, June 24, 1780, ibid., 9:473–74; JA to Joshua Johnson, July 1, 1780, ibid., 9:493–94; JA to A. Lee, Dec. 6, 1780, ibid., 10:395–96; Jay to JA, July 17, 1780, ibid., 10:6; Thomas Digges to JA, June 29, 1780, ibid., 9:486–88; JA to Franklin, Oct. 14, 1780, *WJA* 7:316.

76. JA to Cooper, Feb. 28, 1780, *PJA* 8:374–75; Lee to JA, Sept. 10, 28, 1780, ibid., 10:140–41, 184–85.

77. Edward S. Corwin, *French Policy and the American Alliance of 1778* (Princeton, 1916), 284; Richard B. Morris, *The Peacemakers: The Great Powers and American Independence* (New York, 1965), 90; Orville T. Murphy, *Charles Gravier, Comte de Vergennes: French Diplomacy in the Age of Revolution, 1719–1787* (Albany, 1982), 324, 331, 333–89, 397; Orville T. Murphy, "The View from Versailles: Charles Gravier Comte de Vergennes's Perceptions on the American Revolution," in Ronald Hoffman and Peter J. Albert, eds., *Diplomacy and Revolution: The Franco-American Alliance of 1778* (Charlottesville, 1981), 133, 135–36, 138, 140–42; Dull, *French Navy and American Independence*, 197; W. J. Eccles, "The French Alliance and American Vic-

tory," in John Ferling, ed., *The World Turned Upside Down: The American Victory in the War of Independence* (Westport, Conn., 1988), 154, 161–62; Gregg L. Lint, "Preparing for Peace: The Objectives of the United States, France and Spain in the War of the American Revolution," in Ronald Hoffman and Peter J. Albert, eds., *Peace and the Peacemakers: The Treaty of 1783* (Charlottesville, 1986), 36–38; Stinchcombe, *American Revolution and the French Alliance*, 63–65.

78. Lint, "Preparing for Peace," Hoffman and Albert, *Peace and the Peacemakers*, 33, 36; Eccles, "French Alliance," in Ferling, *World Turned Upside Down*, 152–53; JA to AA, Dec. 18, 1780, *AFC* 4:35; *Boston Patriot*, May 18, 1811, *WJA* 1:655; *DAJA* 2:446.

79. JA to President of Congress, April 18, 1780, *PJA* 9:148–52; JA to Carmichael, April 8, 1780, ibid., 9:113–15; JA to Dumas, Oct. 4, 1780, ibid., 10:252–53; JA to Knox, Feb. 28, 1780, ibid., 8:375; JA to Samuel Adams, Feb. 28, 1780, ibid., 8:374; Morris, *Peacemakers*, 92, 149–50, 188; Stinchcombe, *American Revolution and French Alliance*, 154.

80. Vergennes to JA, June 21, 1780, *PJA* 9:457–58; JA to Huntington, June 26, 1780, ibid., 9:477–78; Hutson, *JA and Diplomacy*, 171n.

81. Hutson, *JA and Diplomacy*, 57–63.

82. JA to AA, June 23, 1780, *AFC* 3:369–70; JA to TJ, June 29, 1780, *PJA* 9:482–83; JA to Mercy Warren, June 23, 1780, *Warren-Adams Letters: Being Chiefly a Correspondence among John Adams, Samuel Adams, and James Warren*, MHS, *Collections* (Boston, 1917, 1923), 2:206; Alan Valentine, *Lord North* (Norman, Okla., 1967), 2:208–18; Ian R. Christie, *Wilkes, Wyvill, and Reform: The Parliamentary Reform Movement in British Politics, 1760–1785* (London, 1962), 75–101.

83. JA to Vergennes, May 12, July 13, 17, 23, 26, 27, 1780, *PJA* 9:303–05, 520–28; 10:1–3, 17, 42–47, 48–50.

84. Vergennes to JA, July 29, 1780, ibid., 10:57; Franklin to Vergennes, Aug. 3, 1780, in A. H. Smyth, ed. *Writings of Benjamin Franklin* (New York, 1905–1907), 8:123–24; Franklin to President of Congress, Aug. 9, 1780, ibid., 8:126–28; Stourzh, *Franklin and American Diplomacy*, 157; Stinchcombe, *American Revolution and the French Alliance*, 155–58.

85. TJ to Madison, July 26, *PTJ* 3:507; TJ to Mazzei, May 31, 1780, ibid., 3:405; TJ to La Luzerne, August 31, 1780, ibid., 3:577–78.

86. Franklin to Huntington, Aug. 9, 1780, Smyth, *Writings of Franklin*, 8:128; *DAJA* 2:446.

87. GW to TJ, Aug. 14, 1780, *WW* 19:374; GW to President of Congress, Aug. 20, 1780, ibid., 19:402.

88. GW to Reed, Aug. 20, 1780, ibid., 19:400; GW to President of Congress, Aug. 20, 1780, ibid., 19:402–10.

Chapter 8

1. Vergennes to Lafayette, Aug. 7, 1780, April 19, 1781, Stanley J. Idzerda, et. al., eds., *Lafayette in the Age of the American Revolution: Selected Letters and Papers* (Ithaca, 1977–), 3:129; 4:47.

2. GW to PC, July 30, 1780, *WW* 19:280; Freeman, *GW* 5:186.

3. John Shy, "George Washington Reconsidered," in Henry S. Bausam, ed., *The John Biggs Cincinnati Lectures in Military Leadership and Command*, 1986 (Lexington, Va., 1986), 39–52.

4. TJ to La Luzerne, April 12, 1781, *PTJ* 5:422.

5. Nelson, *General Gates*, 170–75, 197–202; *JCC* 12:1042–48; 13:11–13; GW to H. Laurens, Nov. 11, 1778, *WW* 13:223–44; GW to Conrad Gerard, May 1, 1779, ibid., 14:470–73; GW to G. Morris, May 8, 1779, ibid., 15:24–25.

6. GW to Congress, Nov. 11, 1778, *WW* 13:223–24; GW to H. Laurens, Nov. 14, 1778, ibid., 13:254–57; *JCC* 13:11–13.

7. Eccles, "French Alliance and American Victory," in Ferling, *World Turned Upside Down*, 152, 159.

8. GW, "Memorandum," July 15, 1780, *WW* 19:174–76; Lee Kennett, *The French Forces in America*, 1780–1783 (Westport, Conn., 1977), 45–56.

9. "Conference at Hartford," Sept. 22, 1780, *WW* 20:76–81; GW to James Duane, Oct. 4, 1780, ibid., 20:118; GW to Cadwalader, Oct. 5, 1780, ibid., 20:122.

10. "Conf. at Hartford," Sept. 22, 1779, *WW* 20:76–81.

11. GW to President of Congress, Aug. 20, 1780, *WW* 19:403.

12. "Conference at Hartford," Sept. 22, 1780, ibid., 19:76–81.

13. GW to John Cadwalader, Oct. 5, 1780, ibid., 20:122; GW to John Mathews, Oct. 4, 1780, ibid., 20:115; GW to J. Laurens, April 9, 1780, ibid., 21:438.

14. Gates to TJ, Aug. 3, 1780, *PTJ* 3:525; TJ to Gates, Aug. 4, 15, 1780, ibid., 3:526–27, 550.

15. Higginbotham, *War of American Independence*, 359; Nelson, *Gates*, 230–35; TJ to GW, Sept. 3, 1780, *PTJ* 3:593–94; TJ to Gates, Sept. 3, 1780, ibid., 3:588; TJ to Huntington, Sept. 3, 1780, ibid., 3:589; "Estimate of Militia Strength," [ca. Sept. 4], 1780, ibid., 3:599–601; Peterson, *TJ*, 197–98; Selby, *Revolution in Virginia*, 216.

16. GW to TJ, Sept. 11, 1780, *PTJ* 3:639; TJ to Huntington, Sept. 3, 1780, ibid., 3:589–90.

17. TJ to Huntington, Nov. 3, 1780, *PTJ* 4:92; Selby, *Revolution in Virginia*, 216–17, 221.

18. TJ to GW, Oct. 22, 1780, *PTJ* 4:60; Page to TJ, Dec. 9, 1780, ibid., 4:192; Mason to TJ, Oct. 6, 1780, ibid., 4:19.

19. TJ to Harrison, Nov. 24, 1780, ibid., 4:15; "Gen. Greene's Requisition for the Southern Army," Nov. 20, 1780, ibid., 4:133–34.

20. GW to TJ, Nov. 8, Dec. 9, 1780, ibid., 4:105, 195; TJ to Harrison, Dec. 11, 1780, ibid., 4:197; TJ to Clark, Dec. 25, 1780, ibid., 4:233–34.

21. Selby, *Revolution in Virginia*, 222–25; Malone, *TJ* 1:338; Randall, *TJ*, 332–23; TJ, "Diary of Arnold's Invasion," *PTJ* 4:258–59; "Depositions Concerning Jefferson's Conduct during Arnold's Invasion," [1796], ibid., 4:271–72.

22. Selby, *Revolution in Virginia*, 223–24; Cunningham, *In Pursuit of Reason*, 70; TJ, "Diary of Arnold's Invasion," *PTJ* 4:258; Randall, *TJ*, 333.

23. Selby, *Revolution in Virginia*, 223–24; Malone, *TJ* 1:340–41; TJ, "A narrative of the late incursion made by the enemy," *Virginia Gazette*, Jan. 13, 1781, in *PTJ* 4:269; TJ to J. P. G. Muhlenberg, Jan. [29-] 31, 1781, ibid., 4:487–88.

24. Peterson, *TJ* 201, 210–11; Malone, *TJ* 1:342–43; Selby, *Revolution in Virginia*, 267.

25. Peterson, *TJ*, 216–17; Malone, *TJ* 1:344–45; TJ, "Circular Letter to Members of the

Assembly," Jan. 23, 1781, *PTJ* 4:433–34; TJ to Gates, Feb. 17, 1781, ibid., 4:637; Freeman, *GW* 5:256–57.

26. Kennett, *French Forces in America*, 98–101.
27. *PTJ* 5:275–76n; GW to TJ, Feb. 6, 1781, ibid., 4:543; Shelby, *Revolution in Virginia*, 270.
28. Weedon to Steuben, April 1, 1781, *PTJ* 5:276n; Greene to Steuben, April 6, 1781, ibid., 5:276–77n; Greene to TJ, March 27, 1781, ibid., 5:258.
29. Selby, *Revolution in Virginia*, 272–74.
30. TJ to GW, May 9, 28, 1781, *PTJ* 5:623–24; 6:32–33; Frey, *Water from the Rock*, 165.
31. JA to Edmund Jenings, Jan. 3, 1781, AFP, reel 354; JA to Sigourney, Ingraham, and Bromfield, April 9, 11, 13, 1781, ibid. reel 102; JA to President of Congress, Aug. 14, 1780, *WJA* 7:245; JA to Livingston, Feb. 21, 1781, ibid., 7:528; JA to AA, April 28, 1781, *AFC* 4:108; JA to Franklin, April 27, 1781, *RDC* 3:390.
32. JA to Carmichael, April 8, 1780, *PJA* 9:113–15; JA to President of Congress, Dec. 31, 1780, ibid., 10:465–66; JA to Digges, Oct. 14, 1780, ibid., 10:267; JA to Hendrik Calkoen, Oct. 16, 1780, ibid., 10:228; JA to Jenings, April 15, 1780, ibid., 9:141–42; JA to Jenings, April 27, 1781, AFP, reel 96; JA to Dumas, Jan. 25, 1781, ibid., reel 102; JA to Dana, March 15, 1781, ibid., reel 102; JA, "Memorial to the States General," April 19, 1781, *RDC* 4:370–76; JA, "Memorial to the Prince of Orange," April 19, 1781, ibid., 4:376–77.
33. GW to PC, Dec. 22, 1780, Jan. 6, 1781, *WW* 21:1, 65; GW to Pickering, Dec. 29, 1780, Jan. 25, 1781, ibid., 21:36, 141; GW, "Circular to the New England States," Jan. 5, 1781, ibid., 21:62; GW to Wayne, Jan. 3–9, 1781, ibid., 21:55–58; GW to Howe, Jan. 22, 1781, ibid., 21:128–29; Carl Van Doren, *Mutiny in January* (New York, 1943); James Kirby Martin, "'A Most Undisciplined, Profligate Crew': Protest and Defiance in the Continental Ranks, 1776–1783," in Ronald Hoffman and Peter J. Albert, eds., *Arms and Independence: The Military Character of the American Revolution* (Charlottesville, 1984), 115–31.
34. JA to President of Congress, June 23, 26, July 11, Aug. 6, 1781, *RDC* 4:514–15, 517–19, 560–61; JA to Knox, Sept. 19, 1779, *PJA* 8:152; JA to Franklin, Aug. 25, 1781, *WJA* 7:465; GW to Greene, Feb. 2, 1781, *WW* 21:172; Thomas Digges to JA, Oct. 10, Nov. 8, 17, Dec. 12, 1781, AFP, reel 353; Gerry to JA, Jan. 10, 1781, reel 354; Cranch to JA, Jan. 18, 1781, ibid., reel 354; Rush to JA, Jan. 21, 1781, ibid., reel 354; William Tudor to JA, Feb. 5, 1781, ibid., 354; A. Lee to JA, Dec. 17, 1780, ibid., reel 353; Lovell to JA, Jan. 2, 1781, *LDCC* 16:537.
35. JA to Joseph Ward, April 15, 1809, AFP, reel 118.
36. JA to Vergennes, July 13, 16, 19, 1781, *RDC* 4:571–73, 576–77, 591–94.
37. JA to AA, April 28, May 11, July 11, 1781, *AFC* 4:108, 122, 170.
38. JA to Mercy Warren, July 30, 1807, in "Correspondence between John Adams and Mercy Otis Warren Relating to Her History of the American Revolution," Massachusetts Historical Society, *Collections*, 5th Ser. (Boston, 1878), 4:388; JA to Livingston, Feb. 21, 1782, *WJA* 7:523; JA to McKean, Oct. 15, 1781, *RDC* 4:779–80; Benjamin Waterhouse to Levi Woodbury, Feb. 20, 1835, Woodbury Papers, Vol. 16, Library of Congress; Volpe, 'Graves' Disease, "Braverman and Utiger, *Werner and*

Ingbar's The Thyroid, 6th ed., 654–55; Terry F. Davies, "The Pathogenesis Thyroidal Graves' Disease," in Braverman and Utiger, *Werner and Ingbar's The Thyroid*, 7th ed., 525–34; Henry B. Burch, "Ophthalmopathy," ibid., 536–52; Vahab Fatourechi, "Localized Myxedema and Thyroid Acropachy," ibid., 553–58; Jeffrey D. Bernhard, "The Skin in Thyrotoxicosis," ibid., 595–97; Whybrow, "Behavioral and Psychiatric Aspects," ibid., 696–700; Marjorie Safran and Louis E. Braverman, "Thyrotoxicosis and Graves' Disease," *Hospital Practice*, 20 (1985): 34–36; De Groot, *The Thyroid*, 362–85; Melvin Bleecher, "Antireceptor Autoimmune Diseases—Part One," *Diagnostic Medicine*, 6 (1983): 67–68.

39. AA to JA, Oct. 21, 1781, *AFC* 4:230; Cranch to JA, July 16, 1781, ibid., 4:179; Lovell to JA, June 21, 1781, *LDC* 17:339–40; *Boston Patriot*, May 15, 1811, in *WJA* 1:649; Franklin to JA, Aug. 16, 1781, ibid., 7:456.

40. JA to AA, Oct. 9, 1781, Aug. 14, 1783, *AFC* 4:224; 5:222–23.

41. JA to AA, Oct. 9, Dec. 2, 18, 1781, Jan. 4, 1782, April 16, May 20, June 10, July 9, 17, 26, Aug. 14, 1783, *AFC* 4:224, 249, 265, 272; 5:125, 126, 163–64, 170, 198, 203, 218, 222–23; JA to AA2d, Aug. 13, 1783, ibid., 5:224; JA to Cranch, July 2, 1782, April 3, 1784, ibid., 4:340; 5:315; AA to Elizabeth Shaw, Dec. 14, 1784, ibid., 6:29; JA to McKean, Oct. 15, 1781, *RDC* 4:779–80; JA to Dana, April 28, 1782, AFP, reel 107; JA to Dana, Dec. 14, 1781, *WJA* 7:493.

42. That JA might have been saved during this medical emergency by physicians lacking modern therapies may be illustrated by what occurred when smallpox broke out among the Moqui Indians in Arizona in 1898. The university-trained physician who treated many of the Moqui possessed neither medicines to cure smallpox nor to prevent secondary bacterial infections; this physician—as was true of JA's doctors—could provide only food, water, warmth, and reassurance to his patients. Nevertheless, only five percent of his patients perished, whereas nearly sixty percent of those who declined to be treated by the physician died during the epidemic. See Alfred W. Crosby, "Virgin Soil Epidemics as a Factor in the Aboriginal Depopulation in America," *WMQ* 33 (1976): 296.

43. JA to President of Congress, Oct. 15, 1781, *RDC* 4:779–80; JA to Ambrose Serle, Dec. 6, 1781, AFP, reel 102; JA to Jenings, Oct. 9, 1781, ibid., reel 102; JA to AA, Dec. 2, 1781, *AFC* 4:250–51; JA to Franklin, Aug. 25, 1781, *WJA* 7:465.

44. GW to H. Laurens, Jan. 15, April 9, 1781, *WW* 2:108–09, 438–39.

45. GW to Gen. Cadwallader, Oct. 5, 1780, ibid., 20:121–22; GW to Rochambeau, Feb. 14, 15, 19, 24, 1781, ibid., 21:225, 229–32, 247, 285; GW to Destouches, Feb. 22, 1781, ibid., 21:278; GW to GW to Col. Laurens, April 9, 1781, ibid., 21:438; GW to Lund Washington, March 28, 1781, ibid., 21:386; Freeman, *GW* 5:271, 278–79. GW lied to Rochambeau about the purloined letter, telling him that he had not kept a copy of his original letter; he also said that the British had altered what he wrote in the original. See GW to Rochambeau, April 30, 1781, *WW* 22:16.

46. GW to Lund Washington, April 30, 1781, ibid., 22:14–15; Freeman, *GW* 5:282–83; Flexner, *GW* 2:420–21; Robinson, *Slavery in the Structure of American Politics*, 121.

47. TJ to GW, May 28, 1781, *PTJ* 6:32–33; GW to Joseph Jones, June 7, 1781, *WW* 22:179.

48. GW to La Luzerne, May 23, 1781, *WW* 22:103–04; GW to PC, May 27, 1781, ibid., 22:120; "Conference with Rochambeau," May 23, 1781, ibid., 22:105–07.
49. Flexner, *GW* 2:429–30; Kennet, *French Army in America*, 108.
50. GW to Noah Webster, July 31, 1788, *PGW:Confed Ser* 6:413–15.
51. GW to Rochambeau, May 27, Jun 4, 13, 1781, *WW* 22:120, 157, 207–208; GW to Lafayette, May 31, 1781, ibid., 22:143; GW to Col. Laurens, Jan. 15, 1781, ibid., 21:108.
52. GW to Webster, July 31, 1788, *PGW: Confed Ser* 6:415; Franklin and Mary Wickwire, *Cornwallis: The American Adventure* (Boston, 1970), 338; Willcox, *Portrait of a General*, 403–04.
53. TJ to GW, May 28, 1781, *PTJ* 6:32.
54. Selby, *Revolution in Virginia*, 275–76.
55. TJ to Lafayette, May 29, 1781, *PTJ* 6:35–36.
56. Malone, *TJ* 2:356; Cunningham, *In Pursuit of Reason*, 72.
57. Malone, *TJ* 2:358.
58. TJ to Edmund Randolph, Sept. 15, 1781, *PTJ* 6:116–17.
59. GW to Rochambeau, June 4, 19, 30, 1781, *WW* 22:157, 234, 293; GW to PC, June 6, July 6, 1781, ibid., 22:168, 329–31; Freeman, *GW* 5:297–99; Kennett, *French Forces*, 107, 115–17.
60. GW to PC, July 10, 1781, *WW* 22:356; GW to Lafayette, July 13, 30, 1781, ibid., 22:368, 431–32; GW to R. H. Lee, July 15, 1781, ibid., 22:383–84; GW to J. A. Washington, July 15, 1781, ibid., 22:386; GW to Greene, July 30, 1781, ibid., 22:430, 437.
61. Freeman, *GW* 5:305.
62. Dull, *French Navy*, 243; Selby, *Revolution in Virginia*, 294.
63. Dalzell and Dalzell, *GW's Mount Vernon*, 100–23; Wall, *GW*, 85–101.
64. John Alden, *A History of the American Revolution* (New York, 1969), 470–71.
65. GW to William Heath, Sept. 23, 1781, *WW* 23:132.
66. Robert Middlekauf, *This Glorious Cause: The American Revolution,* (1763–1789 (New York, 1982), 566, 568; Sheer, *Private Yankee Doodle*, 230–32.
67. James Thacher, *A Military Journal of the American Revolution . . . to the Disbanding of the American Army* (Hartford, 1862), 283.
68. Ward, *War of the Revolution* 2:886–95; Wickwire, *Cornwallis*, 374–84; Kennett, *French Army*, 149.
69. GW to Scammel, Sept. 26, 1781, *WW* 23:142; GW to Weedon, Sept. 20, 1781, ibid., 23:186; GW to PC, Oct. 12, 1781, ibid., 23:213; GW, General Orders, Oct. 6, 10, 1781, ibid., 23:182–83, 205.
70. Flexner, *GW* 2:460; Robinson, *Slavery in the Structure of American Politics*, 123.
71. Freeman, *GW* 5:378–93;; Scheer, *Private Yankee Doodle*, 240–41; Thacher, *Journal*, 288–90.
72. GW to PC, Oct. 19, 27 [-29], 1781, *WW* 241, 295–97; GW, General Orders, Oct. 20, 1781, ibid., 23:245; GW to Thomas Nelson, Oct. 27, 1781, ibid., 23:271–72; *DGW* 3:433–35.
73. GW to Nelson, Oct. 27, 1781, *WW* 23:271; GW to Lafayette, Nov. 15, 1781, ibid., 23:340; Wall, *GW*, 170.

74. TJ to James Monroe, Oct. 5, 1781, *PTJ* 6:127.

75. Nicholas to TJ, July 31, *PTJ* 6:105–06; Archibald Cary to TJ, June 19, 1781, ibid., 6:97; "Charges Advanced by George Nicholas, with Jefferson's Answers," [after 31 July], 1781, ibid., 6:106–09.

76. "TJ's Account and Attendance Record ... October 1781," ibid., 6:135; "Charges Advanced," [after 31 July], 1781, 6:106–09.

77. Higginbotham, *War of American Independence*, 383; Ian R. Christie, *The End of North's Ministry* (London, 1958), 319; Bradford Perkins, "The Peace of Paris: Patterns and Legacies," in Hoffman and Albert, *Peace and the Peacemakers*, 219–20.

78. JA to Livingston, Feb. 14, 1782, *WJA* 7:511; JA to William Jackson, Dec. 1, 1781, *AFC* 4:248; JA to AA, Dec. 2, 1781, ibid., 4:249; Vergennes to Lafayette, Dec. 1, 1781, Idzerda, *Selected Letters of Lafayette*, 4:446.

79. Jonathan R. Dull, *A Diplomatic History of the American Revolution* (New Haven, 1985), 138.

80. Duc de la Vauguyon to JA, March 14, April 17, 1781, *WJA* 7:378, 388–90; JA to Livingston, Feb. 21, 1782, ibid., 7:528; JA to PC, May 7, 1781, *RDC* 4:313–15, 463–64; JA to Franklin, April 13, 1781, ibid., 4:390; Hutson, *JA and Diplomacy*, 104–16.

81. JA to AA, March 22, May 14, July 1, Aug. 15 [?], 1782, *AFC* 4:300, 323, 338, 361; Hutson, *JA and Diplomacy*, 108; Smith, *JA* 1:489.

82. JA to Jay, Aug. 10, 1782, AFP, reel 107.

83. Dull, *Diplomatic History*, 140–41.

84. Ibid., 147–48; Bemis, *Diplomatic History of the American Revolution*, 215–27; Jay to JA, Sept. 28, 1782, *WJA* 7:641; *DAJA* 3:17n.

85. JA to Mercy Warren, Aug. 8, 1807, Adams, "Adams-Warren Letters," 4:427; JA to A. Lee, Oct. 10, 1892, AFP, reel 107; JA to Jackson, Nov. 17, 1782, ibid., reel 110; JA to Livingston, Oct. 31, 1782, *WJA* 7:653; Hutson, *JA and Diplomacy* 123; Shaw, *Character of JA* 170–72.

86. *DAJA* 3:37–38, 47; Hutson, *JA and Diplomacy*, 118.

87. JA to PC, Dec. 28, 1780, Aug. 6, 1781, *RDC* 4:213, 623; JA to Franklin, Aug. 17, 1780, *WJA* 7:247–48; JA to Ralph Izard, Sept. 25, 1778, *PJA* 7:73–74.

88. *Boston Patriot*, May 11, 15, 1811, *WJA* 1:651; JA to A. Lee, Oct. 10, 1782, AFP, reel 107; JA to Jackson, Nov. 17, 1782, ibid., reel 110; JA to AA, April 16, 1783, *AFC* 5:126; *DAJA* 3:37–38.

89. Herbert E. Klingelhofer, "Mathew Ridley's Diary During the Peace Negotiations of 1782," *WMQ* 20 (1963): 123; *Boston Patriot*, July 27, 1811; *DAJA* 3:4 on, 47, 82; Frank Monaghan, ed., *The Diary of John Jay during the Peace Negotiations of 1782* (New Haven, 1934), 14; JA to Livingston, Nov. 8, 1782, *WJA* 8:5.

90. *DAJA* 3:40; Morris, *The Peacemakers*, 291, 351, 357; Charles Ritcheson, "Britain's Peacemakers, 1782–1783: 'To an Astonishing Degree Unfit for the Task?'" in Hoffman and Albert, *Peace and the Peacemakers*, 70–100.

91. *DAJA* 3:82.

92. TJ to Thomas McKean, Aug. 4, 1781, *PTJ* 6:112; TJ to Randolph, Sept. 15, 1781, ibid., 6:116–17.

93. *DAJA* 3:82, 85.

94. *DAJA* 3:82. Historian James H. Hutson has observed that Franklin publicly uttered the commissioners' intent as a means of "trying to advertise to the British a 'split' between France and America to encourage their generosity." See Hutson, *JA and Diplomacy*, 182–83n. On the American team also see James H. Hutson, "The American Negotiators: The Diplomacy of Jealousy," in Hoffman and Albert, *Peace and the Peacemakers*, 52–69. On the differences among the commissioners, see Perkins, "Peace of Paris," ibid., 213–15.

95. *DAJA* 3:43–44.

96. Morris, *The Peacemakers*, 362.

97. "Ridley's Diary," *WMQ* 28:132.

98. JA to Jackson, Nov. 17, 1782, AFP, reel 110; JA to John Quincy Adams, Feb. 25, 1815, ibid., reel 122; JA to James Lloyd, March 12, 1815, ibid., reel 122.

99. Bernard Bailyn, "John Adams," in *Faces of Revolution: Personalities and Themes in the Struggle for American Independence* (New York, 1990), 15; *WJA* 1:58n; *Boston Patriot*, July 31, 1811.

100. Morris, *The Peacemakers*, 363, 377; *DAJA* 3: 48–51.

101. Morris, *The Peacemakers*, 361, 378; *Boston Patriot*, July 31, 1811.

102. *DAJA* 3:50, 83.

103. JA to AA, [ca. Aug. 15, 1782], Jan. 22, 1783, *AFC* 4:361; 5:74. For casualty figures in this war, see Howard H. Peckham, *The Toll of Independence: Engagements and Battle Casualties of the American Revolution* (Chicago, 1974), 130; Mackesy, *War for America*, 368; Rodney Atwood, *The Hessians: Mercenaries from Hessen-Kassel in the American Revolution* (Cambridge, Eng., 1980), 255. Peckham concluded that American deaths in service totaled 25,324. However, this figure does not include naval or civilian casualties, and is likely incomplete on militia losses, especially as a result of disease.

104. *DAJA* 3:50. JA also noted in his diary that Vergennes's remark "would kill Franklin" if he ever learned of it. See ibid., 3:53.

105. GW to Secretary of War, Oct. 2, 1782, *WW* 25:226–29.

106. Hamilton to GW, Feb. 13, 1783, Syrett and Cooke, *Papers of Hamilton*, 3:253–55.

107. *JCC* 24:295–97.

108. Hamilton to GW, Feb. 13, Syrett and Cooke, *Papers of Hamilton* 3:253–55.

109. Josiah Quincy, ed., *The Journal of Major Samuel Shaw* (Boston, 1843), 101–05; GW, "To the Officers of the Army," March 15, 1783, *WW* 26:222–27.

110. Quincy, *Journal of Shaw*, 105; Freeman, *GW* 5:435–36. On the Newburgh Conspiracy, see: Richard H. Kohn, *Eagle and Sword: The Federalists and the Creation of the Military Establishment in America, 1783–1802* (New York, 1975), 17–39; Royster, *Revolutionary People at War*, 333–41; Nelson, *Gates*, 269–77; C. Edward Skeen, "The Newburgh Conspiracy Reconsidered," *WMQ*, 31 (1974): 273–90; Richard H. Kohn, "Rebuttal," ibid., 31:290–98.

111. GW to Carleton, April 9, 1783, *WW* 26:307.

112. GW, "Circular to the States," June 8, 1783, ibid., 26:483–96.

113. Robinson, *Slavery in the Structure of American Politics*, 125–26; Quarles, *Negro in the American Revolution*, 172.

114. Royster, *Revolutionary People at War*, 257; GW, To the Citizens of New Brunswick, Dec. 6, 1783, *WW* 27:260.
115. Freeman, *GW* 5:465–68.
116. "Pocket Day Book," GWP, ser. 5, reel 116, no. 549; "Military Expenses," ibid., ser. 5, reel 116, no. 475.
117. James Tilton to Gunning Bedford, Dec. 25, 1783, *LDCC* 21:232. On GW's expense account see John C. Fitzpatrick, ed., *Account of Expenses while Commander in Chief* (Boston, 1917).
118. James McHenry to Margaret Caldwell, Dec. 23, 1783, *LDCC*, 21:221; TJ to Benjamin Harrison, *PTJ* 6:419; GW, "Address to Congress," Dec. 23, 1783, *WW* 27:284–85; Freeman, *GW* 5:469–78.
119. Garry Wills, *Cincinnatus: George Washington and the Enlightenment* (Garden City, N. Y., 1984), 13.
120. McHenry to Caldwell, Dec. 23, 1783, *LDCC* 21:221.

Chapter 9

1. TJ to Madison, Sept. 6, 1789, *PTJ* 15:394–97.
2. Zagarri, *David Humphreys' "Life of General Washington,"* xiv–li. On rare occasions, Washington was targeted for criticism for his conduct of the war. For an example of an attack on GW's military leadership, see Thomas Paine, "Letter to George Washington," July 30, 1796, in Foner, *Complete Writings of Paine*, 2:691–723. In his private correspondence, GW alluded only to his role in the siege of Yorktown, as mentioned in the previous chapter.
3. GW to Ramsay, June 3, 1790, *PGW:Pres Ser* 5:469; GW to Gordon, Feb. 25, 1791, *WW*, 31:224–25; GW to Smith, May 8, 1792, ibid., 32:41; GW to Snowden, Dec. 4, 1793, ibid., 33:170; GW to William Heath, May 20, 1797, *PGW:Retirement Ser* 1:149.
4. GW, Farewell Address, Sept. 19, 1796, *WW* 35:214–38.
5. GW to Stuart, July 26, 1789, *PGW:Pres Ser* 3:323; GW to Col. Lewis Nicola, May 22, 1782, *WW*, 24:272.
6. GW, Farewell Address, Sept. 19, 1796, ibid., 35:214–38; GW to Madison, March 31, 1787, ibid., 29:191; GW, First Inaugural Address, April 30, 1789, *PGW: Pres Ser* 2:173–77; GW to Henry Lee, Jr., Oct. 31, 1786, *PGW:Confed Ser* 4:318–19.
7. GW to Lund Washington, Feb. 24 [26], 1779, *WW* 14:147–49.
8. Flexner, *GW*, 4:122, 124; GW to Oliver Wolcott, Sept. 1, 1796, *WW* 35:201–2; GW to Joseph Whipple, Nov. 28, 1796, ibid., 35:296–98; GW to George Lewis, Nov. 13, 1797, ibid., 36:70; GW to John Francis Mercer, Sept. 9, 1786, *PGW: Confed Ser* 4:243.
9. GW to Lafayette, Dec. 8, 1784, *PGW: Confed Ser* 2:175.
10. Pleasants to GW, Dec. 11, 1785, *PGW:Confed Ser* 3:450.
11. GW to Arthur Young, Nov. 9, 1794, *WW* 34:21; GW to Tobias Lear, May 6, 1794, ibid., 23:358.
12. Between 1783–1799 GW inherited one slave, accepted one as payment for a debt, and purchased one, a bricklayer, to fill his need for a skilled artisan. See Duncan MacLeod, *Slavery, Race, and the American Revolution* (Cambridge, Eng., 1974), 133–34.

13. GW, Last Will and Testament, [1799], *WW* 37:276–77; Dalzell and Dalzell, *GW's Mount Vernon*, 221–22.

14. JA to Samuel Dexter, March 23, 1801, *WJA* 9:580–81; JA to Charles Gadsden, April 16, 1801, ibid., 9:585; JA to Trumbull, July 18, 1805, AFP, reel 118.

15. Ellis, *Passionate Sage*, 63.

16. JA to John Trumbull, July 27, 1805, AFC, reel 118; JA to B. Rush, Jan. 25, July 23, 1806, Nov. 11, 1807, March 14, 1809, March 19, 1812, Schutz and Adair, *Spur of Fame*, 47, 48, 59, 97–98, 135, 212; JA to Waterhouse, May 9, 1813, Ford, *Statesman and Friend*, 98; Smith, *JA*, 2:1130–31. JA never forgave GW for the role he had played in the selection of general officers to command the provisional army created in 1798 during the Quasi-War crisis. Thereafter, his views on GW were colored both by vanity and bitterness. While JA's rancor did not alter his views of GW's service during the War of Independence, it caused him to portray President Washington as a somewhat incompetent puppet of Hamilton. See Ferling, *JA*, 424–25.

17. Ellis, *American Sphinx*, 166–67; Ellis, *Passionate Sage*, 31; TJ to JA, Nov. 25, 1791, *AJL* 1:252; *PTJ* 20:284–87n; JA to Uriah Forrest, June 20, 1797, *WJA* 8:546–47; JA to Rush, April 18, 1808, Schutz and Adair, *Spur of Fame*, 107; JA to Cranch, May 23, 1801, AFP, reel 118.

18. JA to James Lloyd, March 12, May 31, 1815, *WJA* 10:138, 155; JA to Malcolm, May 20, 1812, AFC, reel 118; JA to B. Rush, Oct. 25, 1809, Schutz and Adair, *Spur of Fame*, 159; JA to MOW, July 20, 1807, Adams, "Correspondence between JA and Warren," MHS, *Colls.*, 4:337.

19. JA to TJ, July 30, 1815, *AJL* 2:451; JA to B Rush, July 3, 1812, Schutz and Adair, *Spur of Fame*, 228; JA to Joseph Ward, April 15, 1809, AFP, reel 118; JA to McKean, July 30, 1815, *WJA* 10:171; JA to Tudor, June 5, 1817, June 1, 1818, ibid., 10:264, 314; JA to Richard Henry Lee, III, Feb. 24, 1821, ibid., 10:396; JA to Jedidiah Morse, March 4, 1815, ibid., 10:133–34.

20. JA to Hezekiah Niles, Feb. 13, 1818, *WJA* 10:282; JA to TJ, Aug. 24, 1815, *AJL* 2:455; JA to Madison, July 25, 1818, AFP, reel 123.

21. JA to Hezekiah Niles, Feb. 13, 1818, *WJA* 10:282. JA divulged a similar interpretation to TJ: "What is meant by the Revolution? The War? That was no part of the Revolution. It was only an Effect and Consequence of it. The Revolution was in the minds of the People, and this was effected from 1760 to 1775, in the course of fifteen Years before a drop of blood was drawn at Lexington. See JA to TJ, Aug. 24, 1815, *AJL* 2:455.

22. JA to Robert Woln, Nov. 19, 1822, AFP, reel 124; JA to Lloyd, April 24, 1815, ibid., reel 122; JA to R. Rush, July 22, 1816, ibid., reel 122; JA to Francis Vanderkemp, Aug. 23, 1806, ibid., reel 118; JA to Tudor, June 1, 1817, ibid, reel 123; JA to Niles, Feb. 13, 1818, *WJA* 10:364–65; JA to Wirt, Jan. 23, 1818, ibid., 10:277–79; *DAJA* 2:119.

23. JA to Waterhouse, Aug. 17, 1817, Ford, *Statesman and Friend*, 137; JA to TJ, May 27, 1819, *AJL* 2:541.

24. TJ to JA, July 9, 1819, *AJL* 2:543–44; JA to TJ, July 13, 1813, June 22, 1819, ibid., 2:356, 542.

25. Maier, *American Scripture*, 169–70, 172–73, 181.

26. TJ to JA, Jan. 11, 1817, *AJL* 2:506; TJ to J. B. Stuart, May 10, 1817, Lipscomb and Bergh, *WTJ* 15:113; TJ to William Wirt, April 12, 1812, Ford, *WTJ* 9:338–41; Malone, *TJ*, 6:225–30.

27. JA to Niles, Feb. 13, 1818, *WJA* 10:282; JA to TJ, Aug. 24, 1815, *AJL* 2:455; TJ to JA, Jan. 11, 1816, Sept. 12, 1821, ibid., 2:458, 575; TJ to Roger C. Weightman, June 24, 1826, Ford, *WTJ* 10:390–92.

28. Quarles, *Negro in the American Revolution*, 6, 16; JA to AA, Aug. 11, 1777, *AFC* 2:304; JA to Joseph Ward, Jan. 8, 1810, AFP, reel 118; JA to Robert J. Evans, June 8, 1819, *WJA* 10:380.

29. JA to TJ, May 22, 1785, *AJL* 1:21.

30. JA to TJ, Feb. 3, 1821, ibid., 2:571.

31. Peter Kolchin, *American Slavery, 1619–1877* (New York, 1993), 85–92.

32. JA to TJ, Dec. 16, 1816, Dec. 21, 1819, ibid., 2:502, 551; JA to Coleman, Jan. 13, 1817, AFP, reel 123; JA to Evans, June 8, 1819, *WJA* 10:379–80.

33. JA to Evans, June 8, 1819, *WJA* 10:379–80; JA to TJ, Dec. 21, 1818, Feb. 3, 1821, *AJL* 2:551, 571; JA to Tudor, Nov. 20, 1819, AFP, reel 124; JA to Cushman, March 16, 1820, ibid., reel 124; JA to Louisa Catherine Adams, Dec. 23, 1819, Jan. 29, 1820, ibid., reel 124; Ellis, *Passionate Sage*, 140–41.

34. Finkleman, "Jefferson and Slavery," in Onuf, *Jeffersonian Legacies*, 198–202; Malone, *TJ*, 6:448–49; Brodie, *TJ*, 286, 431, 457; Douglas R. Egerton, *Gabriel's Rebellion: The Virginia Slave Conspiracies of 1800 and 1802* (Chapel Hill, 1993), 153–62.

35. Lucia Stanton, "'Those Who Labor for My Happiness': Thomas Jefferson and His Slaves," in Onuf, *Jeffersonian Legacies*, 148, 152–53; Finkleman, "Jefferson and Slavery," ibid., 204–07.

36. John Miller, *The Wolf by the Ears: Thomas Jefferson and Slavery* (New York, 1977), 205–6.

37. TJ to Coles, Aug. 25, 1815, Merrill Peterson, ed., *The Portable Thomas Jefferson* (New York, 1975), 544–47.

38. Ibid.; TJ to John Holmes, April 22, 1820, Lipscomb and Bergh, *WTJ* 15:248–50; MacLeod, *Slavery, Race, and the American Revolution*, 145; William Cohen, "Thomas Jefferson and the Problem of Slavery," *Journal of American History* 56 (1969), 519. In the letter to Holmes cited above, TJ is quoted as having written "the wolf by the ears," but in the original he wrote "wolf by the ear." See Finkleman, "Jefferson and Slavery," in Onuf, *Jeffersonian Legacies*, 221n.

39. Brodie, *TJ*, 466; Cohen, "JA and Slavery," *Journal of American History*, 56:519. Soon after his demise, 130 slaves were auctioned at Monticello. See Stanton, "'Those Who Labor for My Happiness,'" in Onuf, *Jeffersonian Legacies*, 147, 152; Paul Finkleman, "Jefferson and Slavery: 'Treason Against the Hopes of the World,'" in ibid., 203–04.

40. Eugene Foster, "Jefferson fathered slave's last Child," *Nature* 396 (Nov. 5, 1998): 27–28; Eric S. Lander and Joseph J. Ellis, "Founding father," ibid., 13–14. In a response to queries about his controversial article, Foster indicated that although the DNA results "could not be conclusive," he believed the "objective data" realized from the testing made it overwhelmingly likely that Jefferson was "implicated in the paternity of illegitimate children with his slave Sally Hemings." See *Nature* 397 (Jan. 7, 1999): 32.

41. Annette Gordon-Reed, *Thomas Jefferson and Sally Hemings: An American Controversy* (Charlottesville, 1997), 91, 101; Brodie, *Jefferson*, 216–18, 228, 240–42, 248, 277, 292–93, 352–53; Miller, *Wolf by the Ears*, 162–76; Stanton, "'Those Who Labor for My Happiness,'" in Onuf, *Jeffersonian Legacies*,147–71; Finkleman, "Jefferson and Slavery," in ibid., 204–06.

42. Gordon-Reed, *Thomas Jefferson and Sally Hemings*, 49, 134–35, 149, 160, 183, 189; Bear, *Jefferson at Monticello*, 4.

43. TJ to Maria Cosway, Oct. 12, 1786, *PTJ* 10:445–46, 450. Much has been written on this episode. A good starting point is in the differing assessments offered in Brodie, *Jefferson*, 252–92, and Ellis, *American Sphinx*, 93–97. Brodie is more persuasive than most scholars in suggesting that Jefferson and Cosway saw much of one another during her second stay in Paris between August and December 1787.

44. TJ to Cosway, Oct. 12, 1786, *PTJ* 10:447–49.

45. Ibid., 10:449.

46. TJ to John Holmes, April 22, 1820, Ford, *WTJ* 10:157–58.

47. William E. Gienapp, "The Crisis of American Democracy: The Political System and the Coming of the Civil War," in Gabor S. Boritt, ed., *Why the Civil War Came* (New York, 1996), 206; JA to TJ, Dec. 21, 1819, *AJL* 2:551.

48. TJ to Holmes, April 22, 1820, Ford, *WJA* 10:157–58.

49. TJ to JA, Jan. 11, 1816, March 25, 1826, *AJL* 2:458–59, 614; TJ to John Taylor, May 28, 1816, Ford, *WTJ* 10:38.

50. Rush to JA, Feb 17, 1812, Schutz and Adair, *Spur to Fame*, 211n; JA to TJ, Nov. 15, 1813, *AJL* 2:402; JA to David Sewall, May 22, 1821, *WJA* 10:399; Ellis, *American Sphinx*, 245,250–57.

51. Wood, *Radicalism of the American Revolution*, 366–68.

52. Ellis, *American Sphinx*, 261, 275–77.

53. Ibid.

Epilogue

1. Martha Washington to ?, Sept. 18, 1799, Fields, *"Worthy Partner,"* 321.

2. Tobias Lear, *Letters and Recollections of George Washington . . . with a diary of Washington's last days, kept by Mr. Lear* (New York, 1906), 130–36; "Statement of Attending Physicians," Dec. 19, 1799, reprinted in Freeman, *GW*, 7:640–41; "A Comparative Critique on Washington's Last Illness," ibid., 7:637–47; Creighton Barker, "A Case Report," *Yale Journal of Biology and Medicine*, 9 (1936–37): 185–87; Fielding O. Lewis, "Washington's Last Illness," *Annals of Medical History*, 4 (1932): 245–48; Walter A. Wells, "The Last Illness and Death of George Washington," *Virginia Medical Monthly*, 53 (1926–27): 629–42.

3. JA to TJ, Feb. 3, 1812, *AJL* 2:296; JA to Vanderkemp, Dec. 15, 1809, AFP, reel 118; JA to Thomas Boylston Adams, June 29, 1801, ibid., reel 118; JA to B. Rush, Feb. 27, 1805, Schutz and Adair, *Spur of Fame*, 24.

4. JA to B. Rush, July 23, 1806, Schutz and Adair, *Spur of Fame*, 60, 61; JA to Mercy Warren, July 11, 20, Aug. 19, 1807, "Correspondence between JA and Mercy Otis

Warren," MHS, Colls., 4:322, 336, 470; JA to Vanderkemp, Oct. 18, 1814, AFP, reel 122; JA to Thomas B. Adams, Sept. 15, 1801, ibid., reel 118; JA to McKean, June 21, 1812, ibid., reel 118.

5. Levin, *AA*, 458–87.

6. JA to John Quincy Adams, May 20, 1816, AFP, reel 122; JA to Louisa Catherine Adams, April 27, May 8, 1820, ibid., reel 124; JA to Susanna Clark, Sept. 9, 1820, ibid., reel 124; JA to John Farmer, Jan. 16, 1823, ibid., reel 124.

7. TJ to B. Rush, Jan. 16, 1811, Ford, *WTJ* 9:294.

8. Ellis, *American Sphinx*, 231; Malone, *TJ*, 6:15–16.

9. Malone, *TJ*, 6:305, 404, 447–48; Hamilton W. Pierson, *The Private Life of Thomas Jefferson* (New York, 1862), 70; TJ to B. Rush, Aug. 17, 1811, Ford, *WTJ*, 9:328; TJ to William Duane, Oct. 18, 1812, ibid., 9:367–68; TJ to Charles Thomson, Jan. 9, 1816, ibid., 10:6; TJ to Vine Utley, March 21, 1819, ibid., 10:125–27; TJ to JA, Oct. 7, 1818, Aug. 15, 1820, Oct. 12, 1823, *AJL* 2:528, 565, 599.

10. TJ to Vanderkemp, Jan. 11, 1825, Ford, *WTJ* 10:336–37; TJ to William Giles, Dec. 25, 1825, ibid., 10:351; TJ to Nathaniel Macon, Feb. 21, 1826, ibid., 10:378; TJ to Page, ND, Randolph, *Domestic Life of TJ*, 303; TJ to Maria Cosway, Dec. 20, 1820, ibid., 374; Andrew Burstein, *The Inner Jefferson: Portrait of a Grieving Optimist* (Charlottesville, 1995), 247, 264–66; TJ to Martha J. Randolph, Dec. 3, 1816, *FLTJ* 418; TJ to Thomas J. Randolph, Feb. 8, 1826, ibid., 469–70; TJ to JA, Nov. 13, 1818, Oct. 12, 1823, *AJL* 2:529, 599; Malone, *TJ*, 6:447.

11. TJ to Nicholas Lewis, July 29, 1787, *PTJ* 11:640; TJ to Martha Jefferson, Jan. 5, 1808, Bear, *Family Letters*, 319; Malone, *TJ*, 6:34–42, 123–25, 301–05, 308–15, 448–52; Herbert E. Sloan, *Principle and Interest: Thomas Jefferson and the Problem of Debt* (New York, 1995), 13–26, 218–23.

12. *WJA* 1:636.

13. Randolph, *Domestic Life of TJ*, 423–29.

14. Barry Schwartz, *George Washington: The Making of an American Symbol* (New York, 1987), 91–103.

15. Merrill D. Peterson, *The Jefferson Image in the American Mind* (New York, 1960), 4; L. H. Butterfield, "The Jubilee of Independence, July 4, 1826," *Virginia Magazine of History and Biography* 61 (1953): 135–38.

16. Butterfield, "Jubilee of Independence," *Virginia Magazine of History and Biography*, 61:136; Merrill D. Peterson, *Adams and Jefferson: A Revolutionary Dialogue* (New York, 1976), 3; Daniel Webster, "Adams and Jefferson," Aug. 2, 1826, in Daniel Webster, *The Writings and Speeches of Daniel Webster* (Boston, 1903), 1:324.

17. JA to William Sumner, March 29, 1809, AFP, reel 118.

18. JA to TJ, Nov. 15, 1813, *AJL* 2:402.

19. GW, General Orders, June 30, July 2, 1776, *PGW:RevWar Ser* 5:155, 180; TJ to JA, Sept. 12, 1821, *AJL* 2:575; Bernard Bailyn, *Faces of Revolution: Personalities and Themes in the Struggle for American Independence* (New York, 1990), 29.

20. TJ to Dr. Walter Jones, Jan. 2, 1814, Ford, *WTJ* 9:448–50; JA to AA, June 18, 1777, *AFC* 2:268.

21. TJ to Samuel Wells Adams, May 12, 1819, Ford, *WTJ* 10:131; TJ to Jones, Jan. 2, 1814, ibid., 9:448–50; TJ to Madison, Jan. 30, 1787, *PTJ* 11:94.
22. JA to Waterhouse, Aug. 16, 1812, Ford, *Statesman and Friend*, 81.
23. Richard Blanco, "Continental Army Hospitals and American Society, 1775–1781, in Maarten Ultee, ed., *Adapting to Conditions: War Society in the Eighteenth Century* (Tuscaloosa, Ala., 1986), 150–73; Mary C. Gillett, *The Medical Department, 1775–1818* (Washington, 1981); Holly A. Mayer, *Belonging to the Army: Camp Followers and Community during the American Revolution* (Columbia, S.C., 1996); Ronald Hoffman and Peter J. Albert, eds., *Women in the Age of the American Revolution* (Charlottesville, 1989); Ronald Hoffman, Thad Tate, and Peter J. Albert, eds., *An Uncivil War: The Southern Backcountry During the American Revolution* (Charlottesville, 1985). For an excellent summary, see Harry M. Ward, *The American Revolution: Nationhood Achieved, 1763–1788* (New York, 1995), 227–58.
24. AA to John Quincy Adams, Jan. 19, 1780, *AFC* 3:268.
25. JA to Moses Gill, June 10, 1775, *PJA* 3:21; JA to Niles, Feb. 13, 1818, *WJA* 10:283.
26. Webster, "Adams and Jefferson," *Writings and Speeches of Webster*, 1:306–307.

Select Bibliography

George Washington, Thomas Jefferson, and John Adams assumed that historians someday would scrutinize their activities, but they never imagined the enormous literature that would result. Only one or two other figures in American history—certainly Abraham Lincoln and probably Franklin D. Roosevelt, as well—have been the subject of as much study as Washington and Jefferson; Adams too has been the focus of numerous scholars.

Modern editions of the papers of these three Founders exist alongside older, but still useful, compilations of their correspondence. The comprehensive modern editions, which are under the direction of professional editors and feature annotation and editorial comment, are a decided improvement over the earliest editions.

From the outset *The Papers of George Washington* (Charlottesville, 1981–) under the editorial guidance of W. W. Abbot and his successor, Dorothy Twohig, made the wise decision to simultaneously publish papers from various periods in Washington's life. The result is *The Colonial Series*, now complete, that spans his first forty-two years, *The Revolutionary War Series*, *The Confederation Series*, also complete and that covers the 1784–1789 period, *The Presidential Series*, and *The Retirement Series*, which focus on his last thirty months and will be complete within a few months of the publication of this book. *The Diaries of George Washington* (6 vols., Charlottesville, 1976–1979), edited by Donald Jackson and Dorothy Twohig, is available as well.

The definitive modern edition of Jefferson's papers has proceeded at a considerably slower pace. In a half-century of publication *The Papers of Thomas Jefferson* (Princeton, 1950–), under the direction of Julian P. Boyd, et al., eds., has now brought its subject only to 1794. However, important supplements exist. Jefferson's correspondence with his daughters can be found in

Edwin M. Betts and James A. Bear, Jr., eds., *The Family Letters of Thomas Jefferson* (Columbia, Mo., 1966). Other significant collections included Dickinson W. Adams, ed., *Jefferson's Extracts from the Gospels* (Princeton, 1983), Lestor Cappon, ed., *The Adams–Jefferson Letters* (Chapel Hill, 1959), which contains Jefferson's correspondence with both John and Abigail Adams, Edwin Morris Betts, ed., *Thomas Jefferson's Garden Book, 1766–1826* (Philadelphia, 1944), Douglas L. Wilson, ed., *Jefferson's Commonplace Book* (Princeton, 1989), and James A. Bear and Lucia C. Stanton, eds., *Jefferson's Memorandum Books: Accounts, with Legal Records and Miscellany, 1767–1826* (2 vols, Princeton, 1997).

The Massachusetts Historical Society owns and is publishing Adams's papers in segmented stages. L. H. Butterfield, ed., *Diary and Autobiography of John Adams* (4 vols., Cambridge, Mass., 1961) appeared first, followed by L. H. Butterfield, et al., eds., *Adams Family Correspondence* (Cambridge, Mass., 1963–), which primarily consists of letters between Adams and his wife and children. On Adams's legal career, see Kinvin Wroth and Hiller Zobel, eds., *Legal Papers of John Adams* (4 vols., Cambridge, Mass., 1966). For his activities as a public official, see Robert J. Taylor, et al., eds., *Papers of John Adams* (Cambridge, Mass., 1977–).

As none of these projects is likely to be completed until deep into the twenty-first century, older editions remain essential for scholarship. John C. Fitzpatrick, ed., *The Writings of Washington from the Original Manuscript Sources, 1754–1799* (39 vols., Washington, D.C., 1931–1944) is essential for those interested in Washington's war and presidential years. For letters addressed to Washington during these periods, see Jared Sparks, ed., *Correspondence of the American Revolution: Being Letters of Eminent Men to George Washington* (4 vols., Washington, D.C., 1853) and Stanislaus M. Hamilton, ed., *Letters to Washington and Accompanying Papers* (5 vols., Boston, 1898–1902).

Two early editions of Jefferson's papers are to be recommended. See Paul L. Ford, ed., *The Writings of Thomas Jefferson* (10 vols., New York, 1892–1899) and A. A. Lipscomb and A. E. Burgh, eds., *The Writings of Thomas Jefferson* (20 vols., Washington, 1900–1904). In addition, the following collections are useful: Gilbert Chinard, ed., *The Correspondence of Jefferson and Du Pont de Nemours* (Baltimore, 1931); Gilbert Chinard, ed., *The Letters of Lafayette and Jefferson* (Baltimore, 1929); and Richard Beale Davis, ed., *Correspondence of Jefferson and Francis Walker Gilmer, 1814–1826* (Columbia, S. C., 1946).

For Adams one should consult Charles F. Adams, ed., *The Works of John Adams, Second President of the United Stares: With a Life of the Author* (10 vols., Boston, 1850–1856), which contains not only many of his published writings, but his speeches, addresses, and letters that relate to public affairs. For other Adams materials, see Charles F. Adams, ed., *Letters of John Adams, Addressed to His Wife* (2 vols., Boston, 1841); John A. Schutz and Douglass Adair, eds., *The Spur of Fame: Dialogues of John Adams and Benjamin Rush, 1805–1813* (San Marino, Cal., 1966), which among other things provides a window into Adams's mind during his initial years of retirement, as does Worthington C. Ford, ed., *Statesman and Friend: Correspondence of John Adams with Benjamin Waterhouse, 1784–1822* (Boston, 1927); [Anon.], *Correspondence between the Hon. John Adams, Late President of the United States, and the late William Cunningham, Esq.* (Boston, 1823); and Charles F. Adams, ed., "Correspondence between Mercy Warren Relating to Her History of the American Revolution," Massachusetts Historical Society, *Collections*, 5th ser., vol 4 (Boston, 1878). James H. Hutson, ed., *Letters from a Distinguished American: Twelve Essays by John Adams on American Foreign Policy* (Washington, D.C., 1978), is a compilation of pieces written by Adams for the British press during the war years, and *Warren–Adams Letters: Being Chiefly a Correspondence among John Adams, Samuel Adams, and James Warren*, Massachusetts Historical Society, *Collections* (2 vols., Boston, 1917, 1925) is good primarily on the 1770s and 1780s.

The Library of Congress possesses many of Washington's papers. They are available on microfilm. However, the most complete collection of Washington's papers—or at least of photostatic copies of his papers—can be found at the Alderman Liberary of the University of Virginia. The Adams Family Papers are housed at the Massachusetts Historical Society in Boston. They too are available on microfilm. The Library of Congress, Massachusetts Historical Society, and the University of Virginia contain the largest collections of Jefferson materials. These collections have been microfilmed as well.

Washington has been the subject of innumerable biographies. The most comprehensive are those of Douglas Southall Freeman, J. A. Carroll, and M. W. Ashworth, *George Washington: A Biography* (7 vols., New York, 1948–1957) and James Thomas Flexner, *George Washington* (4 vols., Boston, 1965–1972). Readers might also wish to consult the following single-volume studies: Marcus Cunliffe, *George Washington: Man and Monument* (New York, 1959); North Callahan, *George Washington: Soldier and Man* (New York, 1972); Robert F. Jones, *George Washington* (Boston, 1979); John Alden,

George Washington: A Biography (Baton Rouge, 1984); John Ferling, *The First of Men: A Life of George Washington* (Knoxville, 1988); and Willard Sterne Randall, *George Washington: A Life* (New York, 1997).

A small volume would be required to list only the best books on specialized aspects of Washington's life. However, no reader would be ill advised to look into Edmund S. Morgan's *The Genius of George Washington* (New York, 1980) and *The Meaning of Independence: John Adams, George Washington, and Thomas Jefferson* (Charlottesville, 1975), which contain reflective short essays on its three subjects. Three especially good works are available on Washington's pre-American Revolution years. Readers should see Bernhard Knollenberg, *George Washington: The Virginia Period, 1732–1775* (Durham, N.H.,1964), Paul K. Longmore, *The Invention of George Washington* (Berkeley, 1988), and the several essays contained in Warren Hofstra, ed., *George Washington and the Virginia Backcountry* (Madison, 1998). The following are indispensable on Washington as a soldier: Marcus Cunliffe, "George Washington's Generalship," in George A. Billias, ed., *George Washington's Generals* (New York, 1964); Dave Richard Palmer, *The Way of the Fox: American Strategy in the War of Independence* (Westport, Conn., 1975); Don Higginbotham, *George Washington and the American Military Tradition* (Athens, Ga., 1985), and John Shy, "George Washington Reconsidered," in Henry S. Bausum, ed., *The John Biggs Cincinnati Lectures in Military Leadership and Command, 1986* (Lexington, Va., 1986). An excellent study of Washington's character and leadership is Richard Brookhiser, *Founding Father: Rediscovering George Washington* (New York, 1996). The best study of Washington at home is that of Robert F. and Lee Baldwin Dalzell, *George Washington's Mount Vernon: At Home in Revolutionary America* (New York, 1998).

Two final works on Washington are of considerable importance. On Washington's understanding of power and leadership, nothing surpasses Garry Wills, *Cincinnatus: George Washington and the Enlightenment* (Garden City, N.Y., 1984). Perhaps the best study of Washington in the popular mind during his final years and later is that of Barry Schwartz, *George Washington: The Making of an American Symbol* (New York, 1987).

Jefferson has also been the subject of numerous biographies and specialized studies. Perhaps the best starting place is Merrill D. Peterson, ed., *Thomas Jefferson: A Reference Biography* (New York, 1986), which contains stimulating essays on virtually every aspect of Jefferson's life, thought, and politics, as well as a good bibliography. Also of importance is Peter Onuf, "The

Scholars' Jefferson," *William and Mary Quarterly* 50 (1993): 671–99, which is good on both bibliography and historiography, and additionally raises questions and lines of inquiry with regard to Jefferson. Dumas Malone, *Jefferson and His Time* (6 vols., Boston, 1948–1981), is the most extensive life history. Several other multivolume biographies are good. Henry S. Randall's *Life of Thomas Jefferson* (3 vols., New York, 1858) is useful principally because the author interviewed family members and other contemporaries of Jefferson. Alf Mapp's *Thomas Jefferson* (2 vols., New York, 1987–1991) is sound, as is Marie Kimball's trilogy, *Jefferson: The Road to Glory, 1743–1776* (New York, 1943), *Jefferson: War and Peace, 1776–1784* (New York, 1947), and *Jefferson: The Scene of Europe, 1784–1789* (New York, 1950). A reliable and readable older work is Nathan Schachner, *Thomas Jefferson* (2 vols., New York, 1951).

Single-volume biographies of Jefferson abound. The most comprehensive is Merrill D. Peterson, *Thomas Jefferson and the New Nation: A Biography* (New York, 1970). Readers will find much that is useful in Noble E. Cunningham, *In Pursuit of Reason: The Life of Thomas Jefferson* (Baton Rouge, 1987). Two more recent works are Willard Sterne Randall, *Thomas Jefferson: A Life* (New York, 1993) and Norman K. Risjord, *Thomas Jefferson* (Madison, Wisc., 1994). No biographer did more with the private side of Jefferson than Fawn Brodie in *Thomas Jefferson: An Intimate History* (New York, 1974), although Andrew Burstein, *The Inner Jefferson: Portrait of a Grieving Optimist* (Charlottesville, 1995) should be consulted. Kenneth Lockridge, *On the Sources of Patriarchal Rage: The Commonplace Books of William Byrd and Thomas Jefferson and the Gendering of Power in th Eighteenth Century* (New York, 1992), is a fascinating study of young Jefferson's outlook toward females. Jack McLaughlin's *Jefferson and Monticello: The Biography of a Builder* (New York, 1988) provides innumerable insights into Jefferson's world atop his mountain. Provocative interpretive analyzes can be found as well in Page Smith, *Jefferson: A Revealing Biography* (New York, 1976) and Joseph Ellis, *American Sphinx: The Character of Thomas Jefferson* (New York, 1997).

Much has been written in recent years on Jefferson and slavery, portions of which are crucial to understanding Washington and Adams as well. To put matters in the proper context, readers should begin with two works by David Brion Davis, *The Problem of Slavery in Western Culture* (Ithaca, 1966) and *The Problem of Slavery in the Age of Revolution, 1770–1823* (Ithaca, 1975), and continue with the trailblazing classic by Winthrop Jordan, *White over Black: American Attitudes Toward the Negro, 1550–1812* (Chapel Hill, 1968);

Paul Finkleman, ed., *Slavery and the Founders: Race and Liberty in the Age of Jefferson* (Armonk, N.Y., 1996), an important collection of essays, Gary Nash, *Race and Revolution* (Madison, Wisc., 1990), and Annette Gordon-Reed's *Thomas Jefferson and Sally Hemings: An American Controversy* (Charlottesville, 1997), which not only is indispensable on the topic of Jefferson's relationship with his female slave, but lays bare the disturbing historiography of the issue. The following are also of considerable importance: John C. Miller, *The Wolf by the Ears: Thomas Jefferson and Slavery* (New York, 1977); Paul Finkelman, "Jefferson and Slavery: 'Treason Against the Hopes of the World,' " in Peter Onuf, ed., *Jeffersonian Legacies* (Charlottesville, 1993) and Lucia C. Stanton, "'Those Who Labor for My Happiness': Thomas Jefferson and His Slaves," in the same volume; Robert McColley, *Slavery and Jeffersonian Virginia* (Urbana, Ill., 1964); David Brion Davis, *Was Jefferson an Authentic Enemy of Slavery? An Inaugural Lecture Delivered before the University of Oxford* (Oxford, Eng., 1978); and William Cohen, "Thomas Jefferson and the Problem of Slavery," *Journal of American History* 56 (1969–70): 503–26. A learned and thoughtful defense of Jefferson can be found in Douglas L. Wilson, "Thomas Jefferson and the Character Issue," *Atlantic Monthly* 279 (Nov. 1992): 57–74.

Works on Jefferson as a political theorist, scientist, architect, and educator, among other topics, are too numerous to list. Fortunately, excellent bibliographic guides exist on Jefferson. See Frank Shuffleton, ed., *Thomas Jefferson: A Comprehensive, Annotated Bibliography of Writings About Him, 1826–1980* (New York, 1983) and *Thomas Jefferson, 1981–1990: An Annotated Bibliography* (New York, 1980).

Jefferson has also been the subject of an important television documentary, *Thomas Jefferson: A Film by Ken Burns* (Florentine Films, 1996). However, anyone watching the film should also consult Jan Lewis and Peter S. Onuf, "American Synecdoche: Thomas Jefferson as Image, Icon, Character, and Self," *American Historical Review* 103 (1998): 125–36.

Although Adams has been the subject of considerably less scholarship than Washington and Jefferson, a sizeable body of works has accumulated. Fortunately, a bibliographical guide on Adams exists in Greenwood Press' "Bibliographies of the Presidents of the United States" series. See John Ferling, ed., *John Adams: A Bibliography* (Westport, Conn., 1994). Only two comprehensive modern biographies are available: Page Smith, *John Adams* (2 vols., New York, 1962) and John Ferling, *John Adams: A Life* (Knoxville, 1992). An older work by a gifted scholar, Gilbert Chinard, *Honest John Adams*

(Boston, 1933), was marred because it was completed prior to the opening of many of Adams's papers. Two excellent studies of Adams's temperament and personality are available. See Peter Shaw, *The Character of John Adams* (Chapel Hill, 1976), and Joseph Ellis, *Passionate Sage: The Character and Legacy of John Adams* (New York, 1993).

Abigail Adams has been the subject of more biographies than her husband, and the best not only tell the story of her life, but open a window onto his. See Charles W. Akers, *Abigail Adams: An American Woman* (Boston, 1980); Phyllis Lee Levin, *Abigail Adams: A Bibliography* (New York, 1987); Lynn Withey, *Dearest Friend: A Life of Abigail Adams* (New York, 1981); and two works by Edith B. Gelles, *Portia: The World of Abigail Adams* (Bloomington, Ind., 1992) and *First Thoughts: Life and Letters of Abigail Adams* (New York, 1998).

Several specialized studies on Adams are significant. On Adams's decision to pursue the law, and his career as a lawyer, see Richard D. Brown, *Knowledge Is Power: The Diffusion of Information in Early America, 1700–1865* (New York, 1989), which includes a wonderful chapter contrasting young Adams and Robert Treat Paine. See also Daniel R. Coquillette, "Justinian in Braintree: John Adams, Civilian Learning and Legal Elitism, 1758–1775," in *Law in Colonial Massachusetts*, Colonial Society of Massachusetts, *Publications*, 62 (1984): 359–418, and Hiller B. Zobel, *The Boston Massacre* (New York, 1970).

Surprisingly little has been written on Adams and the American Revolution through July 1776. An intriguing article is that of John W. Ellsworth, "John Adams: The American Revolution as a Change of Heart," *Huntington Library Quarterly* 28 (1965): 293–300. Also good is Bernhard Knollenberg, "John Dickinson and John Adams: 1774–1776," *American Philosophical Society Proceedings* 107 (1963): 138–44. Richard B. Morris's "John Adams: Puritan Revolutionary," in that author's collection of essays, *Seven Who Shaped Our Destiny* (New York, 1973), is excellent. A good section on Adams is contained in John M. Head, *A Time to Rend: An Essay on the Decision for American Independence* (Madison, Wisc., 1968). For an inquiry into Adams's physical well-being and how it affected him as a public official before and after 1776, see John Ferling and Lewis E. Braverman, "John Adams's Health Reconsidered," *William and Mary Quarrterly* 55 (1998): 83–104.

The literature on Adams as a political thinker is far more extensive. The best starting point is John R. Howe, *The Changing Political Thought of John Adams* (Princeton, 1966). Several provocative studies by C. Bradley Thomp-

son are essential reading; see *John Adams and the Spirit of Liberty* (Lawrence, Kan., 1998); "Young John Adams and the New Philosophic Rationalism," *William and Mary Quarterly* 55 (1998): 259–80 and "John Adams and the Coming of the French Revolution," *Journal of the Early Republic* 16 (1996): 361–88. Significant additional studies include Zoltan Haraszti, *John Adams and the Prophets of Progress* (Cambridge, Mass., 1952); Richard Gummere, "The Classical Politics of John Adams," *Boston Public Library Quarterly* 9 (1957): 167–82; Correa M. Walsh, *The Political Science of John Adams* (New York, 1915); Edward Ryerson, "On John Adams," *American Quarterly* 6 (1954): 253–58; Helen S. Saltman, "John Adams's Earliest Essays: The Humphrey Ploughjogger Letters," *William and Mary Quarterly* 37 (1980): 125–35; Steven G. Kurtz, "The Political Science of John Adams: A Guide to His Statecraft," *William and Mary Quarterly* 25 (1968): 605–13; Randall B. Ripley, "Adams, Burke and Eighteenth Century Conservatism," *Political Science Quarterly* 80 (1965): 216–35; Dorothy M. Robathan, "John Adams and the Classics," *New England Quarterly* 19 (1946): 91–98; and Francis N. Thorpe, "The Political Ideas of John Adams," *Pennsylvania Magazine of History and Biography* 44 (1920): 1–46.

On Adams and America's early governments, see Timothy H. Breen, "John Adams's Fight Against Innovation in the New England Constitution, 1776," *New England Quarterly* 40 (1976): 501–20; George C. Homans, "John Adams and the Constitution of Massachusetts," *American Philosophical Society Proceedings* 125 (1981): 286–91; John Selby, "Richard Henry Lee, John Adams, and the Virginia Constitution of 1776," *Virginia Magazine of History and Biography* 84 (1976): 387–400; Charles Warren, "John Adams and American Constitutions," *Washington University Bulletin* 26 (1926); L. H. Butterfield, "A Government of Laws and Not of Men," *Harvard Magazine* 77 (Nov. 1977): 19–20; Bruce Miroff, "John Adams: Merit, Fame, and Political Leadership," *Journal of Politics* 48 (1986): 116–32; George A. Peek, "John Adams on the Nature of Men and Government," *Michigan Alumnus Quarterly Review* 58 (Autumn 1951): 70–76; Clinton Rossiter, "Homage to John Adams," *Michigan Alumnus Quarterly Review* (Spring 1958): 228–38.

On Adams's role during the war, and on the American navy in particular, see Frederick H. Hayes, "John Adams and American Sea Power," *American Neptune* 25 (1965): 35–45, and Carlos G. Calkins, "The American Navy and the Opinions of One of its Founders, John Adams, 1735–1826," *United States Naval Institute Proceedings* 37 (1911): 453–83. On Adams as a diplomat the best in-depth study is that of James H. Hutson, *John Adams and the Diplo-*

macy of the American Revolution (Lexington, Ky., 1980). For a somewhat different approach, see John Ferling, "John Adams: Diplomat," *William and Mary Quarterly* 51 (1994): 227–52. Gregg L. Lint is the author of an important essay, "John Adams on the Drafting of the Treaty Plan of 1776," *Diplomatic History* 2 (1978): 313–20. Several fine essays can be found in Lawrence S. Kaplan, ed., *The American Revolution and "A Candid World,"* (Kent, Ohio, 1977) and two works edited by Ronald Hoffman and Peter J. Albert, *Diplomacy and Revolution: The Franco-American Alliance of 1778* (Charlottesville, 1981) and *Peace and the Peacemakers: The Treaty of Paris of 1783* (Charlottesville, 1986). On Adams in Holland, see L. H. Butterfield, "John Adams and the Beginnings of Netherlands-American Friendship," in his *Butterfield in Holland: A Record of L. H. Butterfield's Pursuit of the Adamses Abroad in 1959* (Cambridge, Mass., 1961). For Adams's contentious relationship with Benjamin Franklin, see William B. Evans, "John Adams's Opinion of Benjamin Franklin," *Pennsylvania Magazine of History and Biography* 92 (1968): 220–38 and Robert Middlekauff, *Benjamin Franklin and his Enemies* (Berkeley, 1996).

For additional secondary and primary works that pertain to Adams's life and career following the termination of the war, see the bibliographical guide cited previously and the notes that accompany this study. Full citation of a particular work may be found in the list of abbreviations that precede the notes or in its first appearance in the notes.

Even a select list of the literature on the American Revolution and War of Independence would require a lengthy volume. However, any reader just stepping into the thicket of the historiography of this period would be advised to start with the following studies. Merrill Jensen is the author of the best study of the politics of the protest movement to July 1776. See his *The Founding of a Nation: A History of the American Revolution, 1763–1776* (New York, 1968). Jensen's *The American Revolution Within America* (New York, 1974) is also the ablest brief assessment of the varied motives of the Founders and the degree of change brought about by the upheaval. Two classic studies on the ideas of the Founders are essential reading. See Bernard Bailyn, *Ideological Origins of the American Revolution* (Cambridge, Mass., 1967) and Gordon S. Wood, *The Creation of the American Republic, 1776–1787* (Chapel Hill, 1969). Pauline Maier is the author of a study of the protest movement that, if possible, grows better with time. See her *From Resistance to Revolution: Colonial Radicals and the Development of American Opposition to Britain, 1765–1776* (New York, 1972). Her recent study of the Declaration of

Independence, *American Scripture: Making the Declaration of Independence* (New York, 1997), is equally vital. The best work on the meaning of the times is that of Gordon Wood, *The Radicalism of the American Revolution* (New York, 1992).

Excellent surveys of the war can be found in Don Higginbotham, *The War of American Independence: Military Attitudes, Policies, and Practice, 1763–1789* (New York, 1971); James Kirby Martin and Mark E. Lender, *A Respectable Army: The Military Origin of the Republic, 1763–1789* (Arlington Heights, Ill., 1982), Robert Middlekauff, *The Glorious Cause: The American Revolution, 1763–1789* (New York, 1982), Marshall Smelser, *The Winning of Independence* (Chicago, 1972), and Christopher Ward, *The War of the Revolution* (2 vols., New York, 1952). The British side is well covered in Piers Mackesy, *The War for America, 1775–1783* (Cambridge, Mass., 1964). A wonderful collection of essays treats Washington's principal general officers and his foes in George A. Billias, ed., *George Washington's Generals* (New York, 1964) and *George Washington's Opponents* (New York, 1969). On the intertwining of the army, war, and society, see Charles Royster, *A Revolutionary People at War: The Continental Army and the American Character, 1775–1783* (Chapel Hill, 1979). Finally, for two interpretive volumes on the outcome of the war, see Eric Robson, *The American Revolution: In Its Political and Military Aspects, 1763–1783* (New York, 1966) and the collection of essays in John Ferling, ed., *The World Turned Upside Down: The American Victory in the War of Independence* (Westport, Conn., 1988).

Index